HISTORICAL ATLAS OF THE U.S. NAVY

The Naval Institute

Historical Atlas of the U.S. Navy

By Craig L. Symonds

Cartography by William J. Clipson

Naval Institute Press
Annapolis, Maryland

Naval Institute Press
291 Wood Road
Annapolis, MD 21402

First Naval Institute Press paperback edition, 2001
ISBN 1-55750-984-0

The Library of Congress has cataloged the hardcover edition as follows:
Symonds, Craig L.
The Naval Institute historical atlas of the U.S. Navy / Craig L. Symonds ; cartography by William J. Clipson.
p. cm.
Covers the period 1775 through May 1991.
Includes index.
ISBN 1-55750-797-X
1. United States—History, Naval—Maps. I. Clipson, William J. II. United States Naval Institute. III. Title. IV. Title: Historical atlas of the U.S. Navy.
G1201.S1S8 1995 <G&M>
359'.00973'022—dc20 94-22911

Printed in the United States of America on acid-free paper ♾
08 07 06 05 04 8 7 6 5 4 3

For my students at the U.S. Naval Academy

"LEADERSHIP AND LEARNING
ARE INDISPENSABLE TO EACH OTHER."

—JOHN F. KENNEDY

22 NOVEMBER 1963

Contents

Part IV: Pirates, Explorers, and War with Mexico, 1815–1860 • 57

Part V: The Civil War, 1861–1865 • 77

Part VI: Retrenchment and Renaissance, 1865–1900 • 105

Part VII: A Global Navy and a World War, 1901–1939 • 119

Part VIII: World War II, 1939–1945 • 137

Part IX: The Cold War Navy, 1946–1980 • 191

Introduction and Acknowledgments

NEARLY THIRTY YEARS AGO, while browsing in my hometown public library, I chanced upon an oddly shaped pair of volumes entitled *The West Point Atlas of American Wars,* edited by Vincent J. Esposito. As one who had been captivated by World War II films, as well as television programs such as the Army's *Big Picture* and the Navy's *Victory at Sea,* I found these two volumes thrilling. I traced the movements of military units across the battlefields of America, Canada, Mexico, Europe, and the islands of the Pacific. But as someone who was particularly interested (even then) in the Navy, I wondered why there was not such a volume depicting the movements of ships and fleets: an atlas of American *naval* warfare. In the hope that others, too, have perceived such a need, I offer this volume.

I should note at the outset that unlike the West Point atlas, which is again available in a new edition, this book is not in any way official. The views expressed herein do not represent those of the Naval Academy or the Department of the Navy. Nor does this book pretend to be a comprehensive history of the Navy, for not all issues of interest to naval historians lend themselves to cartographic display. Moreover, the design of the book, with one page of text facing each map, necessarily limited the narrative for each map to one thousand words, a circumstance that strongly encouraged brevity. In partial compensation, I have introduced each of the ten sections with a short essay that offers background and context for the maps that follow. I have made a particular effort to include thumbnail sketches of the principal players: presidents, Navy secretaries, admirals, unit commanders, and the occasional junior officer or enlisted man who found himself at the fulcrum of history. Nevertheless, much had to be left out. Throughout the project I struggled between a desire to be inclusive and a determination to keep the book to a manageable (and affordable) size.

A few words of explanation are necessary here. Because this is a *naval* atlas, the "maps" should properly be called "charts." The use of that term, however, implies a precision that is simply not possible on maps of the scale necessary to make naval operations comprehensible at a glance, which is the goal of this volume. As a result, I have used "map" despite the lubberly connotations that word may suggest to some. Second, though I have employed the military style of dating (4 June 1942), I have used civilian time throughout (10:25 A.M.). My reason for doing so was only partly because this was the format suggested by the Naval Institute Press. In addition, I did not want to impede the novice student of naval history by requiring any reader to stop and calculate: "Let's see, 1445 is . . . uh, 2:45 P.M."

Like the other works on which I have collaborated with Bill Clipson, our partnership in this project was a singular joy. Bill is a skilled perfectionist who rendered the 154 maps on 94 plates to my specifications. If any error has managed to find its way onto any map, I am solely responsible. Whenever possible, the raw material for these maps was drawn from original or official sources, but like any historian I am indebted to those who have preceded me, particularly Dudley Knox, Samuel Eliot Morison, my friend and colleague E. B. "Ned" Potter, and other less famous historians who conducted or supervised the primary research on which much of this book is based. While I cannot acknowledge here all of those whose work made my own task easier, the community of naval scholars will forgive me, I hope, if I simply offer an inclusive thank you.

Likewise, I owe thanks to many active naval historians who encouraged me or offered suggestions concerning this work. James Bradford of Texas A&M University offered not only his encouragement but also many excellent suggestions to improve the manuscript. My colleagues at the Naval Academy were invaluable: Frederick Harrod convinced me to make several additions that significantly strengthened the book; Robert W. Love Jr. carefully read the section on World War II and offered his often-emphatic suggestions; and LCDR Tom Cutler's reading of the sections on both World War II and Vietnam also improved the book. Gene Smith of Texas Christian University brought several old maps to my attention, and Ernest Tucker helped me locate several sites in the Persian Gulf. Former colleagues CDR Mike Lipari and LCDR Joe Stanik provided both information and advice and brought my work to the attention of the excellent historians at the Naval Historical Center, including Steven Hill, Roy Grossnick, Michael Crawford, Robert Schneller, Curtis Utz, Jeffrey Barlow, Robert Cressman, Richard A. Russell, and particularly Edward J. Marolda. From the outset, Paul Wilderson was a supportive and helpful editor. Finally, I owe a debt of gratitude to my colleagues in the History Department of the Naval Academy for their willingness to shoulder the heavier teaching loads that are the price of a sabbatical program, thereby making possible the sabbatical semester during which I conducted much of the work for this project.

Like all my work, this volume was possible at all only because of the support and encouragement of my wife, Marylou, to whom I owe more than I can state here.

KEY TO MAP SYMBOLS

COLOR KEY

BLUE	UNITED STATES (or any coalition in which U.S. forces participated)
RED	BRITAIN CONFEDERATE STATES OF AMERICA (MAPS # 30-41) NORTH KOREA (MAPS # 79-81) NORTH VIETNAM (MAPS # 85-89) IRAQ (MAPS # 93-94)
LIGHT BLUE	FRANCE ISRAEL (MAP # 82)
ORANGE	SPAIN JAPAN (MAPS # 54-69)
BLACK	GERMANY ITALY IRAN (MAP # 92)

TERRAIN

SAND BAR

MUD FLATS

PACK ICE

SWAMP OR MARSH
(not navigable)

WOODS OR JUNGLE

CORAL REEF

MAP SYMBOLS

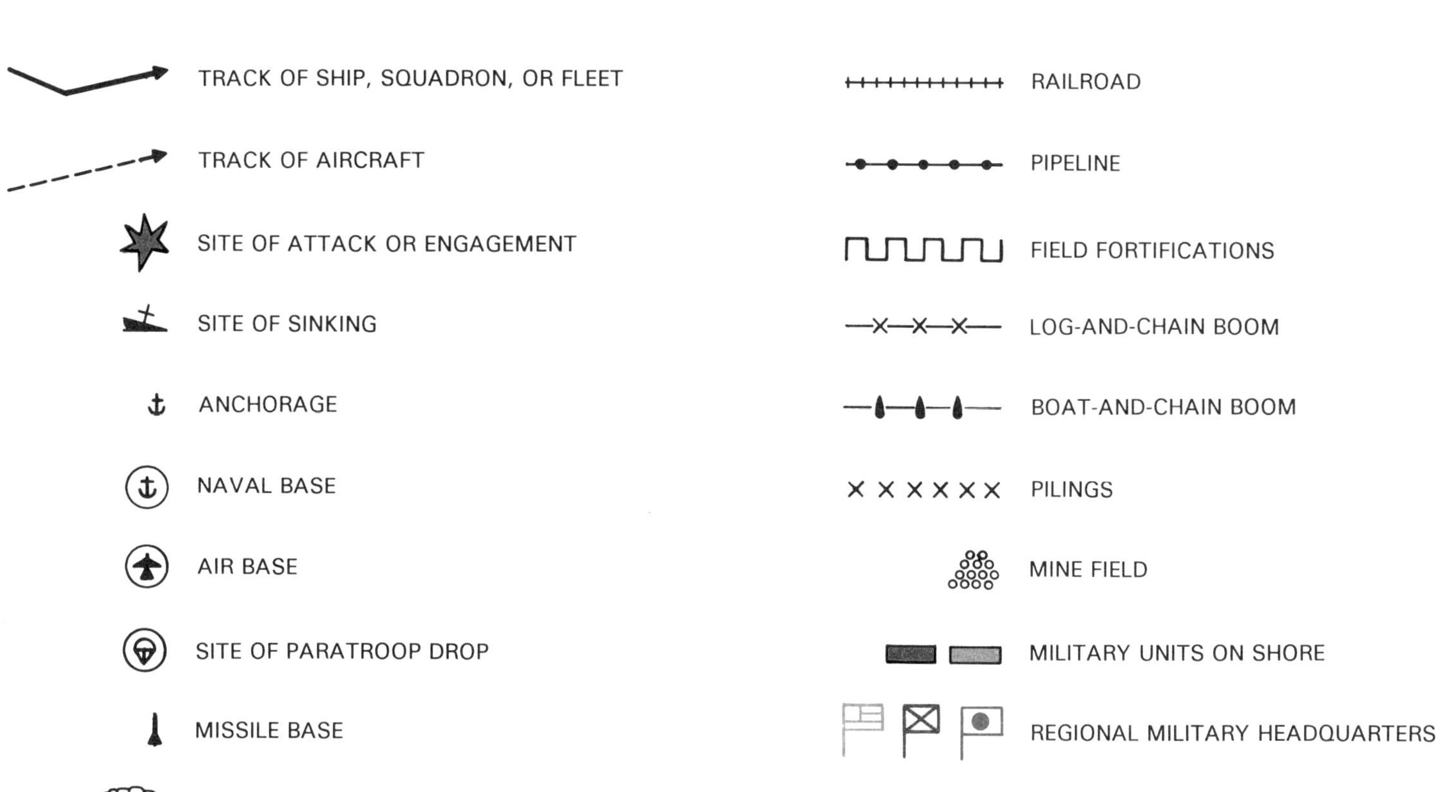

Historical Atlas of the U.S. Navy

Part I

The American Revolution 1775–1783

THOUGH AMERICANS CELEBRATE the thirteenth day of October 1775 as the official "birthday" of the U.S. Navy, it is difficult to trace the beginnings of an American Navy to a single event or date. Nor can it be fairly said that the Navy was the creation of any one person, despite claims made on behalf of several people for the title of "father of the U.S. Navy." Rather, an American Navy emerged fitfully and experimentally in the midst of war as the product of military and political circumstances. American naval forces in the War of Independence took many forms, most of them designed to meet a specific need at a particular moment. Ironically and tellingly, the most ambitious efforts, such as the founding of the Continental Navy by Congress (the event that took place on 13 October 1775), were the least successful. On the whole, the history of American naval forces in the War of Independence is a tale of innovation and perseverance rather than strategic insight or applied doctrine.

Perhaps the most remarkable thing about the early history of an American Navy is that it managed to exist at all. After all, Britain's Royal Navy was not only the most powerful naval force in the world, it was arguably the most efficient and successful instrument of war ever created. For two hundred years before Lexington and Concord the British had engaged in nearly continuous naval wars with Spain (1584–1603), Holland (1652–74), and most recently France (since 1689). In the process, Britain had emerged as the dominant political and military power in Europe, and the Royal Navy had matured into the nation's premier instrument of war, an instrument with a unique subculture, powerful traditions, and a strong sense of professionalism.

British ships-of-the-line go into action under topsails during the Battle of the Capes on 5 September 1781 (see map 8). The majestic ship-of-the-line was the dominant weapon of naval warfare in the eighteenth century, and this engagement between British and French fleets off the entrance to the Chesapeake Bay was the decisive naval battle of the American Revolution. (Painting by V. Zveg, official U.S. Navy photo)

The backbone of the Royal Navy was its fleet of ships-of-the-line—the battleships of the eighteenth century. Their designation as "ships-of-the-line" derived from the unchallenged assumption that the most efficient and deadly formation for a fleet of sailing warships was the line ahead. Such a formation allowed a fleet to bring all of its broadsides to bear simultaneously on the enemy. A ship "of the line" was any vessel strong enough, and powerful enough, to hold a place in the line of battle. These ships were beautiful things, both aesthetically and scientifically. They were ship-rigged, which is to say that each vessel boasted three masts—the central mainmast towering as much as two hundred feet above the surface of the sea—and each mast was crossed with yards supporting square sails that when handled well (no mean feat) drove the ship's wooden hull through the water at speeds of up to twelve knots. Dependent only on the wind for propulsion, the ships were virtually energy independent. Except for food, water, and gunpowder, they could stay at sea, theoretically at least, indefinitely.

The armament of a ship-of-the-line consisted of two or more horizontal decks of iron cannons that fired solid iron balls weighing from eighteen to thirty-two pounds a distance of several miles, though the ideal range was much shorter. Indeed, most ship captains of the age believed that the optimum range for a ship duel was a "half pistol shot"—about one hundred yards—from which distance an enemy vessel was hard to miss. A ship-of-the-line might carry between 60 and 120 such guns, but by the outbreak of the American Revolution, convention had established 74 as the proper number of guns for a battleship. A single broadside from a seventy-four–gun ship-of-the-line sent more than eight hundred pounds of iron hurtling toward an enemy vessel to smash into its wooden hull and create giant splinters of wood that flew across decks crowded with men. No wonder it was necessary to spread sand over the polished wooden decks before a fight so that the bare-footed sailors did not slip in the gore.

These elegant machines of war were crowded places. It took hundreds of men to cast loose or take in the sails or come about to a new course, and hundreds more to man the heavy guns that weighed several tons each. Each ship, therefore, carried a crew of between five hundred and one thousand men, all of whom lived and worked in a hull no longer than two hundred feet at the waterline. Such crowding necessitated rigid discipline and powerful traditions so sacred as to constitute a separate culture. The officers, frequently of the middle class, with perhaps the occasional doctor's or lawyer's son, maintained an august and absolute supremacy over the British tars, many of whom were pressed into service, but others of whom voluntarily spent their entire lives in the Royal Navy. The severe Articles of War maintained discipline within the ranks, listing all sorts of offenses and specifying punishments from the stoppage of the daily grog ration for minor oversights to flogging or death for a long list of major transgressions. Brutal it may have been, but the Royal Navy sustained Britain as the dominant military and political power in Europe for two centuries.

The American colonists did not set out to challenge this awesome power when they began to protest Parliamentary policy in the 1760s. It seemed to them that as British citizens—a designation in which they took some pride—it would hardly be necessary to go to war to obtain the kind of consideration they believed was their birthright. Indeed, they had become accustomed to enjoying the benefits of British citizenship without many of the obligations. For half a century Britain had practiced a deliberate policy of benign neglect toward its American colonies. Sir Robert Walpole, British prime minister from 1721 to 1742, had established the policy in the belief that it was best, as he put it, to let sleeping dogs lie. The few laws that Parliament had passed concerning the governance and regulation of the colonies were almost never enforced. Though few Americans in that age disputed Parliament's right to assert imperial authority, the fact that Parliament had never bothered to do so led most Americans to take it for granted that it never would. Instead, Americans established their own local instruments of government and over time became virtually self-governing.

Britain emerged victorious from the latest of its wars with France—the Seven Years' War or what Americans called the French and Indian War—in 1763. Alas, the expense of its interminable wars, however successful, had rendered the nation virtually bankrupt. Moreover, an Indian rebellion that same year, and the fear that the citizens of former French and Spanish colonies were reluctant subjects at best, led to a decision to station troops in America permanently, a move that promised even more expenses. Government officials estimated the cost of defending and operating the British Empire in North America at £300,000 a year. Current taxes brought in only about £100,000, and Parliament believed it was only just that Americans themselves should pay the remaining £200,000.

To achieve this end, Parliament enacted a series of revenue acts, beginning in 1764. The first of these was a tax levied on imported molasses, from which sugar was made. It was designed to raise £100,000 per year by reviving an old law that had obligated the colonists to pay a duty of 6 pence per barrel on molasses, but that had never been enforced. The new act halved the duty but made it clear that this time inspectors would enforce collection. Colonial merchants grumbled and either paid the tax grudgingly or turned to smuggling, an activity that carried no social disapprobation because few believed the tax to be fair.

Battle action on the main gun deck of a ship-of-the-line is reenacted for a modern film. This photo gives some sense of the crowded conditions on board a warship in the age of sail, but it lacks the choking smoke from guns firing black powder and the din of noise that made some sailors think that a battle at sea was probably much like hell. When the ship was not in action, the sailors would live, eat, and sleep among the guns, slinging their hammocks from hooks in the overhead. (U.S. Naval Institute)

The Boston Tea Party: Americans thinly disguised as Indians dump tea into Boston Harbor from the deck of an East Indiaman on the night of 16 December 1773. This act provoked harsh repressive measures from the British government and marked a turning point in the relationship between Britain and the colonies. (National Archives)

The shot heard 'round the world: A ragged line of "minutemen" face British regulars on Lexington Green on 19 April 1775 in the battle that began the American Revolution. This action provoked thousands of citizen-soldiers to turn out and drive the British back into Boston, where the peculiar geography of Boston Harbor kept them immobile (see map 1). (National Archives)

A year later Parliament passed another revenue bill designed to raise an additional £100,000 per year. This law required the colonials to affix an official stamp—like a notary's seal—on wills, titles, and other legal documents. Opposition to the Stamp Act was immediate and widespread and caught the British quite by surprise. Many Americans granted Parliament the right to enact "external" taxes, such as duties on imports or exports, but denied its right to establish "internal" taxes, collected within the colonies. Stunned by the response, Parliament backed down, repealing the Stamp Act and replacing it a few years later with the Townshend Acts, which specified duties on imported lead, paper, paint, glass, and tea.

Once again Americans objected. Though applied to trade goods, Americans recognized at once that the Townshend Acts were not intended to regulate trade but to raise revenue. As such it did not matter that they were "external" taxes—they were unacceptable. This time, however, the government stood firm. In 1768 the government dispatched troops to Boston. The inevitable clash between British "lobsterbacks" and colonial civilians took place in Boston on 5 March 1770 when British soldiers fired into a crowd that had been taunting them and pelting them with stones.

An uneasy truce ensued that lasted for five years. Then in 1773 the government of Lord North, seeking to bolster the flagging prospects of the East India Tea Company, approved a request to ship tea from India directly to the American colonies without the previously required stop in England. Because of the saving in shipping costs and duties in England, the Indian tea would cost less than untaxed tea smuggled in from the Dutch East Indies. But Boston consumers decided it was the principle that mattered here. If Britain were allowed to enforce a monopoly on tea, it might extend the principle to other commodities. Bostonians refused to allow the tea to land, and on 16 December 1773, rather thinly disguised as American Indians, they threw most of the tea into Boston Harbor.

This lawlessness provoked the so-called "Intolerable Acts," which clamped Boston under virtual martial law. The British government declared Boston Harbor closed and made a major general, Thomas Gage, the new governor of Massachusetts. Early in April of 1775 Gage learned that colonials in the countryside were collecting arms, including cannon, in an apparent attempt to develop the means of military resistance. He decided to send an armed column to seize these arms. On 19 April this column marched to Lexington, about a dozen miles from Boston, and encountered four score militiamen lined up on the town common in passive defiance of British authority. Someone fired a shot, and the "rabble" was quickly routed. The British marched on to Concord and conducted a fruitless search for the arms cache. But for the rest of the day and into the night, while the British marched back toward Boston, other Massachusetts militiamen—hundreds, thousands of them—fired at the British from ambush all along the route of march and nearly annihilated the column before, exhausted to the point of collapse and missing 273 of their number, it returned to Boston.

The war had begun.

Map 1

Washington's Navy

April 1775–March 1776

By retreating from Lexington and Concord, Gage's army effectively surrendered the hinterland around Boston to the rebels. Throughout April and May, as word of the fighting spread, the number of American militiamen outside Boston increased until between fifteen thousand and eighteen thousand men were camped in a huge semicircle around the Boston peninsula. But while the American rabble controlled the countryside, Boston's peculiar geography provided a sanctuary for Gage's 6,500-man garrison. The narrow neck (1) that connected Boston to the mainland doomed to failure any overland attack aimed at driving the British from the city.

Of course, if the Americans could not get in, neither could the British get out; they were virtual prisoners in the city they occupied. Prisoners, that is, except for British command of the sea, for thanks to the Royal Navy, Gage's army could be supplied and reinforced at will. Gage could also take advantage of the mobility offered by sea power to outflank his besiegers with an amphibious movement. But Gage showed no inclination to do so; having been burned by the outcome of his expedition to Lexington and Concord, he seemed satisfied to remain in Boston and let higher authority determine his next step.

On 25 May a British frigate arrived in Boston with a reinforcement of a kind: three British major generals—William Howe, Henry Clinton, and John Burgoyne. Their arrival demonstrated that the government in London was not pleased with the embarrassing circumstances in which Gage now found himself. All three British generals urged Gage to adopt a more aggressive posture. In particular, they suggested that he use his amphibious capability to occupy and fortify Dorchester Heights south of the city (2) and/or Breed's and Bunker's Hills (3) north of the city. Gage agreed. But learning of the British plans from sympathizers in Boston, the Americans immediately set to work to fortify those heights themselves. They began with Breed's Hill on the Charlestown Peninsula.

All night on 16 June American militiamen dug fortifications on Breed's Hill, and at dawn, when this effort became visible to British warships in Boston Harbor, HMS *Lively* opened fire. In Boston the four British generals decided to send 1,500 men to seize the American redoubt on Breed's Hill. The ensuing fight (which has gone down in history as the Battle of Bunker Hill) was a British victory only in a technical sense. Though the British drove the Americans from their redoubt, they sustained more than a thousand casualties in the process, more than double that of the Americans.

Two weeks after this fight, George Washington arrived in the American camp to assume command of what was now designated the Continental Army. Washington appreciated at once the limitations placed on his tactical options, not only by the local geography but also by severe shortages in military equipment. The besieging Americans had no heavy field guns and only whatever gunpowder the volunteers had brought with them. Washington appealed to the Continental Congress for guns and powder, but the incipient nation had no military infrastructure capable of producing munitions in large quantities even if the Continental Congress could pay for them, which it could not. Seeking pragmatic solutions to his dilemma, Washington did two things. First he sent COL Henry Knox to Fort Ticonderoga in upstate New York to oversee the transfer of heavy guns from that fort to Boston. And second, he adopted the suggestion of COL John Glover of Massachusetts to charter Glover's seventy-eight–ton fishing schooner, the *Hannah* (at a dollar per ton per month), for the purpose of raiding British shipping.

Washington had no intention of establishing an American Navy in any traditional sense—the *Hannah*'s purpose was simply to forage for the Army. Commanded by an Army officer and manned by soldiers, the *Hannah* was to seek out British supply vessels and confiscate military equipment. In a brief career, the *Hannah* captured only one ship (which turned out to belong to an American Patriot) before being chased aground by a British warship in October. But other vessels chartered in the same way had more luck. The most prominent of these was the schooner *Lee* commanded by CAPT John Manley. In November Manley captured the British ordnance brig *Nancy* filled with 2,500 muskets, several cannon, and more than thirty tons of shot. That same month Washington asked Congress to authorize the formation of admiralty courts so that the prizes taken by his chartered vessels could be legally condemned. Over the six months of the American siege of Boston, the eleven vessels of "Washington's Navy" captured a total of fifty-five prizes.

In January 1776 Colonel Knox returned to Boston at the head of an artillery train that had been dragged on sledges over the winter snows from Fort Ticonderoga, and on 2 March the Americans began erecting a battery on Dorchester Heights (2), from which the American guns would dominate the city. Though he had already decided to evacuate Boston on 20 March, Brigadier General Howe, who had replaced Gage in October, ordered an amphibious attack on the position. But his heart was not in it, and a storm on 4 March gave him an excuse to cancel it. Instead, he decided to evacuate the city three days early, on 17 March.

The Americans had been able to sustain their "siege" of Boston largely because of Washington's ability to hold the volunteer American Army together over a cold winter and his willingness to employ creative and innovative tactics to supply that army, including the use of seagoing raiders. Moreover, the success of "Washington's Navy" boosted the efforts of naval-minded members of the Continental Congress who sought to create a national naval force.

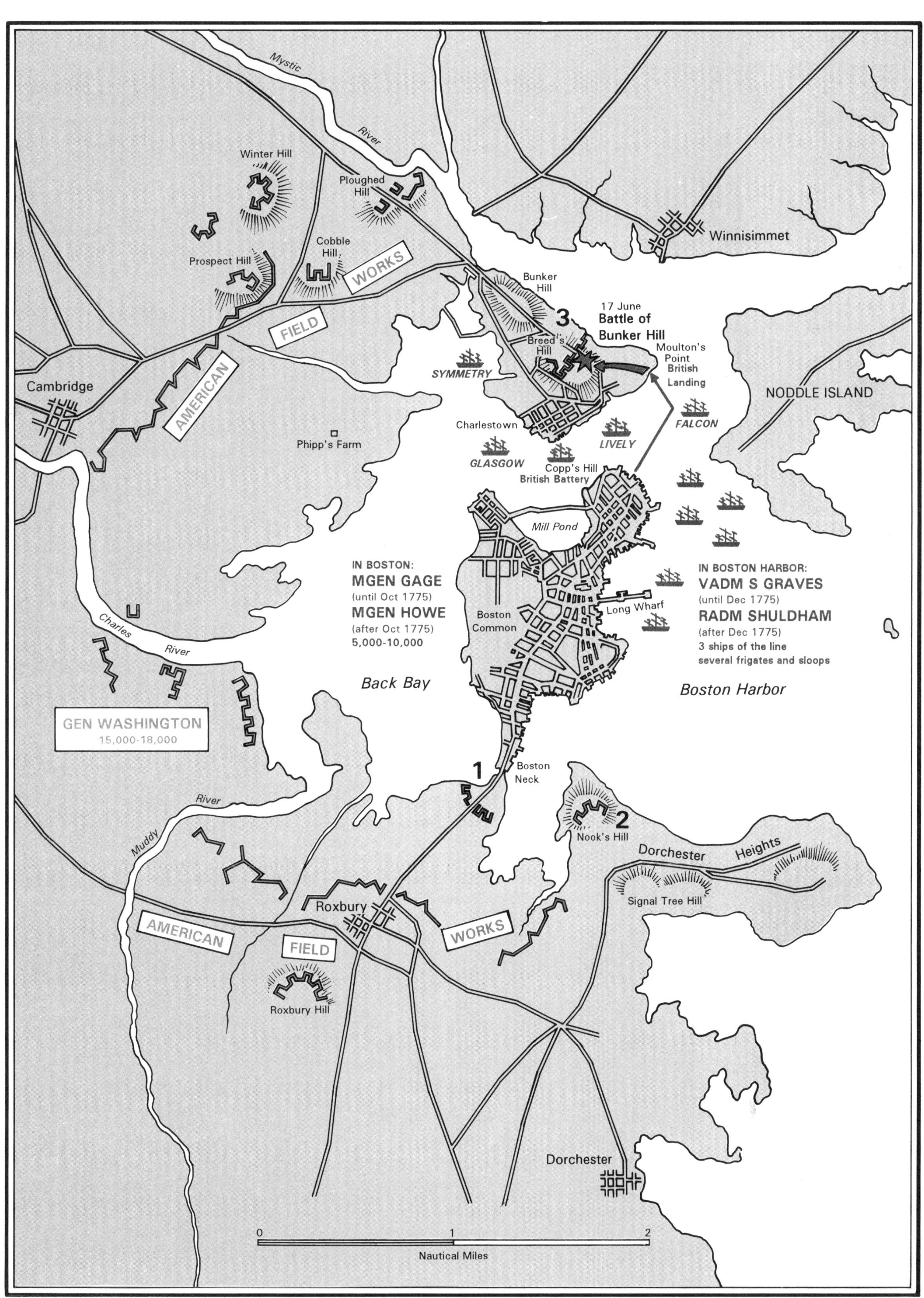

Mystic
River
Winter Hill
Ploughed Hill
Cobble Hill
Prospect Hill
WORKS
FIELD
AMERICAN
Winnisimmet
Bunker Hill
3
17 June
Battle of Bunker Hill
Breed's Hill
Moulton's Point
British Landing
SYMMETRY
NODDLE ISLAND
Cambridge
Charlestown
FALCON
LIVELY
Phipp's Farm
GLASGOW
Copp's Hill
British Battery
Mill Pond
IN BOSTON:
MGEN GAGE
(until Oct 1775)
MGEN HOWE
(after Oct 1775)
5,000-10,000
Boston Common
Long Wharf
IN BOSTON HARBOR:
VADM S GRAVES
(until Dec 1775)
RADM SHULDHAM
(after Dec 1775)
3 ships of the line
several frigates and sloops
Charles River
Back Bay
Boston Harbor
GEN WASHINGTON
15,000-18,000
1
Boston Neck
River
Muddy
2
Nook's Hill
Dorchester Heights
Signal Tree Hill
Roxbury
AMERICAN
FIELD
WORKS
Roxbury Hill
Dorchester
0
1
2
Nautical Miles

MAP 2

THE CONTINENTAL NAVY

MARCH 1776–MARCH 1777

Inspired by Washington's example in Massachusetts, and prompted by representatives from New England, the Continental Congress established a Naval Committee on 13 October 1775—celebrated today as the official "birthday" of the U.S. Navy. Congress enjoined this committee to oversee the purchase of a number of armed vessels for the struggle against Britain and to draft a set of Navy regulations, thus creating what came to be known as the "Continental Navy."

As befitted an impecunious budget, this first American Navy was modest enough. It consisted of only two ships, the *Alfred* and *Columbus,* each mounting twenty-four cannon, and six sloops and schooners that carried between six and eighteen guns each. Moreover, it was unclear what the mission of this tiny armada would be. No naval force the Americans could buy or build could hope to challenge the Royal Navy for command of the sea. The only realistic duties of an American Navy would be either to defend Patriot trade and property from raids by British Loyalists, or to attack British commerce. While commerce raiding was sure to be popular with the officers and men of an American Navy, protecting Patriot property from British seizure was more politically urgent. Lord Dunmore, the former Loyalist governor of Virginia, was already conducting raids on Patriot estates throughout the Chesapeake Bay area (1). Support for the Patriot cause in general, and for the Continental Congress in particular, would dissipate quickly if Congress failed to make a serious effort to stop him.

In pursuit of this objective, Congress appointed Esek Hopkins, younger brother of one of the influential members of the Naval Committee, to command of the Continental Navy with the rank of commodore and ordered him to drive Lord Dunmore's squadron from Virginia's waters. After accomplishing that objective, Hopkins was to cruise the waters off the Carolina Capes (2), where other armed British vessels had been harassing American merchants. Hopkins dutifully put to sea from Philadelphia in January 1776, but once at sea he took advantage of a loophole in his orders to bypass the Chesapeake, and he sailed instead directly to the Bahamas.

A few days out, two of the eight American vessels collided and had to turn back for repairs. With the remaining six, Hopkins arrived off Nassau (3) in March. He landed a party of sailors and marines under CAPT Samuel Nicholas and secured the forts guarding the harbor, then he looked around for supplies. The British commander had managed to carry off most of the powder and shot, but Hopkins ordered that the fort's artillery be loaded on board the American vessels. With fifty-eight pieces of heavy ordnance as booty, Hopkins prepared to return to America. En route, his squadron came upon the British brig *Glasgow,* which managed to escape into Newport after a long chase despite overwhelming American superiority. Though Hopkins did bring back some much-needed ordnance from his raid, Patriots in the southern states felt abandoned. Disappointed, Congress first censured Hopkins and later dismissed him from the Navy.

This inauspicious beginning did not dissuade Congress from making a more far-reaching effort to develop the Continental Navy. Even before Hopkins embarked on his adventure to the Bahamas, Congress had approved the construction of thirteen new frigates, which would constitute the backbone of its Navy. The decision to build frigates suggests that Congress had more in mind than merely defending American merchants or harassing British trade. Sloops and schooners could do that. Frigates were ship-rigged, flush-decked warships mounting between thirty-two and forty-four guns and were the cruisers of the eighteenth century. Considering Congress's inability to raise revenue by taxing, the decision to authorize thirteen frigates was extremely ambitious. Yet the tragic history of those vessels emphasizes the difficulty of attempting to create a navy in the midst of war without a mature naval industry.

Two of the frigates were built in New York (4), but when Lord Howe's British Army landed there in August 1776, both ships had to be burned to prevent their capture. Three more were lost when Howe captured Philadelphia (5) in 1777, and two more suffered the same fate when the British took Charleston, South Carolina (6), in May 1780. Thus seven of the thirteen frigates never even got to sea. The other six fared little better. The *Virginia* was captured while attempting to run the British blockade, and the *Warren* was burned by its own crew while fleeing from a British squadron in Penobscot Bay (7). The other four American frigates were all captured at sea. One of them, the *Hancock,* was taken into British service as the *Iris* and later captured her sister ship, the *Trumbull.* Only the *Randolph* could claim a brief moment of glory when it fought the much larger British *Yarmouth,* 64, for most of an hour before the *Randolph*'s magazine exploded, blowing the ship into tiny fragments and killing all but 4 of its crew of 315.

The record of these thirteen frigates is not the complete history of the Continental Navy, of course. Other vessels made important contributions to the Patriot war effort, especially as commerce raiders, and the exploits of men like John Paul Jones (see map 5) gladdened the hearts of American Patriots. But on the whole the Continental Navy was a terrible disappointment. After the war John Adams wrote a friend that when he contemplated the history of the Continental Navy, it was difficult for him to avoid tears. The Royal Navy's superiority in the traditional weapons of naval warfare was simply too great for the Americans to achieve any meaningful success with a baker's dozen of frigates.

Lake Huron
80°
BRITISH CANADA
Lake Ontario
Lake Erie
Lake Champlain
Lake George
MAINE (MASS.)
7
Penobscot Bay
WARREN burned
(August 1779)
90°
N.H.
Portsmouth
NEW YORK
Albany
Hudson River
MASS.
Boston
Cape Cod
CONN.
R.I.
Newport
PENNSYLVANIA
4
40°
N.J.
New York (2 frigates)
captured by British, August 1776
5
Philadelphia (3 frigates)
captured by British, September 1777
Baltimore
MD.
DEL.
Cape May
VIRGINIA
1
Richmond
Cape Charles
Cape Henry
NORTH CAROLINA
2
35°
Cape Hatteras
Cape Lookout
Wilmington
Cape Fear
SOUTH CAROLINA
6
Charleston (2 frigates)
captured by British, May 1780
GEORGIA
Savannah
COMMO HOPKINS
Atlantic
Ocean
30°
St. Augustine
SPANISH FLORIDA
Gulf of Mexico
GREAT BAHAMA ISLAND
GREAT ABACO ISLAND
BAHAMA ISLANDS
Strait of Florida
25°
3
Nassau
ANDROS ISLAND
NEW PROVIDENCE ISLAND
ELEUTHERA ISLAND
CAT ISLAND
0
100
200
300
Nautical Miles

Map 3

Benedict Arnold's Navy (Valcour Island)

11 October 1776

In the late summer of 1775, while the American Army besieged the British in Boston and Congress contemplated the creation of a Continental Navy, Washington offered the command of an American expedition to Quebec in British-held Canada to COL Benedict Arnold. Many Americans believed that the Canadians would be eager to join in a war against British "tyranny," and Arnold willingly accepted the opportunity. After an arduous overland march, Arnold's six hundred men met another force of three hundred Americans under BGEN Richard Montgomery outside Quebec (1) in December. Their joint attack on the Canadian citadel, in a snowstorm on New Year's Eve 1775, was a disaster. Arnold was wounded, Montgomery killed, and half the American force taken prisoner. Arnold tried to maintain a siege of Quebec with the survivors, but when British reinforcements arrived in the spring, he had no choice but to fall back.

The arrival of reinforcements allowed the British to assume the offensive. MGEN Sir Guy Carleton now commanded some eleven thousand men, and in June he began moving up the St. Lawrence. The Americans fought an unsuccessful delaying action at Trois-Rivières (2) on 8 June, but soon they were in full retreat, falling back to Sorel (3) and then southward up the Richelieu River to the southern end of Lake Champlain at Crown Point (4). On 17 June Congress appointed MGEN Horatio Gates to command this exhausted and demoralized force, but few doubted the result if Carleton's army managed to catch up with the small American force.

The key was Lake Champlain. A passable road ran along its western shore, but an enemy in control of the lake could cut that road. Aware of this, Carleton halted his advance at St. Johns (5) on the Richelieu River to construct a squadron of vessels to gain control of Lake Champlain. He arranged to have a ship-rigged vessel, the *Inflexible,* dismantled on the St. Lawrence and carried in sections to Lake Champlain to be reassembled. In addition, the British built two schooners (of twelve and fourteen guns, respectively), a gondola (seven guns), twenty gunboats, and a giant raftlike vessel called a *radeau* that carried heavy twenty-four pounders and a crew of three hundred and that was appropriately named *Thunderer.*

To confront this armada, the Americans had only four small gunboats on Lake Champlain. Recognizing at once the inadequacy of this naval force, Arnold requested permission from Gates to build an American Navy on the lake. Infusing the project with the energy of his dynamic personality, Arnold brought together blacksmiths, riggers, and sailmakers at the head of the lake at Skenesboro (6). The raw material of Arnold's navy was all around them in the standing timber of the New York forests. Through July and August the Americans cut the timber, shaped it, then framed and rigged an entire naval squadron. They built a half dozen gundalows (flat-bottomed, single-masted vessels each carrying three guns and a crew of forty-five) and an equal number of galleys (slightly larger vessels carrying eight to ten guns and a crew of seventy to eighty). By the end of August Arnold was at sea in command of this flotilla, sailing north to challenge the British for control of the lake.

For a month Arnold drilled his green crews in the curiosities of their strange craft—themselves built mostly of green wood. Then on 11 October lookouts spotted the British squadron moving south. Arnold positioned his flotilla in the lee of Valcour Island, an unoccupied and heavily forested island off the western coast of the lake (see inset). Carleton's ships had already passed the island when British lookouts sighted the masts of Arnold's two dozen vessels. With the wind out of the north, Carleton had to beat to windward to close with the smaller American force. As a result, the ungainly *Thunderer* was unable to close the range and played no part in the battle. The Americans concentrated their fire on the schooner *Carleton* and eventually forced the British to tow it out of range. Even so, the superior firepower of the ship-rigged *Inflexible* overpowered the American vessels, though darkness fell before the British could complete their victory.

Arnold was now in a desperate situation. With the dawn, the British would certainly be able to complete the destruction of the American squadron at their leisure. Escape was the only option to surrender. But the wind prevented an escape around Valcour Island to the north, and the British squadron blocked the route south. Nevertheless, in the dark and fog of the early morning hours the American vessels slipped past the British in the shallow waters along the forested coastline. When dawn revealed that the quarry had flown, Carleton set off in pursuit, and the result was a running fight southward. Arnold played out the game as long as he could, but one by one his vessels were forced to beach themselves as the British drew within range. Only five of Arnold's vessels made it to Crown Point.

In this "Battle of Valcour Island" Arnold lost eleven of his sixteen vessels and surrendered control of Lake Champlain to the British. But his energy in challenging the British for supremacy on the lake had not been wasted, for Carleton decided that the time he had devoted to winning command of the lake made it too late in the season to initiate a full-fledged campaign into New York. He withdrew to St. Johns to await the spring. He could not know that by spring the military circumstances in New York would be dramatically different—that the American Army, so vulnerable in 1776, would have become a much tougher obstacle. The spring campaign of 1777, made possible by Arnold's sacrifice at Valcour Island, would culminate in the British defeat at Saratoga.

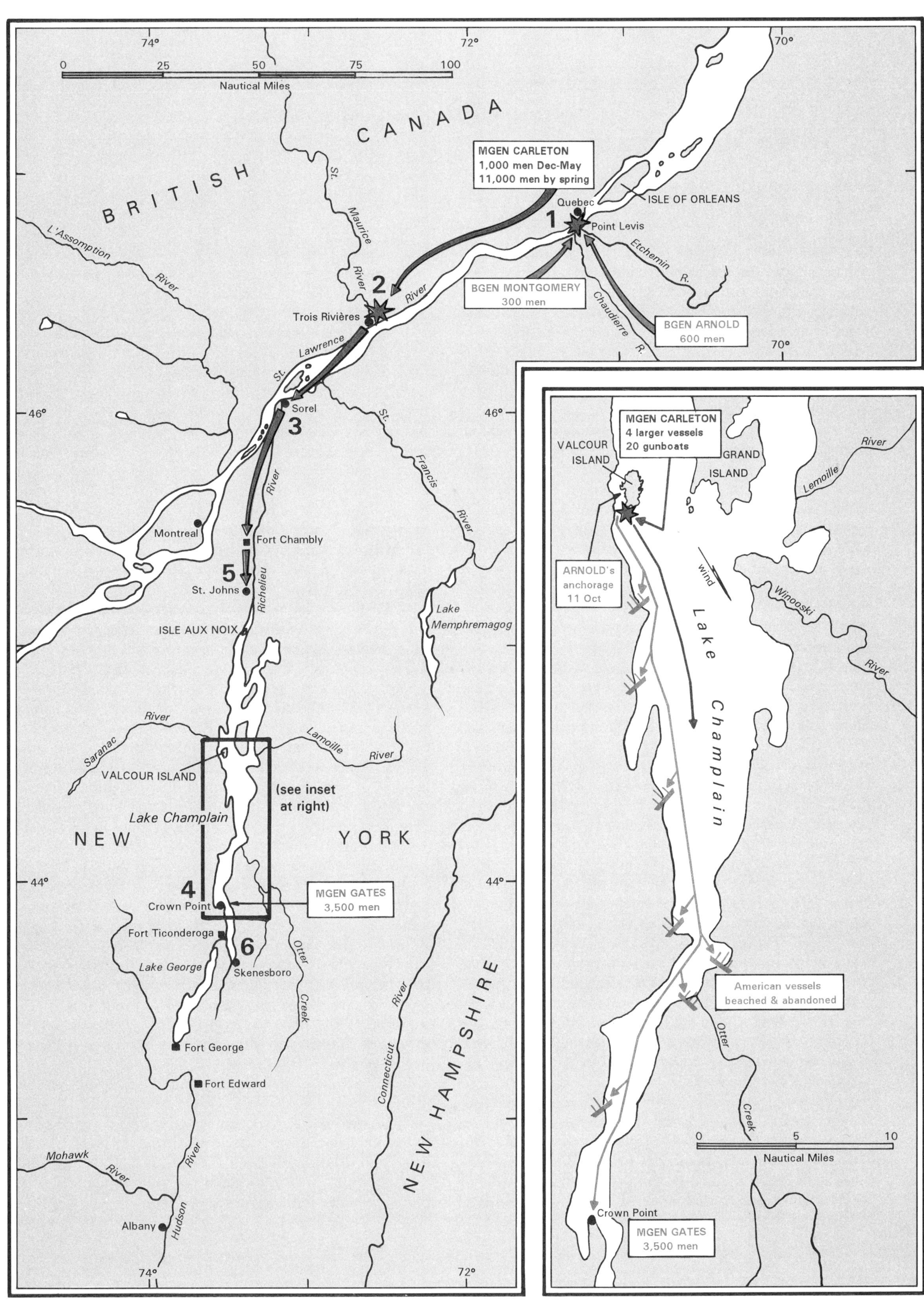

0
25
50
75
100
Nautical Miles
74°
72°
70°
46°
44°
BRITISH CANADA
MGEN CARLETON
1,000 men Dec-May
11,000 men by spring
Quebec
ISLE OF ORLEANS
1
Point Levis
Etchemin R.
BGEN MONTGOMERY
300 men
Chaudierre R.
BGEN ARNOLD
600 men
St. Maurice River
2
Trois Rivières
St. Lawrence River
L'Assomption River
Sorel
3
St. Francis River
Montreal
Fort Chambly
5
St. Johns
Richelieu River
ISLE AUX NOIX
Lake Memphremagog
Saranac River
Lamoille River
VALCOUR ISLAND
(see inset at right)
Lake Champlain
NEW YORK
4
Crown Point
MGEN GATES
3,500 men
Fort Ticonderoga
6
Lake George
Skenesboro
Otter Creek
Fort George
Fort Edward
Connecticut River
NEW HAMPSHIRE
Mohawk River
Hudson River
Albany
MGEN CARLETON
4 larger vessels
20 gunboats
VALCOUR ISLAND
GRAND ISLAND
River
Lemoille
ARNOLD's anchorage 11 Oct
wind
Winooski River
Lake Champlain
American vessels beached & abandoned
Otter Creek
0
5
10
Nautical Miles
Crown Point
MGEN GATES
3,500 men

Map 4

The States' Navies

1777–1779

Though Congress had established a Continental Navy, most individual colonies—now states—felt that a naval force committed to the protection of the ports and harbors within their own borders would better serve their particular interests. Massachusetts and Rhode Island were the first states to establish their own naval forces, but eventually eleven of the thirteen states did so, most notably Virginia, Connecticut, Pennsylvania, Maryland, and South Carolina. Though many of these navies did good service, they were simply too small to fulfill the difficult assignments they were given.

Virginia's was the largest of the state navies, but the gunboats and barges of its tiny "fleet" were unable to provide a realistic deterrent to the Royal Navy. When Esek Hopkins bypassed the Chesapeake to sail for the Bahamas in January 1776 (see map 2), the Virginia State Navy tried to take up the slack, but with little success. Lord Dunmore, leader of the Tory force that had been pillaging Patriot homes in the Bay area, discontinued his escapades, but his decision was due less to the efforts of the Virginia Navy than to his own shortage of supplies and volunteers.

A year later a British fleet under RADM Lord Richard Howe invaded the Chesapeake with a fleet of warships and transports carrying an army commanded by his brother, MGEN Sir William Howe (1). This British armada of some two hundred ships sailed leisurely up the Bay to the head of the Elk River, where the soldiers disembarked for an overland march to Philadelphia, defeating Washington's army at the Battle of the Brandywine (2) en route. Throughout the campaign the Virginia and Maryland State Navies could do no more than scurry out of the way. The results were similar in 1781 when Benedict Arnold, having changed sides and joined the British, brought another enemy fleet into the Bay. Ignoring the ineffective efforts to stop him, Arnold sailed boldly up the James River to Richmond, which he put to the torch.

The simple fact was that no individual state possessed the resources to construct a naval force sufficient to stand up to the Royal Navy. In addition, the state navies almost never operated outside local waters and seldom cooperated with one another. Though the Maryland and Virginia State Navies pledged to "cheerfully cooperate . . . in every Measure that may contribute to our Mutual Defence against the invaders," only in rare cases did state navies work together effectively.

One time when state navies did cooperate, though not with any great success, was in the American naval expedition to Penobscot Bay (3), on the coast of what is now Maine but which was then part of Massachusetts. The British had established a refuge for Loyalists at Castine on the edge of Penobscot Bay (see inset), and in midsummer 1779 they sent two regiments to garrison the town and construct a small fort. The Massachusetts General Court authorized the use of "such armed vessels, State or National, as could be prepared" to drive off the enemy.

Massachusetts committed its entire state navy, which consisted of two brigantines (the *Active* and *Tyrannicide*), and the State of New Hampshire, in a rare show of cooperation, committed its only warship, the *Hampden.* Responding to pleas for help from Massachusetts, Congress agreed to send three Continental Navy vessels—the frigate *Warren,* the sloop *Providence,* and the brig *Diligent.* In addition to these six warships, Massachusetts convinced the owners of sixteen privateers to join the expedition with the promise that the owners would be compensated for any losses incurred and would share in any prize money that was won. Thus twenty-two armed vessels, plus another eighteen transports loaded with one thousand Massachusetts militiamen, set sail on 24 July 1779 to evict the British from Penobscot Bay.

Despite the impression of efficiency and cooperation suggested by the speed of these preparations, the Penobscot expedition is a sobering case study of the pitfalls inherent in any military operation that lacks a clear command structure. Though there was a single commander—the Continental Navy's COMMO Dudley Saltonstall—he could not exercise effective control over his disparate naval forces, and worse, he could not issue orders to the Massachusetts militia under BGEN Solomon Lovell. The result was a series of fruitless councils of war in which Saltonstall urged the militia to drive the British soldiers from the small fort and Lovell urged the naval forces to attack the three British warships in the harbor.

On 11 August 250 Massachusetts militiamen made a half-hearted demonstration against the British fort, but when 50 British regulars marched out to confront them, the militia fled back to the safety of their own fortifications (4). Saltonstall decided to attempt a naval attack, but before he could do so, a British naval squadron consisting of a ship-of-the-line, three frigates, and three sloops sailed into the bay (5) and provoked panic among the American fleet. The Americans fled upriver, eventually grounding their ships in the narrowing river and disappearing into the forests. All forty ships were lost, including the frigate *Warren,* which its own crew burned to prevent it from falling to the British.

Saltonstall was censured at a court-martial and dismissed from the service. While he no doubt deserved his fate, an inability to exercise effective command over the mixed bag of national, state, and private vessels that made up his "fleet" had handicapped him throughout the campaign. Like the Continental Navy, the individual state navies were a disappointment to the advocates of American independence.

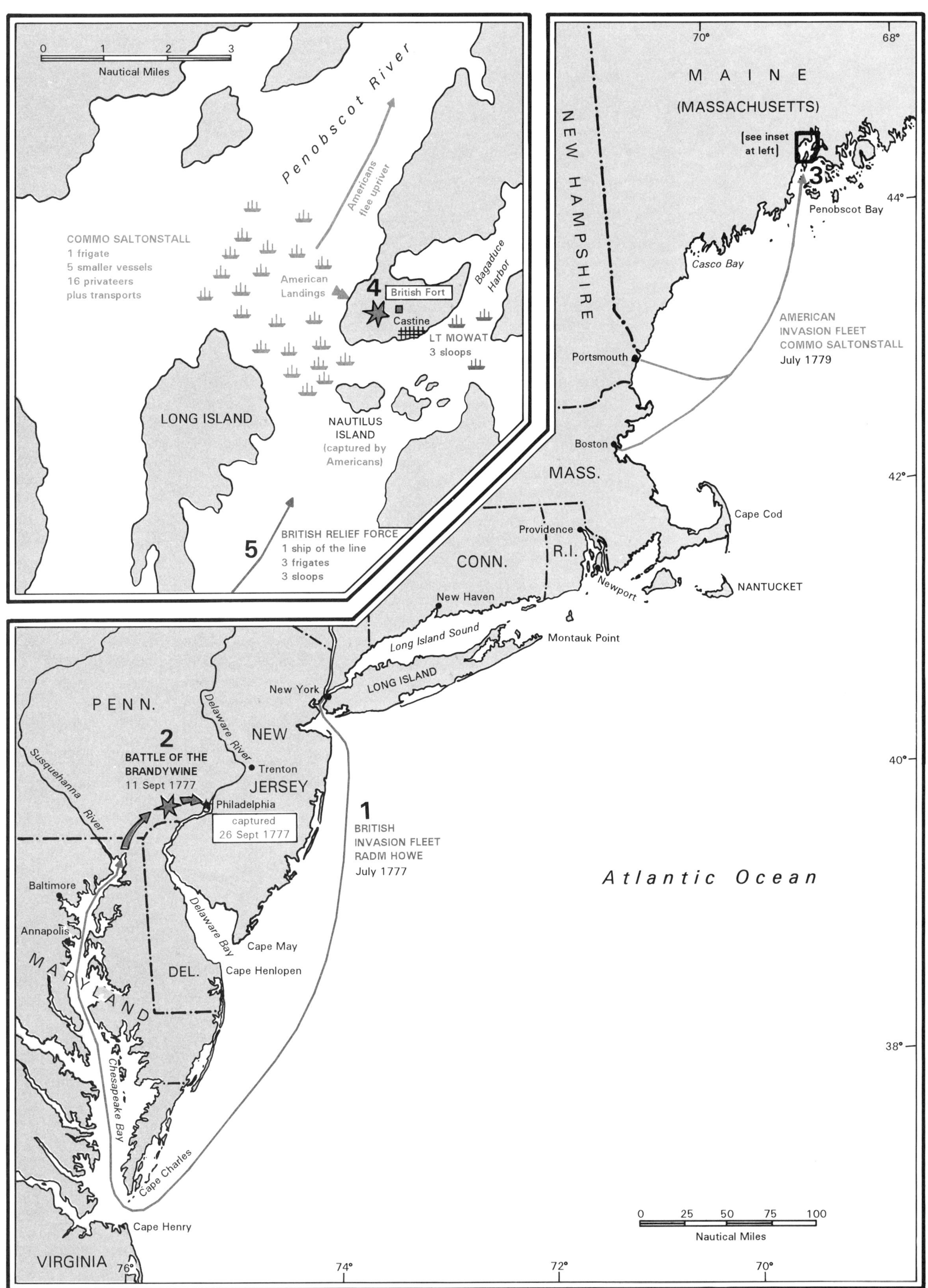

0
1
2
3
Nautical Miles
Penobscot River
Americans flee upriver
COMMO SALTONSTALL
1 frigate
5 smaller vessels
16 privateers
plus transports
American Landings
4
British Fort
Castine
Bagaduce Harbor
LT MOWAT
3 sloops
LONG ISLAND
NAUTILUS ISLAND
(captured by Americans)
5
BRITISH RELIEF FORCE
1 ship of the line
3 frigates
3 sloops
70°
68°
M A I N E
(MASSACHUSETTS)
[see inset at left]
3
44°
Penobscot Bay
NEW HAMPSHIRE
Casco Bay
AMERICAN INVASION FLEET
COMMO SALTONSTALL
July 1779
Portsmouth
Boston
MASS.
42°
Cape Cod
Providence
R.I.
CONN.
Newport
NANTUCKET
New Haven
Long Island Sound
Montauk Point
New York
LONG ISLAND
PENN.
NEW JERSEY
Delaware River
2
BATTLE OF THE BRANDYWINE
11 Sept 1777
Trenton
Susquehanna River
Philadelphia
captured
26 Sept 1777
1
BRITISH INVASION FLEET
RADM HOWE
July 1777
40°
Atlantic Ocean
Baltimore
Annapolis
MARYLAND
Delaware Bay
Cape May
DEL.
Cape Henlopen
38°
Chesapeake Bay
Cape Charles
Cape Henry
0
25
50
75
100
Nautical Miles
VIRGINIA
76°
74°
72°
70°

Map 5

In British Waters (The Battle of Flamborough Head)

February 1778–September 1779

Of all the naval efforts employed by the American rebels, the one that contributed most to the eventual American success was the war against British merchant shipping, much of which was conducted by a host of privately owned vessels known as privateers. Privateers were not pirates (though their victims often called them such), for they carried a privateering commission that was, quite literally, a license to steal. In addition, armed merchantmen could apply for what was known as a "letter of marque" that authorized them to take prizes as well, should the opportunity arise. Because Britain possessed the largest merchant fleet in the world, the seas thronged with potential victims.

This kind of warfare, often referred to by its French term as *guerre de course* (literally "war on commerce"), threatened Britain's transatlantic supply lines and brought the war home to the British public in a very real way. Maritime insurance rates at Lloyd's of London more than doubled as the number of privateers grew (eventually Congress issued more than two thousand letters of marque), and political support for the ministry's war policy eroded with every capture. In the end, the American rebels achieved their objective of independence not because they defeated Britain's Army or Navy but because the British government lost the political support necessary to continue the war. Commerce raiders—including privateers—played a major role in helping to erode that public support.

American privateers occasionally operated out of French ports as well. Through France was legally neutral until 1778, French authorities frequently turned a blind eye when American privateers used their ports to refit and resupply. Following the American victory at Saratoga in 1777, the French signed an alliance with the Americans, after which all French ports were opened to American privateers—and to Continental Navy warships as well. Among the more successful raiders of British commerce were Lambert Wickes and Gustavus Conyngham of the Continental Navy—and, of course, John Paul Jones. One of the ships that brought the news of Saratoga to the French court was Jones's Continental Navy sloop *Ranger,* 18. When Jones arrived in Quiberon Bay (1) on 14 February 1778, French warships in the harbor fired the first official salute to the U.S. flag ever offered by a foreign government. After completing his diplomatic mission, Jones took the *Ranger* into the waters around Britain, where he enhanced his reputation as an enterprising and determined commander. No privateer, Jones was not after booty. Glory was his coin. Sailing into the Irish Sea, where no enemy had dared to venture in a hundred years, Jones landed a small force at Whitehaven Bay (2), spiking the guns of the fort, and then continued on to St. Mary's Island (3), where he attempted to kidnap a British peer, the Earl of Selkirk, whom he planned to exchange for American prisoners of war. Frustrated in that objective when it turned out that the earl was not at home, Jones continued north and defeated a British sloop-of-war, the *Drake,* 20, in the North Channel (4) before circumnavigating Ireland to return to France.

There Jones petitioned Benjamin Franklin to use his influence to obtain another command for him. The best Franklin could do was an old French East Indiaman—a broad-beamed hermaphrodite vessel designed to carry cargo as well as to fight. Jones supervised significant modifications to the ship, and in honor of Franklin's "Poor Richard's Almanac" he christened it the *Bonhomme Richard.* In August of 1779 Jones set out from L'Orient in command of a small squadron consisting of his own ship, one American and one French frigate, and four smaller vessels, to sail around the British Isles. After taking a dozen prizes, half of them in the passage between the Orkney and Shetland Islands (5), the squadron dispersed, and Jones led three ships into the Firth of Forth (6), intending to capture the city of Leith and hold it for ransom. A strong gale in the confined waters of the firth compelled him to cancel the operation and continue south.

On 23 September 1779 in the North Sea off Flamborough Head (7), Jones's three vessels encountered a British convoy from the Baltic. While the British merchantmen fled for port, Jones squared off against the larger of the two British escorts, the frigate *Serapis,* and the French frigate took on the other escort, a twenty-gun sloop. The American frigate *Alliance* lingered briefly in the vicinity, firing broadsides into friend and foe alike, and then left the scene, for which her commander, a Frenchman named Pierre Landais, was subsequently stripped of his commission.

Early in the battle one of the *Bonhomme Richard*'s main deck guns exploded, suggesting that the eighteen pounders were unreliable, and Jones resolved to close with the enemy and take it by boarding. With his own hands he lashed the two ships together. In a lengthy night battle the *Bonhomme Richard* was battered so badly that the commander of the *Serapis,* Richard Pearson, asked if Jones had struck, whereupon Jones bellowed back, "I have not yet begun to fight!" Eventually a fire on the *Serapis,* ignited by an American hand grenade, threatened to reach the ship's magazine, and it was Pearson who was forced to strike. American sailors joined the British crew of the *Serapis* in fighting the fire while the *Bonhomme Richard* continued to take on water. After two days with the pumps manned constantly, Jones reluctantly ordered the crew to abandon ship, and on 25 September the *Bonhomme Richard* went down. Jones reached the Texel (8) in the *Serapis* with American colors flying over the British ensign.

Like the exploits of the privateers, Jones's heroics literally within sight of the British coast brought the war home to British citizens in a particularly dramatic way.

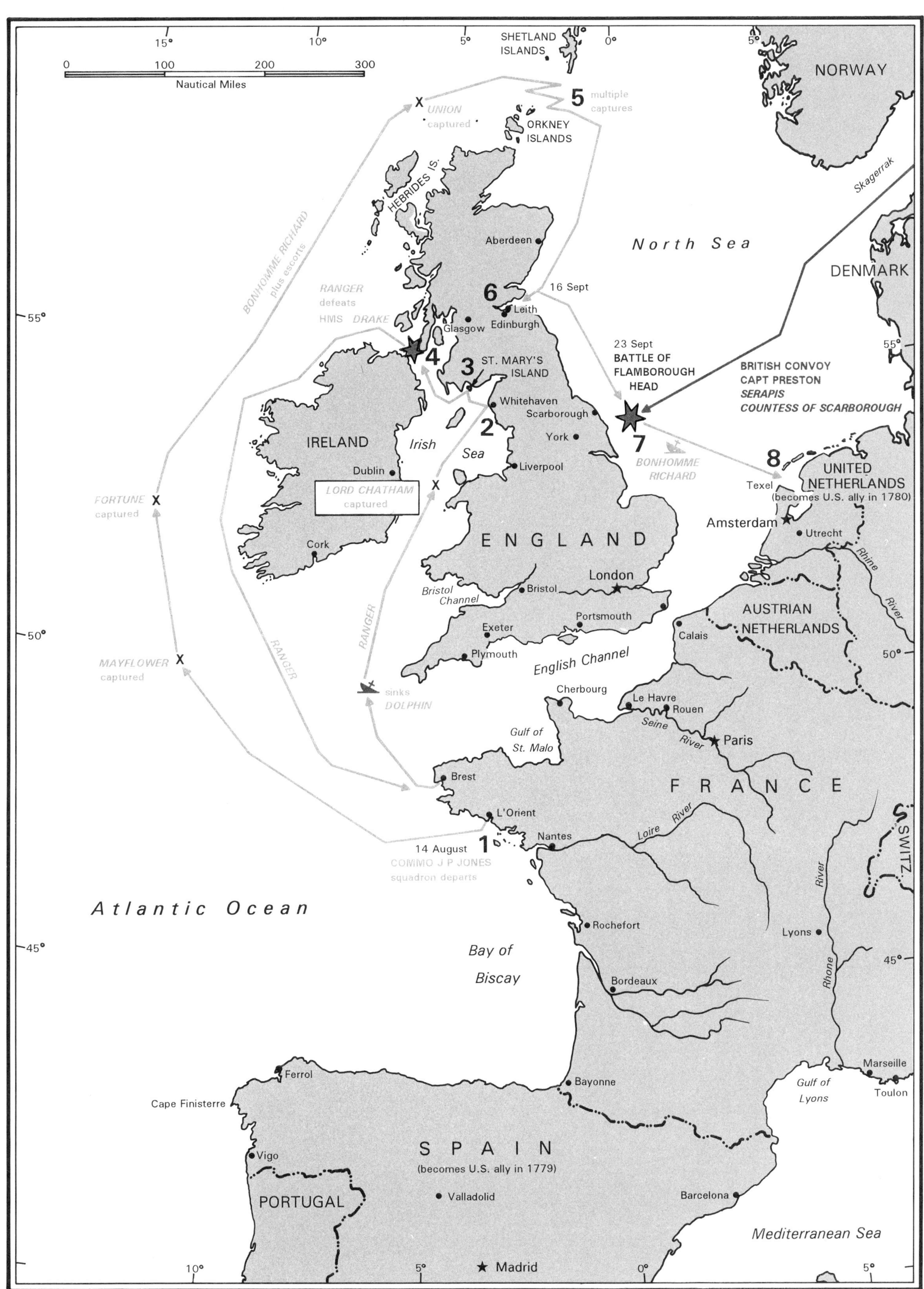

SHETLAND ISLANDS
NORWAY
Nautical Miles
5 multiple captures
UNION captured
ORKNEY ISLANDS
HEBRIDES IS.
BONHOMME RICHARD plus escorts
Skagerrak
North Sea
Aberdeen
DENMARK
RANGER defeats HMS DRAKE
6
16 Sept
Leith
Edinburgh
Glasgow
4
3 ST. MARY'S ISLAND
23 Sept
BATTLE OF FLAMBOROUGH HEAD
BRITISH CONVOY
CAPT PRESTON
SERAPIS
COUNTESS OF SCARBOROUGH
Whitehaven
Scarborough
2
IRELAND
Irish Sea
York
7
BONHOMME RICHARD
8
UNITED NETHERLANDS (becomes U.S. ally in 1780)
Texel
Dublin
Liverpool
LORD CHATHAM captured
FORTUNE captured
Amsterdam
Utrecht
Cork
ENGLAND
Rhine River
London
Bristol Channel
Bristol
AUSTRIAN NETHERLANDS
RANGER
Portsmouth
Exeter
Calais
MAYFLOWER captured
Plymouth
English Channel
sinks DOLPHIN
Cherbourg
Le Havre
Rouen
Seine River
Paris
Gulf of St. Malo
Brest
FRANCE
L'Orient
Loire River
Nantes
1
14 August
COMMO J P JONES squadron departs
SWITZ.
Atlantic Ocean
Rochefort
Lyons
Bay of Biscay
Bordeaux
Rhone River
Marseille
Toulon
Ferrol
Bayonne
Gulf of Lyons
Cape Finisterre
SPAIN (becomes U.S. ally in 1779)
Vigo
PORTUGAL
Valladolid
Barcelona
Mediterranean Sea
Madrid

MAP 6

CHARLESTON

FEBRUARY–MAY 1780

The American alliance with France forced British planners to reassess their strategy. Facing an expanded war, and unhappy with the lack of military progress in the northern and middle colonies, British policymakers curtailed their efforts to pacify New England and sought to change their fortunes by mobilizing pro-British sentiment in the southern colonies. Perhaps by organizing, arming, and supplying the Loyalists in the Carolinas and Georgia, the British could regain the upper hand in the war. As a base for the conduct of this new campaign, the British selected Charleston, South Carolina.

A British invasion armada left New York City for Charleston on 26 December 1779. It consisted of fourteen warships under VADM Marriot Arbuthnot and ninety transports bearing an army of 8,500 under the command of GEN Sir Henry Clinton. The expedition did not get off to a good start. Winter storms off Cape Hatteras scattered the British vessels literally all over the Atlantic. (One transport loaded with Hessian troops washed ashore on the coast of Cornwall in England.) Not until the first week of February 1780 was most of the British fleet reassembled in Tybee Roads almost one hundred miles south of Charleston.

The British did not attempt to force their way into Charleston Harbor in a *coup de main* because they had tried such a tactic four years earlier in 1776. Clinton had been the Army commander then, too, and he had landed his forces on Long Island (1) north of the city, while the naval commander, COMMO Peter Parker, anchored his ships off Fort Moultrie (2) on Sullivan's Island, intending to smash it into submission. Two of Parker's ships went hard aground on the bar (3), and American gunfire set a third ablaze. In addition, Fort Moultrie proved more resilient to the British cannonade than anyone had suspected, thanks mainly to its walls of spongy palmetto logs. Parker and Clinton had been forced to give up and return to New York.

This time, therefore, there would be no direct assault from the sea. Instead, the British fleet would act merely to cork the bottle of Charleston Harbor while the Army took Charleston by siege. While Arbuthnot's fleet took up positions outside the harbor's entrance, Clinton's 8,500 men marched overland from Edisto Inlet, thirty miles to the south. They crossed the Stono River (4), then after capturing Fort Johnson (5) on 6 March, they turned north to cross the Ashley River (6) and approach Charleston from the northwest, pinning the defenders inside the city.

The American defenders had a few thousand militiamen, under the command of MGEN Benjamin Lincoln, and a fleet of seven warships, including two frigates, commanded by COMMO William Whipple (7). Both Lincoln and Whipple knew that their position was not a strong one. The very geography that offered them good defensive positions also ensured that there would be no escape once a superior enemy occupied both the harbor's entrance and the land behind the city. The militarily correct move would have been to evacuate the city and save what they could of the soldiers and their equipment. But to abandon Charleston to its fate would have alienated southern Patriots and aided the British in their long-term goal to win the allegiance of the southern states. Lincoln, therefore, called for reinforcements and prepared to fortify the city. Some 2,500 Continental regulars joined him in March, raising his land strength to more than 5,000, still only about half the strength of Clinton's army, now augmented to nearly 10,000 men.

Whipple's small squadron of warships, including two of the Continental Navy's thirteen original frigates, was substantial by American standards, but it stood no chance against Arbuthnot's fleet, and so on 20 March, after removing the guns and other useful military equipment, Whipple scuttled his ships across the mouth of the Cooper River and transferred the crews to the shore fortifications. Meanwhile, Clinton closed in on the city from the landward side, and Arbuthnot did the same on the seaward side when, on 8 April, seven British frigates found a way over the bar and past Fort Moultrie to anchor off the city.

There was still one narrow escape route to the north across the Cooper River (8), which was blocked by Whipple's sunken ships and a log-and-chain boom. Lincoln asked the city council for permission to abandon the city and preserve his army, but the city fathers begged him to stay and save them. The issue was soon rendered moot when, in mid-April, Loyalist cavalry occupied Monck's Corner twenty miles north of the city, cutting the last avenue of escape.

In the formal tradition of siege warfare, Clinton notified Lincoln on 8 May that his army was in position to assault the city. Lincoln stalled and tried to bargain for terms, but Clinton held all the cards and refused to negotiate. After a terrifying all-night bombardment on 9 May, the city fathers who had pleaded with Lincoln to stay and save them now begged him to capitulate to prevent the destruction of the city. On 12 May Lincoln surrendered both the city and his army. It remains to this day the third largest U.S. military capitulation in history behind Bataan in World War II and Harpers Ferry in the Civil War.

The British had secured their base for the southern campaign, and for a few weeks at least it appeared that the predicted Loyalist support would indeed help the British turn the war around. Clinton returned to New York in June, leaving MGEN Charles Cornwallis behind with orders to pacify the countryside. But instead of leading to victory, Cornwallis's southern campaign would end in disaster at the small Virginia seaport of Yorktown.

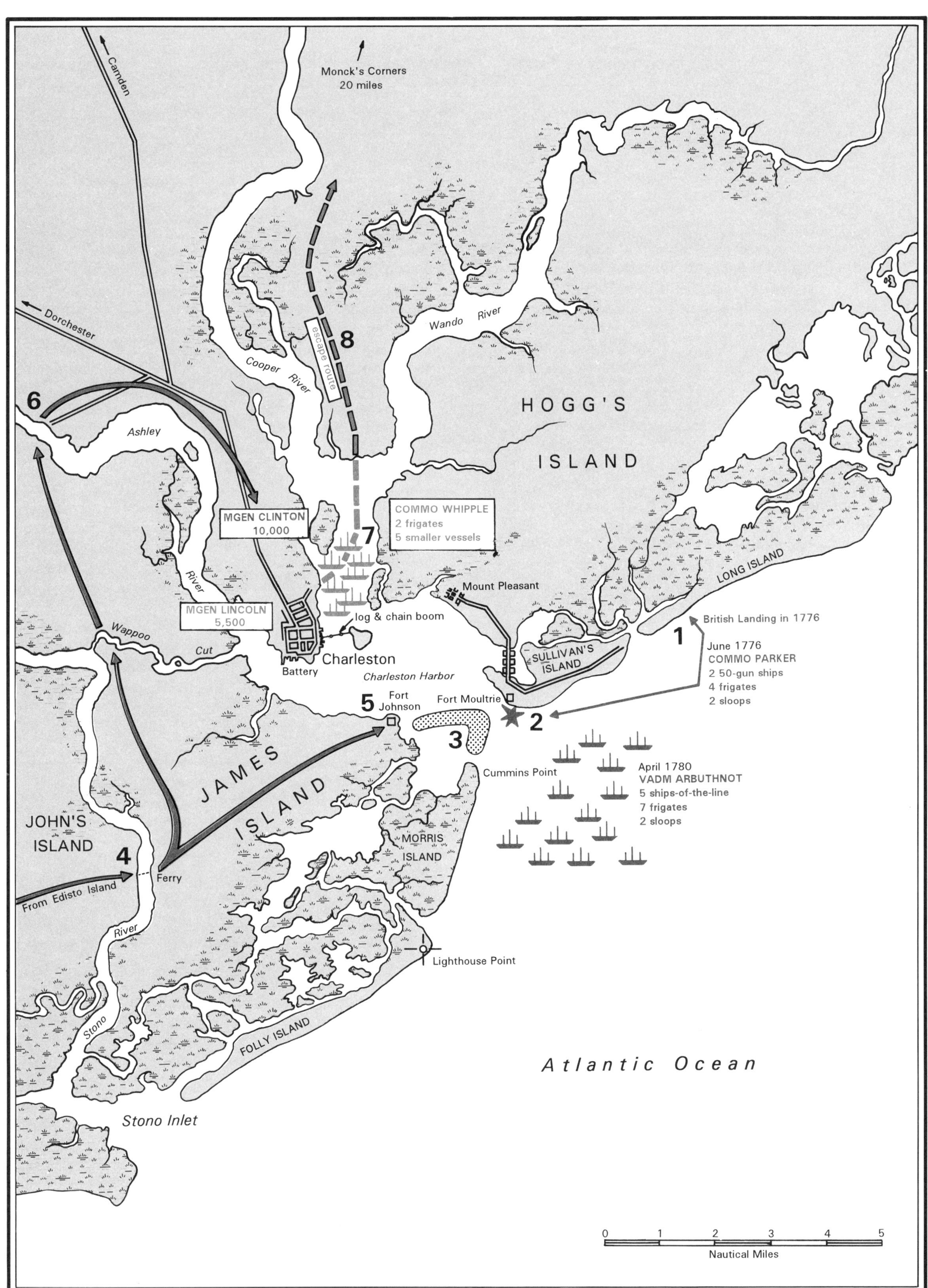

Camden
Monck's Corners
20 miles
Dorchester
escape route
8
Cooper River
Wando River
6
Ashley
HOGG'S
ISLAND
MGEN CLINTON
10,000
COMMO WHIPPLE
2 frigates
5 smaller vessels
7
River
Mount Pleasant
LONG ISLAND
MGEN LINCOLN
5,500
log & chain boom
Wappoo
Cut
Charleston
Battery
Charleston Harbor
British Landing in 1776
1
June 1776
COMMO PARKER
2 50-gun ships
4 frigates
2 sloops
SULLIVAN'S
ISLAND
Fort Moultrie
5
Fort
Johnson
2
3
Cummins Point
April 1780
VADM ARBUTHNOT
5 ships-of-the-line
7 frigates
2 sloops
JAMES
ISLAND
JOHN'S
ISLAND
MORRIS
ISLAND
4
Ferry
From Edisto Island
River
Lighthouse Point
Stono
FOLLY ISLAND
Atlantic Ocean
Stono Inlet
0
1
2
3
4
5
Nautical Miles

Map 7

The Yorktown Campaign

August–September 1781

The naval force that played the most important role in achieving American independence was not American at all; it was the French battle fleet of RADM François J. P. Comte de Grasse. Washington knew that as long as the Royal Navy commanded the sea, the British Army could never be pinned down and destroyed except when it ventured inland, as Burgoyne had done at Saratoga. Whenever British land forces got into trouble, they headed for the coast, where the Royal Navy could supply them, reinforce them, or if necessary evacuate them. Ever since the Americans had secured an alliance with France, Washington had hoped to bring the Franco-American Army and the French Navy together simultaneously to achieve local superiority. Alas, such a convergence was dauntingly difficult, given the communications capabilities of armies and navies in the eighteenth century. Washington first hoped to achieve a concentration against the British garrison in New York City, but circumstances led him instead to the Chesapeake Bay.

The sequence of events began with Cornwallis's campaign in the Carolinas. That officer found his orders to pacify the countryside beyond Charleston complicated by the need to garrison British outposts and deal with partisans like Thomas Sumter and Francis Marion (the Swamp Fox), as well as the small army of regulars skillfully commanded by MGEN Nathaniel Greene. But he dutifully embarked on a lengthy land campaign that occupied the summer and fall of 1780 and the winter of 1780–1781. Winning a few small victories, though often at heavy cost, Cornwallis worked his way north through the Carolinas and into Virginia, ending up at Yorktown (1) in need of supplies and support.

Meanwhile, Washington learned that de Grasse was planning to bring his fleet from the Caribbean to American waters in the fall. At once he began to develop plans for a combined operation against British-occupied New York, and he urged MGEN Jean Baptiste Comte de Rochambeau to bring his four thousand–man French Army from Newport to join him. Rochambeau started his army marching southward in the first week of July (2). Even with Rochambeau's forces, however, Washington could amass no more than 9,000 men, not enough to dislodge Clinton's 14,500, and so with some reluctance he agreed to attempt instead a concentration against Cornwallis's army in Virginia.

On 14 August Washington received a letter from de Grasse informing him that his fleet would arrive in the Chesapeake Bay at the end of the month. Exactly a week later Washington left behind a small force of 2,500 under MGEN William Heath to watch New York and started south with an army of 7,000 men—4,000 of them Rochambeau's army—on a long trek from the Hudson River highlands across New Jersey and through Philadelphia to the headwaters of the Elk River (3). Soon afterward French COMMO Jacques M. Comte de Barras put to sea from Newport with six ships-of-the-line and four frigates, plus eighteen transports carrying Rochambeau's artillery train (4). The campaign against Cornwallis would work only if all these forces—French and American, land and naval—came together at the same time without mishap.

The key element, de Grasse's fleet of twenty-eight ships-of-the-line, was already en route, having left the West Indies two weeks earlier on 5 August. The British commander in the Caribbean, ADM Sir George Rodney, knew of de Grasse's departure but assumed that the French admiral would leave half his force behind to protect French colonies in the Lesser Antilles. Accordingly, Rodney decided to send his second in command, RADM Sir Samuel Hood, with only fourteen ships-of-the-line, in pursuit. Then Rodney sailed for England with four ships-of-the-line, vessels that might have changed history if they had gone with Hood instead.

Though Hood did not know where de Grasse was headed, there were only two possibilities: the Chesapeake or New York. Setting a direct course for Virginia, Hood arrived at the entrance to the Chesapeake on 25 August (5), unaware that the French fleet had taken a longer route, stopping briefly at Havana. Hood looked into the Chesapeake, saw no sign of the French, and concluded that de Grasse was headed for New York. Without delay he set sails once again and headed north, looking into the Delaware Bay (6) en route.

Someone standing on the Cape Henry headland on 26 August might have seen the last British warship disappear over the horizon to the north just as the first ships of de Grasse's fleet came up from the south (7). By 30 August the French fleet was safely anchored in Lynnhaven Bay just inside Cape Henry. De Grasse had some 2,500 French soldiers on board, and these, combined with the small force of Americans already in Virginia under the Marquis de Lafayette, would be sufficient to hold Cornwallis in place until the French fleet could ferry the rest of the Franco-American Army from the northern end of the Chesapeake Bay to the Yorktown peninsula. Cornwallis was trapped.

Meanwhile, Hood arrived at New York (8) on 28 August to discover that the French were not there either. He leaped to the correct conclusion that he had outsailed de Grasse and that the French had headed for the Chesapeake after all. Moreover, he also learned that Commodore de Barras had sailed from Newport, and presumably he, too, was bound for the Chesapeake. Hood convinced the British naval commander in New York, RADM Thomas Graves (who was senior), that the American feints and maneuvers outside New York were merely a ruse and that the Chesapeake was the crucial theater. On 1 September Graves brought five of his eight ships-of-the-line over the bar to join Hood's fourteen, and the combined British fleet headed south for a confrontation with de Grasse.

MASS.
Providence
Hartford
MGEN COMTE de ROCHAMBEAU 4,000
NEW YORK
Hudson River
2
CONNECTICUT
Newport
15 August De BARRAS sails
New Haven
0 25 50 75
Nautical Miles
Long Island Sound
GEN WASHINGTON 5,000
MGEN CLINTON 14,500
PENNSYLVANIA
LONG ISLAND
Morristown
New York
4
Middlebrook
RADM GRAVES 8 ships-of-the-line
8
Sandy Hook
Princeton
28 August RADM HOOD arrives
RADM COMTE de BARRAS
6 ships-of-the-line
4 frigates
18 transports (with siege guns)
Trenton
Susquehanna River
Philadelphia
Chester
Wilmington
NEW JERSEY
3
Baltimore
Delaware Bay
Annapolis
DELAWARE
6
MARYLAND
HOOD 14 ships-of-the-line
Chesapeake Bay
Atlantic Ocean
LAFAYETTE 5,000
1
Yorktown
CORNWALLIS 7,500
Cape Charles
5
25 Aug RADM HOOD looks into Chesapeake Bay
Cape Henry
VIRGINIA
7
RADM HOOD
14 ships-of-the-line
from the West Indies
Albemarle Sound
NORTH CAROLINA
ADM COMTE de GRASSE
28 ships-of-the-line
from the West Indies
76°
74°
72°
40°
38°
36°

MAP 8

THE BATTLE OF THE CAPES

5 SEPTEMBER 1781

From their ships at anchor in Lynnhaven Bay (1), French lookouts spotted the topsails of the British fleet approaching from the north at 9:30 A.M. on 5 September. Though de Grasse was anxious to come to grips with the enemy, the tide was still coming in, and he, therefore, waited three hours for the tide to turn before giving the order to get under way. The twenty-four French ships-of-the-line then slipped their cables and set courses to round Cape Henry, seemingly trying to outdo one another in demonstrating their eagerness for battle. As a result, the French vessels bunched up about the headland and came straggling out of the Bay in an undisciplined mass, one group of five ships well ahead of the rest. Worse yet, from the French view, the rear division of ships failed to clear Cape Henry on a single tack and had to come about to gain an offing before following the rest of the fleet. This left a rather large gap in the French "line." Nevertheless, by 2:00 P.M. the French fleet was at sea, heading almost due east on the port tack to gain sea room. De Grasse's flagship, the giant three-decker *Ville de Paris,* was more or less in the middle of the pack.

Watching these maneuvers from the quarterdeck of his flagship, the *Barfleur,* Hood could see the battle developing in his mind's eye. He claimed later that he saw this as the moment when Graves should have hoisted the signal for "general chase," which would have sent the British fleet swooping down on the disorganized French ships while they were still jockeying for position around Cape Henry. Though the formal "Fighting Instructions," first set down nearly eighty years earlier, called for the fleet to remain in a disciplined line, Hood was one of several flag officers who believed those rules too rigid and confining. Now he saw an opportunity to mass on the French van while contrary winds held back the trailing ships in the French line.

Instead of "general chase," however, at about 2:00 P.M. Graves hoisted the signal to "wear together." The purpose of this maneuver was to reverse both the fleet's course and the order of ships in the line. In obedience to Graves's signal, each ship simultaneously turned south, then east, backing the main-topsail to kill headway, and then sheeting home on the port tack (2). But the maneuver was not an easy one, and it took an hour and a half before all nineteen ships were again in line, heading east toward the open sea on a parallel track with the French. The maneuver achieved what Graves had wanted: he continued to hold the weather gage and had placed his fleet opposite his enemy on a parallel track. But the execution of this maneuver afforded the French the time they needed to sort out their battle line.

At 3:45 P.M., with the two fleets now on parallel courses a mile or two apart (see lower map), Graves hoisted the signal "to bear down and engage." The appropriately named RADM Francis Drake, commanding the British van, did just that (3), opening fire at 4:15. But Graves's flagship, the *London,* continued to fly the signal for maintaining the line ahead, meaning that each captain was to keep his ship a strict cable's length behind the vessel in front of him. Hood, whose ships now made up the rear division, was inclined to take that signal literally. As long as Graves flew the signal to maintain line ahead, Hood felt obligated to hold his place in the line, benignly following the ships in front of him (4).

At about the time that the van ships opened fire, Graves hauled down the line-ahead signal, but ten minutes later he hoisted "line ahead, close action," intending for all ships in the fleet to engage their opposite number in the French line. But it was a signal that was subject to misinterpretation. Whether from pique or stubbornness, Hood remained where he was. Finally, at 5:20 Graves replaced this signal with the less ambiguous "close action," and Hood at last brought his division of ships into the fight. But less than an hour later the French took advantage of holding the lee gage to bear away. The battle died out at about 6:30 as the two fleets separated in the gathering dusk.

Though neither commander knew it at the time, the battle was over. For two more days the fleets maneuvered within sight of each other in blustery weather. Several British ships had been badly battered—one, the *Terrible,* was leaking so badly it had to be abandoned. Meanwhile, de Grasse maneuvered his fleet to seize the windward gage, thus gaining the initiative. But his strategic objective was not to destroy the enemy, it was to hold the Chesapeake Bay—something Graves apparently never figured out. On 11 September de Grasse ordered his fleet to return to Cape Henry, and there he discovered that de Barras had successfully brought his squadron into the Bay, safely delivering Rochambeau's siege artillery and increasing the French battle fleet to thirty ships-of-the-line. Graves had little choice now but to return to New York and leave Cornwallis to his fate.

A modest tactical victory for the French, the Battle of the Capes was nevertheless the decisive naval engagement of the war, for it led directly to Cornwallis's eventual surrender. Hemmed in by the Franco-American Army on land and de Grasse's fleet at sea, Cornwallis knew the game was up. A month after the battle, on 17 October, he asked for terms. His surrender two days later did not necessarily mean the end of the war, but news of the disaster made it impossible for the prowar ministry to retain power in the House of Commons. The prime minister, Lord North, saw it at once. When he heard of Cornwallis's surrender at Yorktown, he threw up his hands and cried, "Oh God, it is all over!"

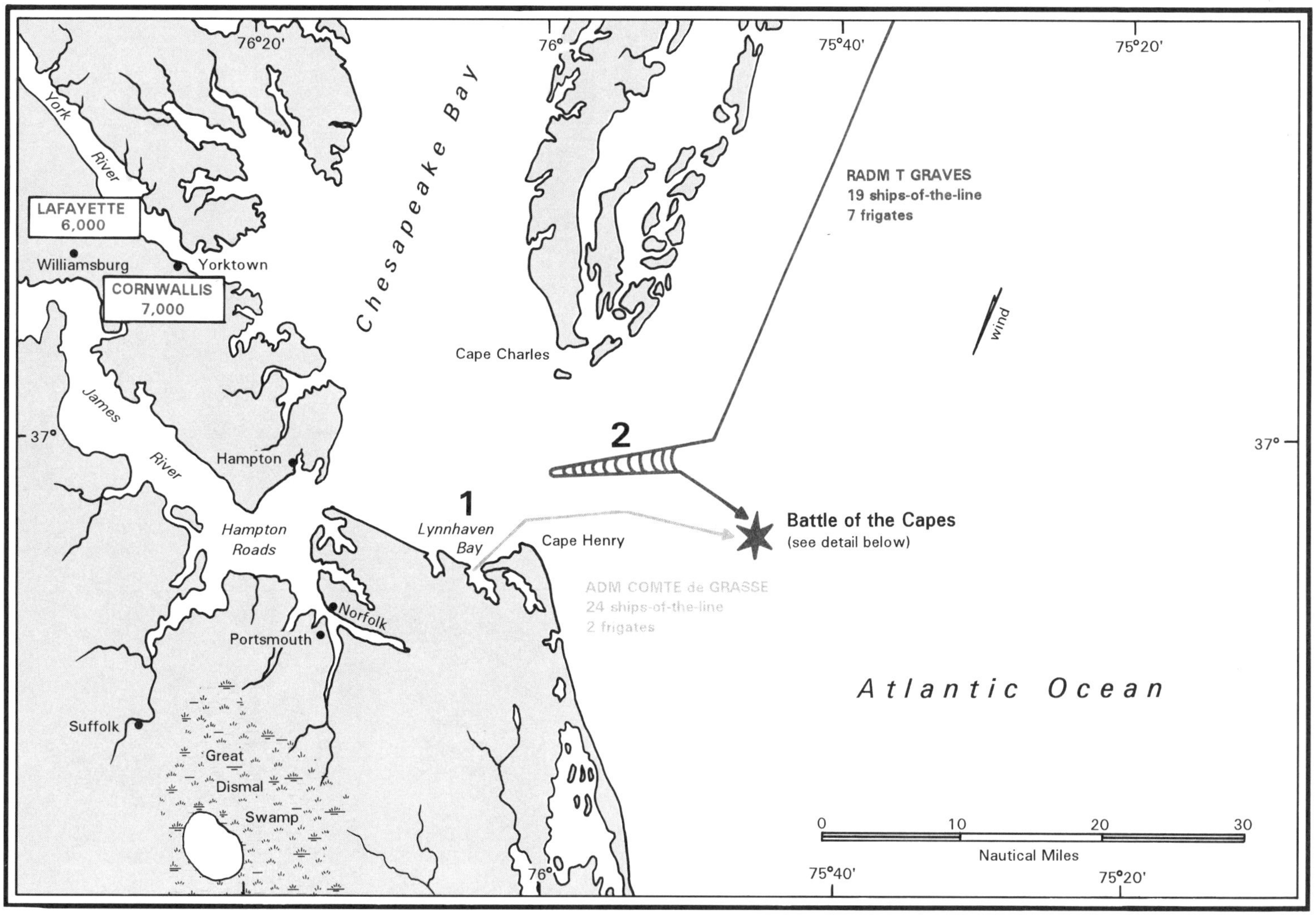

76°20'
76°
75°40'
75°20'
York River
Chesapeake Bay
RADM T GRAVES
19 ships-of-the-line
7 frigates
LAFAYETTE
6,000
Williamsburg
Yorktown
CORNWALLIS
7,000
wind
Cape Charles
James River
37°
2
Hampton
37°
1
Lynnhaven Bay
Hampton Roads
Cape Henry
Battle of the Capes
(see detail below)
ADM COMTE de GRASSE
24 ships-of-the-line
2 frigates
Norfolk
Portsmouth
Atlantic Ocean
Suffolk
Great Dismal Swamp
0 10 20 30
Nautical Miles
76°
75°40'
75°20'

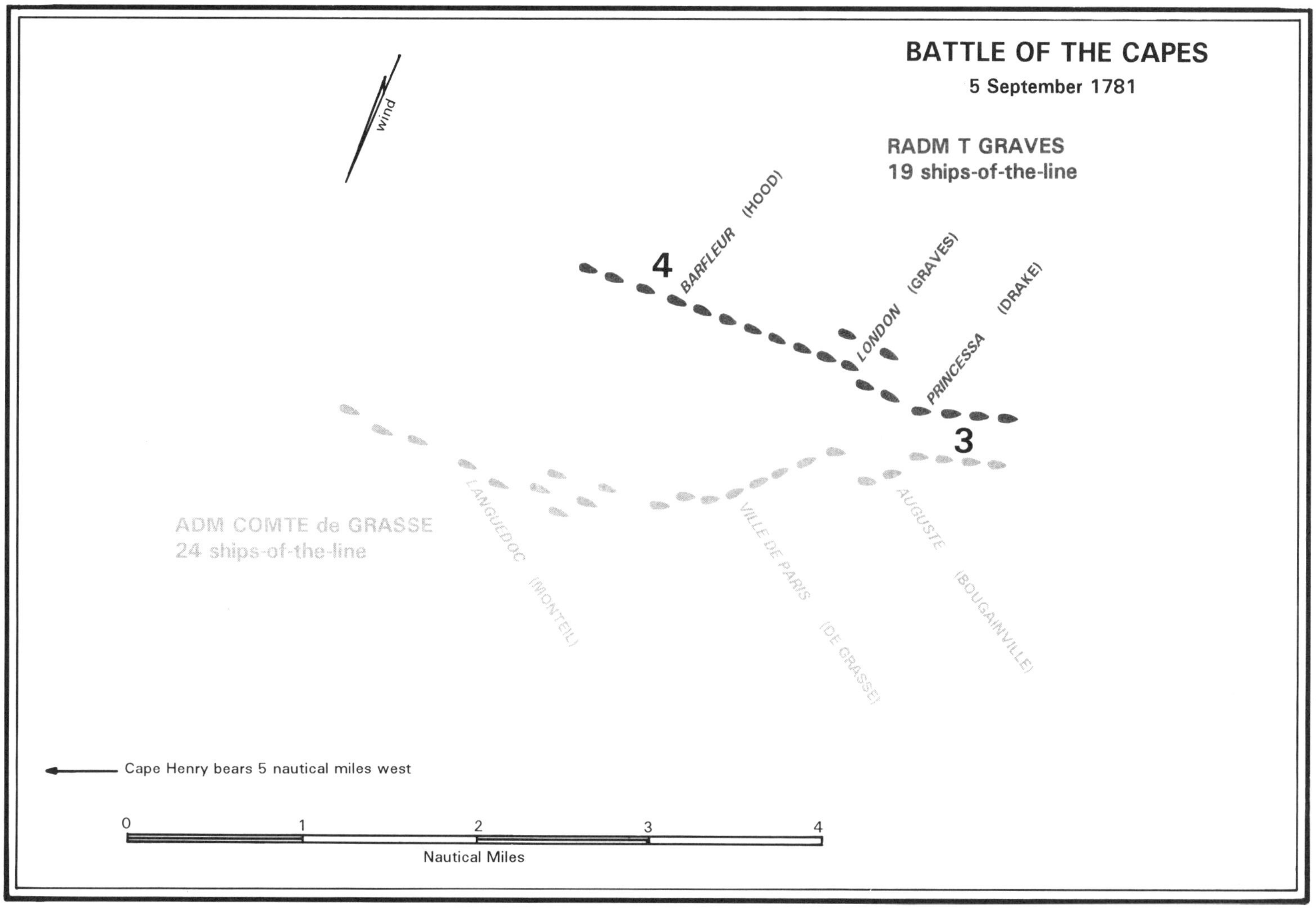

BATTLE OF THE CAPES

5 September 1781

wind

RADM T GRAVES
19 ships-of-the-line

4
BARFLEUR (HOOD)
LONDON (GRAVES)
PRINCESSA (DRAKE)
3

ADM COMTE de GRASSE
24 ships-of-the-line

LANGUEDOC (MONTEIL)
VILLE DE PARIS (DE GRASSE)
AUGUSTE (BOUGAINVILLE)

Cape Henry bears 5 nautical miles west

0 1 2 3 4
Nautical Miles

PART II

The Age of Sail 1783–1812

THE WAR WON AND INDEPENDENCE SECURED, it seemed to most Americans that the need to sustain a military establishment or a naval force had ended as well. The Articles of Confederation, drafted during the war and ratified in March 1781, said almost nothing about a Navy. That document declared that no individual state could maintain a private navy or issue letters of marque "unless such state be infested by pirates." As for a national Navy, the Articles specified only that nine of the thirteen states had to approve the construction or purchase of ships of war or the appointment of a commander in chief. Beyond that, the Articles were silent on the issue. Within a single decade, however, dissatisfaction with this instrument of government led to the adoption of the Constitution, Article I, Section 8 of which specified that Congress had power "to provide and maintain a Navy." Indeed, in the *Federalist Papers* Alexander Hamilton argued that this was one of the strengths of the Constitution, and he envisioned a day when American ships-of-the-line would hold the balance of power between England and France.

Though the ratification of the Constitution in 1789 gave Congress the *authority* to establish a Navy, it was by no means clear to most Americans that there was any immediate *need* to do so. It was hard for most Americans to imagine who or what might constitute a military threat to the new nation. Hamilton notwithstanding, most Americans shared the Whig prejudice against standing armies in peacetime, seeing them more as potential instruments of tyranny than as a means of national defense. Likewise, most conceived of national navies as expensive and unnecessary baubles of big government. Ships-of-the-line, they believed, were tools of empire, not defenders of democracy. Americans believed that the key to the nation's security was the militia, symbolized by the minuteman of Lexington—the citizen soldier who would spring to arms in time of danger and muster on the village common.

The frigate Philadelphia *bursts into flame in Tripoli Harbor within sight of the bashaw's castle. The Tripolitans had seized the* Philadelphia *after it grounded on an uncharted sandbar in October 1803, and LT Stephen Decatur led a volunteer crew that stole into the harbor late on the evening of 16 February 1804 and set the ship afire, an exploit that Britain's Lord Nelson called the most daring act of the age (see map 11). (Library of Congress)*

Partly as a result of such views, the nation divested itself of what remained of its small Navy in the 1780s. The few surviving vessels of the Continental Navy were sold off or, in the case of the ship-of-the-line *America,* given away to France as a gesture of thanks, and by 1785 the Navy had simply ceased to exist. Though a few people bemoaned the fact, the disappearance of the Navy caused hardly a stir of debate.

In the next decade, however, events in the Mediterranean and Europe inaugurated a national debate about the need for a national naval force. The outbreak of the French Revolution in 1789, the same year the U.S. Constitution was ratified, led in due course to a renewal of the Anglo-French warfare that had been commonplace in Europe for a century. Once again Britain mobilized its fleet, clamped a blockade on the French coast, and sought allies who could carry on a ground war against its historic enemy. Hamilton saw this as an opportunity for the United States to cast its weight in the balance of power, align with Britain, and emerge as at least a minor power. Others wondered if the United States was not morally and legally bound to come to the aid of France in accordance with the terms of the Treaty of 1778. Thomas Jefferson in particular believed that the revolutionary movement in France was ideologically compatible with American ideals. President Washington wanted most of all to avoid any involvement, and he chose neutrality, accepting Alexander Hamilton's view that the 1778 treaty with France had been made with the French monarchy, which no longer existed. Most Americans were relieved. They saw the renewal of the Anglo-French war as one more reason to keep Europe at arm's length.

Alexander Hamilton was the chief spokesman for those who favored the construction of a fleet of warships modeled on that of the Royal Navy. Hamilton argued that an American fleet of ships-of-the-line would force both Britain and France to offer concessions to secure American friendship. (National Archives)

Thomas Jefferson believed that the primary function of an American Navy should be defensive. He was willing to use force against the Barbary powers (see maps 10–11) but was wary of building the kind of fleet that would make the United States a player in the game of European power politics. (National Archives)

But despite Washington's desire to avoid entanglement, circumstances made that impossible. In December of 1793 Portugal announced that it would join the British-led coalition to check the growth of French power. This decision affected the United States because up to that moment Portugal had concentrated its naval forces in the Strait of Gibraltar, keeping the corsairs of the North African city-states, particularly Algiers, out of the Atlantic sea-lanes. To concentrate on the war against France, however, the Portuguese Navy planned to abandon its war with Algiers. As a result, the raiders of the Barbary Coast would be free to attack American merchant ships not only in the Mediterranean but in the Atlantic as well. Only days later Washington asked Congress to take up the matter. Quickly, Congress resolved "that a naval force, adequate to the protection of the commerce of the United States against the Algerine corsairs, ought to be provided."

The Naval Act of March 1794 marked the rebirth of the U.S. Navy. It authorized the construction of six frigates—four of forty-four guns and two of thirty-six guns. Critics of a standing Navy supported the bill because it created a naval force with a specific object—pacification of the Algerine "pirates." These critics also inserted a clause specifying that if ongoing negotiations produced a peace with Algiers before the ships were completed, "no farther proceeding be had under this act."

Joshua Humphreys headed a trio of designers responsible for the construction of the six frigates, and he produced truly remarkable vessels. Larger than European frigates of the time, the Humphreys frigates also carried a greater spread of sails and more and heavier guns. While British frigates generally carried thirty-two or thirty-six guns, each firing a ball weighing eighteen pounds, Humphreys's frigates carried up to fifty guns, most of them twenty-four pounders, giving the American vessels more than twice the broadside throw weight of a British frigate. The hulls were constructed of tough Georgia live oak and built so strongly as to be nearly invulnerable to all but the heaviest shot.

But constructing such vessels took time and money—indeed more time and money than Congress had anticipated. Two years later none of the vessels was yet nearing completion, and in the meantime negotiations between the United States and Algiers had resulted in a treaty. The new agreement obligated the United States to pay a small annual tribute to Algiers in exchange for an Algerine agreement not to attack American merchant ships. Such an accommodation was typical of the relationship between European powers and the North African city-states, and only a few objected that it compromised national honor. The more pressing question was: what about the six frigates? Having poured so much money into them, Congress was reluctant to cancel the project altogether. But opponents of a standing Navy would charge duplicity if Navalists in Congress now insisted that the frigates be completed in spite of the onset of peace. In the end, the two sides reached a compromise: three of the six frigates would be finished—though they would not be manned or fully equipped—and there the matter stood until the next national crisis two years later.

The United States managed to sustain a precarious neutrality while the great powers of Europe slugged it out on land and sea. France demonstrated its revolutionary fervor by raising great armies and winning important battles on land, such as the one at Valmy in 1792, while the British reasserted their command of the sea with naval victories such as the Glorious First of June (1794). Having unilaterally renounced its treaty with

France, the United States watched the war from the sidelines, but Britain's command of the sea meant that American merchants could continue their profitable trade with Britain, especially after the ratification of an Anglo-American trade treaty (Jay's Treaty) in 1794. The French, of course, were unhappy with the hairsplitting interpretation that Americans had applied to the alliance of 1778, and they saw little distinction between British merchant ships supplying British garrisons and American ships doing the same. As a result, the French government authorized its warships and privateers—those few that managed to escape the British blockade—to seize any merchant ship trading with British ports. At the same time the French government signaled its unhappiness with the United States by refusing to receive the new American ambassador, Charles Cotesworth Pinckney.

Hoping to avoid an open break with France, President Adams sent a delegation of three men to Paris to seek an accommodation, but when representatives of the French government (identified in the official documents only as X, Y, and Z) demanded a payment of a quarter million dollars for an audience with the French foreign minister, Charles Maurice de Talleyrand, the three Americans had to confess that such funds were not available. News of the French demand enraged Congress, which responded defiantly, quickly passing a resolution to complete all six of the frigates that had been authorized in 1794. Other bills, passed in quick succession, authorized the purchase of sixteen small sloops-of-war and, most far-reaching of all, the establishment of a Navy Department.

Over the next decade, the Navy thus established would fight two undeclared naval wars—against the French in the Caribbean (1798–1800) and against Tripoli in the Mediterranean (1801–1805). As many had feared, the United States would also be drawn into the war in Europe. In these conflicts, the U.S. Navy experienced its first trials by fire and developed the traditions and leadership that would lay the foundation for future greatness.

The U.S. Frigate Constellation *was the first of the six frigates authorized by Congress in 1794 to be commissioned in 1797. Known as the "Yankee racehorse," the* Constellation *was reputedly the fastest of the Humphreys-designed frigates, and under the command of CAPT Thomas Truxtun it won two important victories during the Quasi War (see map 9). (Painting by P. Melville, official U.S. Navy photo)*

Edward Preble was the hero of the Barbary Wars. By maintaining a blockade of Tripoli and directing several vigorous attacks on the city, he laid the groundwork for a satisfactory peace. Because he served as a role model for the junior officers in his squadron, many of them came to think of themselves as "Preble's Boys." (U.S. Naval Academy Museum)

MAP 9

THE QUASI WAR

APRIL 1798–OCTOBER 1800

During the debate over how to respond to the French demand for a substantial payment to ensure an audience with the French foreign minister, outraged congressmen coined the slogan "Millions for defense, but not one cent for tribute." Of course, this saying ignored the fact that the United States had been paying tribute to several of the Barbary States for years. Nevertheless, the outrage was real enough, and in April Congress authorized American warships to seize "armed vessels under authority or pretense of authority from the Republic of France." Congress stopped short of an open declaration of war, however, and as a result the conflict that ensued has gone down in history as the Quasi War, though it was real enough to those who fought in it.

The first clash of the war resulted in a modest American victory when the sloop *Delaware,* 20, commanded by Stephen Decatur (father of the more famous Stephen Decatur of the Barbary Wars), captured the French privateer *Croyable,* 18, off the coast of New Jersey in July. Soon afterward, however, the scene of war shifted to the Caribbean, and except for a brief foray into the Far East by the *Essex* in 1800, the Caribbean remained the principal seat of the war.

COMMO John Barry led the first American squadron into the Caribbean early in July, but other vessels followed within weeks, and by the end of the year there were thirteen U.S. Navy warships plus eight revenue cutters (forerunners of the U.S. Coast Guard) deployed in four squadrons throughout the West Indies. Barry commanded the largest squadron based in Prince Rupert's Bay on the British island colony of Dominica (1), strategically situated between the French islands of Martinique and Guadaloupe. Though the United States was not officially allied to Britain in this war, the British were only too happy to help the Americans fight the French and even shared their signal codes. Another substantial squadron, commanded by COMMO Thomas Truxtun in the *Constellation,* 38, operated out of St. Christopher (2), while smaller squadrons patrolled the Windward Passage between Cuba and Haiti (3), and the northern coast of Cuba (4).

This remarkable mobilization of naval forces was possible in large part because of the leadership of the first Secretary of the Navy, forty-seven-year-old Marylander Benjamin Stoddert, who presided with enthusiasm and efficiency over the naval buildup. In addition to ensuring the completion of the six original 1794 frigates, Stoddert initiated construction of six more frigates and three sloops, and in the course of the war he orchestrated the conversion of some forty merchant vessels into warships. By 1800 the U.S. Navy boasted a total of fifty-five warships supported by a score of revenue cutters.

Though John Barry was the senior U.S. Navy officer during the Quasi War, the hero of the war was Thomas Truxtun, a former privateersman who was a skilled navigator and shiphandler with a reputation as a stern disciplinarian. On 9 February 1799, while on independent patrol just north of St. Kitts (5), Truxtun's *Constellation,* 38, encountered the French frigate *Insurgente,* 36. Though the two vessels were nominally equal, the *Insurgente* was handicapped from the outset by a sudden squall that carried off its main topmast, seriously reducing its maneuverability. During the fight, the French gunners fired on the uproll in an effort to wreck the *Constellation's* rigging, while the Americans shot low, striking the enemy's hull and inflicting serious casualties. The *Insurgente's* missing topmast affected her speed, and Truxtun forged ahead, crossing the Frenchman's bow and pouring a raking broadside down the length of the crippled frigate. Within an hour it was over. The French captain struck his flag, and an American prize crew took possession. While the *Constellation* had suffered only three casualties, seventy Frenchmen had been killed or wounded in the fight.

Dramatic as this victory was, Truxtun would soon outdo himself. Almost exactly a year later, still commanding the *Constellation,* Truxtun encountered the *Vengeance,* 50, some 150 miles west of Dominica (6). The *Vengeance* had a 40 percent advantage in weight of broadside, but Truxtun was convinced he could compensate with faster and more accurate fire. For more than five hours the two ships slugged it out in rough seas. Once again the French fired into the rigging and the Americans aimed at the French hull. So punishing were the American broadsides that the French captain tried three times to strike his flag, but amidst the noise of battle and in the gathering dark he could not make his intentions known. At length the French fire so weakened the *Constellation's* mainmast that it toppled and went over the side. As the American frigate drifted away to jury-rig a new mainmast, the *Vengeance* made off into the dark. Though Truxtun had not secured his prize, there was no doubt he had dominated the fight. The *Vengeance* had suffered more than one hundred casualties (compared with forty American casualties), and when it limped into port at Curaçao (7) five days later, its captain reported that he had fought an American ship-of-the-line.

The war ended with the Treaty of Môrtefontaine, signed in September 1800 and ratified in July 1801. In it the French agreed to accept the American interpretation of the Treaty of 1778 and to stop interfering with American merchant shipping. There was one more major engagement in the war before news of the treaty reached the Caribbean. On 12 October 1800, five hundred miles northeast of Guadaloupe (8), the American frigate *Boston,* 28, defeated and captured the French *Le Berceau,* 24. This victory, combined with those of Truxtun and the dozens of smaller successes won by U.S. vessels throughout the Caribbean, imbued the fledgling Navy with a sense of confidence and ensured its survival.

Benjamin Stoddert was America's first Secretary of the Navy and was largely responsible for the nation's rapid mobilization during the Quasi War with France. As the only administrator in the new department, Stoddert assumed strategic as well as managerial direction of the war. (Official U.S. Navy photo)

COMMO Thomas Truxtun commanded the frigate Constellation *in the two most dramatic ship duels of the Quasi War. A strict disciplinarian, he was also touchy on matters of personal honor and declined a subsequent command when the Navy Department refused to appoint a flag captain to serve under him. (Painting by Bass Otis, official U.S. Navy photo)*

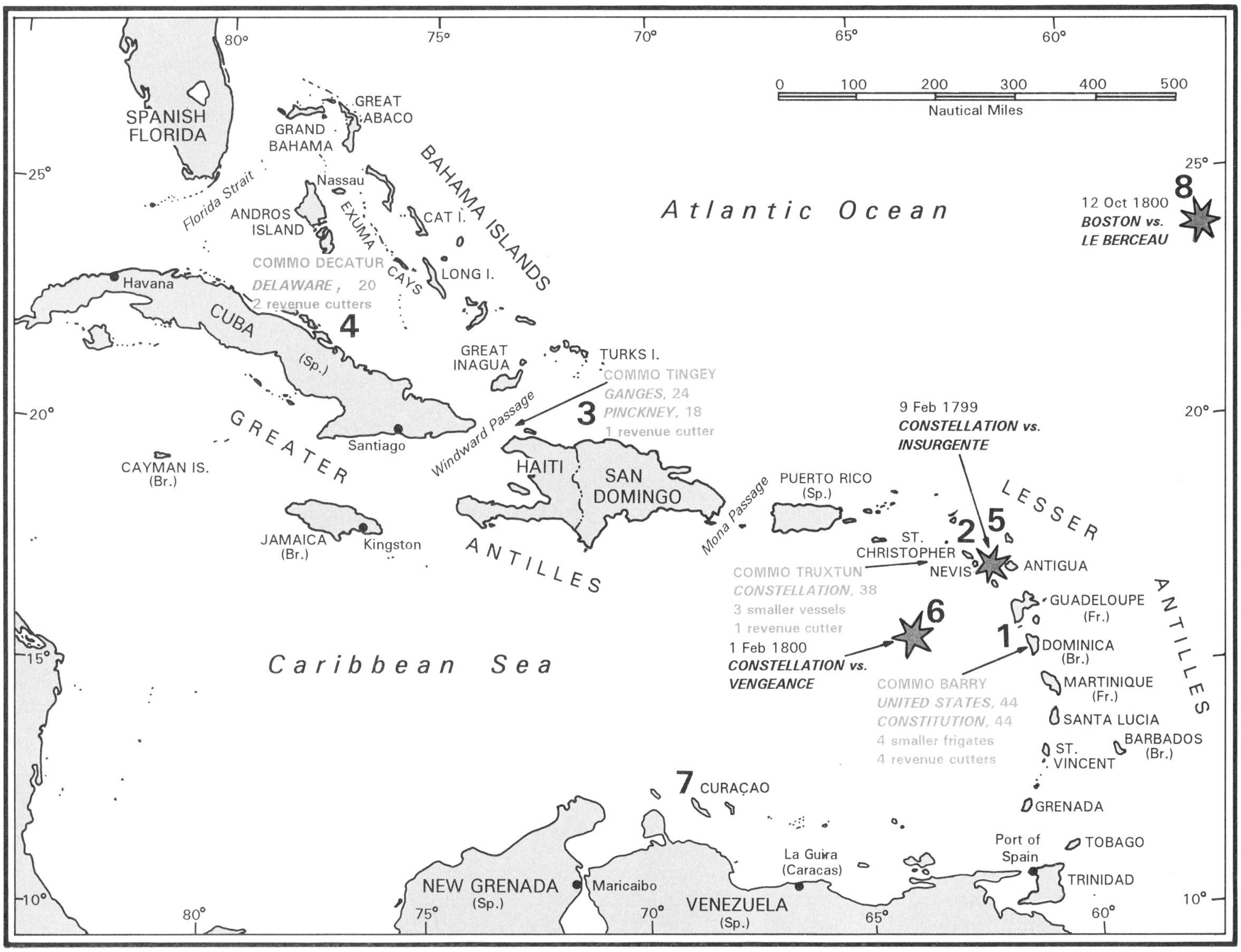

80° 75° 70° 65° 60°
0 100 200 300 400 500
Nautical Miles
25° 20° 15° 10°
SPANISH FLORIDA
GRAND BAHAMA
GREAT ABACO
Nassau
Florida Strait
ANDROS ISLAND
EXUMA CAYS
CAT I.
LONG I.
BAHAMA ISLANDS
Atlantic Ocean
8
12 Oct 1800
BOSTON vs. LE BERCEAU
Havana
CUBA (Sp.)
COMMO DECATUR
DELAWARE, 20
2 revenue cutters
4
GREAT INAGUA
TURKS I.
COMMO TINGEY
GANGES, 24
PINCKNEY, 18
1 revenue cutter
3
Windward Passage
Santiago
GREATER ANTILLES
CAYMAN IS. (Br.)
HAITI
SAN DOMINGO
JAMAICA (Br.)
Kingston
Mona Passage
PUERTO RICO (Sp.)
9 Feb 1799
CONSTELLATION vs. INSURGENTE
LESSER ANTILLES
ST. CHRISTOPHER
NEVIS
2 5
ANTIGUA
COMMO TRUXTUN
CONSTELLATION, 38
3 smaller vessels
1 revenue cutter
6
1 Feb 1800
CONSTELLATION vs. VENGEANCE
GUADELOUPE (Fr.)
1
DOMINICA (Br.)
COMMO BARRY
UNITED STATES, 44
CONSTITUTION, 44
4 smaller frigates
4 revenue cutters
MARTINIQUE (Fr.)
SANTA LUCIA
ST. VINCENT
BARBADOS (Br.)
GRENADA
Caribbean Sea
7 CURAÇAO
TOBAGO
Port of Spain
TRINIDAD
La Guira (Caracas)
NEW GRENADA (Sp.)
Maricaibo
VENEZUELA (Sp.)

Map 10

The Barbary Wars I

July 1801–September 1803

Throughout the naval war with France, the United States continued to make annual payments to several North African states in conformance with treaty arrangements made in 1796. The United States was not the only maritime nation to do so. Most of the European powers had calculated that it was both cheaper and easier to make annual payments to the rulers of these small states than it was to provide constant armed escorts for their merchantmen. As for the Muslim states of North Africa, war against the "infidel" Christians was always justified, and if it could be made profitable, so much the better.

West to east, there were four North African states that engaged in this form of naval extortion. The largest of them was the Empire of Morocco (1) across the strait from Gibraltar. Though Muslim like the rest of North Africa, Morocco was independent of the Ottoman Empire and was ruled by its own sultan (emperor), Moulay Suleiman, the most pacific of the North African rulers. Farther east, three much smaller city-states were all loosely bound to Selim III, grand seignor of the Ottoman Empire. Algiers (2) was ruled by a potentate known as a "dey," a word that translates loosely as "uncle"; Tunis (3) was ruled by a bey, from the Turkish word for gentleman; and Tripoli (4) was ruled by a pasha (or bashaw), who in 1800 was a wily and unscrupulous man named Yusuf Karamanli.

American problems with these four governments began almost from the moment of independence. Once American ships ceased to fly the British ensign, raising the Stars and Stripes in its place, they forfeited the protection of the Royal Navy. The 1796 treaties had bought a few years of peace at a modest cost—the treaty with Tripoli, for example, had cost the United States just $56,000 and required no annual fee. In the fall of 1800, however, Yusuf Karamanli decided that this was no longer adequate, and he notified the U.S. consul, James L. Cathcart, that continued peace depended on a new treaty that stipulated an annual payment of tribute. Cathcart's report of these demands arrived in the United States in mid-March 1801, only days after the inauguration of a new president, Thomas Jefferson.

Jefferson had consistently opposed tribute payments. He argued that a naval squadron sufficient to maintain peace in the Mediterranean was probably cheaper than making payments and was at least a fixed cost, whereas tribute payments were subject to constant upward revision—as Yusuf Karamanli's demands demonstrated. The news from Tripoli, therefore, confirmed Jefferson in his decision to send a naval "squadron of observation" to the Mediterranean. Jefferson's idea was to rotate a new squadron there every year, thus maintaining a constant American presence along the North African coast.

The first American squadron, three frigates and a sloop-of-war all under the command of COMMO Richard Dale, arrived at Gibraltar (5) on 1 July 1801. There Dale learned that Tripoli had declared war on 10 May. Leaving one of his frigates (the *Philadelphia*) behind to watch a Tripolitan ship in Gibraltar Harbor, Dale took the rest of his squadron to Tripoli (see lower map). The harbor at Tripoli was well protected by a rocky reef (6), a difficult approach, and the guns of a large citadel (7) and several smaller forts overlooking the harbor. Lacking clear instructions to conduct an offensive war, and unwilling to assume the responsibility himself, Dale acted tentatively and defensively, escorting American ships from place to place and maintaining a half-hearted blockade.

There were some bright spots during Dale's eight-month tenure of command. On 1 August LT Andrew Sterrett, in command of the *Enterprise,* 12, defeated the polacre *Tripoli,* 14, in a three-hour fight that left sixty of the Tripolitan's crew of eighty killed or wounded while the Americans did not suffer a single casualty. Lacking the authority to take prizes (Congress had still not declared war), Sterrett ordered the *Tripoli's* guns thrown overboard and sent the vessel limping back into port, where her captain received a hostile welcome from a furious bashaw who ordered him beaten and forced him to ride through the city sitting backwards on an ass.

Dale returned to the United States in April 1802 and resigned from the Navy. His replacement, COMMO Richard Morris, arrived at Gibraltar in June. News of the Tripolitan declaration of war had convinced Congress to authorize additional ships for the Mediterranean, and by midsummer Morris commanded a fleet of seven frigates and a sloop. But Morris proved an even greater disappointment than Dale. His decision to bring his wife and child to the scene of the war suggests that he did not anticipate a particularly violent tour of duty. In spite of clear orders to "proceed with the whole squadron under your command and lie off Tripoli," Morris decided that convoying American merchant ships around the Mediterranean was a better use of his force. Though he sent CAPT Alexander Murray in the *Constellation* to watch Tripoli, Morris himself did not arrive there for nearly a year, and then the only success the Americans could claim was a small expedition to burn a number of coasting grain ships east of Tripoli (8). In September 1803 Morris was suspended from command and recalled to the United States. A subsequent court of inquiry censured him for lack of diligence, and Jefferson dismissed him from the Navy.

In two years the Navy had been unable to take the war to Tripoli and convince Yusuf Karamanli that a war with the United States was not likely to be profitable. In June 1803, however, the course of the war changed dramatically with the arrival of a new U.S. commander in the Mediterranean—COMMO Edward Preble.

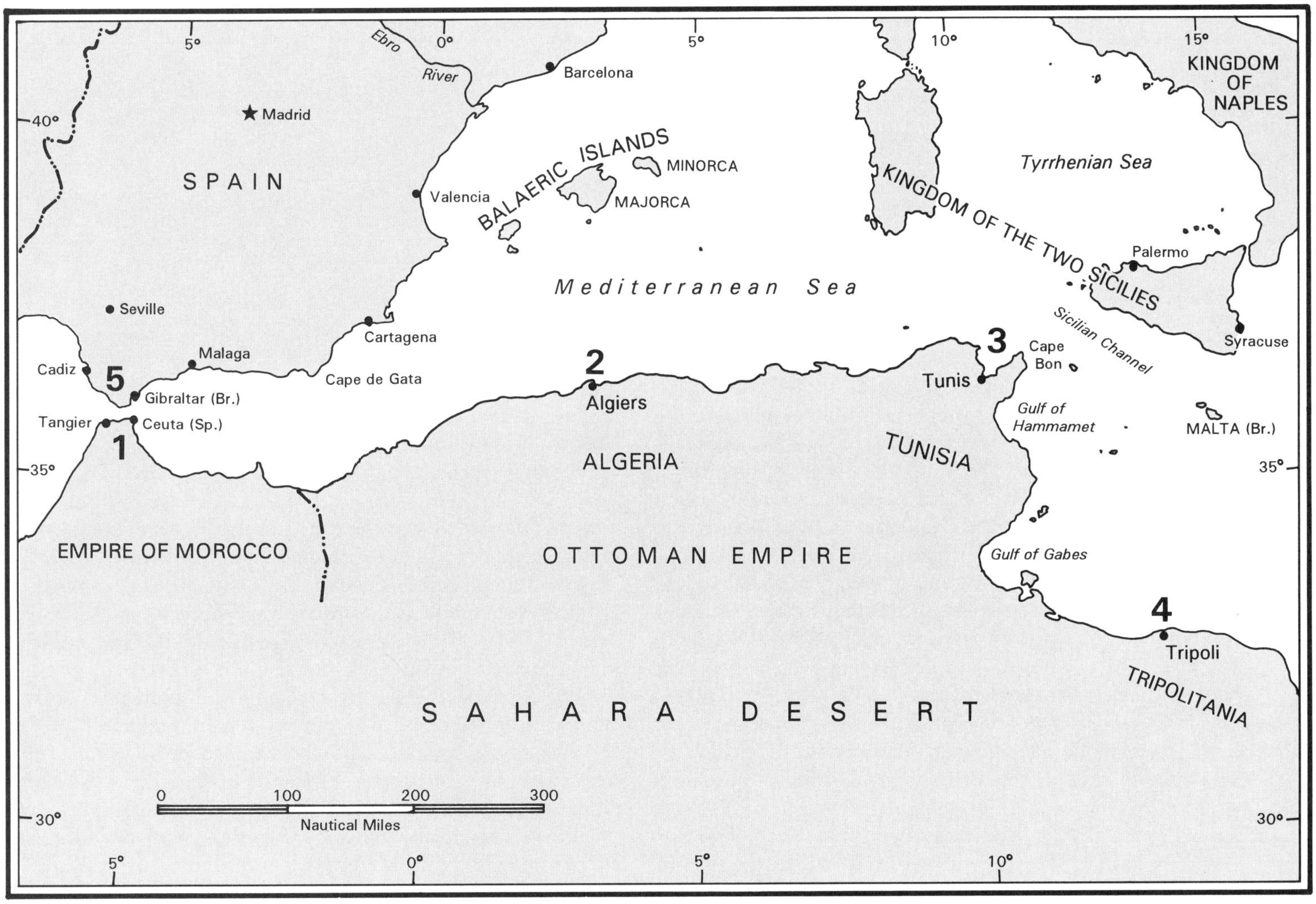

5° 0° 5° 10° 15°
Ebro River
Barcelona
KINGDOM OF NAPLES
40°
Madrid
SPAIN
BALAERIC ISLANDS
MINORCA
MAJORCA
Valencia
KINGDOM OF THE TWO SICILIES
Tyrrhenian Sea
Palermo
Mediterranean Sea
Seville
Cartagena
Sicilian Channel
Syracuse
Cadiz
5
Malaga
Cape de Gata
2
3
Cape Bon
Tunis
Gibraltar (Br.)
Algiers
Tangier
Ceuta (Sp.)
1
Gulf of Hammamet
MALTA (Br.)
ALGERIA
TUNISIA
35°
35°
EMPIRE OF MOROCCO
OTTOMAN EMPIRE
Gulf of Gabes
4
Tripoli
TRIPOLITANIA
SAHARA DESERT
0 100 200 300
Nautical Miles
30°
30°
5° 0° 5° 10°

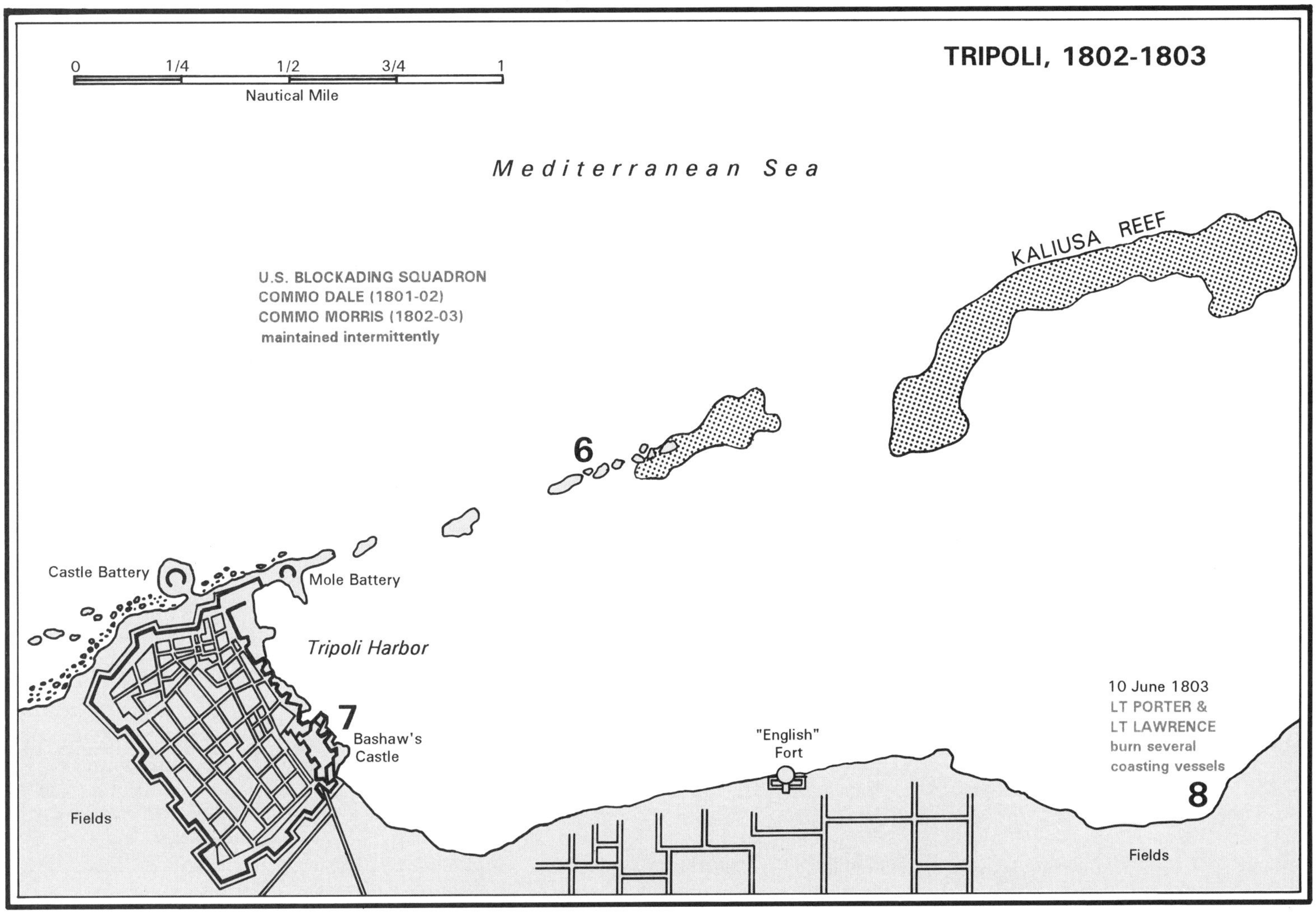

TRIPOLI, 1802-1803

0 1/4 1/2 3/4 1
Nautical Mile

Mediterranean Sea

KALIUSA REEF

U.S. BLOCKADING SQUADRON
COMMO DALE (1801-02)
COMMO MORRIS (1802-03)
maintained intermittently

6

Castle Battery
Mole Battery
Tripoli Harbor
7
Bashaw's Castle
"English" Fort
10 June 1803
LT PORTER &
LT LAWRENCE
burn several
coasting vessels
8
Fields
Fields

MAP 11

THE BARBARY WARS II

SEPTEMBER 1803–JULY 1805

After arriving at Gibraltar in September 1803, Preble sent the frigate *Philadelphia* and the sloop *Vixen* ahead to resume the blockade of Tripoli while he resolved a misunderstanding with the Empire of Morocco. That task satisfactorily accomplished, Preble set a course for Tripoli. En route he received appalling news: on 31 October William Bainbridge had run the *Philadelphia* hard aground on the uncharted Kaliusa Reef off the entrance to Tripoli Harbor (1). In an attempt to lighten ship, Bainbridge had ordered the ship's guns thrown overboard and had even had the foremast cut away, all to no avail. Unable to defend the ship, Bainbridge had decided that he had no option but to surrender. Two days later heavy swells floated the *Philadelphia* free of the reef, and the Tripolitans took possession of the ship, which now lay anchored under the guns of the citadel (2).

Shaken by this news, Preble contemplated his options. A cutting-out expedition to recapture the ship and sail out with it was unrealistic; the best that might be accomplished was somehow to destroy it. LT Stephen Decatur offered a plan to do exactly that. In December Decatur's ship the *Enterprise* had captured a Tripolitan ketch, the *Mastico,* which the Americans renamed the *Intrepid.* Decatur now suggested that he be allowed to lead a volunteer crew into the harbor in the *Intrepid* to burn the *Philadelphia* at its moorings. On the evening of 16 February 1804 the *Intrepid* limped into the harbor, posing as a vessel in distress, with more than eighty American volunteers hidden below decks (3). At 10:00 P.M. the vessel coasted up to the *Philadelphia,* and an Arabic-speaking pilot on board requested permission to tie up alongside. Not until the *Intrepid* was only a few yards away did the Tripolitans discover the ruse. Too late. Decatur and his men sprang aboard the *Philadelphia,* all shouting at once. Cutting down the guards, the Americans placed their inflammables, set them afire, then retreated to the *Intrepid.* As they made their way out of the harbor, with shot from the guns of the fort raining about them, flames on board the *Philadelphia* streamed up the rigging, and soon the entire vessel was ablaze.

The destruction of the *Philadelphia* removed a heavy weight from Preble's shoulders and won Decatur a captain's commission at the age of twenty-five, but it brought the Americans no closer to their objective. To convince Karamanli to accept peace, Preble planned to launch a direct attack on the city, and to do that he needed more shallow-draft vessels that could fight their way into the harbor. Preble borrowed six gunboats and two bomb ketches from Ferdinand IV, king of the Two Sicilies, who was also at war with Tripoli. With these small vessels, Preble directed a series of furious assaults throughout the month of August 1804.

The first attack took place on 3 August. Under Decatur's aggressive command, the American gunboats took on the Tripolitan gunboat fleet in two hours of furious hand-to-hand fighting (4) while the bomb ketches lobbed shells into the city and Preble's *Constitution* engaged the shore batteries. Decatur captured three enemy gunboats by boarding; three more were sunk; and the Americans suffered only fourteen casualties, though one of them was Decatur's younger brother James. Over the next four weeks Preble ordered four more attacks, including two at night that terrified the city's residents and sent many of them fleeing into the countryside. After each assault Preble sent Yusuf Karamanli a message suggesting negotiations and offering payments of $40,000, then $50,000, in exchange for the American prisoners from the *Philadelphia.* Karamanli scorned all such offers, and Preble continued to pound the city.

On 3 September 1804 Preble watched as the *Intrepid* was once again the centerpiece of a daring operation. LT Richard Somers guided the vessel, loaded this time with explosives, into the harbor where the *Intrepid's* volunteer crew intended to ground the vessel beneath the walls of the citadel, light the fuse to the explosives, and then escape in small boats. But the vessel was barely into the harbor's entrance when it exploded in a giant fireball, killing everyone on board (5). Though the cause of the explosion was unknown, Preble chose to believe that the Americans had been detected and had blown themselves up to avoid capture and to take a few of the enemy with them.

Less than a week later COMMO Samuel Barron arrived off Tripoli with substantial American reinforcements. Because Barron was senior, Preble chose to return home rather than remain in a subordinate position. Barron continued the American blockade, but he halted the naval attacks. Instead, he sanctioned a scheme proposed by the American consul at Tunis, William Eaton, to replace Yusuf Karamanli on the bashaw's throne with his older brother Hamet. Eaton found Hamet in Egypt and assembled a ragtag army of Europeans and Arabs, bolstered by half a dozen marines from the brig *Argus,* for a harrowing five hundred–mile journey along the coast toward Tripoli's back door (see lower map). In late April Eaton and Hamet reached Derna (6), which they captured in cooperation with the American brigs *Argus* and *Hornet* and the schooner *Nautilus.* Fearful now for his throne, Yusuf Karamanli accepted the latest American offer of $60,000 for the release of the American prisoners, and he approved a new treaty that did not require tribute payments. The American objective now accomplished, the United States abandoned its support of Hamet, to Eaton's great disgust.

The application of naval force in the Mediterranean had won a satisfactory peace with the North African city-states. At the same time, it had provided a testing ground for a generation of young officers who would be proud to call themselves "Preble's boys."

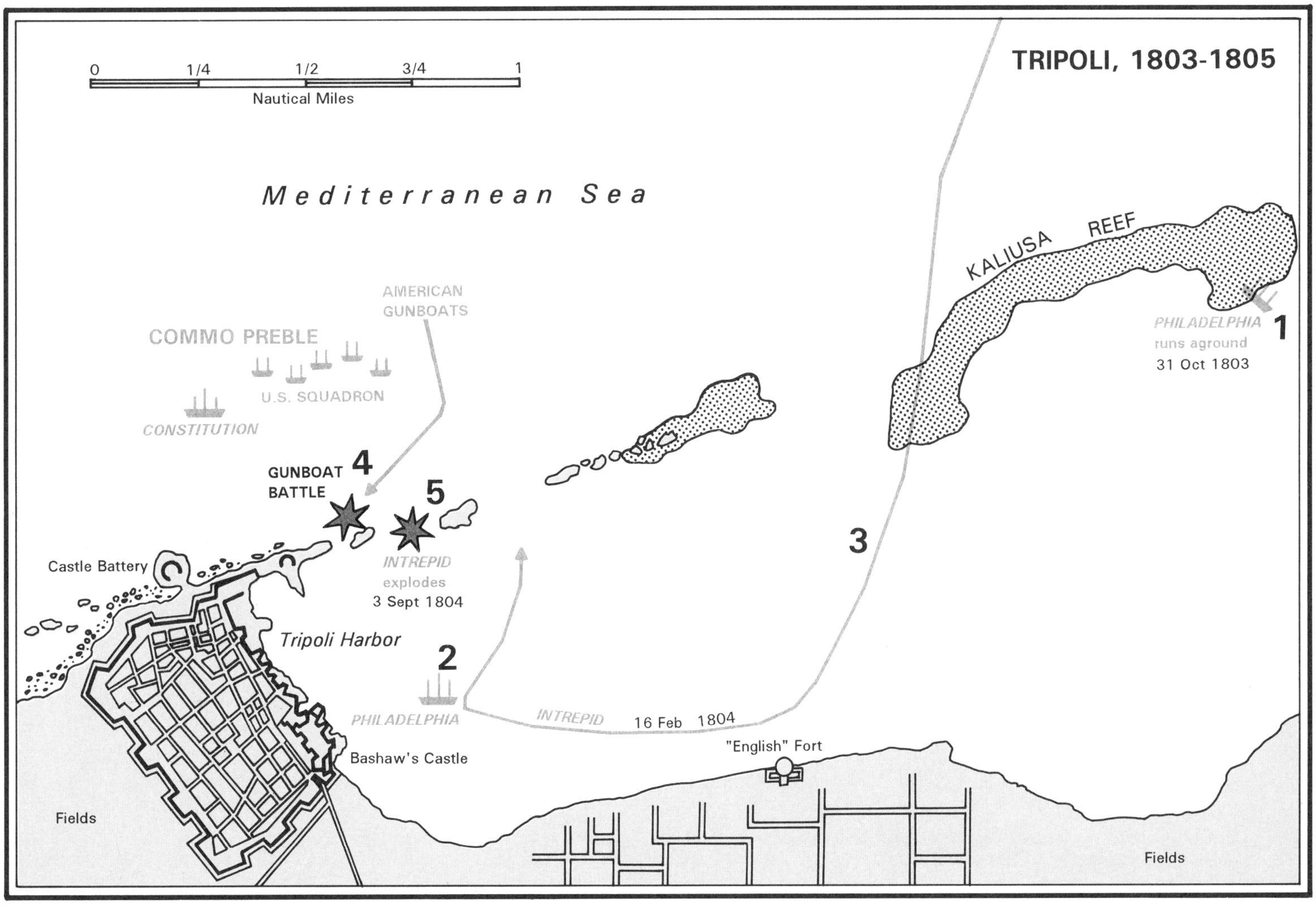

TRIPOLI, 1803-1805

0 1/4 1/2 3/4 1
Nautical Miles

Mediterranean Sea

KALIUSA REEF

PHILADELPHIA runs aground 31 Oct 1803 1

AMERICAN GUNBOATS

COMMO PREBLE

U.S. SQUADRON

CONSTITUTION

GUNBOAT BATTLE 4

5

INTREPID explodes 3 Sept 1804

3

Castle Battery

Tripoli Harbor

2

PHILADELPHIA

INTREPID 16 Feb 1804

Bashaw's Castle

"English" Fort

Fields

Fields

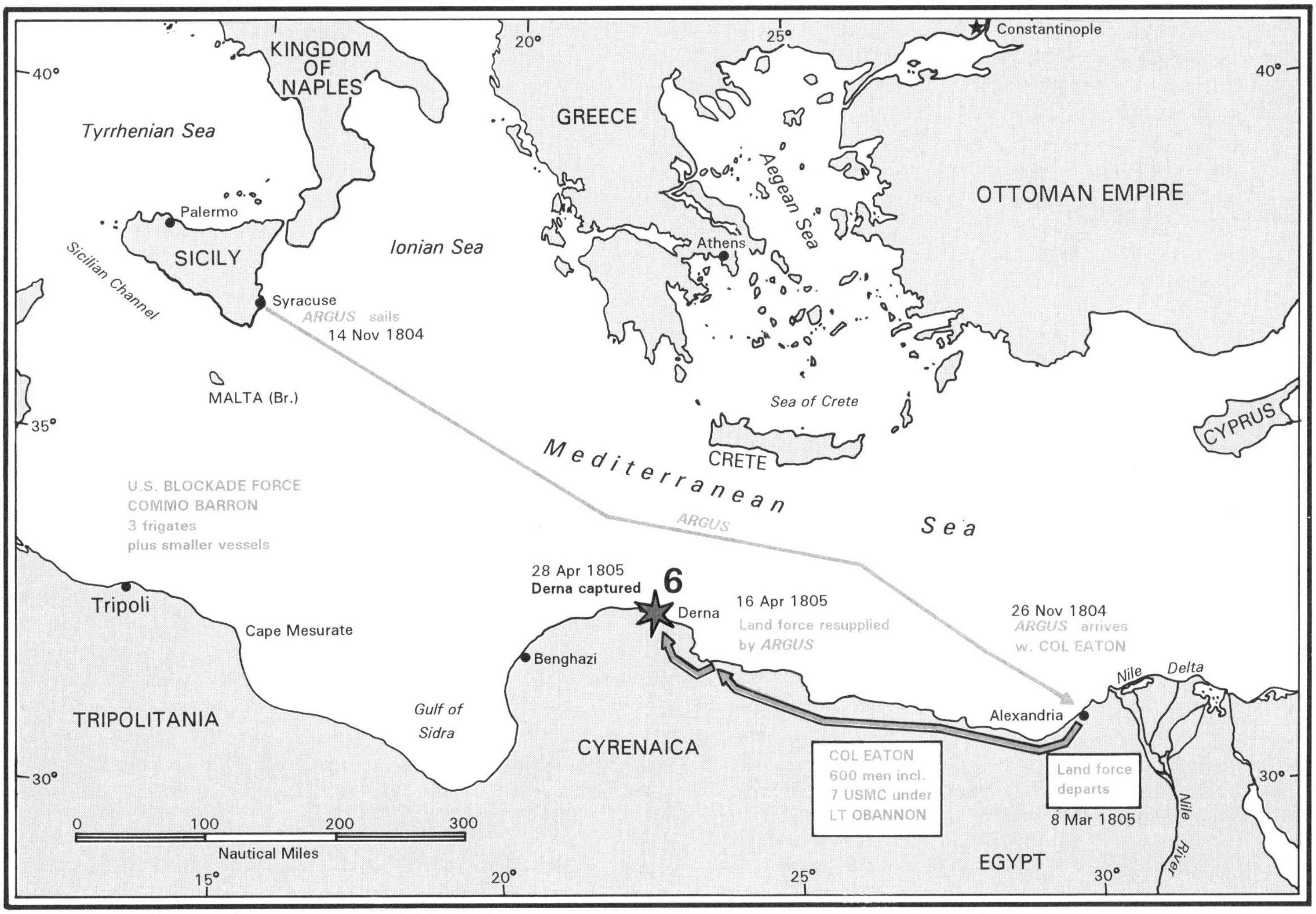

KINGDOM OF NAPLES

20°

25°

Constantinople

40°

40°

Tyrrhenian Sea

GREECE

Aegean Sea

OTTOMAN EMPIRE

Palermo

SICILY

Ionian Sea

Athens

Sicilian Channel

Syracuse

ARGUS sails 14 Nov 1804

MALTA (Br.)

Sea of Crete

35°

CYPRUS

CRETE

Mediterranean Sea

U.S. BLOCKADE FORCE
COMMO BARRON
3 frigates
plus smaller vessels

ARGUS

28 Apr 1805
Derna captured 6

Derna

16 Apr 1805
Land force resupplied by ARGUS

26 Nov 1804
ARGUS arrives
w. COL EATON

Tripoli

Cape Mesurate

Benghazi

Nile Delta

Gulf of Sidra

Alexandria

TRIPOLITANIA

CYRENAICA

COL EATON
600 men incl.
7 USMC under
LT OBANNON

Land force departs
8 Mar 1805

Nile River

30°

30°

0 100 200 300
Nautical Miles

15° 20° 25° 30°

EGYPT

MAP 12

TRAFALGAR

21 OCTOBER 1805

While America's small Navy pacified the bashaw of Tripoli, the Anglo-French war entered its second decade. A peace agreement signed at Amiens in 1802 turned out to be no more than a respite, as both sides sought to strengthen their forces for the next round. The French first consul, Napoleon Bonaparte, sanctioned an ambitious naval building program, while Britain's prime minister, William Pitt, sought allies for another anti-French coalition. To the surprise of few, the war resumed in 1803. Again the United States watched from the sidelines. But events in 1805 would create a climate that made it impossible for the United States to avoid involvement.

For much of the European war, the French had won victories against Britain's allies on land while the British controlled the sea, but this time Napoleon (who declared himself emperor in 1804) planned an amphibious campaign to conquer Britain itself. The key was to gain control of the English Channel long enough to allow French transports to ferry an army from Boulogne to Dover. While Napoleon assembled an army at Boulogne (1), ADM Pierre Villeneuve was to break out of Toulon (2) and sail for the Atlantic via the Strait of Gibraltar, picking up Spanish squadrons at both Cartegena (3) and Cadiz (4) en route. Then this combined fleet of some twenty-three ships-of-the-line would sail for the West Indies, join more Franco-Spanish forces there, and recross the Atlantic to join the main French fleet under ADM Honoré J. A. Ganteaume at Brest (5). This would give the French and Spanish nearly fifty ships-of-the-line in the English Channel, enough to hold the Strait of Dover—temporarily at least—against the Royal Navy's Channel Fleet under Admiral Lord Cornwallis.

All went well through the early stages. Villeneuve slipped away from Toulon on 30 March and sailed from Cadiz for the West Indies on 9 April, with ADM Horatio Nelson in hot pursuit. But in the West Indies Villeneuve could not add to his twenty ships-of-the-line, and upon returning to Europe, instead of heading for the Channel, he fought an indecisive battle off Cape Ferrol (6) with a fleet of eighteen ships-of-the-line under ADM Sir Robert Calder and then entered the harbor at Vigo, Spain (7). Napoleon ordered Villeneuve to sail at once for the Channel, but he headed instead for Ferrol (8) to refit his battered vessels, and on 15 August he sailed not north but south, arriving at Cadiz five days later with twenty-nine ships-of-the-line.

His invasion plans in tatters, Napoleon gave up on his grand scheme and decided instead to march against England's continental allies, Austria and Russia. Learning that Napoleon planned to relieve him, Villeneuve decided to put to sea once again and risk everything on a great battle with the English fleet off Cadiz.

That fleet was now under the command of ADM Viscount Horatio Lord Nelson, who had pursued Villeneuve across the Atlantic and back. The diminutive Nelson had lost an arm and an eye in the service of his country and earned a notorious reputation for his affair with Lady Emma Hamilton, the wife of a British diplomat, but he was without doubt the greatest sailor of his age. Nelson had spent years in considering the kind of tactics that would allow him to achieve a decisive victory at sea. Rather than merely placing his own battle line alongside that of the enemy, he planned to break through the enemy line just ahead of its center, massing his own fleet against the center and rear of the enemy fleet, while the wind kept the enemy van out of the fight. Nelson discussed these ideas with his captains in spirited dinner conversations, using cutlery to illustrate fleet maneuvers on the tablecloth. Thus it was that as Nelson's fleet awaited Villeneuve's appearance off Cape Trafalgar, every ship's captain knew what was expected of him. Just in case there was any lingering doubt, Nelson had instructed them, "No captain can do very wrong if he places his ship alongside that of an enemy."

At dawn on 21 October, twenty miles west of Cape Trafalgar (9), lookouts on the English ships spotted the topsails of Villeneuve's thirty-three ships-of-the-line. Nelson formed his own fleet of twenty-seven ships-of-the-line into two columns and bore down on the enemy. Villeneuve reversed course and formed a line of battle, awaiting the British attack. To give the officers on his ships something to consider while the two fleets came together, Nelson ordered his signal officer to spell out a message in flag hoist: "England expects that every man will do his duty." After the battle began, Nelson raised another signal and kept it flying throughout the battle: "Engage the enemy more closely."

The battle unfolded much as Nelson had envisioned (see lower map). The lead ship of each division broke through the enemy line, and the superior gunnery of the British ships did the rest as one after another the French and Spanish ships struck. At the height of the battle Nelson was walking his quarterdeck with his flag captain when he was struck down by a sharpshooter's ball and fell mortally wounded. But the battle was already won. In the most decisive naval battle in history, the Royal Navy virtually annihilated the combined fleets of France and Spain. Nelson's victory at Trafalgar confirmed Britain's position as ruler of the sea.

Five weeks later Napoleon won an equally decisive battle on land, defeating the combined armies of Austria and Russia at Austerlitz (10, upper map). That victory, plus other victories over Prussia that followed, gave him undisputed command of the continent. With France in command of the land and Britain in command of the sea, the two rival nations could assail one another only through economic warfare—a circumstance that put the United States directly in the middle.

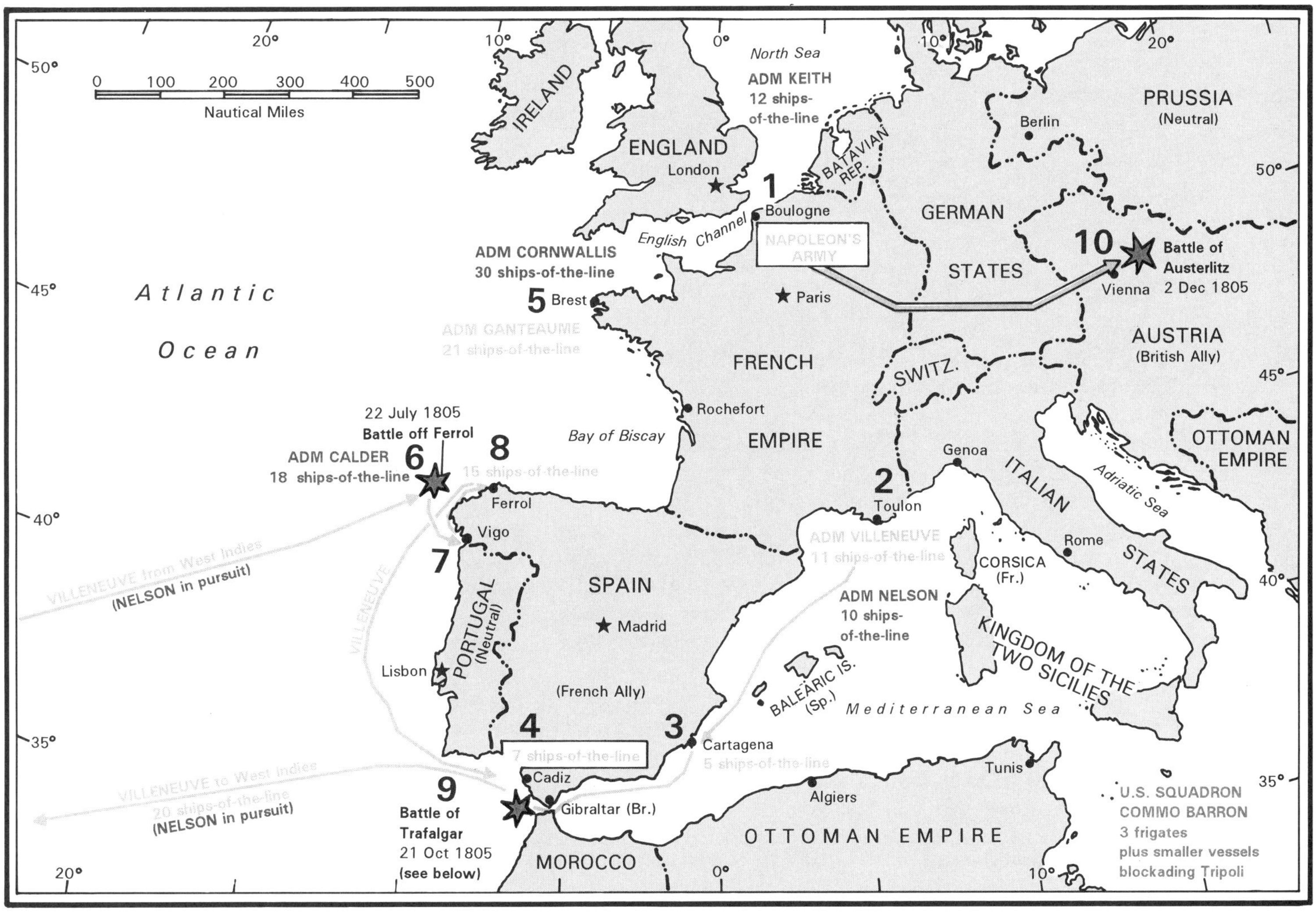

0 100 200 300 400 500
Nautical Miles

20° 10° 0° 10° 20°
50° 45° 40° 35°

IRELAND
ENGLAND
London
North Sea
ADM KEITH
12 ships-of-the-line
BATAVIAN REP.
PRUSSIA
(Neutral)
Berlin
1
Boulogne
English Channel
NAPOLEON'S ARMY
GERMAN STATES
10
Battle of Austerlitz
2 Dec 1805
Vienna
ADM CORNWALLIS
30 ships-of-the-line
5 Brest
ADM GANTEAUME
21 ships-of-the-line
Paris
Atlantic Ocean
FRENCH EMPIRE
SWITZ.
AUSTRIA
(British Ally)
Rochefort
Bay of Biscay
22 July 1805
Battle off Ferrol
ADM CALDER
18 ships-of-the-line
6
8
15 ships-of-the-line
Ferrol
Vigo
7
Genoa
2
Toulon
ITALIAN STATES
Adriatic Sea
OTTOMAN EMPIRE
Rome
ADM VILLENEUVE
11 ships-of-the-line
CORSICA
(Fr.)
VILLENEUVE from West Indies
(NELSON in pursuit)
VILLENEUVE
PORTUGAL
(Neutral)
SPAIN
Madrid
(French Ally)
ADM NELSON
10 ships-of-the-line
Lisbon
BALEARIC IS.
(Sp.)
KINGDOM OF THE TWO SICILIES
Mediterranean Sea
4
7 ships-of-the-line
3
Cartagena
5 ships-of-the-line
Cadiz
Tunis
VILLENEUVE to West Indies
20 ships-of-the-line
(NELSON in pursuit)
9
Battle of Trafalgar
21 Oct 1805
(see below)
Gibraltar (Br.)
Algiers
OTTOMAN EMPIRE
MOROCCO
U.S. SQUADRON
COMMO BARRON
3 frigates
plus smaller vessels
blockading Tripoli

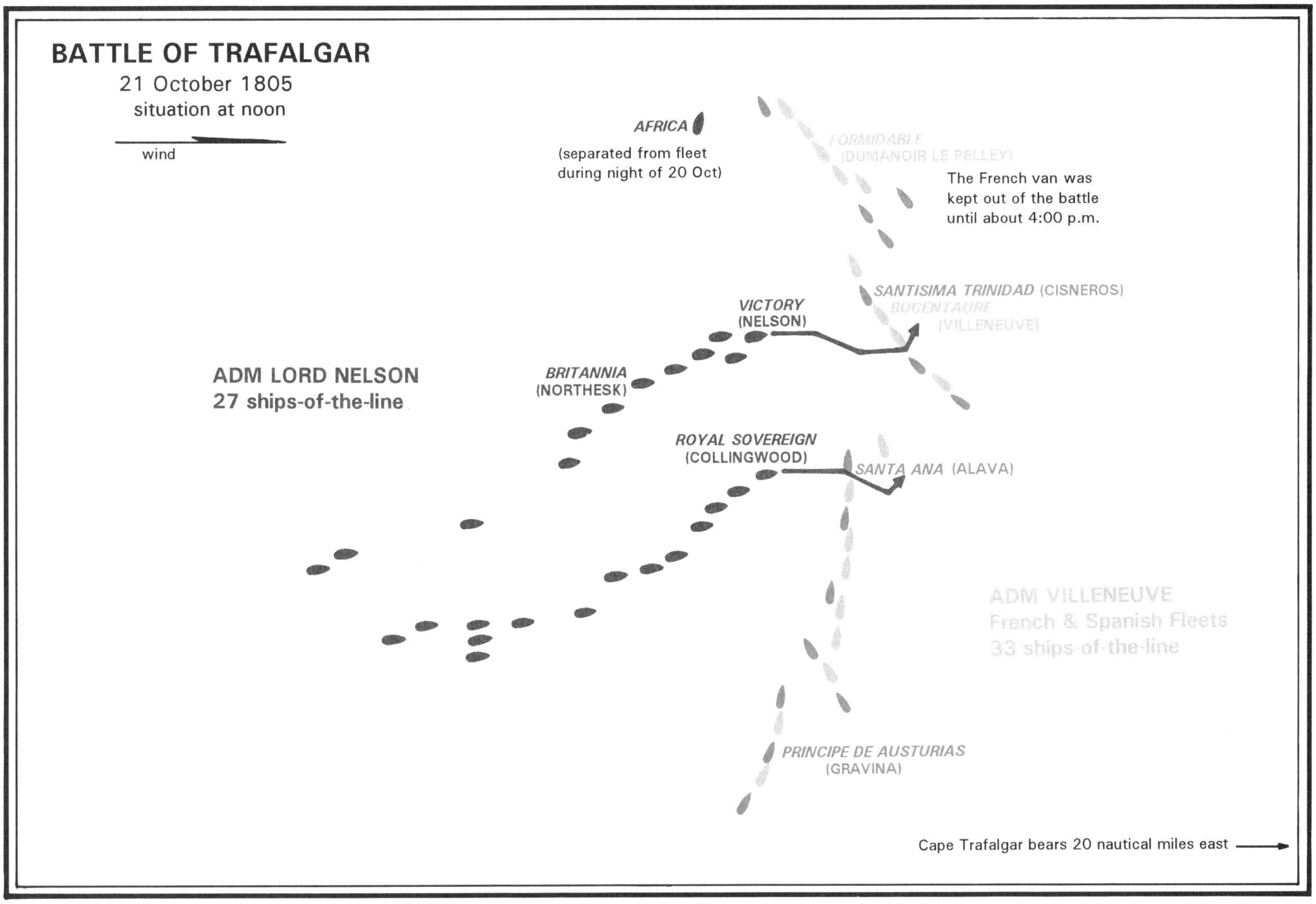

BATTLE OF TRAFALGAR

21 October 1805
situation at noon

wind

AFRICA
(separated from fleet during night of 20 Oct)

FORMIDABLE
(DUMANOIR LE PELLEY)

The French van was kept out of the battle until about 4:00 p.m.

SANTISIMA TRINIDAD (CISNEROS)
BUCENTAURE
(VILLENEUVE)

VICTORY
(NELSON)

BRITANNIA
(NORTHESK)

ADM LORD NELSON
27 ships-of-the-line

ROYAL SOVEREIGN
(COLLINGWOOD)

SANTA ANA (ALAVA)

ADM VILLENEUVE
French & Spanish Fleets
33 ships-of-the-line

PRINCIPE DE AUSTURIAS
(GRAVINA)

Cape Trafalgar bears 20 nautical miles east

Map 13

The *Chesapeake-Leopard* Affair

23 June 1807

The great battles of 1805—Trafalgar in October and Austerlitz in December—confirmed England as ruler of the sea and solidified Napoleon's position as ruler of the continent. To break this stalemate between sea power and land power, Napoleon sought to strangle Britain's island economy by denying British merchant ships access to European ports. In 1806, therefore, Napoleon issued a proclamation from the Prussian capital of Berlin, announcing that all nations friendly to France must close their ports to English ships (the Berlin Decree); a year later he extended the ban to require neutral nations to follow suit (the Milan Decree). Britain retaliated against the French economic offensive by issuing an "Order in Council" forbidding neutral nations from trading with France or its allies. These declarations put the United States directly in the middle of the power struggle.

At first the edicts had little impact on American merchants for the simple reason that France lacked the naval power to enforce its demands. In contrast, British ships dominated the sea-lanes, and because the British were better customers anyway, most American merchants simply continued to trade with British ports as usual. British warships regularly visited the American coast and even used American harbors to resupply and refit. In the late summer of 1806 two French frigates fleeing a British squadron straggled into the Chesapeake Bay. Determined to keep them bottled up, the British maintained a watch off the entrance to the Chesapeake all winter. The proximity of neutral ports proved too much of a temptation for several British sailors, who deserted from the Royal Navy and lost themselves in the American melting pot. A few even signed enlistment papers with the American Navy, joining the ship's company of the frigate *Chesapeake*, 38.

Because Britain's very survival depended on its ability to man its ships, it had a policy of hunting down deserters and executing them as a deterrent to others. Thus Britain's ministers protested vigorously that the *Chesapeake* had enlisted British deserters. Alas, a misunderstanding about the identity of the suspected men led to some fateful confusion. Though American naval officers believed that all the disagreements had been resolved, the British North American commander, VADM George Berkeley, ordered all his captains to search the *Chesapeake* for British deserters if ever they encountered the ship outside American territorial waters.

In the spring of 1807 the *Chesapeake* was in the Washington Navy Yard, preparing for a year-long cruise off the Barbary Coast. In the second week of May the *Chesapeake* got under way and transited slowly down the Potomac to drop anchor on 5 June in Hampton Roads (1), where the loading of supplies would be completed. The *Chesapeake's* commander was CAPT Charles Gordon, but the ship also flew the broad pennant of COMMO James Barron, younger brother of Samuel Barron who had presided over the final negotiations with Tripoli in 1805. While Gordon had responsibility for the workaday tasks of preparing the vessel for sea, Barron was ultimately responsible for its readiness and performance.

After much delay, and with its decks still encumbered with barrels and piles of stores for the long cruise, the *Chesapeake* got under way from Hampton Roads at 7:15 A.M. on 22 June. At 9:00 it passed Lynnhaven Bay (2), where two British frigates lay at anchor, maintaining their vigil. As the *Chesapeake* passed, the two British frigates could be seen signaling to each other. A third ship, several miles north of Cape Henry (3), signaled as well, apparently in reply, and headed out to sea. At noon the next day this third vessel appeared to be bearing down on the *Chesapeake,* and at 3:30 (23 June) this ship, the *Leopard,* 50, sailed up on the *Chesapeake's* lee quarter only sixty yards away (4). An officer on board hailed the American frigate, claiming to have dispatches to deliver. Barron invited the *Leopard* to send a boat, and soon afterward a British lieutenant climbed on board, carrying the order from Vice Admiral Berkeley to search the *Chesapeake.*

Barron had been informed of the dispute over deserters, but he believed it had been resolved—information which he politely gave the young lieutenant while explaining that he could not allow his ship to be searched. The lieutenant returned to the *Leopard,* and soon afterward the *Leopard's* captain, Salisbury Humphreys, began hailing the American frigate, warning Barron that he was determined to fulfill his orders to search the American frigate. Only now did Barron give the order to clear for action, something the *Leopard* had done before coming alongside. Barron tried to stall for time, but the *Leopard's* captain was insistent. Then, without further warning, the British ship fired a broadside. The Americans found they could not return fire, partly because of the encumbrances littering the gun deck, but also because no matches or powder horns for priming the guns had been prepared. The *Leopard* fired several more broadsides—seven altogether—and still the *Chesapeake* failed to return fire. Finally, LT William Allen managed to fire a single gun, using a hot coal from the ship's galley. Barron then ordered the *Chesapeake's* flag struck.

The British lieutenant returned to the wrecked *Chesapeake,* and ignoring Barron's claim that his ship was a prize of war, he conducted a search of the ship, during which he found the men he was seeking. Its mission accomplished, the *Leopard* sailed away, and the *Chesapeake* limped back into port.

Six months later a naval court of inquiry found Barron guilty of "negligent performance of duty" and suspended him from the Navy for five years. The episode embittered many American naval officers and all but eradicated the sense of professional pride they had developed in the Mediterranean.

The unlucky Chesapeake, *which suffered the ignominy of being stopped and boarded by the* Leopard *in 1807, was also the only American frigate to be bested in a ship-to-ship frigate duel during the War of 1812. (U.S. Naval Institute)*

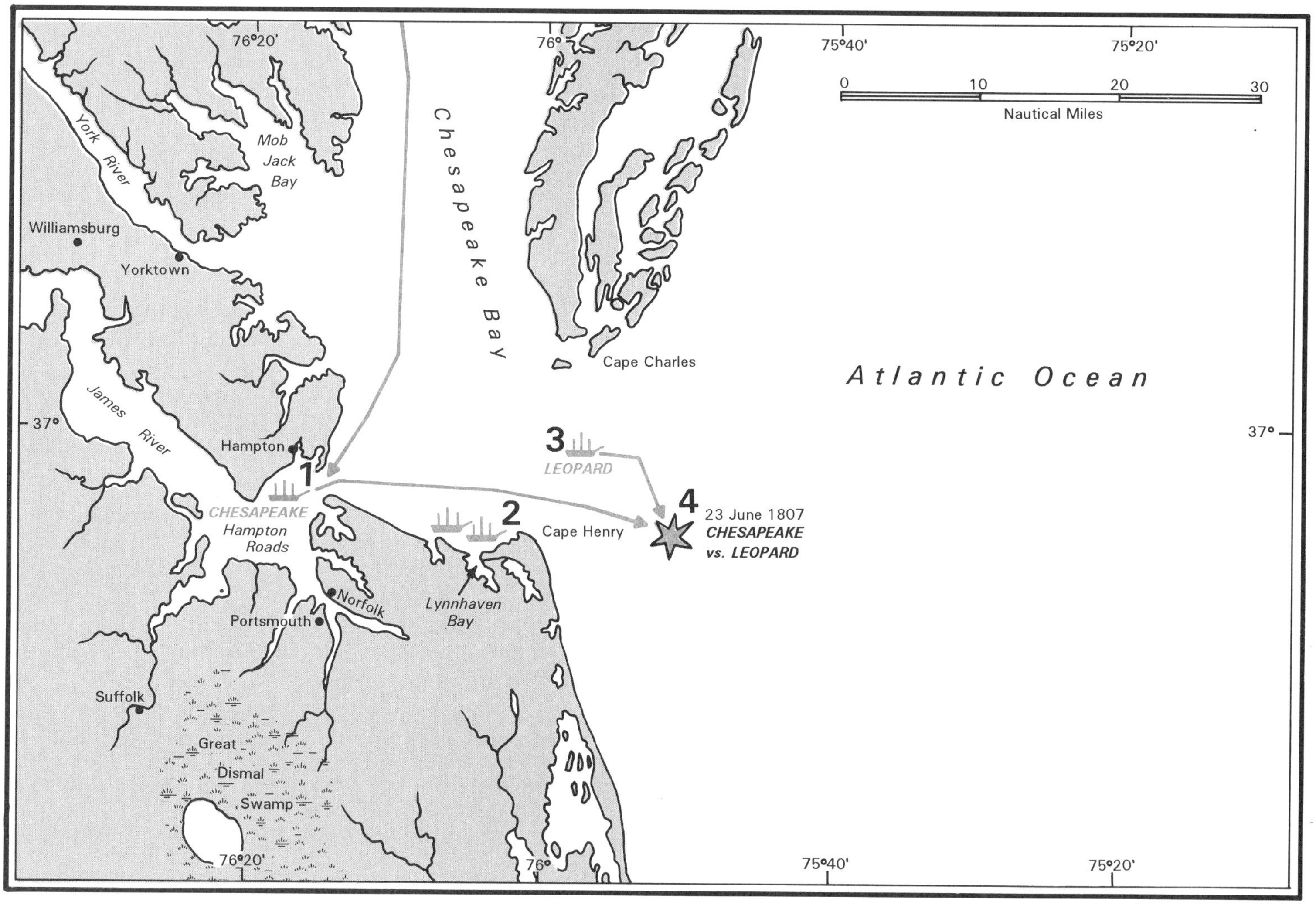

Map 14

The Gunboat Navy

1807–1809

Like most Americans, Thomas Jefferson was outraged by the high-handedness of the *Leopard's* attack on the *Chesapeake,* but he was even more concerned that the incident might propel the United States into a war with Britain. His initial response to the crisis, therefore, was to prevent an open rupture in Anglo-American relations. To assuage American anger (and prevent additional confrontations), he banned British warships from American ports and demanded an official explanation from the British government. These steps—and the passage of time—eventually succeeded in defusing the crisis. After years of negotiations, the British apologized and returned the one survivor of the four men who had been taken from the *Chesapeake.* (Two had been hanged as deserters, and the other had died of natural causes.)

More far-reaching was Jefferson's advocacy of an embargo of American trade, a policy Congress dutifully enacted into law in December of 1807. Though Jefferson's political enemies portrayed the embargo as an act of national cowardice, the president saw it as an appropriate response to the kind of economic warfare that England and France were practicing. Jefferson believed that Europe was more dependent on American goods than America was on European goods, and that if denied access to American goods by the embargo, both England and France would, in time, be forced to repeal their restrictive trade policies.

Jefferson also concerned himself with military preparations. His principal concern was how the United States could best defend itself against overt violations of its neutrality. One option was to build a conventional fleet of ships-of-the-line that might act as a deterrent to further British imperiousness. Such a policy might have been viable when most of the Royal Navy was busy blockading the French and Spanish fleets, but after Nelson's victory at Trafalgar, challenging the Royal Navy for command of the sea seemed hopeless. Jefferson's alternative was to forward a theory of national defense that was unpopular at the time with most U.S. naval officers, and that remains controversial to this day—that of the Gunboat Navy.

Gunboats of the nineteenth century were small, open vessels between sixty and eighty feet long and were propelled by oars or sweeps, though they could sail fairly well in moderate seas when rigged as sloops or schooners. What defined them was their armament: each boat carried one or two large-caliber guns, twenty-four or thirty-two pounders, most often mounted in the eyes of the boat. The heavy ordnance (each gun weighed about seven thousand pounds) in so small a vessel made most gunboats unstable for duty on the high seas, but such was not their function. They were intended for the defense of harbors or inlets, where their shallow draft and maneuverability would give them a presumed advantage over much larger enemy warships.

Jefferson saw several tangible advantages in such craft. Because they were exclusively defensive, they posed no challenge to Britain's command of the sea and were, therefore, unlikely to provoke a preemptive strike by the Royal Navy, such as the one Admiral Nelson had carried out against the Danish fleet in 1801. Because they could be manned quickly in a crisis by a special category of militia, they were unlikely to provoke opposition from those Americans who continued to suspect a standing military force. Unlike a conventional fleet, gunboats could be parceled out along the coast to provide at least some protection to all the states that demanded it. Finally, at a projected price of $3,000 to $5,000 a copy, they were cheap—though the actual cost proved to be closer to $10,000.

For the rest of Jefferson's administration (1807–1809) a combination of forts, floating batteries, and gunboats constituted the nation's primary coastal-defense force. The map at right depicts the distribution of gunboats at their height, in the summer of 1809 when the nation had 172 of them. Ironically, the primary function of gunboats in this period was not to defend U.S. harbors from an enemy naval force but to enforce the embargo. It was not only an unpopular job, it was an impossible job. Even with 172 gunboats in commission, they were far too few to guard every port, harbor, inlet, and river mouth. Also, the duty of chasing, detaining, and arresting American merchants was distasteful to naval officers and made the gunboats extremely unpopular with the local citizens. As in the years prior to the outbreak of the American Revolution, smuggling became more or less socially acceptable in many locations, especially Massachusetts and New Orleans.

Following the inauguration of James Madison as president in March 1809, the United States began to move away from the gunboat doctrine. Though Congress authorized an additional one hundred of the boats, no more were built. Most of the existing boats were placed "in ordinary," awaiting the outbreak of a national crisis, and by December of 1811 only sixty-three gunboats remained in active service.

Though American naval officers accepted service in the gunboat flotilla, few of them embraced the concept with any enthusiasm. Nearly all preferred service in seagoing warships, and many of those who commanded gunboats or gunboat flotillas criticized their own vessels as "cockleshells." Despite Stephen Decatur's heroism in the gunboat battles off Tripoli, service in harbor-defense craft provided few opportunities for personal glory or professional advancement. But the most damning indictment of the gunboats was that when a national crisis did arrive with the outbreak of war in 1812, they proved unable to fulfill their advertised function of protecting America's ports and harbors.

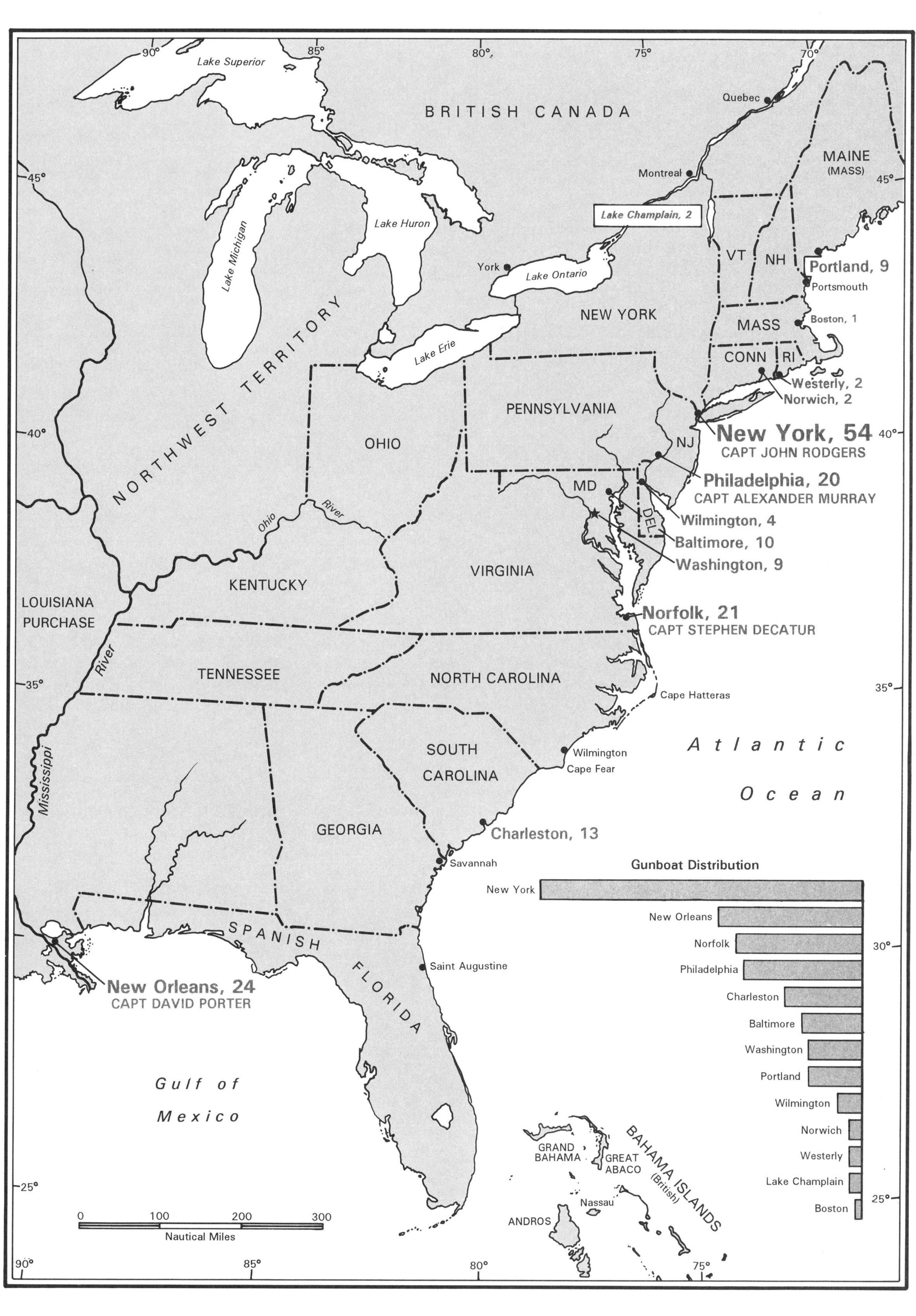

BRITISH CANADA
Lake Superior
Lake Michigan
Lake Huron
Lake Ontario
Lake Erie
Quebec
Montreal
York
Lake Champlain, 2
MAINE
(MASS)
VT
NH
Portland, 9
Portsmouth
NEW YORK
MASS
Boston, 1
CONN
RI
Westerly, 2
Norwich, 2
NORTHWEST TERRITORY
PENNSYLVANIA
OHIO
New York, 54
CAPT JOHN RODGERS
NJ
Philadelphia, 20
CAPT ALEXANDER MURRAY
MD
DEL
Wilmington, 4
Baltimore, 10
Washington, 9
Ohio River
KENTUCKY
VIRGINIA
LOUISIANA PURCHASE
Norfolk, 21
CAPT STEPHEN DECATUR
TENNESSEE
NORTH CAROLINA
Mississippi River
Cape Hatteras
SOUTH CAROLINA
Wilmington
Cape Fear
Atlantic Ocean
GEORGIA
Charleston, 13
Savannah
SPANISH FLORIDA
Saint Augustine
New Orleans, 24
CAPT DAVID PORTER
Gulf of Mexico
GRAND BAHAMA
GREAT ABACO
BAHAMA ISLANDS (British)
Nassau
ANDROS
0 100 200 300
Nautical Miles
90°
85°
80°
75°
70°
45°
40°
35°
30°
25°
Gunboat Distribution
New York
New Orleans
Norfolk
Philadelphia
Charleston
Baltimore
Washington
Portland
Wilmington
Norwich
Westerly
Lake Champlain
Boston

Part III

The War of 1812
1812–1815

JAMES MADISON TOOK THE OATH of office as the fourth president of the United States in March 1809. By then it was evident that the American embargo was not going to bring England and France to their knees; indeed, the two European superpowers hardly seemed to notice it. New England merchants, on the other hand, felt the effects keenly. U.S. exports had dropped from $108 million in 1807 to $22 million in 1808, though the latter figure could probably be enlarged considerably to reflect the value of unreported smuggling. Whereas it was still possible to defend the embargo on the grounds that it prevented American merchant ships from sailing into harm's way, domestic opposition to it was so strong by 1809 that the new president decided to try another tack.

In one of his first acts, therefore, Madison approved a repeal of the general embargo and backed a congressional alternative called the Non-Intercourse Act, which authorized Americans to trade with any nation *except* Britain and France. This retained the principle of economic sanctions while allowing U.S. merchants to reopen trade with the outside world. Naval officers were pleased that they would no longer spend most of their time in trying to prevent American merchants from exporting their goods. The bill also succeeded in muting the cries of protest from New England, but as a means of influencing the behavior of the great powers, it was as ineffective as the embargo. More than a few vessels departing Boston or Newport declared for a neutral port, then set sail for English or French ports once they were at sea.

The U.S. Frigate Constitution *duels with the British* Guerrière *in August 1812. In this painting by Michelle Corne, the* Guerrière's *mizzenmast has gone over the side; the other two masts would soon follow, leaving the* Guerrière *a defenseless hulk. This was the first of several frigate duels early in the war that undermined the British tradition of invincibility at sea (see map 16). (U.S. Naval Academy Museum)*

A year later, in May of 1810, the Madison administration tried another ploy. Discarding the Non-Intercourse Act, Congress passed what was known as Macon's Bill Number 2, a curious and confusing piece of legislation that reopened trade with both European belligerents but pledged the United States to reimpose sanctions against the enemy of whichever nation first repealed its own restrictive trade acts. Thus if Britain acted first by repealing the Orders in Council, the United States would reward the British by reimposing trade restrictions on France, and if Napoleon repealed the Berlin and Milan Decrees, the United States would reimpose restrictions on England. Because Napoleon was unable to enforce his so-called Continental System on the United States anyway, he had nothing to lose by taking Congress up on its offer. In August 1810, therefore, he accepted (officially at least) the American offer. Though Napoleon's sincerity was open to question, Madison took his retraction at face value and reimposed nonimportation against England in February of 1811.

Other events that year conspired to bring the United States and England closer to war. The voracious demand for manpower in the Royal Navy led zealous British ship captains to press into service anyone who might once have been a British citizen. British warships almost routinely stopped American merchant vessels to examine their crews. Any likely hand with a tattoo or a pigtail, who bore the scars of a cat-of-nine-tails on his back, or who spoke with a likely accent might be declared to be a British citizen and hauled off to serve in His Majesty's Navy. This practice of impressment was more of a nuisance than a threat to America's national security, but it kept the level of animosity between the two nations at a high level and provoked occasional violent confrontations.

One such occurred in May of 1811, when the British frigate *Guerrière,* 38, seized an American citizen off a merchant vessel just outside New York Harbor. Learning of the incident, CAPT John Rodgers put to sea in the U.S. frigate *President,* 44, hoping to encounter the *Guerrière* and demand that the man

Impressment: A British naval officer looks over a surly crew on board an American merchantman as he prepares to press one or more men into the Royal Navy. This practice was a constant irritant in the relations between the United States and Britain in the years prior to the outbreak of the War of 1812. (U.S. Naval Academy Museum)

COMMO Oliver Hazard Perry was only twenty-eight years old when he won the crucial American victory on Lake Erie on 10 September 1813 (see map 18). Sadly, his promising career ended only five years later when he succumbed to yellow fever after completing a diplomatic mission to Venezuela. (U.S. Naval Academy Museum)

COMMO Thomas Macdonough commanded the American squadron that won the Battle of Plattsburg on Lake Champlain on 11 September 1814 (see map 20). Like Perry, Macdonough won fame with his singular victory, and also like Perry, disease cut his career short when he died at sea of tuberculosis in 1825. (Official U.S. Navy photo)

be returned. In this mood, Rodgers discovered himself close aboard an unidentified British vessel in the dark and fog off Long Island late on the evening of 16 May. It was, in fact, the British sloop-of-war *Little Belt,* 22. Rodgers exchanged shouted enquiries with the unidentified British vessel and, unsatisfied with the answers he got, ordered his ship to open fire. The *Little Belt* fired back and got much the worst of the exchange, suffering nine killed and twenty-three wounded before the identity of each ship was established with the coming of dawn. Rodgers then offered assistance, but it was refused, and the *Little Belt* limped off to refit at Halifax. Many American naval officers viewed the event as suitable revenge for the *Chesapeake-Leopard* affair.

Anglo-American relations suffered on the western frontier as well. A thousand miles to the west in the thinly populated Northwest Territory, most Americans held the British government in Canada largely responsible for continued raids by hostile Indians against American settlements. In the largest outbreak of frontier violence since Pontiac's rebellion of 1763, six hundred Shawnees attacked an army of one thousand regulars and militia led by GEN William Henry Harrison in the Battle of Tippecanoe on 7 November 1811 and inflicted some two hundred casualties before being routed. Though there was no evidence of direct British involvement, many Americans began to argue that no peace on the frontier would be possible until British influence was eradicated from North America.

Such arguments provided ammunition to a group of Southern and Western congressmen who argued on the floor of Congress that since the economic sanctions had failed, war was now the inevitable last resort. Known as the War Hawks, they were generally young men inspired by a strong sense of nationalism and convinced that only an assertive stand could cure Britain's evident disrespect for the United States. They argued that because Britain was committed to an apparently endless war with Napoleonic France, it could not garrison Canada with a force large enough to protect it from an American invasion. Seizing Canada would enable the United States to use it either as a hostage for British good behavior or as the means of eliminating British influence from North America.

By November of 1811 the crisis with Britain had become so severe that President Madison felt compelled to call for military preparations in his annual address to Congress. Congress enthusiastically passed a series of bills augmenting the ten thousand–man Army with an additional twenty-five thousand recruits, authorizing a militia force of another fifty thousand, and appropriating nearly $2 million for ordnance. But Congress saw no need to expand the small U.S. Navy because any such effort, it was argued, would be futile. Citing the Royal Navy list of July 1811, War Hawks pointed out that Britain possessed more than a thousand warships, a number that was growing all the time. While it was true that most of these vessels were tied down in fighting the French, the War Hawks noted as well that the Halifax Squadron by itself contained 111 British ships, including 7 ships-of-the-line, 2 razees, and 31 frigates. Despite their eagerness for war, the Southern and Western delegates concluded that "we cannot contend with Britain upon the ocean."

As a result, prowar Republicans from the South and West helped defeat a proposal to build ten new frigates. Ironically, many of the supporters of the bill opposed war with Britain but nevertheless sought to gain an appropriation for a permanent expansion of the Navy. When the bill to construct ten frigates failed, these supporters offered substitute bills that would have authorized six vessels, then four, then three—but each time the proposal was defeated. The only naval bill Congress adopted was a small authorization to fit out the existing frigates and a half million dollars to improve coastal fortifications. If the War Hawks were bent on war, they were also bent on fighting it on their own terms.

In April of 1812 the congressional War Hawks pushed through a sixty-day embargo, not as an instrument of economic pressure but as a preliminary step toward war. Designed to ensure that American shipping was safely in port when war was declared, this embargo had exactly the opposite effect as American merchants frantically sought to get their ships to sea before it took effect. The descent toward war grew steeper in May when the American sloop-of-war *Hornet* returned from London with the latest dispatches. These showed no softening of the British position, and on 1 June Madison sent what amounted to a war message to Congress. Even now, sentiment for war was not overwhelming. Many people opposed war altogether. Others, who agreed that the time for military measures had come, argued for a limited war fought only at sea, much like the Quasi War of 1798–1800. But the War Hawks controlled the debate, and in the end the motion for war passed both houses, though by less than overwhelming margins. The vote was 79–49 in the House and 19–13 in the Senate, where a shift of three votes would have forced the vice president to break a tie.

The Senate vote took place on 17 June. The day before, in London, the British Foreign Secretary announced to the House of Commons that it was suspending the Orders in Council. The British government had decided it was not profitable to allow a continuing deterioration in Anglo-American relations during the war with Napoleon. But the decision came too late; by the time the news reached the United States, war had been declared, and the impetus of events made a reconsideration impossible.

Naval Battle of New Orleans: The five gunboats of LT Thomas ap Catesby Jones on Lake Borgne under attack by forty-five small boats from the British naval squadron in December 1814. Though Jones's force was eventually overwhelmed, the fight on Lake Borgne delayed the British advance and gave MGEN Andrew Jackson intelligence of the British route of attack (see map 21). (Mariner's Museum, Newport News, Virginia)

Map 15

Cruise of the U.S. Fleet

21 June–31 August 1812

With the American declaration of war, the tiny U.S. Navy of seventeen ships found itself arrayed against the greatest naval power on earth, boasting more than eight hundred commissioned warships. Of course, the mismatch was considerably mitigated by virtue of the fact that most of the Royal Navy had to remain in European waters to blockade the French fleet, but any objective observer in June of 1812 would have concluded that the British had little to fear from what they derisively dismissed as "a handful of fir-built frigates."

Even before the declaration of war, Navy Secretary Paul Hamilton surveyed his senior officers for advice about how best to deploy the American warships in the event of war. CAPT John Rodgers, whose seniority made him the highest-ranking officer in the U.S. Navy at the time, answered Hamilton's inquiry by suggesting that the country should concentrate its naval forces into one or two squadrons that should put to sea at once upon the outbreak of war and attempt to catch the British unprepared. Rodgers argued that the United States should send one squadron to cruise the waters around Britain and retain the other in home waters for defensive purposes. Of course, Rodgers's certainty of commanding at least one of the squadrons, because he was the senior U.S. Navy officer, may have influenced his proposals.

Other U.S. Navy officers offered different views. Stephen Decatur and William Bainbridge each argued that the American frigates should be distributed singly or in pairs over a broad area not only to inflict maximum damage on Britain's warships but "to annoy the trade of Great Britain." Decatur in particular emphasized the importance of *guerre de course* and urged single-ship deployments that would allow complete freedom of action to individual commanders.

Hamilton sided with Rodgers and organized two squadrons of five warships each, one under Rodgers and one under Decatur. When news of the congressional declaration of war reached New York on 21 June, Rodgers set sail at once with his own vessel, the *President,* 44, plus two other frigates and two sloops. The *Constitution,* then in Boston Harbor, was to join Rodgers as soon as possible, but it ran into a strong British squadron under CAPT Philip Broke and barely escaped back into port. Even so, Rodgers's squadron represented the largest concentration of U.S. naval forces since the war in the Mediterranean.

Rodgers's principal objective was to intercept the British Jamaica convoy that had left the Caribbean in May. Two days out of New York, Rodgers met an American brig whose master told him that he had seen the Jamaica convoy northwest of Bermuda four days earlier. Rodgers cracked on sail and shaped a course to the southeast to intercept. But within a matter of hours his lookouts sighted a solitary vessel to the northeast that proved to be the British frigate *Belvidera,* 32, under the command of CAPT Richard Byron. Though Byron could not possibly have known of the American declaration of war, the appearance of a strong U.S. squadron made him cautious, and when Rodgers changed course to close, the *Belvidera* turned and fled. A long chase ensued (1). The *Belvidera* set every possible sail and lightened ship by discarding its drinking water. Rodgers was unwilling to follow suit because he was just embarking on what he hoped would be a long voyage. Several times Rodgers ordered the *President* to fall off just enough to allow him to try a long-range broadside, but none of them succeeded in crippling the *Belvidera,* and each time he tried this tactic he lost ground until eventually the British frigate managed to escape.

After this disappointment, Rodgers turned south again (2), hoping to pick up the Jamaica convoy. But the British had a long head start. Twice Rodgers encountered vessels that reported seeing the convoy, and once the Americans spotted what appeared to be the effluence of the convoy, including orange peelings and coconut shells, but throughout a chase of nearly three weeks, much of it in heavy fog and mist, he never sighted the convoy itself. On 13 July, only three hundred miles from the English Channel (3), Rodgers called off the pursuit.

Hoping to find better hunting in the busy sea-lanes between the Canary and Azores Islands, Rodgers took his squadron south toward the Spanish island colony of Madeira (4), and from there he shaped a course to the northwest to pass close to the Portuguese Azores. Though this was one of the busiest sea-lanes in the Atlantic, his vessels sighted no other sails en route. Resignedly, Rodgers headed for the United States where, after an uneventful crossing, he arrived in Boston (5) on 31 August.

In his report, Rodgers claimed that his cruise across the Atlantic and back was not so fruitless as it seemed at first glance. He argued that "our being at sea obliged the enemy to concentrate a considerable portion of his most active force, and thereby prevented his capturing an incalculable amount of American property." Indeed, the news that Rodgers's squadron was loose in the Atlantic had compelled CAPT Philip Broke to attach his four-ship squadron (the same squadron that had chased the *Constitution* back into port) to a homeward-bound convoy for its protection rather than continue to hover off the American coast to snatch up American merchant vessels returning to port.

Though Rodgers's argument may have been valid, the absence of tangible victories, combined with the ambition of the Navy's other ship captains, led the Navy Department to abandon the doctrine of concentrated force and adopt instead the suggestion of Decatur and Bainbridge that American frigates be deployed individually.

COMMO John Rodgers was the senior U.S. Navy officer during the War of 1812. Though his transatlantic cruise in the summer of 1812 was barren of any signal success, his voyage may have compelled the British to delay the establishment of an effective blockade. Rodgers was also the founder of a family of famous naval officers: his son RADM John Rodgers served with distinction in the Union Navy during the Civil War and in the postwar era. (Painting by J. W. Jarvis, U.S. Naval Academy Museum)

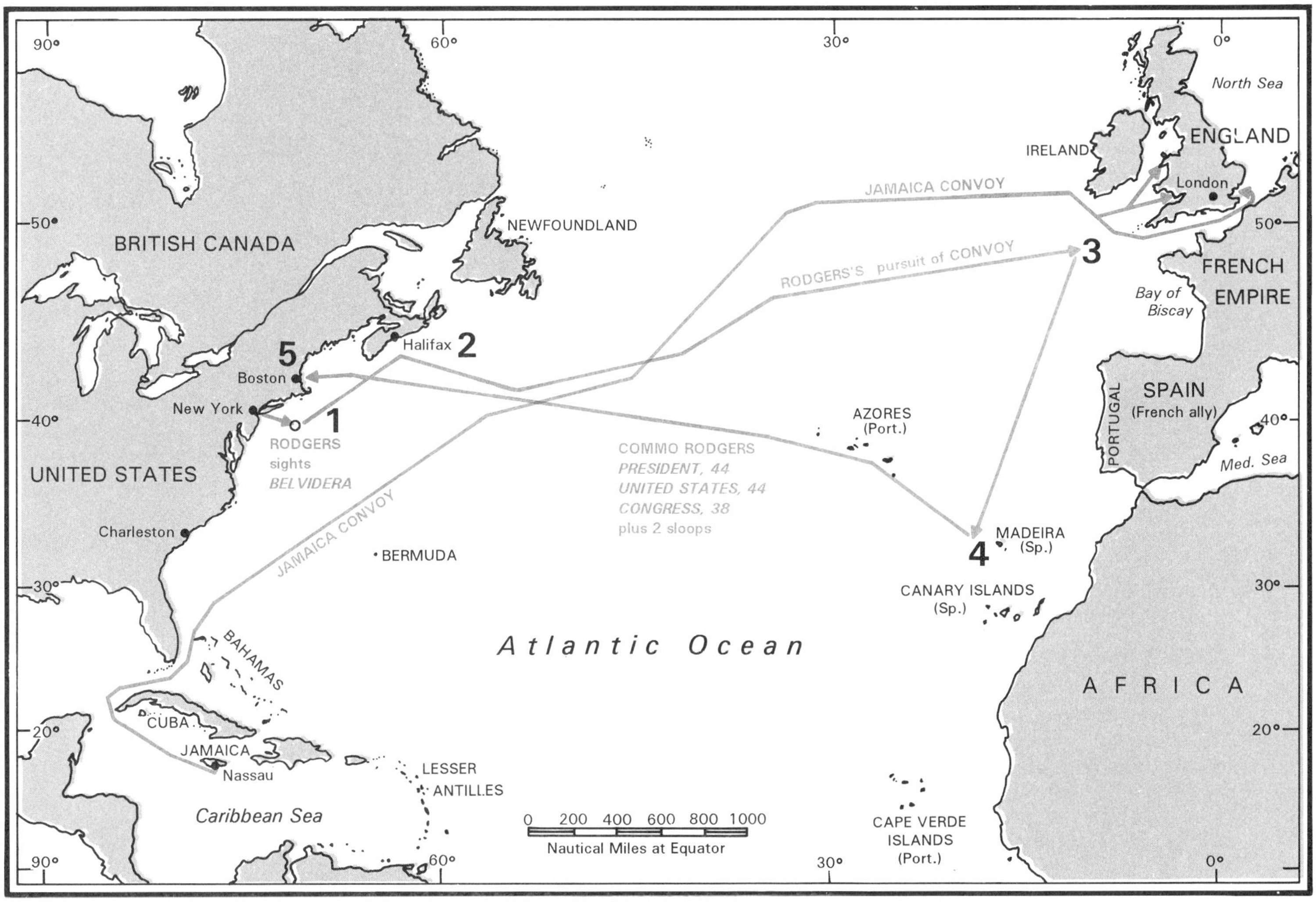

MAP 16

FRIGATE DUELS

AUGUST–DECEMBER 1812

The day before Rodgers's squadron returned to Boston Harbor, the frigate *Constitution* arrived there with the news that it had defeated a British frigate in single combat. This victory was the first of three such in the first six months of war—victories that were strategically insignificant, but that elevated American morale and cracked the facade of British naval invincibility.

Though CAPT Isaac Hull had been unable to join up with Rodgers's squadron in June, he put to sea again in August in hopes of damaging the British merchant trade off Halifax. After capturing several merchant ships in the vicinity of Cape Race (see map A), Hull decided to head south. Four days later lookouts on the *Constitution* sighted a lone ship heading west under easy sail. Hull ordered the *Constitution* to bear down on the stranger, which proved to be the British frigate *Guerrière*, CAPT James Dacres (see map B).

As the *Constitution* approached, the *Guerrière* wore ship twice to cross the bows of the American vessel as it approached, delivering raking broadsides each time. Hull yawed left and right to minimize the effect of these broadsides, then closed the range and came up on the *Guerrière's* port quarter. The two ships fought broadside-to-broadside for twenty minutes until the *Guerrière's* mizzenmast suddenly gave way and went over the side. That proved to be the turning point in the fight. The drag of the mizzenmast in the water slowed the *Guerrière* and allowed Hull to pull ahead to cross the bow of the British vessel and deliver a raking broadside at close range. At 6:30 P.M. the *Guerrière's* other two masts toppled, and with his enemy helpless, Hull withdrew from the fight to make repairs. At 7:30 he maneuvered his ship across the bow of the dismasted British frigate, which struck its flag. Hull burned the wrecked British frigate and set course for Boston, returning on 30 August to a hero's welcome one day before Rodgers's squadron came into port.

Five weeks later Rodgers was again at sea with a powerful squadron consisting of two frigates and the sloop-of-war *Wasp*. At the same time, however, Stephen Decatur also put to sea with two more frigates and the sloop-of-war *Argus*. In conformance with new policy, Decatur soon parted company with the rest of his squadron and began a solitary patrol in the heavy frigate *United States*, 44. On 25 October, just after daybreak, lookouts on the *United States* spotted a sail to the southeast that proved to be the British frigate *Macedonian*, CAPT John Carden (see map C). At 8:30 A.M. Decatur wore around onto the starboard tack, and the *Macedonian* hauled up closer to the wind so that the ships were running nearly parallel, with Decatur's ship in the lead. Decatur wore again, and the two ships passed each other on opposite courses about a mile apart. Decatur's move forced Carden to follow suit, and once again the British ship took on the role of pursuer even though the American frigate was the more powerful vessel. To unmask his port broadside, Decatur steered slightly into the wind, his course forming a gentle arc to the south, while the *Macedonian* tried to close the range by sailing along the chord of the arc. But this meant that Decatur could fire repeated broadsides into the bow of the British frigate, to which Carden could not reply. The American broadsides so damaged the *Macedonian's* rigging that it lost headway, and by the time it closed the *United States*, it had been badly battered. Soon afterward Carden was forced to strike. Decatur brought his prize into New York where, like Hull, he was greeted with a hero's welcome.

The third American victory took place in late December off the coast of Brazil. In September CAPT William Bainbridge, who had replaced Hull in command of the *Constitution*, departed Boston, accompanied by the sloop *Hornet*. The small frigate *Essex*, which departed separately from the Delaware Bay a few days later, was supposed to join him, but the *Essex* never caught up with the squadron. Finding no sign of the *Essex* at the planned rendezvous sites in the Cape Verde Islands and Fernando de Noronha, Bainbridge proceeded toward Cape Frio near Rio de Janeiro.

On 29 December the *Constitution's* lookouts spotted two ships sailing in company, but they separated almost at once, one heading for shore, the other moving to intercept the American frigate. Bainbridge headed east to gain sea room, then came about and advanced toward the strange vessel, which was the British frigate *Java*, 38, CAPT Henry Lambert (see map D). Bainbridge sought to close swiftly and slug it out, but Lambert patiently maneuvered so as to cross astern of the *Constitution* and deliver a raking broadside, which wounded Bainbridge, among others. Soon afterward, however, the *Java* missed its tack, and Bainbridge was able to close. An hour-long slug match ensued in which the *Constitution's* heavier weight of broadside made itself manifest. All three of the *Java's* masts went over the side. Bainbridge drew off to repair his own rigging, and then, as Hull had done, he placed the *Constitution* across the bows of the dismasted British frigate in a silent but unmistakable gesture of dominance, forcing the British ship to strike.

Though in each case the American frigate was substantially more powerful than its opponent, the tradition of British naval invincibility was so strong that the American successes seemed near miraculous. The victories provided a substantial boost to American morale and provoked the British Lords of the Admiralty to order its frigate captains to avoid future single-ship encounters with American frigates.

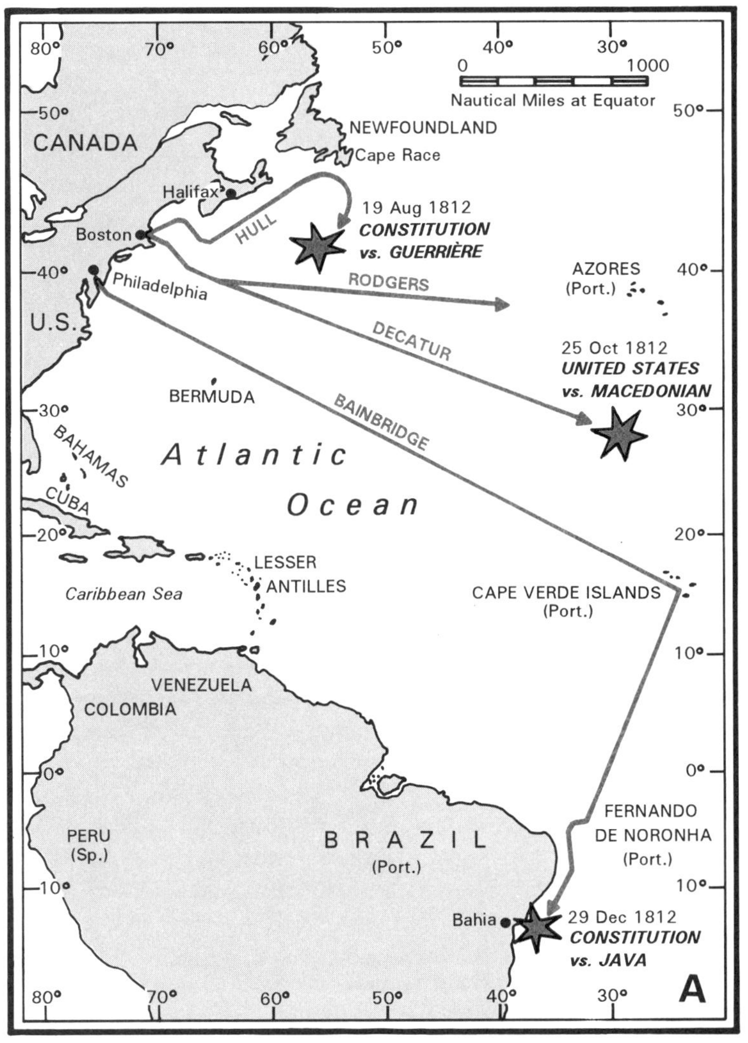

Nautical Miles at Equator
0
1000
CANADA
NEWFOUNDLAND
Cape Race
Halifax
Boston
HULL
19 Aug 1812
CONSTITUTION
vs. GUERRIÈRE
Philadelphia
RODGERS
AZORES
(Port.)
U.S.
DECATUR
25 Oct 1812
UNITED STATES
vs. MACEDONIAN
BERMUDA
BAINBRIDGE
BAHAMAS
Atlantic
Ocean
CUBA
LESSER
ANTILLES
Caribbean Sea
CAPE VERDE ISLANDS
(Port.)
VENEZUELA
COLOMBIA
FERNANDO
DE NORONHA
(Port.)
PERU
(Sp.)
B R A Z I L
(Port.)
Bahia
29 Dec 1812
CONSTITUTION
vs. JAVA
A

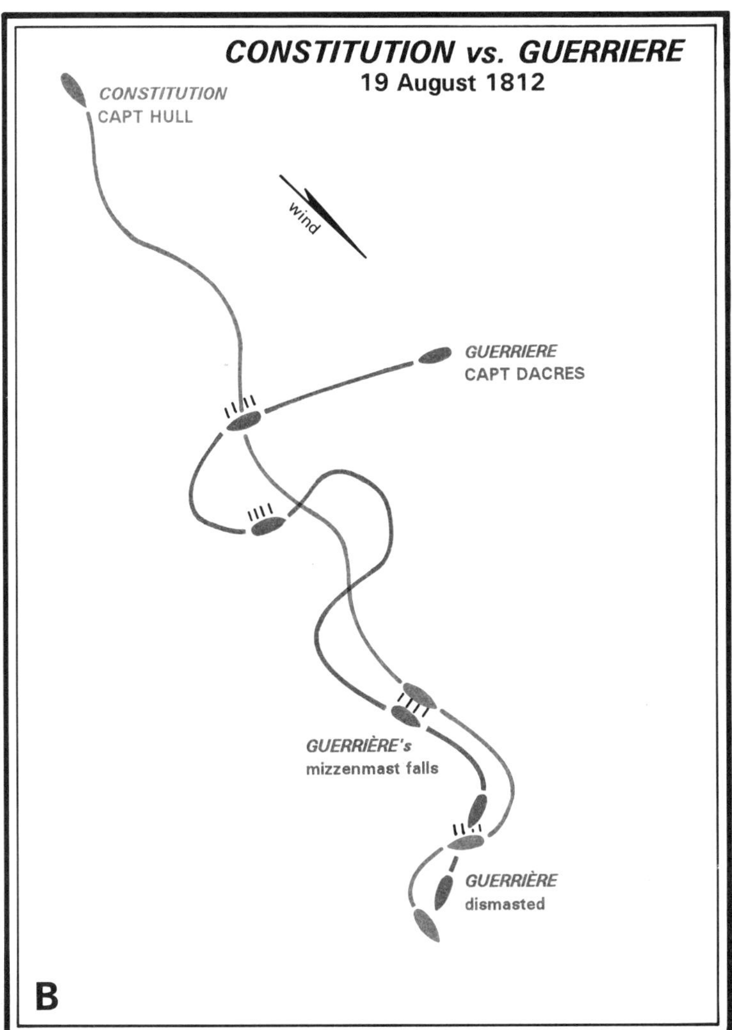

CONSTITUTION vs. GUERRIERE
19 August 1812
CONSTITUTION
CAPT HULL
wind
GUERRIERE
CAPT DACRES
GUERRIÈRE's
mizzenmast falls
GUERRIÈRE
dismasted
B

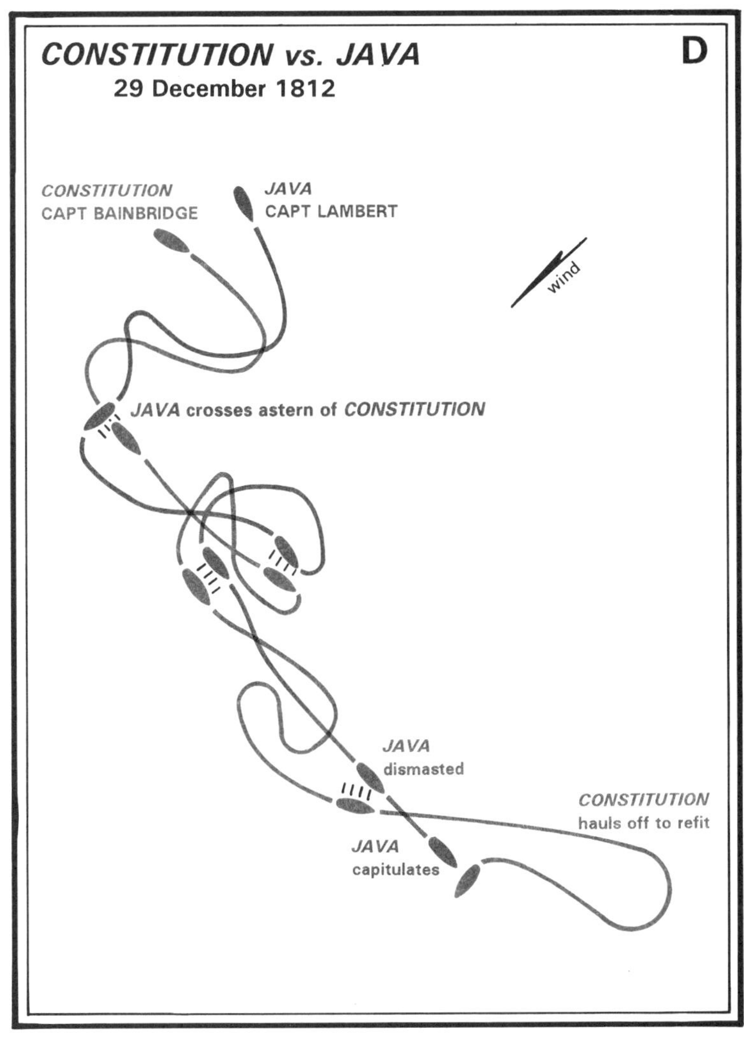

CONSTITUTION vs. JAVA
29 December 1812
D
CONSTITUTION
CAPT BAINBRIDGE
JAVA
CAPT LAMBERT
wind
JAVA crosses astern of CONSTITUTION
JAVA
dismasted
CONSTITUTION
hauls off to refit
JAVA
capitulates

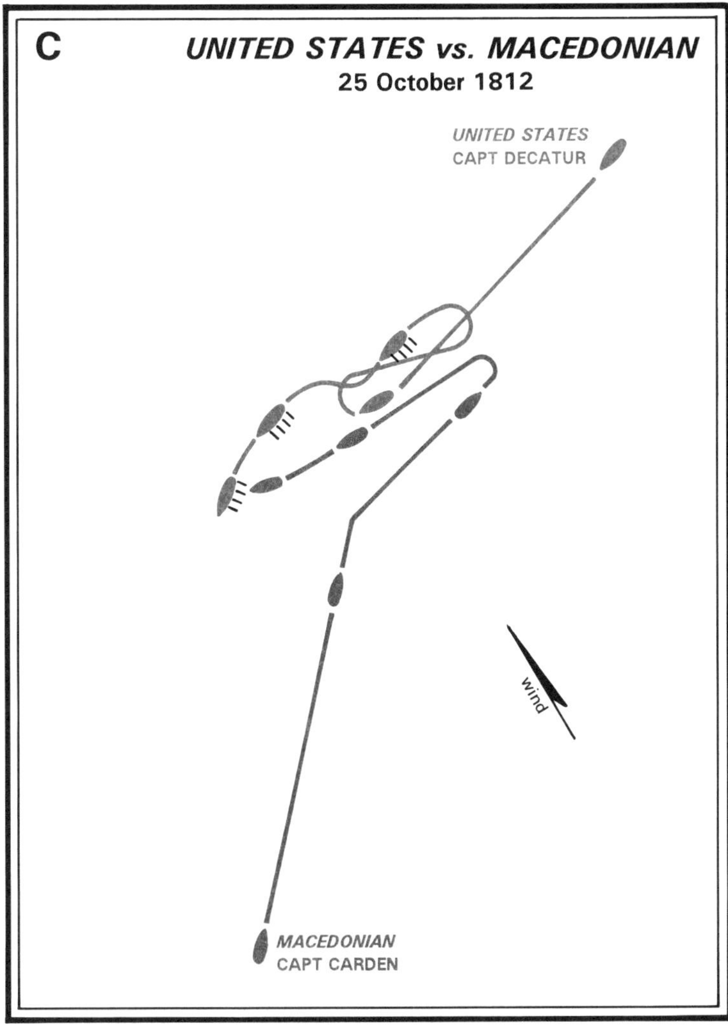

C
UNITED STATES vs. MACEDONIAN
25 October 1812
UNITED STATES
CAPT DECATUR
wind
MACEDONIAN
CAPT CARDEN

MAP 17

THE CRUISE OF THE *ESSEX*

DECEMBER 1812–MARCH 1814

The cruise of the American frigate *Essex,* commanded by David Porter, is one of the most remarkable stories of the War of 1812. Departing the Delaware Bay in September, the *Essex* was supposed to rendezvous with Bainbridge's squadron either at the Cape Verde Islands (1) or at Fernando de Noronha (2). But at each place Porter found that Bainbridge had already come and gone. Porter, therefore, headed south toward the next rendezvous at Cape Frio (3), but the irresistible attraction of a large British convoy lured him away, and he chased it for several hundred miles, taking one prize. Porter arrived next at Santa Catarina Island (4) but again found no sign of Bainbridge or the squadron. Finally, in late January, Porter learned from a passing Portuguese merchantman that Bainbridge had fought and won a battle with a British frigate (which was correct) and that the third vessel of the squadron, the *Hornet,* had been lost (which was incorrect). Assuming that his was the only vessel left of the original squadron, Porter decided to take his ship around Cape Horn into the Pacific, where he would raid British shipping in that previously inviolate sea.

The *Essex* approached Cape Horn in February and safely transited Le Maire Strait between the "horn" of Tierra del Fuego and the outermost island of De los Estados. Passing the strait proved to be the easy part. On the Pacific side of the strait the *Essex* encountered terrible storms (5) that threatened to sink her. After five days the weather finally abated, and the *Essex* headed up the western coast of South America to Mocha Island (6), where Porter stopped to take on fresh meat and water before proceeding to Valparaiso (7), where he arrived on 4 March 1813.

After repairing the effects of the storm, Porter left Valparaiso and headed north for the whaling grounds near the Galapagos Islands (8). There Porter found easy pickings, capturing eight prizes within two months, including several American whalers that the British had taken previously. In mid-June Porter took his prizes into Tumbes, Peru (9). There, he converted the largest of his prizes into a twenty-gun raider that he christened the *Essex Junior,* giving the command to LT John Downes. The *Essex Junior* convoyed four of the prizes to Valparaiso, and Porter took the *Essex* plus two armed whalers back to the Galapagos.

At Valparaiso, Downes learned that the British were sending three warships to track down the *Essex,* and he returned to the Galapagos to warn Porter. The news forced Porter to change his plans. After a summer in the South Pacific, the *Essex* was encumbered by a foul bottom and weakened rigging. If he expected to fight three British warships, one of which was reputed to be a thirty-six–gun frigate, what Porter needed was a place to refit without fear of being discovered. In early October, therefore, Porter announced to his crew that the *Essex,* the *Essex Junior,* and the four prizes would head for the Marquesas Islands in the South Pacific (10).

Porter, his officers, and his men spent seven weeks in this South Pacific paradise. Porter ordered that a fort be built, raised the American flag, and claimed the island (Nuku Hiva) for the United States. The natives welcomed this bit of imperialism (later disavowed by President Madison) largely because Porter agreed to help them in their local tribal wars. But the purpose of Porter's visit was to repair his ships. The *Essex* was emptied of its guns and stores and careened on the beach. Native workers helped the crew scrape and recopper the bottom, using copper sheeting taken from one of the British whalers. The interior of the ship was fumigated to drive out most of the rats, and the ship's worn rigging was replaced. The crew was allowed evening liberty on the island, one quarter of them at a time, and became so enamored of the place, and particularly of its women, that in December when the repairs were completed and it was time to go, there was so much grumbling that Porter feared a mutiny.

After a brief stop at Mocha Island, Porter returned to Valparaiso on 3 February. He might have been wiser to return immediately to the Atlantic with his prizes, but Porter sought a victory that would punctuate his Pacific adventure. On 8 February two British warships entered Valparaiso Harbor—the frigate *Phoebe,* 36, and the *Cherub,* 28. Ashore, Porter met with the British commander, CAPT James Hillyar, and suggested that the *Essex* and *Phoebe* fight a ship-to-ship dual, but Hillyar declined. The four warships—two British and two American—remained in Valparaiso Harbor for most of two months.

The impasse was broken on 28 March when the *Essex* lost its anchor in a gale and had to run for the open sea. Both British vessels followed. Outside the harbor, strong winds carried away the main-topmast of the *Essex,* and Porter sought refuge in a small bay south of Valparaiso (11). Though Porter was in neutral waters, the two British frigates closed, firing deliberate broadsides from beyond the effective reach of Porter's short-range carronades. For several hours they pounded the *Essex* from long range while Porter was unable to fight back. Nearly half the crew of the *Essex* was killed or wounded before Porter finally admitted that the situation was hopeless. He told those of his crew who wished to chance it to swim for shore, and he struck his flag.

Though it ended in disaster, Porter's Pacific odyssey demonstrated the ability of a warship in the age of sail to operate independently for long periods, and the devastating impact that a single warship could have on maritime trade or, in this case, a whaling fleet.

GREENLAND
ICELAND
ALASKA
Hudson's Bay
BRITISH CANADA
IRELAND
North Atlantic Ocean
OREGON
North Pacific Ocean
LOUISIANA PURCHASE
UNITED STATES
MEXICO
Boston
New York
Philadelphia
ESSEX departs
AZORES (Port.)
CANARY ISLANDS (Sp.)
Gulf of Mexico
BAHAMA ISLANDS
CUBA
Caribbean Sea
LESSER ANTILLES
1
CAPE VERDE ISLANDS (Port.)
AFRICA
VENEZUELA
COLOMBIA
8
GALAPAGOS ISLANDS
9
Tumbes
2
FERNANDO DE NORONHA (Port.)
10
25 Oct - 13 Dec 1813
ESSEX refits
ESSEX captures 12 prizes
PERU (Sp.)
BRAZIL (Port.)
MARQUESAS ISLANDS
3
Rio de Janeiro
ESSEX pursues British convoy
4
SANTA CATARINA ISLAND
PITCAIRN ISLAND
11
28 March 1814
ESSEX vs. PHOEBE & CHERUB
7
Valparaiso
Buenos Aires
6
MOCHA ISLAND
CHILE
ARGENTINA
South Pacific Ocean
South Atlantic Ocean
Strait of Magellan
FALKLAND ISLANDS
Le Maire Strait
0 500 1000 1500 2000
Nautical Miles at Equator
ESSEX battles storms
5
Drake Strait
120°
90°
60°
30°
0°

MAP 18

THE GREAT LAKES (BATTLE OF LAKE ERIE)

10 SEPTEMBER 1813

Many of those who had voted for war in June of 1812 had expected that the first military action of the war would be an American conquest of Canada. In pursuit of that goal, American BGEN William Hull (the uncle of Isaac Hull) prepared to invade Upper Canada in the summer of 1812 with an army of some two thousand militiamen (1). Though Hull's army was vastly superior to British land forces in the area, he soon convinced himself that he was in jeopardy of being cut off by hostile Indians to the west and by a British naval squadron on Lake Erie. Falling back on Detroit, Hull withstood a brief siege before losing his nerve and surrendering the town on 16 August, an act for which he was later court-martialed and sentenced to be shot, though President Madison commuted the execution. The British took advantage of their success at Detroit to launch an invasion of their own (2) that carried them to the banks of the Sandusky River in Ohio by the summer of 1813.

Meanwhile, the Navy Department sent COMMO Isaac Chauncey to take command of both Lake Erie and Lake Ontario and to supervise the construction of naval squadrons on both lakes. Chauncey assumed personal command of the Lake Ontario squadron based at Sackett's Harbor (3) and dispatched LT Jesse Elliot to Presque Isle (4) to take command of the squadron on Lake Erie. Chauncey put to sea in the spring of 1813, and ignoring the major British naval base at Kingston (5), he sailed instead to York (6), now Toronto, which he captured and put to the torch on 27 April. In May the British naval commander on Lake Ontario, COMMO Sir James Yeo, returned the favor, unsuccessfully attacking Sackett's Harbor.

Throughout the summer and fall Chauncey and Yeo engaged in several long-range skirmishes, including clashes near the mouth of the Genesee River (7) and the so-called Burlington Races (8), but the only significant losses to either side came when two American schooners were lost to a storm on 8 August and two others were captured on 10 August. Indeed, for the rest of the war the Anglo-American war on Lake Ontario consisted primarily of a naval building contest in which each side tried unsuccessfully to gain naval superiority. Before the end of the war the British had launched a 102-gun battleship, and the Americans had two 120-gun ships under construction.

While Chauncey and Yeo skirmished indecisively on Lake Ontario, naval forces on Lake Erie fought one of the most important battles of the war. In the spring of 1813 Master Commandant Oliver Hazard Perry arrived at the American naval base of Presque Isle to succeed Lieutenant Elliot in command of the American squadron on Lake Erie (Elliot stayed on as Perry's second in command). Perry inherited a squadron of two twenty-gun brigs and nine smaller vessels, but his greatest problem was manpower. When the Navy Department sent new recruits west for the lake squadrons, Chauncey kept most of them for his ever-expanding fleet on Lake Ontario. Perry appealed to the new Army commander, MGEN William Henry Harrison, who sent to Perry all those in his army who would admit to having sea experience, plus one hundred sharpshooters. Thus outfitted, Perry sailed from Presque Isle on 6 August and established an advance base at Put-In-Bay in the Bass Islands (9), from which his force could constitute a threat to British communications between Detroit and Malden. Perry's move forced the hand of the commander of the British squadron at Malden (10), CAPT Robert H. Barclay. Despite a 50 percent inferiority in broadside throw weight, Barclay decided to sortie and attempt to regain command of the lake.

The two squadrons met on 10 September (see lower map). Perry had the weather gauge, and because most of his guns were short-range carronades, he sought to close quickly with the enemy and batter him into submission. Directing the rest of his squadron to follow, he steered a course to approach the British squadron at an acute angle (A) so as to minimize the effect of British raking fire. In his haste to close the range, however, Perry's flagship, the *Lawrence,* soon opened a gap over the rest of the American squadron. Worse, Lieutenant Elliot in the *Niagara* showed no particular eagerness to catch up, and the *Lawrence* took the brunt of the British fire. From noon until 2:00 P.M. the *Lawrence* fought the British squadron virtually alone, and still Elliot did not bring the *Niagara* into the fight. Finally, with his rigging shot to pieces and 80 percent of his crew killed or wounded, Perry ordered himself rowed over to the *Niagara* (B). Climbing aboard, Perry sent Elliot to take charge of bringing the small schooners into the fight, then he steered the *Niagara* across the bows of the two British vessels that had been dueling with the *Lawrence* and compelled their surrender (C).

Small in comparison with the great fleet engagements of the Napoleonic wars, the Battle of Lake Erie had a strategic significance out of all proportion to its size. It forced the British to give up their invasion of Ohio and allowed Harrison's American army to assume the offensive. Knowing that news of the American naval victory was crucial to Harrison, Perry grabbed a piece of paper (actually the back of an old envelope) and scrawled a quick note to him: "We have met the enemy, and they are ours: Two Ships, two Brigs, one Schooner & one Sloop." With command of the lake, Perry transported Harrison's army to intercept the retreating British, and the Americans fought and won a tactical victory at the Battle of the Thames (11) on 5 October 1813. Though Perry's victory did not lead to an American conquest of Canada, it did reverse the tide of battle on the western frontier and forestalled any British claim to the Northwest Territory.

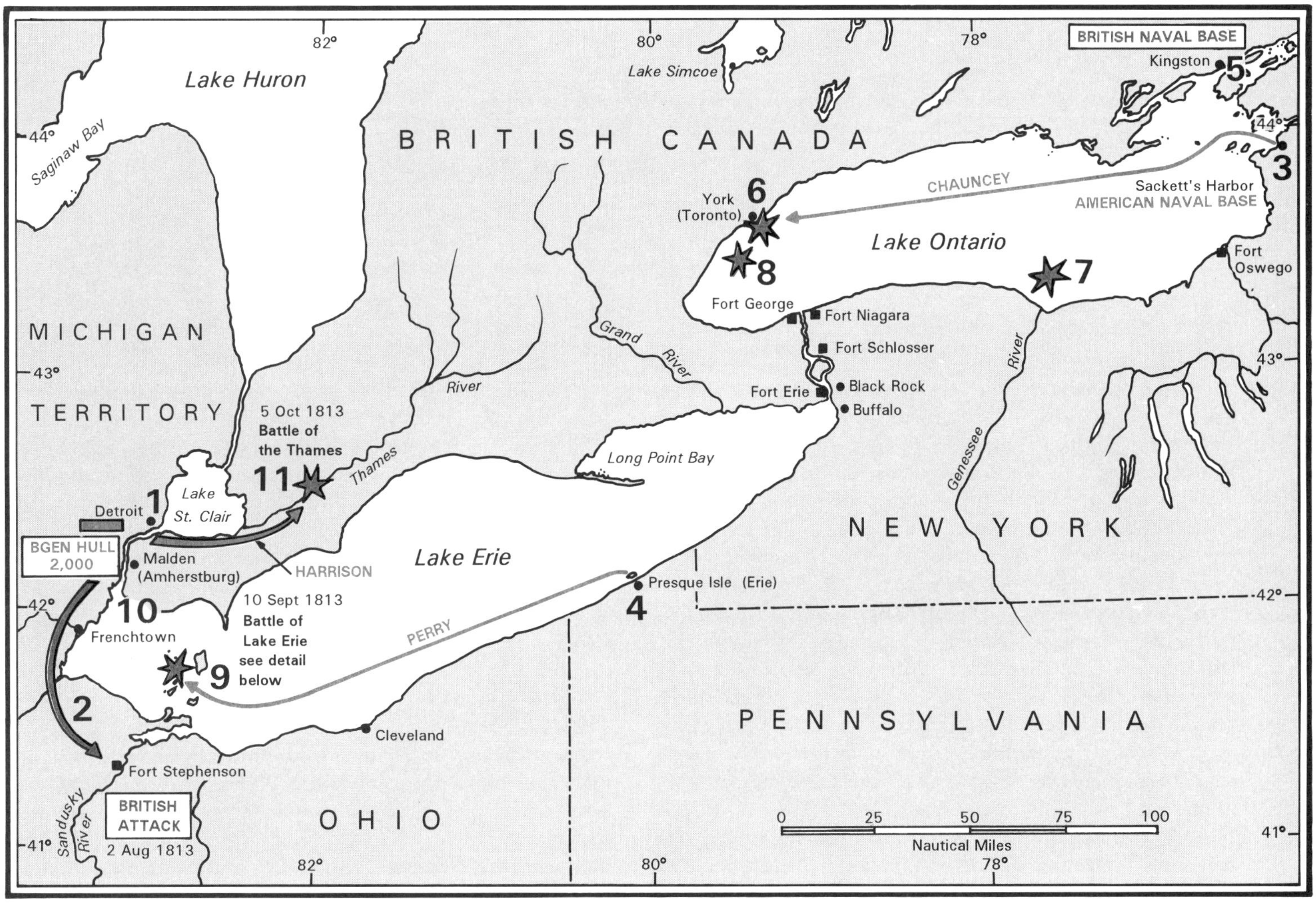

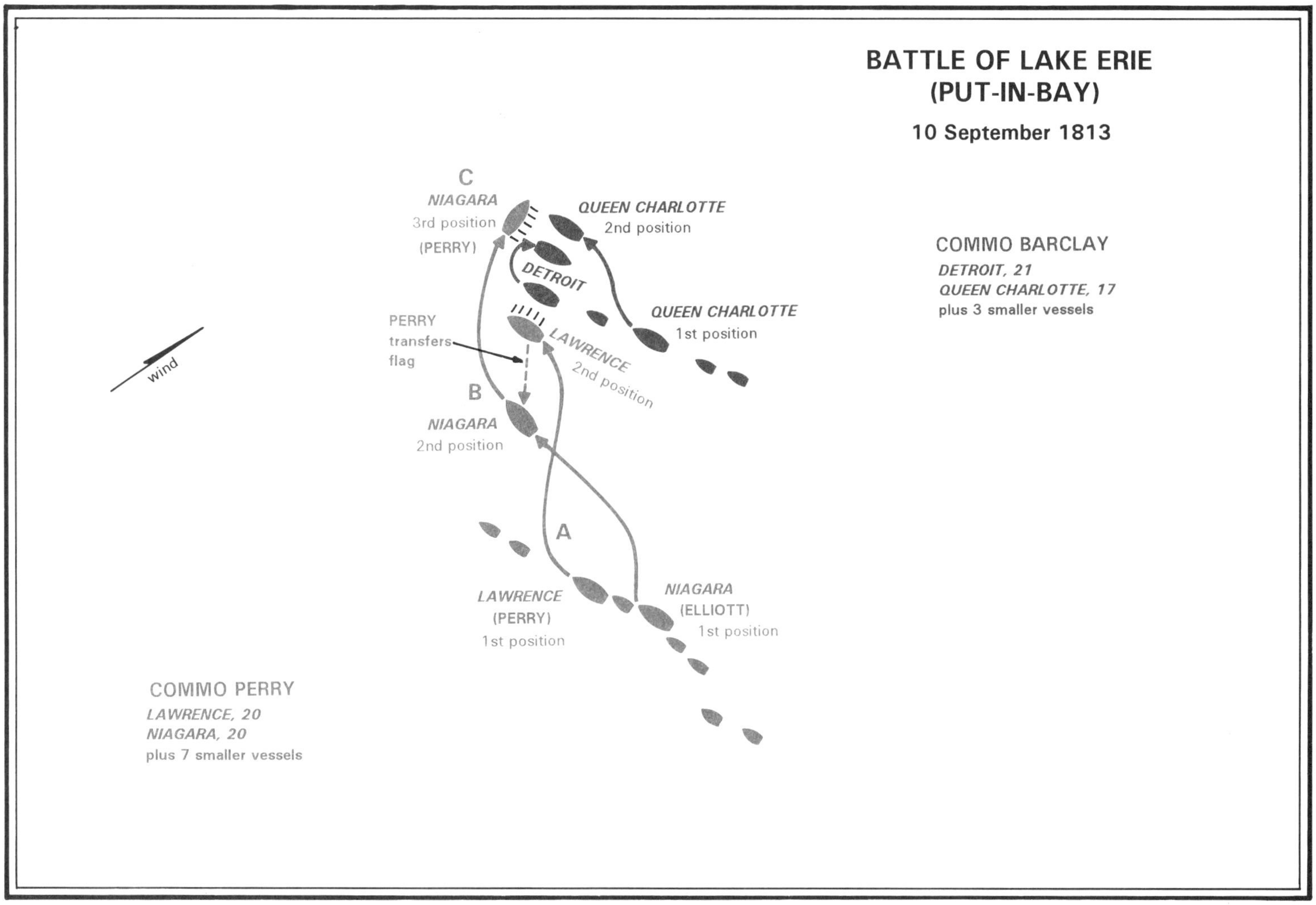

BATTLE OF LAKE ERIE (PUT-IN-BAY)

10 September 1813

Map 19

The Chesapeake Bay

Summer 1814

To Europeans, America's war with Britain on the Canadian frontier was only a sideshow of the gigantic conflict that was reaching a crisis in Europe in the fall of 1813. A month after Perry's victory on Lake Erie, Britain's European allies won a major victory over Napoleon at Leipzig in the so-called Battle of Nations (16–19 October 1813). Soon the armies of France were in retreat on all fronts, and in March 1814 the allied armies entered Paris. The Bourbon kings were restored to the throne of France, Napoleon was exiled to the island of Elba, and the long war between England and France was apparently at an end. From America's point of view, this was a disastrous turn of events, for with the defeat of France, all the power of the British Empire could now be concentrated on the war in America.

That summer, American armies along the Canadian frontier made one last effort to secure a foothold in enemy territory. In July of 1814 a 3,500-man army under MGEN Jacob Brown crossed the Niagara River, captured Fort Erie, and fought the Battles of Chippewa (5 July) and Lundy's Lane (25 July), both of which the United States claimed as victories but neither of which was decisive. Brown's men repelled several vigorous British efforts to retake Fort Erie, but at the end of the campaign season he abandoned the fort and withdrew across the river. With British troop strength in Canada topping thirty thousand, the initiative passed to the redcoats.

The first target of the 1814 British counteroffensive was the Chesapeake Bay. Originally intended as a diversion to draw American strength and attention away from the Canadian frontier, the British campaign in the Chesapeake Bay demonstrated just how weak and disorganized American defenses were. The campaign began in the spring when a British fleet appeared in the Chesapeake and established a base on Watts Island in Tangier Sound (1). The American flotilla of two gunboats and a dozen barges under the command of COMMO Joshua Barney dropped down from Baltimore to Drum Point (2) to defend the upper Chesapeake, but British naval forces under ADM Alexander Cochrane forced Barney to retire up the Patuxent River to St. Leonard's Creek (3). There, British and American barges fought a general engagement on 10 June in which the Americans lost a barge and the British an eighteen-gun schooner. Two weeks later, on 26 June, Barney successfully fought his way out of St. Leonard's Creek, but he remained trapped in the cul-de-sac of the Patuxent River. Hemmed in by the narrowing estuary, and outflanked by British forces on land, Barney eventually had to abandon his ships at Pig Point (4) opposite Upper Marlborough. The inability of Barney's flotilla to do more than annoy the British invasion fleet was convincing testimony to the limitations of gunboats to stand up to traditional warships.

By August the British had assembled a substantial force in the Chesapeake Bay: twenty warships under Cochrane and an army of four thousand regulars commanded by MGEN Robert Ross. On 19 August British ships escorted the army up the Patuxent River to Benedict, Maryland (5), where it landed. Belatedly, the Americans made frantic efforts to pull together an army to defend the capital. By 24 August they had gathered some seven thousand men at Bladensburg (6) under the overall command of MGEN William Winder. Most of the troops were raw militiamen, but five hundred regulars and five hundred sailors and marines from Barney's gunboat flotilla bolstered those troops.

The Battle of Bladensburg was an American disaster. The American command structure was so confusing that officers issued contradictory orders; the American lines were too far apart for mutual support; and despite numerical superiority, the American militia stood only briefly before fleeing the field, hastened on its way by the terrifying Congreve rockets. Only the courageous stand of Barney's gunners prevented a rout. The British entered Washington that night and set fire to the abandoned public buildings—including the Capitol and the White House—in retaliation for the destruction of York (Toronto) the previous year. In addition to the damage to the city itself, the U.S. Navy suffered a severe blow when American Navy CAPT Thomas Tingey set fire to the Washington Navy Yard and to two new warships, the frigate *Columbia* and the sloop *Argus,* to prevent them from falling into British hands.

After their easy victory, the British reembarked and proceeded up the Chesapeake Bay toward Baltimore. MGEN Ross landed his army at North Point (7) on 12 September, and that same day his force defeated a body of American militia in the Battle of North Point (8), where a sniper killed Ross himself. That night the British deployed within sight of the city. While the British Army threatened the city from the north, Admiral Cochrane's ships commenced a bombardment of Fort McHenry (9), the city's principal harbor fortification. The American defenders could not respond because Cochrane kept his ships outside the range of conventional artillery and lobbed mortar shells into the fort. On board one of the British ships, Francis Scott Key watched the bombardment with some anxiety. Several of the mortar shells (bombs) whose fuses were cut too short burst over the fort, and occasionally the red glare of a Congreve rocket would streak from one of the ships toward the fort. With the dawn, Key was so delighted to see the oversize flag of Fort McHenry still flying that he wrote the poem that would later become the lyrics for the national anthem. That same morning the British land force began its retreat to North Point.

The successful defense of Baltimore notwithstanding, the British depredations in the Chesapeake Bay in the summer of 1814 demonstrated vividly that the war had turned against the Americans.

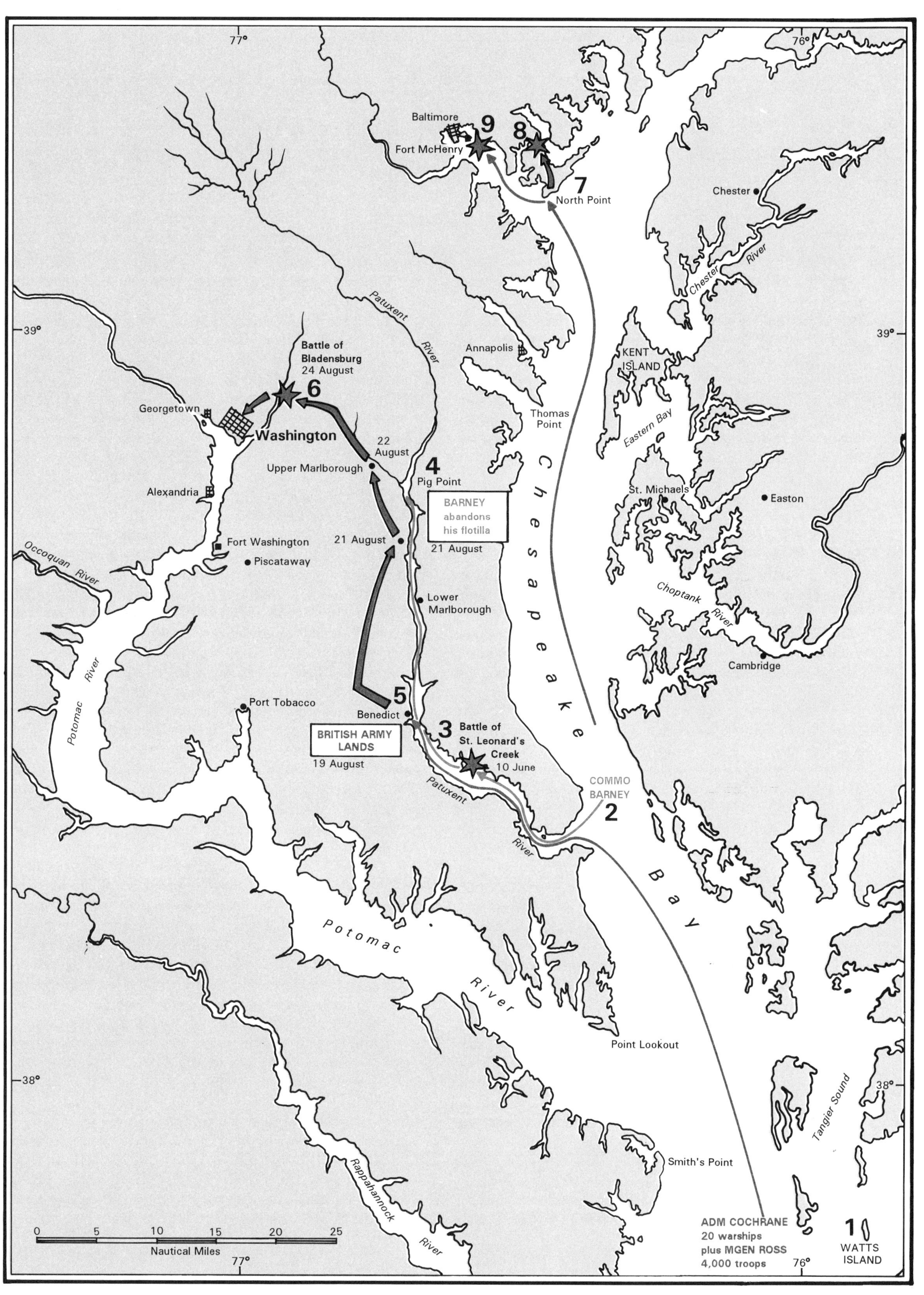

77°
76°
Baltimore
9
8
Fort McHenry
7
North Point
Chester
Chester River
Patuxent River
39°
Annapolis
KENT ISLAND
Battle of Bladensburg
24 August
6
Georgetown
Washington
Thomas Point
Eastern Bay
22 August
Upper Marlborough
4
Pig Point
Chesapeake Bay
BARNEY abandons his flotilla
21 August
St. Michaels
Easton
21 August
Fort Washington
Piscataway
Alexandria
Occoquan River
Lower Marlborough
Choptank River
Cambridge
Potomac River
Port Tobacco
5
Benedict
3
Battle of St. Leonard's Creek
10 June
BRITISH ARMY LANDS
19 August
COMMO BARNEY
2
Patuxent River
Potomac River
Point Lookout
38°
Tangier Sound
Smith's Point
Rappahannock River
0 5 10 15 20 25
Nautical Miles
ADM COCHRANE
20 warships
plus MGEN ROSS
4,000 troops
1
WATTS ISLAND

MAP 20

THE BATTLE OF LAKE CHAMPLAIN

11 SEPTEMBER 1814

The British offensive in the Chesapeake Bay was supposed to have been a diversion for the nearly simultaneous British invasion of New York along the traditional eighteenth-century military route from Canada to Lake Champlain (see map 3). Even as Washington burned, MGEN Sir George Prevost crossed the U.S. border on the last day of August 1814 with an army of eleven thousand men and marched south along the western bank of Lake Champlain. His objective was the town of Plattsburg (1), which he planned to hold as a bargaining chip in the peace negotiations.

The American Army at Plattsburg consisted of 1,500 regulars and perhaps 3,000 militia, all under the command of BGEN Alexander Macomb. Though Macomb's subordinates urged him to withdraw in the face of this overwhelming force, Macomb was determined to defend the town. He placed his men behind the Saranac River (2) and waited for the invaders. Though Prevost was confident that he could sweep Macomb's force aside, he knew he could not sustain himself in Plattsburg without command of the lake to maintain his communications with Canada. Just as in 1776, therefore, the fight between British and American naval squadrons on Lake Champlain would determine the fate of the campaign.

The American fleet on Lake Champlain consisted of four larger vessels and ten barges carrying a total of eighty-six guns and was commanded by thirty-year-old Master Commandant Thomas Macdonough. The British force of four larger vessels and twelve gunboats boasted about the same number of total guns (eighty-seven) but had a significant advantage in long guns, which had greater range and accuracy than the American carronades. Like Perry on Lake Erie, Macdonough's best hope was to force a close action, but the young American commander knew that his ships' crews were made up of inexperienced sailors who might stand manfully by their guns but who lacked the nautical skills to maneuver effectively in the open waters of the lake. He, therefore, decided to anchor his fleet off Plattsburg, guarding Macomb's right flank, and fight a battle of static defense.

Macdonough prepared his position with some care (see inset). He made sure that all of his vessels were securely anchored bow (A) and stern (B) so as to create a stable firing platform, but he also rigged cables leading to kedge anchors (C)—lines running fore and aft that could be used to wind the ship, that is, spin the vessel about in place like a top (D). This would allow the American ships to present either their starboard or port battery to the enemy.

The British naval commander, CAPT John Downie, was no more confident of the skill of his sailors than Macdonough, but his advantage in long guns made a running fight in the open lake his best hope. He certainly did not want to have to fight the American squadron in the confined waters of Plattsburg Harbor. But Prevost (perhaps remembering Burgoyne's experience at Saratoga) was concerned about getting bogged down in the American wilderness, and he urged Downie to attack.

On 11 September (the day before the Battle of North Point near Baltimore) Downie's squadron rounded Cumberland Head (3) in front of a following wind and then hauled the sheets to turn into the bay. When the British vessels cleared Cumberland Head, the looming bulk of that headland killed the wind, and Downie's vessels drifted slowly toward the American battle line, much more slowly than Downie would have wished. Once alongside, however, the battle became an old-fashioned slugfest at close range. This was the kind of battle at which British crews excelled: firing rapidly into an enemy hull.

The key to the battle was the match between the two flagships: Macdonough's *Saratoga,* 26, and Downie's *Confiance,* 37. The British vessel was both larger and more powerfully armed, and its broadsides soon began to tell on the smaller American vessel. The American advantage in short-range heavy-caliber carronades evened the score slightly. Alas for Downie, one American shot struck a British twenty-four–pound gun square on the muzzle and drove it backward into Downie and killed him. The shot flying across the deck of the *Saratoga* and rigging falling from the tops nearly killed Macdonough as well. After an hour of very heavy fighting at close range, both ships were badly damaged, and the rate of fire slowed dramatically. At that moment Macdonough ordered his crew to cut the lines to the bow and stern anchors and haul in on the lines to the kedge anchors, allowing the *Saratoga* to present a fresh battery (see inset).

On the *Confiance* the young lieutenant who had succeeded Downie to command attempted to duplicate Macdonough's maneuver, but because he had not prepared kedge anchors, he was unable to do so and succeeded only in presenting Macdonough with the *Confiance*'s bow, allowing the Americans to rake the British vessel fore to aft. Soon afterward the *Confiance* struck, and the rest of the British squadron soon followed suit. It was as complete a victory as Perry's on Lake Erie, and perhaps in recognition of that Macdonough penned a similar report: "The Almighty has been pleased to Grant us a Signal Victory on Lake Champlain in the Capture of one Frigate, one Brig and two sloops of war of the enemy."

With his naval squadron destroyed, Prevost lost his enthusiasm for the campaign and withdrew northward, leaving a large supply of military stores behind. Almost exactly one year to the day after Perry's victory on Lake Erie, an American freshwater naval squadron had reversed the tide of war along the New York–Canadian frontier and forced the withdrawal of another British Army from U.S. territory.

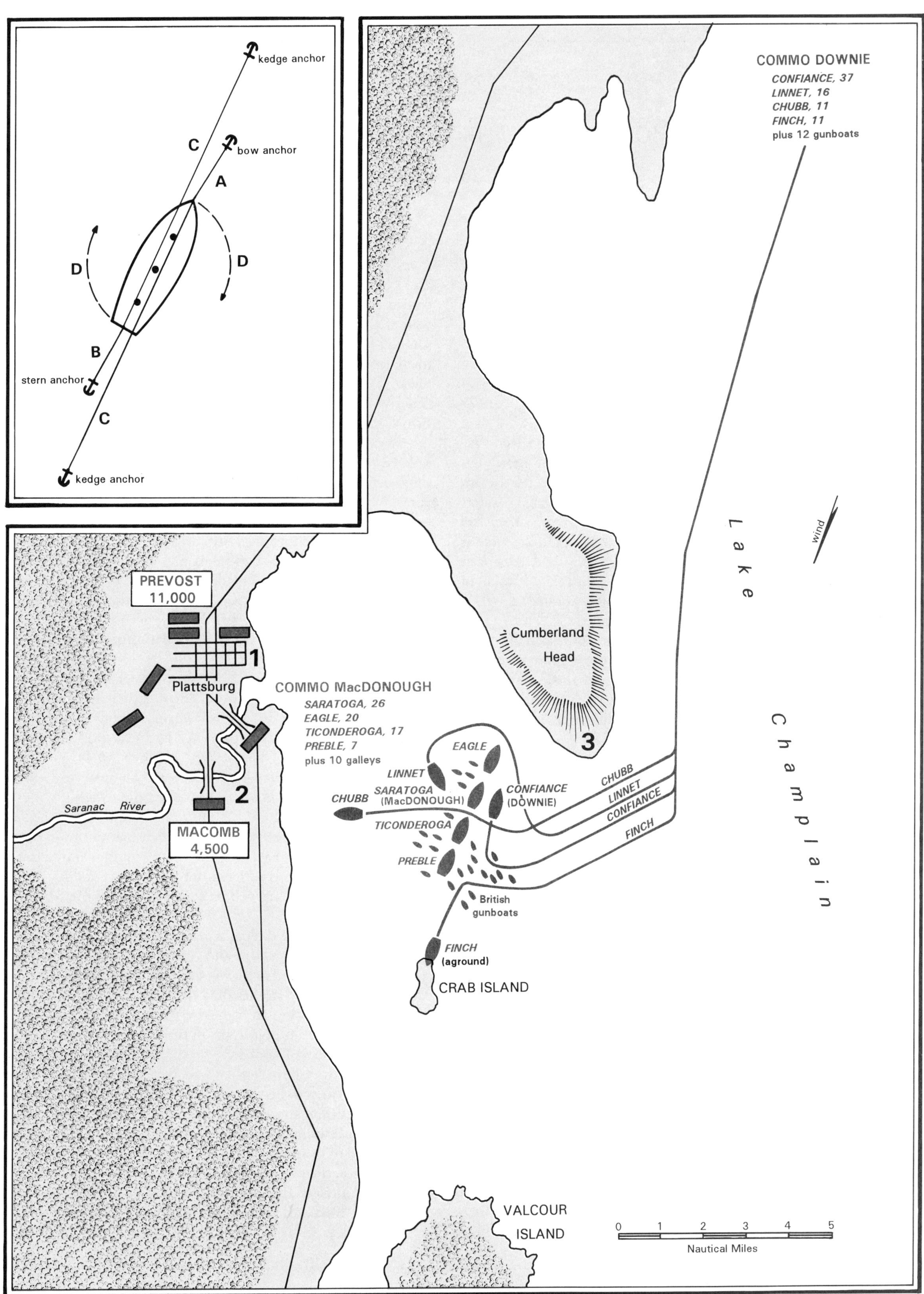
kedge anchor
C
bow anchor
A
D
D
B
stern anchor
C
kedge anchor
COMMO DOWNIE
CONFIANCE, 37
LINNET, 16
CHUBB, 11
FINCH, 11
plus 12 gunboats
wind
Lake Champlain
PREVOST
11,000
1
Plattsburg
Cumberland Head
3
COMMO MacDONOUGH
SARATOGA, 26
EAGLE, 20
TICONDEROGA, 17
PREBLE, 7
plus 10 galleys
EAGLE
LINNET
SARATOGA (MacDONOUGH)
CONFIANCE (DOWNIE)
CHUBB
TICONDEROGA
PREBLE
CHUBB
LINNET
CONFIANCE
FINCH
2
Saranac River
MACOMB
4,500
British gunboats
FINCH (aground)
CRAB ISLAND
VALCOUR ISLAND
0 1 2 3 4 5
Nautical Miles

MAP 21

LAKE BORGNE AND THE BATTLE OF NEW ORLEANS

DECEMBER 1814–JANUARY 1815

While Prevost's army invaded the United States from the north, another British Army was preparing to invade from the south. In November 1814 Admiral Cochrane's fleet escorted a British Army of ten thousand men under LGEN Sir Edward Pakenham from Jamaica into the Gulf of Mexico, where Pakenham established an advance base on Cat Island (1). Pakenham's orders were to capture and occupy New Orleans (2), thereby cutting off American trade down the Mississippi, and to hold the city as a counterweight in the peace negotiations that were already under way in Ghent, Belgium.

Rather than thread his way up the Mississippi River, Pakenham decided to approach New Orleans via the nearly enclosed bay known as Lake Borgne (3). Because the British ships-of-the-line and frigates could not enter the shallow waters of Lake Borgne, the British gathered together some forty-five barges and ship's longboats, each mounting one gun, to serve as an invasion flotilla. Blocking their way was a small American squadron consisting of five gunboats mounting a total of twenty-three guns, which was under the command of LT Thomas ap Catesby Jones. Jones had planned to fall back to the narrows between Lake Borgne and Lake Pontchartrain called the Rigolets (4), where he could count on support from land batteries. Alas, a dying wind and an ebb tide made that impossible, and Jones was forced to fight it out with the British flotilla near the entrance to Lake Borgne at Malheureux Island (5) on 14 December 1814.

Like Macdonough at Plattsburg, Jones established a stationary battle line, and to advance, the British had to row laboriously into the wind. The Americans were able to do significant damage to the British during their approach, but once the British closed the range, their superior numbers began to tell. One by one the American gunboats were forced to strike, and Jones and his entire command were taken prisoner. Despite his defeat, Jones's sacrifice served to delay the British, giving the American forces at New Orleans not only more time to prepare their defenses but foreknowledge of the British approach route.

The lead elements of Pakenham's army advanced across Lake Borgne, through Bayou Bienvenu and Bayou Mazant, to the plantation of Jacques Villere (6) on the eastern bank of the Mississippi eight miles south of New Orleans (see lower map). Here Pakenham established his headquarters and supervised the concentration of his army, which had to be shuttled from the fleet anchorage along his lengthy line of communications.

Meanwhile, the American defense of New Orleans had become the concern of MGEN Andrew Jackson, a fiery-tempered and determined officer with plenty of frontier fighting experience. No stickler for regulations, Jackson accepted all volunteers who expressed a willingness to serve, including a company of free blacks made up of refugees from San Domingo and the Baratarian pirates under the infamous Jean Lafitte. Jackson also had two warships available: the ship-rigged *Louisiana,* 22, and the schooner *Carolina,* 14. On the night of 23 December Jackson led a mixed force of 1,800 men, accompanied by the two warships, to the British outpost at Villere's plantation and launched a surprise attack (7) that inflicted some 275 casualties on the British, though Jackson was eventually forced to retreat, having suffered more than 200 casualties of his own. The two warships played a major role in this American success, firing grapeshot from close range into the British ranks on shore.

Determined to eliminate the American ships, Pakenham ordered a furnace built to enable his gunners to fire "hot shot"—heated cannon balls designed to set wooden vessels afire. With these the British routed the two American ships during a second attack on 27 December; the *Carolina* blew up when flames reached its magazine. To neutralize the *Louisiana,* Pakenham ordered that boats be manhandled over the bayous from Lake Borgne so that British troops could be ferried across the river to attack the American outpost on the western bank (8). These troops would then use the American artillery to contain the *Louisiana* and to enfilade the main American line on the eastern bank of the river.

The British launched their main attack on 8 January 1815 (9). Some 5,300 redcoats boldly assailed the American defensive line manned by Jackson's mixed force of 4,700 militia and volunteers, who were protected by an earth and log barricade behind a canal. The attackers took horrible losses while crossing the open boggy fields in the teeth of a fierce and accurate fire. Few British soldiers even reached the American lines. The main assault lasted only about an hour, and at the end of it the British had suffered two thousand casualties (more than 37 percent), including Pakenham, who was cut in half by a cannon ball; the Americans suffered only thirteen casualties. Pakenham's successor determined to accept defeat and retreat the way he had come.

Though none of the participants of this campaign could have known it, the American and British negotiators at Ghent had agreed to peace terms two weeks earlier—on Christmas Eve 1814. In effect, the peace restored the status quo ante bellum. The United States did not "win" the War of 1812, for it failed to achieve either of its objectives on the battlefield: Canada remained unconquered, and though the British did repeal the hated Orders in Council, they had done so before the war started. Nevertheless, because of the American frigate victories in 1812, because of the victories on Lakes Erie and Champlain, and because of the nearly simultaneous arrival along the eastern seaboard of the news of the victory at New Orleans and the news of peace, the psychological impact was to create a sense of victory in American minds. That sentiment boosted American morale and enhanced the prospects of the U.S. Navy in the postwar years.

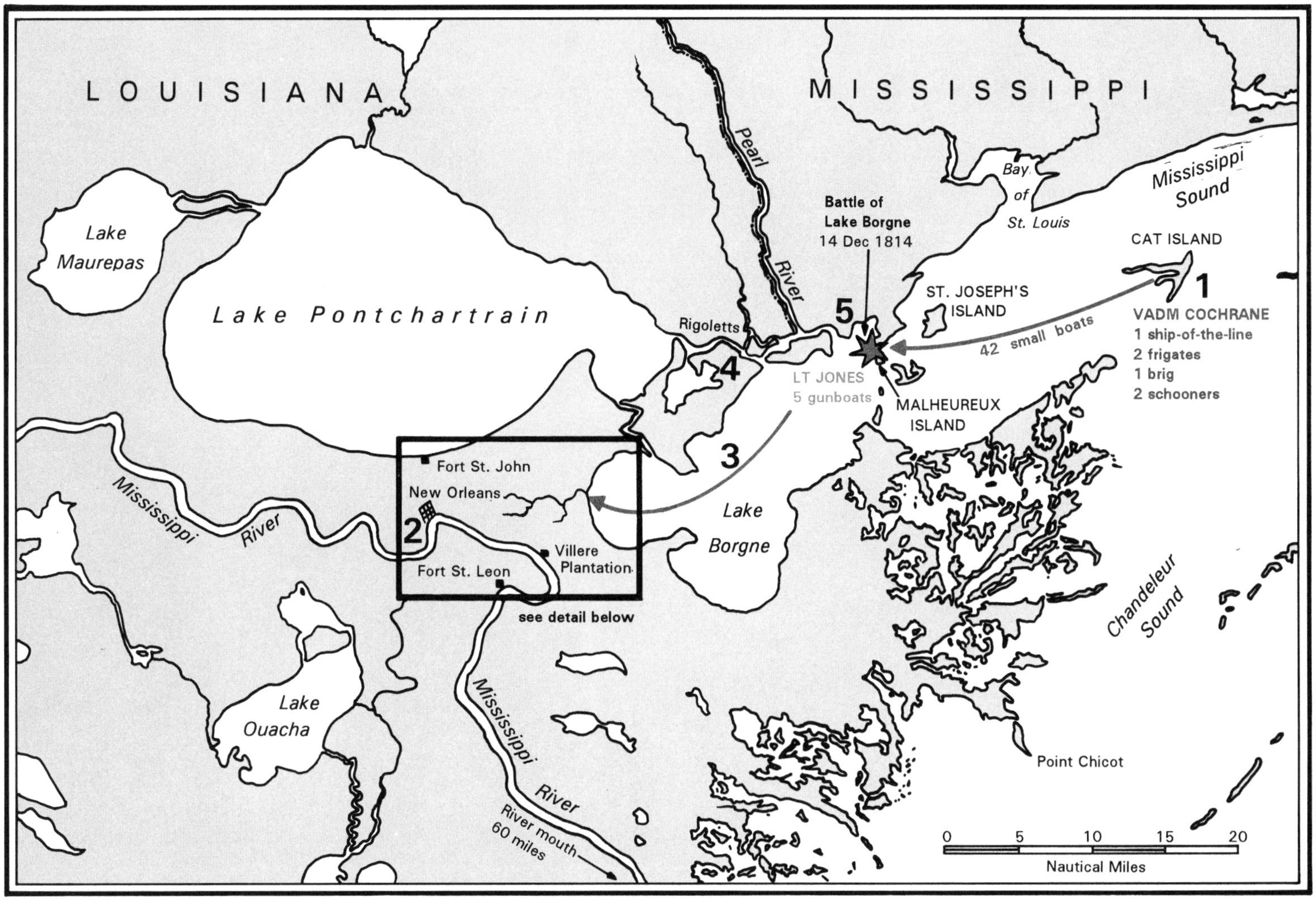

LOUISIANA

MISSISSIPPI

Pearl River

Bay of St. Louis

Mississippi Sound

Battle of Lake Borgne
14 Dec 1814

CAT ISLAND

Lake Maurepas

Lake Pontchartrain

Rigoletts

5

ST. JOSEPH'S ISLAND

42 small boats

1

VADM COCHRANE
1 ship-of-the-line
2 frigates
1 brig
2 schooners

4

LT JONES
5 gunboats

MALHEUREUX ISLAND

3

Fort St. John

New Orleans

2

Mississippi River

Lake Borgne

Villere Plantation

Fort St. Leon

see detail below

Chandeleur Sound

Lake Ouacha

Mississippi River

River mouth 60 miles

Point Chicot

0 5 10 15 20
Nautical Miles

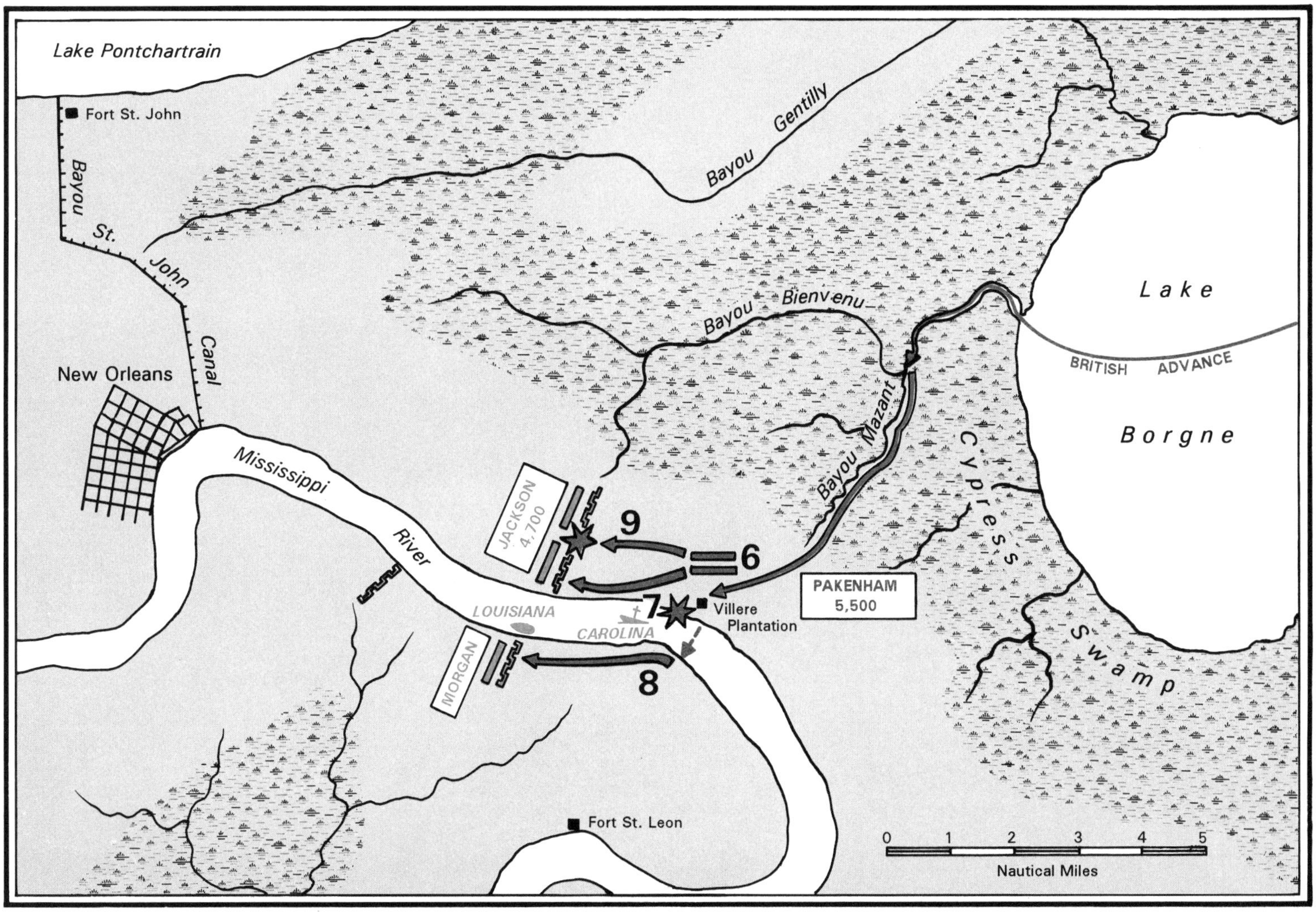

Lake Pontchartrain

Fort St. John

Bayou St. John Canal

Bayou Gentilly

Bayou Bienvenu

Lake Borgne

BRITISH ADVANCE

New Orleans

Mississippi River

Bayou Mazant

Cypress Swamp

JACKSON 4,700

9

6

PAKENHAM 5,500

7

Villere Plantation

LOUISIANA

CAROLINA

MORGAN

8

Fort St. Leon

0 1 2 3 4 5
Nautical Miles

PART IV

Pirates, Explorers, and War with Mexico 1815–1860

THE BURST OF NATIONALISM that followed the news of peace in 1815 marked the onset of an "Era of Good Feelings" characterized by economic resurgence, territorial expansion, and a growing nationalism that finally collapsed amidst the sectional confrontations of the 1850s. The period began with the revival of American trade to Europe as exports increased from just less than $7 million in 1814 to more than $93 million in 1818, and it ended with a naval mission to open Japan that offered a promise of increased trade with Asia as well. In between, an American scientific and exploring expedition circumnavigated the globe, and a one-sided victory over Mexico brought 150,000 square miles of new land into the national domain.

At the very outset of this era, the United States committed itself to a dramatic expansion of the Navy. The American frigate victories during the War of 1812 had had little impact on the outcome of the war, but they had gratified the public mind and helped convince Congress to commit the unprecedented sum of $10 million to the construction of a peacetime fleet of ships-of the-line. With the "Act for the Gradual Increase of the Navy," passed in April of 1816, Congress authorized the single largest naval expansion in American history up to that time: nine new ships-of-the-line and twelve new heavy frigates. Like the Humphreys frigates, the new vessels authorized by this legislation were to be the best of their class. Though rated at 74 guns, these American ships-of-the-line would each carry 80 to 100 guns, and the largest of them, the *Pennsylvania,* would boast more than 120. Similarly, all the frigates would be of the forty-four–gun variety, carrying up to sixty guns each. When all of this building was completed, it would make the United States a naval power of the first rank.

The U.S. gunboats Spitfire *and* Scorpion, *part of the squadron commanded by COMMO Matthew C. Perry, steam upriver toward the Mexican city of Tabasco on 16 June 1847 (see map 26). The U.S. war with Mexico was the first in which the U.S. Navy made widespread use of steam warships, and the first in which it conducted a major amphibious operation. (Franklin D. Roosevelt Library)*

Ironically, however, none of these vessels ever fired a shot in anger. In large part this was because the missions that the U.S. Navy was called upon to perform in the four decades after 1816 required smaller, quicker, and handier vessels. In this period of burgeoning commerce and expanding boundaries, the mission of the U.S. Navy focused largely on the protection of trade. Beginning with a renewal of the conflict with the "pirates" of the North African coast (see map 22), the U.S. Navy focused most of its effort on patrolling those areas where American trade was threatened—the Caribbean, the African coast, the Brazilian coast, and, increasingly, the Pacific (see maps 23–24). In all these areas the huge ships-of-the-line authorized in 1816 proved to be inappropriate and inefficient for the jobs they were asked to do. Hollywood notwithstanding, most pirate ships were not "ships" at all but small, handy, fore-and-aft rigged vessels with one or two guns. They could outsail and outmaneuver the giant two-deck battleships, and they could escape into shoal water or into river mouths where no ship-of-the-line could follow. To meet this challenge, Congress in 1821 halved the appropriation for ships-of-the-line and spent the money thus saved on small sloops more appropriate to the duties of the U.S. Navy in the 1820s and 1830s.

Another reason the American ships-of-the-line never went to war as combatants was that advances in naval technology soon made them obsolete. Steam propulsion had become a practical reality even before the end of the War of 1812. Robert Fulton, the American inventor of steam propulsion, designed and built a steam-powered naval battery for the defense of New York Harbor during the last year of the war. This vessel, the *Demologos,* never saw action, but it foreshadowed the next generation of warships. Throughout the 1820s and 1830s the maritime nations of Europe as well as the United States experimented with various types of steam propulsion, provoking a debate between the advocates of paddlewheel steamers and

The USS Pennsylvania, *the last and largest American ship-of-the-line ever built, was rated at 120 guns but carried as many as 140. Authorized along with eight other American battleships in a burst of naval enthusiasm following the War of 1812, the* Pennsylvania *was laid down in 1822 though not completed until 1837. (U.S. Naval Historical Center)*

those who promoted screw propellers. At the same time, advances in naval ordnance substantially increased the firepower of shipboard batteries. The smooth-bore cannons firing solid shot that had dominated naval warfare for three centuries gradually gave way to rifled guns capable of firing explosive shells. As a result of all these changes, when the United States went to war with Mexico in 1846 (see maps 26–27), the ships-of-the-line authorized in 1816 were already dinosaurs.

Administratively, the management of the Navy was turned over to a Board of Navy Commissioners (established on 7 February 1815) consisting of three captains who provided advice to the Secretary of the Navy. This system functioned with mixed success until 1842, when Congress abolished the Board and replaced it with the so-called Bureau System. Under this arrangement, administrative responsibilities were divided up among five specialty bureaus (Ordnance and Hydrography; Yards and Docks; Construction, Equipment, and Repair; Provisions and Clothing; and Medicine and Surgery), each headed by an active-duty captain who assumed primary responsibility for that particular aspect of the Navy establishment. The Bureau system proved somewhat more efficient than the Board of Navy Commissioners, and its establishment was a milestone in the emergence of a self-sustaining institutional structure.

The precise role and responsibilities of naval officers also developed in important ways during this period. Officers who commanded vessels on distant stations had occasionally been compelled to make decisions of a diplomatic nature—Preble's role in the Mediterranean had been, at least in part, diplomatic as well as military. With the nation's naval forces spread out over the globe in the period 1815–1860, such duties became commonplace. Out of touch with Washington in an era before telegraphic communications, naval officers frequently had to make decisions affecting, or even defining, national policy. Occasionally, officers overstepped their authority—for example, David Porter's misadventure at Fajardo (map 23)—but on other occasions naval officers proved to be America's most successful diplomats, as in Matthew Perry's mission to Japan (map 29).

In addition, the Navy's changing technology created a need for officers who had detailed knowledge of the engineering plant, and in 1837 the Navy created a special career path for engineering officers. Line officers often resented or deprecated engineering officers, who were denied command opportunities, until the two categories were finally merged at the end of the century.

Finally, this era witnessed an important change in the way officers were identified and commissioned. Up to 1845 young men became U.S. Navy officers either by direct commission in time of national emergency or, more generally, by obtaining an appointment as a midshipman and going to sea to learn their profession from the bottom up. This was a tradition inherited from the Royal Navy in which "young gentlemen," almost always in their teens, were effectively apprenticed to ships' captains to learn navigation and leadership on the job. After a period of years, and upon the recommendation of his commanding officer, a young gentleman could sit for an exam that, if passed, would make him a lieutenant. From that point on, seniority and performance determined his rise through the ranks. Because an appointment as a midshipman was generally the result of political influence, social prominence, or both, this system tended to maintain a social hierarchy within the officer corps.

The idea of establishing a naval school for the education and instruction of naval officers as an alternative to this system was as old as the country, but its advocates had never been able to overcome the opposition of traditionalists who argued that the school of the sea provided the best education or that such a school would foster a "naval aristocracy." In the 1840s, however, several factors came together to bring this system into question. The first was the increased technological challenge of a steam-powered navy. The second was the "mutiny" aboard the U.S. brig *Somers* in November 1842.

The *Somers* was a training ship whose crew consisted entirely of volunteer "boys" who, it was hoped, would be encouraged to make enlisted service in the Navy a career. Halfway through the cruise the ship's commanding officer, CAPT

The side-wheel steamer Mississippi*: If the* Pennsylvania *was the epitome of the sailing ship-of-the-line, the* Mississippi, *commissioned in 1841, was the archetype of the new generation of steam-driven warships. It served as COMMO Matthew Perry's flagship during the Mexican War (see map 26) and was part of his squadron during his mission to Japan in 1853 (see map 29). (Official U.S. Navy photo)*

Alexander Slidell Mackenzie, learned that one of his midshipmen, nineteen-year-old Philip Spencer, was plotting a mutiny. Mackenzie acted quickly, arresting Spencer and several of his accomplices and clapping them in irons. But the *Somers* was weeks from land, and Spencer's presence in the ship created a palpable tension among the young crewmen. Mackenzie decided that the circumstances were so precarious that he had to act decisively. He convened a court-martial that found Spencer and two others guilty, and Mackenzie ordered them hanged from the yardarm of the *Somers*.

Mackenzie's actions would have been controversial in any case, but the fact that Philip Spencer was the son of the Secretary of War made them more so. A subsequent court of inquiry and court-martial exonerated Mackenzie and validated his decisions, but the entire episode called into question the wisdom of training young men—teenage boys—in the harsh school of the sea. This event gave added impetus to the advocates of a naval college, and in 1845 Secretary of the Navy George Bancroft established such a school at the Army's Fort Severn in Annapolis, Maryland.

Only a year later the United States embarked on a war with Mexico. The ostensible cause of this war was a dispute over the location of the boundary between Texas, recently annexed by the United States, and Mexico, from which Texas had won its independence in 1836. Skeptical Whigs believed that the Democratic president, James Knox Polk of Tennessee, had contrived a war deliberately to augment the national territory into which the institution of slavery might expand. Whatever the merit of such charges, the subsequent American victory did bring a huge new western territory into the national domain and set the stage for sectional confrontation about the status of slavery in that new territory.

Though the Navy's role in the war with Mexico was relatively modest, the war witnessed the first U.S. blockade of a foreign coast, the first large-scale amphibious landing, and the acquisition of California—which made the United States a two-ocean power.

COMMO David Porter commanded the frigate Essex *during its Pacific odyssey in 1813–1814 (see map 17) and also commanded the so-called "mosquito squadron" in the Caribbean, 1823–1824 (see map 23). A bold fighter, he was a poor diplomat, and in 1824 he was suspended from the service for his ill-judged actions at Fajardo, Puerto Rico. Angry at what he considered unfair treatment, he resigned his commission and accepted a job as commander in chief of the Mexican Navy. (Painting by R. S. Wiles, Corcoran Gallery of Art)*

COMMO Matthew C. Perry in a formal portrait taken by the famous photographer Matthew Brady after Perry's return from Japan in 1853. The younger brother of Oliver Hazard Perry, Matthew Perry proved that naval officers could serve as effective diplomatic representatives overseas. (Library of Congress)

Map 22

Back to the Med

May–August 1816

On 23 February 1815, only eight days after Congress ratified the Treaty of Ghent ending the war with Britain, President Madison sent Congress a message recommending war with Algiers. During the War of 1812 the British had encouraged the new dey at Algiers, Hajj Ali, to resume attacks on American shipping. Though pickings were slim due to the British blockade, Algerine corsairs did capture the *Edwin,* a brig out of Salem, near the end of the war. Madison was eager to return an American naval presence to the Mediterranean to put a stop to such attacks.

American naval officers were as eager for war as Madison, and no one more so than CAPT Stephen Decatur. Having been forced to surrender the frigate *President* to a British squadron in the last year of the war, Decatur burned with an ambition to erase what he, at least, considered a stain on his professional record. "I have lost a noble ship, sir," he wrote to a fellow officer after the *President* had been captured, "but I shall satisfy the world there has been no loss of honor." Decatur believed that command of a successful expedition to chastise the dey of Algiers would give him an opportunity to do just that.

Alas for Decatur, Secretary of the Navy Benjamin Crowninshield had already promised command of the expedition to CAPT William Bainbridge, commandant of the Boston Navy Yard, who was preparing his new flagship, the seventy-four–gun *Independence,* for a Mediterranean cruise. Bainbridge, however, encountered the all-too-common delays associated with completing a new warship for sea, and Crowninshield, therefore, authorized a *second* squadron for Mediterranean service to outfit in New York, offering the command to Decatur. Driven by a determination to regain his honor, Decatur applied his considerable energy to the task of getting his squadron under way, appropriating both ships and men originally intended for Bainbridge's command, while Bainbridge wrestled with the logistic difficulties of gun carriages that didn't fit his guns. As a result, Decatur put to sea first on 20 May and arrived off Gibraltar on 12 June while Bainbridge was still shipping the *Independence's* main-battery guns.

Decatur flew his flag in the frigate *Guerrière,* 44, and commanded a squadron of ten ships mounting 220 guns, the largest the U.S. Navy had ever sent to sea. In addition to power, however, Decatur also had luck on his side. At Cadiz (1) he learned that the Algerine squadron had recently reentered the Mediterranean from an Atlantic cruise, and he lost no time in port, setting sail at once to seek it out. On 17 June near Cape de Gatt (2), with the coast of Spain just visible on the northern horizon, the lookout in the *Constellation* spotted a strange sail that proved to be the *Mashouda,* flagship of the Algerine Navy, with its admiral, Rais Hammida, on board. Hammida foolishly offered battle and cleared for action. CAPT Charles Gordon in the *Constellation* immediately closed and opened the fight with a broadside, but before he could fire again, Decatur brought the *Guerrière* into the fight, sailing between the two combatants to pour another broadside into the *Mashouda.* The *Ontario* and *Epervier* also entered the fight, and the four American vessels pounded the *Mashouda* for more than two hours until the Algerine warship was a virtual wreck with 140 wounded and 20 killed, including Hammida.

Two days later off Cape Palos (3), four ships of Decatur's squadron encountered the Algerine armed brig *Estudio,* 22, which ran itself aground on the Spanish coast in trying to escape. The Americans sent in boats and seized the vessel with most of its crew. Decatur reassembled his squadron and, together with the two prizes, set a course for Algiers (4), where he arrived on 28 June. Decatur's seizure of a significant portion of the Algerine Navy immeasurably enhanced the American bargaining position, and the dey resisted only briefly before agreeing to a new treaty that eliminated tribute payments and obligated him to give up his hostages.

After this success, Decatur took his squadron to both Tunis (5) and Tripoli (6), where he demanded indemnity from the rulers of both cities for their failure to abide by the laws of neutrals during the war with Britain. Receiving satisfaction at both cities, Decatur returned to Gibraltar in July, where he welcomed the arrival of the second American squadron under Bainbridge, nine ships mounting 230 guns. Alas for that "hard luck" officer, there was little now for him to accomplish. Decatur and his squadron had already achieved all of the objectives of the mission. Nevertheless, Bainbridge and his squadron retraced Decatur's route, visiting Algiers, Tunis, and Tripoli, where the appearance of another powerful American squadron, so soon after the visit of the first, underscored the ability of the United States to protect its interests and its commerce in the Mediterranean.

There was, however, an epilogue. When the U.S. minister returned to Algiers in April 1816 with a signed copy of the treaty negotiated during Decatur's visit, the dey refused to accept it and insisted once again on a return to the tribute system. The United States refused and prepared a third naval squadron for service in the Mediterranean, this one commanded by COMMO Isaac Chauncey. But the United States was not the only nation whose patience had been exhausted by Algerine threats, and before Chauncey arrived, an Anglo-Dutch fleet under Lord Exmouth arrived off Algiers in August 1816 and bombarded the city so thoroughly that the power of the dey was broken. The United States maintained a squadron of observation in the Mediterranean for most of the next forty-five years (see map 24), but the Barbary States of North Africa would never again pose a serious threat to American commerce in the Mediterranean.

COMMO Stephen Decatur, hero of two wars, personified the dashing young naval officer in the age of sail. Determined to erase the humiliation of losing his last command during the War of 1812, he raced to the Mediterranean in 1815 and compelled the Barbary states to accept peace on American terms. Five years later Decatur died as a result of wounds suffered in a duel with James Barron. (U.S. Naval Institute)

COMMO William Bainbridge was Decatur's rival during the 1815 expedition to the Mediterranean. A survivor of several professional disasters, including the surrender of the Philadelphia *in 1803, he arrived in the Mediterranean with his squadron only after Decatur had secured all the objectives of the campaign. Ironically, Bainbridge served as Decatur's second in the 1820 duel that took Decatur's life. (U.S. Naval Academy Museum)*

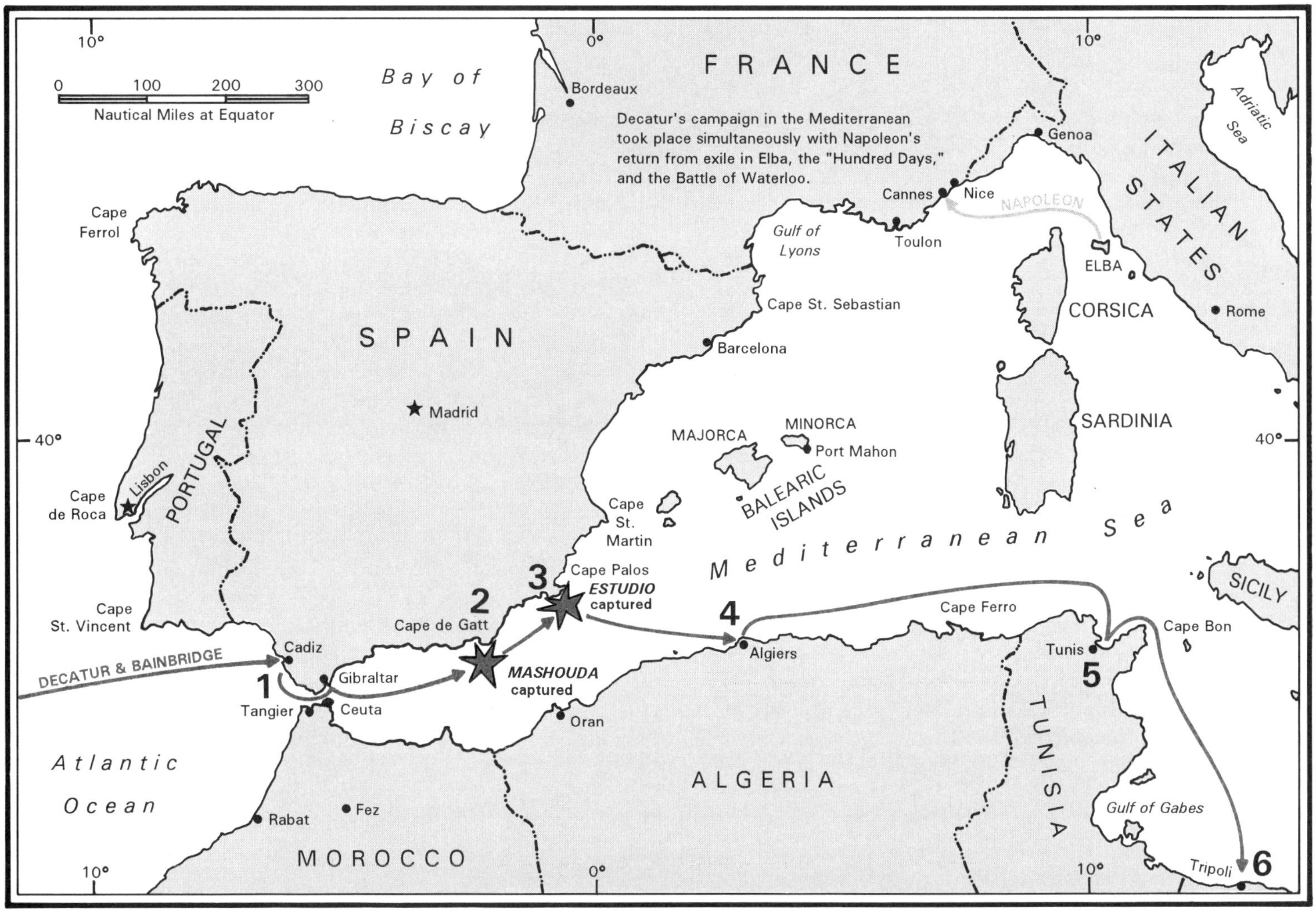

Decatur's campaign in the Mediterranean took place simultaneously with Napoleon's return from exile in Elba, the "Hundred Days," and the Battle of Waterloo.

0 100 200 300
Nautical Miles at Equator

10° 0° 10°
40° 40°

Bay of Biscay
FRANCE
Bordeaux
Genoa
Adriatic Sea
ITALIAN STATES
Cannes
Nice
NAPOLEON
Gulf of Lyons
Toulon
ELBA
Cape St. Sebastian
CORSICA
Rome
Cape Ferrol
SPAIN
Barcelona
PORTUGAL
Madrid
Lisbon
Cape de Roca
MINORCA
MAJORCA
Port Mahon
BALEARIC ISLANDS
SARDINIA
Cape St. Martin
Mediterranean Sea
Cape Palos
3 ESTUDIO captured
2 Cape de Gatt
MASHOUDA captured
4 Algiers
Cape Ferro
Cape Bon
SICILY
Tunis
5
Cape St. Vincent
Cadiz
DECATUR & BAINBRIDGE
1 Gibraltar
Tangier
Ceuta
Oran
TUNISIA
Atlantic Ocean
ALGERIA
Gulf of Gabes
Rabat
Fez
MOROCCO
Tripoli
6

Map 23

Pirates of the Caribbean

1810–1824

Though Americans routinely described the corsairs of the Barbary Coast as "pirates," a more serious piratical problem for American merchants was found in the Gulf of Mexico and the Caribbean Sea. Piracy in the West Indies dated to the seventeenth century and included such feared buccaneers as Henry Morgan and Blackbeard. But long after these freebooters had been swept from the sea, piracy remained a going concern for a wide variety of opportunists.

One such opportunist was the French-American Jean Lafitte, who presided over a colony of smugglers at Grand Terre in Barataria Bay (1) in the Mississippi River delta (see upper map). After 1810, when Colombia declared its independence from Spain, followed a year later by Venezuela, Lafitte obtained a Colombian letter of marque and thereafter justified his piracy as "privateering." For its part, Spain reacted to the Colombian and Venezuelan declarations by proclaiming their coastlines to be under blockade. Because Spain lacked the ships to make such a blockade effective, American merchants continued to trade with Cartagena and La Guira (Caracas), and Lafitte used this as a justification to capture and loot American ships, or indeed any ships trading in the Caribbean basin. Lafitte won a pardon from President Madison for his role in the defense of New Orleans (see map 21) but was soon back to his old habits, and in 1817 he managed to get himself named governor of Texas by the revolutionary government of Mexico, in which capacity he carried on his piratical activities from Campeche (Galveston) (2).

By 1818 the scene of piratical activity had shifted to the Caribbean (see lower map), and that year the United States dispatched COMMO Oliver Hazard Perry to Venezuela to urge the revolutionary government there to exercise more discretion in issuing letters of marque. Though Perry was successful in his mission, it cost him his life when he fell victim to yellow fever.

The next year the United States tried a different approach, passing a law authorizing U.S. Navy ships to convoy American merchantmen in the Caribbean and to attack pirates operating in the West Indies. COMMO James Biddle was the first commander of the West India Squadron. His squadron of four frigates, two sloops, two brigs, and four schooners operated out of Key West (3) and the Danish island of St. Thomas (4). But Biddle soon discovered that most of his ships were simply too big to deal effectively with the tiny pirate vessels that invariably fled into shoal waters or beached themselves on Spanish territory upon the approach of an American warship. Though it was in Spain's interest to help eliminate piracy, Spanish authorities were jealous of their territoriality, and more often than not, local governors refused to grant permission for American vessels to pursue pirates on Spanish territory. Command of the West India Squadron, therefore, was an assignment that demanded delicate diplomatic skills as well as a determination to pursue pirates.

In February of 1823 COMMO David Porter succeeded Biddle in command (see illustration, p. 59). Porter's strengths were courage and audacity, as evidenced in his campaign in the Pacific in 1812–1814 (see map 17). But Porter was not known for his diplomatic subtlety, and though he proved effective in combating piracy, his tendency to act precipitously would land him in serious trouble. His first actions in the Caribbean were both sound and effective. He retired the squadron's larger vessels, replacing them with ten Chesapeake Bay schooners—small fifty-ton vessels not unlike those the pirates themselves used. Porter also obtained a Hudson River paddlewheel ferryboat, which he named the *Sea Gull,* the first U.S. Navy steam warship to see action.

Porter achieved early and dramatic success with his "mosquito squadron." Over the next eighteen months his vessels captured or recaptured a total of seventy-nine vessels. But the summer climate wreaked havoc on Porter's health, and like Perry, he fell ill to yellow fever. During much of 1823 and 1824 Porter attempted to direct his squadron from Washington. When he returned to the West Indies in October of 1824, he learned from a subordinate of an incident that Porter, at least, considered grounds for immediate action.

The facts were these: Merchants on the Danish island of St. Thomas had reported a theft from a warehouse. Suspecting that the stolen goods had been transported to Fajardo in Spanish Puerto Rico (5), LT Charles Platt of the *Beagle* had gone to Fajardo with another American officer, both of them dressed in civilian clothes. There they were arrested as suspected spies and detained for several hours by Spanish authorities before being released. When Porter heard the tale, he was enraged. He led a three-ship squadron to Fajardo, landed an armed party, and threatened to destroy the town unless he received an immediate apology. The local governor apologized, and Porter and his landing party returned to their ships.

Such behavior was not particularly unusual in the nineteenth-century Navy; over the next five decades, dozens of naval officers would behave similarly, "chastising" local communities for real or perceived insults to the American flag. Seldom were they called to account. But Porter was tried by court-martial and found guilty of exceeding his orders as well as of insubordination. Sentenced to a six-month suspension, he chose instead to resign his commission and accept command of the Mexican Navy. What made Porter's case different was that he had not assailed some South Sea island tribe or Asian warlord; he had challenged the authority of a European power, and in doing so he had rocked the boat of international diplomacy.

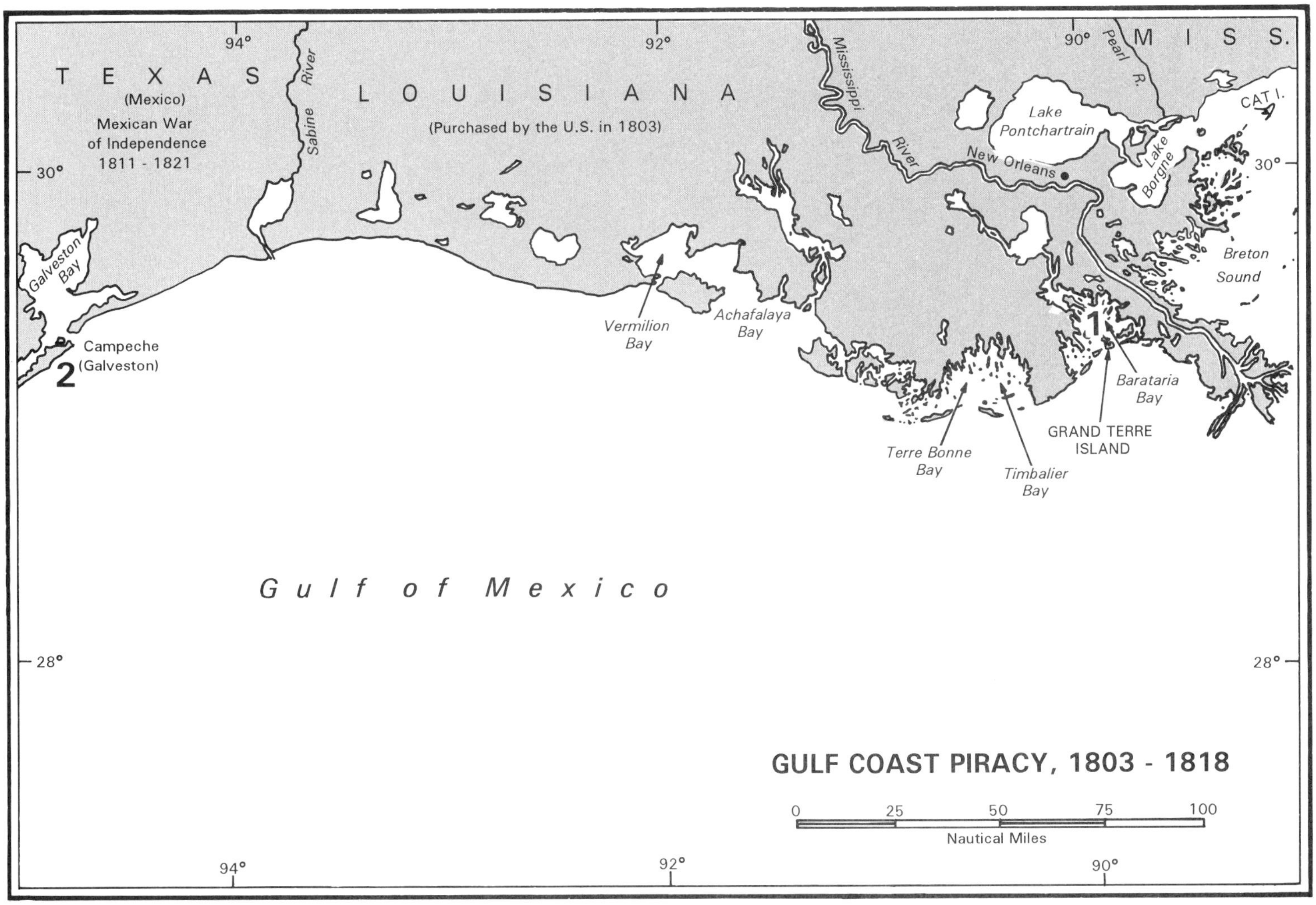

GULF COAST PIRACY, 1803 - 1818

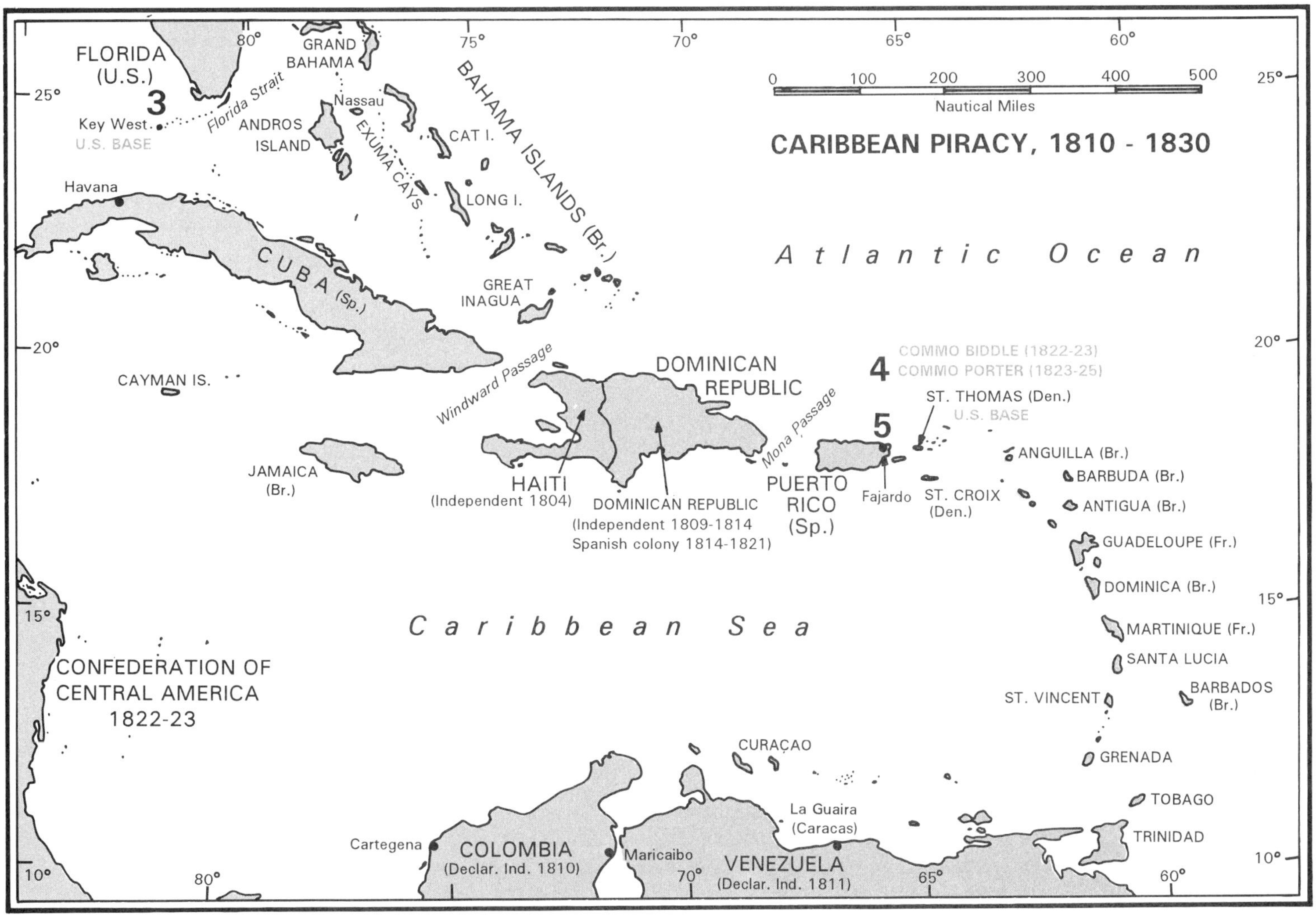

TEXAS
(Mexico)
Mexican War
of Independence
1811 - 1821

LOUISIANA
(Purchased by the U.S. in 1803)

MISS.

Sabine River
Mississippi River
Pearl R.
Lake Pontchartrain
New Orleans
Lake Borgne
CAT I.
Breton Sound
Galveston Bay
2 Campeche (Galveston)
Vermilion Bay
Achafalaya Bay
Terre Bonne Bay
Timbalier Bay
1 Barataria Bay
GRAND TERRE ISLAND

Gulf of Mexico

94° 92° 90° 30° 28°

0 25 50 75 100
Nautical Miles

CARIBBEAN PIRACY, 1810 - 1830

0 100 200 300 400 500
Nautical Miles

80° 75° 70° 65° 60° 25° 20° 15° 10°

FLORIDA
(U.S.)
3 Key West
U.S. BASE
Florida Strait
GRAND BAHAMA
Nassau
ANDROS ISLAND
EXUMA CAYS
CAT I.
LONG I.
BAHAMA ISLANDS (Br.)
GREAT INAGUA
Havana
CUBA (Sp.)
CAYMAN IS.
JAMAICA
(Br.)
Windward Passage
HAITI
(Independent 1804)
DOMINICAN REPUBLIC
DOMINICAN REPUBLIC
(Independent 1809-1814
Spanish colony 1814-1821)
Mona Passage
PUERTO RICO
(Sp.)
Fajardo
4 COMMO BIDDLE (1822-23)
COMMO PORTER (1823-25)
5 ST. THOMAS (Den.)
U.S. BASE
ST. CROIX
(Den.)
ANGUILLA (Br.)
BARBUDA (Br.)
ANTIGUA (Br.)
GUADELOUPE (Fr.)
DOMINICA (Br.)
MARTINIQUE (Fr.)
SANTA LUCIA
ST. VINCENT
BARBADOS
(Br.)
GRENADA
TOBAGO
TRINIDAD

Atlantic Ocean

Caribbean Sea

CONFEDERATION OF
CENTRAL AMERICA
1822-23

CURAÇAO
La Guaira
(Caracas)
Cartegena
COLOMBIA
(Declar. Ind. 1810)
Maricaibo
VENEZUELA
(Declar. Ind. 1811)

MAP 24

DISTANT STATIONS

1815–1860

From 1815 until the outbreak of the American Civil War, distant-station patrol was the primary function of the U.S. Navy. Out of touch with the United States for months at a time, officers and men of the Navy protected American commercial interests abroad and often acted as diplomatic representatives.

(1) THE MEDITERRANEAN SQUADRON (ESTABLISHED 1815)

Thomas Jefferson sent the Navy's first "Squadron of Observation" to the Mediterranean in 1801 (see map 10), but most naval historians date the birth of the Mediterranean Squadron from 1815. The squadron's official purpose was to guard against a resurgence of piracy in Algiers until the French occupied Algeria in 1830 and made it a French colony. After that the Mediterranean Squadron survived, in part at least, because Mediterranean service was such delightful duty. The U.S. squadron generally boasted a ship-of-the-line as a flagship, which was accompanied by two or three frigates and one or two smaller vessels (see illustration at top right). Based at Port Mahon on Minorca, this squadron cruised leisurely from port to port to "show the flag." An officer recalling his Mediterranean service remarked that "to be ordered to a ship on the European [Mediterranean] station was simply to be included as a member of a perpetual yachting party."

(2) THE WEST INDIA SQUADRON (ESTABLISHED 1821)

Like the Mediterranean Squadron, the West India Squadron was born out of concern for piratical attacks on American commerce (see map 23). And as in the Mediterranean, the Navy's effectiveness against the pirates and a change in political circumstances ended the need for a permanent U.S. presence after 1830, by which date Colombia and Venezuela had ended their wars with Spain and with each other. In 1842, therefore, the West India Squadron merged with the Home Squadron, which generally spent winters in the Caribbean and summers in the Chesapeake Bay or Newport.

(3) THE AFRICAN SQUADRON (ESTABLISHED 1821; REESTABLISHED 1842)

In April of 1818 Congress declared the international trade in slaves to be illegal and authorized the president to use warships to interdict it. Dutifully, the Navy established an African Squadron in 1821. If duty in the Mediterranean was the best assignment in the Navy, service on the African Station was the worst. The slave trade centered on the Guinea coast of equatorial West Africa, where the tropical climate was a constant threat to health. Scientists in the nineteenth century believed that evil humors in the air transferred diseases like yellow fever, and the high mortality of Europeans off the West African coast convinced officers and men alike that the very air they breathed threatened their lives. As a result, the Navy disbanded the African Squadron after only two years.

But the British stuck to it. Their war on slavery began in 1815 when they inserted a clause against slavery in the Treaty of Vienna, and soon afterward the Royal Navy began regular patrols off West Africa. Slave smugglers, attempting to escape these warships, often found it useful to fly the American flag. Aware of American touchiness about violations of its flag on the high seas, the British were reluctant to stop and search such vessels, and whenever they did so the United States protested vehemently, even though the flag was being used for illegal purposes. To defuse the situation, the two nations hammered out the Webster-Ashburton Treaty in 1842. Britain agreed not to stop or search American-flag vessels, and the United States agreed to reestablish its African Squadron, which it maintained until the outbreak of the Civil War in 1861.

(4) THE PACIFIC SQUADRON (ESTABLISHED 1821)

The expansion of American trade into the Pacific led to inevitable pleas from American merchants and from the substantial American whaling fleet for protection. The Pacific Squadron generally consisted of a frigate or ship-of-the-line as a flagship and of one or two smaller ships, usually sloops. The flagship cruised up and down the South American coast from Valparaiso, Chile, to the isthmus of Panama, while the sloop made occasional runs out to Hawaii. After the Mexican-American War added California to the national domain (see map 27), the Pacific Squadron operated more frequently out of San Francisco, and eventually it was split into two groups: a North Pacific Squadron in San Francisco and a South Pacific Squadron at Panama.

(5) THE BRAZIL SQUADRON (ESTABLISHED 1826)

Though U.S. trade with Brazil itself was modest, an American presence in Rio de Janeiro was important because it was a port of call for virtually all vessels bound for the Pacific via Cape Horn or for the Indian Ocean via the Cape of Good Hope (see, for example, the cruise of the *Susquehanna,* map 28). The trigger for the establishment of the Brazil Squadron in 1826 was a demand from American merchants caught in the middle of a war between Brazil and Argentina over what is now Uruguay. Later (1838–1842) a U.S. naval presence was important in insulating American merchant vessels from the ambitions of Juan Manuel Rosas, the dictator at Buenos Aires.

(6) THE EAST INDIA SQUADRON (ESTABLISHED 1835)

U.S. trade with the Far East was limited, but for those who risked the long voyage to trade fur, sandalwood, and cotton goods for Chinese silks and tea, the results were very profitable. Indeed, stories about the riches of the Far East created a national myth about the vast potential of the China market. In an effort to turn the myth into reality, the United States sent a diplomatic envoy to China in 1835 with an escort of two warships under the command of COMMO Edmund P. Kennedy, thus establishing the East India Squadron. Throughout the 1840s and 1850s U.S. Navy ships made routine visits to Canton, Hong Kong, Foochow, Shanghai, Manila, and Singapore.

Ships of the U.S. Mediterranean Squadron, including the ship-of-the-line North Carolina, *leave Port Mahon, Minorca, in 1825. Of the half dozen overseas stations where the U.S. Navy operated between the War of 1812 and the Civil War, the Mediterranean was by far the most desirable. Service there consisted mainly of a series of port visits along the French and Italian Riviera and, for the officers in particular, was as much social as professional. (Watercolor by A. Carlotta, Naval Historical Foundation)*

Map 25

The Great United States Exploring Expedition

August 1838–July 1842

The idea of an American scientific and exploring expedition had been popular for many years before it became a reality. The purpose was primarily scientific—to determine if the southern polar ice shelf concealed land, perhaps even a continent, and to chart the little-known islands of the South Pacific. Congress authorized $300,000 for the expedition in 1836, but the preparations lagged, and several officers declined offers to command it until a relatively junior lieutenant, Charles Wilkes, accepted.

The six vessels of Wilkes's command (three sloops, one brig, and two schooners) left Norfolk (1) on 18 August 1838, and after brief stops in the Madeiras, Rio de Janeiro, and Rio Negro, they headed south to Orange Harbor on the eastern shore of Tierra del Fuego (2), where they arrived on 26 January 1839 (early summer in the southern hemisphere). There, Wilkes divided his squadron, ordering two ships to survey the straits and islands near Cape Horn, two (under his own command) to explore Palmer's Land (3), and two to penetrate the ice shelf to the southeast (4). Ice, fog, and cold made exploration difficult for all the vessels, and by mid-April the squadron was back at Orange Harbor, having accomplished little—except for the loss of the small schooner *Sea Gull,* which disappeared off Cape Horn.

The squadron then headed north to Valparaiso, Chile (5), and thence to Callao, Peru (6). At Callao, Wilkes decided to send the sloop *Relief* home with mineral and botanical samples. The remaining four vessels headed into the Pacific to explore the islands of the South Sea. For most of four months Wilkes's ships explored the Tuamotu Islands, Samoa, Tonga, and Fiji, ending up in Sydney, Australia (7), in December 1839, ready to make another attempt at the southern ice shelf.

The squadron headed south for its second attempt at the ice shelf on Christmas Day 1839. In the treacherous ice-strewn seas and thick fog of the southern latitudes, the four ships became separated, but each explored the fringe of ice from Cape Adare (8) to Cape Poinsett (9). On 19 January 1840 Midshipman Henry Eld and one of the scientists, William Reynolds, sighted land in the distance, naming two high peaks after themselves. At the time Wilkes dismissed the sighting and insisted that the heights were icebergs. Ten days later, however, Wilkes himself sighted a dark band of rock behind the sea ice, and for several weeks afterward land could be seen regularly to the south as the ships cruised eastward. On 12 February Wilkes wrote in his journal of his discovery of an Antarctic continent. When Wilkes returned to Sydney in March, he learned that a French exploring vessel claimed to have sighted Antarctic land on the afternoon of 19 January—which predated his own sighting on 28 January. Wilkes then recalled that Reynolds and Eld had spied mountains on the *morning* of the nineteenth, and he now decided that they had been correct after all.

The U.S. squadron rendezvoused on the northeastern shore of New Zealand's North Island (10) before sailing to Tonga and Fiji. While the expedition was surveying Fiji (11) in July, natives killed two American crewmen, and Wilkes retaliated by attacking the village of the perpetrators, killing eighty-seven natives and burning the town. Then he forced the survivors to demonstrate their subjugation by crawling to him on their hands and knees to beg forgiveness.

From Fiji the squadron sailed for Hawaii (12) in August, stopping to survey several islands en route. The squadron spent several months in refitting while Wilkes solved a problem of expiring enlistments by intimidating most of the men to reenlist, ordering that the members of the Marine detachment who refused to do so should be flogged until they changed their minds. Throughout the fall and winter of 1840 the U.S. squadron used Hawaii as a base to explore several islands of the Central and South Pacific, including Samoa, Tahiti, and the Marshall Islands (13).

In the spring of 1841 the squadron quit Hawaii and headed for British Columbia (14), arriving on 28 April. While engaged in mapping and sounding the coastline, the *Peacock* grounded on 18 July and went down with the loss of one hundred lives. During the late summer LT George F. Emmons led a party of thirty-nine men from the squadron on a trek to explore the Columbia River (15). They traveled overland for more than two months and reunited with the squadron at San Francisco on the last day of October.

In November 1841 the squadron left California and recrossed the Pacific, stopping again at Hawaii before continuing to Manila in the Philippines (16), where it arrived on 12 January 1842. The three surviving ships of the squadron then proceeded south to Singapore and on through the Sunda Strait into the Indian Ocean (17). After rounding the Cape of Good Hope (18) in April, Wilkes in the *Vincennes* reached St. Helena (19) in May and continued on to New York, arriving in late June. The other two ships of the squadron sailed from Cape Town to Rio and then to New York, where they arrived on 2 July.

In four years the Great U.S. Exploring Expedition sailed more than 85,000 miles and charted 280 islands as well as 1,500 miles of the Antarctic continent. The vast collection of scientific samples Wilkes brought back eventually comprised the core of what would become the Smithsonian Institution, and a five-volume *Narrative* of the voyage made an important contribution to scientific knowledge. But Wilkes's overbearing personality and his vendetta against most of his subordinate officers tarnished the expedition, despite its achievements. Sadly, the epilogue to this remarkable voyage was his lengthy court-martial and years of unprofessional bickering.

The U.S. sloop-of-war Vincennes *surrounded by the Antarctic ice during the cruise of the Great United States Exploring Expedition. Despite the notable geographic and scientific discoveries, the friction generated by LT Charles Wilkes's tyrannical style of command overshadowed the expedition. (Official U.S. Navy photo)*

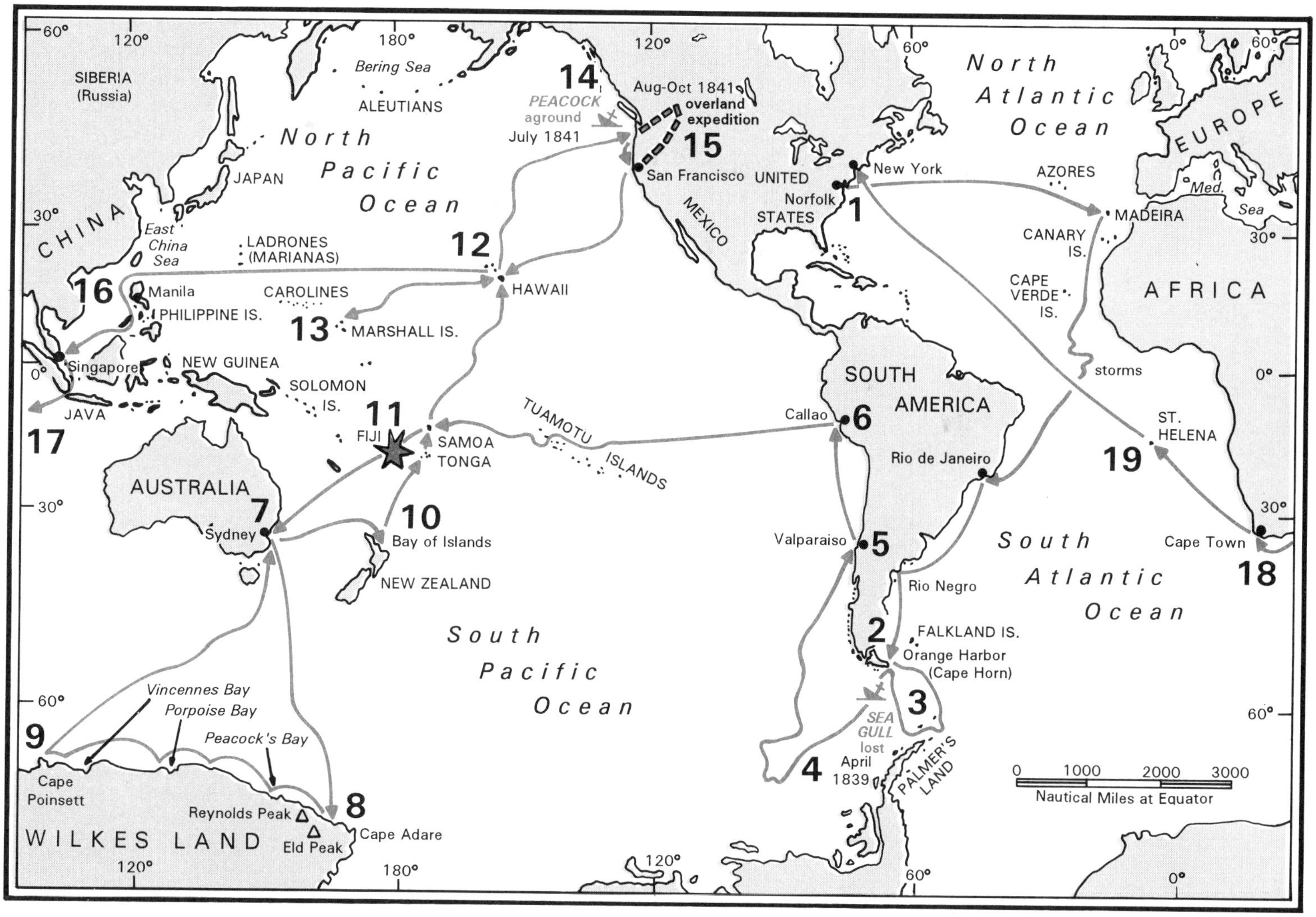

60° 120° 180° 120° 60° 0° 60°
SIBERIA (Russia)
Bering Sea
ALEUTIANS
14
PEACOCK aground July 1841
Aug-Oct 1841 overland expedition
15
San Francisco
North Pacific Ocean
JAPAN
CHINA
East China Sea
LADRONES (MARIANAS)
12
HAWAII
16
Manila
PHILIPPINE IS.
CAROLINES
13
MARSHALL IS.
Singapore
NEW GUINEA
SOLOMON IS.
JAVA
17
11
FIJI
SAMOA
TONGA
TUAMOTU ISLANDS
AUSTRALIA
7
Sydney
10
Bay of Islands
NEW ZEALAND
South Pacific Ocean
9
Vincennes Bay
Porpoise Bay
Peacock's Bay
Cape Poinsett
Reynolds Peak
Eld Peak
8
Cape Adare
WILKES LAND
UNITED STATES
MEXICO
New York
Norfolk
1
North Atlantic Ocean
AZORES
MADEIRA
CANARY IS.
CAPE VERDE IS.
EUROPE
Med. Sea
AFRICA
storms
SOUTH AMERICA
Callao
6
Rio de Janeiro
Valparaiso
5
Rio Negro
2
FALKLAND IS.
Orange Harbor (Cape Horn)
3
SEA GULL lost April 1839
4
PALMER'S LAND
St. HELENA
19
Cape Town
18
South Atlantic Ocean
30° 0° 30° 60°
0 1000 2000 3000
Nautical Miles at Equator

Map 26

War with Mexico: The Gulf Coast

May 1846–May 1848

In April of 1836 American settlers in the Mexican province of Texas secured their independence by defeating the army of GEN Antonio Lopez de Santa Anna at the Battle of San Jacinto. Almost at once they began to petition the United States for admission as a state. But not until the administration of President James Knox Polk (1845–1853) did the nation agree to admit Texas to the Union. Soon afterward, the United States and Mexico began to quarrel over the location of the boundary between Texas and Mexico. On 25 April 1846 a large Mexican force ambushed an American patrol in the disputed territory, and Polk asked Congress to declare war. With some misgivings, Congress voted for war on 13 May. That same day Polk ordered a blockade of the Mexican coast.

For the U.S. Navy, the ensuing conflict was a novel experience. Mexico had only two important warships at the start of the war, and believing that they could have little impact on the outcome, the Mexican government sold them to the British. Mexico's other warships, all small craft, were used in harbor defense. As a result, the U.S. Navy was the dominant naval force in the war. Instead of trying to break a blockade, it sought to enforce one; rather than defend a coast, it sought to attack one.

In 1846 there were half a dozen important ports on the Mexican Gulf Coast. From north to south they were Tampico, Tuxpan, Vera Cruz, Alvarado, Tabasco, and Carmen. The two most important were Vera Cruz (1), where Cortes had landed in 1519 and which was the gateway to Mexico City, and Alvarado (2) at the entrance to the Papaloapan River and host to four of Mexico's remaining warships. In recognition of this, the American commander, COMMO David Connor, established a fleet base in the protected anchorage of Anton Lizardo (3), halfway between these two cities.

Connor's Gulf Squadron consisted of eleven vessels—two frigates, two steamers, four sloops, and three brigs. But it lacked adequate small craft for inshore work. Coastal sandbars protected all of the Mexican ports except Vera Cruz, keeping the large U.S. steamers beyond effective range. Connor discovered the importance of this during three unsuccessful attempts to capture Alvarado during the summer and fall of 1846 (see map at lower right). In each case only a few U.S. vessels made it over the bar, and each time Mexican batteries forced Connor to turn back. Eventually, Alvarado fell to a combined army-navy operation in the spring of 1847.

The Navy enjoyed greater success in an October 1846 attack on Tabasco (4), also known as San Juan Batista and now called Villahermosa. Connor's second in command, COMMO Matthew C. Perry, who commanded the expedition, left the large steamer *Mississippi* off the entrance and used the shallow-draft *Vixen* to tow two schooners over the bar. Once across, the Americans seized the port town of Frontera (5), capturing a Mexican brig and three gunboats in the harbor. Then they steamed seventy miles up the Grijalva River to Tabasco (see illustration, p. 56). Perry landed his marines and seized Tabasco, but recognizing the impracticality of holding it, he withdrew that night after shelling the town in response to scattered harassing fire from the buildings.

The Gulf Squadron enjoyed another easy success the next month when Connor took a powerful force to Tampico (6), which the Mexicans abandoned. This time the Americans held the town as a base for future operations against the interior. A month later a smaller force under Perry duplicated Connor's success at the Yucatan port city of Carmen (7). Carmen proved to be a valuable source of fresh fruit for the U.S. squadron, which had suffered several outbreaks of scurvy during the blockade.

While the Navy maintained a blockade of the Gulf Coast, the Army under MGEN Zachary Taylor won several large-scale battles north and south of the Rio Grande. Despite that, Santa Anna showed no willingness to terminate the war. As a result, President Polk determined to open a new front by landing an American force at Vera Cruz for a march on Mexico City.

The landing at Vera Cruz (see map at lower left) was the largest amphibious landing in history, and it remained such until the World War I landings at Gallipoli. Connor and the Army commander, MGEN Winfield Scott, proved to be an effective team in this unprecedented operation. In early March 1847 Army transports brought ten thousand soldiers and sixty-four specially designed surfboats (constructed in three different sizes so that they could nest inside one another on the decks of the transports). On 9 March the soldiers clambered into the boats and maneuvered with some difficulty into a line abreast off the beach near Sacrificios Island (8). At 5:30 P.M. Scott gave the order to land. The surfboats, manned by sailors, each carried forty soldiers to the beach, where two thousand men splashed ashore more or less simultaneously. There was no opposition, and the exuberant soldiers planted the American flag on the dunes behind the beach (9).

Over the next two weeks Scott's army advanced inland and surrounded Vera Cruz from the landward side. On 22 March Scott demanded the city's surrender, and after his demand was rejected, he opened a bombardment of the city, supported by the guns of the fleet as well as a battery of six heavy naval guns that had been brought ashore (10). Unable to stand up to such a pounding, the city capitulated on 29 March. With the aid of the Navy, Scott had secured his foothold for the conquest of Mexico. From Vera Cruz he marched westward to Mexico City in a campaign that lasted a year and a half. After the fall of Mexico City in September 1848, Scott ordered that U.S. Marines assume the guard in the National Palace—the Halls of Montezuma.

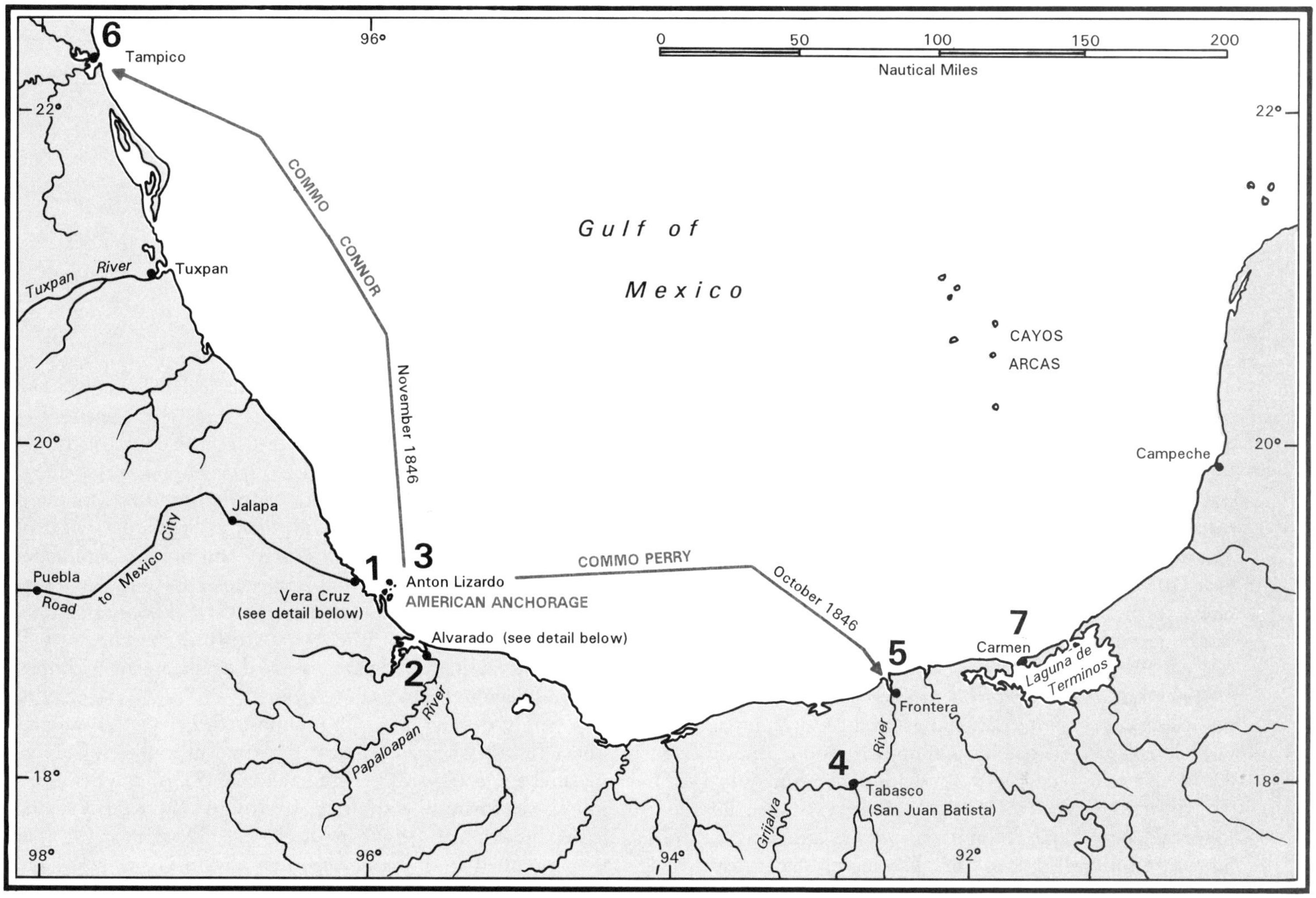

6
Tampico
96°
0 50 100 150 200
Nautical Miles
22°
22°
COMMO CONNOR
November 1846
Gulf of
Mexico
Tuxpan River
Tuxpan
CAYOS
ARCAS
20°
20°
Campeche
Jalapa
Road to Mexico City
Puebla
1
3
Anton Lizardo
AMERICAN ANCHORAGE
Vera Cruz
(see detail below)
COMMO PERRY
October 1846
Alvarado (see detail below)
2
7
Carmen
Laguna de Terminos
5
Frontera
Papaloapan River
River
Grijalva
4
Tabasco
(San Juan Batista)
18°
18°
98°
96°
94°
92°

LANDINGS AT VERA CRUZ
9 March 1847
Gulf of
Mexico
Galleguilla
Reef
Blanquilla
Reef
Gallega Reef
Bay of
Vera Cruz
San Juan
de Ulloa
Vera
Cruz
SOMERS
lost
5 Dec 1846
Pajaros
Reef
NAVAL
BATTERY
ARMY
BATTERY
10
8
SACRIFICIOS
ISLAND
SCOTT'S
HQ
U.S. TRANSPORTS
AMERICAN
LINES
Landing Beach
9
0 1 2
Nautical Miles

ENTRANCE TO
ALVARADO
0 1 2
Nautical Miles
sand bar
MEXICAN
SHORE
BATTERIES
Alvarado
ANCHORAGE
Papaloapan
River

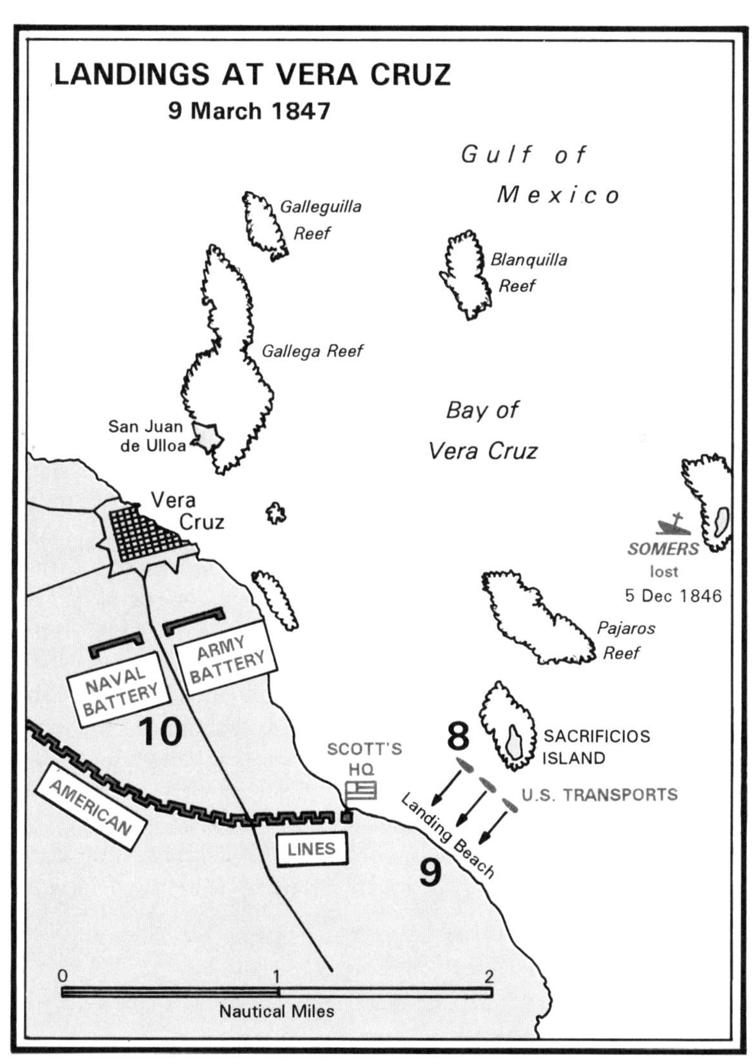

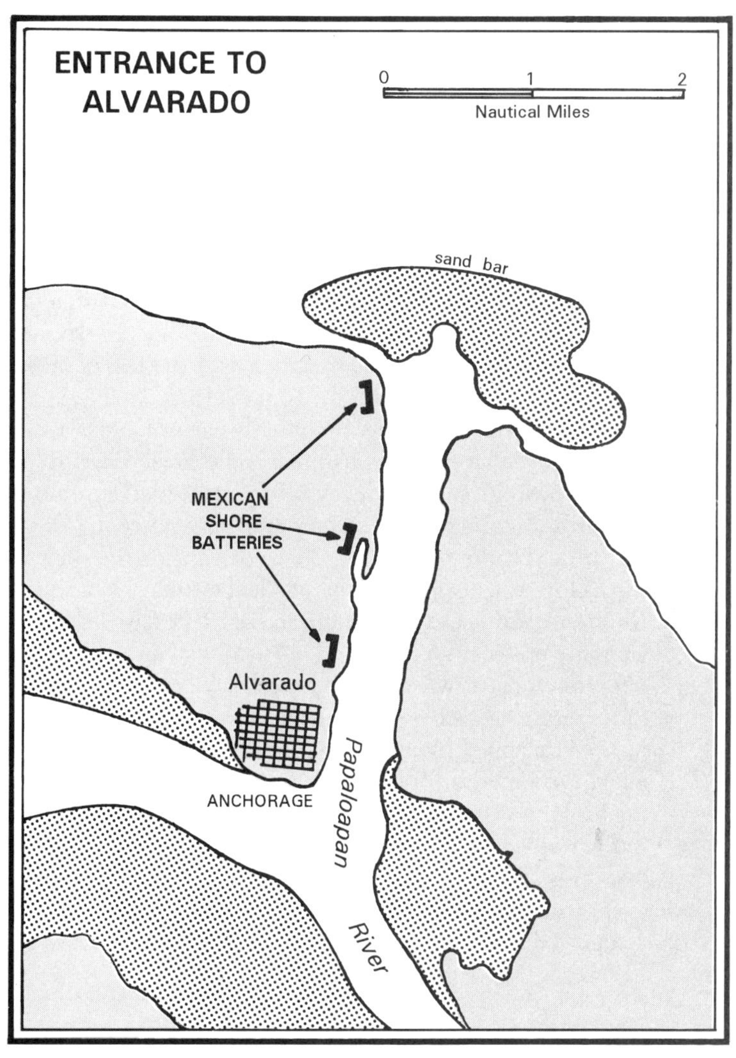

MAP 27

WAR WITH MEXICO: THE CALIFORNIA COAST

JULY 1846–JANUARY 1847

The Mexican province of California had been an object of American interest long before the outbreak of war. Sparsely populated and loosely governed, it had a long Pacific seacoast that offered the promise of access to the imagined wealth of the Pacific and the fulfillment of what many Americans assumed was the nation's "manifest destiny" to dominate the North American continent. When in the fall of 1842 COMMO Thomas ap Catesby Jones, commanding the Pacific Squadron, heard rumors of the imminent outbreak of war, he immediately sailed north from Callao to seize Monterey (1). Learning afterward that the rumor was false, he apologized and returned control of the town to Mexican authorities. Though Congress officially censured him for his rashness, he had demonstrated the vulnerability of this rich and isolated Mexican province.

Jones's censure provided an object lesson to his successor, COMMO John Sloat, who commanded the American Pacific Squadron when war *did* break out four years later. Recalling Jones's fate, Sloat was determined to avoid any overt act until he received official orders from Washington. Sloat dispatched the sloop *Portsmouth* to Monterey from his base at Mazatlan (2) in March 1846 with orders to protect American lives. But only after he learned of the Battles of Palo Alta and Resaca de la Palma did Sloat finally sail for California himself, arriving at Monterey on 5 July in the frigate *Savannah.*

By then the situation in California had become extraordinarily complicated due to the activities of LCOL John C. Fremont. The "Pathfinder" operated under a commission from the government to survey the Arkansas and Red Rivers, but he had ignored his orders and instead led his party into California in 1845. By June of 1846 he had associated himself with a group of rebellious American settlers, and on 4 July, the day before Sloat arrived at Monterey, Fremont raised the flag of an independent California Republic at Sonoma (3).

Learning of these events upon his arrival, Sloat assumed (incorrectly) that Fremont had received official orders to commence hostilities and, therefore, issued orders to his own squadron to seize both Monterey and San Francisco (4). On 7 July a U.S. landing party of 225 sailors and marines from the three-ship American squadron marched into the town square at Monterey and raised the American flag. Two days later a similar scene was acted out in San Francisco. Having thus committed himself, Sloat was shocked a week later when Fremont told him that he had acted on his own. Worried now that he might have overstepped his authority, Sloat breathed a sigh of relief when the American frigate *Congress* arrived in Monterey, bearing his long-expected replacement, COMMO Robert F. Stockton. Pleading ill health, Sloat turned the direction of events over to Stockton.

Stockton was as precipitate as Sloat had been cautious. He recognized Fremont's armed band as "the California battalion of United States troops," transported it to San Diego (5) to extend the war to southern California, and declared open warfare against the Mexican commandant GEN José María Castro. Rejecting Castro's offer to negotiate, Stockton led an armed column into Los Angeles (6) on 13 August. Mexican resistance collapsed two days later, and Stockton returned to Monterey. But by refusing to negotiate with Castro, Stockton had sown the seeds of future revolt. Those seeds sprouted in September when the armed population of Los Angeles drove the U.S. garrison out of the city. Stockton brought the *Savannah* and *Congress* to San Pedro in October but decided his landing party of sailors and marines was inadequate to the task, and he withdrew to San Diego to build up his forces.

In December a small American force of 150 soldiers under BGEN Stephen W. Kearny arrived in southern California after a ten-week march from Santa Fe (7). After a fierce but indecisive skirmish with Mexican troops (8), Kearny's men joined Stockton's force at San Diego on 12 December. Together they mounted an overland campaign toward Los Angeles, and after a short battle at San Gabriel they entered the city on 10 January 1847.

Almost at once Commodore Stockton and Brigadier General Kearny began to argue over who had authority to establish a civil government in California. Though Kearny's orders came from the president, Stockton dismissed them as out of date and refused to recognize Kearny's authority. On 22 January COMMO William B. Shubrick arrived at Monterey in the old razee *Independence* (the same ship Bainbridge had taken to the Mediterranean thirty years before), and he and Kearny worked out a satisfactory division of responsibility. Bolstered by Shubrick's support, Kearny preferred charges against Stockton and Fremont, both of whom left California and returned to Washington to plead their cases.

If Sloat had been overly cautious while in command, Stockton had proved too reckless. Sloat's failing was that he had been unwilling to shoulder personal responsibility at a time when uncertain communications with the government in Washington made difficult decisions a natural part of a commodore's job. Stockton's error was insufficient consideration for the long-term political solution in California. Overly presumptuous and eager to assert his command authority, he came very near to losing what he had gained. In the end, the American conquest of California was due more to the small size of the Mexican garrison than to American strategy or command leadership. In any case, the American acquisition of California, confirmed in the Treaty of Guadaloupe-Hidalgo, would have a profound impact on the nation's history, beginning almost at once with the discovery of gold near Sutter's Mill (9) on 24 January 1848.

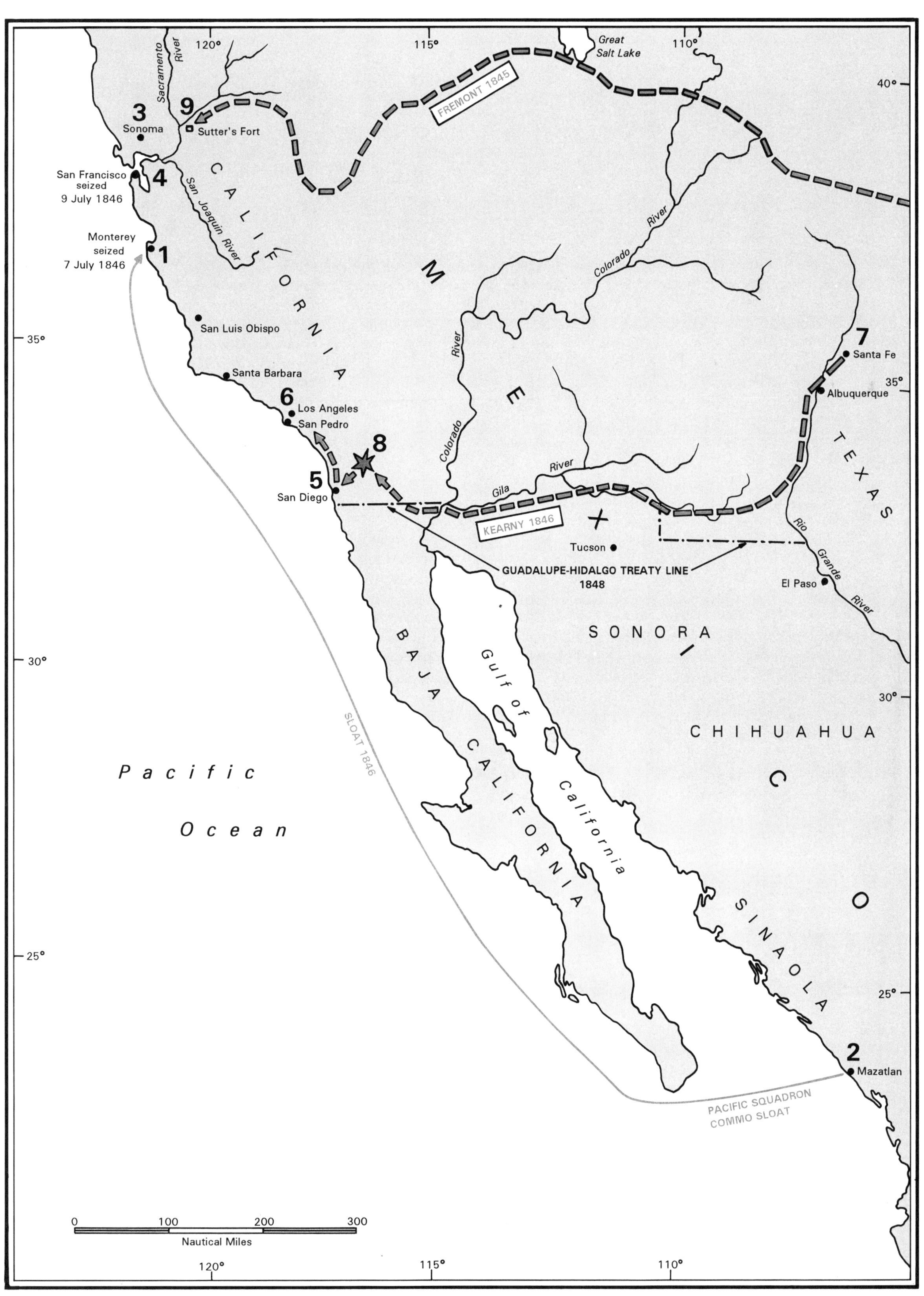

Great Salt Lake
120°
115°
110°
40°
35°
30°
25°
Sacramento River
FREMONT 1845
3
9
Sonoma
Sutter's Fort
San Francisco seized 9 July 1846
4
San Joaquin River
C A L I F O R N I A
Monterey seized 7 July 1846
1
M E X I C O
Colorado River
Colorado River
San Luis Obispo
Santa Barbara
6
Los Angeles
San Pedro
8
5
San Diego
Gila River
KEARNY 1846
7
Santa Fe
Albuquerque
T E X A S
Tucson
GUADALUPE-HIDALGO TREATY LINE 1848
Rio Grande River
El Paso
S O N O R A
B A J A C A L I F O R N I A
Gulf of California
C H I H U A H U A
S I N A O L A
SLOAT 1846
Pacific Ocean
2
Mazatlan
PACIFIC SQUADRON COMMO SLOAT
0
100
200
300
Nautical Miles

MAP 28

SAILS VS. STEAM: THE CRUISE OF THE *SUSQUEHANNA*

JUNE 1851–FEBRUARY 1852

During the blockade of Vera Cruz, both Connor and Perry had been hampered by the fact that the nearest U.S. naval base was nine hundred nautical miles to the northeast at Pensacola, Florida. This was a particular problem for U.S. Navy steam ships. Even those vessels equipped with both a distiller (to desalinate the water) and a condenser (to recapture "used" steam) operated at a standard pressure of only about 10–15 psi (pounds per square inch)—which yielded a fuel efficiency of about five miles per ton of coal burned. Assuming a five hundred–ton bunker capacity, this gave U.S. Navy warships a steaming range of about 2,500 miles. Sending these ships on an 1,800-mile round-trip to Pensacola to recoal consumed almost as much fuel as the ship could carry. Connor and Perry, therefore, chartered a number of merchant ships to use as colliers.

For most Navy vessels, however, the solution to this technological and logistic dilemma was to rely on sails while cruising to and from a duty station and to fire up the boilers only when the tactical circumstances warranted. But it was an unhappy compromise in many ways. The top-hamper of masts and spars reduced the ship's speed when under steam, and the drag of the paddlewheels (or screw propeller) did the same when the vessel was under sail. Naval policy makers were aware of these facts, but they were constrained by the limits of the contemporary technology and the absence of American overseas coaling stations.

The maiden voyage of the U.S. steam frigate *Susquehanna* just two years after the end of the war with Mexico underscored the problems of relying exclusively on steam. Launched in the spring of 1850, the *Susquehanna* was a side-wheel steamer 257 feet long displacing 2,450 tons—making it considerably larger than the biggest ship-of-the-line. Its steam plant was of the newest design, boasting both a distiller and a condenser. Under the command of CAPT John H. Aulick, the *Susquehanna* steamed out of Hampton Roads in June of 1851, bound for Asian waters, where it would become the flagship of the East India Squadron.

The *Susquehanna* departed Norfolk (1) on 8 June with a full bunker of coal, but Aulick could not shape a course directly for the Cape of Good Hope (more than 6,000 miles away), for the *Susquehanna's* steaming range was only about 3,500 miles. Instead, therefore, Aulick steered almost due east for Funchal in Portuguese Madeira (2). The *Susquehanna* arrived at Funchal on 26 June after a passage of eighteen days, and that same day its crew began taking on coal. It was a particularly messy job: bags of coal were hoisted over the side and dumped into wicker baskets that were then trundled along the deck to chutes leading to the bunkers. Of course, coal dust settled on everything and everyone. Over the next ten days the crew was employed almost constantly in coaling ship and by the end of that time had loaded a total of 380 tons. Assuming that this topped off the coal bunkers in the *Susquehanna,* this meant that the ship had managed a creditable seven and a half miles per ton of coal burned from Norfolk to Funchal.

After an Independence Day celebration aboard ship on 4 July, the *Susquehanna* departed Funchal the next day. Even with a full bunker, Aulick could not reach the Cape of Good Hope (still 4,200 miles away) on a single leg, and so he headed southwest for Rio de Janeiro (3), where the *Susquehanna* arrived on 26 July. There, Aulick ordered some minor repairs, which took most of two weeks, before loading coal. From the thirteenth to the twenty-seventh of September the logbook of the *Susquehanna* read simply, "Crew employed in coaling ship." On the twenty-seventh the *Susquehanna* departed Rio and headed for the Cape of Good Hope, 3,300 miles to the east (4).

On 15 October the *Susquehanna* reached Cape Town, where the crew spent another twelve days in loading four hundred tons of coal. Then the vessel zigzagged across the Indian Ocean, stopping briefly at French Mauritius (5) to recoal (six days, 250 tons) and again at Zanzibar (6), where the sultan was able to provide only 20 tons of coal, which the crew supplemented with "1100 sticks of wood." The *Susquehanna* arrived at Colombo, Ceylon (7), on Christmas Day with its coal bunkers nearly depleted, and over the next twelve days (with a break on New Year's Day) the ship loaded a full five hundred tons.

Steaming east again, the *Susquehanna* made stops at Pulo Penang (8) off the Malay coast, where local laborers assisted the crew in loading coal (375 tons), then ran through the Strait of Malacca to Singapore (9), where another 30 tons were loaded. Finally, in February of 1852 the *Susquehanna* turned north for the run through the South China Sea to Hong Kong (10), arriving on 5 February. There, Aulick topped off again, loading 246 tons of coal in seven days.

The *Susquehanna's* maiden voyage had covered 18,500 miles and lasted eight months. More to the point, the trip had consumed 2,500 tons of coal (*and* 1,100 sticks of wood!), and the crew had been actively engaged in coaling ship for fifty-four days, roughly one fourth of the total time spent in transit. Not incidentally, the coal had cost an average of $10 per ton for a total of $25,000 at a time when a Navy captain's annual salary was $3,500. Finally, none of the ports where the *Susquehanna* had stopped to recoal had been American territory—to use a modern phrase, the *Susquehanna* had been dependent on foreign sources of energy. In short, the *Susquehanna's* cruise proved that a dependence on coal for long voyages was expensive, time-consuming, and strategically insecure. Technological advances over the next several decades would reduce the impact of many of these problems, but at midcentury the United States had little alternative but to continue to rely on ships with both sails and steam plants.

The side-wheel steamer Susquehanna *on its circuitous route toward the Far East in 1851 to serve as the flagship of the East Asia Squadron. The limited range of its coal-fired steam plant necessitated frequent stops for coaling en route. The* Susquehanna *subsequently served as COMMO M. C. Perry's flagship during his mission to Japan (see map 29). (Official U.S. Navy photo)*

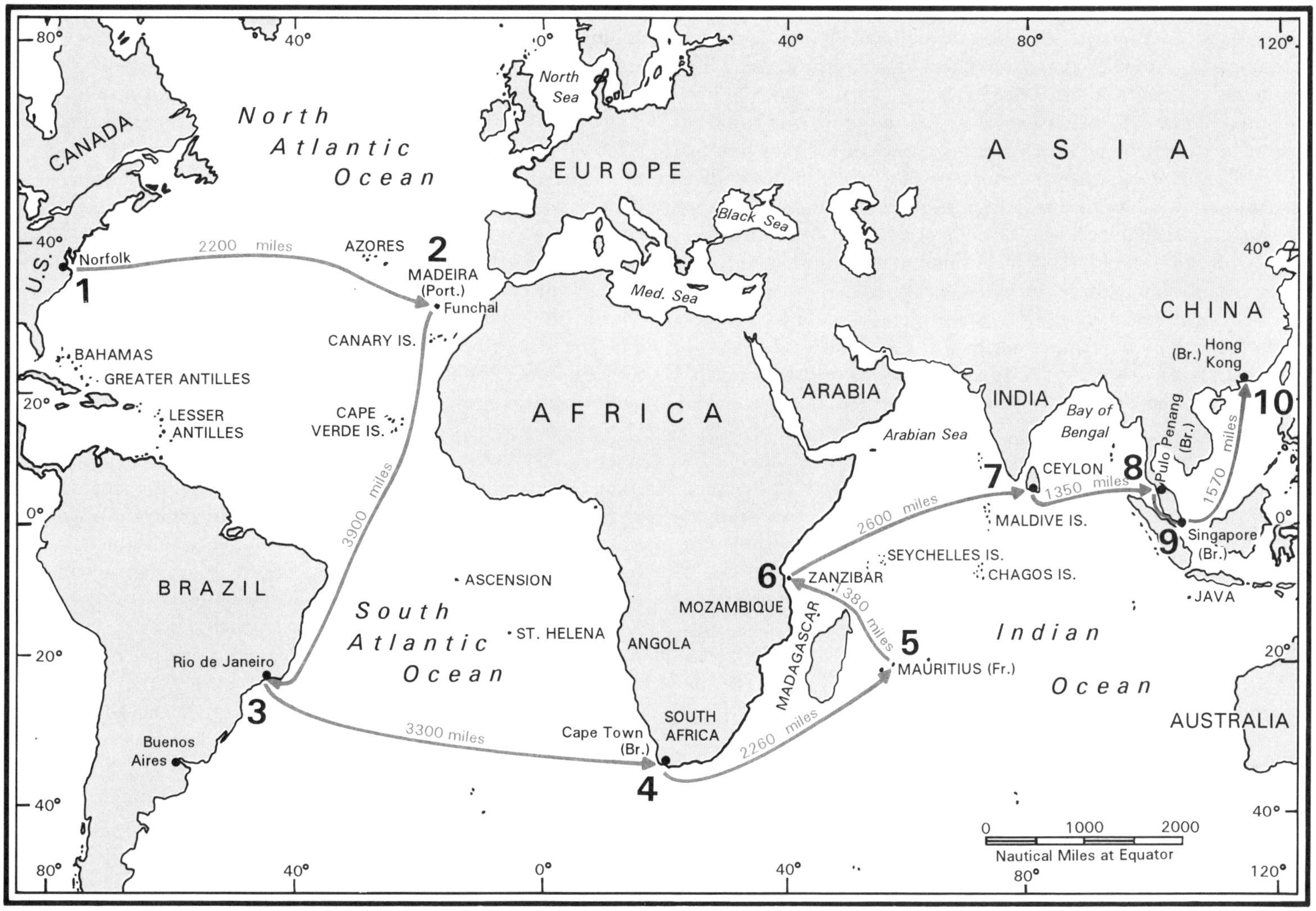

MAP 29

PERRY'S MISSION TO JAPAN

NOVEMBER 1852–MARCH 1854

On 24 November 1852 the steam frigate *Mississippi* left Norfolk and steamed east on the same track taken by its sister ship the *Susquehanna* eighteen months earlier. The *Mississippi's* commander was COMMO Matthew C. Perry, whose assignment was to take command of the East India Squadron and negotiate a change in Japan's policy of strict isolationism. Specifically, he was charged with three objectives: Japanese agreement to protect American seamen who were either shipwrecked on Japan's coast or driven into Japanese ports by bad weather; a similar agreement to allow the establishment of American coaling and supply stations at selected Japanese ports; and permission for U.S. vessels to enter one or more Japanese ports for trade. Considering the Japanese abhorrence of outside contact, this was an extremely ambitious assignment.

The *Mississippi* arrived at Hong Kong (1) on 6 April 1853 after a four-and-a-half-month passage, and two weeks later Perry transferred his flag to the *Susquehanna* at Shanghai (2). On 17 May his four-ship squadron—each of the steamers towing a sloop—left Shanghai for Okinawa (3), where it arrived on 26 May. Perry treated his dealings with the regent for the young monarch of the Ryukyus as a rehearsal for his forthcoming negotiations with the Japanese. He refused to meet with lower-ranking officials, and when he visited the monarch's castle at Naha on 6 June, he traveled in a sedan chair built for him by the *Susquehanna's* carpenter. Impressed by Perry's posture of dignity and firmness, the king's regent agreed to provide aid to any Americans shipwrecked on Okinawa. Perry next took his squadron to Peel Island (Chichi Jima) in the Bonins (4), where he scouted out locations for a possible American coaling station.

Perry returned to Okinawa at the end of June and prepared for the most important part of his mission—the visit to Japan. His four-ship squadron departed Naha on 2 July and anchored in the Uraga Channel at the entrance to the Bay of Edo (Tokyo Bay) six days later (5). His arrival provoked considerable alarm in Japan. For two centuries the Japanese had not allowed foreign vessels—let alone warships—to enter any port except Nagasaki (6), where the Dutch maintained a trading "factory." The fact that Perry's were the first steamships the Japanese had seen increased the shock.

Local authorities urged Perry to leave immediately; foreigners, they told him, could visit only Nagasaki. Once again combining firmness with restraint, Perry replied that he had a letter from the president of the United States for the emperor and that he could deliver it only to a person of high rank. Moreover, he announced that he would not leave until he had accomplished this task and implied that if bureaucratic impediments delayed him for too long he might be forced to land an armed contingent and deliver the letter in person. Aghast, the Japanese agreed to a ceremony on shore at Kurihama (inset, 7) where Perry would turn the letter over to the local governor. The ceremony took place on 14 July, and Perry left two days later, promising to be back in a few months for an answer.

After a stop at Okinawa, Perry returned to Shanghai and Canton, where American merchants urged him to forsake the Japanese mission to protect their interests on the China coast during the bloody Taiping Rebellion (1851–1864). But Perry did not lose sight of his primary mission, and after being reinforced in August he planned a swift return to Japan. In January 1854 Perry's reinforced squadron left Shanghai and rendezvoused at Okinawa before steaming north to the Bay of Edo, where he arrived on 13 February. The squadron now consisted of three steam frigates (the *Susquehanna, Powhatan,* and *Mississippi*), four armed sloops, and two storeships, one of which was loaded with gifts for the emperor—which Perry hoped would encourage the Japanese to reassess their trade policy.

During Perry's absence the Shogunate had decided to compromise with the insistent Americans. They would agree to aid castaways and allow the establishment of coaling stations at selected ports, but they would not open the country to trade. Thus when Perry returned, much of the tension that had characterized his first visit was gone. Of course, there were still a few problems to overcome. It took three weeks just to decide where the negotiations would be held. Perry insisted on Edo (Tokyo), which was sacred to the Japanese, and the Japanese insisted on Uraga. They compromised on Yokohama (8), at that time only a small village but destined to become a great seaport. On 8 March Perry went ashore amidst great pomp and ceremony. The Japanese agreed to offer hospitality to shipwrecked Americans and offered the ports of Hakodate (9) and Shimoda (10) as sites for American coaling stations. Perry raised the question of trade, but on this the Japanese stood firm. As a fallback position, Perry suggested that a permanent American consul should reside in Japan, and after some reluctance the Japanese agreed. Perry suspected (correctly) that the presence of an American consul would lead eventually to the establishment of trade. On 12 March the Americans came ashore again with their cargo of gifts, the most spectacular of which was a small-gauge railroad, complete with track, engine, and cars, which chugged around a small oval track at twenty miles per hour.

The Treaty of Kanagawa, signed on 31 March 1854, proved to be the opening wedge that brought medieval Japan into the modern world. By a combination of firmness and restraint, of calculated pomp and a respect for local customs, Perry had demonstrated that naval officers in the nineteenth century could be effective diplomats as well as warriors.

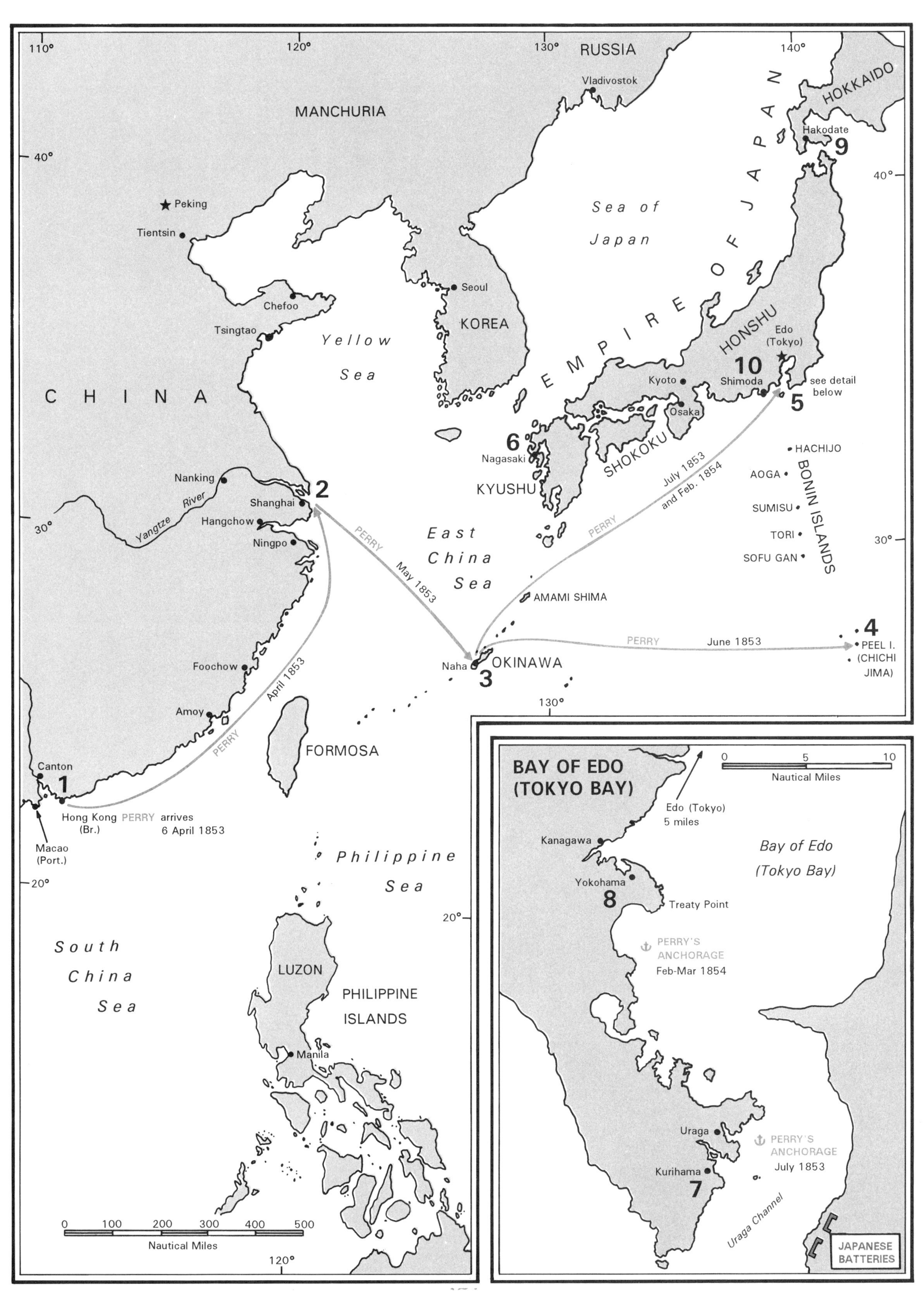
RUSSIA
MANCHURIA
Vladivostok
HOKKAIDO
Hakodate
9
Peking
Tientsin
Sea of Japan
EMPIRE OF JAPAN
Chefoo
Seoul
Tsingtao
KOREA
Yellow Sea
CHINA
HONSHU
Edo (Tokyo)
10
Kyoto
Shimoda
see detail below
5
Osaka
6
Nagasaki
SHOKOKU
KYUSHU
HACHIJO
AOGA
BONIN ISLANDS
SUMISU
TORI
SOFU GAN
Nanking
2
Shanghai
Yangtze River
Hangchow
Ningpo
PERRY
May 1853
East China Sea
July 1853 and Feb. 1854
AMAMI SHIMA
4
PERRY
June 1853
PEEL I. (CHICHI JIMA)
Naha
OKINAWA
3
Foochow
April 1853
Amoy
FORMOSA
Canton
1
Hong Kong (Br.)
PERRY arrives 6 April 1853
Macao (Port.)
Philippine Sea
South China Sea
LUZON
PHILIPPINE ISLANDS
Manila
0 100 200 300 400 500
Nautical Miles
BAY OF EDO (TOKYO BAY)
0 5 10
Nautical Miles
Edo (Tokyo) 5 miles
Kanagawa
Bay of Edo (Tokyo Bay)
Yokohama
8
Treaty Point
PERRY'S ANCHORAGE Feb-Mar 1854
Uraga
PERRY'S ANCHORAGE July 1853
Kurihama
7
Uraga Channel
JAPANESE BATTERIES

PART V

The Civil War 1861–1865

THE CIVIL WAR WAS THE GREATEST—that is to say the largest and most pervasive—conflict in American history. It was a total war—arguably the only total war in which the United States has ever been engaged. In no other conflict was so large a percentage of American manpower mobilized for war; in no other conflict were so many American cities and farms the scenes of military action and destruction; in no other conflict, save the Revolution, was the very survival of the nation so much in doubt. Finally, in no other conflict were so many lives lost. Counting casualties from both sides, the number of combatants killed in the Civil War exceeded those of all other American wars added together—including both world wars—from the American Revolution to the war in Vietnam.

It was primarily a land war; only a small fraction of the nearly six hundred thousand who lost their lives in the war were sailors. But the Union Navy was nevertheless an important element in the final outcome. A naval blockade helped seal the Confederacy off from the outside world, diplomatically as well as economically; Union command of the sea meant that Northern armies could move by ocean transport and river steamers; and the Navy was an equal partner in Union victories on the western rivers, establishing a precedent for effective interservice cooperation.

The cause of the war was slavery. That is not to say that every soldier or sailor who fought in the war did so because he held some personal conviction about the rightness or wrongness of "the peculiar institution." Men fought for the Union, for the flag, for home and hearth, for their rights as they understood them. Both sides, ironically enough, fought for "freedom." But of all the issues that divided North from South, slavery was the one that evoked the deepest emotional response, and the one in which genuine compromise proved impossible.

The Union Fleet of Flag Officer Samuel F. Du Pont steams in a circle while shelling Fort Walker in Port Royal Sound, South Carolina, on 7 November 1861. Army transport ships offshore await the outcome. By compelling the surrender of Fort Walker (and Fort Beauregard on the opposite headland), Du Pont demonstrated that steam warships firing explosive ordnance could stand up to shore fortifications (see map 32). (Official U.S. Navy photo)

By 1860 both sides had drawn the lines so firmly that retreat was unthinkable. The new Republican Party insisted that slavery be barred from the western territories acquired from Mexico; Southerners declared that slave ownership was an inalienable right. The election of Abraham Lincoln in 1860 signaled to Southerners that they had lost control of the government. Without waiting to see what policies Lincoln might propose, South Carolina called a state convention and declared its secession from the Union on 20 December 1860. Six other states quickly followed, and when Lincoln took the oath of office on 4 March 1861, Jefferson Davis of Mississippi had already been named the provisional president of a seven-state southern Confederacy.

From the first day of Lincoln's administration the nation's attention focused on Fort Sumter, a pentagonal brick fortification still under construction on a man-made island in the middle of Charleston Harbor. Sumter was unquestionably within the waters of South Carolina, but it was a Federal fort, built with Federal money, and manned by Federal troops. Even if one accepted the principle of secession (which Lincoln did not), the legal status of Fort Sumter was murky at best. To officials of the self-proclaimed southern Confederacy, the American flag flying above Fort Sumter was a mute but constant challenge to Confederate sovereignty, and they insisted that the Federal government evacuate the fort. But Lincoln had no intention of doing so, and he notified the governor of South Carolina that he was sending a vessel with food and medical supplies for the garrison. In response, Jefferson Davis ordered the Confederate commander at Charleston, BGEN Pierre G. T. Beauregard, to demand the immediate surrender of the fort, and if a surrender was not forthcoming, to reduce the fort with artillery. Confederate batteries opened up a few minutes past 4:30 A.M. on 12 April 1861.

Bombardment of Fort Fisher: Though the U.S. Navy numbered fewer than ninety ships at the outset of the Civil War, it grew rapidly to a force of nearly seven hundred vessels, forty-four of which participated in the bombardment of Fort Fisher at the entrance to the Cape Fear River, North Carolina, in January 1865 (see map 40). (Official U.S. Navy photo)

The outbreak of hostilities made Lincoln a war president, and he turned to MGEN Winfield Scott, the nation's foremost military hero, for strategic advice. Scott responded by offering the president a three-part plan:

1. Create a large field army in the vicinity of the nation's capital to hold the Confederacy's main army in check.

2. Maintain a strict naval blockade of the Confederate coastline to prevent the Southern states from exporting their cotton or importing munitions of war.

3. Conduct a combined Army-Navy operation to seize control of the Mississippi River and thereby split the Confederacy in half.

Critics thought Scott's proposals too passive and attacked the plan as suggestive of an anaconda, the South American reptile that slowly strangles its prey. But despite such criticism, Scott's "Anaconda Plan" became the blueprint for Federal strategy during the war, and it is noteworthy that two of the three elements of that plan involved the Navy.

The Union Navy established and maintained a blockade of the Southern coastline throughout the entire war (map 30). As a corollary to its blockade strategy, the Navy seized a number of Confederate ports, not only to deny their use to the Confederacy but to obtain coaling stations for the blockading fleet. Beginning with Hatteras Inlet, North Carolina (map 31), and Port Royal, South Carolina (map 32), the Navy occupied sections of the Confederate coastline until by 1864 there were only three major ports left open to the Confederacy. Two of these fell in the last year of the war: Mobile, Alabama (map 39), and Wilmington, North Carolina (map 40). Only Charleston held out to the end, finally capitulating when MGEN William T. Sherman cut it off from the landward side.

Naval superiority gave the Union the advantage of mobility, as Federal commanders moved whole armies by sea. McClellan's move to the Virginia peninsula (map 33) was the most evident example of this, but the Navy also helped transport MGEN Ambrose Burnside's army to the coast of North Carolina and MGEN Benjamin Butler's army of occupation to New Orleans. And the Navy was crucial in combined operations on the inland rivers, as in the seizure of Forts Henry and Donelson on the Tennessee River (map 34) and the pivotal Vicksburg campaign (map 37).

The Civil War also witnessed the first combat use of a number of new technologies in propulsion, ordnance, and armor. For the Navy, as well as for the nation, the American Civil War was a watershed. Whereas in the 1850s the U.S. Navy was a sailing navy with auxiliary steam, by 1865 it was primarily a steam navy with auxiliary sails. The increased accuracy and explosive power of naval ordnance gave ships a new advantage over shore fortifications, an advantage demonstrated dramatically at Hatteras Inlet and Port Royal on the Atlantic coast (maps 31 and 32) and Fort Henry on the inland rivers (map 34). And most striking of all, the use of armor plate and the advent of the rotating turret dramatically changed both the defensive capability and the silhouette of naval warships. John Paul Jones would have recognized the USS *Susquehanna* as a ship of war, but he would not have known what to make of the USS *Monitor.*

Such technological achievements were possible because the Union possessed an industrial infrastructure that could mass-produce and sustain a modern steam navy. Lacking such facilities, the Confederacy adopted the traditional strategy of the weaker naval power: a reliance on commerce raiding and experimentation with innovations of its own. The most famous Confederate raider was the CSS *Alabama* (map 41), which met its doom off the coast of France after a legendary career. The South also experimented with a whole range of naval innovations, including submarines, torpedo boats, and underwater mines, which the Federals called "infernal machines." The most notable such innovation was the CSS *Virginia* (formerly the USS *Merrimack*), which threatened to destroy the entire Federal blockading squadron in Hampton Roads before being checked by the USS *Monitor* (map 33).

In the American Civil War the naval officers on both sides were men who shared a common professional heritage. They had served together in the crowded wardrooms of frigates and sloops on distant stations around the world from the Barbary Coast to the Far China Station, where they had represented the United States to foreign powers and minor princes. Nevertheless, of the 1,554 naval officers on duty in December 1860, 373 of them (24 percent) resigned to "go South." Once shipmates, they were now enemies, and it was not unusual for opposing commanders to know one another personally. For them, this was genuinely a Civil War.

Secession forced many naval officers into a crisis of conscience. One was CAPT Franklin Buchanan, who had been the first superintendent of the U.S. Naval Academy at Annapolis. A Marylander, Buchanan submitted his resignation in the expectation that his state was about to secede. When Maryland instead remained in the Union, Buchanan tried to withdraw his resignation. But Navy Secretary Gideon Welles wanted no half-hearted patriots in his navy and ordered Buchanan struck from the Navy List. Buchanan went South to become the Confederacy's first admiral. Another who faced a personal crisis was Tennessee-born CAPT David Glasgow Farragut, who had spent virtually all his adult life in the U.S. Navy. While Buchanan went South, Farragut chose to stay by the flag, and in July 1862 he became the Union's first admiral. Some families were torn in half. Brothers Thomas and Percival Drayton of South Carolina found themselves firing at one another in November of 1861, Thomas in command of a Confederate fort on Hilton Head Island and Percival commanding the U.S. steam sloop *Pocahontas* (see map 32).

A final note on naval ranks: In the U.S. Navy, captain remained the highest rank available. This proved awkward when the commander of a Navy squadron had to work in partnership with an Army major general. To give Navy officers parity with Army officers, Congress created the rank of flag officer in April 1861 (abbreviated FLG OFCR on maps 30–36). Fifteen months later, in July 1862, Congress established the rank of rear admiral and designated the Tennessean David G. Farragut as the first American to hold that rank.

RADM Franklin Buchanan had been the first superintendent of the U.S. Naval Academy, where the superintendent's house is named for him. In 1861 Buchanan resigned his commission in the expectation that his native Maryland would secede. When Maryland instead stayed in the Union, Buchanan tried to recall his resignation. Rebuffed by Secretary of the Navy Gideon Welles, Buchanan accepted service as an admiral in the Confederate Navy and commanded the CSS Virginia *on its maiden voyage (see map 33). (Library of Congress)*

RADM David Glasgow Farragut: While the Marylander Buchanan served the Confederacy, the Tennessean Farragut was the first American to be promoted to the rank of rear admiral in the U.S. Navy. His promotion was a reward for the successful capture of New Orleans (see map 36), but he is best remembered for his aggressive-ness at Mobile Bay, where he is supposed to have said, "Damn the torpedoes, full speed ahead" (see map 39). (Library of Congress)

MAP 30

THE UNION BLOCKADE

1861–1865

On 19 April 1861, even before Major General Scott submitted his so-called Anaconda Plan, President Lincoln declared a naval blockade of the seceded states, asserting that "a competent force will be posted so as to prevent entrance and exit of vessels." His reference to "a competent force" was deliberate. International law held that merely declaring a blockade was not enough; it became binding only when the blockading power stationed a naval squadron off shore strong enough to prevent vessels from entering or leaving. Because the Confederacy claimed a coastline that stretched 3,500 miles from Alexandria, Virginia, to Brownsville, Texas, it was evident that even if the entire U.S. Navy were committed to the blockade, it would not be "competent" to guard such a coastline. The first task at hand, therefore, was a dramatic expansion of the Navy.

The government went on a buying spree, snapping up merchant steamers, ferryboats, and even pleasure yachts (including the *America,* original winner of the America's Cup). All these vessels were armed with a few pieces of naval ordnance, commissioned as warships, and sent south on blockade duty. Within four months the number of active commissioned warships in the Navy doubled (from 42 to 82), and by the end of 1861 the Navy List boasted 264 ships. By the end of the war the U.S. Navy consisted of 671 vessels, almost two-thirds of which were converted merchantmen. To command and administer this growing armada, a Federal Strategy Board, headed by Flag Officer Samuel F. Du Pont, recommended the establishment of four blockade squadrons, as shown at right.

Early in the war the Union blockade was little more than a "paper blockade." In May and June 1861 several vessels passed in and out of the South's major ports, bringing in rifles and other munitions of war and leaving with full cargoes of cotton, without ever seeing a Federal blockading vessel. During this period the Confederacy missed a good opportunity to build up overseas credits by shipping out as much cotton as possible. Instead, the Confederate government declared an embargo on its own cotton exports in the hope that the resulting cotton famine in England would create economic pressure for England to enter the war. It was a terrible miscalculation. England had stockpiled cotton beforehand and found alternate sources in India and Egypt. By the time the Confederacy lifted its self-imposed embargo in 1863, the Union blockade had become much more effective.

Blockade duty was excruciatingly boring for the officers and men of the blockading squadrons. Day after day they sat anchored off a Southern port, keeping steam up in anticipation of an attempt to run the blockade, but with little to do besides stare at the distant shoreline. Only occasionally did the frantic chase of a swift blockade runner or a berry-picking expedition ashore break the routine. Night was the most dangerous time. That was when blockade runners were most likely to test the vigilance of the blockaders. Because of that, the ships of the blockading squadrons shifted their anchorages after dark to confound those on shore who might attempt to signal the location of the blockaders to vessels over the horizon.

The U.S. Navy claimed that in the course of the war a total of 1,149 vessels were captured while attempting to run the blockade and another 351 were destroyed. But many of those were small coastal barges and sailing ships. The real threat to the integrity of the blockade came from steam ships. By mid-1862 a regular pattern of blockade running had developed. Merchant ships from England off-loaded their cargoes at Bermuda (1), Nassau (2), or Havana (3). From these neutral ports, specially designed blockade runners, shallow-draft steamships with low silhouettes, painted gray to blend with the sea, made the quick run into a Confederate port on dark, moonless nights. Although 210 of them were captured and 85 others destroyed, more than three-fourths of all attempts were successful.

From Bermuda, blockade runners headed for Wilmington, North Carolina (4), or Charleston, South Carolina (5). From Nassau, the center of the blockade-running industry, ships headed mainly for Charleston, Savannah (6), or Fernandina, Florida (7). Cargoes destined for the Confederacy's Gulf Coast stopped in Havana, from which they made for Mobile (8) or Galveston (9). Brownsville, Texas (10), offered particular problems for the Union blockaders. The international boundary bisected the Rio Grande River, and neutral ships off-loaded their cargoes at Matamoros, Mexico, for subsequent reshipment into the Confederacy. The United States protested this obvious ruse, but with little success. Still, this particular port of entry was inefficient for the Confederacy because of the long trek from Brownsville to points east.

Throughout the war the Confederate government repeatedly asserted that the Union blockade was ineffective. It made this claim because effectiveness was the measure of legitimacy, and of course to encourage additional attempts to run the blockade. But whereas the Union blockade was never impermeable, neither was it entirely ineffective. The Confederacy never lost a battle due to a lack of munitions or supplies, and the scarcity of many nonmilitary goods in the wartime South was due in large part to the Confederacy's poor internal transportation system. Still, the Union blockade created genuine hardships for the Confederate population, and it sealed off the South from would-be sympathizers in Europe who might otherwise have had an opportunity to develop closer diplomatic and economic relations with the Confederacy.

The Confederate steamer Nashville *running the Union blockade early in the war. The Confederates hoped to convert the* Nashville *into a warship, but its deck would not bear the weight of heavy ordnance. Renamed the* Thomas L. Wragg, *it served during most of the war as a privateer and blockade runner. (Mariner's Museum, Newport News, Virginia)*

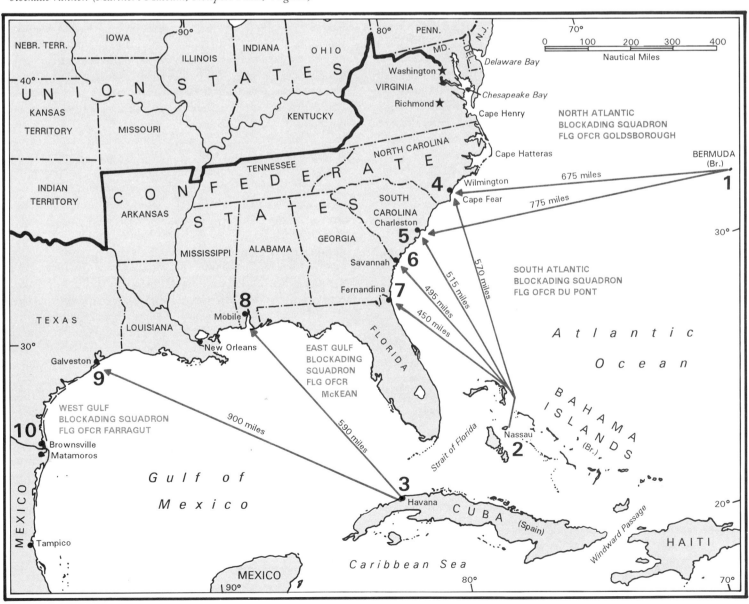

MAP 31

HATTERAS INLET AND ROANOKE ISLAND

AUGUST 1861 AND FEBRUARY 1862

Early in the war Confederate privateers and warships of the North Carolina Navy captured a number of prizes off Cape Hatteras (1), and Secretary of the Navy Gideon Welles resolved to do something to neutralize this threat. His solution was an expedition to stop up the entrances to Pamlico Sound: Oregon Inlet (2), Hatteras Inlet (3), and Ocracoke Inlet (4). In August 1861 Welles ordered Flag Officer Silas Stringham to command an expedition to Hatteras Inlet, the largest and most important of the inlets, ten miles southwest of Cape Hatteras.

Stringham's squadron consisted of two large steamers (the *Minnesota* and *Wabash*), three smaller steam warships, and the sloop *Cumberland,* plus two Army transports carrying 860 soldiers under the command of BGEN Benjamin Butler. Stringham departed Hampton Roads on 26 August and arrived off Hatteras Inlet the next day. The Confederates had built two sand-and-log forts to guard the inlet, both of them on the northern headland. Fort Hatteras, the larger of the two, mounted ten guns and overlooked the channel; Fort Clark, about a mile to the north, mounted only five guns.

The Union plan for attacking these forts was straightforward. While Stringham bombarded the forts with his heavier warships, the three small steamers would cover a landing by Butler's troops a few miles north of Fort Clark. After the naval bombardment had softened up the forts, Butler's men would advance overland to capture them. While the plan was reasonable enough, the soldiers had never received any amphibious training, and there was no time for a rehearsal.

The *Minnesota, Wabash,* and *Cumberland,* joined later by the *Susquehanna* from the blockading squadron, began shelling Fort Clark at 10:00 A.M. on 28 August. At 12:25 P.M. the Confederate defenders lowered their flag and abandoned the fort, falling back to Fort Hatteras. Two miles up the beach, however, the landing of Federal troops was not going so well. Loaded into surfboats at 6:45 A.M., the troops began heading for shore soon afterward, but their boats proved unmanageable in the heavy Atlantic chop, and several of them swamped or wrecked on the beach. By the afternoon only 325 of Butler's men had managed to struggle ashore. They occupied the abandoned Fort Clark but could go no farther that day.

The next morning (29 August) the Federal fleet turned its attention to Fort Hatteras. Shoal water off the point made it difficult to get within range, and only the largest 10-inch guns, fired at maximum elevation, could reach the fort. Still, those weapons outranged all of the Confederate guns, and after several hours of being bombarded without an opportunity to reply, the Confederate commander, Flag Officer Samuel Barron, capitulated. (Barron was the son of the commodore of the same name who fought in the Barbary Wars.)

Having seized the forts at Hatteras Inlet, the Federals might have exploited their success by passing through the inlet and wreaking havoc among the unprotected communities of Pamlico Sound. Instead, however, Stringham and Butler sped back to Washington and New York to report the news of their victory. The Federal Navy did not make another aggressive move in Pamlico Sound for most of five months. Given this respite, the Confederates evacuated their fortifications at the other two inlets and concentrated their defenses on Roanoke Island (5), hoping to block Federal access to Albemarle Sound.

The initiative for the eventual Federal move against Roanoke Island came from the Army. MGEN George B. McClellan, contemplating an amphibious move to the Virginia peninsula in the spring (see map 33), believed it would be useful if a Federal division moved inland from Pamlico Sound to threaten the Confederacy's rail connections south of Norfolk. For this task he designated the division of MGEN Ambrose Burnside, whose three brigades of New Englanders were composed of men familiar with small boats. Escorted by a naval squadron under Flag Officer Louis M. Goldsborough (Stringham's replacement), Burnside's division was to seize Roanoke Island and then move inland to interrupt rail and canal transportation in North Carolina.

Because the large Union warships could not cross the bar at Hatteras Inlet, Goldsborough's attacking squadron consisted of seventeen small gunboats mounting a total of fifty-four guns. This flotilla approached the Confederate positions on Roanoke Island on 7 February (see inset). The Union gunboats traded salvos with the Confederate forts ashore and with a small flotilla of Confederate gunboats under COMMO William F. Lynch. In quick order Lynch's gunboats were driven off, and not long afterward the forts, too, were silenced. Burnside's division of ten thousand men landed on Roanoke Island with little difficulty, partly because of the calm waters of Pamlico Sound but also because of excellent planning and cooperation between Army and Navy officers. Each of Burnside's brigades was assigned a steamer to tow the surfboats ashore while another gunboat stood off to provide fire support. The Confederates on Roanoke Island capitulated, and Burnside took two thousand prisoners.

Subsequently, Goldsborough's gunboats escorted Union forces to Elizabeth City (6), which connected to Norfolk by canal, and to Newbern (7), which had rail connections to Raleigh. In April Burnside captured Morehead City (8) and Beaufort (9), closing both of those ports as well. By the spring of 1862 the entire North Carolina coast from the Virginia line to Cape Fear was in Union hands. The only North Carolina port left open to Confederate blockade runners was Wilmington on the Cape Fear River, 150 miles south of Cape Hatteras.

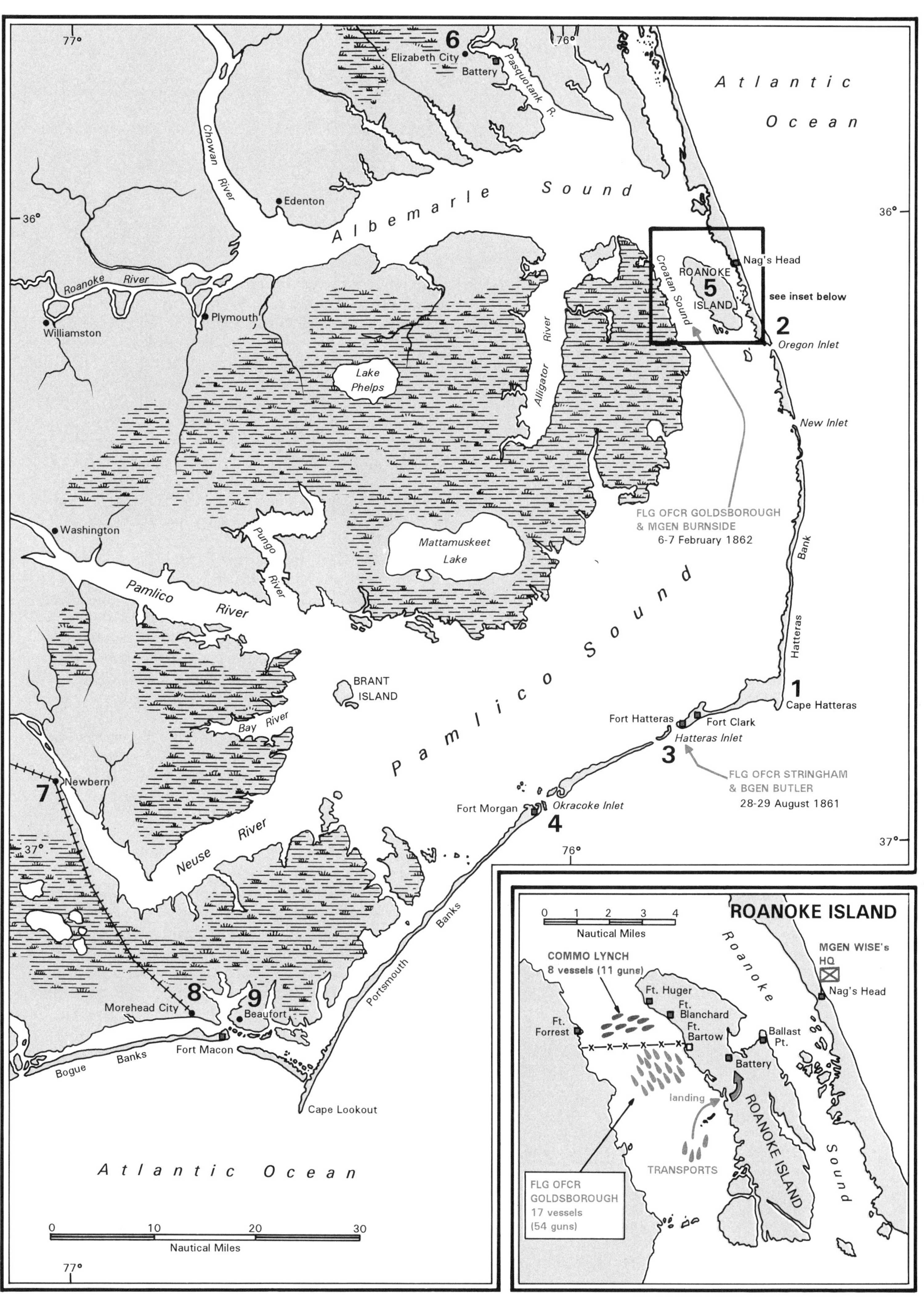

Atlantic Ocean
Albemarle Sound
Pamlico Sound
Elizabeth City
Battery
Pasquotank R.
Chowan River
Edenton
Roanoke River
Plymouth
Williamston
Lake Phelps
Alligator River
Croatan Sound
ROANOKE ISLAND
Nag's Head
see inset below
Oregon Inlet
New Inlet
FLG OFCR GOLDSBOROUGH
& MGEN BURNSIDE
6-7 February 1862
Mattamuskeet Lake
Washington
Pungo River
Pamlico River
Hatteras Bank
BRANT ISLAND
Bay River
Cape Hatteras
Fort Hatteras
Fort Clark
Hatteras Inlet
FLG OFCR STRINGHAM
& BGEN BUTLER
28-29 August 1861
Newbern
Fort Morgan
Okracoke Inlet
Neuse River
Portsmouth Banks
Morehead City
Beaufort
Fort Macon
Bogue Banks
Cape Lookout
Nautical Miles
ROANOKE ISLAND
Nautical Miles
COMMO LYNCH
8 vessels (11 guns)
MGEN WISE's HQ
Ft. Huger
Ft. Blanchard
Ft. Bartow
Ft. Forrest
Ballast Pt.
Battery
landing
Roanoke Sound
TRANSPORTS
FLG OFCR GOLDSBOROUGH
17 vessels
(54 guns)

Map 32

Port Royal

7 November 1861

When the Federal Strategy Board established the Union blockade of the Southern coast in the spring of 1861, it recommended that at least one site within each blockading zone be seized for use as a coaling and repair station. Within the area assigned to the South Atlantic Blockading Squadron there was no better site for such a base than Port Royal Sound, South Carolina (1), situated between Savannah (2) and Charleston (3). Its commodious anchorage could accommodate the whole U.S. Navy, and the offshore islands, fringed by swamps and marshes, offered reasonable protection from an overland attack. In addition, Port Royal Sound (like Pamlico Sound) was a watery knife into the Confederate interior, offering the possibility of cutting the Charleston and Savannah Railroad at Coosawhatchie (4).

Confederate defenses at Port Royal were more imposing than those at Hatteras Inlet (see inset). Fort Walker (5) on Hilton Head was a substantial earth-and-log fort mounting twenty-three guns, while Fort Beauregard (6) on Bay Point mounted twenty guns. In addition, the Confederates had a flotilla of seven small steamers, mostly armed tugs, commanded by COMMO Josiah Tatnall. Once again, however, Confederate defenses proved insufficient to contend with the Federal attacking force, this time under Flag Officer Samuel F. Du Pont. In addition to two large steam frigates (the *Wabash* and *Susquehanna*), Du Pont commanded more than a dozen other armed steamers, a handful of sailing warships, and more than fifty transports and colliers; his entire command consisted of more than seventy-five vessels.

Du Pont's armada departed Hampton Roads on 29 October, but storms off Cape Hatteras slowed its progress, and a gale off South Carolina drove several of the vessels ashore. The gunboat *Isaac Smith* had to throw its guns overboard to keep from foundering. Finally, on 4 November about half the squadron reassembled off Port Royal, and over the next few days most of the rest of the fleet straggled into the anchorage. Because the Confederates had removed all the aids to navigation, the ships of the Federal squadron had to sound and mark the channel, and on 6 November Du Pont ordered a reconnaissance of the Confederate fortifications. Finally, on 7 November all was ready for the assault.

At 9:00 A.M. ten of Du Pont's warships entered Port Royal Sound in single file (7), with the heavy frigates *Wabash* and *Susquehanna* in the lead. The column of ships steamed up the center of the channel, opening fire at 9:30, then swung left and steamed past Fort Walker at eight hundred yards, at which range the Federals' 11-inch guns had a visible impact on the ramparts of the fort. At the same time a Union flanking squadron of five steam gunboats moved farther up the sound to take the fort in a flanking fire. Commodore Tatnall brought his small flotilla out to challenge this invasion, but recognizing the futility of such a duel, he turned into Skull Creek (8) and landed his marines to help in the defense of the fort.

By then the defenders of the fort were beginning to realize that they were badly outgunned. After passing Fort Walker the first time, Du Pont ordered his column of ships to come left again and retrace its course, this time steaming past Fort Walker at six hundred yards (9). At 11:30 a shot from the fleet took down the fort's flagpole, provoking a cheer from the Federal gunners, and a half hour later three more newly arrived Federal warships joined in the cannonade. One of the new arrivals was the USS *Pocahontas* under CDR Percival Drayton, whose older brother, BGEN Thomas F. Drayton, was the Confederate commander at Fort Walker.

After the third pass the Federal gunners had disabled many of the fort's guns, and the defenders were down to five hundred pounds of powder. Accepting the inevitable, Brigadier General Drayton gave his approval to evacuate the fort. CAPT John Rodgers (son of the naval officer of the same name who fought in the War of 1812) led a landing party ashore and raised the American flag over South Carolina soil at 2:20 P.M. The fall of Fort Walker led the Confederates to abandon Fort Beauregard as well.

The seizure of Port Royal had long-term repercussions for both sides. The Confederate commander on the South Carolina coast was none other than Robert E. Lee, and he concluded that the superiority of Federal warships over shore fortifications made it futile to try to defend the Confederacy at the water's edge. Rather than contest the shoreline, therefore, he recommended that the Confederacy hold only a few important and easily defensible ports (like Wilmington and Charleston) and surrender the rest of the coastline to the enemy.

The Federals drew much the same conclusion—to their long-term detriment. It was particularly gratifying to Secretary Welles that the Navy had succeeded in taking possession of Port Royal Sound while the twelve thousand–man division of soldiers under BGEN Thomas W. Sherman bobbed uncomfortably in transports offshore. He concluded that Du Pont's victory proved that steam-powered warships firing explosive shells could overwhelm enemy shore fortifications. As Du Pont would discover, Welles did not sufficiently appreciate the difference between the earth-and-log forts at Port Royal and reinforced masonry structures like Fort Sumter in Charleston Harbor. Welles's desire to see the Navy take the lead in seizing the Southern coastline contributed to a sense of rivalry between the Army and Navy. On several occasions over the next three years, rather than seeking to cooperate, the two services all too often engaged in a fierce rivalry.

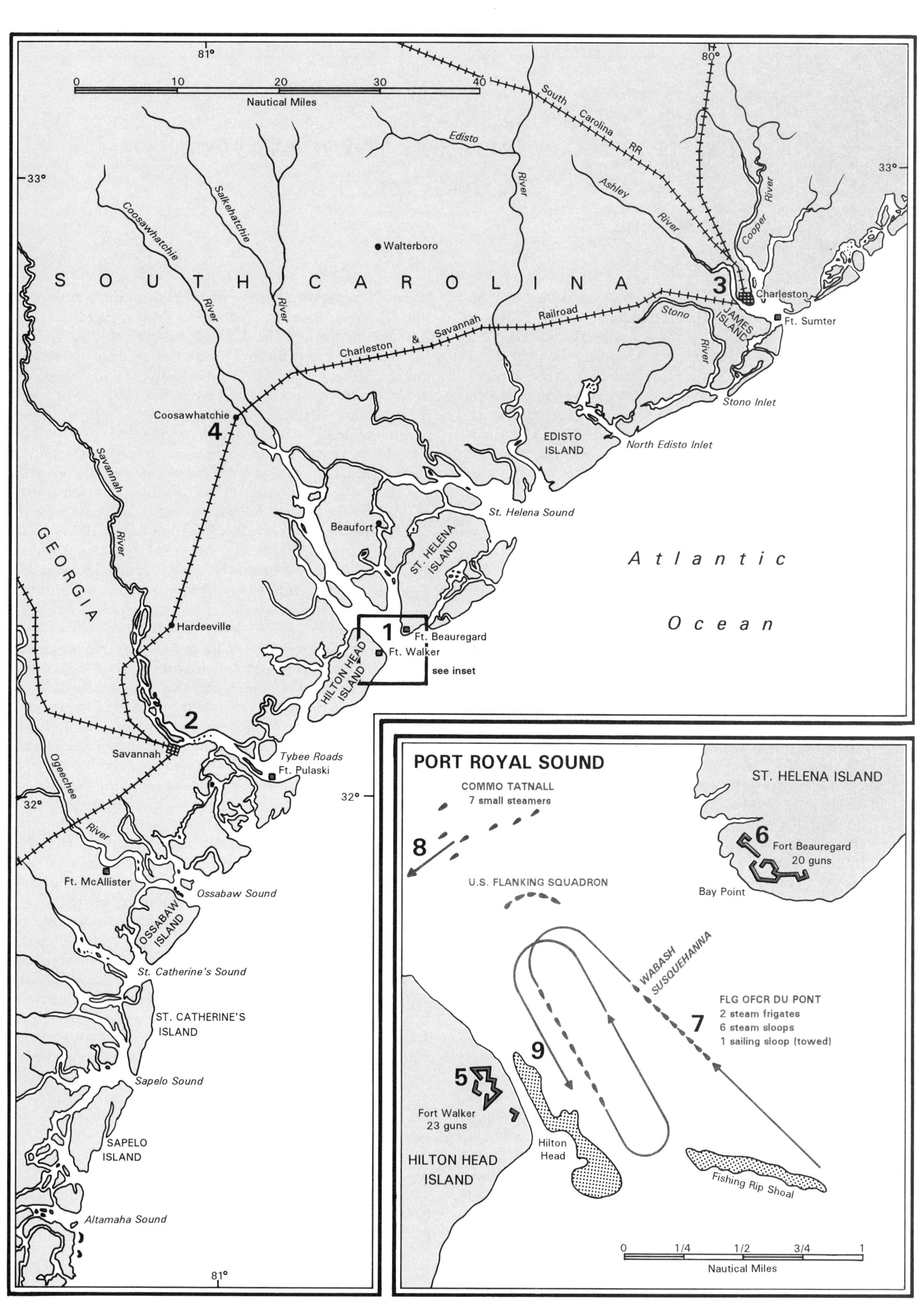

81°
0
10
20
30
40
Nautical Miles
80°
33°
33°
South Carolina RR
Edisto River
Salkehatchie River
Coosawhatchie River
Ashley River
Cooper River
Walterboro
S O U T H C A R O L I N A
3
Charleston
Stono River
JAMES ISLAND
Ft. Sumter
Charleston & Savannah Railroad
Stono Inlet
Coosawhatchie
4
EDISTO ISLAND
North Edisto Inlet
Savannah River
St. Helena Sound
GEORGIA
Beaufort
ST. HELENA ISLAND
Atlantic
Ocean
Hardeeville
1
Ft. Beauregard
Ft. Walker
HILTON HEAD ISLAND
see inset
2
Savannah
Tybee Roads
Ft. Pulaski
Ogeechee River
32°
32°
Ft. McAllister
Ossabaw Sound
OSSABAW ISLAND
St. Catherine's Sound
ST. CATHERINE'S ISLAND
Sapelo Sound
SAPELO ISLAND
Altamaha Sound
81°
PORT ROYAL SOUND
COMMO TATNALL
7 small steamers
8
ST. HELENA ISLAND
6
Fort Beauregard
20 guns
Bay Point
U.S. FLANKING SQUADRON
WABASH
SUSQUEHANNA
FLG OFCR DU PONT
2 steam frigates
6 steam sloops
1 sailing sloop (towed)
7
9
5
Fort Walker
23 guns
HILTON HEAD ISLAND
Hilton Head
Fishing Rip Shoal
0
1/4
1/2
3/4
1
Nautical Miles

MAP 33

BATTLE OF HAMPTON ROADS: *MONITOR* VS. *VIRGINIA*

9 MARCH 1862

After the humiliating Union defeat on the banks of Bull Run in July 1861, President Lincoln appointed MGEN George B. McClellan to command the Army, and in November McClellan assumed command of all Union armies. Over the ensuing fall and winter McClellan developed a strategic plan to take advantage of Union naval superiority by transporting his army to the Virginia coast, then moving quickly inland to capture Richmond before the Confederates could react (see inset). However, the appearance of a single Confederate warship in Hampton Roads—the CSS *Virginia*—threatened this campaign even before it began.

The existence of this warship was no surprise to Union authorities. They knew that the Confederates had occupied the Gosport Navy Yard (1) in April 1861 after the Union Navy abandoned it. They knew, too, that the Confederates had recovered the partially burned hull of the U.S. steam frigate *Merrimack* from the stone dry dock, reconfigured it as an ironclad, and rechristened it the *Virginia.* As a result, Navy Secretary Welles contracted with Swedish-born inventor John Ericcson to build an ironclad warship for the Union Navy. Welles gave Ericcson only one hundred days to build his vessel, which Ericcson called the *Monitor.* Time was crucial, for if the *Merrimack-Virginia* proved operationally successful, it could make Hampton Roads untenable for the Union Navy and checkmate McClellan's move to the Virginia peninsula.

The *Virginia* sortied for the first time at 10:00 A.M. on 8 March (2). An odd-looking warship, it was in effect an iron fort on a frigate's hull. Its heavy casemate superstructure was constructed of twenty-four inches of pine and oak covered by four inches of iron plate and was so heavy that the *Virginia* could manage a top speed of only five knots. Once in the relatively open water of Hampton Roads, the *Virginia's* commander, CAPT Franklin Buchanan, steered for the point of land off Newport News (3), where the Union's forty-four–gun frigate *Congress* lay at anchor. At 2:00 P.M. Buchanan opened fire and, bypassing the *Congress,* he steadied on a course to ram the frigate *Cumberland.* The *Virginia* struck the *Cumberland* on its port bow, burying its four-foot iron ram so deeply into the frigate that when the *Cumberland* began to sink, it threatened to take the *Virginia* down too. Instead, the ram broke off, and the *Cumberland* went down with the loss of 121 men.

Witness to these events, CAPT William Smith of the *Congress* sought to move his vessel out of range, but it grounded on the shoals and became a hapless, immobile target to the guns of the *Virginia* and its smaller consorts until 4:30 P.M., when Smith was forced to strike his flag. Ignoring the surrender, Union batteries on shore continued to fire, preventing the Confederates from taking possession of the vessel. Furious at what he considered a breach of honor, Buchanan foolishly climbed out onto the exposed deck of the *Virginia* to fire a musket at the offending batteries, and while thus engaged he was wounded in the leg. The *Virginia's* renewed shelling set the *Congress* afire, and it finally blew up near midnight, with the loss of 120 men. Meanwhile, the newer steam frigate *Minnesota* moved to intercept the *Virginia.* But it, too, grounded (4), and the two ships exchanged long-range fire until dusk, when the *Virginia* retired to its anchorage off Sewall's Point (5).

Buchanan's wound forced him to relinquish command to LT Catesby ap R. Jones, who was at the conn when the *Virginia* got under way at 8:00 A.M. the next morning. Jones intended to finish off the grounded *Minnesota* and then destroy the rest of the Union fleet in Hampton Roads. But when the *Virginia* moved out into the roadstead, Jones found the *Monitor,* which had arrived overnight, brashly blocking his path. The duel between the two ironclads began at 8:45 A.M. and lasted for three and a half hours. The two ships maneuvered carefully around each other at close range. LT John Worden, captain of the *Monitor,* fired fifty-five rounds from his two 11-inch Dahlgren guns housed in the *Monitor's* revolutionary rotating turret, but the shot made no significant impression on the casemate of the *Virginia.* For its part, the *Monitor* proved equally resistant to Confederate shot, though Worden was rendered temporarily blind when a shell exploded against the slit of the pilothouse while he was looking out. Jones tried to ram his opponent, but the *Virginia* had lost its ram and was unable to get up a good head of steam at such close range. At 12:15 P.M., with his engines straining and his crew physically exhausted, Jones ordered the *Virginia* to return to its anchorage at Sewall's Point. Though the battle was a tactical draw, the arrival of the *Monitor* meant that the Union Navy could remain in Hampton Roads and that McClellan could proceed with his peninsular campaign.

McClellan's army arrived the next month. In April nearly 400 chartered vessels transported more than 120,000 men, 15,000 animals, and 1,200 wagons to Fort Monroe (6). But McClellan's hope of outflanking Confederate defensive lines on the peninsula by sending warships up the James or York Rivers proved vain. The *Virginia's* looming presence blocked the James, and Union Navy officers were unwilling to run past the Confederate shore batteries (7) into the York. Disappointed, McClellan set out to take Yorktown by old-fashioned siege tactics (8). Eventually, his own slow-footed progress, and vigorous Confederate counterattacks outside Richmond, destroyed his campaign and led to his recall.

Neither of the ironclads survived the year. The *Virginia* was destroyed by its own crew on 11 May because it could not ascend the James River to Richmond after the Confederates evacuated Norfolk. The *Monitor* went down ten months later, on 31 December, in a storm off Cape Hatteras.

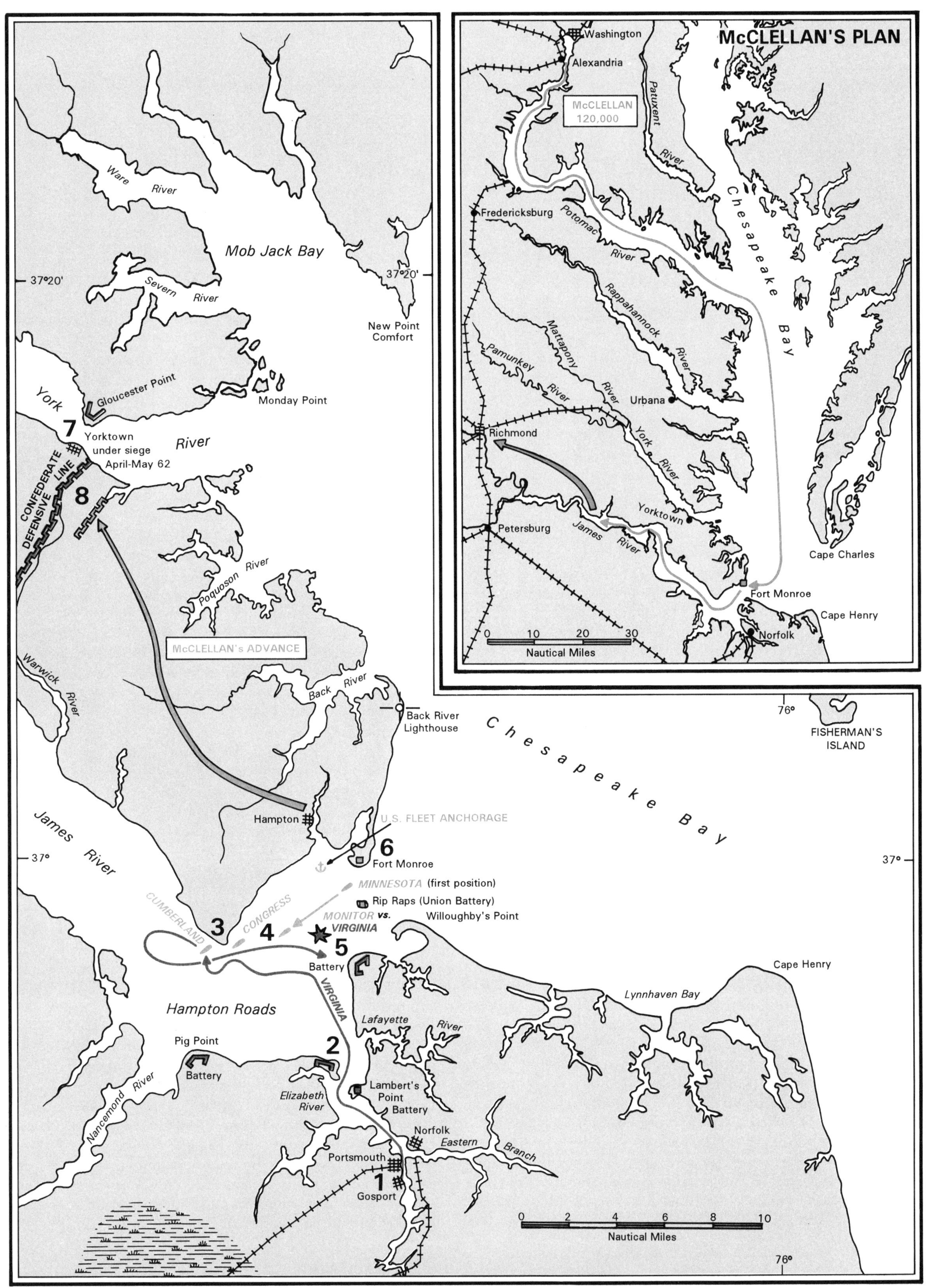
McCLELLAN'S PLAN
Washington
Alexandria
McCLELLAN
120,000
Patuxent
River
Chesapeake
Bay
Fredericksburg
Potomac
River
Rappahannock
River
Mattapony
River
Pamunkey
River
Urbana
York
River
Richmond
Yorktown
Petersburg
James
River
Cape Charles
Fort Monroe
Cape Henry
Norfolk
0
10
20
30
Nautical Miles
Ware
River
Mob Jack Bay
37°20'
Severn
River
New Point
Comfort
Gloucester Point
Monday Point
York
7
Yorktown
under siege
April-May 62
River
CONFEDERATE
DEFENSIVE
LINE
8
Poquoson
River
McCLELLAN's ADVANCE
Warwick
River
Back
River
Back River
Lighthouse
76°
FISHERMAN'S
ISLAND
Chesapeake
Bay
James
River
Hampton
U.S. FLEET ANCHORAGE
6
Fort Monroe
37°
MINNESOTA (first position)
Rip Raps (Union Battery)
CUMBERLAND
CONGRESS
MONITOR vs. VIRGINIA
Willoughby's Point
3
4
5
Battery
VIRGINIA
Cape Henry
Lynnhaven Bay
Hampton Roads
Lafayette
River
Pig Point
Battery
2
Nancemond
River
Elizabeth
River
Lambert's
Point
Battery
Norfolk
Eastern
Branch
Portsmouth
1
Gosport
0
2
4
6
8
10
Nautical Miles

MAP 34

THE RIVER WAR: FORTS HENRY AND DONELSON

4–16 FEBRUARY 1862

During the first months of the Civil War it was not clear that the U.S. Navy would play any role in the war on the inland rivers. At first, even Navy Secretary Welles considered the western rivers to be the Army's domain. Welles sent CDR John Rodgers to Cincinnati in May to develop a riverine naval force on the Ohio River, but his function was primarily that of an adviser to the Army. Rodgers purchased three river steamers (the *Conestoga, Lexington,* and *Tyler*) and supervised their modification into gunboats. By the end of the summer these so-called "woodclads" were at Cairo, Illinois (1), the unofficial headquarters of the Union's riverine flotilla.

In September 1861 Welles sent CAPT Andrew H. Foote to command the flotilla at Cairo and contracted with James Eads for the construction of seven ironclad river gunboats. Built along lines recommended by Naval Constructor Samuel Pook, these came to be known as "Pook's Turtles," and the first of them joined the naval flotilla in November. That same month Foote was promoted to flag officer to give him nominal equality with major generals in the theater, though he remained under the operational control of the Army. In effect, Union Army and Navy commanders in the western theater worked within what amounted to a unified-command system. The strategic direction of Foote's flotilla belonged to the Union theater commander in the West, MGEN Henry W. Halleck, who also had responsibility for two Union field armies: one under MGEN Don Carlos Buell in central Kentucky (off the map) and one under BGEN Ulysses S. Grant at Paducah (2).

Command of the rivers was crucial to military success in the West, for they provided the primary means of military transport and logistic support. The southward-flowing Mississippi was obviously the most important, but Union forces could also use the Tennessee or Cumberland Rivers to penetrate the South's defenses. In recognition of this, the Confederate commander in the West, GEN Albert Sidney Johnston, ordered that substantial fortifications be built on the banks of all three rivers. The principal Confederate bastion on the Mississippi was at Columbus (3), where MGEN Leonidas Polk commanded an army of seventeen thousand men. The best site to block the Tennessee and Cumberland Rivers was probably the Birmingham narrows (4), where the rivers were less than three miles apart. But because Kentucky had attempted to maintain its neutrality in the first months of war, the Confederates had instead built separate forts just over the Tennessee line: Fort Henry (5) on the Tennessee and Fort Donelson (6) on the Cumberland.

In January 1862 Grant and Foote each wired Halleck at St. Louis to express their opinion that Fort Henry was vulnerable to a combined attack, and to request permission to attempt its capture. Their request coincided with one from President Lincoln demanding offensive action, and Halleck gave them the go-ahead. Thirteen transports ferried Grant's two divisions to a landing site a few miles north of Fort Henry, while Foote's gunboats prepared to shell the fort from the river (see map at lower left).

The Confederate commander at Fort Henry, BGEN Lloyd Tilghman, doubted the ability of his fort to stand up to a determined attack. Not only was Fort Henry poorly sited on low ground adjacent to the river, but the river was thirty feet higher than normal and threatened to flood his gun positions and magazines. When Foote's gunboats approached on 6 February, therefore, Tilghman sent all but eighty of his three thousand men toward Fort Donelson and prepared to defend the fort as long as possible with his artillery alone.

The duel between the gunboats and the fort began at 12:30 on 6 February. Foote opened fire at 1,700 yards and rapidly closed the range to 600 yards. The *Essex,* a converted ironclad, was knocked out of the fight when it took one shot through the stack and another in the boiler—which killed ten and wounded twenty-six. But over the next hour and a half the more powerfully armed gunboats overwhelmed the Confederate battery until only four of its seventeen guns were still working. Satisfied that honor had been served, Tilghman lowered his flag at 1:50 P.M., and Grant's soldiers arrived a half hour later to raise the American flag in its place.

After Fort Henry capitulated, Foote sent his wooden gunboats upstream to burn the railroad bridge (7) that connected Bowling Green with Memphis, and he sent the *Carondelet,* the least damaged of his ironclads, on a roundabout journey to Fort Donelson, which was Grant's next objective. The *Carondelet* arrived at Fort Donelson on 12 February and opened a one-ship bombardment. Three more ironclads arrived on the fourteenth, as did Grant's army after an overland march from Fort Henry. But Fort Donelson proved to be much tougher than Fort Henry (see map at lower right). It was sited on high ground, and the plunging shot of its batteries proved devastating to Foote's gunboats, which suffered more than thirty hits each and had to retire out of range (8). Moreover, Fort Donelson was manned by a garrison of seventeen thousand, a force nearly as large as Grant's. But no fort is stronger than the will of its commander, and after calling a council of war, Confederate MGEN John B. Floyd decided to evacuate. He ordered the garrison to fight its way out. But after his men had opened an escape route (9) in fierce fighting on 15 February, he lost his nerve and ordered a retreat back into the fort. Floyd himself managed to escape across the river, as did a handful of others, but he left behind BGEN Simon B. Buckner to endure the ignominy of capitulation. When Buckner asked Grant for terms, the Union general's reply made him famous: "No terms except unconditional and immediate surrender can be accepted."

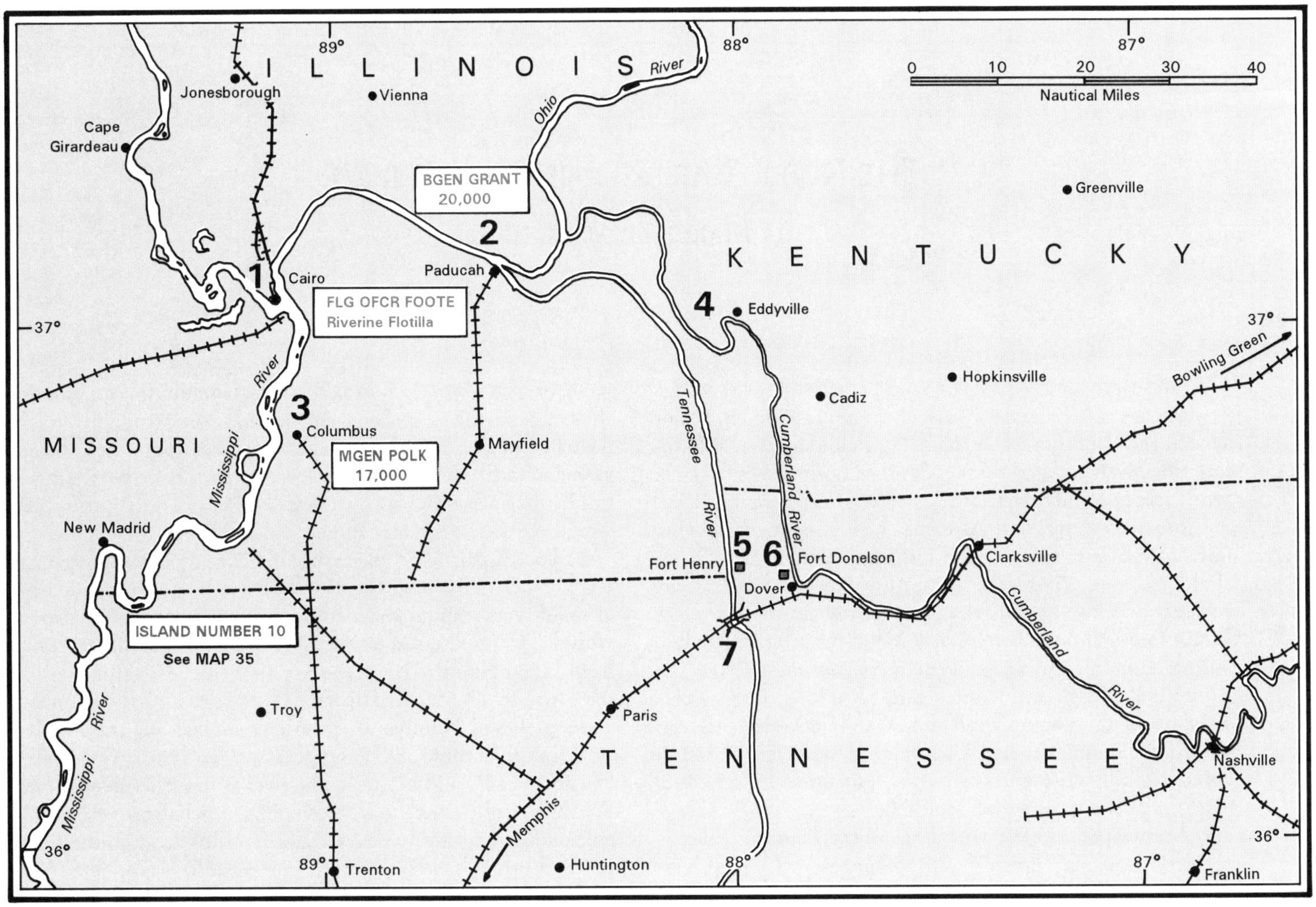

ILLINOIS
MISSOURI
KENTUCKY
TENNESSEE
89°
88°
87°
37°
36°
0 10 20 30 40
Nautical Miles
Jonesborough
Vienna
Cape Girardeau
Ohio River
BGEN GRANT
20,000
2
Greenville
1
Cairo
Paducah
FLG OFCR FOOTE
Riverine Flotilla
4
Eddyville
Hopkinsville
Bowling Green
Cadiz
3
Columbus
Mississippi River
Mayfield
MGEN POLK
17,000
Tennessee River
Cumberland River
New Madrid
5
6
Fort Henry
Fort Donelson
Dover
Clarksville
ISLAND NUMBER 10
See MAP 35
7
Cumberland River
Troy
Paris
Nashville
Memphis
Trenton
Huntington
Franklin

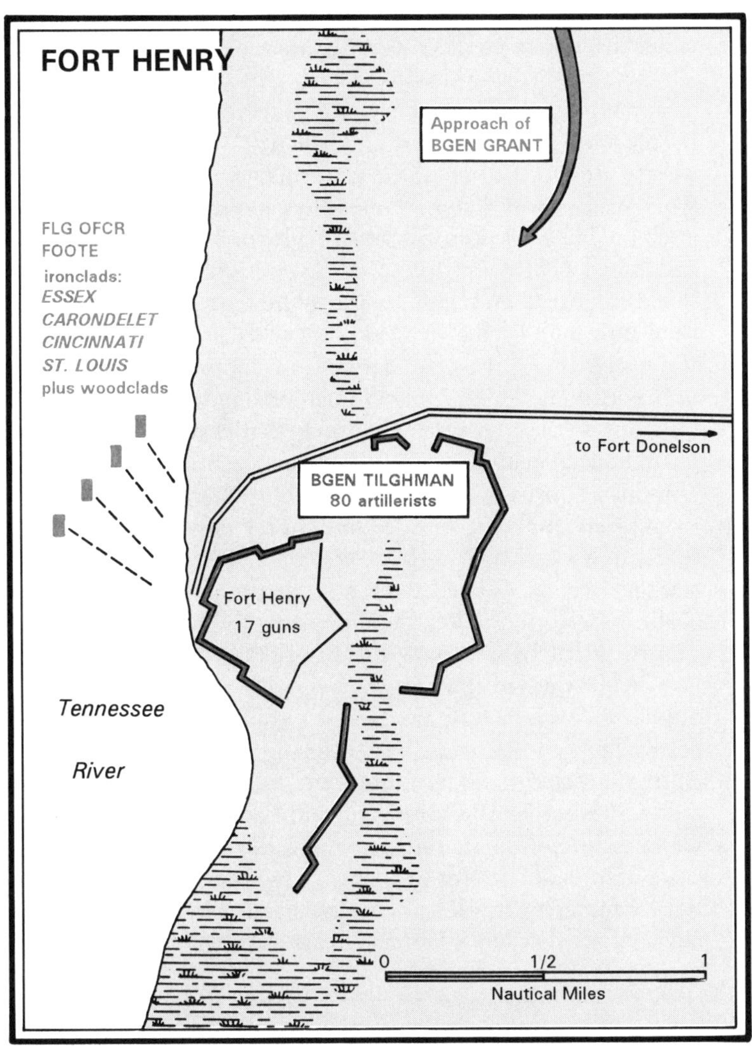

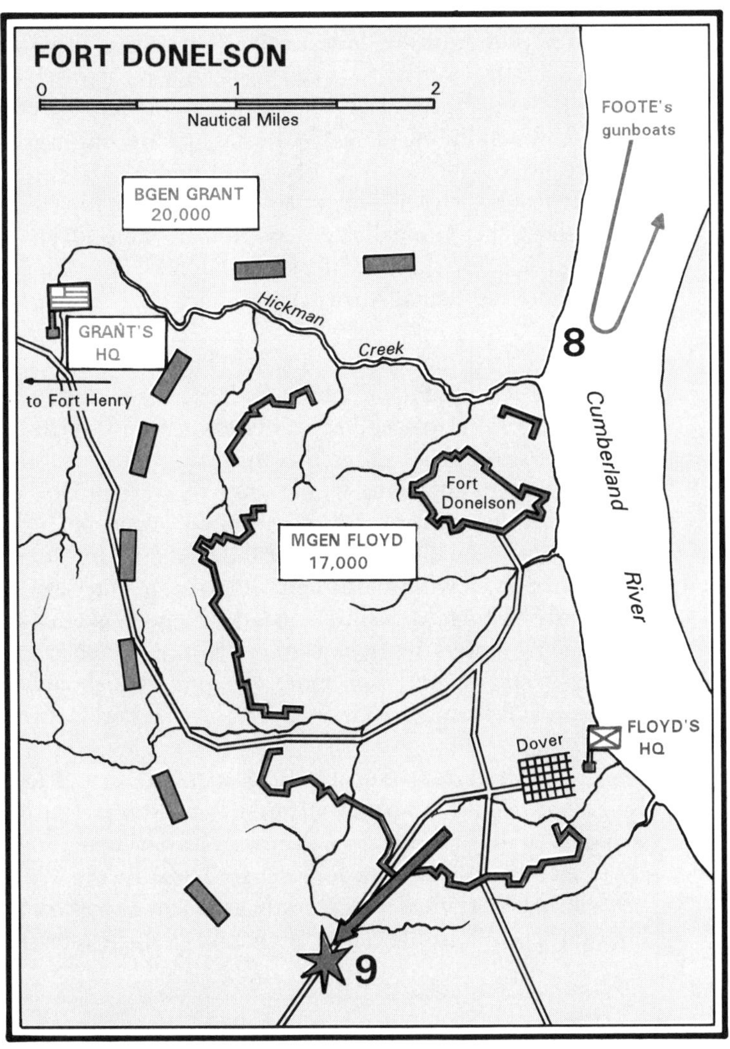

MAP 35

THE RIVER WAR: ISLAND NUMBER 10

14 MARCH–7 APRIL 1862

The capture of Forts Henry and Donelson drove a wedge between the Confederate forces at Columbus under Major General Polk and those at Bowling Green under General Johnston. Effectively isolated from each other, both armies fell back from their positions in Kentucky, through Tennessee, all the way into Mississippi and Alabama. Grant followed, moving south up the Tennessee River to Pittsburg Landing near Shiloh Church. There on 6 April he was surprised by a Confederate attack that was so vigorous it threatened to destroy his army. Grant's forces avoided being pushed into the river in part because of support from the gunboats *Lexington* and *Tyler,* whose gunfire helped halt the Confederate advance at dusk. Reinforced overnight, Grant counterattacked the next day and won back all the ground he had lost. Though the Battle of Shiloh was strategically indecisive, its twenty-four thousand casualties suggested how costly the war would be.

Meanwhile, Major General Halleck was anxious to initiate a Union advance down the Mississippi as well. The principal obstacle there was the Confederate bastion at Island Number 10, so named because it was the tenth island in the Mississippi south of the Ohio River. There, on a hairpin turn in the river, the Confederates had erected formidable defenses: both on the island itself (1) and on the Tennessee side of the river (2). In addition, the Confederates had a floating battery moored to the western tip of the island (3) and a small squadron of river gunboats under CDR George N. Hollins. Altogether, the Confederates committed more than fifty heavy guns to the defenses at Island Number 10, making it a much more substantial barrier than either Fort Henry or Fort Donelson.

Foote was much less anxious than Halleck to take on this obstacle. The pounding his flotilla had taken at Fort Donelson had required him to spend several weeks at Cairo in effecting repairs. Moreover, he realized that there was an important difference between attacking Confederate defenses on the Tennessee and Cumberland and those on the Mississippi. When the *Essex* had been damaged during the fight for Fort Henry, it had drifted *north* with the current into friendly waters. But on the south-flowing Mississippi, wounded vessels would drift into enemy waters to their certain capture. These circumstances would make Foote more cautious in the operation against Island Number 10 than he had been at Forts Henry or Donelson.

Foote departed Cairo on 14 March and arrived in the vicinity of Island Number 10 the next day. He hoped to avoid a slugfest with the Confederate batteries by having ten mortar boats shell the island from long range. These vessels were essentially flat-bottomed barges with casemate superstructures but no overhead. In the center of each was a single mortar capable of firing a 13-inch projectile on an arcing trajectory over the bends in the river. Foote opened his bombardment on 16 March, and later that day he committed his ironclad gunboats as well. Both sides suffered damage in the artillery exchange, but by the end of the day it was evident that Island Number 10 would not fall to artillery alone.

Foote's partner in the combined Union operation against Island Number 10 was MGEN John Pope, who commanded an army of twenty thousand men. In February Pope advanced to within striking distance of New Madrid ten miles downstream from Island Number 10 on the Missouri side (4), and he seized the town on 13 March. This effectively sealed off the Confederates at Island Number 10 from any support via the Mississippi, but they could still be supplied overland from Tiptonville (5), and Pope could not cross the river without naval support. Pope, therefore, urged Foote to send his ironclads past the Confederate batteries so that they could ferry his army to the Tennessee shore. When Foote put this proposal to his captains, two of them volunteered to attempt it, but Foote vetoed the idea. Instead, he supported an Army project to construct a canal across the loop in the river to bypass the Confederate works (6). The resulting canal proved wide enough to allow small vessels to pass through but not the ironclad gunboats, and finally Foote relented and agreed to allow CDR Henry Walke in the *Carondelet* to attempt a run past the Confederate batteries.

Walke chose 4 April, a moonless and rainy night, for the attempt. He reinforced his vessel with timbers and hay bales and lashed a coal barge to the vessel's port side as an additional shield against Confederate gunfire. The Confederate batteries were only one of the dangers. On a black night the heavy *Carondelet* could easily run aground in the twisting river with no navigational lights. Only by memorizing the image left on his retina by the intermittent lightning flashes could Walke navigate the channel. Of course, those same lightning flashes also illuminated his vessel for the enemy, but for the first hour the Confederate lookouts failed to spot him. Halfway past the batteries, however, a sudden blaze of flame from the *Carondelet's* stack alerted the Confederates, and their gunners opened fire. Walke ordered full power and completed the run at full speed. He arrived safely off New Madrid at 1:00 A.M. on 5 April.

After this success the *Pittsburg* (LT Egbert Thompson) duplicated Walke's feat, and the two ironclads successfully escorted Pope's army across the Mississippi to Tiptonville on 7 April. Outflanked and outnumbered, the Confederate garrison at Island Number 10 capitulated, and Pope took six thousand Confederate prisoners. That same day, 125 miles to the southeast, Grant launched his successful counterattack at Shiloh. In both campaigns, it was the effective combination of land and naval power that made Union success possible.

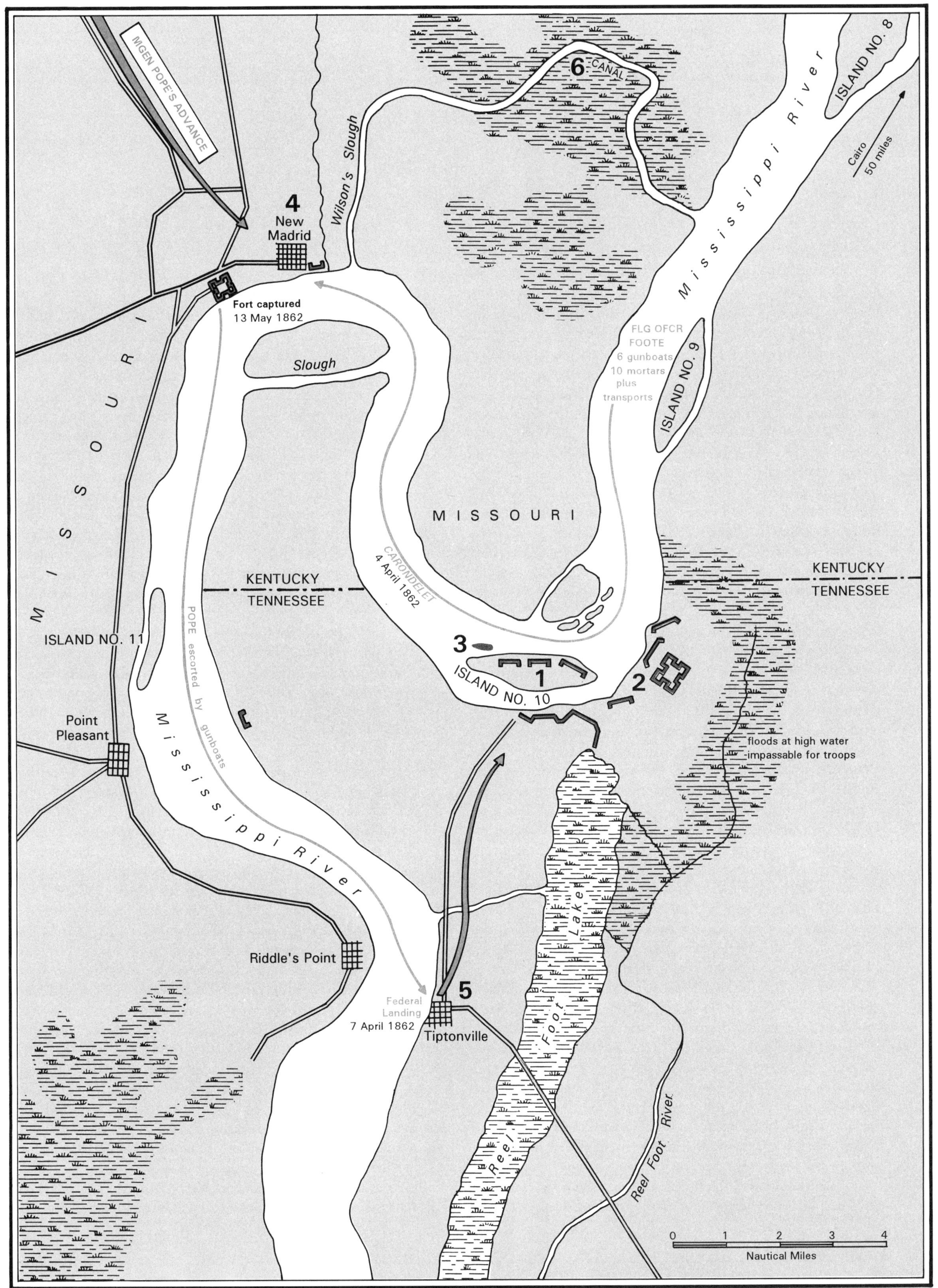

MGEN POPE'S ADVANCE
4
New Madrid
Fort captured
13 May 1862
Wilson's Slough
6
CANAL
ISLAND NO. 8
Mississippi River
Cairo
50 miles
Slough
FLG OFCR
FOOTE
6 gunboats
10 mortars
plus
transports
ISLAND NO. 9
MISSOURI
MISSOURI
CARONDELET
4 April 1862
KENTUCKY
TENNESSEE
KENTUCKY
TENNESSEE
ISLAND NO. 11
POPE escorted by gunboats
3
1
ISLAND NO. 10
2
floods at high water
impassable for troops
Point Pleasant
Mississippi River
Riddle's Point
Federal
Landing
7 April 1862
5
Tiptonville
Reel Foot Lake
Reel Foot River
0
1
2
3
4
Nautical Miles

Map 36

The River War: New Orleans

15–25 April 1862

While Foote teamed with Grant and Pope to assail Confederate defenses in the upper Mississippi Valley, Flag Officer David Glasgow Farragut tested Confederate defenses at the mouth of the great river. Impressed by the dominance of Du Pont's warships over Confederate fortifications at Port Royal Sound, Secretary of the Navy Welles and Assistant Secretary Fox urged a naval assault on New Orleans. Though ten thousand Army troops under BGEN Benjamin Butler would support Farragut, they were designated as a garrison force to occupy whatever enemy fortifications Farragut's ships could overcome with their firepower.

In February 1862 Farragut established an advance base at Ship Island (1). He could not approach New Orleans via Lakes Borgne or Pontchartrain as the British had done in 1814 because his was to be a purely naval attack and his oceangoing warships could not navigate the shallow waters of Lake Borgne. Instead, he would advance upriver from the Head of Passes (2) to Plaquemine Bend (3) and use long-range mortars to shell the Confederate forts there into submission. Then, presumably, his oceangoing warships could run past the forts and up the river to New Orleans (4).

Farragut's first problem was getting his oceangoing screw steamers over the bar at the various mouths of the river. Not until 15 April was his squadron safely assembled at the Head of Passes, where it was joined by six gunboats and twenty mortar schooners under CDR David Dixon Porter (son of David Porter). The next day Farragut steamed upriver and anchored just east of Plaquemine Bend (see lower map). Two days later, on 18 April, the Federal mortar schooners opened fire on the Confederate forts with their 13-inch mortars. Fourteen of the bomb vessels concentrated their fire on Fort Jackson (5), while six others along the eastern bank targeted Fort St. Philip (6). This latter group came under heavy fire from the gunners in Fort Jackson and were soon withdrawn to join the rest of the flotilla along the western bank, where thick woods along the riverbank made it difficult for the Confederates to respond.

For five days Federal bombs rained down on Fort Jackson. The exploding shells destroyed the flammable wooden structures inside the fort and drove the garrison into protected casemates but did not significantly reduce the fort's firepower. At the same time several of Porter's gunboats tested the strength of the ship-and-chain boom the Confederates had erected across the river (7). On the twentieth two of the gunboats succeeded in cutting the boom, and on 23 April, even though the forts had not been silenced, Farragut decided that it was time to make his next move.

Farragut ordered his squadron to get under way at 2:00 A.M. on 24 April. The gunboat *Cayuga* led the flotilla, followed by the twenty-three–gun screw steamer *Pensacola.* The *Cayuga* passed through the boom without mishap, but CAPT H. W. Morris of the *Pensacola* slowed to fire a broadside at Fort Jackson, then steamed up to Fort St. Philip, where he stopped long enough to deliver two broadsides from such close range that the gunners on both sides shouted curses at one another (8). Morris's bold gesture temporarily drove the Confederate gunners from their guns, but it slowed the progress of the flotilla through the narrow opening, causing the ships to bunch up, and the billowing smoke made visibility difficult for officers of the deck attempting to steer by starlight.

Nevertheless, the flotilla forged ahead. Farragut's flagship, the *Hartford,* ran aground above Fort St. Philip and caught fire when it was struck by a fire raft, though the disciplined crew got the fire under control, and the *Hartford* was soon refloated. Once past the forts, the Federal warships faced a small but dangerous flotilla of Confederate gunboats. The most serious threat of all was the Confederate ironclad *Louisiana,* whose engines were not yet operational but which did significant damage as a floating battery. In addition, the Confederate ram *Manassas* struck the *Brooklyn* before it was driven ashore and destroyed. By dawn most of Farragut's flotilla was safely above the forts, and the surviving Confederate vessels were fleeing upriver. Growing daylight had kept three Union ships from attempting the run, three others had run aground, and all of the Union vessels had suffered some damage from enemy shells.

Barely pausing to assess the damage, Farragut left Porter behind to deal with the forts and steamed upriver toward New Orleans. Near Chalmette (9, upper map), where Jackson had repelled the British in January 1815, the Confederates opened fire with shore artillery, but Farragut's ships steamed ahead and enfiladed the Confederate lines. That same day (25 April) he anchored off Jackson Square and demanded the city's surrender. The spring floods had raised the river level so that Farragut's warships looked down on the city, and even though Butler's troops were still ninety miles downriver, securing the surrender of the Confederate forts, the civil authorities in New Orleans bowed to Farragut's demand. Two weeks later the screw sloop *Richmond* steamed up to Baton Rouge (10, upper map) and compelled its surrender as well.

A month later, a thousand miles to the north, Foote's successor in command of the Mississippi flotilla, Flag Officer Charles Henry Davis, ran by Fort Pillow in Tennessee and accepted the surrender of Memphis after a battle with another outgunned Confederate riverine squadron. Confederate control of the Mississippi was slipping away. By the fall of 1862 only Port Hudson, Louisiana, and Vicksburg, Mississippi, held the two halves of the Confederacy together.

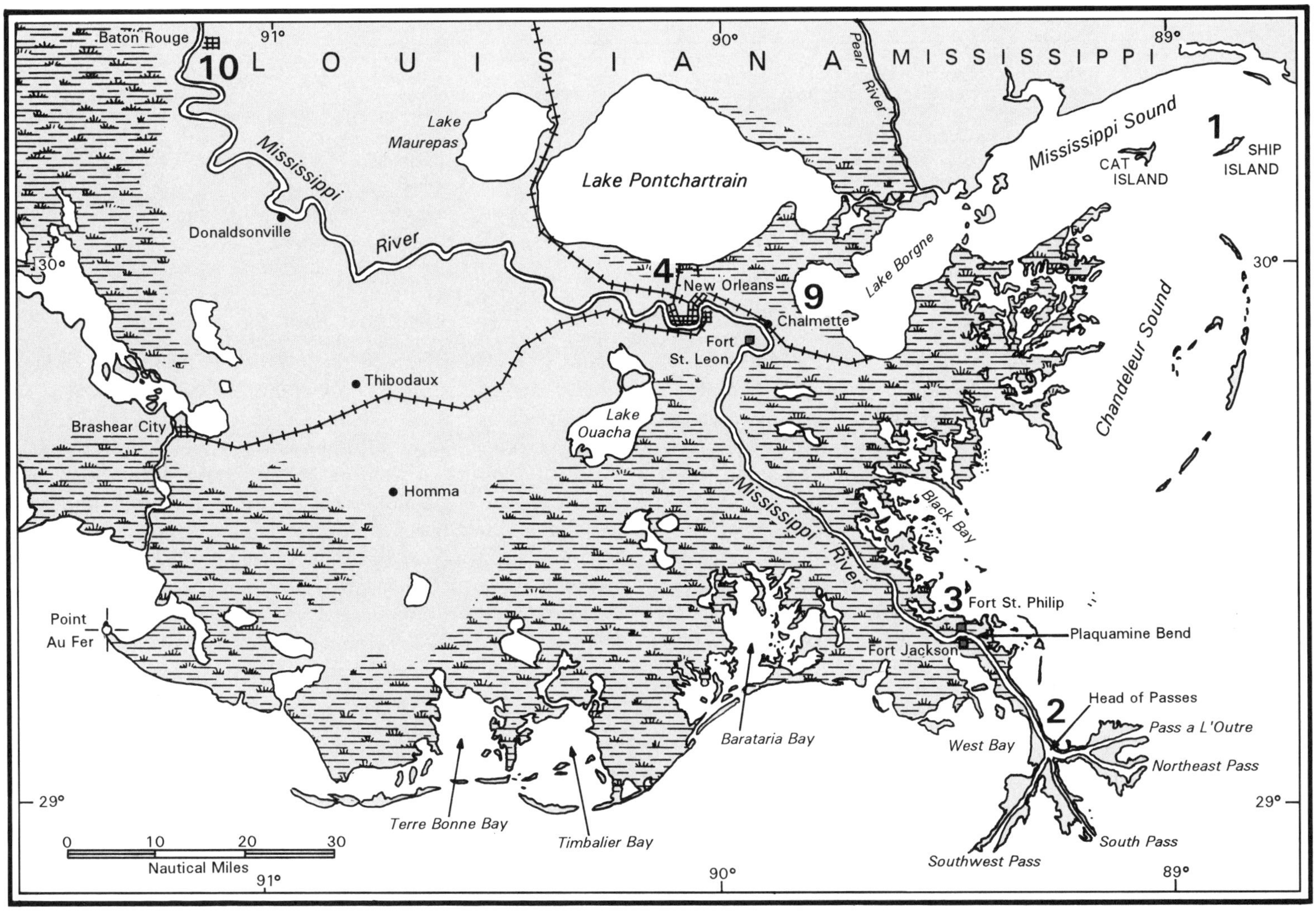

Baton Rouge
91°
90°
89°
10 LOUISIANA
MISSISSIPPI
Pearl River
Lake Maurepas
Lake Pontchartrain
Mississippi River
Mississippi Sound
1 SHIP ISLAND
CAT ISLAND
Donaldsonville
30°
4 New Orleans
9
Lake Borgne
Chalmette
Chandeleur Sound
Fort St. Leon
Thibodaux
Brashear City
Lake Ouacha
Homma
Black Bay
3 Fort St. Philip
Plaquamine Bend
Fort Jackson
Point Au Fer
Barataria Bay
2 Head of Passes
Pass a L'Outre
West Bay
Northeast Pass
29°
Terre Bonne Bay
Timbalier Bay
South Pass
Southwest Pass
0 10 20 30
Nautical Miles

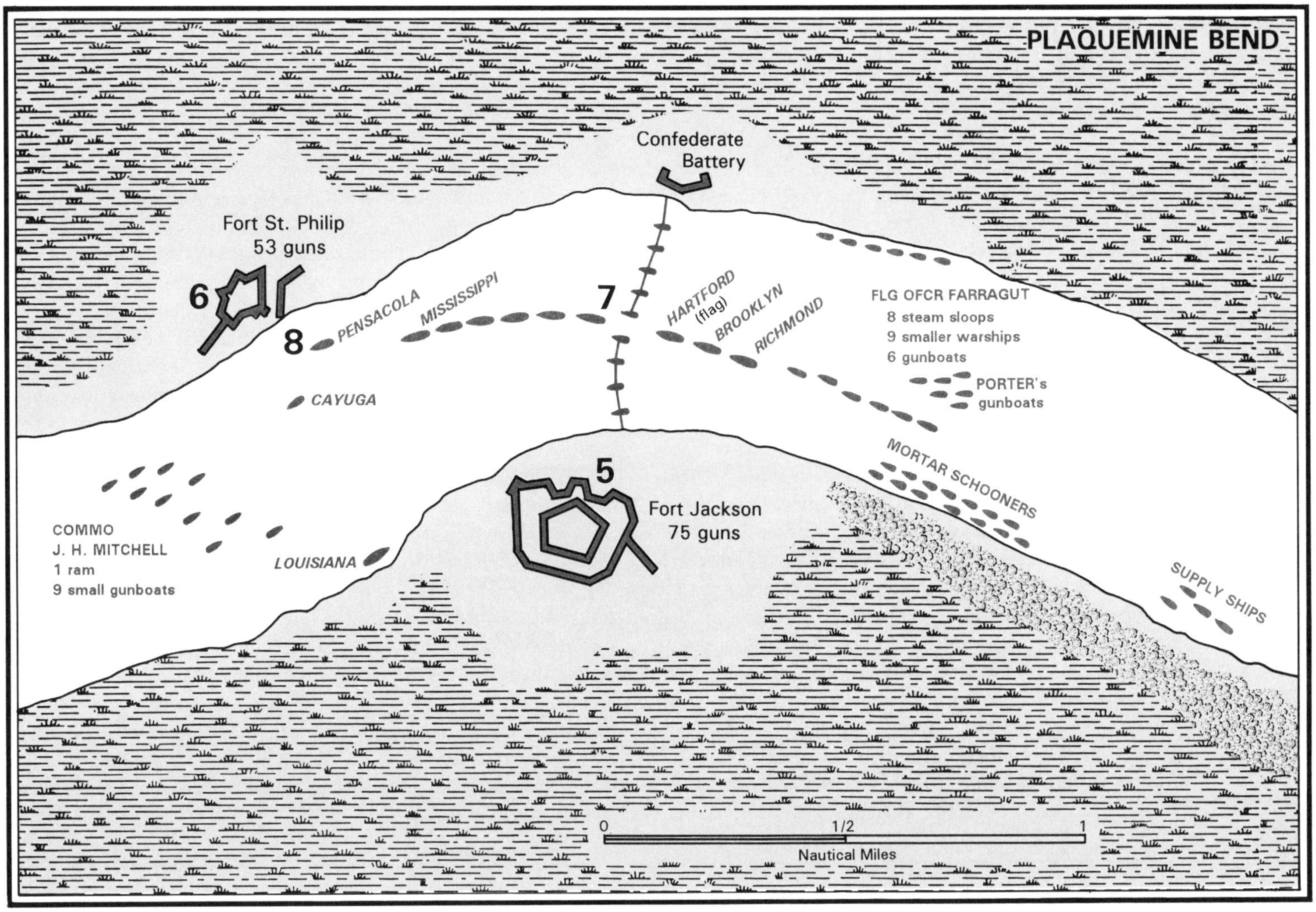

PLAQUEMINE BEND

Confederate Battery
Fort St. Philip
53 guns
6
7
8
PENSACOLA
MISSISSIPPI
HARTFORD (flag)
BROOKLYN
RICHMOND
FLG OFCR FARRAGUT
8 steam sloops
9 smaller warships
6 gunboats
CAYUGA
PORTER's gunboats
MORTAR SCHOONERS
5
Fort Jackson
75 guns
COMMO
J. H. MITCHELL
1 ram
9 small gunboats
LOUISIANA
SUPPLY SHIPS
0 1/2 1
Nautical Miles

MAP 37

THE RIVER WAR: VICKSBURG

DECEMBER 1862–JULY 1863

Along with the Battle of Antietam (September 1862), which triggered the Emancipation Proclamation, and the fall of Atlanta (September 1864), which ensured Lincoln's reelection, the Union's capture of Vicksburg and the simultaneous Confederate defeat at Gettysburg in July 1863 marked decisive turning points in the war. Significantly, in no other operation of the Civil War was the importance of effective Army-Navy cooperation demonstrated more clearly.

What made Vicksburg so important was its peculiar geography. Situated on a two-hundred-foot-high bluff on the eastern bank of the Mississippi, it completely dominated a hairpin turn in the river so that vessels had to run past several miles of Confederate batteries. Moreover, those bluffs ran north and south along the eastern bank of the Yazoo and Mississippi Rivers, making Vicksburg almost impregnable to any assault from the water. After his victory at New Orleans, Farragut steamed upriver to Vicksburg in June 1862, when the Confederates had only ten guns in place on the bluffs. Farragut managed to run past the batteries without suffering any serious damage, but he could not compel the city's surrender, and in the months afterward Confederate engineers set to work expanding and strengthening the fortifications so that by 1863 the eastern bank of the river bristled with gun emplacements. With some pride, Confederates called Vicksburg the Gibraltar of the West.

The team responsible for the Union's capture of Vicksburg was MGEN Ulysses S. Grant and Acting RADM David Dixon Porter. In the fall of 1862 President Lincoln called Major General Halleck to Washington to become his military chief of staff, and Grant succeeded to command of the Department of Tennessee. At the same time Flag Officer C. H. Davis became chief of the Bureau of Navigation, and Welles reached down past all the captains in the Navy to elevate Porter, then a commander, to acting rear admiral and command of the Mississippi Squadron. Grant and Porter were each exceptional men, but what made their campaign successful was less their individual brilliance than their ability to cooperate.

Grant knew that the key to eventual Union success was somehow to get a Federal army onto the bluffs *behind* Vicksburg. With that in mind, his first attempt to assail the citadel was a move southward through central Mississippi to approach Vicksburg from the east. But when Confederate cavalry cut his rail communications twice in December, he gave up that line of approach and returned to the river. A second option was to assail the bluffs east of the river *above* Vicksburg. That, too, failed when Grant's lieutenant, MGEN William T. Sherman, was repulsed at Haynes' Bluff (1) on 27 December. Sherman's men suffered 1,800 casualties and inflicted only 187.

Grant arrived at Milliken's Bend (2) north of Vicksburg in late January 1863. Through the winter months Union forces spent a lot of time and energy in trying to find a way *around* Vicksburg. This included explorations up the Yazoo River (3) and Steele's Bayou (4), as well as an attempt to dig a canal across the neck of the hairpin turn in the Mississippi opposite Vicksburg (5). None of these efforts bore fruit. Finally, in the spring of 1863 Grant set in motion his third and successful campaign.

The first part depended entirely on the Navy. On 2 April Grant asked Porter to run his squadron past the Vicksburg batteries. This was a much more daunting prospect than it had been the previous June when Farragut had managed it. Confederate batteries had multiplied tenfold since then. Moreover, there would be no going back. Even if Porter's gunboats could run past the batteries going downstream, it was less likely they could return to Milliken's Bend while fighting the five-knot current. Grant could not order Porter to run past Vicksburg. Strategic direction of the Mississippi Squadron had been transferred from the Army to the Navy in October, and Porter was under no obligation to accept the risky maneuver that Grant proposed. Nevertheless, Porter agreed at once to do it.

Choosing a dark night, Porter made his move on 16 April. Confederate sentries on the bluffs fired warning shots, and daring volunteers from Vicksburg crossed the river in small boats to light bonfires on the western shore to silhouette the Union gunboats on the inky river. For more than an hour Porter's gunboats endured a plunging fire from the bluffs, but they successfully cleared the batteries, losing only one transport and a few barges.

The second phase of Grant's plan required the Army to march along old levees bordering Roundabout Bayou from Milliken's Bend to Hard Times Landing (6). Then Porter's boats were to transport the troops across the Mississippi to Grand Gulf (7). This proved more difficult than expected, for Grand Gulf was nearly as impregnable as Vicksburg. Instead, Porter landed Grant's men ten miles downriver at Bruinsburg (8). From there, Grant's men fought their way inland, winning a skirmish at Port Gibson (9) that forced the Confederates to evacuate Grand Gulf. Grant continued inland, capturing the Mississippi state capital at Jackson on 14 May. Then he turned west, driving the Confederate Army under LGEN John C. Pemberton before him along the Vicksburg and Jackson Railroad. Winning battles at Champion Hill and the crossing of the Big Black River (10), Grant's army forced the Confederate defenders back into the defenses of Vicksburg. After a siege of forty-eight days, Pemberton surrendered both the city and the remnants of his starving army on 4 July 1863.

The Army-Navy partnership had regained the Mississippi for the Union. As Lincoln phrased it: "The father of waters once more flows unvexed to the sea."

That same day that Vicksburg surrendered, Lee began his retreat from Gettysburg.

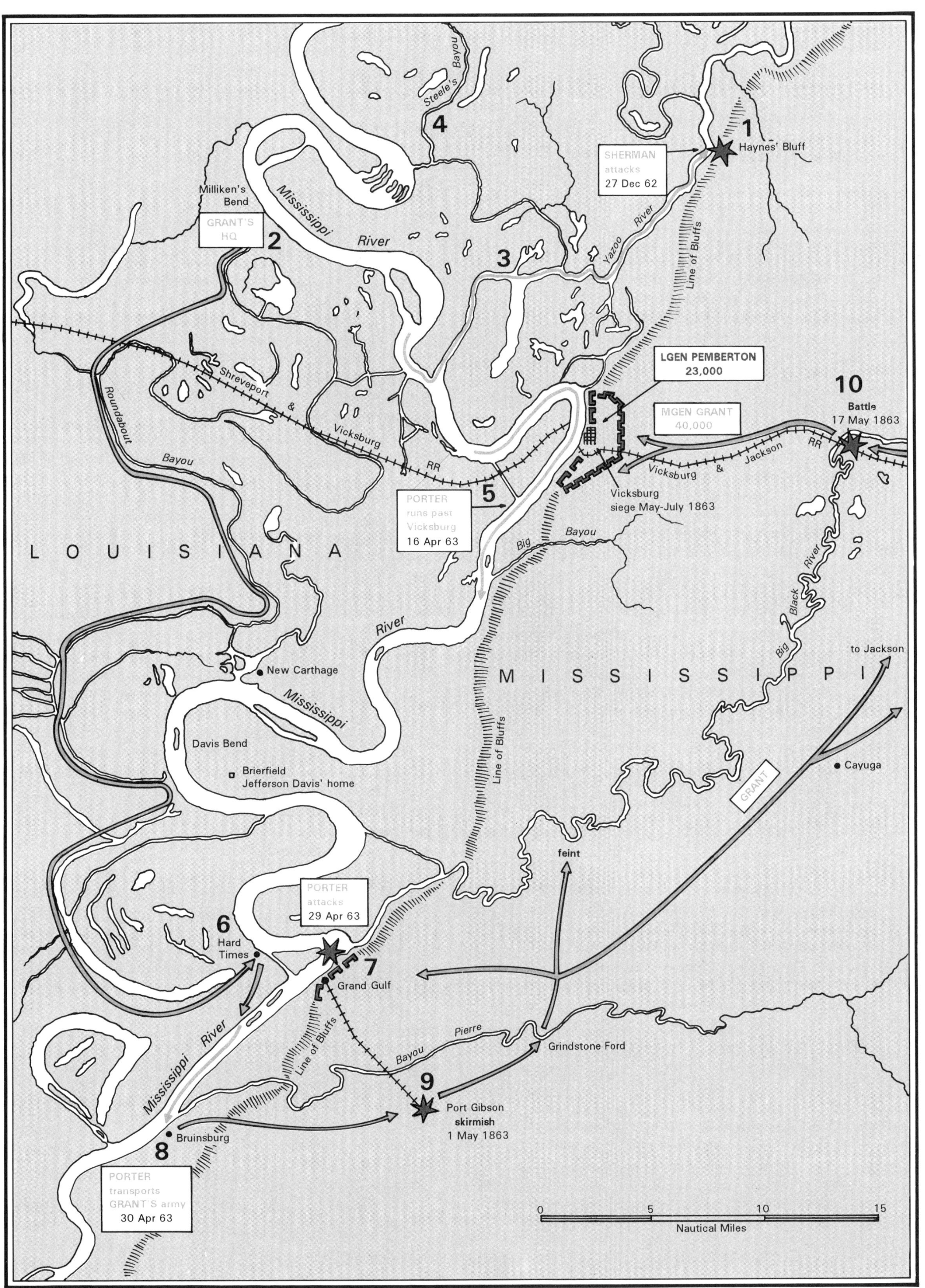

1
Haynes' Bluff
SHERMAN attacks 27 Dec 62
2
Milliken's Bend
GRANT'S HQ
3
4
Steele's Bayou
Mississippi River
Yazoo River
Line of Bluffs
LGEN PEMBERTON 23,000
10
Battle 17 May 1863
MGEN GRANT 40,000
Shreveport & Vicksburg RR
Roundabout Bayou
Vicksburg & Jackson RR
Vicksburg siege May-July 1863
5
PORTER runs past Vicksburg 16 Apr 63
LOUISIANA
Big Bayou
Big Black River
River
New Carthage
Mississippi
MISSISSIPPI
to Jackson
Davis Bend
Brierfield Jefferson Davis' home
Line of Bluffs
GRANT
Cayuga
feint
PORTER attacks 29 Apr 63
6
Hard Times
7
Grand Gulf
Bayou Pierre
Grindstone Ford
Line of Bluffs
Mississippi River
9
Port Gibson skirmish 1 May 1863
Bruinsburg
8
PORTER transports GRANT'S army 30 Apr 63
0 5 10 15
Nautical Miles

Map 38

Charleston

7 April 1863

Because South Carolina had been the first state to secede, and because the first shots of the war had been fired in Charleston Harbor, the city of Charleston had a symbolic importance for both sides. But Charleston's importance was more than symbolic, for its harbor was a center of blockade running. In an effort to interdict that traffic, the Union committed a dozen vessels to the blockade of Charleston by 1863, but runners still managed to get through often enough to be a source of great frustration for the Union's high command. Consequently, Secretary Welles was especially eager to find a way to capture Charleston.

The first serious attempt to do so came in the summer of 1862, when CAPT John B. Marchand, commander of the blockading force off Charleston, took a few of his lighter-draft vessels over the bar at Stono Inlet (1). Marchand reported that an army landed on James Island (2) could seize Fort Johnson (3), which he claimed was the key to Charleston's back door. A Union Army under BGEN Henry W. Benham landed on the banks of the Stono River in June, but a poorly coordinated Federal attack on the Confederate fort at Secessionville (4) on 16 June was unsuccessful.

If the back door to Charleston was shut, Welles wondered why the Navy couldn't kick in the front door. From the first Welles had urged Du Pont to do at Charleston what he had done at Port Royal and batter the Charleston forts into dust with his naval artillery. Welles became even more emphatic in 1863 when Du Pont's South Atlantic Blockading Squadron obtained the services of a number of new ironclads. At the very least, Welles thought, Du Pont could run past Fort Sumter and occupy Charleston Harbor, thus ruining it as a haven for blockade runners.

Du Pont, now a rear admiral, believed Welles's optimism was unfounded. First of all, by 1863 the Confederates had erected a ring of batteries, mounting hundreds of heavy guns, around the harbor. Second, the Confederates had sown the harbor with a large number of torpedoes, or mines, which the Federals called "infernal machines." And third, the South had built a small ironclad fleet of its own. This was brought home to Du Pont with some emphasis on 31 January 1863 when two Confederate ironclads, the *Chicora* and *Palmetto State,* sortied from the harbor and attacked the Union blockading fleet. Two Union vessels were badly damaged and struck their flags, though with the coming of dawn both ships limped off and rehoisted their flags, a clear violation of the laws of sea warfare.

Far from dissuading Welles of the wisdom of a naval attack on Charleston, the Confederate sortie in January made him all the more anxious. He believed that the monitors—several more of which had been built since Ericcson's original—were the secret weapon of the war and that nothing could stand up to them. Du Pont agreed that the ironclads were relatively invulnerable, but he argued that they were also relatively weak offensive weapons. To test his theory, Du Pont sent three monitors to attack Fort McAllister on the Ogeechee River south of Savannah (see map 32). On 3 March the monitors fired several hundred rounds at Fort McAllister without inflicting any serious damage. Nevertheless, Welles remained insistent, and Du Pont dutifully prepared for a naval attack on Fort Sumter.

Du Pont's ironclad fleet crossed the bar off Charleston on 6 April and ran into the harbor the next day. To counter the feared torpedoes, the lead vessel (the monitor *Weehawken*) was equipped with another of Ericcson's inventions: an antitorpedo raft complete with grappling hooks to dislodge the feared mines. Alas, the hooks became entangled with the *Weehawken*'s anchor chain and slowed the whole column. Worse, the currents in the narrow channel pushed Du Pont's flagship, the *New Ironsides,* toward the shallows, and Du Pont had to anchor to avoid grounding. Coincidentally, he anchored directly over a large Confederate mine, but the *New Ironsides* escaped disaster because the mine's electrical triggering device failed to operate. The rest of the monitors passed into the harbor and engaged the forts, concentrating most of their fire on Fort Sumter (5). The fight lasted from 3:00 to 5:00 in the afternoon. In those two hours the slow-firing monitors managed to get off only 214 shots, 55 of which struck their target. On the other hand, each of the monitors was pounded by a hail of heavy shot from the forts. The *Patapsco* was hit forty-seven times, the *Nantucket* fifty-one times, and the *Weehawken* fifty-three times. Worst hit of all was the *Keokuk,* a new-design ironclad with two nonrotating towers, which was struck ninety times and sank the next day.

Du Pont withdrew at 5:00 P.M., intending to renew the fight the next day. But after hearing his captains' damage reports, he instead determined to call off the attack altogether. Welles was not convinced that Du Pont had done all that he could. Upon learning that the admiral did not intend to renew the attack, Welles ordered RADM John A. Dahlgren to replace Du Pont in July.

The change in command made little difference. Like Du Pont, Dahlgren appreciated the futility of pitting his monitors against the Confederate forts. Instead, he teamed up with MGEN Quincy A. Gilmore in a combined operation against Fort Wagner (6) and Battery Gregg (7). Fort Wagner fell on 6 September after a long and bloody siege that included the heroic sacrifice of the 54th Massachusetts, and Union forces shelled Sumter from Battery Gregg for most of a year. But though Sumter was reduced to a pile of rubble, Charleston held out until the last months of the war and capitulated only when it was cut off to the east by Sherman's march northward through South Carolina.

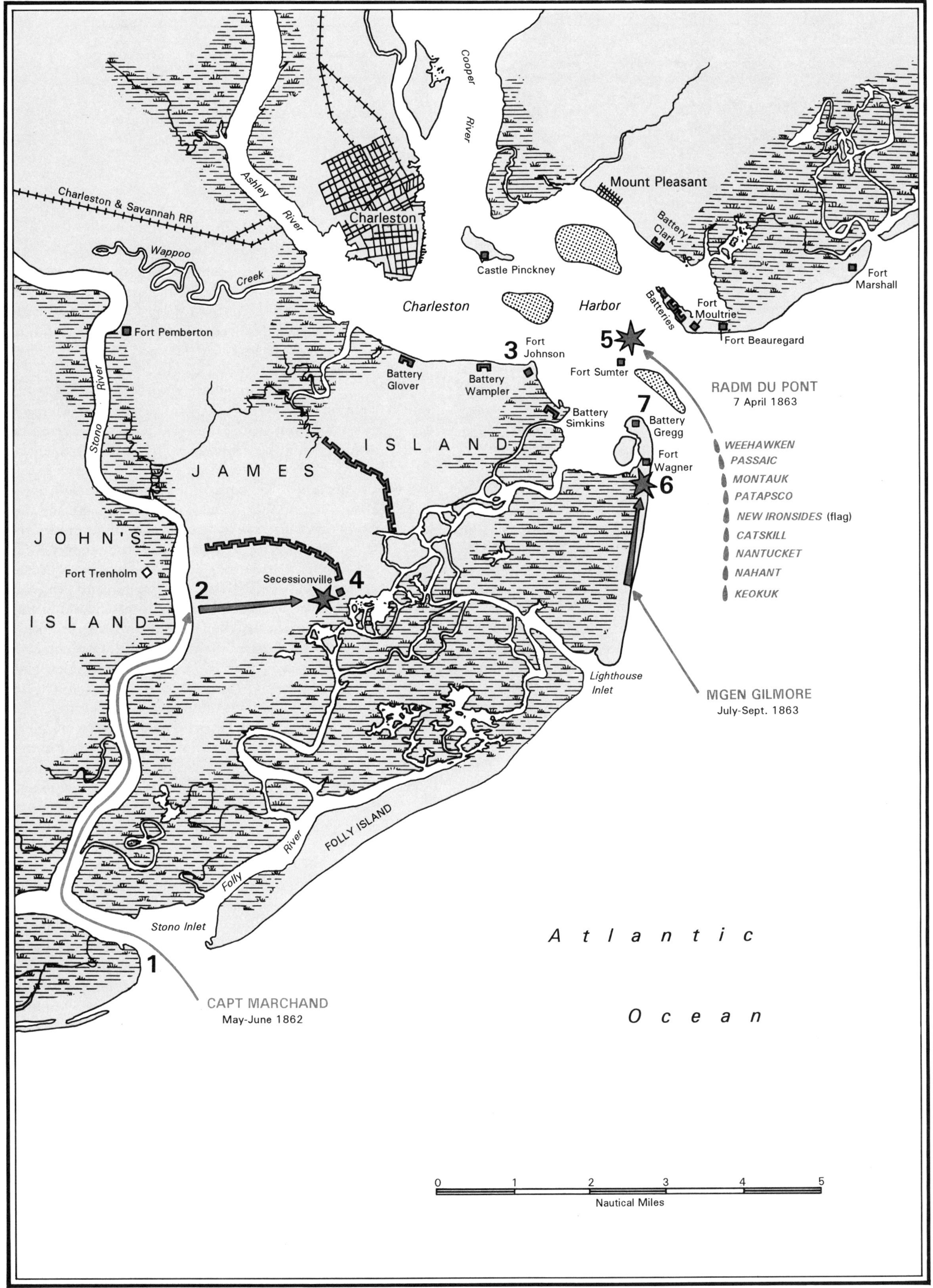

Cooper River
Ashley River
Charleston & Savannah RR
Charleston
Mount Pleasant
Battery Clark
Wappoo Creek
Castle Pinckney
Fort Marshall
Charleston Harbor
Batteries
Fort Moultrie
Fort Beauregard
Fort Pemberton
3 Fort Johnson
5
Fort Sumter
Battery Glover
Battery Wampler
RADM DU PONT
7 April 1863
7
Battery Simkins
Battery Gregg
Stono River
ISLAND
JAMES
Fort Wagner
6
WEEHAWKEN
PASSAIC
MONTAUK
PATAPSCO
NEW IRONSIDES (flag)
CATSKILL
NANTUCKET
NAHANT
KEOKUK
JOHN'S
ISLAND
Fort Trenholm
Secessionville
2
4
Lighthouse Inlet
MGEN GILMORE
July-Sept. 1863
FOLLY ISLAND
Folly River
Stono Inlet
Atlantic Ocean
1
CAPT MARCHAND
May-June 1862
0 1 2 3 4 5
Nautical Miles

MAP 39

MOBILE BAY

5 AUGUST 1864

David Glasgow Farragut became the nation's first admiral in July 1862 as a reward for his capture of New Orleans. Not one to rest on his laurels, he intended to turn at once to the capture of Mobile, the most active port for blockade runners on the Gulf Coast. But the need to secure the lower Mississippi and the difficulty of coordinating plans with the Army delayed his attempt for two years. Finally, in the summer of 1864 Farragut got his opportunity.

Mobile Bay is shaped like an arrowhead embedded in Alabama's Gulf Coast (see upper map). Mobile itself (1) is at the head of the bay some twenty miles from the entrance. From the city, the Mobile and Ohio Railroad connected Mobile with Mississippi and points west, while across the bay the Mobile & Great Northern Railroad, built in 1862, connected the city to Atlanta and points east. Mobile, in short, was both an important haven for blockade runners and a crucial link in the Confederacy's collapsing internal-transportation system.

Nature had protected the city well. At the entrance to Mobile Bay a long spit of land projected from the eastern flank of the bay, and only two narrow ship channels interrupted a series of small islands that constituted a barrier across the broad mouth of the bay (see lower map). On the tip of that spit of land the Confederates built Fort Morgan (2), a star-shaped fort that, along with Fort Gaines on Dauphin Island (3), guarded the main ship channel. Fort Powell on Cedar Point (4) guarded the narrower and shallower Grant's Pass. The Confederate commander of these defenses was RADM Franklin Buchanan, who had commanded the *Virginia* on its maiden sortie. To supplement the forts, Buchanan ordered that pilings be driven into the sea bottom opposite Fort Gaines (5) and that a large number of torpedoes (mines) be placed so that the navigable channel was only five hundred yards wide.

If an enemy managed to survive these obstructions, Buchanan had the *Tennessee,* a casemate ironclad similar to the *Virginia*—except that its iron plating was two inches thicker. In May 1864 Buchanan took the *Tennessee* over the bar at Mobile and into the lower bay. He planned to run through the blockade and attack Fort Pickins and Pensacola. But deterred by both the size of Farragut's blockading fleet and his uncertainty about the *Tennessee's* seaworthiness, he decided instead to remain in the bay and use the *Tennessee* for defense.

To deal with the forts and especially with the *Tennessee,* Farragut asked Welles for a number of ironclads of his own. Welles sent him two from the East Coast (the *Tecumseh* and *Manhattan*) and two from Porter's Mississippi Squadron. Characteristically, Farragut laid his plans carefully. The four monitors would lead the way in a column to starboard of the main fleet. The *Tecumseh* and *Manhattan* would lead, followed by the two smaller river ironclads. Farragut's wooden sloops would proceed in a parallel line to port, with each large warship screening a smaller gunboat lashed to its port side. Farragut wanted to lead this column in the *Hartford,* but his staff convinced him that it would be better to let the *Brooklyn* go first because it had more forward-firing guns and was fitted with a mine-sweeping device.

The Union fleet got under way at 5:30 A.M. on 5 August, and an hour later the monitors opened fire on Fort Morgan. Buchanan steamed out in the *Tennessee* to engage Farragut's wooden ships. Seeing the *Tennessee* as his appropriate target, CDR T. A. M. Craven in the *Tecumseh* steered a course to intercept her. His change of course took him into a newly sown mine field; and at 7:30 the *Tecumseh* struck a torpedo, and the iron ship went down in less than a minute, taking 93 of its 124-man crew down with it (6). A witness to this disaster, CAPT James Alden in the *Brooklyn,* saw floating objects in the water ahead and ordered his engines backed to stop forward progress. Farragut, in the *Hartford,* veered to port to pass ahead of the *Brooklyn* on a course that took him directly into the mine field. Alden called across that there were mines ahead, to which Farragut is supposed to have replied: "Damn the torpedoes. Full speed ahead." The *Hartford* charged into the bay, followed by the rest of the fleet, without encountering any other mines.

Waiting was Buchanan in the *Tennessee.* Farragut's gunboats dealt with the *Tennessee's* small wooden consorts, but the *Tennessee* nearly proved itself equal to the whole Union fleet. After the initial run into the bay, Farragut had planned to anchor and send the hands to breakfast, but Buchanan disrupted those plans by charging into the Federal fleet at 8:45 to take on Farragut's entire fleet. The *Lackawanna* and *Hartford* each rammed the *Tennessee,* as did the *Monongahela* a bit later, but all these wooden ships did more damage to themselves than they did to their opponent. The monitor *Chickasaw* repeatedly fired its 11-inch guns into the *Tennessee* from a range of about fifty yards—which had a cumulative weakening effect—and one of the *Manhattan's* 15-inch shells actually broke through the *Tennessee's* armor plate. After more than an hour, with the *Tennessee's* steering chains cut, and many of its gunports jammed shut from the shelling, Buchanan had little option but to surrender.

With Buchanan's fleet out of the way, the Federals turned their attention to the forts. Fort Powell and Fort Gaines, cut off from the mainland by Farragut's victory, capitulated quickly. Fort Morgan held out for two weeks, surrendering on 23 August only after a siege. Though Mobile itself remained in Confederate hands, possession of the forts made it useless as a seaport. With Farragut's victory, only Charleston, South Carolina, and Wilmington, North Carolina, remained open to Confederate blockade runners.

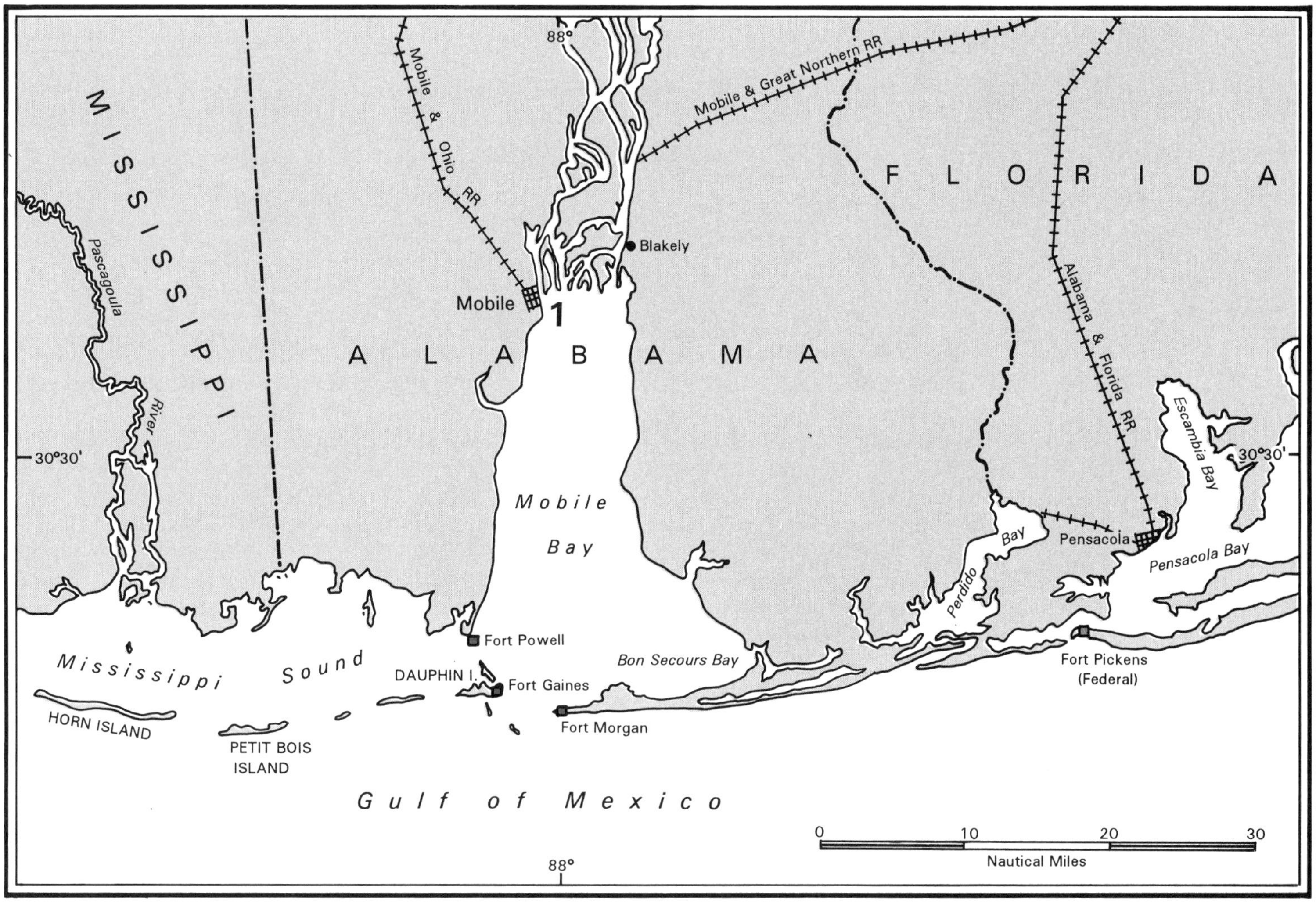

MISSISSIPPI
ALABAMA
FLORIDA
88°
Mobile & Ohio RR
Mobile & Great Northern RR
Alabama & Florida RR
Pascagoula River
Blakely
Mobile
1
30°30'
Mobile Bay
Escambia Bay
Perdido Bay
Pensacola
Pensacola Bay
Fort Powell
Bon Secours Bay
Mississippi Sound
DAUPHIN I.
Fort Gaines
Fort Morgan
Fort Pickens (Federal)
HORN ISLAND
PETIT BOIS ISLAND
Gulf of Mexico
0 10 20 30
Nautical Miles
88°

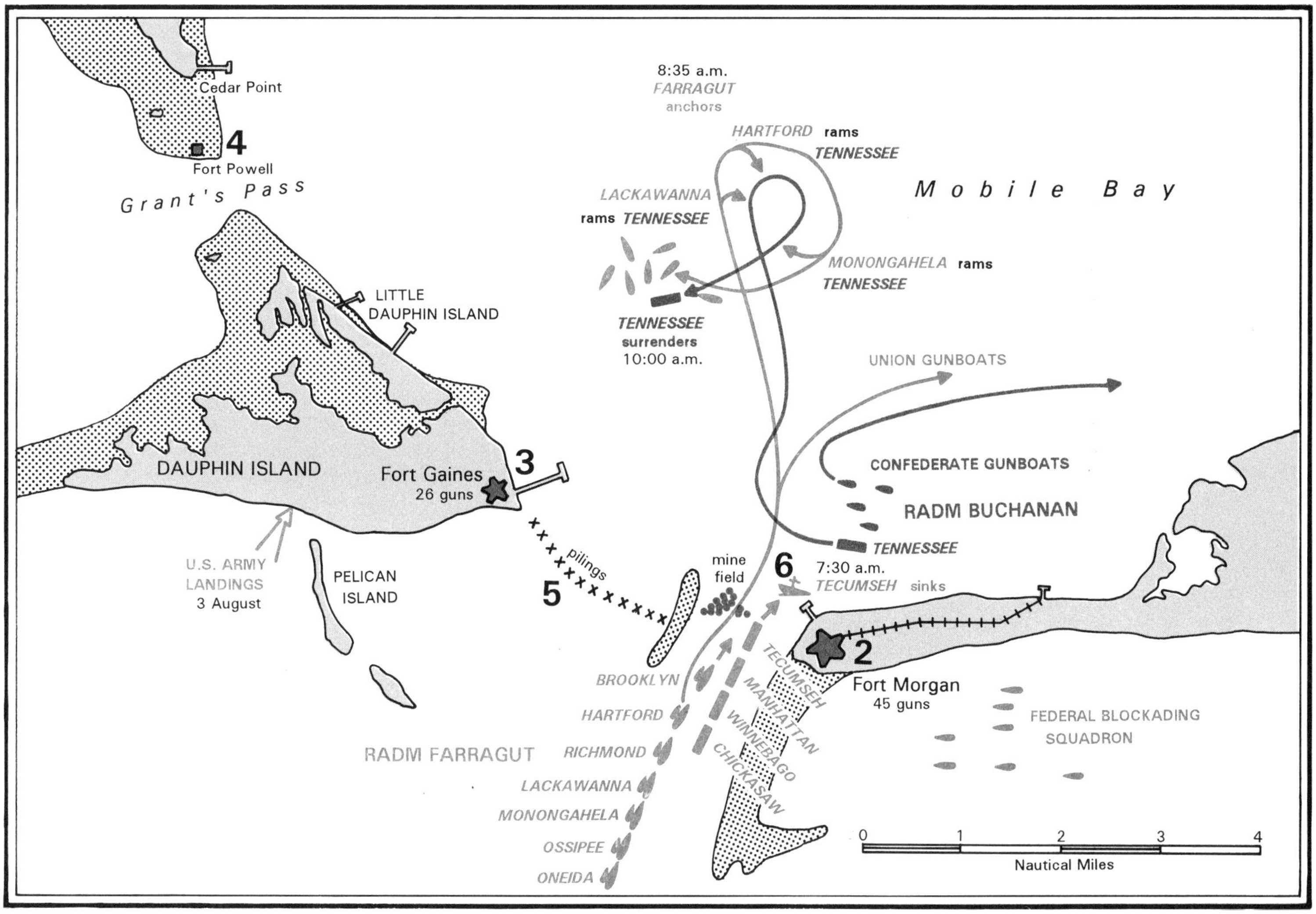

Cedar Point
4
Fort Powell
Grant's Pass
LITTLE DAUPHIN ISLAND
DAUPHIN ISLAND
Fort Gaines
26 guns
3
U.S. ARMY LANDINGS
3 August
PELICAN ISLAND
pilings
5
8:35 a.m.
FARRAGUT anchors
HARTFORD rams TENNESSEE
LACKAWANNA rams TENNESSEE
MONONGAHELA rams TENNESSEE
TENNESSEE surrenders 10:00 a.m.
Mobile Bay
UNION GUNBOATS
CONFEDERATE GUNBOATS
RADM BUCHANAN
TENNESSEE
mine field
6
7:30 a.m.
TECUMSEH sinks
2
Fort Morgan
45 guns
TECUMSEH
MANHATTAN
WINNEBAGO
CHICKASAW
BROOKLYN
HARTFORD
RICHMOND
LACKAWANNA
MONONGAHELA
OSSIPEE
ONEIDA
RADM FARRAGUT
FEDERAL BLOCKADING SQUADRON
0 1 2 3 4
Nautical Miles

MAP 40

WILMINGTON (FORT FISHER)

FEBRUARY–MARCH 1865

Even more than Charleston, the city of Wilmington, North Carolina, was critical to the Confederate war effort because of its direct rail communications with Richmond. So important was this link between the Confederate capital and the outside world that Secretary Welles believed the Confederates could not hold Richmond without it. But the Navy could not take it alone. Like Mobile, Wilmington was twenty miles up a protected estuary, in this case the Cape Fear River, and was guarded by a series of shore fortifications at the entrance (see inset). Naval forces might be able to run past the formidable guns of Fort Fisher, but they could not take the fort itself without an army to occupy the defenses. In the fall of 1864 Lieutenant General Grant, now appointed to command of all Union armies, agreed to support a combined attack on Fort Fisher.

The naval commander was RADM David Dixon Porter, who took over command of the North Atlantic Blockading Squadron on 1 October 1864. The Army commander was to have been MGEN Godfrey Weitzel, but because the attack took place in MGEN Benjamin Butler's Department, Butler decided to take personal charge. In particular, Butler advocated blowing the fort off the face of the earth with a giant bomb. Porter agreed to give it a try, and the next several weeks were spent in gathering 235 tons of gunpowder and stuffing it (with great care) into the steamer *Louisiana.* On 23 December a volunteer crew ran the *Louisiana* ashore near the northeastern salient of Fort Fisher (1) and set the fuse. Uncertain of how devastating the explosion would be, Porter took his fleet several miles offshore. But despite a spectacular explosion, the results were a huge disappointment. The explosion did virtually no damage to the fort. Rocked from their sleep, a few Confederates supposed that some ship's boiler had exploded.

With the failure of this gambit, the Union's forces fell back on a more conventional approach. On Christmas Eve Porter's fleet began a steady bombardment of the Confederate defenses. Thousands of shells—Porter reported that the fleet fired 115 rounds per minute—fell on the ramparts and inside the parade ground. Porter was convinced that nothing could survive the pounding his warships dished out. The Confederate defenders did not bother to fire back and fled into their bombproof shelters. Meanwhile, three thousand of Butler's fifteen thousand–man army were landed several miles up the beach with the intention of taking the fort by storm after Porter's gunners had silenced the enemy guns. But despite the volume of naval gunfire, the results did not impress Butler. When Porter's ships lifted fire on 26 December, Butler could see the Confederate defenders climb out of their bombproofs and man their guns. Instead of ordering an attack, he ordered his army to reembark and took himself back to Washington, declaring that the fort was impregnable.

Porter was furious. He begged Grant for another body of troops and, most of all, for another commander. Grant complied, sacking Butler and sending MGEN Alfred H. Terry to Fort Fisher. Terry arrived on 12 January 1865, and Porter began another bombardment of the fort the next day. The map at right shows the location of the forty-four vessels Porter committed to this second bombardment. The four heavy monitors and the *New Ironsides* (2) concentrated their attention on the northeastern salient of the fort, and each vessel was assigned a specific battery to silence. After the first bombardment, Porter had learned that many captains had told their gun crews simply to fire at the fort's flagpole. This time, Porter gave each captain a specific target. The results were dramatic. While only three of the fort's seventy-five guns had been damaged during the first shelling on 23–24 December, this time all but two were put out of action.

Porter's fleet also contributed a landing party to the ground assault. Four hundred marines joined 1,600 sailors armed with pistols and cutlasses, the traditional weapons of a boarding party, and were ordered to storm the fort's northeastern salient. In creating this force, Porter may have been motivated by service partisanship. After Butler's departure, he had written Welles, "I don't believe in anybody but my own good officers and men. I can do anything with them, and you need not be surprised to hear that the webfooters have gone into the forts." While Porter's landing party attacked along the beach (3), Major General Terry's four thousand soldiers assaulted the northwestern corner of the fort (4). A withering fire from the fort's two thousand defenders met the sailors and marines, who never got closer than three hundred yards, but their attack focused the attention of the Confederates on the seaward approach and allowed Terry's division to break into the fort along the riverfront. The battle did not end when the Union soldiers gained the fort. The Confederates fought yard-by-yard, defending each gun emplacement in severe hand-to-hand fighting. Finally, after 9:00 P.M., following more than six hours of fighting and with 35 percent casualties, the fort's commander, COL William Lamb, raised the white flag.

The fall of Fort Fisher forced the Confederates to abandon both Fort Caswell and Smith's Island (see inset), leaving the approaches to the Cape Fear River in Union hands. Wilmington itself fell to Union forces six weeks later on 22 February. In the meantime, several blockade runners ran into the Cape Fear River, only to be snatched up by the waiting Union Navy. With Wilmington closed, the logistic base from which the Confederates could draw support was dramatically restricted. At Richmond, Grant had forced Lee into a static defense of the city, and Major General Sherman was marching north through the Carolinas toward Richmond's back door. Only a miracle could save the Confederacy now.

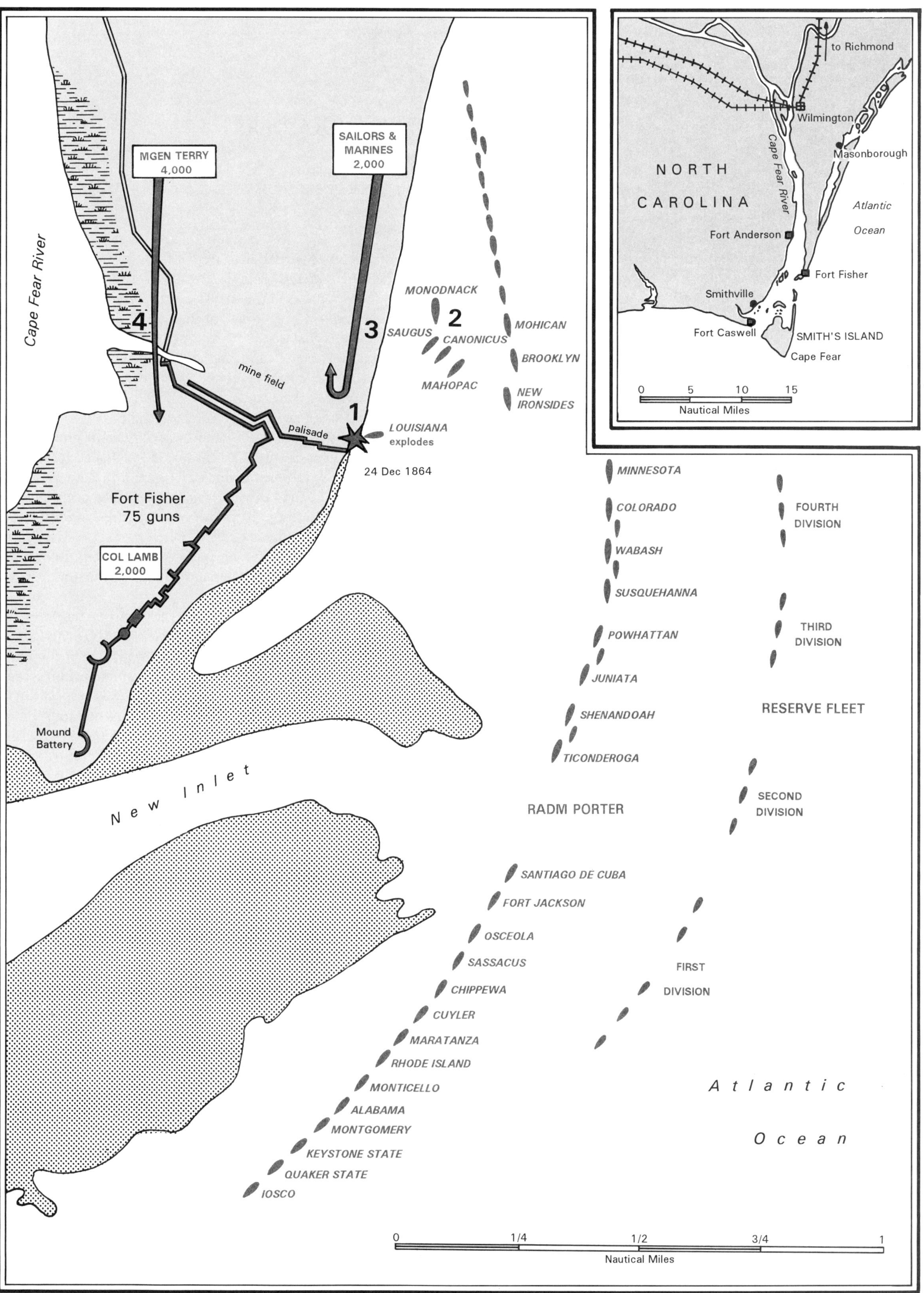

MGEN TERRY
4,000
SAILORS & MARINES
2,000
Cape Fear River
4
3
2
1
MONODNACK
SAUGUS
CANONICUS
MAHOPAC
MOHICAN
BROOKLYN
NEW IRONSIDES
mine field
palisade
LOUISIANA explodes
24 Dec 1864
Fort Fisher
75 guns
COL LAMB
2,000
Mound Battery
New Inlet
MINNESOTA
COLORADO
WABASH
SUSQUEHANNA
POWHATTAN
JUNIATA
SHENANDOAH
TICONDEROGA
RADM PORTER
FOURTH DIVISION
THIRD DIVISION
RESERVE FLEET
SECOND DIVISION
FIRST DIVISION
SANTIAGO DE CUBA
FORT JACKSON
OSCEOLA
SASSACUS
CHIPPEWA
CUYLER
MARATANZA
RHODE ISLAND
MONTICELLO
ALABAMA
MONTGOMERY
KEYSTONE STATE
QUAKER STATE
IOSCO
Atlantic
Ocean
0
1/4
1/2
3/4
1
Nautical Miles
to Richmond
Wilmington
Masonborough
NORTH
CAROLINA
Cape Fear River
Atlantic
Ocean
Fort Anderson
Fort Fisher
Smithville
Fort Caswell
SMITH'S ISLAND
Cape Fear
0
5
10
15
Nautical Miles

MAP 41

CONFEDERATE COMMERCE RAIDERS

1862–1865

As a new nation with no preexisting navy, and lacking the industrial base to produce modern warships in large numbers, the Confederacy relied heavily on commerce raiding, the traditional naval strategy of a nonnaval power against a maritime nation. This had been the principal naval weapon of the United States against Britain in two wars, and because of that the United States had declined to sign the Declaration of Paris in 1856 proclaiming privateering to be illegal. That decision haunted the Union government when the Confederacy began to issue letters of marque in 1861. Confederate privateers, however, proved disappointing: daring Confederate ship owners soon discovered that they could make more money as blockade *runners* than as commerce *raiders.*

The most effective instruments of commerce raiding for the Confederacy were commissioned warships of the C.S. Navy. Of the roughly three hundred Union merchant ships captured at sea by Confederate commerce raiders, only fifty or so were taken by privateers, most of them in the early months of the war. And of the 255 captured and destroyed by Confederate warships, 162 of them (63 percent) were taken, directly or indirectly, by only three ships: the *Florida, Alabama,* and *Shenandoah,* all acquired in England by the Confederacy's principal agent there, James D. Bulloch.

The *Florida* was the first to go to sea. Built at Liverpool as the *Oreto,* it sailed in March 1862 as a merchant ship with English officers and crew. Bulloch dispatched another ship loaded with a cargo of naval guns and munitions to meet the *Oreto* in the Bahamas, and at remote Green Cay the *Oreto* was converted to the Confederate armed sloop *Florida* and began a career as a commerce raider under CAPT John N. Maffitt. After a lengthy hiatus in Mobile occasioned by the outbreak of yellow fever and Maffitt's need to acquire a crew, the *Florida* began a lengthy cruise in January 1863, during which it captured and destroyed thirty-nine Union merchant vessels, two of which he converted to Confederate raiders that made twenty-three more captures.

In October 1864 the *Florida* ran into Bahia, Brazil, to recoal and refit and was discovered there by CAPT Napoleon Collins in the USS *Wachusett.* In a deliberate violation of Brazilian neutrality, Collins attacked the Confederate raider in the middle of the night on 7 October, ramming it and firing its forward guns until the *Florida* struck. The Brazilian government protested, and Collins was formally censured. But the *Florida* was never returned to Brazilian authorities. Instead, the vessel sank mysteriously in Hampton Roads on 28 November, almost certainly the result of deliberate sabotage.

The most famous and successful of the Confederate raiders was the *Alabama,* which sailed from Liverpool on 29 July 1862 under the pretext of going on a trial run. Instead, it made for the Portuguese Azores, where it took on armament, stores, and an international crew of Englishmen and Portuguese. The *Alabama's* captain was Raphael Semmes, who had taken eighteen prizes in the small steamer *Sumter* and who now began the most storied voyage of the war (see upper map).

Semmes's goal was not to take prizes but to destroy Union commerce. Instead of capturing ships and sending them into port with a prize crew, therefore, he burned the ships he captured after taking their crews on board the *Alabama* as prisoners. In a cruise that lasted one month short of two years, Semmes scoured three oceans and took sixty-eight prizes, four of which he used as cartels to rid himself of his accumulated prisoners, and sixty-four of which he burned. In January 1863 he fought and defeated the USS *Hatteras* off Galveston (1). His exploits raised maritime insurance rates in the United States and encouraged hundreds of U.S. merchant vessels to change their national registry. At one point Welles committed more than two dozen Union warships to the search for the elusive *Alabama.*

In June 1864 Semmes brought the *Alabama* into port at Cherbourg, France. There he encountered the USS *Kearsarge* under CAPT John A. Winslow. True to his cultural ethos, Semmes offered to fight the *Kearsarge* ship-to-ship, even though he knew that some of his ordnance was suspect after two years at sea. On 19 June 1864 the two ships met four miles outside Cherbourg (2) and fought a classic duel, circling each other and trading blows. Winslow had prepared well by draping anchor chains over the sides of the *Kearsarge* and covering them with wood planking—a provision that Semmes later declared unfair. But the real difference in the fight was that several of the *Alabama's* shells failed to explode, including one that lodged in the sternpost of the *Kearsarge* and that would likely have been fatal. Instead, it was the *Alabama* that began taking on water, and Semmes gave the order to abandon ship. Semmes and forty of his men escaped capture by swimming to a nearby pleasure yacht, the *Deerhound,* owned by an Englishman sympathetic to the South.

The saga of the *Shenandoah* under LT James I. Waddell is the most curious of all (see lower map). Purchased in England by Bulloch in the fall of 1864, the *Shenandoah* began a cruise that circumnavigated the globe, in the course of which it captured and destroyed thirty-eight vessels, devastating the American whaling industry in the Bering Sea (3). Out of touch with land, Waddell continued his cruise in the Pacific long after the war ended in April 1865. Not until Waddell spoke the British bark *Baracouta* (4) on 2 August 1865—more than three months after Appomattox—did he accept the news of defeat. Even then he took the ship around Cape Horn and back to Liverpool rather than surrender to a Union warship. The *Shenandoah* hauled down its flag in November 1865, symbolizing the end of America's bloodiest war.

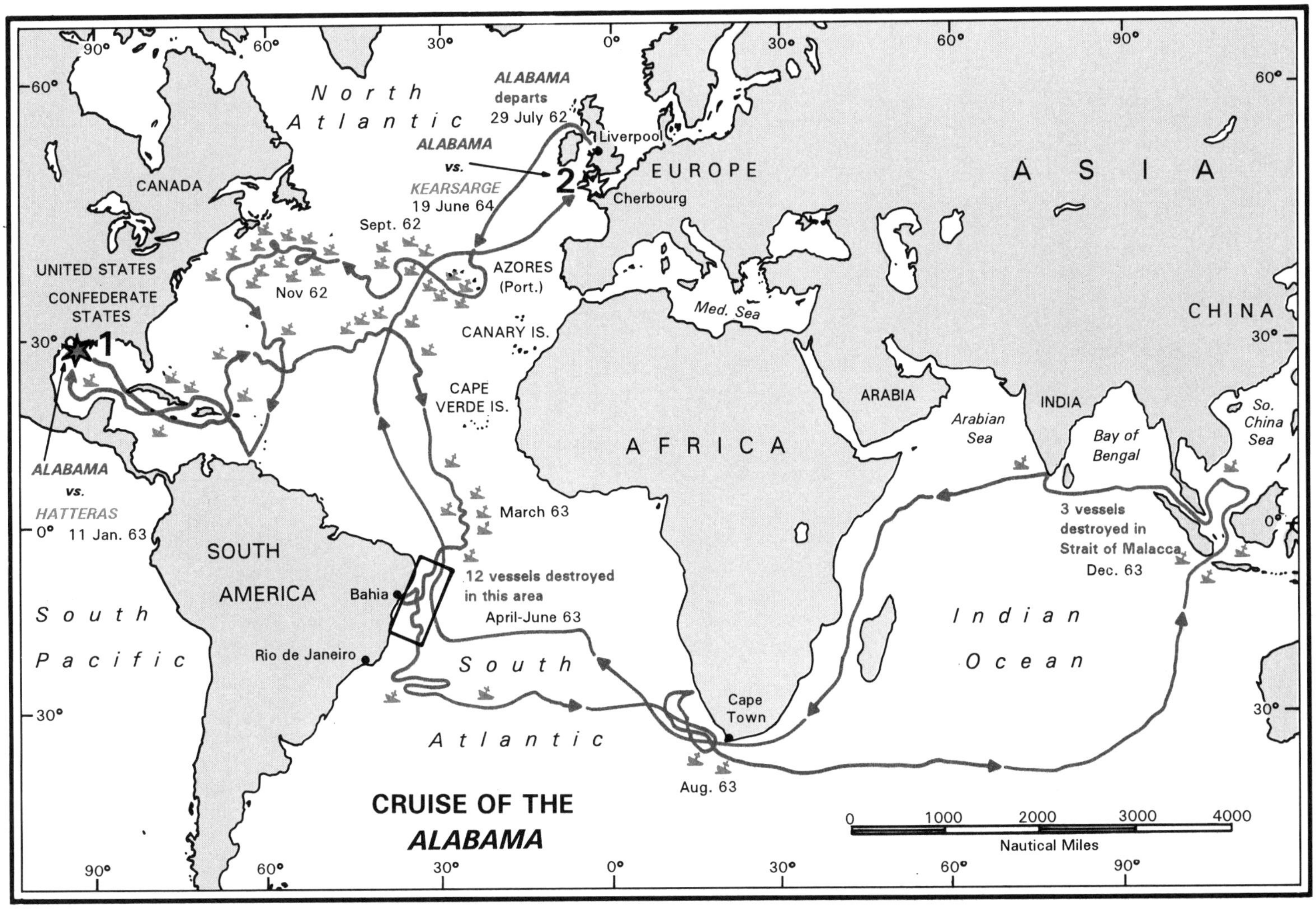

CRUISE OF THE *ALABAMA*

North Atlantic

ALABAMA departs 29 July 62

Liverpool

ALABAMA vs. *KEARSARGE* 19 June 64

2

Cherbourg

EUROPE

ASIA

CANADA

Sept. 62

UNITED STATES

CONFEDERATE STATES

Nov 62

AZORES (Port.)

Med. Sea

CHINA

1

CANARY IS.

CAPE VERDE IS.

ARABIA

INDIA

Arabian Sea

Bay of Bengal

So. China Sea

AFRICA

ALABAMA vs. *HATTERAS* 11 Jan. 63

March 63

3 vessels destroyed in Strait of Malacca Dec. 63

SOUTH AMERICA

Bahia

12 vessels destroyed in this area April-June 63

South Pacific

Rio de Janeiro

South Atlantic

Indian Ocean

Cape Town

Aug. 63

0 1000 2000 3000 4000 Nautical Miles

90° 60° 30° 0° 30° 60° 90°

CRUISE OF THE *SHENANDOAH*

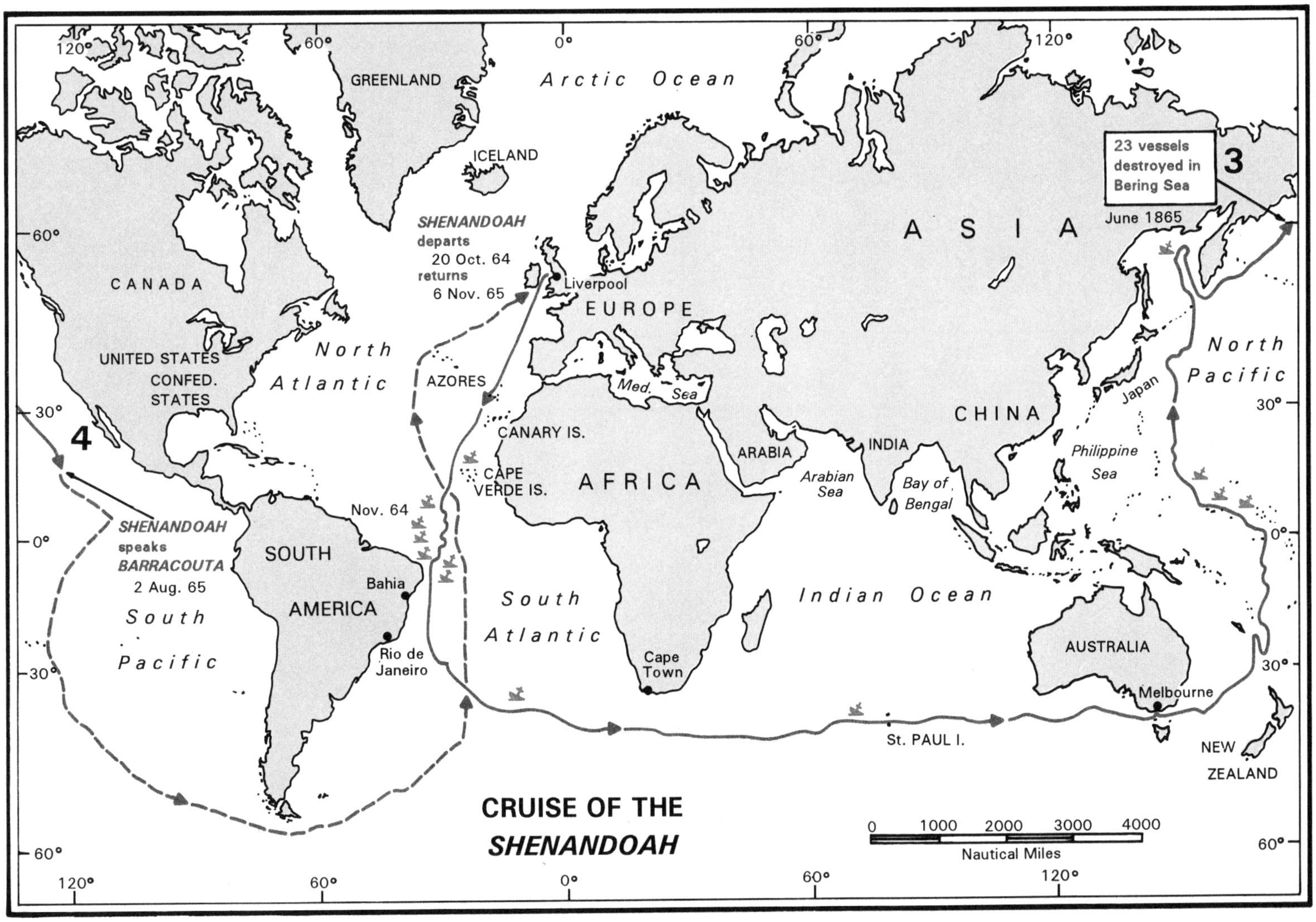

GREENLAND

Arctic Ocean

ICELAND

23 vessels destroyed in Bering Sea

3

June 1865

ASIA

SHENANDOAH departs 20 Oct. 64 returns 6 Nov. 65

Liverpool

CANADA

EUROPE

North Atlantic

UNITED STATES

CONFED. STATES

AZORES

Med. Sea

North Pacific

Japan

CHINA

4

CANARY IS.

CAPE VERDE IS.

AFRICA

ARABIA

INDIA

Arabian Sea

Bay of Bengal

Philippine Sea

Nov. 64

SHENANDOAH speaks *BARRACOUTA* 2 Aug. 65

SOUTH AMERICA

Bahia

South Atlantic

Indian Ocean

South Pacific

Rio de Janeiro

Cape Town

AUSTRALIA

Melbourne

St. PAUL I.

NEW ZEALAND

0 1000 2000 3000 4000 Nautical Miles

120° 60° 0° 60° 120°

GIRARD POINT ELEVATORS

PART VI

Retrenchment and Renaissance 1865–1900

The history of the U.S. Navy in the last third of the nineteenth century can be usefully divided into two very distinct eras. From 1865 to 1890 the U.S. Navy suffered through a period of retrenchment. Not only did the nation demobilize quickly after Appomattox, it stopped building new warships altogether and thereby failed to keep pace with the dramatic advances in naval technology being adopted by the navies of Europe. Then in the last decade of the century the Navy experienced a stunning renaissance, characterized by the construction of a new generation of steel-hulled warships and the emergence of a new philosophy of naval power to explain and justify that expansion. Not surprisingly, most naval historians have criticized the shortsightedness of American policy from 1865 to 1890 and applauded the wisdom of U.S. policy from 1890 to 1900. But American naval policy in each era was appropriate to the national needs of the time and successfully supported U.S. national interests.

RETRENCHMENT

The most notable element of the nation's naval demobilization after Appomattox was the rapid elimination of warships from the Navy's active list. In five years (1865–1870) the number of Navy vessels on active service declined from nearly seven hundred to only fifty-two. Often cited to demonstrate an inappropriate and even foolish destruction of the nation's naval might, the numbers are misleading. Though more than 700 warships served in the Union Navy at one time or another, the number on active service at any one time probably never reached 600, and 418 of them were converted merchant ships, tugs, or ferry boats purchased by the Navy Department during the war for service on the blockade. Though useful against unarmed blockade runners, these vessels had no practical utility in a postwar navy, and virtually all of them were sold off or scrapped.

In addition, many of the special-service warships built during the war had limited value in the postwar era. The one hundred or so vessels of the Mississippi River Squadron could not be expected to perform effectively in support of American interests overseas, nor could the fifty-two coastal monitors serve in any capacity other than as harbor-defense craft. In 1866 Assistant Secretary Gustavus Vasa Fox crossed the Atlantic in the monitor *Miantonomah* as if to demonstrate that those terrible machines of war could be used effectively against a European enemy. But the crossing was considered something of a stunt, and it was generally recognized that monitors had a limited utility on the open sea. Most of them were laid up in ordinary at League Island, near Philadelphia, to await a future national emergency. They were mobilized only once, in 1873, with disappointing results (see map 42).

The general demobilization also claimed some of the newest U.S. Navy vessels. A few were discarded because they had been built in a hurry, often of unseasoned timber, and found to be unfit for further service. Others had been designed to fulfill a specific need that no longer existed, such as the fast (seventeen-knot) *Wampanoag* designed by the Navy's chief engineer Benjamin Isherwood to chase down and destroy the *Alabama.* To be sure, some perfectly good warships were decommissioned as well, but if one subtracts the converted merchantmen, the riverine craft, and the monitors from the vaunted seven hundred–ship Navy, it is not hard to conclude that the fifty-two ships retained for active service in 1870 probably represented most of those that could be used effectively in the postwar world.

Another indictment of the U.S. Navy in this era is that it

The old Navy and the new: A mothballed monitor from the Civil War rusts quietly at anchor at the League Island Navy Yard, Philadelphia, opposite the new battleship Iowa, *launched in 1897. During the thirty-five years that separated these two vessels, the world's navies underwent a technological revolution, one in which the United States lagged behind until the last decade of the century. (Library of Congress)*

A line of monitors laid up at League Island Navy Yard, Philadelphia. Though a few monitors were retained for active service in the post–Civil War era, the majority were laid up in ordinary to await an emergency. Their low freeboard and marginal buoyancy made them largely inappropriate for the duties the U.S. Navy was called upon to perform in the late nineteenth century. (U.S. Naval Institute)

RADM Alfred Thayer Mahan was the leading philosopher of naval power and an influential voice for American naval expansion in the 1890s. Mahan deduced a general theory of warfare from the British experience in its wars against the Dutch and French, 1660 to 1815. His argument that a fleet of battleships would ensure national greatness provided the advocates of naval expansion with a philosophical underpinning for their program. (Official U.S. Navy photo)

failed to incorporate the latest advances in naval technology. While the naval powers of Europe developed fleets with a distinctly modern look—steel hulls, armored decks, and gun turrets—the U.S. Navy continued to rely on wooden-hulled screw sloops armed in some cases with smooth-bore guns and propelled much of the time by sails. In part the Navy's continued reliance on older vessels was simple economy, but in part, too, the nation's lack of overseas coaling stations compelled the U.S. Navy to rely on sail power long after European navies had abandoned it. To fulfill its primary mission of protecting American interests overseas, the U.S. Navy of the late nineteenth century had to be "long-legged," that is, capable of operating at great distances from a friendly port. Only in the late 1880s did the Navy's chief engineer, George W. Melville, introduce a triple-expansion engine with a fuel efficiency that enabled coal-burning warships to steam 7,500 miles on a single 500-ton load of coal. Not coincidentally, that is also when the United States began to build its first steam and steel warships, and the first American warship to boast a triple-expansion engine was also its first battleship—the *Maine,* commissioned in 1895.

Finally, the U.S. Navy languished in this era because the American public, and hence its leaders, focused on internal problems and opportunities. Reconstruction issues dominated the public consciousness until well into the 1870s, and afterward the opportunities of westward expansion seemed more important to most Americans than problems overseas. The golden spike, hammered down at Promontory Point, Utah, in 1869, completed the transcontinental railroad, and tens of thousands of Americans moved west. To those Americans, protection from Indian uprisings was of more immediate consequence than some unspecified overseas adversary. As for most Americans, the Navy was simply not a high priority.

The end result of all these factors was such that in 1876 a British critic could sneer that "there never was such a hapless, broken-down, tattered, forlorn apology for a navy as that possessed by the United States."

Renaissance

The change came gradually rather than suddenly. In 1881 Secretary of the Navy William H. Hunt submitted a report in which he asserted that the Navy's aging wooden sloops could no longer ensure protection of American commercial interests overseas. That report provided the impetus for a congressional appropriation in March 1883 authorizing the construction of four new steel-hulled warships—three armored cruisers and a dispatch vessel—with modern steam plants. Because of the first letters of their names—*Atlanta, Boston, Chicago,* and *Dolphin*—they were universally known as the "ABCD" ships. They still had a distinctly nineteenth-century look with their flush decks and towering masts, but they had all-steel double hulls with watertight compartments and were fully equipped with electricity.

As further evidence of a sea change, the very next year (1884) COMMO Stephen B. Luce opened the doors of the

The new steel Navy is represented in this 1889 photograph of the so-called "Squadron of Evolution," better known as the ABCD ships. The cruiser Chicago *is in the forefront, followed by the* Atlanta *and* Boston. *Though modern for their day, the full suite of sails and the guns mounted in broadside suggest their transitional character. (Official U.S. Navy photo)*

Naval War College in Newport, Rhode Island, the purpose of which was to sensitize midcareer naval officers to the broader questions of national policy and the application of naval power. Two years later Congress authorized the construction of the first American steel-hulled battleships, the *Maine* and *Texas,* both with triple-expansion engines and both commissioned nine years later in 1895.

The one person most closely associated with the American naval renaissance was RADM Alfred Thayer Mahan. The son of noted strategist Dennis Hart Mahan, who was a longtime professor of civil and military engineering at West Point, the younger Mahan was one of the first instructors Luce selected for the faculty at the Naval War College. There, Mahan developed a series of lectures in which he postulated that a strong navy—specifically, a fleet of ships-of-the-line—had been the key instrument that had made Britain a great power. In 1890 Mahan collected these lectures into a book, added a general introduction summarizing the elements of sea power, and published the whole as *The Influence of Sea Power Upon History, 1660–1783.*

Mahan's book was an instant success. It received glowing reviews at home, including one from a positively gushy Theodore Roosevelt, and provoked equal enthusiasm abroad. It elicited such a reaction not only because it explained the past, but also because it offered a blueprint for seizing and holding national power in the future. Here at last was a formula for national greatness: command of the sea, which ensured national wealth, belonged to that nation that produced the dominant "fleet in being" capable of driving the enemy fleet from the seas. All else—colonies, trade, wealth, and power—resulted from that first principle. Mahan's book was translated into several languages and eventually became required reading for both Japanese and German naval officers.

Mahan's book did not *cause* a change in American naval policy but provided an intellectual rationale for a policy that was in the midst of change. The year before Mahan's book was published, Navy Secretary Benjamin F. Tracy submitted an ambitious building program to Congress, making a case in terms that anticipated most of Mahan's arguments.

ADM George Dewey, the victor of the Battle of Manila Bay (see map 43), was also the first man to be promoted to the rank of four-star admiral in the U.S. Navy. Dewey's fame rested on his success in one battle, but he remained a respected figurehead in the Navy, serving as president of the General Board from 1900 until his death in 1917. (Official U.S. Navy photo)

In 1890 Congress authorized the construction of three more American battleships—the *Indiana, Massachusetts,* and *Oregon.* All five of the new American battleships were commissioned in 1895–1896, and a sixth, the *Iowa,* in 1897. A year later the United States took this modern fleet to war against Spain on behalf of Cuban independence. In what one contemporary called "a splendid little war," the U.S. Navy won dramatic and one-sided battles over Spanish fleets in both the Atlantic and Pacific, and in the process the nation acquired overseas obligations and became a recognized world power. For both the Navy and the nation, the Spanish-American War was a coming of age from which there was no turning back.

Map 42

Defending American Interests Overseas

1866–1893

For a quarter of a century after the end of the Civil War the Navy's primary responsibility was to protect American lives and to support American commercial interests abroad. In pursuit of those goals, U.S. naval officers on distant stations often used force to chastise brigands or intimidate foreign governments, particularly in Asia and Latin America. As in the antebellum era, ship captains were generally independent decision makers in these small-scale incursions, simultaneously making and enforcing national policy.

An early example of this kind of activity occurred off the Chinese coast in June of 1867. Learning that the inhabitants of a village on the island of Formosa (1) had killed the crew of an American merchant vessel, CDR George C. Belknap led a landing party of 180 men from two U.S. Navy steam sloops (the *Wyoming* and *Hartford*) in burning the village to the ground, killing scores of villagers in the process.

In addition to protecting American lives, naval officers often used force to redress perceived insults to the flag. Perhaps the most overt example of such a case occurred in the spring of 1871 when the five-ship squadron of RADM John Rodgers escorted American ambassador Frederick Low to Korea (2). Like Japan, Korea was an isolationist country known as the "hermit kingdom," and Low's assignment was to induce Korea to open its ports to U.S. trade. Rodgers's powerful escort was intended to contribute to Low's mission in much the same way that Perry's squadron had helped to open Japan (see map 29).

Rodgers anchored in Inchon Harbor on 30 May. The next day one of the Korean forts fired on the USS *Palos,* and Rodgers responded by bombarding the Korean forts with his entire squadron. The forts soon ceased firing, but Rodgers demanded an apology. When he didn't get one, he landed a party of seven hundred sailors and marines along with seven light guns. Advancing under the cover of naval gunfire, the American landing party stormed three harbor forts, killing 243 Korean soldiers while suffering casualties of 3 killed and 7 wounded. Convinced that American honor had been served, Rodgers reembarked his landing party and sailed away. Rodgers had made his point, but he had also failed in his mission. An American rapprochement with Korea had to wait until 1878 when COMMO Robert W. Shufeldt arrived in the *Ticonderoga* to lay the groundwork for an eventual treaty.

Two years after Rodgers's bombardment of the Inchon forts, the U.S. Navy proved much less intimidating in responding to another crisis when Spanish authorities in Cuba (3) executed fifty-three men who had been caught smuggling guns to Cuban revolutionaries in the steamer *Virginius.* Several of those executed were American citizens, including the captain of the *Virginius,* a former U.S. naval officer and Naval Academy graduate named Joseph Fry. When the United States attempted to mobilize its fleet to demonstrate its readiness and resolve, the mothballed monitors and other assorted vessels assembled at Key West made a less-than-convincing armada. In the end, the crisis was resolved without resort to force, but the weak American mobilization demonstrated how far the U.S. fleet had deteriorated in less than a decade.

American intervention was more effective in Panama (4), where a railroad connected the Caribbean port of Panama City to the Atlantic port of Aspinwall (Colón). A province of Colombia, Panama was in a nearly constant state of rebellion in the late nineteenth century, and U.S. warships frequently landed troops there to maintain peace and keep the railroad running. In the spring of 1885 four American warships landed a battalion of marines in Panama, and it was soon reinforced by another battalion from the United States, with CDR Bowman H. McCalla in overall command. McCalla virtually occupied Panama and kept the railroad open until units of the Colombian Army arrived to relieve him.

While the Colombians professed gratitude for McCalla's services, U.S. intervention in Latin America also provoked resentment of American high-handedness. That resentment boiled over in October of 1891 when a liberty party from the cruiser *Baltimore* participated in a saloon brawl in Valparaiso, Chile (5), that left two American sailors dead. Like the *Virginius* affair, the incident in the True Blue Saloon provoked angry war talk in the United States, but again the crisis was resolved short of war, and American policy makers were sobered by the realization that Chile's Navy was more powerful than that of the United States.

The inability of the United States to mount a credible naval threat to Spain in 1873 or to Chile in 1891 was frustrating to advocates of American naval power. But this period also witnessed a few straws in the wind that foreshadowed a more active future role for the U.S. Navy in the Pacific. In 1867 the United States purchased Alaska (6) from Russia and annexed Midway (7). A decade later the United States concluded a treaty with the Kingdom of Samoa (8) for naval basing rights at Pago Pago. When Germany expressed interest in Samoa as well and sent a naval squadron there in 1889, the United States responded by sending a squadron of its own. After a violent hurricane all but destroyed both squadrons in March 1889, the United States, Britain, and Germany agreed to a shared protectorate. Finally, a revolution in Hawaii (9) demonstrated growing American influence there as well. In January 1893 American pineapple growers in Hawaii overthrew the monarchy, declared themselves a republic, and petitioned for annexation to the United States. The country was not yet ready for such a move in 1893, and President Cleveland declined to act, but American interest in the world beyond its shores was growing, and a new era of American activism and expansionism was about to begin.

Arctic Ocean
RUSSIA
6
ALASKA
purchased by U.S.
1867
Bering Sea
Sea of Okhotsk
ALEUTIANS
CANADA
North Pacific Ocean
MANCHURIA
2
Sea of Japan
Inchon
JAPAN
Tokyo
KOREA
RADM RODGERS
captures Inchon forts
1871
CHINA
1
FORMOSA
U.S. Landing
1867
Hong Kong
Philippine Sea
PHILIPPINES
(Sp.)
LADRONES
(Sp.)
CAROLINE IS.
MARSHALL IS.
7
MIDWAY
annexed by the U.S.
1867
HAWAII
Republic established
1893
9
Seattle
UNITED STATES
Washington
New York
Norfolk
San Francisco
Los Angeles
Charleston
MEXICO
VIRGINIUS
episode
1873
3
Havana
CUBA
4
U.S. INTERVENTION
1885
Colon
Panama City
COLOMBIA
GALAPAGOS
EQUADOR
PERU
Callao
NEW GUINEA
SOLOMONS
8
SAMOA
Pago Pago
American
co-protectorate
1889
FIJI
Coral Sea
AUSTRALIA
Sydney
Melbourne
Tasman Sea
NEW ZEALAND
South Pacific Ocean
5
Valparaiso
Incident at the
True Blue Saloon
1891
CHILE
WILKES LAND
0 1000 2000 3000 4000
Nautical Miles
120° 150° 180° 150° 120° 90°
60° 30° 0° 30° 60°

MAP 43

BATTLE OF MANILA BAY

1 MAY 1898

The natural empathy that Americans felt for colonial societies seeking their independence was particularly strong in favor of Cuban revolutionaries in the 1890s, due largely to the sympathetic treatment the American press gave the rebels. American "yellow journalism" portrayed Spain as a ruthless tyrant suppressing the natural Cuban instinct for freedom. Thus, when an explosion aboard the battleship *Maine* on 15 February 1898 sent it to the bottom of Havana Harbor, most Americans were quick to conclude that Spain had somehow engineered the disaster. In fact, the *Maine* was almost certainly the victim of a not-uncommon accident in the age of coal-fired steamers: an explosion of coal dust in the fuel bunkers. Nevertheless, the emotional reaction to this disaster provoked a war hysteria in the United States and led to a formal declaration of war against Spain on 25 April.

That same day Secretary of the Navy John D. Long telegraphed COMMO George Dewey, commanding the American Asiatic Squadron at Hong Kong: "Proceed at once to Philippine Islands. Commence operations at once, particularly against the Spanish fleet. You must capture vessels or destroy. Use utmost endeavors." The message did not catch Dewey by surprise. The Assistant Secretary, Theodore Roosevelt, had already alerted Dewey that the Spanish Squadron in Manila would be his primary objective. That squadron had little to do with the liberation of Cuba, of course, but influenced in part by the writings of Alfred Thayer Mahan, Roosevelt and Long believed it was necessary to destroy Spanish naval power worldwide to ensure American command of the sea.

Dewey waited only to hear the latest intelligence reports from Manila Bay before putting to sea from Mirs Bay north of Hong Kong on 27 April (see map A). His fleet consisted of four cruisers (two of which were armored or "protected" cruisers), two gunboats, and one revenue cutter, mounting a total of 117 guns, including ten 8-inch guns. The Spanish fleet under RADM Don Patricio Montojo consisted of only one modern cruiser, the *Reina Cristina,* which at 3,500 tons was only half the size of Dewey's *Olympia,* plus one old wooden cruiser and five gunboats mounting eighty-six guns altogether, the largest of which were the six 6.2-inch guns of the *Reina Cristina.* Still, three factors made Dewey concerned about the coming encounter: first, Montojo would have the opportunity to fight at anchor with the heavy guns of the Manila batteries to support him; second, the Spanish were reported to have sown mines in Manila Bay; and third, the American fleet would be fighting some six hundred miles from the British base at Hong Kong. If for any reason Dewey suffered a reverse, he would have difficulty either sustaining the fleet in Philippine waters or retiring to Hong Kong, which, as a neutral port, he could not use to refit anyway.

Arriving off the western coast of Luzon on 30 April, Dewey sent the *Boston* and *Concord* to reconnoiter Subic Bay (see map B), and finding it empty, he continued south, arriving off the entrance to Manila Bay that same afternoon. Learning that Montojo's fleet was still inside, he gave orders to enter the bay that night through Boca Grande Passage south of Corregidor Island. Dewey had served under Farragut as a junior officer and later claimed that he was thinking of Farragut's bold dash into Mobile Bay as his own squadron transited Boca Grande Passage that night. The Spanish batteries on El Fraile tried a few ranging shots, which the Americans answered, but the U.S. fleet successfully passed into the bay without damage. By dawn on 1 May Dewey's squadron was inside the bay, where the Spanish fleet lay waiting (see map C).

Montojo's fleet was anchored in a stationary battle line in Cañacao Bay near the Cavite Navy Yard (1). Montojo might have placed his fleet off Manila (2), where the 9.4-inch guns of the city's shore batteries could have supported his outgunned vessels, but he chose not to do so because he knew that American shots passing over his fleet would kill civilians in Manila. As dawn broke over Manila Bay, the two fleets sighted one another, and Dewey at once steamed to the attack. The Spanish began firing long before the Americans came within range, but the U.S. ships held their fire until 5:40 A.M. when Dewey turned to his flag captain, CAPT Charles Gridley, and remarked laconically, "You may fire when you are ready, Gridley."

If Dewey's run into Manila Bay suggested Farragut's run past the Mobile forts in 1864, his tactics inside the bay were reminiscent of Du Pont at Port Royal Sound. Steaming in line ahead, with the *Olympia* in the lead, Dewey's fleet traced a series of elliptical ovals (3) at three thousand yards, each ship firing as the target came to bear. American marksmanship was poor; throughout the battle, only 141 of the 5,859 American shots fired struck their targets (2.4 percent). But Spanish marksmanship was worse. After five passes, every Spanish vessel had been hit at least once, and several were on fire, while no U.S. vessel had yet been struck. After two hours Dewey received a report that some U.S. ships had only 15 percent of their ammunition left, and much alarmed, he ordered a withdrawal (4). Only after he had drawn off did Dewey learn that only 15 percent of the ammunition had been *expended*! After sending the hands to breakfast, Dewey renewed the unequal contest at 11:00 A.M.

The Spanish resisted heroically, fighting their vessels till they sunk, but there was never any doubt of the outcome. All of the Spanish vessels except two small launches were either sunk or burned, including the *Reina Cristina* (5), which suffered more than 50 percent casualties before going down. No American ship was even slightly damaged, and only seven Americans reported themselves wounded. In one day Dewey's fleet had swept Spanish naval power from the Pacific.

A
0 100 200 300 400
Nautical Miles
120°
CHINA
Foochow
Amoy
Canton
Hong Kong (Br.)
Mirs Bay
FORMOSA
20°
HAINAN
DEWEY
Philippine Sea
LUZON
Manila
PHILIPPINES (Sp.)
South China Sea
PALAWAN
10°
Sulu Sea
MINDANAO
BORNEO
Celebes Sea
110°
120°

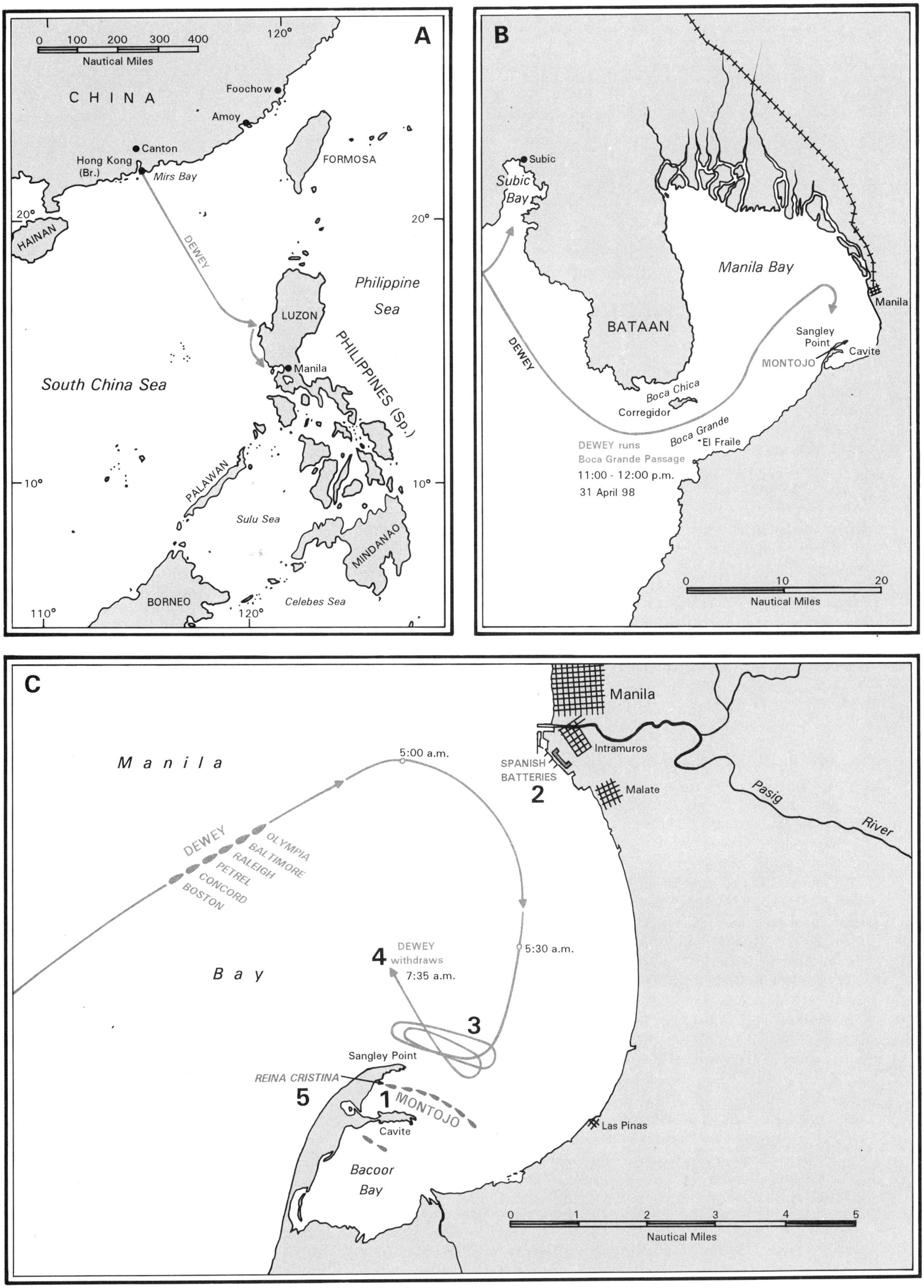

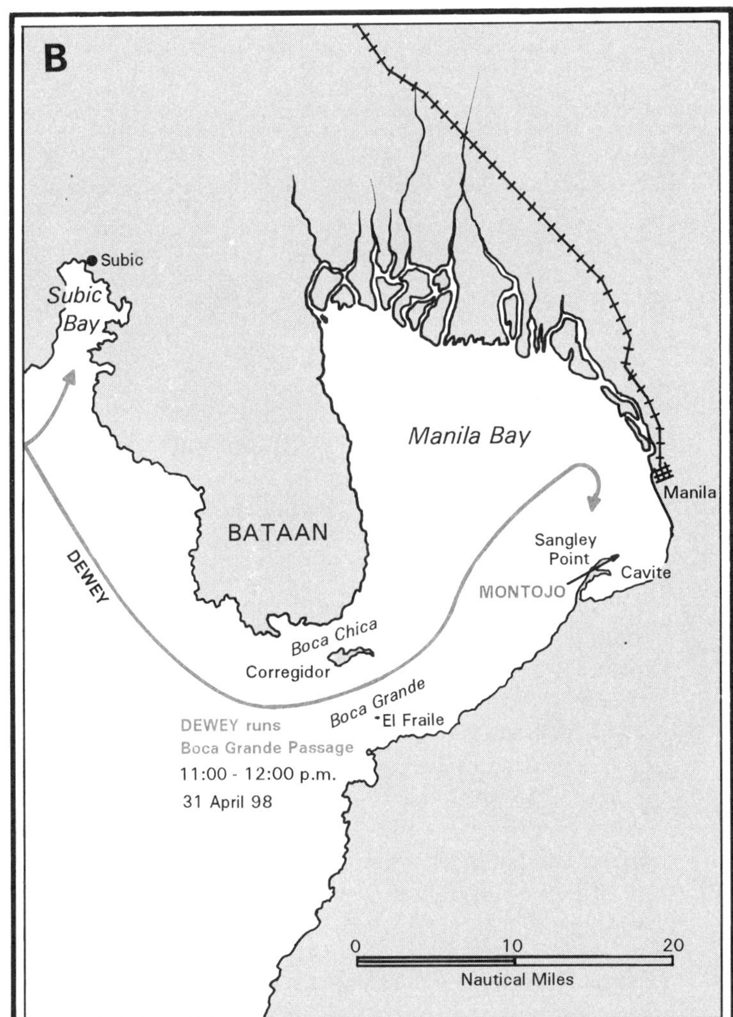
B
Subic
Subic Bay
Manila Bay
Manila
BATAAN
DEWEY
Sangley Point
Cavite
MONTOJO
Boca Chica
Corregidor
Boca Grande
El Fraile
DEWEY runs
Boca Grande Passage
11:00 - 12:00 p.m.
31 April 98
0 10 20
Nautical Miles

C
Manila
Intramuros
SPANISH BATTERIES
2
Malate
Pasig River
5:00 a.m.
Manila Bay
DEWEY
OLYMPIA
BALTIMORE
RALEIGH
PETREL
CONCORD
BOSTON
DEWEY withdraws
4
7:35 a.m.
5:30 a.m.
3
Sangley Point
REINA CRISTINA
5
1
MONTOJO
Cavite
Las Pinas
Bacoor Bay
0 1 2 3 4 5
Nautical Miles

MAP 44

THE SEARCH FOR CERVERA

APRIL–JULY 1898

The news of Dewey's one-sided victory at Manila set Americans to rejoicing, but their uncertainty about the intentions of Spain's Atlantic fleet under ADM Pascual Cervera muted their joy. To many Americans, it seemed conceivable that Cervera might cross the Atlantic and strike at any one of a half dozen cities along the U.S. East Coast. The commander of the American Home Squadron, RADM William T. Sampson, could not adopt Dewey's plan and take the fight to the enemy, for most of Sampson's warships could not carry sufficient coal to cross the ocean and fight an enemy fleet in its own waters. Then, too, Sampson's steaming off to look for Cervera at his base in the Cape Verde Islands would uncover the U.S. coast to a surprise Spanish raid. Instead of taking the fight to Cervera, therefore, Sampson would have to wait for Cervera to come to him. Throughout the month of May, the questions that dominated every conversation were Where was Cervera? and What would he do?

The most likely scenario was that Cervera would head for Cuba, which was, after all, the prize for which the two nations contended (see upper map). Accordingly, Sampson established his base at Key West (1) only eighty nautical miles from Cuba. But to assuage the fears of East Coast citizens, the Navy Department established a second squadron at Hampton Roads under COMMO Winfield S. Schley (rhymes with sky).

Cervera's force of four cruisers and three destroyers left St. Vincent in the Cape Verde Islands at midnight on 28 April. Thanks to the transatlantic cable, the Americans knew of his departure, but they did not know where he was headed. Though civilians along the U.S. East Coast looked to sea daily, expecting to see him off Boston or New York, American naval authorities believed that he was headed for Havana (2) on the northern coast of Cuba or Cienfuegos (3) on the southern coast.

Sampson hoped to intercept Cervera in the Windward Passage (4), but after waiting there for more than a week, he began to suspect that Cervera had gone instead to San Juan, Puerto Rico (5). On 10 May, therefore, Sampson took his own fleet to San Juan, where his ships traded salvos with the harbor forts while looking into the bay. Both sides sustained little damage in this exchange, and the Americans saw no sign of Cervera's fleet. Then on 14 May Sampson learned that Cervera had arrived at Curaçao (6), where he was taking on coal. That far south, it was unlikely that Cervera was headed for any U.S. city, and the Navy Department released Schley to join Sampson at Key West (7). Sampson, too, headed for Key West to recoal, and he met there with Schley on 19 May.

That same day Cervera's squadron entered Santiago Harbor (8). Cervera had intended to make for Puerto Rico, but at Curaçao he had learned of Sampson's attack on San Juan and decided it was a good opportunity to make a dash for a Cuban port. He would have headed for Cienfuegos but did not have enough coal, so he ended up at Santiago. The citizens of that city cheered Cervera's arrival, but their jubilation turned to apprehension when they realized that this relatively small squadron represented all that Spain was able to commit to the war, and that Cervera's ships had arrived low on coal and food, bringing three thousand more mouths to feed.

The day that Cervera arrived at Santiago, Sampson sent Schley to initiate a blockade of Cienfuegos (9). Schley arrived there on 21 May, and spotting what looked to him like the masts of warships in the harbor, he decided that he had found Cervera. Meanwhile, Sampson had been informed by telegraph that Cervera was at Santiago. He sent orders to Schley to take his big ships to Santiago at once. But unconvinced that Sampson's intelligence was accurate, Schley delayed, and he did not arrive off Santiago until 26 May. That same day the USS *Oregon* arrived in Key West after a harrowing voyage around Cape Horn, and Sampson added her to his squadron and set out for Santiago himself.

The five days that Santiago lay unguarded (20–25 May) turned out to be Cervera's only chance to escape, for Santiago was a cul-de-sac, and once the U.S. blockade was in place, he was trapped (see lower map). Sampson joined Schley off Santiago on 1 June and divided the blockading squadron into two groups, one under his own command to guard the eastern approaches (10) and another under Schley to guard the western approaches (11). On 3 June Sampson attempted to "cork the bottle" by sinking one of his own colliers in the harbor's entrance, but despite the heroism of its volunteer crew, it succeeded only in blocking a side channel (12). Then on 6 June Sampson tried a direct approach, bombarding the Spanish forts at the harbor's mouth and lobbing shells over the headland toward the enemy fleet. This, too, proved disappointing, and the next day Sampson recommended bringing a division of Army troops to capture the batteries at the harbor's mouth to allow the Navy to enter Santiago Bay to confront Cervera.

U.S. Army troopships arrived off Santiago on 20 June, and two days later fifteen thousand men under MGEN William T. Shafter landed on the Cuban coast at Daiquiri twenty miles west of Santiago. Much confusion marked the landing, but there was no resistance, and the next day the Army began to move inland. Instead of striking west for the batteries, however, Shafter's force drove north toward the city of Santiago (13). This alarmed the governor general at Santiago, Ramón Blanco, who suggested to Cervera that he should attempt to fight his way out. Cervera noted that half his crew was helping fight the Americans on land and offered this comment: "To attempt to leave this port would mean our absolute, immediate destruction." Nevertheless, when American forces captured the high ground outside Santiago on 1 July, Blanco ordered Cervera to "leave at once."

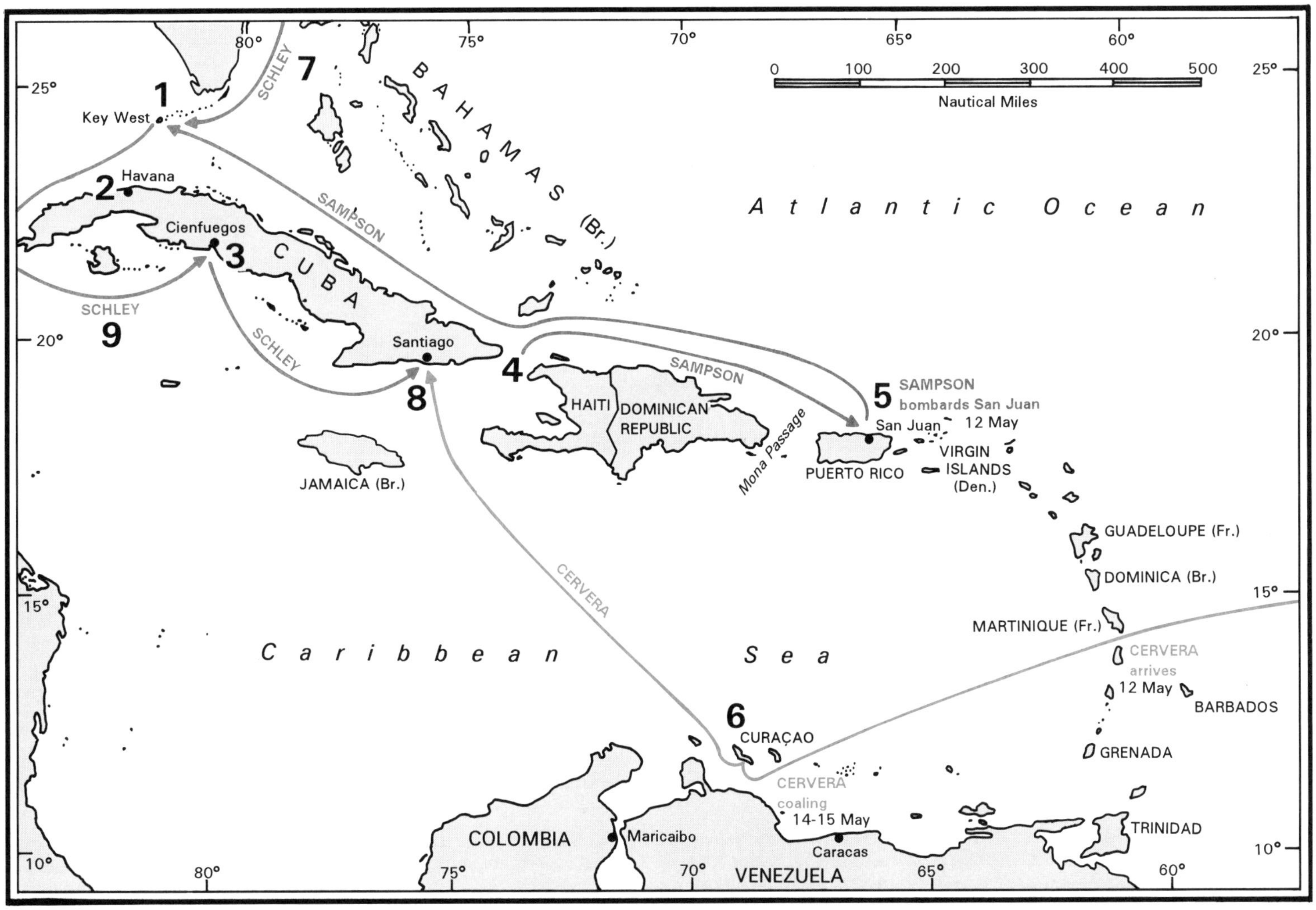

80° 75° 70° 65° 60°

25° 20° 15° 10°

0 100 200 300 400 500

Nautical Miles

1 Key West

2 Havana

3 Cienfuegos

4

5 SAMPSON bombards San Juan 12 May

6 CURAÇAO

7 SCHLEY

8 Santiago

9 SCHLEY

CUBA

SCHLEY

SAMPSON

SAMPSON

BAHAMAS (Br.)

Atlantic Ocean

HAITI

DOMINICAN REPUBLIC

Mona Passage

San Juan

PUERTO RICO

VIRGIN ISLANDS (Den.)

JAMAICA (Br.)

GUADELOUPE (Fr.)

DOMINICA (Br.)

MARTINIQUE (Fr.)

CERVERA arrives 12 May

BARBADOS

GRENADA

TRINIDAD

CERVERA

Caribbean Sea

CERVERA coaling 14-15 May

COLOMBIA

Maricaibo

Caracas

VENEZUELA

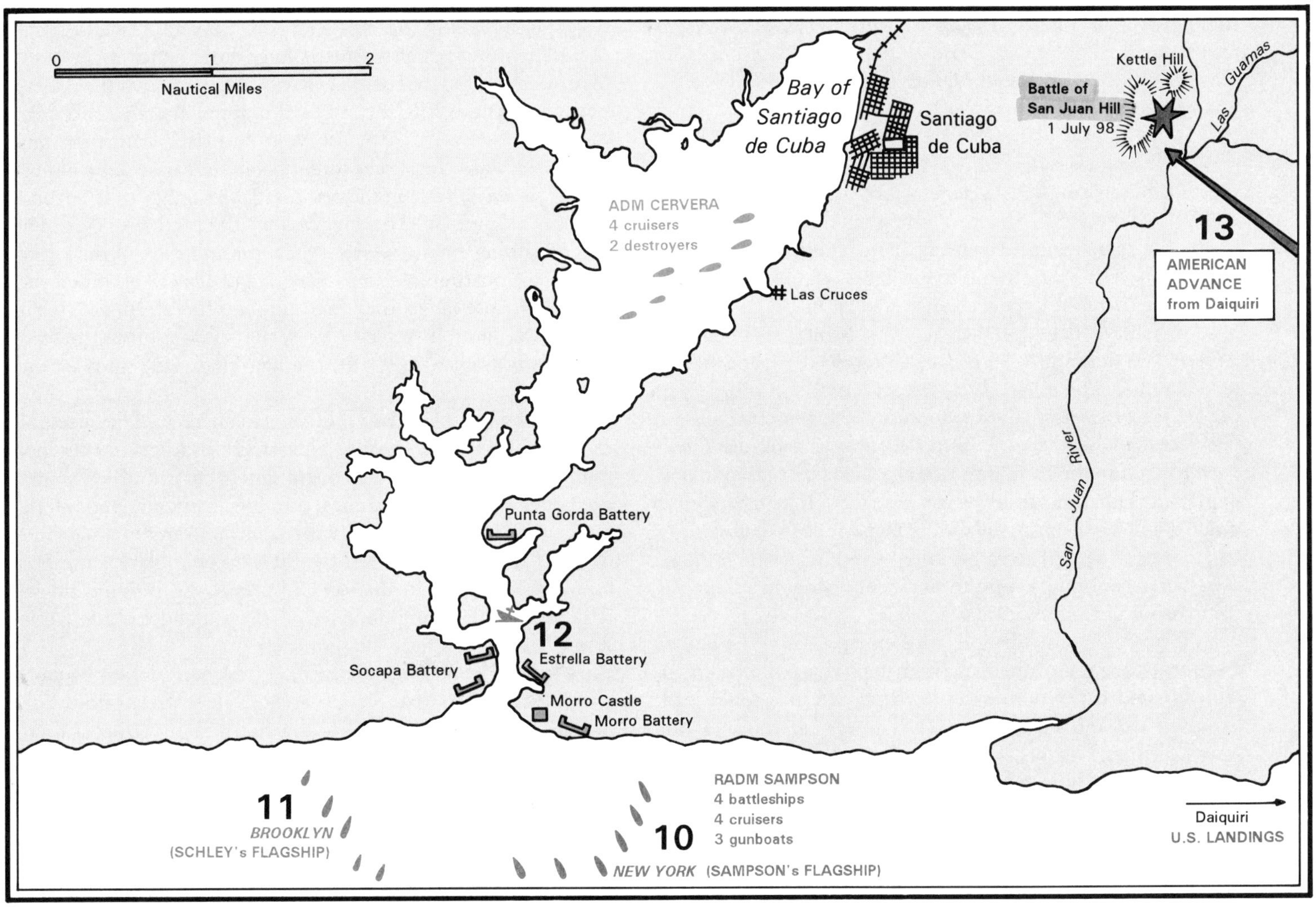

0 1 2

Nautical Miles

Bay of Santiago de Cuba

Santiago de Cuba

Battle of San Juan Hill 1 July 98

Kettle Hill

Las Guamas

ADM CERVERA
4 cruisers
2 destroyers

Las Cruces

13 AMERICAN ADVANCE from Daiquiri

San Juan River

Punta Gorda Battery

12 Estrella Battery

Socapa Battery

Morro Castle

Morro Battery

RADM SAMPSON
4 battleships
4 cruisers
3 gunboats

11 BROOKLYN (SCHLEY's FLAGSHIP)

10 NEW YORK (SAMPSON's FLAGSHIP)

Daiquiri U.S. LANDINGS

Map 45

Battle of Santiago

3 July 1898

Though the situation at Santiago looked grim to the Spanish, things looked little better to Major General Shafter. His troops had suffered heavy losses at San Juan Hill (1) and in the fighting for El Caney (2), and disease in the ranks had weakened the survivors. His troops were less than a mile from Santiago, but Shafter feared they could go no farther, nor was he even sure that they could safely retreat to the coast. As a result, he sent Rear Admiral Sampson a message, begging him to use his fleet "to force the entrance to avoid future losses among my men." Ironically, though the Army had been sent to Cuba to open the channel for the Navy, Shafter was now asking the Navy to force its way through the mined channel to save the Army. Sampson decided that he had to meet with Shafter to discuss their options, and on 3 July he steamed east (3) in the *New York* toward the Army base at Siboney. That same morning the battleship *Massachusetts* had departed the blockade, bound for Guantanamo Bay where it was scheduled to take on coal.

These events seemed fortuitous to Cervera, who had ordered his fleet to get steam up on all boilers the night before, and who had dispatched the gunboat *Alvarado* at dawn to retrieve the mines from the ship channel. With two of the American capital ships missing from the blockade, and with Governor General Blanco ordering him to "leave at once," it was now or never.

The third of July was a Sunday, and the officers and men of the U.S. blockading fleet were in their dress whites for inspection by divisions when at 9:30 A.M. the *Iowa* fired a gun and hoisted No. 250: "Enemy coming out." All the U.S. ships in the blockade sounded general quarters and fired up their boilers. The first Spanish ship to emerge was Cervera's flagship, the *María Teresa.* At 9:35 it steamed straight out of the channel toward Schley's flagship, the *Brooklyn.* Schley assumed that Cervera was attempting to ram and ordered the helmsman to turn hard to starboard (4). But Cervera was not seeking a fight; the *María Teresa* turned west to run along the coast toward Cienfuegos. Worse, Schley's turn to starboard took the *Brooklyn* directly into the path of the *Texas,* which had turned to port in pursuit. The commander of the *Texas,* CAPT John W. Philip, ordered all engines back full and barely avoided a collision. In an attempt to recover from his initial error, Schley ordered the *Brooklyn* to continue its turn to starboard, swinging around the compass until it, too, was headed west.

One by one the Spanish ships emerged from the harbor and turned west, and the American ships charged after them, their forward batteries firing as fast as their crews could load. Sampson had ordered the *New York* to reverse course at the sound of the first shot, and he, too, joined the general chase. Though he started from some distance back, the superior speed of his vessel closed the range quickly.

Cervera had ordered his two destroyers to launch torpedo attacks on the American battleships to allow the Spanish cruisers to escape. But the destroyers were the last to emerge from the bay, and they had little chance to execute their mission. Both Spanish destroyers came under steady fire from the U.S. gunboat *Gloucester* under LCDR Richard Wainwright, as well as from the larger U.S. vessels. A 13-inch shell from the *Indiana* hit the *Pluton,* killing most of the engine-room crew and nearly cutting the vessel in half, and soon afterward the *Furor* struck its flag to the *Gloucester.* The Spanish destroyers had made it only five miles beyond the mouth of the harbor (5).

Meanwhile, Cervera's larger ships steamed west, with shell splashes tearing up the water all around them. As the faster American vessels closed the range, the American firing became more accurate, and soon smoke could be seen billowing from several of the ships. The *María Teresa* was the first to suffer a mortal wound. An 8-inch shell started a fire on the stern and also cut the fire mains. Unable to fight the fire, Cervera had to order the ship's magazine flooded. As the *María Teresa* slowed, more and more American shells began to strike home, and the vessel began to sink (6). At 10:15 A.M. Cervera struck his flag.

The other Spanish cruisers fared little better. Their only hope was in speed, but in that they could not match the American vessels, especially the armored cruisers *Brooklyn* and *New York.* One by one the Spanish vessels suffered damaging hits and turned into the shore, running aground to avoid sinking. The *Oquendo* ran up on the beach at 10:35 only a mile beyond the *María Teresa* (7). The *Vizcaya* was next, and as one of only two remaining enemy vessels it drew the attention of the entire American squadron. As the *Brooklyn* and *Oregon* pounded the *Vizcaya* at close range, the *Texas* and *Iowa* fired from astern. At 11:15 A.M., afire in several places, the *Vizcaya* turned toward shore and beached itself (8), finished off by the guns of the *Iowa.*

Now only the *Cristóbal Colón* remained (9). The fastest of the Spanish ships, it steamed west at fifteen knots, its engine-room gang encouraged by frequent shots of brandy. But though the *Colón* led the American fleet on a fifty-five–mile chase along the Cuban coast, the superior speed of the American warships doomed the Spanish vessel. By 1:00 P.M. the black gang was both exhausted and inebriated, and with shells from the *Brooklyn* and *Oregon* finding the range, the commander of the *Colón* struck his flag and headed ashore.

As at Manila, a materially superior American fleet had virtually destroyed its Spanish opponent while suffering almost no damage to itself. In addition to the destruction of four cruisers and two destroyers, the Spanish lost more than 300 killed and 150 wounded, as well as 1,800 taken prisoner, including Cervera. The American fleet lost one killed and one wounded.

The wreck of the Spanish cruiser Vizcaya *off the coast of Cuba after the Battle of Santiago. For U.S. Navy warships, the battle was much like a shooting gallery as the smaller, slower Spanish vessels unsuccessfully attempted to break out of the harbor. (Official U.S. Navy photo)*

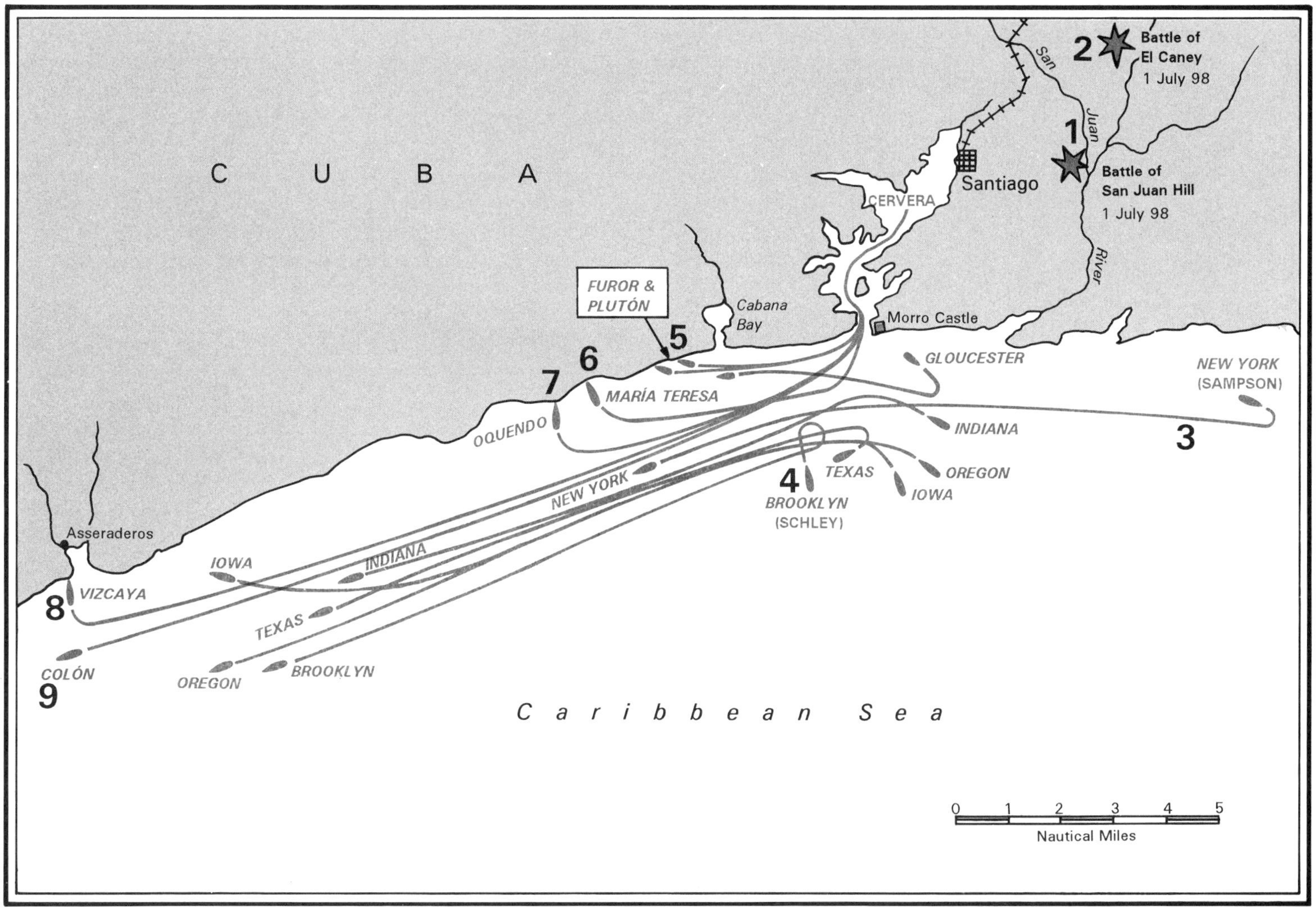

MAP 46

THE BOXER REBELLION

MAY–OCTOBER 1900

American victory in the war with Spain symbolized the emergence of the United States as a world power and brought with it an American overseas empire. Though the American declaration of war had included a clause by which the United States forswore any territorial claims in Cuba, the treaty transferred both Guam and Puerto Rico from Spain to the United States. Even more important was the American decision to annex the Philippines, for which the United States paid Spain an indemnity of $20 million. A few Americans opposed this move as the first step toward imperialism, which they claimed to be incompatible with democratic government, but most were swept away by the heady taste of empire, and President McKinley decided that American stewardship of the Philippines was a national obligation.

The Filipinos were disappointed to discover that they had exchanged a Spanish master for an American one and initiated a fierce rebellion (1899–1901) under the leadership of GEN Emilio Aguinaldo. It struck some as ironic that the United States had gone to war in 1898 to help the Cubans win their independence and then went to war in 1899 to prevent the Filipinos from getting theirs. After two years of fierce fighting, American forces succeeded in capturing Aguinaldo—which effectively ended the war, although sporadic fighting continued for many months.

In a related development almost overlooked at the time, the United States quietly annexed the Republic of Hawaii in July 1898. Combined with the U.S. acquisition of Guam in the treaty with Spain and the Navy's occupation of Wake Island, the United States now possessed a series of stepping stones across the Pacific (see upper map): from Hawaii (1) to Midway (2), Wake (3), Guam (4), and Manila (5). This maritime highway led to the shores of China, a market that American businessmen endowed with mythic potential.

But the United States was not the only nation interested in China. Indeed, during the previous half century European powers had carved up much of that Asian nation, each claiming exclusive trading rights in particular ports. British Hong Kong and Portuguese Macao (6) were only the most overt European enclaves along the Chinese coast. Left out of the early race for the best ports, the United States in 1899 announced its preference for a policy that came to be known as the "Open Door," which asserted the right of equal access to Chinese ports for all western countries.

Of course, during all of this diplomatic maneuvering about which nation could trade in which ports, no one bothered to ask the Chinese. In part this was because the Imperial Chinese government exerted little effective control over much of the country and was unable to resist western encroachment. In 1900 the passivity of the Chinese government to growing western influence provoked an organization opposed to both the government and the foreigners to take action. This organization was "The Righteous and Harmonious Fists," known to westerners as the Boxers. The Boxers' goal was to drive foreigners out of China altogether. At first the empress claimed that she opposed the Boxers, but their influence grew so strong that in the end she had little option but to cooperate with them.

By the spring of 1900 the power of the Boxers had grown so great in the Chinese capital of Peking that the American minister, Edwin Conger, felt compelled to wire a request for help to the commander of the U.S. Asiatic Squadron (see lower map). Most of the European ministers made similar requests, and by the first week of June a mixed force of some 450 Americans, British, French, Italians, Germans, Japanese, and Russians had arrived at Peking (7) to defend the legations. The American contingent consisted of forty-eight marines and five sailors from the cruiser *Newark,* all under Marine CAPT John T. Myers.

To support this small force, British ADM Sir Edward Seymour led a column of more than 2,000 men, including 112 Americans, out of Tientsin (8) along the rail line toward Peking on 11 June. His advance, and the shelling of the Taku forts (9) by allied warships on 17 June, convinced the empress that this was a foreign invasion, and she ordered the Imperial Army to resist. Seymour's force got as far as Land-fang (10) before it was forced to fall back to Tientsin, where it was itself besieged. Meanwhile, on 21 June the Boxers, aided now by Imperial troops, began a series of attacks against the walled quarter of Peking where the foreign legations were housed (11). For fifty-five days the 450 men who had arrived in June, aided by every able-bodied westerner in the legation quarter, fought off repeated attacks while hoping that a relief column could fight its way to the city.

In July the western powers assembled a second relief column of more than five thousand men, including an American contingent of one thousand U.S. Marines under COL R. W. Meade, that fought its way into Tientsin and relieved Seymour's force on 14 July. Then on 4 August an army of more than eighteen thousand, including five hundred U.S. Marines and two thousand U.S. Army soldiers under MGEN Adna Chaffee, set out on a hard-fought ten-day campaign along the Pei Ho River (12), reaching Peking on 14 August.

U.S. participation in the multinational effort to rescue the besieged diplomats in Peking offered further evidence of America's emergence from its traditional insularity. Noteworthy, too, was the prominence of Japanese forces in the relief expedition. Like the United States, Japan was an emerging naval power that would stun the world in 1905 by winning a naval war with Russia and becoming the dominant naval power in the western Pacific.

120°
150°
180°
150°
120°
Peking
Tientsin
CHINA
Sea of Japan
JAPAN
Tokyo
Yellow Sea
Pacific Ocean
UNITED STATES
San Francisco
Los Angeles
San Diego
Nanking
Shanghai
East China Sea
30°
Foochow
Amoy
BONINS
MIDWAY (U.S.)
2
1100 miles
1350 miles
2100 miles
6
FORMOSA
Hong Kong (Br.)
Macao (Port.)
Philippine Sea
MARIANAS
3
WAKE (U.S.)
1350 miles
1
Honolulu
HAWAII (U.S.)
5
LUZON
Manila
15°
1500 miles
PHILIPPINES (U.S.)
4
GUAM (U.S.)
So. China Sea
CAROLINE ISLANDS
MARSHALL ISLANDS
MINDANAO
BORNEO
0
500
1000
1500
2000
Nautical Miles

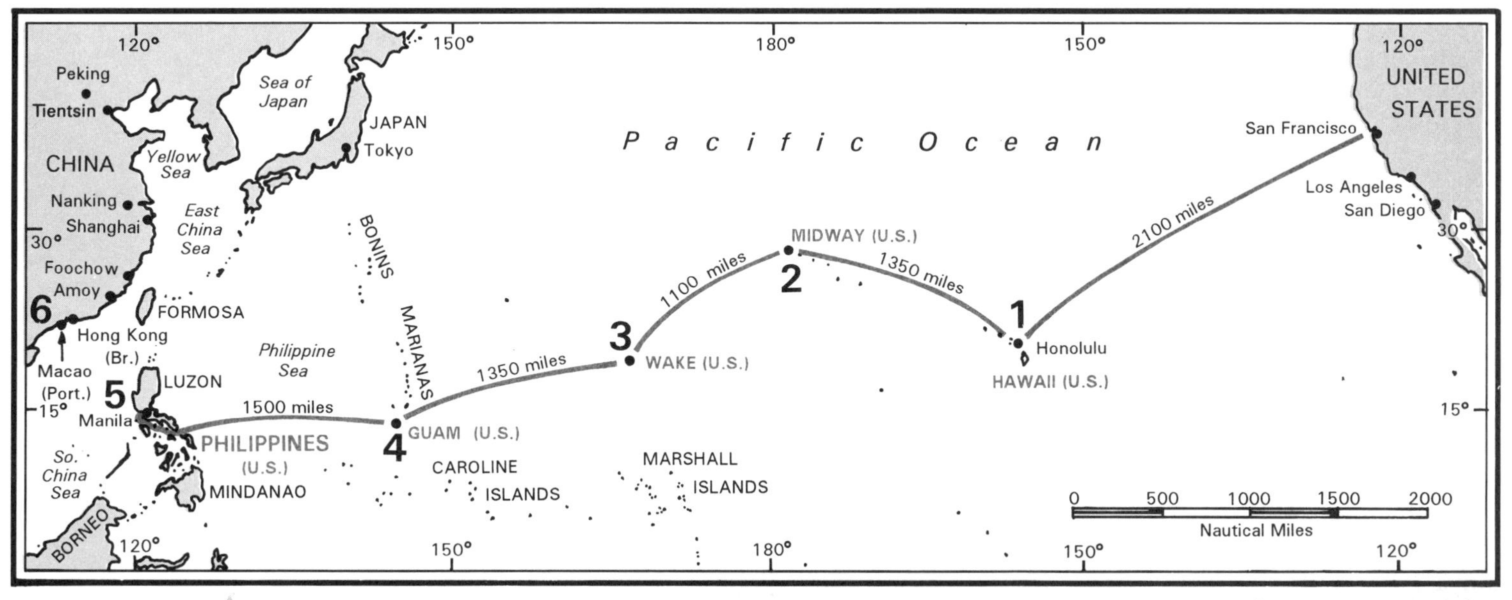

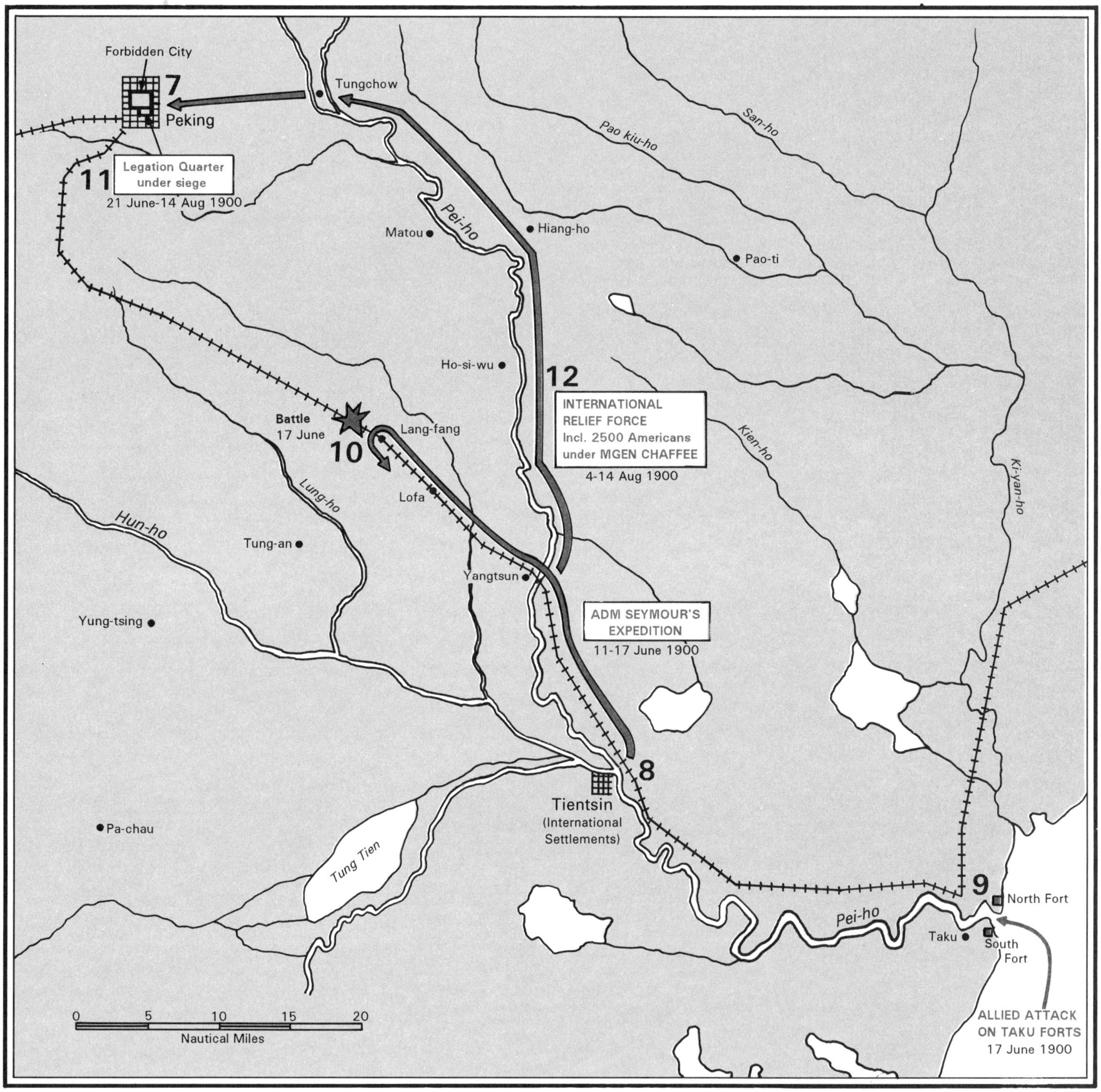

Forbidden City
7
Peking
Tungchow
Legation Quarter under siege
21 June-14 Aug 1900
11
San-ho
Pao kiu-ho
Pei-ho
Matou
Hiang-ho
Pao-ti
Ho-si-wu
12
INTERNATIONAL RELIEF FORCE
Incl. 2500 Americans under MGEN CHAFFEE
4-14 Aug 1900
Battle
17 June
Lang-fang
10
Kien-ho
Ki-yan-ho
Lung-ho
Lofa
Hun-ho
Tung-an
Yangtsun
ADM SEYMOUR'S EXPEDITION
11-17 June 1900
Yung-tsing
8
Tientsin
(International Settlements)
Pa-chau
Tung Tien
9
North Fort
Pei-ho
Taku
South Fort
ALLIED ATTACK ON TAKU FORTS
17 June 1900
0
5
10
15
20
Nautical Miles

PART VII

A Global Navy and a World War 1901–1939

ON 6 SEPTEMBER 1901 a self-proclaimed anarchist named Leon Czolgosz shot and mortally wounded President William McKinley, putting forty-two-year-old Theodore Roosevelt in the White House. Author of a naval history of the War of 1812 and a former Assistant Secretary of the Navy, Roosevelt was an enthusiastic navalist. During his first term as president, U.S. expenditures for the Navy nearly doubled—from $60 million to $117 million, and from 11.5 percent of the federal budget to 21 percent. Most of the money went toward the construction of battleships, and the fruits of that spending appeared in 1906–1907 when the U.S. commissioned no fewer than ten new battleships, giving the Navy a total of seventeen, with three more under construction. In December 1907 Roosevelt dispatched sixteen of these ships on a cruise from the Atlantic to the Pacific via the Strait of Magellan, and thence around the world. Because the American battleships were painted a peacetime white, this voyage has always been known as the cruise of the Great White Fleet (see map 47).

Even as Roosevelt's Great White Fleet put to sea, however, every ship in it—indeed, every battleship in the world—was already obsolete. The reason was that almost two years earlier, in February 1906, the British had launched HMS *Dreadnought*, the first capital ship in the world with no secondary battery. Until the appearance of the *Dreadnought*, every battleship had carried a mixed battery of naval guns. Typically, U.S. battleships had four 12-inch guns for use at maximum range (about eighteen thousand yards), eight 8-inch guns for use at intermediate range, and twelve 6-inch guns for use against torpedo boats or other small targets at close range. For some time naval officers and ship designers had considered that engagements between battle fleets could be decided at ranges of twelve thousand yards (six miles) or more, so the guns of the secondary battery might never come into play. In that case, they wondered, why not dispense with the secondary battery altogether and build battleships with only the biggest-caliber guns? A U.S. Navy lieutenant, Homer Poundstone, actually designed such a vessel as early as 1901, and Congress approved the construction of the USS *Michigan*, an all-big-gun battleship, in 1904. But it was the British who first produced such a ship.

President Theodore Roosevelt, an enthusiastic navalist, poses with the commander of the U.S. battle fleet, RADM Robley "Fighting Bob" Evans, prior to the departure of the "Great White Fleet" in 1907 (see map 47). Roosevelt's successful sponsorship of naval expansion heralded the emergence of the United States as a naval power and coincided with a burgeoning arms race in Europe. (Library of Congress)

The *Dreadnought* was laid down in October 1905, built in the strictest secrecy, and launched in record time less than five months later. With its ten 12-inch guns mounted in five turrets, the *Dreadnought* had an immense advantage at long range over any predreadnought battleship. At distances beyond twelve thousand yards, HMS *Dreadnought* would be able to employ all ten of its heavy guns, whereas other battleships, such as the USS *Rhode Island* (launched the same month), could respond with only four. So significant was this milestone that from 1906 onward naval officers routinely labeled all battleships as either dreadnoughts or predreadnoughts, assigning the latter a secondary role.

It is both typical and ironic that the British took the lead in this naval revolution. As the world's foremost naval power, Britain had often initiated revolutionary advances in naval ordnance and engineering. On the other hand, it was precisely because Britain was the world's foremost naval power that it stood to lose the most from a naval revolution that rendered all existing battleships obsolete. Nevertheless, Britain's leaders, including its energetic First Sea Lord, Sir John "Jacky" Fisher, knew that the revolution was coming and decided that it was better to anticipate change than react to it.

For the newer naval powers—the United States, Germany, and Japan—this revolution signaled an opportunity. With the elimination of Britain's overwhelming lead in battleship hulls, it became possible to contemplate challenging

HMS Dreadnought, *launched in 1906, redefined the capital ship. Whereas earlier battleships carried a mixed battery of naval guns, the* Dreadnought *boasted a main battery of ten 12-inch guns, thus rendering obsolete all existing battleships. Its appearance in 1906 helped spark a naval-arms race between Britain and Germany. (Official U.S. Navy photo)*

Britain for naval supremacy. The nation that took up the challenge was the empire of the German kaiser, William II. Thus it was that the appearance of the *Dreadnought* in 1906 contributed to a full-blown naval-arms race between Britain and Germany. In February 1908 Germany announced that it was amending its naval-construction program. Whereas in 1900 the kaiser's government had projected the construction of thirty-eight battleships, it now declared an intention to build no fewer than fifty-eight of the new dreadnoughts.

The specter of such a naval power on its continental flank led Britain to strain every sinew to maintain naval superiority. Winston Churchill, who became First Lord of the Admiralty in September 1911, vowed to outbuild Germany two for one. In addition, Britain consolidated its fleet in home waters, virtually abdicating the Pacific to Japan, with whom it had signed a treaty in 1902, and it drew closer to France—Germany's principal enemy in Europe.

The naval-arms race in Europe affected strategic planning in the United States as well. Britain's abandonment of the Pacific, combined with Japan's victory over the Russian Baltic Fleet at the Battle of Tsushima in May 1905, left Japan as the dominant power in the western Pacific. Both the United States and Japan realized that they were likely to become rivals for supremacy in the Pacific, and the United States developed its first contingency plan for a Pacific war against Japan—code-named Plan Orange—in 1911 (see map 53).

The United States launched its first dreadnought, the USS *Michigan,* in January 1910. Three more were commissioned that same year, and ten more over the next five years. These dreadnoughts were substantially larger and better protected than those built only a few years earlier. The last American predreadnought, the USS *Idaho,* commissioned in 1908, displaced 13,000 tons and carried four 12-inch guns, whereas the USS *Pennsylvania,* commissioned only eight years later in 1916, displaced 32,000 tons and carried twelve 14-inch guns with a range of 25,000 yards, or 12.5 nautical miles.

Another important technological change that occurred in this era was the shift from coal to oil. The first U.S. dreadnought, the *Michigan,* was a coal burner, but two of the four dreadnoughts commissioned in 1910 were designed to burn oil as well as coal. The *Nevada* (1916) was the first U.S. battleship to burn only oil. Naval engineers had been aware for some time that oil was more efficient, offered greater cruising range, and increased a ship's speed by as much as 20 percent. But not until the discovery of the vast Spindletop Oil Fields in Texas in 1901 was it evident that the United States possessed sufficient oil resources to avoid a dependence on imported oil for the fleet. The problem was even more serious for Britain, which inaugurated the oil-fueled *Queen Elizabeth* class of battleships in 1912. Unlike the United States, Britain had no domestic sources of oil, and it had an apparently unlimited supply of coal (taking "coal to Newcastle" is still an expression of superfluity). But British planners in 1912 were willing to trade energy independence for the increased manageability of oil and an increase in fleet speed from twenty-one to twenty-five knots.

The naval-arms race in Europe did not cause the First World War, but it contributed to both the hardening alliance system and the growing tension. The spark that ignited the explosion of violence was the assassination of the Austrian Archduke Francis Ferdinand during a visit to the Serbian capital of Sarajevo in July 1914. After obtaining German backing, Austria presented Serbia with a provocative ultimatum. Serbia appealed to Russia, Austria appealed to Germany, and Europe tumbled into war. After a month of rapid advances and violent battles in August, the war settled into a static but astonishingly bloody war on two fronts. Forced to rethink their strategies, the western allies (Britain and France) sought to wear Germany down through constant wasting attacks against German entrenchments in France, while Germany turned east in an attempt to drive Russia out of the war.

Meanwhile, the giant battle fleets built by Britain and Germany in the decade prior to the war spent most of the conflict in watching each other across the North Sea. Only once, in the spring of 1916, did they engage in a major fleet action (see map 49). Meanwhile, however, the kaiser gave his permission for the German Navy to embark on a program of unrestricted submarine warfare in an attempt to starve Britain into defeat. Germany's adoption of *guerre de course* warfare was a

The USS Michigan *was America's first dreadnought-class battleship. It might have been the first such vessel in the world because the plans for the* Michigan *were completed in 1904. But whereas Britain's energetic First Sea Lord, Sir John "Jacky" Fisher, pushed the* Dreadnought *to completion with unprecedented speed and secrecy, the* Michigan *was not commissioned until January 1910. (National Archives)*

U.S. Marines fire from cover as smoke billows around them in Belleau Wood on the Western Front in 1918. The appearance of fresh American troops helped turn the tide of battle in France, and the Marine Corps commandant, MGEN George Barnett, made sure that a Marine contingent accompanied the first U.S. troops to go overseas (see map 51). (Official U.S. Marine Corps photo)

modernized version of the strategy conducted by American privateers in two wars, and by the *Alabama* in the Civil War. But because U-boats often attacked without warning, contemporaries looked upon unrestricted submarine warfare as a new and particularly barbarous kind of warfare. Upon the outbreak of war in 1914, President Woodrow Wilson had asked Americans to adopt a strict neutrality in the war, but by 1916 the U-boat campaign, effective British propaganda, and a general perception that American interests were linked with those of Britain led the United States into a posture of open sympathy for the Allies.

The sinking of the British Cunard liner *Lusitania* in May of 1915 sent a shock wave through the American public, and when a U-boat torpedoed the French passenger liner *Sussex* in March 1916, Wilson sent an angry note to the German ambassador. In response, the German government on 4 May 1916 pledged that it would no longer sink merchant vessels without warning. Nine months later, however, the German government reversed itself. Perceiving the opportunity to deliver a knockout blow to its enemy, Germany reinstituted unrestricted submarine warfare on 1 February 1917. Two days later the United States severed diplomatic ties. On 12 March a German U-boat sank the American merchant steamer *Algonquin,* and a week later several other American ships went down. His patience exhausted, Wilson asked Congress for a declaration of war on 2 April, and four days later Congress complied.

Like the Spanish-American War, America's participation in the Great War of 1914–1918 marked a milestone for both the nation and the Navy—a turning point from which there would be no retreat.

MAP 47

THE GREAT WHITE FLEET

DECEMBER 1907–FEBRUARY 1909

While Theodore Roosevelt presided over the largest peacetime expansion of the Navy in the nation's history, events in both Europe and Asia redefined power relationships in the western Pacific. In the half century since Commodore Perry's visit in 1853, the Empire of Japan had emerged as a modern industrialized state with a powerful navy. Few westerners realized just how powerful the Japanese Imperial Navy was until its spectacular victory over the Russian Baltic Fleet in the Tsushima Strait during the Russo-Japanese War in 1905. When soon afterward Britain recalled most of its Pacific naval forces to home waters in response to the German threat, Japan became the dominant naval power in the western Pacific.

Roosevelt helped mediate the end to the Russo-Japanese War—for which he received the Nobel Peace Prize—but Roosevelt also recognized that Japanese naval power posed a threat to American interests and ambitions in the Pacific. Tensions between the two countries became strained in 1907 as a result of a California law declaring that all "mongolians" (defined as anyone of Asian descent) had to be educated in segregated schools. The Japanese naturally protested this insult, and the Roosevelt administration mediated a compromise wherein California agreed to postpone the segregation of its schools and Japan agreed to restrict immigration.

Though this so-called "gentleman's agreement" defused the immediate crisis, the episode acted as a catalyst to spur Roosevelt toward a project he had long considered: sending the U.S. battle fleet from the Atlantic to the Pacific via the Strait of Magellan. Roosevelt hoped that a visit by the U.S. fleet to the Pacific would have a beneficial effect on future Japanese-American relations. But he had other objectives as well. A primary objective was to test the fleet's capability to operate effectively on such a long voyage. The difficulties that the Russians had encountered in moving their Baltic Fleet from European waters to the western Pacific were not lost on American naval planners. Finally, Roosevelt hoped that favorable press coverage of the cruise would help sustain public support for the Navy and allow him to continue his building program.

The battle fleet departed Hampton Roads (1) on 16 December 1907 under the command of RADM Robley Evans, a veteran of the Civil War who had been wounded in the assault on Fort Fisher. Evans was in questionable health, but Roosevelt was loath to relieve him. As it turned out, Evans spent much of the voyage around South America sick in his cabin while his chief of staff, CAPT Royal S. Ingersoll, ran the fleet.

Besides command problems occasioned by Evans's illness, the most sensitive issue was deciding which ports to visit. Every major city en route had invited the fleet to make a courtesy call. But in the end the deciding factor was not politics but coal. The U.S. fleet of sixteen battleships burned 1,500 tons of coal per day, and it was the ships' bunker capacity that determined the ports of call. As a result, the fleet stopped at Port-of-Spain in Trinidad (2) and Rio de Janeiro (3), where the Brazilians put on an extravagant entertainment, but bypassed Buenos Aires (4), pausing only long enough to exchange a formal salute with the Argentine Navy. Likewise the fleet stopped at the small port of Punta Arenas (5) on the northern shore of the Strait of Magellan but only passed in review without stopping at the major Chilean port of Valparaiso (6).

The people of California greeted the fleet with wild enthusiasm in April of 1908. The biggest reception was at San Francisco (7), where the fleet drew a million visitors. There the ailing Rear Admiral Evans finally stepped aside, turning command over to RADM Charles M. Thomas. But Thomas, too, was ailing, and after only a week in command he was succeeded by RADM Charles S. Sperry, who commanded the fleet for the rest of its voyage.

After visits up and down the West Coast, each stop the occasion for further celebration, the fleet sailed from San Francisco for Hawaii on 7 July. After a refueling stop at Honolulu (8), the fleet made lengthy visits to Auckland, New Zealand (9), and three cities in Australia, where the reception was, if anything, even more extravagant than in California—so much so that Admiral Sperry had a serious problem with desertion. After transiting the Lombok Strait and the Makassar Strait in September, the fleet anchored off Manila (10) on 2 October. A cholera epidemic ashore forced Sperry to cancel shore liberty, and after a week spent in coaling the fleet got under way for its visit to Japan.

En route, the fleet was struck by a typhoon that severely battered the fleet for two days, though no ships were lost, and the fleet safely dropped anchor in Yokohama on 17 October. The Japanese reception was not only gracious but genuinely friendly, with no evidence of the tension that many had anticipated. The American battleships stayed a week at Yokohama and then returned to Manila—half directly, and half via the Formosa Strait in order to stop at Amoy, China. The fleet conducted its regular annual exercise in November, held for the first time in Asian waters, and left Manila on 1 November, heading home via the Strait of Malacca, the Indian Ocean, and the Suez Canal (11).

On all counts the voyage was a great success. The glowing press stories helped Roosevelt win popular support for his naval program as Congress approved the president's request for more battleships and also authorized nine new colliers. It is less evident that the cruise had any decisive impact on Japanese policy makers other than to provide tangible evidence of what they already knew: that the United States was likely to be their principal rival in the Pacific Ocean in the twentieth century.

The Great White Fleet entering Puget Sound on 21 May 1908. The fleet was wildly received at each of its West Coast ports of call, fulfilling Roosevelt's goal of increasing public enthusiasm for naval expansion. (U.S. Naval Historical Center)

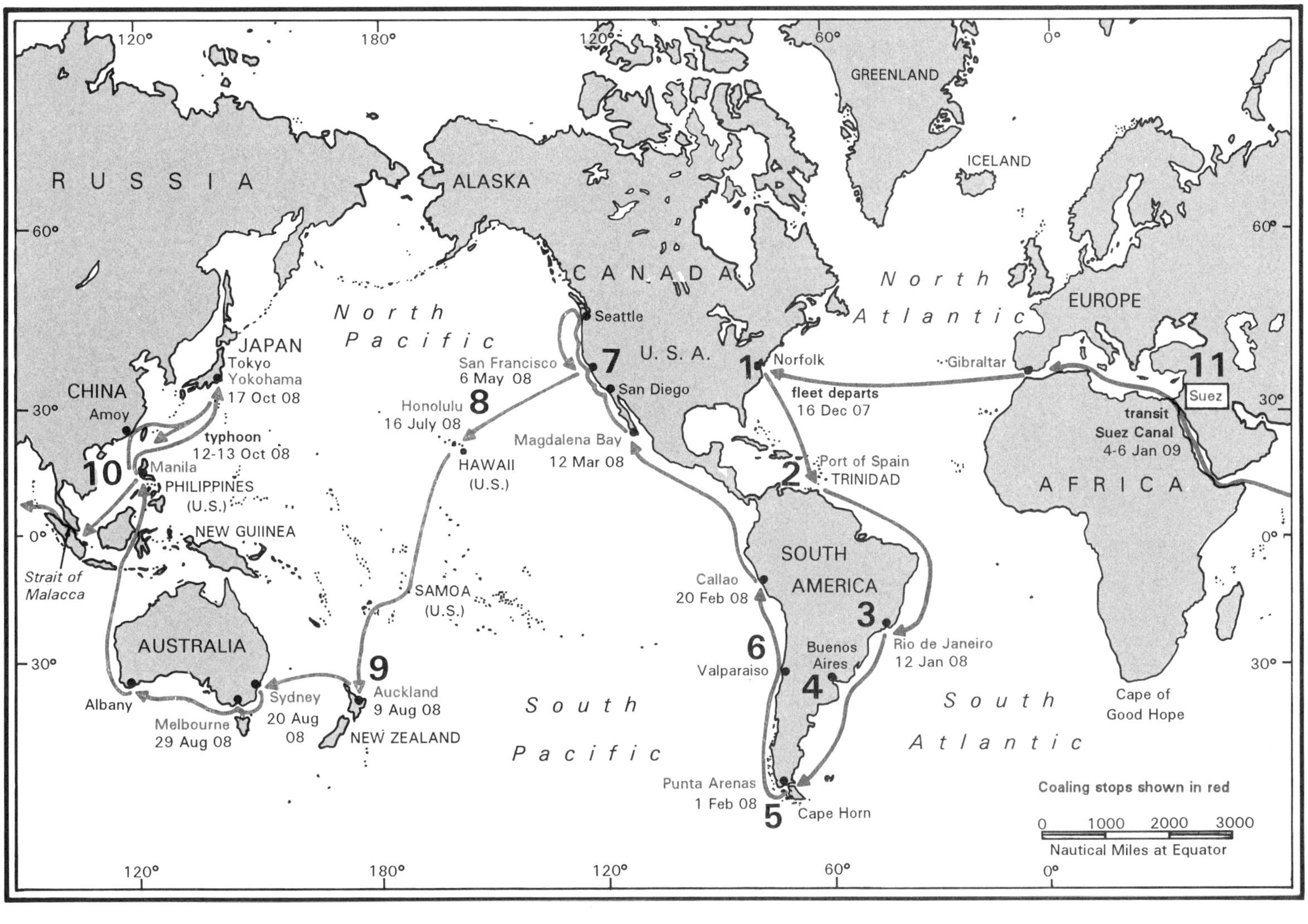

MAP 48

AN AMERICAN LAKE: THE NAVY AND MARINES IN CENTRAL AMERICA 1902–1915

Nowhere was the emergence of the United States as a major power manifested more clearly than in Central America, where the instrument of American intervention was the U.S. Marine Corps. The Marines engaged in a score of operations—some peaceful, other's bloody—to protect American lives and property, to maintain political or financial stability, and even to effect changes in government. The Marines accomplished the difficult missions assigned them, but the policy that directed them left behind a legacy of resentment in Latin America that has lingered for generations.

PANAMA (1903)

The Mahanian doctrine that a nation's battle fleet must never be divided made an isthmian canal a necessity for the United States. A French company headed by Ferdinand de Lessups had attempted to build a canal across Panama (1) in the 1880s but had gone bankrupt. Under Roosevelt, the project took on new urgency, and on 22 January 1903 the United States signed the Hay-Herran Treaty with Colombia, which granted the United States canal rights in Panama (a province of Colombia) as soon as Colombia's lease with the de Lessups Company expired. Then, shockingly, the Colombian Senate rejected the treaty.

Rebellions in Panama had been endemic for fifty years, but the one that broke out in November 1903 was engineered by stockholders in the de Lessups Company who stood to gain if an agreement with the United States were approved. Meanwhile, American warships had been dispatched to Panama with orders to protect U.S. citizens and property, and help keep the peace. A U.S. Marine battalion under MAJ John A. Lejeune landed on 5 November; the United States recognized Panamanian independence on 6 November; and a treaty between the United States and the new Panamanian government was signed on 18 November. Work on the canal began almost at once, but the episode damaged U.S. credibility in Latin America.

VENEZUELA (1902–1904)

A self-absorbed dictator named Cipriano Castro had ruled Colombia's neighbor Venezuela (2) since 1899. In 1902 Castro declared forfeit $12.5 million of Venezuelan debts to European investors. Germany, England, and Italy responded to this declaration by blockading Venezuela's ports. Roosevelt had no sympathy for dictators or debtors; he had warned the nations of Latin America that the Monroe Doctrine did not exempt them from punishment for wrongdoing. But at the same time he did not want European navies exercising gunboat diplomacy in the Caribbean. Roosevelt, therefore, ordered the U.S. Atlantic Fleet under Admiral Dewey to proceed from San Juan, Puerto Rico, to the Venezuelan coast to act as a deterrent to the Europeans as well as to Castro. In the end, all of the powers agreed to Roosevelt's suggestion that they submit their case to the International Court of Justice at the Hague.

Two years later, in December 1904, Roosevelt made explicit what his intervention in Venezuela had implied: The United States, he declared, had the right to exercise "an international police power" among the nations of Latin America. Often referred to as the Roosevelt Corollary to the Monroe Doctrine, this policy provided the justification for continued U.S. intervention.

DOMINICAN REPUBLIC (1904–1905)

The Roosevelt Corollary received an early test in the Dominican Republic (3), where another rebellion prompted the landing of U.S. Marines to protect American lives and property. As the government proved incapable of dealing effectively with the rebellion, and foreign debts mounted, the United States attempted to end the chaos by simply taking over the customs house in Santo Domingo in January 1905. U.S. Navy and Marine Corps officers took charge of the accounts, collected revenues, and applied the money to reducing the nation's overseas debt. The signal was clear: the United States would see to it that Latin American nations met their fiscal obligations.

CUBA (1906–1909)

The United States had gone to war in 1898 to support a Cuban bid for independence from Spain, but the outbreak of another revolution in 1906 led Roosevelt to send six U.S. Marine battalions to Cuba (4) to help the government maintain order and suppress the rebellion. An American "Army of Cuban Pacification" followed this initial commitment, remaining in Cuba until 1909.

NICARAGUA (1909–1912)

A revolution in Nicaragua (5) in December 1909 also prompted the landing of U.S. troops to protect American interests. The United States bolstered the sagging government of Nicaragua with money as well as marines. Then to ensure that the money was repaid, the United States occupied and managed the customs house, as it had in the Dominican Republic. Eventually, COL Joseph H. Pendleton, USMC, commanded a force of more than two thousand marines who fought a full-scale war in Nicaragua in the fall of 1912 before suppressing the opposition. After that, the United States maintained a virtual military occupation of Nicaragua until 1933.

HAITI (1915)

In much the same way, an initial U.S. peacekeeping mission in Haiti (6) led to a permanent occupation. A revolution in that country in 1915 turned particularly ugly on 27 July when the government conducted mass executions in the streets of Port-au-Prince. U.S. Marines went ashore the next day and established a military occupation that would rule Haiti for nineteen years before President Franklin Roosevelt finally terminated it in 1934.

By the time the Panama Canal opened in August 1914, the United States had actively intervened at least once in every nation of the Caribbean littoral. Politically and economically, the United States dominated the region. Militarily, it controlled access to the Caribbean Basin through naval bases at Key West (7) and Guantanamo Bay (8), the latter leased from Cuba in 1903. The Caribbean had become an American lake.

90°
80°
70°
Norfolk Naval Base
Cape Hatteras
UNITED STATES
Cape Fear
Charleston
Savannah
Mobile
New Orleans
Pensacola Naval Base
30°
Atlantic Ocean
Gulf of Mexico
BAHAMAS (Br.)
7
Key West Naval Base
Florida Strait
Bahia Honda Naval Base 1903-1912
Havana
4
CUBA
Occupied by U.S. 1906-1909
Occupied by U.S. 1915-1934
Occupied by U.S. 1916-1924
20°
MEXICO
Santiago
8
Windward Passage
6
3
HAITI
DOMINICAN REPUBLIC
Guantanamo Bay Naval Base
JAMAICA
Kingston
Port-au-Prince
Santo Domingo
Mona Passage
San Juan
PUERTO RICO
VIRGIN ISLANDS
Purchased by U.S. 1917
BRITISH HONDURAS
GUATEMALA
U.S. Intervention 1912
HONDURAS
Caribbean Sea
DEWEY 1902
EL SALVADOR
5
NICARAGUA
Occupied by U.S. 1909-1933
Gulf of Fonseca Naval Base 1914-1933
Managua
2
Caracas
Maricaibo
Cartagena
10°
COSTA RICA
U.S. CANAL ZONE
Colón
1
Panama City
VENEZUELA
REPUBLIC OF PANAMA (1903)
Pacific Ocean
COLOMBIA
0 100 200 300 400 500
Nautical Miles

MAP 49

JUTLAND

31 MAY–1 JUNE 1916

The First World War—what contemporaries called simply the Great War—began in August 1914. For most of four years, while tens of thousands of young men died in the western-front trenches, the huge British and German battle fleets faced each other across the North Sea (see upper map). From their base at Scapa Flow in the Orkney Islands (1), the British maintained a loose blockade of the German coast in the hope that the German High Seas Fleet would be encouraged to sortie so that the Royal Navy could achieve another Trafalgar. For most of the war, however, the German fleet remained at its base at Kiel (2), aware that its very existence as a "fleet in being" kept the British fleet tied down as well.

Elements of the German fleet did venture out now and again. In December 1914 a squadron of German battlecruisers shelled the Yorkshire coast (3), and a month later another squadron of four German battlecruisers put to sea under VADM Franz von Hipper to conduct a similar raid. This time, however, the Royal Navy was waiting. The British had obtained a copy of the German naval code and used it to decode radio intercepts. Thus forewarned of Hipper's sortie, VADM David Beatty put to sea with five British battlecruisers on 23 January to ambush Hipper's force near Dogger Bank (4). In the running fight that ensued, the British sank one German battlecruiser, the *Blücher,* but allowed the other three to escape. Bred as he was in the spirit of Trafalgar, Beatty was disappointed not to have destroyed the entire squadron.

More disappointment was forthcoming. A year after the Dogger Bank action, the German High Seas Fleet received a new commander, VADM Reinhard Scheer, who adopted a more active strategy, periodically sending out patrols in the hope of enticing a British response and springing an ambush. Scheer's Royal Navy counterpart was ADM Sir John Jellicoe, who was eager for a fleet action but also aware that he had more to lose in such an engagement than Scheer. For the Germans, a naval defeat in the North Sea would be disappointing, but for the British it would be disastrous.

On 31 May 1916 Scheer's fleet sortied from Jade Bay near the western terminus of the Kiel Canal (5), with Hipper's five battlecruisers and a substantial destroyer force screening ahead of Scheer's twenty-two battleships, sixteen of them dreadnoughts. Tipped to Scheer's move by radio intercepts, Jellicoe was already at sea with Beatty's advance force of six battlecruisers and four dreadnoughts some seventy miles south of Jellicoe's main fleet of twenty-four dreadnoughts. Counting the destroyer screens of both sides, a total of 250 warships—151 British and 99 German—were at sea on a collision course.

The two battlecruiser forces sighted each other first. Hipper recognized at once the long odds against him, and he fled south, with Beatty charging after him, determined not to let him get away this time. By 4:00 P.M. salvos from both sides were finding their marks at a range of thirteen thousand yards. Then suddenly and spectacularly one of Beatty's battlecruisers, the *Indefatigable,* exploded and sank, and twenty minutes later the *Queen Mary* did the same. With characteristic British understatement, Beatty turned to his flag captain to remark, "There seems to be something wrong with our bloody ships today." Even so, Beatty continued the pursuit until about 4:30, when he sighted the masts of the German battleships coming up from the south. Now it was Beatty's turn to reverse course and flee.

Beatty's four remaining battlecruisers and four dreadnoughts ran north, hotly pursued by Scheer's entire fleet. This phase of the action lasted just over an hour until 6:00 P.M. (see lower map), when Scheer encountered Jellicoe's battle line stretched out across his line of advance in a perfect position to "cap the T" of the German fleet (6). Once again the pursuer became the pursued. Scheer ordered his fleet to execute a battle turn to starboard, his only thought now being to get back safely to Jade Bay. For his part, Jellicoe was eager to cut off Scheer's line of escape and ordered a turn to the south by divisions (7).

In the faltering daylight, neither fleet commander had a clear understanding of the course or dispositions of the other. Attempting to cut across the wake of Jellicoe's fleet, Scheer turned east at 6:55 P.M. (8), but again found himself capped by Jellicoe's battle line (9). Screened by a torpedo attack executed by his destroyers, Scheer turned away again. As darkness fell, the two fleets lost contact. Jellicoe maintained a southerly course until 3:00 A.M. in the hope of blocking Scheer's escape route. Nevertheless, between 10:00 P.M. and 2:00 A.M. Scheer's force cut through the rear of the British fleet (10) and eventually made its way back to base.

For the British public, the outcome of the battle was disappointing. Not only did the enemy escape, but the Royal Navy suffered nearly double the tonnage losses of the Germans, including three new battlecruisers. But if the British did not win decisively, neither did they lose. Though the Germans celebrated a tactical victory, the High Seas Fleet never again came out to challenge the Royal Navy for command of the North Sea.

Not surprisingly, this one great fleet action of World War I became the object of intense scrutiny by the navies of the world. Several nations, including the United States, decided that battlecruisers had demonstrated an unsuspected vulnerability. In addition, the tactics of both commanders at Jutland were subjected to the most detailed analysis. For more than twenty years the Battle of Jutland cast a shadow over the curricula of the world's naval academies and war colleges, including the U.S. Naval War College at Newport, Rhode Island.

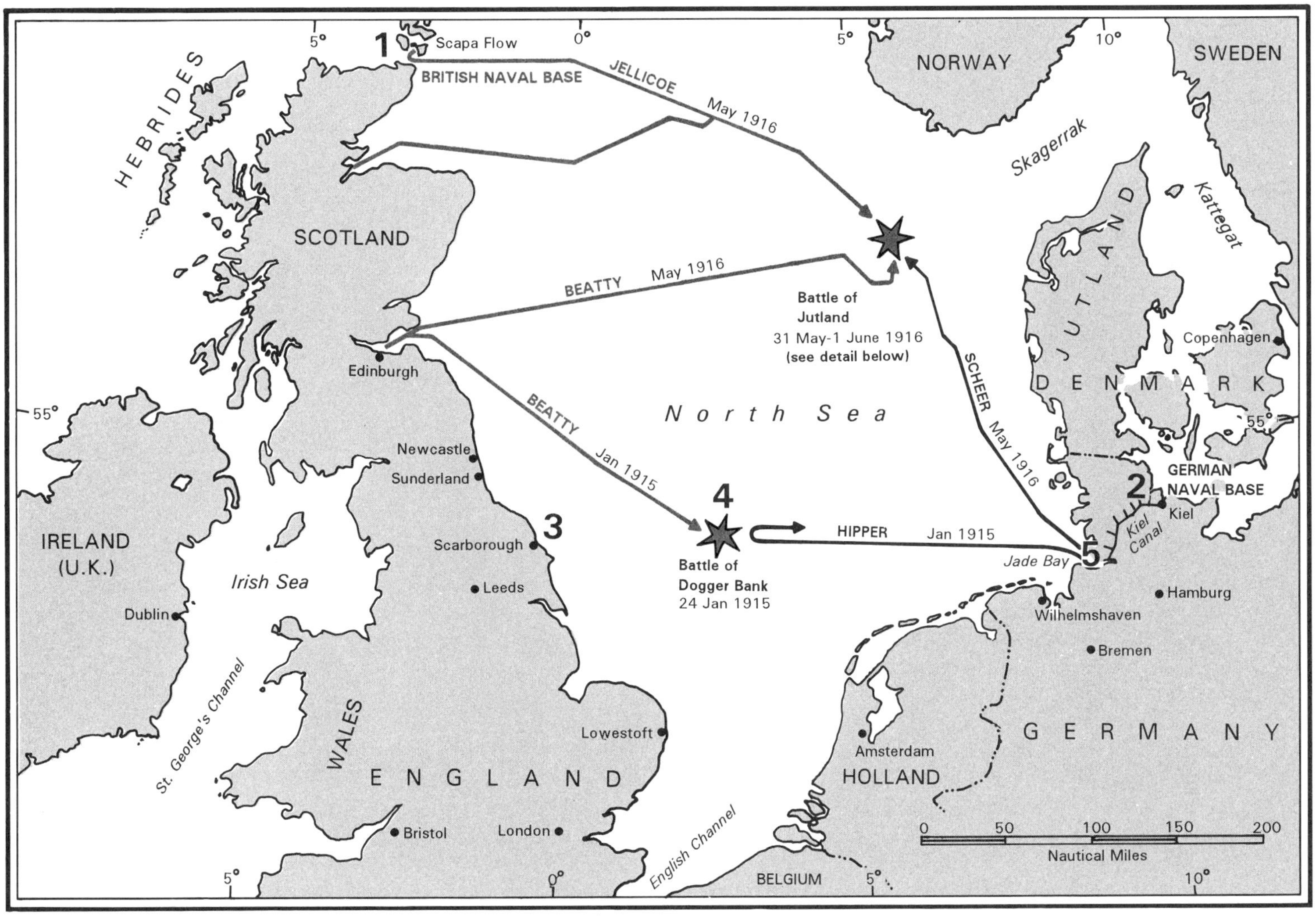

1 Scapa Flow
BRITISH NAVAL BASE
JELLICOE May 1916
HEBRIDES
SCOTLAND
NORWAY
SWEDEN
Skagerrak
Kattegat
JUTLAND
DENMARK
Copenhagen
BEATTY May 1916
Battle of Jutland
31 May-1 June 1916
(see detail below)
SCHEER May 1916
Edinburgh
North Sea
BEATTY Jan 1915
Newcastle
Sunderland
2 GERMAN NAVAL BASE
Kiel
Kiel Canal
4
Battle of Dogger Bank
24 Jan 1915
HIPPER Jan 1915
3
Scarborough
Leeds
Jade Bay 5
Hamburg
Wilhelmshaven
Bremen
IRELAND (U.K.)
Irish Sea
Dublin
St. George's Channel
WALES
ENGLAND
Lowestoft
Amsterdam
HOLLAND
GERMANY
Bristol
London
English Channel
BELGIUM
0 50 100 150 200
Nautical Miles

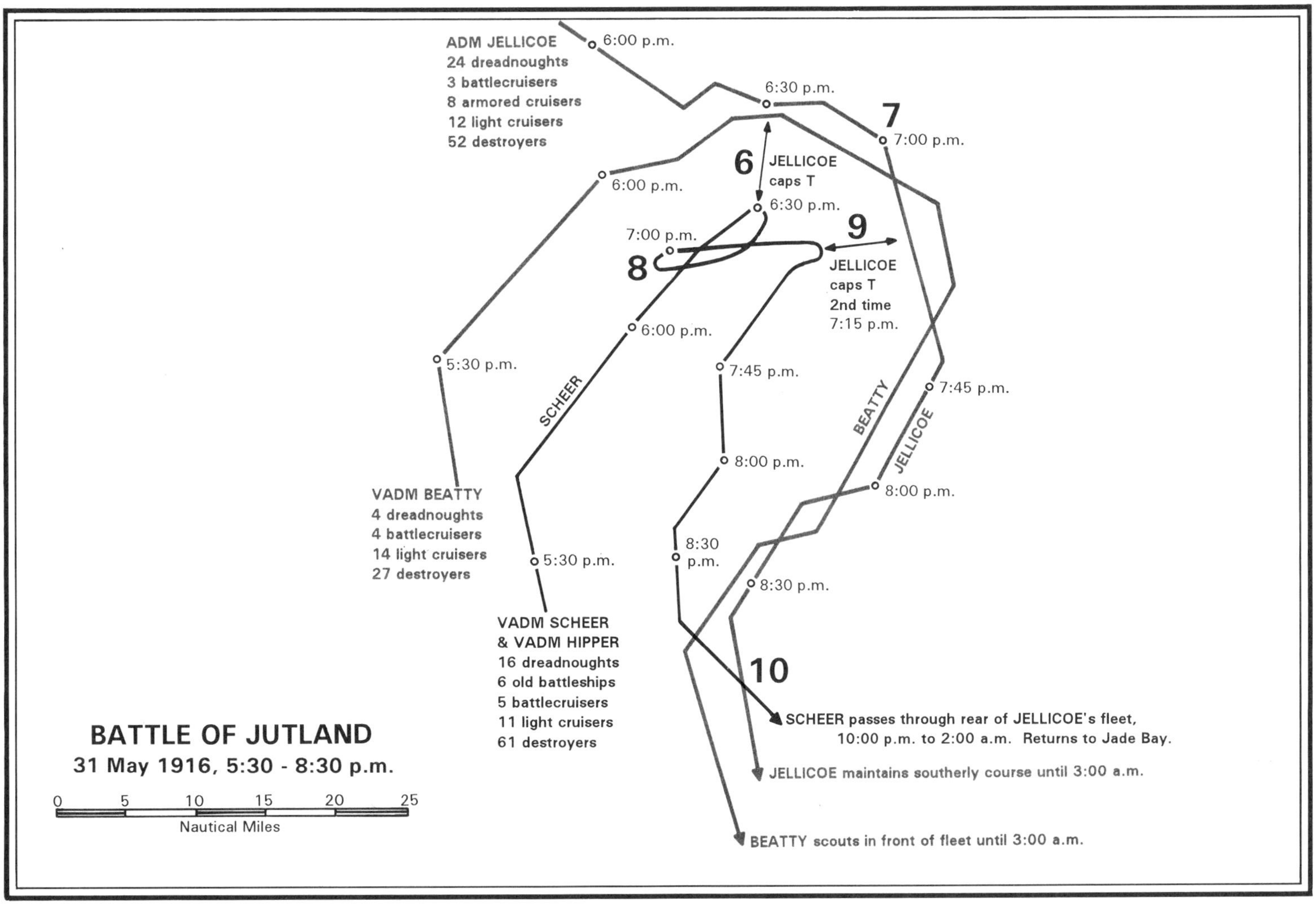

ADM JELLICOE
24 dreadnoughts
3 battlecruisers
8 armored cruisers
12 light cruisers
52 destroyers

6:00 p.m.
6:30 p.m.
7 7:00 p.m.
6 JELLICOE caps T
6:00 p.m.
6:30 p.m.
7:00 p.m.
9
8
JELLICOE caps T 2nd time 7:15 p.m.
6:00 p.m.
5:30 p.m.
7:45 p.m.
SCHEER
7:45 p.m.
BEATTY
JELLICOE
8:00 p.m.
8:00 p.m.

VADM BEATTY
4 dreadnoughts
4 battlecruisers
14 light cruisers
27 destroyers

5:30 p.m.
8:30 p.m.
8:30 p.m.

VADM SCHEER
& VADM HIPPER
16 dreadnoughts
6 old battleships
5 battlecruisers
11 light cruisers
61 destroyers

10
SCHEER passes through rear of JELLICOE's fleet, 10:00 p.m. to 2:00 a.m. Returns to Jade Bay.
JELLICOE maintains southerly course until 3:00 a.m.
BEATTY scouts in front of fleet until 3:00 a.m.

BATTLE OF JUTLAND
31 May 1916, 5:30 - 8:30 p.m.

0 5 10 15 20 25
Nautical Miles

Map 50

Atlantic Convoys

1916–1918

As an island nation, Britain depended for survival not only on defeating the enemy's main battle fleet but also on maintaining trade—the economic lifeline of shipping that fed the people and sustained the national economy. The United States had attempted to sever those lines with *guerre de course* warfare during its wars with Britain in the eighteenth and nineteenth centuries. Though this harassment of British trade had proved a substantial nuisance, the widely respected naval strategist Alfred Thayer Mahan (who died in 1914) had declared that it could never be decisive. In the First World War, however, the Germans came very close to proving Mahan wrong.

When the United States declared war against Germany in April 1917, the British were keeping the extent of German success against British shipping a closely guarded secret. Americans became privy to the secret in April 1917 when American RADM William S. Sims arrived in London to confer with Admiral Jellicoe, now the British First Sea Lord. Sims listened in astonishment as Jellicoe told him that U-boat sinkings since the initiation of unrestricted submarine warfare in February had been so successful that Britain would be forced to capitulate by fall if the trend were not reversed (see graph at lower right). Sims at once cabled Washington to rush destroyers and other antisubmarine craft to British waters, and Destroyer Division Eight under CDR Joseph Taussig arrived at Queenstown (1) on 4 May.

More destroyers would certainly help, but something far more dramatic would have to be done—and soon—to forestall disaster. A number of Royal Navy junior officers recommended a shift in emphasis from patrolling sea-lanes to a wider use of convoys. This group noted that cross-channel shipping, which was escorted in convoys, suffered significantly fewer losses than oceangoing shipping traveling independently. To test the effectiveness of convoys, the officer in command of North Sea shipping instituted convoys between Britain and Norway in April and reported that losses dropped from 25 percent to .25 percent in a month. The Lords of the Admiralty remained skeptical. Convoys, they noted, had to proceed at the speed of the slowest vessel, and bunching a large number of slow ships together would only provide U-boat skippers with an opportunity to sink dozens of vessels at one time. Merchant captains, too, opposed the idea. They believed they had more to fear from collisions in tightly packed convoys than from U-boats.

Sims had always been something of an agitator in the U.S. Navy, eager to seize new ideas. He succeeded in convincing David Lloyd George, the British prime minister, who pressed the Admiralty to attempt convoys as an experiment. Then Sims ran into another obstacle in the form of the U.S. Navy Department. Senior U.S. Navy officers were no more enthusiastic about convoys than senior British officers. They argued that convoys were essentially passive and reactive and left the initiative to the enemy. Only after the exchange of several transatlantic cables did the U.S. Navy agree to try convoys, and the first of them left the United States for Britain in July.

Convoys from the United States generally had only a single warship as an escort as far as the fifteenth degree of longitude, south of Iceland (2), where they met a more substantial escort from Queenstown (now Cobh) in Cork Harbor for the run into a British port. For this most dangerous part of the voyage, each convoy contained twenty to thirty merchant ships and three to six escorts. Each ship was assigned a specific position in the convoy formation, and each captain had to be alert for frequent orders from the escort commander as the formation zigged and zagged to confuse U-boat skippers who might be lining up for a shot, or as the convoy changed course to avoid the reported location of a U-boat. Slower vessels (ten knots) were segregated into convoys of their own, while fast liners, which could make twenty knots or more, generally sailed unescorted, for no U-boat could keep up with them.

The effect of the implementation of this system was immediate and dramatic. Losses dropped from 20 percent in March and April to only .5 percent in June and July. The three dozen destroyers operating out of Queenstown conducted the lion's share of the work in this war-saving effort, steaming out to meet incoming convoys, escorting them to port, then returning to Queenstown to refuel and going out again. It was tedious and uncomfortable work, particularly in winter. But these destroyers broke the back of the U-boat offensive. Confident that they were on the verge of victory in mid-1917, the Germans had cut back on U-boat construction. Only in 1918 did they again begin to turn out U-boats in large numbers, but by then it was too late.

In addition to the protection of trade, a large number of escorts were committed to guarding troop transports in the summer and fall of 1917. Two million Americans, as many as had fought for the Union in the whole of the Civil War, safely crossed the ocean in 1917 to fight on the western front in France. The vast majority of them left from New York and arrived at either Liverpool or Brest.

The great irony of the Allied war against the U-boat menace was that the impressive dreadnought battle fleets, which the United States and Britain had built at great expense, now seemed less important than three dozen small, fast destroyers and a handful of other escorts, some of them converted yachts, that kept open the transatlantic lifeline and brought over the soldiers that would turn the tide on the western front.

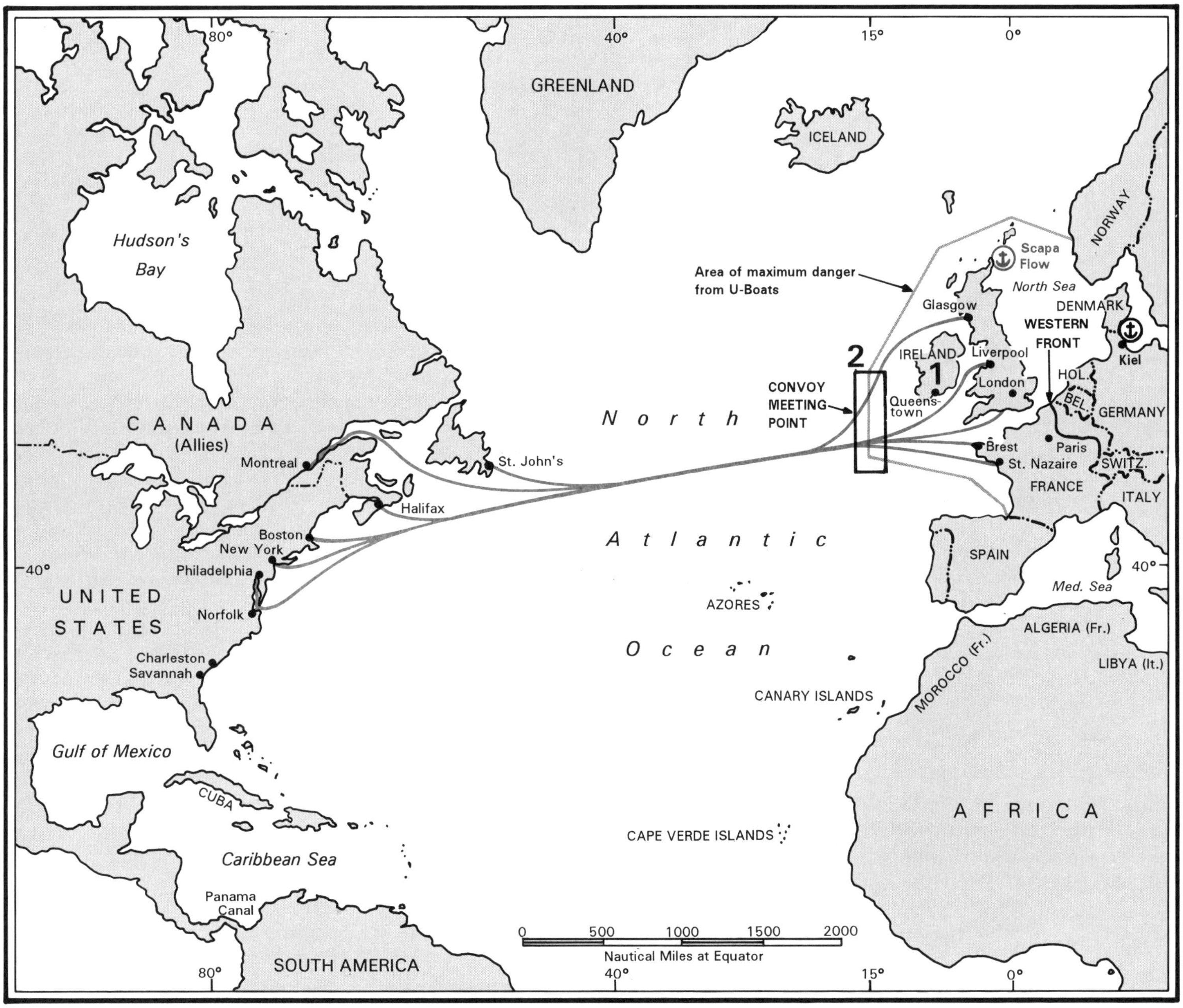

GREENLAND
ICELAND
NORWAY
Hudson's Bay
Scapa Flow
North Sea
Area of maximum danger from U-Boats
Glasgow
DENMARK
WESTERN FRONT
Kiel
2
IRELAND
Liverpool
1
London
HOL.
CONVOY MEETING POINT
Queens-town
BEL.
GERMANY
CANADA (Allies)
North
Brest
Paris
Montreal
St. John's
St. Nazaire
SWITZ.
FRANCE
ITALY
Halifax
Boston
New York
Atlantic
SPAIN
Philadelphia
UNITED STATES
Norfolk
AZORES
Med. Sea
ALGERIA (Fr.)
Ocean
Charleston
Savannah
MOROCCO (Fr.)
LIBYA (It.)
CANARY ISLANDS
Gulf of Mexico
CUBA
AFRICA
CAPE VERDE ISLANDS
Caribbean Sea
Panama Canal
0 500 1000 1500 2000
Nautical Miles at Equator
SOUTH AMERICA
80°
40°
15°
0°
40°

ALLIED SHIPPING LOSSES
1914-1918
During World War I, German U-Boats sank 5,234 Allied ships displacing 12,185,832 tons. Compare to graph on p. 156.
NUMBER OF ALLIED SHIPS SUNK MONTHLY
50
100
150
200
250
300
350
April 1915
LUSITANIA sunk
May 1916
SUSSEX pledge
Feb 1917
Germany announces unrestricted submarine warfare
April 1917
U.S. declares war; convoys begin
May 1917
First U.S. destroyers arrive in Queenstown
July 1917
First regular transatlantic convoys
June 1918
Belleau Wood
Sept 1918
St. Mihiel offensive
1914
1915
1916
1917
1918

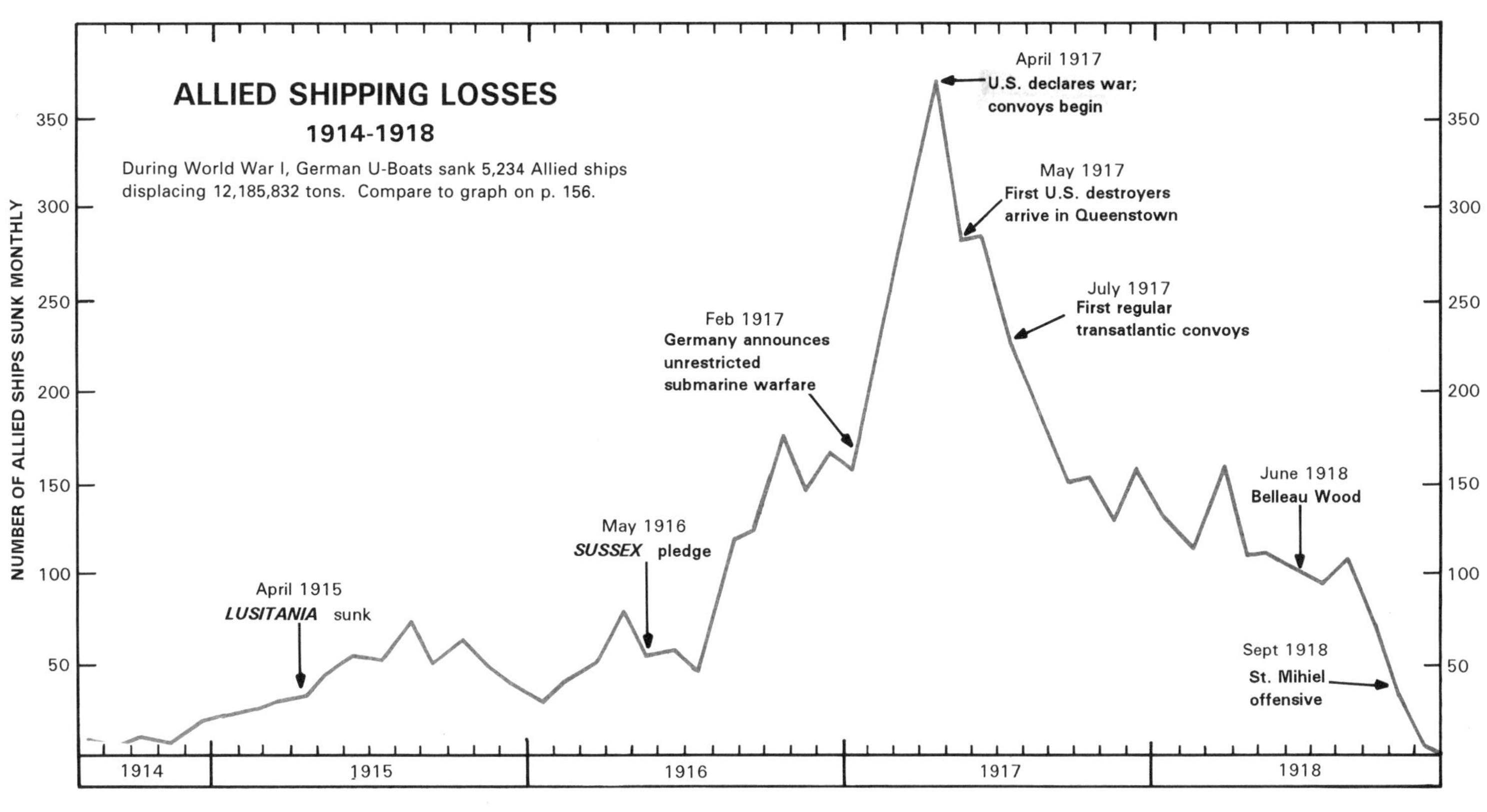

MAP 51

"LAFAYETTE, WE ARE HERE": THE NAVY AND MARINES IN EUROPE

DECEMBER 1917–NOVEMBER 1918

With the important exception of the destroyers operating out of Queenstown, active U.S. participation in the First World War was confined to the last year of the conflict. Even then, the U.S. Navy did not engage in any battles with enemy surface units. Indeed, the mighty dreadnoughts of the U.S. fleet were all but superfluous in the war. The United States would have preferred to operate its battle fleet as a single unit in conformance with Mahanian doctrine, but the British frankly did not need the U.S. dreadnought fleet to contain the Germans, and Britain would have been hard-pressed to sustain such a force at Scapa Flow anyway. Admiral Jellicoe agreed that a division of American battleships would help assure Allied superiority over the German High Seas Fleet, but he asked that the United States send older coal-burning ships because of the difficulty of keeping the fleet supplied with fuel oil. As a result, six battleships under RADM Hugh Rodman (the *New York, Texas, Wyoming, Arkansas, Florida,* and *Delaware*) arrived at Scapa Flow (1) in December 1917. This force was designated Battle Squadron Six of the Grand Fleet, but because the German High Seas Fleet did not again sortie, none of these vessels ever fired a shot in anger. In addition to the six American battleships at Scapa Flow, the United States stationed three more—the *Nevada, Oklahoma,* and *Utah*—at Bantry Bay on the western coast of Ireland in support of the convoys bearing American troops to France.

Another aspect of the naval war closely associated with the U.S. Navy was the ambitious project to erect a mine barrage across the North Sea between the Orkney Islands and Norway (2). Aside from the closely guarded Strait of Dover, this was the only route for German U-boats to take to the prime hunting grounds off Ireland. To seal it off with mines was a daunting prospect and would have been unthinkable but for the invention of the antenna mine, which could be detonated not only by direct contact but by a vessel's striking any part of a long antenna that led to the surface. Even so it was a big job: mines had to be sown every 300 feet at depths of 45, 160, and 240 feet in an area 240 miles across and 15 miles wide. At first, the United States was charged with minelaying only in Area A, but in the end it sowed most of the mines in all three areas.

The mines were built in the United States and shipped from Norfolk to Glasgow (3). Then they were transported overland to Invergorden or Inverness (4), where they were carefully assembled and loaded onto minelayers. CAPT Reginald R. Belknap commanded the fleet of American minelayers, which consisted of two modified cruisers—the *San Francisco* and *Baltimore*—and ten converted merchant steamers. Belknap's squadron began laying mines in June 1918, and by November 1918 it had laid 56,600 mines; British ships had laid 16,300 more. Despite the scale of the operation, the North Sea mine barrage had no significant impact on the war. The mines were known to have sunk only one German U-boat, and on the whole the project was probably not cost effective.

If the Allies were lukewarm about the participation of American dreadnoughts in the naval war, they were desperately eager to welcome American soldiers to the western-front trenches. Bled white after three years of trench warfare, the Allies wanted to feed American units into the front under Allied command as replacements for frontline troops. Americans balked at the idea of U.S. troops serving under foreign command, and no one more so than GEN John J. Pershing, who commanded the American Expeditionary Force (AEF). As a compromise, the United States agreed to send one division of veteran troops to Europe immediately but insisted that it be integrated into an American Army as soon as enough recruits had arrived to form a second division. The commandant of the Marine Corps, MGEN George Barnett, convinced Secretary of War Newton Baker to include a Marine Corps regiment in that first wave of American combat troops, and the 5th Marine regiment arrived in France in June 1917. A second Marine Corps regiment arrived in February 1918 and was brigaded with the first to form the 4th Marine Brigade under BGEN Charles A. Doyen.

The brigade took its place in the western-front trenches in March 1918 as part of the U.S. 2nd Division. In May the Germans attacked along the Aisne River and drove the Allies back some twelve miles, capturing Château-Thierry (5) on the Marne River. The Allied high command sent the U.S. 2nd Division to bolster the front. When the Germans attacked again on 2 June, the 2nd Division held its ground, and on 6 June it counterattacked at Belleau Wood (6) in a fight that lasted the entire month of June. The 4th Marine Brigade demonstrated appalling courage in this fight, taking more than five thousand casualties, including one thousand dead. Newspaper stories about the heroism of the 4th Marine Brigade aided USMC recruiting at home, and Congress authorized the enlargement of the Corps from 30,000 to 75,000 men.

In September MGEN John A. Lejeune, USMC, became the 2nd Division commander, and the 2nd joined the rest of the American First Army at St. Mihiel (7) for its first independent action. The German attacks of the summer had failed to break the Allies, and now it was time for the Allied counteroffensive. The 2nd Division was initially held in reserve during the St. Mihiel offensive, but when the U.S. attack stalled at Mont Blanc, Pershing called on the 2nd to break through. The 2nd Division assaulted Mont Blanc on 3 October and took the heights, again despite horrible casualties; in four days the 4th Marine Brigade lost another 2,300 men. For this action the French government awarded the Croix de Guerre to the 4th Marine Brigade.

The brigade fought literally until the last day of the war and was still attacking at noon on 11 November 1918 when news arrived that an armistice had been signed.

SHETLAND ISLANDS
FAIR ISLE
ORKNEY ISLANDS
AREA B (British)
AREA A (American)
AREA C (British)
NORTH SEA MINE BARRAGE
1
2
Scapa Flow
U.S. BATTLE SQUADRON SIX
NORWAY
Kristiansand
Skagerrak
Nautical Miles
0
50
100
150
HEBRIDES
Invergordon
Moray Firth
4
Inverness
SCOTLAND
3
Glasgow
Edinburgh
Firth of Forth
North Sea
DENMARK
North Channel
Newcastle
Belfast
IRELAND
Irish Sea
Dublin
Scarborough
Leeds
Kingston upon Hull
Liverpool
GERMAN FLEET BASE
Kiel Canal
Jade Bay
Elbe R.
Wilhelmshaven
Bremen
The Wash
Yarmouth
Lowestoft
HOLLAND (occupied)
Amsterdam
St. George's Channel
WALES
ENGLAND
GERMANY
Rhine River
GERMAN U-BOAT BASES
Cardiff
Bristol
London
Bristol Channel
Dover
Zeebrugge
Ostend
Dusseldorf
Cologne
Strait of Dover
Brussels
Exeter
Southampton
Portsmouth
BELGIUM (occupied)
Liège
WESTERN FRONT
English Channel
Meuse R.
LUXEMBOURG
Somme R.
Oise River
GERMAN DRIVE 1918
Cherbourg
Le Havre
6
Aisne R.
Verdun
Metz
CHANNEL ISLANDS
Belleau Wood
5
Seine River
Château Thierry
Marne River
7
Strasbourg
Rhine River
Paris
St. Mihiel Offensive
Brest
FRANCE
Orléans
Basel
Tours
SWITZERLAND
60°
55°
50°
5°
0°
10°

MAP 52

THE TREATY NAVIES

1921–1930

In August 1916, while the United States maintained a precarious neutrality in the European war, the Wilson administration sponsored a gigantic naval-expansion bill designed to ensure that the United States would be able to defend itself in the event of a German victory. The bill authorized the construction of 159 new ships, including 16 capital ships. With an appropriation of $500 million, it was not only the largest naval appropriation in the history of the United States, it was the single largest naval appropriation in the history of the world.

When the United States entered the war as a belligerent the following April, work on the sixteen capital ships was temporarily halted while U.S. yards produced the destroyers and transports necessary to sustain the Atlantic lifeline, but the capital-ship authorization was never rescinded. With the war over, Wilson used the threat of completing the 1916 program as a diplomatic weapon to bludgeon the Allies—particularly Britain—into accepting the League of Nations at Versailles. But he was less successful in selling the League to the U.S. Senate, which rejected the Versailles Treaty and the League of Nations. Unwilling to put its faith in collective security, the United States resumed work on the 1916 program.

But who was the presumed enemy for this fleet? The German Navy no longer existed. Interned at Scapa Flow after the armistice, its officers suspected (rightly) that the British would simply add the High Seas Fleet to the Royal Navy. To prevent that, they sank their own vessels as they lay at anchor on 21 June 1919, thus eliminating in a single day the second largest navy on earth. After that, the only possible opponent for an expanded U.S. dreadnought fleet was Britain itself. The warm relations between the United States and Britain, and a general disillusionment with the tools of war after the great bloodletting of 1914–1918, led many to wonder why America was building a battle fleet aimed at its closest ally. In June 1921 President Warren G. Harding invited Britain, Japan, France, and Italy to send representatives to a conference on naval-arms limitation at Washington. Harding also invited China, Holland, Portugal, and Belgium to participate in collateral discussions on the Far East.

The first session of this conference took place on 21 November 1921, when American Secretary of State Charles Evans Hughes stood to welcome the delegates. His speech was a bombshell. Hughes announced that the United States was prepared to scrap fifteen of its own battleships and to destroy eleven more that were under construction, thus reducing America's battle fleet to eighteen capital ships displacing just over five hundred thousand tons. But he was not through. Britain, he announced, must scrap twenty existing battleships, and Japan would scrap ten battleships plus six others under construction. The delegates were stunned, but Hughes had seized the high ground. Because the meeting was public, newspaper stories around the world praised the American proposal, and though modifications were made as the details were worked out, it remained the core of the final agreement signed almost a year later.

As finally approved, each of the five participating naval powers was allotted a specific number of capital ships and given a total tonnage limit for its capital-ship fleet (see chart). As older ships were replaced, the participating powers were required to keep under the tonnage limits of 525,000 for the United States and Britain, 315,000 for Japan, and 175,000 each for France and Italy—the famous 5:5:3 ratio. The agreement did not impose limits for smaller warships, and the limits on aircraft carriers were set so high that the treaty left plenty of room for growth and experimentation. Indeed, the United States obtained specific permission to convert two of its unfinished battlecruiser hulls into the aircraft carriers *Lexington* and *Saratoga*.

Because the Washington Treaty defined battleships as any vessel that exceeded ten thousand tons in displacement or that had guns larger than 8 inches, most of the participating nations subsequently built a number of so-called "treaty cruisers": vessels of exactly ten thousand tons with 8-inch guns. Eight years later in London, the signatory nations established national tonnage limits for these vessels as well, though Japan's continued emergence as a major power was recognized in a modification of the ratio from 5:5:3 to 10:10:7.

The Washington Conference also helped resolve pending problems in the Pacific. Britain was anxious to extricate itself from its alliance with Japan without angering the Japanese, and Japan sought a nonfortification clause to prevent the United States from turning Guam into an American bastion amidst the islands mandated to Japan by the League of Nations after World War I (see map). A clause in the naval-arms treaty stipulated that "no new fortifications or naval bases shall be established" in the Pacific, though the British received an exception for Singapore, and the United States was authorized to improve its bases in Hawaii. A largely meaningless Four-Power Pact (Britain, Japan, the United States, and France) replaced the Anglo-Japanese alliance, stipulating only that each nation would respect the rights of the others in the Pacific region.

The Four-Power Pact, a so-called Nine-Power Pact respecting the territorial integrity of China, and the "Treaty for the Limitation of Armament" were all signed in February 1922. Delegates also signed a pact outlawing submarine warfare, but because France declined to ratify it, it never went into effect. Though criticized by naval officers, the Washington Naval Disarmament Treaty was a victory for U.S. diplomacy. It maintained America's co-equal status with Britain as the world's greatest naval power, limited the growth of Japan's navy, and saved a considerable sum of money.

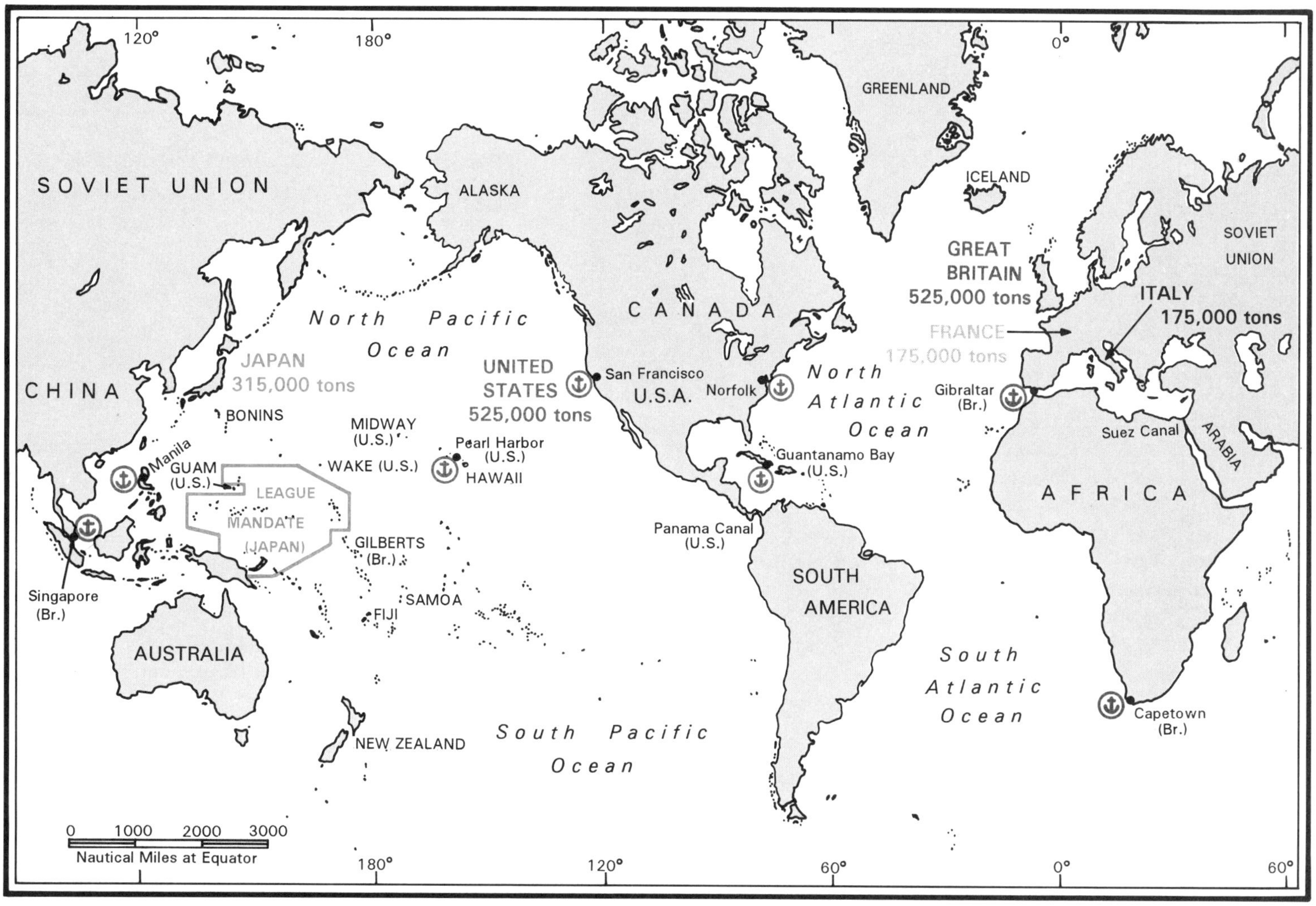

120° 180° 0°
GREENLAND
SOVIET UNION
ALASKA
ICELAND
SOVIET UNION
GREAT BRITAIN 525,000 tons
CANADA
ITALY 175,000 tons
North Pacific Ocean
FRANCE 175,000 tons
JAPAN 315,000 tons
UNITED STATES 525,000 tons
San Francisco
U.S.A.
Norfolk
North Atlantic Ocean
Gibraltar (Br.)
CHINA
BONINS
MIDWAY (U.S.)
Pearl Harbor (U.S.)
HAWAII
Suez Canal
ARABIA
Manila
GUAM (U.S.)
WAKE (U.S.)
Guantanamo Bay (U.S.)
LEAGUE MANDATE (JAPAN)
AFRICA
Panama Canal (U.S.)
GILBERTS (Br.)
Singapore (Br.)
SOUTH AMERICA
SAMOA
FIJI
AUSTRALIA
South Atlantic Ocean
Capetown (Br.)
NEW ZEALAND
South Pacific Ocean
0 1000 2000 3000
Nautical Miles at Equator
180° 120° 60° 0° 60°

CAPITAL SHIPS TO BE RETAINED OR DESTROYED
In Accordance with the "Treaty for the Limitation of Armament," 1922

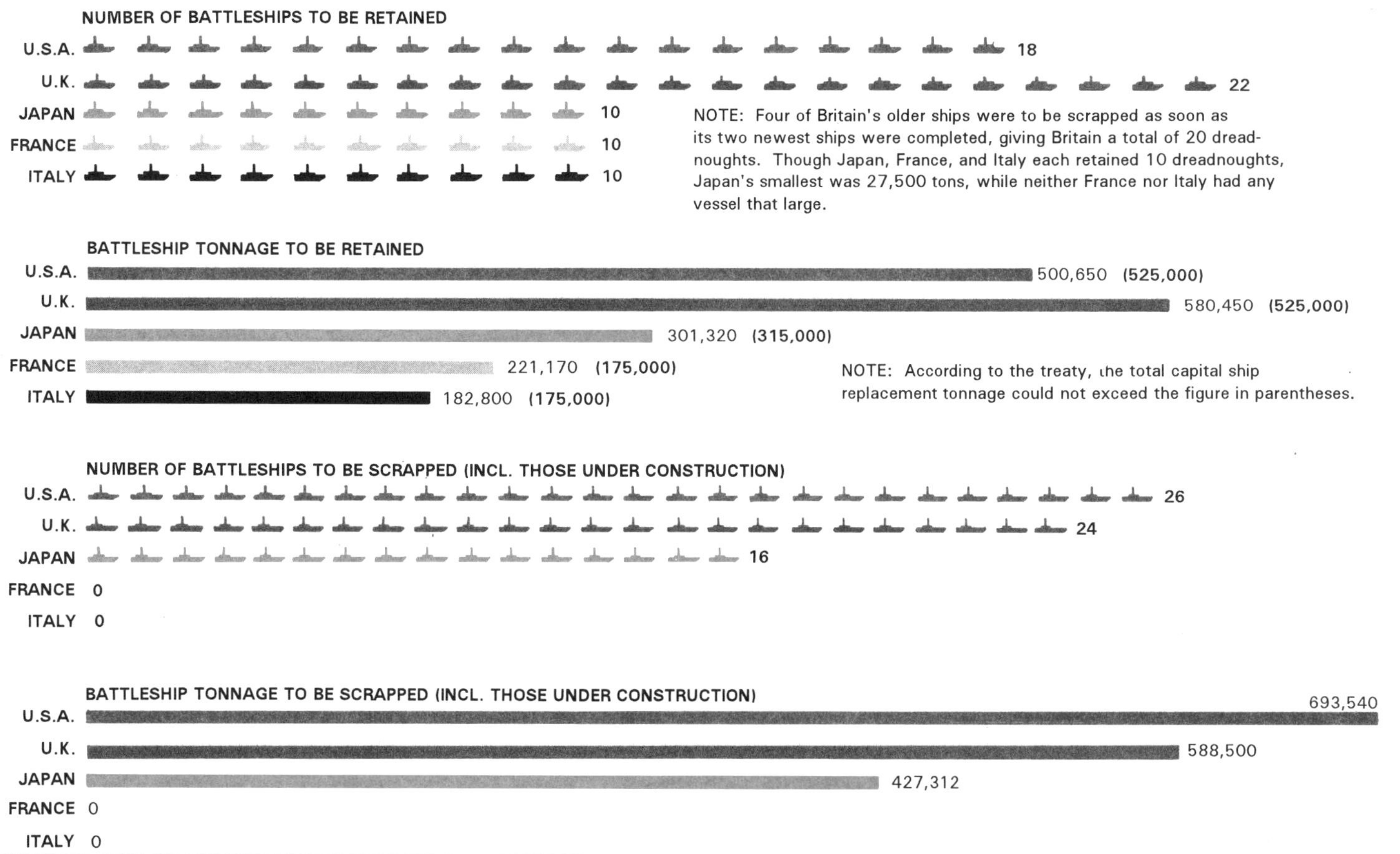

NUMBER OF BATTLESHIPS TO BE RETAINED

U.S.A.	18
U.K.	22
JAPAN	10
FRANCE	10
ITALY	10

NOTE: Four of Britain's older ships were to be scrapped as soon as its two newest ships were completed, giving Britain a total of 20 dreadnoughts. Though Japan, France, and Italy each retained 10 dreadnoughts, Japan's smallest was 27,500 tons, while neither France nor Italy had any vessel that large.

BATTLESHIP TONNAGE TO BE RETAINED

U.S.A.	500,650 (525,000)
U.K.	580,450 (525,000)
JAPAN	301,320 (315,000)
FRANCE	221,170 (175,000)
ITALY	182,800 (175,000)

NOTE: According to the treaty, the total capital ship replacement tonnage could not exceed the figure in parentheses.

NUMBER OF BATTLESHIPS TO BE SCRAPPED (INCL. THOSE UNDER CONSTRUCTION)

U.S.A.	26
U.K.	24
JAPAN	16
FRANCE	0
ITALY	0

BATTLESHIP TONNAGE TO BE SCRAPPED (INCL. THOSE UNDER CONSTRUCTION)

U.S.A.	693,540
U.K.	588,500
JAPAN	427,312
FRANCE	0
ITALY	0

Map 53

Planning for War: Orange to Rainbow

1922–1941

The first version of an American plan for the defeat of Japan in a Pacific war was patched together in 1911. In this plan, as in all of America's contingency war plans, the presumed enemy was identified only by color. Thus, the plan for the defeat of Japan was Plan Orange; the plan for a war against Britain was Plan Red; and the blueprint for a possible war against Germany was Plan Black. Because Japan seemed the most likely enemy after World War I, more attention was lavished on Plan Orange than on all the others combined.

The outline of Plan Orange was simple. It assumed that Orange (Japan) would attempt to expand its resource base in the South Pacific by attacking the American-held Philippines (1). It would be the Army's job to hold Manila Bay as long as possible while the U.S. battle fleet (Blue) assembled at Hawaii and pushed west for an eventual Jutland-like showdown with the Japanese main battle fleet. The naval encounter would take place somewhere in the western Pacific, with the Blue fleet defeating the Orange fleet and then steaming on to rescue the Philippines.

Before 1922 some planners assumed that the Blue fleet would be able to use Guam (2) as an advance base during its move to the western Pacific, but the nonfortification clause in the Washington Treaties made that impossible. After 1922, therefore, more attention was paid to the idea of establishing one or more temporary advance bases within the islands of the Japanese Mandate. In September 1922 the War Plans Division (WPD) of the General Board issued a revised Orange Plan that called for the seizure of Eniwetok (3) in the western Marshall Islands. At about the same time Marine Corps MAJ Earl "Pete" Ellis submitted a paper entitled "Advance Base Operations in Micronesia" that proposed an amphibious doctrine for seizing enemy-held islands. Ellis's paper became the basis of future Marine Corps planning for war in the Pacific in support of Plan Orange.

The problem with a staged advance through Micronesia was that even optimists agreed it would take up to six months before the American relief force could be expected to arrive at Manila. Such a schedule seemed to give up the idea of holding the Philippines. For more than a decade (1923–1933), therefore, planners in the WPD and at the Naval War College debated the relative wisdom of a so-called "Through Ticket to Manila." In this scenario, the fleet would steam nonstop from Pearl Harbor to Manila, refueling at sea, to save the Philippines before they were overwhelmed by the Japanese. A variation on this plan, forwarded in 1928, had the U.S. fleet steaming not to Manila but to Dumanquillas Bay (4) on the southern coast of Mindanao.

The idea of a "Through Ticket to Manila" was discarded in 1933 when CAPT Samuel Woods Bryant became director of the War Plans Division. He presided over modifications to Plan Orange that committed the Navy to the seizure of two advance bases in Micronesia before the leap to the Philippines. The first base would be at Eniwetok, and the second at Truk (5) in the Carolines, which boasted a deep and commodious harbor surrounded by protecting hills. This was also the first version of the Orange Plan that projected bypassing Japanese strong points—which was a key element in the U.S. advance through the Central Pacific in World War II. From Truk the U.S. advance could go in any one of five possible directions, depending on circumstances (see map).

In 1937–1938 U.S. planning underwent a dramatic reconsideration. The Japanese invasion of China and the German annexation of Austria confronted Navy planners with the possibility of a two-front war, and a single-color war plan no longer seemed sufficient. Planners began to construct a series of so-called Rainbow Plans, which posited that the United States might be part of an alliance fighting either Japan (Orange) or Germany (Black) or both. In 1940, the year that France fell to the German blitzkrieg, Plan Orange was formally abandoned in favor of a portfolio of Rainbow Plans.

Rainbow 1 and Rainbow 4 were essentially modified and updated versions of hemispheric defense plans that assumed an Allied collapse. Taken much more seriously were Rainbow 2 and Rainbow 3, which adapted much of the Orange Plan within an Allied framework. Thus, Rainbow 2 assumed that the U.S. Navy would cooperate with Britain (Red) against Japan (Orange) and use both Darwin, Australia (6), and Singapore (7) as advance bases. By 1941 Rainbow 5 seemed the most likely scenario of all. It posited a simultaneous two-front war by the United States in alliance with Britain against both Germany and Japan. The basic premise of Rainbow 5 was that the offensive character of Plan Orange would have to give way before the realization that Germany was the more serious of the two opponents and had to be dealt with first. The Navy was disappointed by the rejection of its offensive strategy but continued to believe that large parts of the original Orange Plan were still valid, particularly the concept of an island-hopping campaign across the central Pacific that would culminate in a showdown with the Japanese fleet.

Critics of Plan Orange claimed that it was largely a sham, repeatedly forwarded by the Navy primarily to justify requests for increased funding. Such criticism was not entirely unfounded, but the twenty-year exercise in planning nevertheless paid valuable dividends by forcing Navy leaders to consider important elements of the Navy's force structure that might otherwise have been ignored, especially long-range air patrol and logistic support. Though formally abandoned in 1940, the ghost of Plan Orange remained with the fleet and became evident in its long Pacific campaign in 1943–1945.

SOVIET UNION
MONGOLIA
MANCHURIA
Vladivostok
Peking
CHINA
KOREA (Japan)
Sea of Japan
Sea of Okhotsk
U.S.S.R.
JAPAN
KURIL IS. (Japan)
Tokyo
JAPAN
Pacific Ocean
Bering Sea
ALASKA
ALEUTIANS (U.S.)
Shanghai
East China Sea
Foochow
Canton
OKINAWA
BONINS (Japan)
MIDWAY (U.S.)
MARCUS (Japan)
WAKE (U.S.)
FORMOSA (Japan)
BURMA
INDOCHINA (Fr.)
SIAM
South China Sea
Manila
1
PHILIPPINES (U.S.)
2 GUAM (U.S.)
MARIANAS
JAPANESE
MANDATE
ENIWETOK
5
TRUK
3
MARSHALLS
CAROLINES
PLAN ORANGE
Pearl Harbor
HAWAII
RAINBOW TWO
4
Dumanquillas Bay
Singapore
7
SUMATRA
BORNEO
JAVA
Suribaya
NEW GUINEA
Rabaul
SOLOMON ISLANDS (Br.)
GILBERTS (Br.)
ELLICE IS. (Br.)
SAMOA
Darwin
6
NEW HEBRIDES (Br.)
FIJI ISLANDS (Br.)
Coral Sea
NEW CALEDONIA (Fr.)
Indian Ocean
AUSTRALIA
Brisbane
Sydney
Melbourne
Auckland
Tasman Sea
NEW ZEALAND
0 500 1000 1500
Nautical Miles at Equator
120°
150°
180°
60°
30°
0°
30°

PART VIII

World War II

1939–1945

THOUGH AMERICAN NAVAL PLANNERS focused most of their attention on a possible naval war with Japan, Adolf Hitler's rise to power in Germany forced them to consider other possible enemies as well. In the spring of 1938 soldiers of a revitalized German Army marched into Austria, preempting a scheduled plebiscite and completing what Germans called the *anschluss*, or reunification of German-speaking peoples. Almost at once, Hitler began to complain publicly that there were Germans in the Republic of Czechoslovakia as well—a nation patched together at Versailles from pieces of the old Hapsburg Empire. Hitler insisted that the Czechs were oppressing these Germans, who lived primarily in the border region known as the Sudetenland, and that they desired to "return" to their homeland, even though this region had never been part of Germany. The Czechs were prepared to fight for their borderlands, but at Munich in September of 1938 British Prime Minister Neville Chamberlain and French Foreign Minister Edouard Deladier abandoned their Czech ally and surrendered to Hitler's demands. The bankruptcy of Hitler's guarantees was revealed the following March when German forces swallowed up the rest of Czechoslovakia without regard for the nationality of its citizens.

The capitulation of the western democracies at Munich preserved peace for less than a year. In 1939 Hitler once again cited an "oppressed" German minority—this time in Poland—as a source of deep dissatisfaction. He insisted that the so-called Polish Corridor, created at Versailles to provide Poland with an outlet to the sea, be returned to Germany. Danzig, he declared, was a German city. This time England and France stood firm; they guaranteed Poland's frontiers, committing themselves to fight if Poland were attacked. Hitler's response startled the world as he signed a nonaggression pact with Soviet Russia. Thus bolstered, he struck at Poland on the first day of September. Hitler may have believed that Britain and France would back down once again, but instead two days later both nations declared war.

The battleship USS Arizona *sinks at its moorings after being hit by several bombs and torpedoes during the surprise Japanese attack on Pearl Harbor on 7 December 1941 (see map 54). The* Arizona *went down quickly after a Japanese bomb detonated its forward magazine. Eleven hundred men lost their lives on the* Arizona, *which was the only U.S. battleship not salvaged from the attack; it remains where it sank and is now a national memorial. (Official U.S. Navy photo)*

The outbreak of war in Europe cast the United States in a role similar to the one it had played in 1914–1917. This time, however, there was no effort to remain neutral in thought as well as deed. Franklin Roosevelt believed that American national interests were inextricably tied to an eventual Allied victory over fascism, and he was eager to support the Allied war effort. At first, it did not seem that any major effort would be necessary. After all, Britain and France between them possessed the world's largest navy and army. But the German seizure of Norway in April 1940 demonstrated Hitler's audacity, and the astounding success of the German *blitzkrieg* in May and June knocked France out of the war. Britain now stood alone against the threat of fascist hegemony in Europe.

These circumstances forced American policy makers to reconsider the nation's defense posture. The Vinson-Trammel Act, passed in 1934, had established an eight-year program to replace existing warships and bring the Navy up to the limits authorized by the Washington Treaty, and a second Vinson Act four years later had authorized another 20 percent increase. Now Congress approved plans that would more than double the size of the fleet. Roosevelt was willing to go even further and offer direct U.S. support of the British, but a majority of Americans continued to oppose such a step.

The fall of France left Britain standing alone against Hitler's Germany, and German occupation of the seaports of Norway and France meant that U-boats had easier access to the principal British trade routes. Desperate for more ships that could act as convoy escorts, Britain appealed to the United States for help. In July 1940 the two nations agreed to an arrangement whereby the United States turned over fifty of its World War I–vintage destroyers to the British in exchange for

ADM Yamamoto Isoroku planned the Japanese attack on Pearl Harbor (see map 54). By 1941 the Japanese high command had concluded that war with the United States was inevitable, and Yamamoto hoped his attack would neutralize the American fleet long enough to allow the Japanese to consolidate their conquests in the western Pacific. The Japanese planned to defend their conquests so fiercely that the Americans, whom they believed lacked the will to fight a long war, would eventually give up and go home. (Painting by Shugaku Homma, U.S. Naval Institute Archives)

basing rights in British western-hemisphere ports. And in December of that year Roosevelt announced "Lend Lease," effectively promising to act as Britain's arsenal, a policy that Congress approved in March 1941. Such behavior was markedly un-neutral, but Roosevelt believed that Hitler's defeat was essential to American national interests, and he was willing to stretch both the letter and the spirit of traditional definitions of neutrality.

In May 1941, in response to continued U-boat success in the Atlantic and the sortie of the German battleship *Bismarck* (see map 62), Roosevelt declared a national emergency. That summer, while Hitler turned his legions loose on Soviet Russia, American destroyers began so-called "neutrality patrols," escorting convoys as far as Iceland, which American forces had occupied. Then in September an American destroyer, the USS *Greer,* while aggressively tracking a submerged German U-boat in the North Atlantic, became a combatant when the German submarine fired a torpedo at it and the *Greer* responded with a depth-charge attack. Two months later the USS *Reuben James,* while escorting a British convoy west of Ireland, became the first American warship to be sunk in the war. Neither of these events prompted a declaration of war, though it certainly looked like war to the American sailors who served on the North Atlantic convoys.

Meanwhile, relations between the United States and Japan were deteriorating as well. With the fall of France in June 1940, French colonies in Asia became easy prey, and in September the Japanese occupied the northern half of French Indochina. Combined with the continued Japanese presence in China, this new aggression strengthened the hand of hardliners in the U.S. State Department, and the United States adopted a series of economic sanctions designed to force the Japanese to change their behavior. First, the United States halted the sale of aviation fuel to Japan and soon afterward extended the embargo to include iron and steel. In response, the Japanese signed a defensive pact with Germany and Italy (the Tripartite Pact), and thus emboldened, they declared a protec-

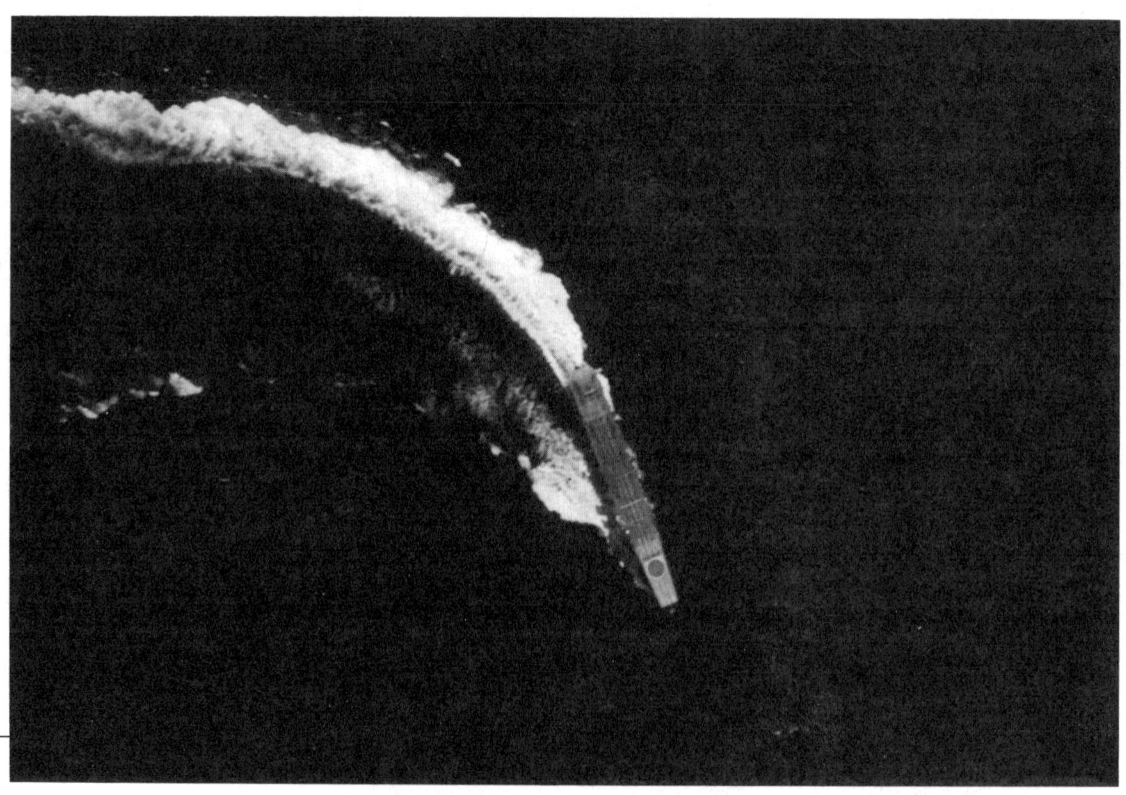

A dive-bomber's eye view of the Japanese carrier Soryu *at the Battle of Midway. American dive-bombers sank all four of the Japanese carriers in the main strike force—the* Soryu *by planes from the carrier* Yorktown *(see map 59). The crushing Japanese defeat at Midway was a major turning point in the Pacific war. (Official U.S. Navy photo)*

torate over all of Indochina in July. That announcement provoked the final crisis.

Japan's startling rise to world prominence had been accomplished within half a century—and the fuel that drove its industrial engine was oil. Like England, Japan had virtually no petroleum resources of its own and could not survive without oil imports, most of which came from the United States. It was a matter of the highest consequence, therefore, when in response to the Japanese occupation of Indochina the United States cut off oil exports to Japan. Japanese leaders had but two options: to swallow their pride and accept American conditions in order to continue to buy American oil, or to defy the United States and find an alternate source of petroleum. Japanese military leaders, who were increasingly calling the shots, were utterly incapable of giving serious consideration to the first option, and they, therefore, looked elsewhere for alternative sources of oil.

Their eyes fell upon the oil-rich islands of the Dutch East Indies. Because Nazi Germany now occupied Holland, the Dutch were in no position to resist Japanese seizure of their colony. The problem was that the American-controlled Philippines lay directly astride the potential lines of communication from the Dutch East Indies to Japan. The Japanese high command found intolerable the notion that the United States would remain in a position to threaten Japan's economic lifeline and concluded that the Philippines, too, must be taken. That, of course, meant war with the United States. In September 1941 Japanese Army and Navy planners determined that unless the United States altered its demands, "We shall immediately decide to open hostilities against the United States, Great Britain, and the Netherlands." That same month Japanese Navy planners submitted an outline for a carrier-based air strike on the U.S. battleship fleet at Pearl Harbor. In October continued pressure by the military forced the resignation of Prince Konoye as prime minister, who was replaced by the leader of the war faction, GEN Tojo Hideki. From that moment war was inevitable.

The originator of the concept of a surprise attack on the American naval base at Pearl Harbor was ADM Yamamoto Isoroku. (During World War II Japanese names were correctly rendered with the family name first—a practice that will be followed here.) Yamamoto had lived and traveled extensively in the United States and had the greatest respect for its seemingly unlimited resources and industrial capability. He believed that war with such a power should be avoided if possible, but that if war was unavoidable only a devastating surprise attack that crippled or destroyed the U.S. fleet would give the Japanese the time needed to conquer and consolidate its resource base in Southeast Asia. His idea seemed overly bold to many Japanese officers, but Yamamoto was adamant. The plan presented by his staffers in September called for a strike by four carriers that would cross the Pacific in the seldom-traveled northern latitudes to avoid detection. Yamamoto approved the plan but increased the strike force from four carriers to six—he would stake everything on one desperate gamble.

In late November, while Japanese diplomats in Washington sought to convince the United States to moderate its position and lift the oil embargo, Japanese naval forces put to sea from their isolated base in the southern Kuriles to rendezvous at sea and begin their fateful journey east.

VADM Marc Mitscher commanded the fast carrier force throughout most of the war in the Pacific. Called Task Force 38 when it was part of Halsey's Third Fleet, and Task Force 58 when it was part of Spruance's Fifth Fleet, the fast carrier force was the striking arm of the U.S. Navy and participated in every major campaign of the central Pacific drive. (Official U.S. Navy photo)

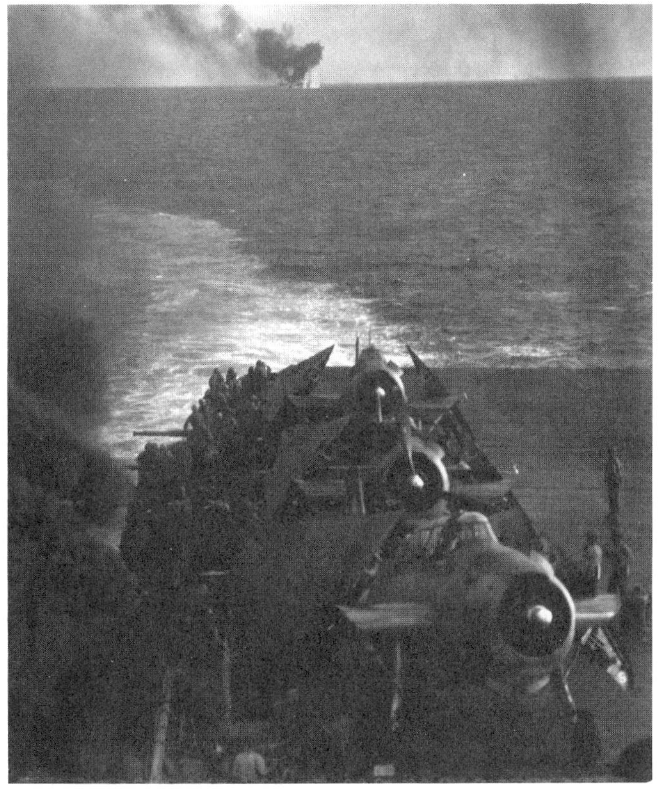

Shell splashes from Japanese surface ships can be seen bracketing the USS Gambier Bay *in this photograph taken from the escort carrier* Kitkun Bay *during the Battle off Samar on 25 October 1944 (see map 75). Part of the gigantic engagement known as the Battle of Leyte Gulf, this battle was the only time in the Pacific war that surface fire sank a carrier. (Official U.S. Navy photo)*

MAP 54

PEARL HARBOR

7 DECEMBER 1941

Commanded by VADM Nagumo Chuichi, the Japanese strike force of six carriers, screened by a light cruiser and nine destroyers and supported by two battleships and two heavy cruisers, sortied from a remote naval base on the island of Etorofu in the Kuriles (1) on 26 November. That same day Secretary of State Cordell Hull informed Japan's envoys in Washington that any long-term settlement to the Far Eastern crisis had to include a Japanese evacuation of China. Informed of the American hard line, Tojo's government issued orders for the military plans to proceed. In addition to Nagumo's Pearl Harbor strike force, other forces moved out of Japanese ports and steamed south toward British possessions in Malaya and toward the Philippines.

American intelligence analysts, noting the increased shipping activity, speculated that the Japanese planned some aggressive action in the Southwest Pacific within the week. On 27 November the Navy issued a "war warning" to its Pacific commands—including Hawaii. No one, however, genuinely expected that Pearl Harbor was a likely target; it was simply unimaginable. Meanwhile, Nagumo's force steamed east along the forty-third parallel, well north of any well-traveled shipping lanes. The Japanese fleet maintained strict radio silence, and even the weather seemed to cooperate, for the heavy cloud cover and rough seas kept Nagumo's strike force enshrouded in a cocoon of secrecy.

On 3 December, 2,100 miles east of the Kuriles and 1,300 miles almost due north of Midway Island, Nagumo turned his fleet to the southeast (2), aiming for a launch position 230 miles north of Oahu. Early in the morning on 6 December Nagumo received the latest intelligence from Pearl Harbor—the American battleships were present, and nothing suggested that the Americans suspected anything out of the ordinary. But there was bad news too—the American carriers were not in port. Greatly disappointed, Nagumo momentarily considered calling off the attack, but his subordinates convinced him to continue.

At 9:00 P.M. Nagumo turned his ships due south (3) and increased speed to twenty-six knots. There was no turning back now. The hands were assembled on the flight decks of the carriers and encouraged by patriotic speeches. Afterward, the battle ensign from Admiral Togo's flagship at the Battle of Tsushima, a sacred icon, was raised to the masthead on Nagumo's flagship, the *Akagi.* At dawn Nagumo ordered two float planes from his cruisers to make a reconnaissance of the American base. They reported that nothing had changed—all was quiet. At 6:00 A.M. Nagumo ordered the strike force to launch (4).

The Pearl Harbor naval base was just coming to life on a Sunday morning (see lower map). Not everyone was asleep. Alerted by the war warning from Washington the week before, the Navy was maintaining routine destroyer patrols off the harbor entrance, and during the night the USS *Condor* had sighted an unidentified submarine periscope. At 6:30, while Nagumo's planes were rolling off the decks of their carriers, the USS *Ward* attacked and sank a midget submarine inside the harbor. The *Ward's* commanding officer reported the sinking, but the duty officer did not relay the information to higher command authority because the telephone communications system was unmanned on a Sunday morning. At 7:02 an Army private manning one of two active radar sets on the northern coast of Oahu reported what appeared to be a flight of inbound aircraft, but the second lieutenant on duty, knowing that B-17 bombers were due in from California, told him to "forget it." Forty minutes later the first wave of 191 Japanese torpedo planes, dive-bombers, and fighters swooped down on the American naval base.

The Japanese pilots knew what to look for and quickly focused on the line of gray hulls along "battleship row" adjacent to Ford Island. The *Oklahoma,* moored outboard of the *Maryland,* took three torpedo hits almost at once and began to capsize. Likewise the *West Virginia,* directly astern of the *Oklahoma* and outboard of the *Tennessee,* took two hits. The *Arizona,* moored inboard of a small repair ship providing little protection, was hit by torpedoes and bombs, one of which struck the forward magazine and caused a spectacular explosion. She sank quickly, taking more than 1,100 officers and men with her. The *California,* at the head of battleship row, also went down, and the inboard ships *Maryland* and *Tennessee* were severely damaged.

A second Japanese wave struck a few minutes before 9:00. The *Nevada,* which had managed to get under way and was headed for the open sea, veered off to the right under the impetus of this new attack and beached itself (5) to avoid sinking in the ship channel. Japanese pilots then concentrated on the USS *Pennsylvania* in dry dock (6), but the Americans were fully alerted now, and this wave failed to duplicate the success of the first attack. By 9:30 it was all over. The Pacific Fleet battleships were all but destroyed: four had been sunk, and two others were badly damaged. But though it was not immediately evident, what the Japanese had missed was almost as important as what they had hit. The American carriers were at sea delivering planes to the garrisons at Wake and Midway and thus were spared. The Pearl Harbor repair facilities were relatively undamaged, and the submarine base and oil-reserve tanks (7) survived unscathed. Then, too, the "infamy" of the surprise attack on a Sunday morning galvanized the slumbering giant of the United States, whose citizens vowed to "Remember Pearl Harbor!"

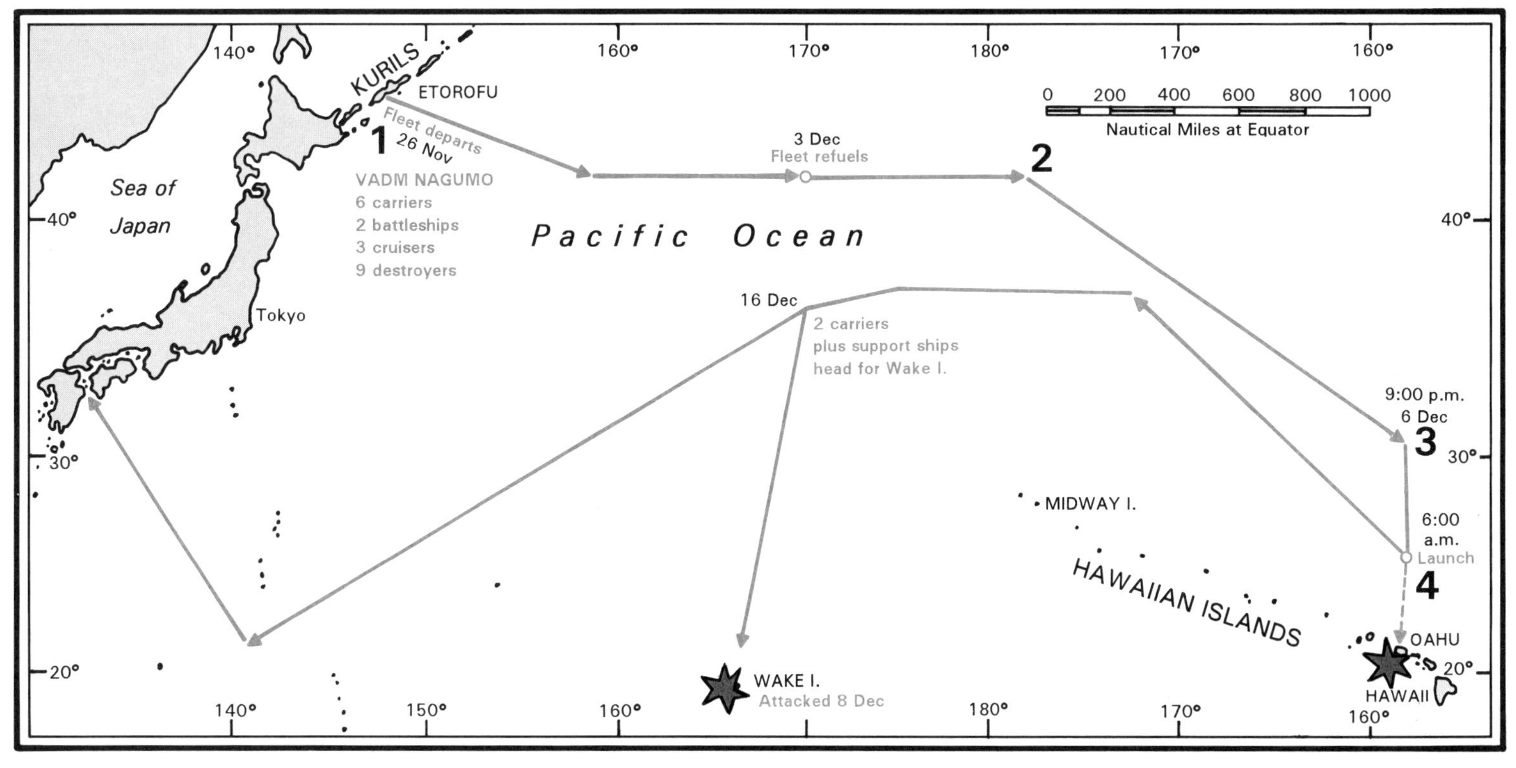

140°
160°
170°
180°
170°
160°
KURILS
ETOROFU
Fleet departs
1
26 Nov
VADM NAGUMO
6 carriers
2 battleships
3 cruisers
9 destroyers
3 Dec
Fleet refuels
2
0 200 400 600 800 1000
Nautical Miles at Equator
Sea of
Japan
Pacific Ocean
40°
Tokyo
16 Dec
2 carriers
plus support ships
head for Wake I.
9:00 p.m.
6 Dec
3
30°
6:00
a.m.
Launch
4
MIDWAY I.
HAWAIIAN ISLANDS
OAHU
HAWAII
20°
WAKE I.
Attacked 8 Dec
140°
150°
160°
180°
170°
160°

Pearl City
East Loch
Whitney
Phoenix
Middle Loch
Dobbin
Aiea Bay
Detroit
Raleigh
Solace
Medura
UTAH
Tangier
Curtiss
NEVADA
ARIZONA
Ford Island Airfield
TENNESSEE
Vestal
MARYLAND
WEST VIRGINIA
OKLAHOMA
Neosho
CALIFORNIA
Ramapo
New Orleans
San Francisco
Honolulu
CinCPACFLT HQ
Avocet
Oglala
Helena
7
West Loch
5
NEVADA
aground
Shaw
6
Oil
Tanks
Submarine
Base
PENNSYLVANIA
U.S. NAVAL STATION
Naval
Hospital
Oil Tank Farm
7
Helm
Hickam Field
PEARL HARBOR
7 December 1941, 7:00 a.m.
0 1/2 1
Nautical Mile
NOTE: Battleships are labelled in CAPITAL LETTERS

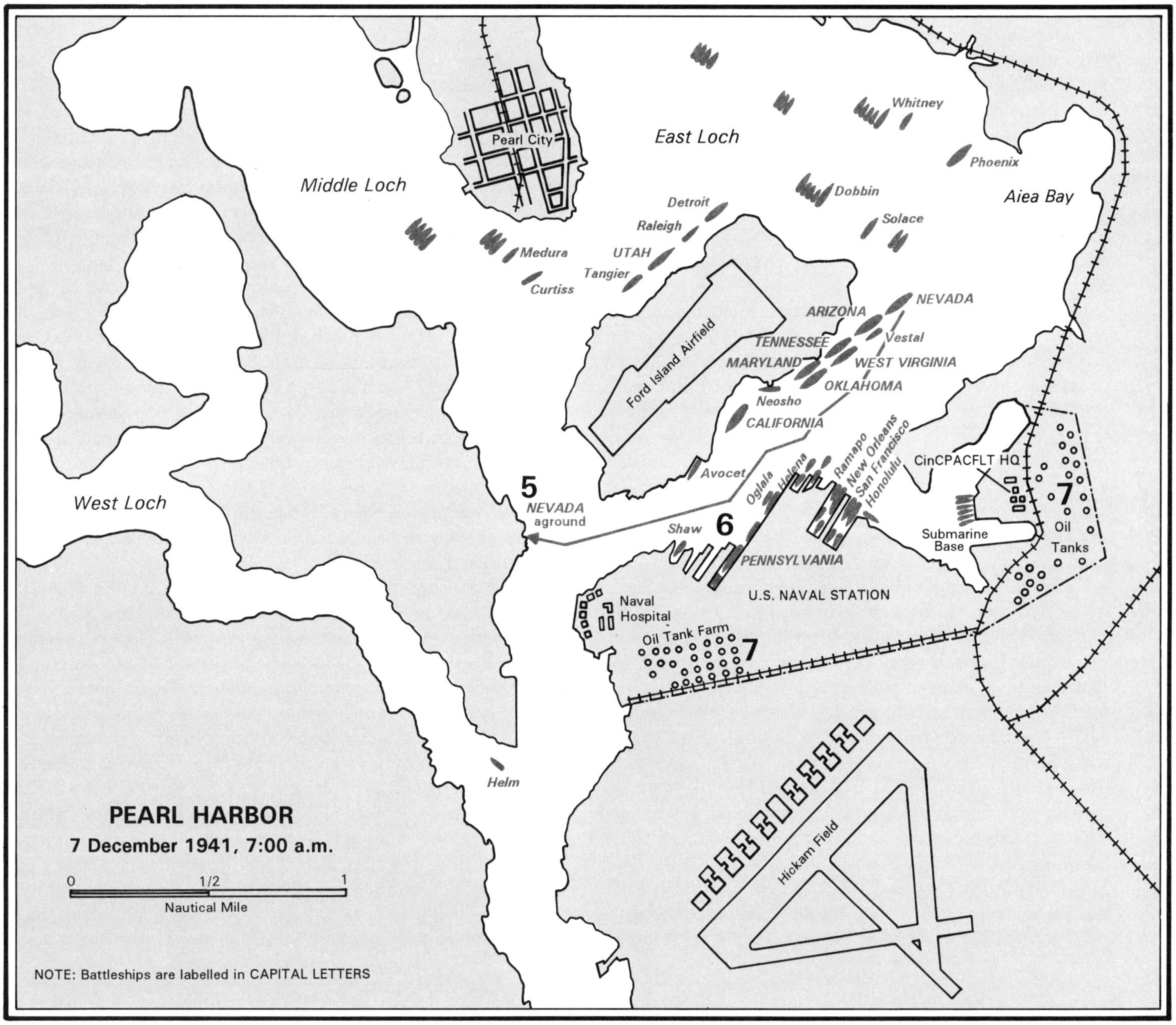

MAP 55

THE RISING SUN

DECEMBER 1941–APRIL 1942

Four days after the Pearl Harbor attack Hitler honored the spirit of the Tripartite Pact by declaring war on the United States. Though not obligated to do so, Hitler may have calculated that because the United States was already providing Britain "all aid short of war," he risked little by formalizing the conflict already under way in the Atlantic. Hitler's declaration brought the United States fully into the war, and despite the frenzy of anti-Japanese sentiment in the United States after the surprise attack, U.S. planners were not prepared to abandon their commitment to a Germany-first strategy. American and British planners alike agreed that Germany was the most dangerous of the Axis powers and that the longer Hitler remained master of Europe, the more dangerous he would become. Therefore, although emotion fed an American desire to go on the offensive in the Pacific, reason and prior commitment compelled a different strategy.

Even without that commitment, the United States could not have launched an early counterattack against Japan for the simple reason that it lacked the assets to do so. With its Pacific Fleet battleship force on the bottom of Pearl Harbor, the United States had to rely on its few aircraft carriers and a handful of submarines to carry on the war in the Pacific. A string of unbroken Japanese victories, therefore, characterized the first five months of the war.

The day after the Pearl Harbor attack Japanese amphibious groups landed on the Malay peninsula (1) at Singora in Siam (Thailand) and at Khota Baru in British-held Malaya, threatening the back door to the British bastion at Singapore (2). The British dispatched a task force composed of the battleship *Prince of Wales* and the battlecruiser *Repulse,* escorted by four destroyers, to attack the enemy transports. The British had already turned back from this sortie when Japanese land-based bombers from Saigon located the task force on 10 December and sank both capital ships (3), further proof of the importance of air cover for surface combatants. Over the next two months the Japanese advanced down the Malay peninsula toward Singapore, which surrendered on 15 February—a devastating blow to British pride.

On the same day the Japanese sank the *Repulse* and *Prince of Wales,* other Japanese forces landed on Luzon (4), the largest of the Philippine islands, and Japan followed up this initial landing with many others over the next two weeks. American and Filipino forces were soon hemmed in on the Bataan peninsula (5), which, according to the Orange Plan long since abandoned, they were to hold until American naval forces fought their way across the Central Pacific to rescue them. President Roosevelt recalled GEN Douglas MacArthur from the Philippines, supposedly to organize a relief expedition in Australia. But there could be no rescue because there were simply not enough American or Allied forces in the Pacific to mount a relief expedition. The eighty thousand men left behind on Bataan under LGEN Jonathan Wainwright held out until early April before capitulating in the largest surrender of American military forces in history. The island of Corregidor in Manila Bay held out until May. The Bataan "Death March" that followed the American surrender rendered it even more horrible, as the Japanese herded their captives on a brutal march to prisoner-of-war camps.

With the devastation of British and American forces in the Southwest Pacific, the Allies decided to pool their remaining resources into a unified command composed of American, British, Dutch, and Australian units—called ABDA. The overall commander of ABDA was Sir Archibald Wavell, a British Army field marshall whose highest priority was the defense of the Malay barrier and, until it fell, the citadel of Singapore. The commander of ABDA naval forces was an American, ADM Thomas Hart, who believed that Singapore was doomed and who was more interested in the defense of Java and Australia.

ABDA naval forces fought several minor skirmishes and one major naval battle. On 27 February 1942 an ABDA task force of five cruisers and nine destroyers, commanded by Dutch ADM K. W. F. Doorman, set out from Surabaya (6), intending to intercept a Japanese invasion force steaming for Java. In the Battle of the Java Sea (7) a Japanese force of four cruisers and fourteen destroyers under RADM Takagi Takeo badly mauled the ABDA force in a confused six-hour surface action. The Allied survivors, the cruisers USS *Houston* and HMAS *Perth,* while passing through the Sunda Strait, fell in with the Japanese invasion fleet in Banten Bay (8) and shot up several transports, thereby somewhat evening the score. The Japanese had the last word, however, when three Japanese cruisers and thirteen destroyers set upon and sank the *Perth* and *Houston,* the *Houston* going down with its flag still flying.

There were a few bright moments for American forces in these dark times. In December the garrison of tiny Wake Island (not on the map) put up a gallant defense and even threw back a Japanese invasion force before eventually capitulating. In January four U.S. destroyers from Kupang in Timor (9) charged into Balikpapan Bay (10) and sank four Japanese transports and a patrol boat. Elsewhere the Japanese victories continued. Borneo, Java, and Sumatra all fell to Japanese invasion forces, and hoping to avoid the same fate, Thailand's government signed an alliance with Japan. The Japanese bombed Darwin in Australia (11), and Vice Admiral Nagumo took his Pearl Harbor strike force of carriers through the Strait of Malacca into the Indian Ocean (12), where it raided British bases in India and Ceylon. By early spring the Japanese had conquered an ocean empire of some ten thousand square miles and had secured the resource base that they hoped would make them both self-reliant and invulnerable.

CHINA
Foochow
Japanese Control
Taipei
Japanese Control
FORMOSA (Japan)
RYUKYU IS.
OKINAWA (Japan)
BURMA invaded 12 Dec
Hanoi
Hong Kong (Br.) falls 25 Dec
HAINAN (Japan)
Rangoon falls Mar 42
SIAM invaded 9 Dec
Bangkok
Andaman Sea
INDOCHINA (Japan)
Saigon
Gulf of Siam
South China Sea
Landings 10 Dec
4
Landings 22 Dec
LUZON
5
BATAAN falls 9 Apr
Manila falls 2 Jan
Landings 12 Dec
PHILIPPINES (U.S.)
PALAWAN
Sulu Sea
MINDANAO falls 10 May
Landings 20 Dec
12
VADM NAGUMO
4 carriers
Mar-Apr 42
Landings 8 Dec
Singora
1
Khota Baru
MALAYA
3
REPULSE & PRINCE OF WALES sunk 10 Dec
Strait of Malacca
2
Singapore (Br.) falls 15 Feb
SUMATRA (Dutch)
Landings 14 Feb
Landings 14 Dec
Landings 17 Jan
Celebes Sea
Landings 23 Dec
NORTH BORNEO (Br.)
Landings 11 Jan
Landings 11 Jan
BORNEO
falls Jan 42
Balikpapan
10
CELEBES
falls Jan 42
Java Sea
8
Battle of Banten Bay 1 Mar
Landings 28 Feb
7
Battle of the Java Sea 27 Feb
Sunda Strait
JAVA (Dutch)
Surabaya
6
Landings 18 Feb
Banda Sea
THE MALAY BARRIER
9
Kupang
TIMOR
EXTENT OF JAPANESE CONQUESTS BY MAY 1942
Indian Ocean
11
Darwin
AUSTRALIA
0 100 200 300 400 500 600
Nautical Miles
100° 110° 120° 130°
20° 10° 0° 10° 20°

MAP 56

DIVIDED AMERICAN COMMAND

JANUARY–MAY 1942

During ABDA's brief history, the various Allied commanders had occasionally bickered over how to deploy their scarce assets. The collapse of ABDA in March 1942 left the Pacific war in the hands of the Americans but did not end political squabbling over priorities. Once the United States assumed sole responsibility for the conduct of the Pacific war, American planners agreed that a return to the Philippines should be the focus of their strategy, but they did not agree about the best way to achieve that objective.

General MacArthur, who had the greatest personal and professional investment in a quick return to the Philippines, argued for the most direct route: from Australia north to New Guinea (1), then along the length of New Guinea to Mindanao (2), a route he called the New Guinea–Mindanao axis. But the Navy had other ideas. For more than thirty years Plan Orange had dominated Navy planning, and its key element was a drive across the Central Pacific (see map 53). Though Plan Orange itself had been formally abandoned, the Navy's long commitment to its principles and the expertise that the Marine Corps had developed in ship-to-shore amphibious operations made the Central Pacific the Navy's preferred route. The Navy envisioned an island-hopping campaign from Hawaii to the Marshalls (3), the Carolines (4), the Marianas (5), and finally the Philippines (6) or possibly Formosa.

MacArthur's performance in defense of the Philippines had been mediocre at best, but in the unhappy winter of 1941–1942 the public seized upon him as a symbol of defiance and strength and made him a hero—at least in the movie newsreels. President Roosevelt encouraged this perception to the extent of conferring a Medal of Honor on MacArthur, who capitalized on his public image to make a bid for supreme command in the Pacific theater. The American chief of naval operations, ADM Ernest J. King, a tough-minded, no-nonsense flag officer, was a fierce defender of the Navy's role and refused to consider placing the Pacific Fleet under the operational command of an Army general, and especially of MacArthur, whom he considered unqualified to direct naval operations. The impasse led to a divided command.

Early in 1942, with the Japanese still expanding southward, the Allied Combined Chiefs of Staff divided the Pacific into two command theaters. MacArthur would command the Southwest Pacific Area (SoWesPac) from his headquarters at Brisbane, Australia, a command that included the continent of Australia and the larger islands of the Southwest Pacific, including the Philippines. His job would be to direct an advance along the New Guinea–Mindanao axis to achieve his return to the Philippines. At the same time Texas-born ADM Chester Nimitz, headquartered at Pearl Harbor, would command the Pacific Ocean Area (POA) and coordinate a drive across the Central Pacific. Each theater commander would control all forces—land, air, and sea—within his theater. At the same time, Allied planners hoped to pressure the Japanese from both China and Burma, thus forcing the enemy to fight on four fronts.

The decision to divide American command in the Pacific violated one of the most fundamental principles of warfare: unity of command. The two-pronged American offensive gave the Japanese an opportunity to concentrate their combined forces against first one and then the other of the American offensives. Moreover, the existence of two independent American commands resulted in a great deal of duplication of effort as each theater boasted its own command structure and logistic-support system. Finally, the two commands competed with each other for scarce resources, especially landing craft and airplanes. The decision to divide command in the Pacific between the Army and the Navy—between MacArthur and Nimitz—was as much the product of political and personality considerations as a careful consideration of strategic and military factors. During the Pacific war the intensity of the competition between the two theaters was so fierce it was sometimes hard to tell who the enemy was: the Japanese or the rival American service.

While these decisions were being confirmed in Washington, two widely separated events in the Pacific set the stage for important and dramatic confrontations between American and Japanese forces. In a mission that was primarily a gesture of American defiance, sixteen Army Air Corps B-25 bombers under the command of LCOL "Jimmy" Doolittle succeeded in bombing Japan's capital city of Tokyo on 18 April (7). In a rare example of interservice cooperation, the land-based planes flew from the deck of the carrier *Hornet* (Rear Admiral Halsey). Doolittle's B-25s dropped their ordnance in "thirty seconds over Tokyo," then flew on to airfields in China. Though the raid did little material damage, it had important strategic consequences. Admiral Yamamoto felt humiliated, fearing that he had failed in his first duty to protect the homeland and the life of the emperor. The raid convinced him to proceed with his plan for a major offensive aimed at Midway, to eliminate the offensive potential of the U.S. fleet.

Other events a thousand miles to the south also influenced Japanese planners. In March carrier-based Navy planes flying over the Owen Stanley Mountains on New Guinea swooped down on Japanese forces in Huon Gulf (8), sinking four ships and damaging nine others. This raid impressed the Japanese with the need to control the waters around New Guinea, and particularly the city of Port Moresby (9). Their decision to seize Port Moresby led to the first fleet action of the war between Japanese and American forces.

A smiling Franklin Roosevelt sits between his two grim-visaged Pacific commanders on board the cruiser Baltimore *in July 1944. GEN Douglas MacArthur (left) and ADM Chester Nimitz (right) differed from each other in outlook and personality as well as service affiliation. (Official U.S. Navy photo)*

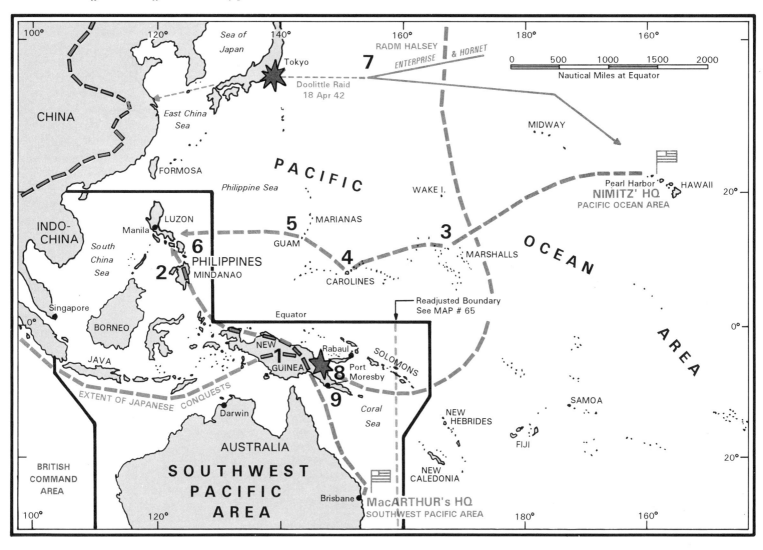

MAP 57

BATTLE OF THE CORAL SEA

7–8 MAY 1942

The Japanese first sought to capture Port Moresby by attacking southward from Buna (1) along the Kokoda Trail over the Owen Stanley Mountains, but tough Australian jungle fighters turned them back. Japanese planners thereupon decided that rather than fight their way over the mountains, they would instead seize Port Moresby by means of an amphibious landing. Nimitz learned of the Japanese plan thanks to a handful of naval officers under the direction of LCDR Joseph Rochefort, who pored over Japanese radio intercepts in a basement room under the 14th Naval District headquarters in Pearl Harbor. In mid-April Rochefort was able to inform Nimitz of the Japanese plan and even predicted that the operation would begin around 3 May.

The news created a dilemma for King and Nimitz. Two U.S. carrier task groups were with Halsey more than two thousand miles to the west, preparing to launch Doolittle's B-25s for the raid on Tokyo, and probably would not be back in time. With the *Saratoga* still refitting on the U.S. West Coast, that left only two carriers that Nimitz might use to counter this Japanese thrust. Nevertheless, King ordered Nimitz to send the *Lexington* from Pearl Harbor to join RADM Frank Jack Fletcher's *Yorktown* force in the Coral Sea (2). MacArthur contributed three cruisers and a handful of destroyers under the command of Australian RADM J. G. Crace.

Like many Japanese operational plans during the war, the blueprint for the capture of Port Moresby was unnecessarily complicated. Despite clear superiority in ships and planes, VADM Inouye Shigeyoshi at Rabaul (3) divided his forces into four groups. The smallest of these, centered around a seaplane tender, would seize Tulagi (4) in the Solomon Islands and establish a seaplane base. The Port Moresby invasion force (5) would steam due south from Rabaul, screened by another force consisting of the light carrier *Shoho* and four cruisers (6) proceeding south from Truk in the Carolines under RADM Goto Arimoto. Finally, the main Japanese strike force (7) of two fleet carriers under RADM Takagi Takeo would swing around the Solomons and enter the Coral Sea from the east.

The Japanese operation began on schedule. On 3 May Japanese forces occupied Tulagi, and the next day Fletcher launched three air strikes against Tulagi from the *Yorktown* (8). The raids did little important damage, and they revealed Fletcher's presence to the enemy, but fortunately Takagi's two heavy carriers were still out of range (9), delayed by orders to deliver fighter planes to Rabaul.

Reunited with the *Lexington* (10), Fletcher moved west with both American carriers toward the anticipated position of the Japanese invasion force in the Jomard Passage (11). Meanwhile, Takagi rounded the easternmost island of the Solomon chain, and he, too, headed west (12). For most of two days each force searched for the other. Both were searching in a fog—almost literally—for a band of foul weather stretched across the Coral Sea, obscuring ships from the searching scout planes of both forces. Peering through the cloud cover at 7:30 A.M. on 7 May, a Japanese scout-plane pilot reported an American carrier and a cruiser to the south (13). Takagi at once launched a full strike to get in the first blow. But the target was not an American carrier—it was the fleet oiler *Neosho* and the destroyer *Sims.* Jumped by overwhelming Japanese forces, both ships succumbed to repeated hits and went down, but they unwittingly kept Takagi's attention away from the real prize—the American carriers.

That same morning one of the *Yorktown's* scout planes also made a false report, identifying enemy cruisers near the Jomard Passage as carriers. Now it was Fletcher's turn to jump at the bait, and he launched a full strike toward this reported contact. But luck favored the Americans because, en route to the two cruisers, the Americans sighted the escort carrier *Shoho* and the Japanese covering force (14). At once they dove to the attack and sent the *Shoho* to the bottom. The jubilant flight commander, LCDR R. E. Dixon, radioed back, "Scratch one flattop!"

The errors of the morning continued into the afternoon. Fletcher had detached Crace's cruiser-destroyer force to watch the outlet from the Jomard Passage, and Takagi's scouts reported Crace's ships as carriers. Once again Takagi ordered an attack, but this time fighters from the *Lexington* intercepted his bombers. The visibility was so poor, and the fighting so confused, that several Japanese pilots actually tried to land on the *Lexington.*

The two carrier forces finally spotted each other on 8 May, and both launched full deck loads of bombers and fighters (15). American bombers missed the *Zuikaku,* hidden by a rainsquall, but badly damaged the *Shokaku,* bending her deck plates so that she could not launch or recover planes. Meanwhile, Japanese pilots put two torpedoes and two bombs into the *Lexington* and made one bomb hit on the *Yorktown.* Both ships were damaged, but neither fatally—or so it seemed. Hours later, however, two internal explosions rocked the *Lexington,* and CAPT Frederick Sherman had to order abandon ship. The *Lexington* had to be "put down" by a torpedo from a U.S. destroyer.

The loss of the *Lexington* was a heavy blow to the Americans, representing as it did 25 percent of America's carrier force in the Pacific. But the American decision to commit the carrier forces to the defense of Port Moresby was justified when the Japanese ordered the invasion force to reverse course and return to Rabaul (16). In that respect, the battle can easily be considered an American strategic victory despite the loss of the *Lexington.* Moreover, neither the *Shokaku* nor the *Zuikaku* would be repaired in time to participate in the upcoming battle for Midway.

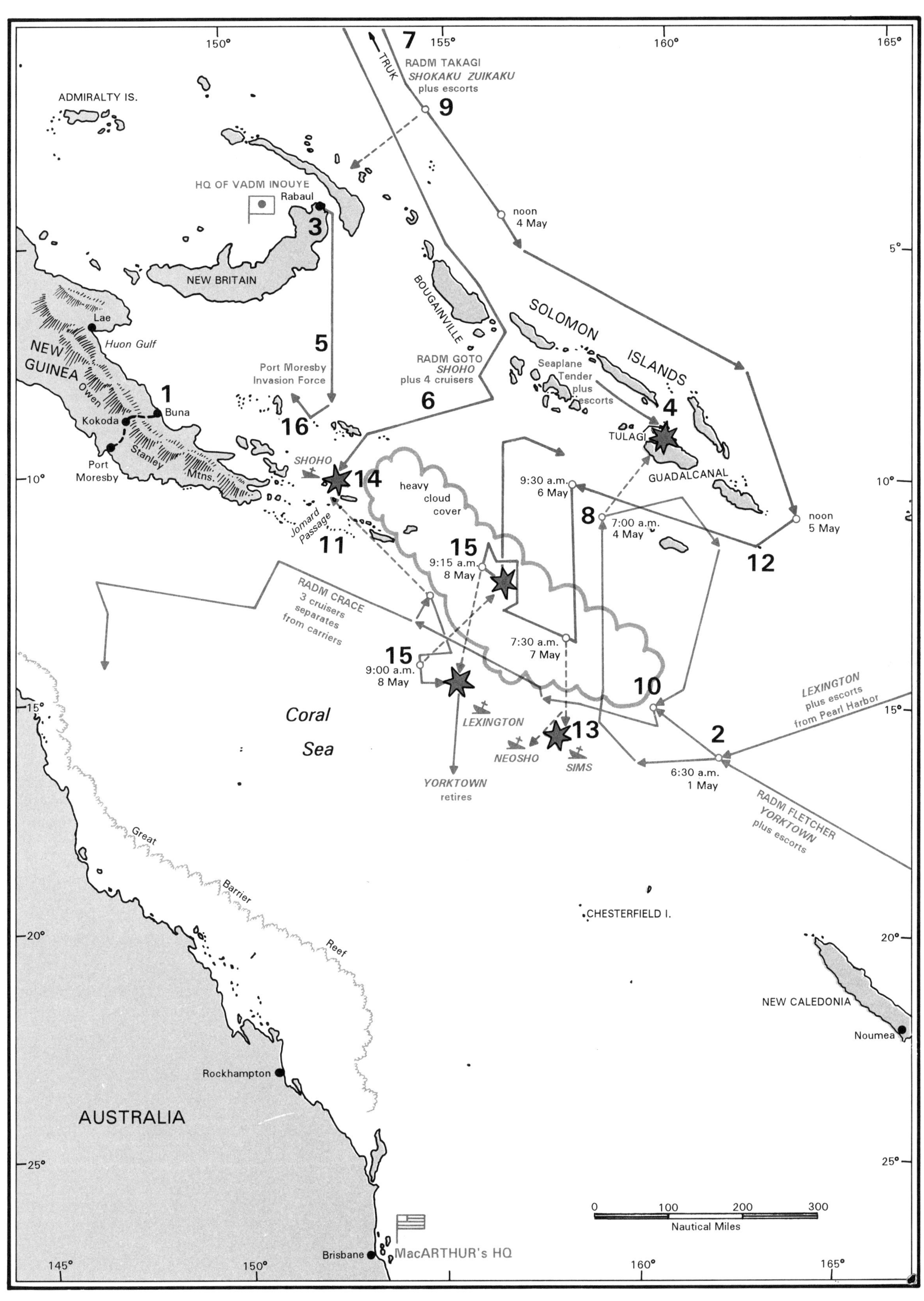

TRUK
7
RADM TAKAGI
SHOKAKU ZUIKAKU
plus escorts
9
ADMIRALTY IS.
HQ OF VADM INOUYE
Rabaul
3
NEW BRITAIN
noon
4 May
BOUGAINVILLE
SOLOMON
ISLANDS
Lae
Huon Gulf
NEW GUINEA
Owen
Stanley
Mtns.
5
Port Moresby
Invasion Force
RADM GOTO
SHOHO
plus 4 cruisers
6
1
Buna
Kokoda
Port Moresby
16
Seaplane
Tender
plus
escorts
4
TULAGI
GUADALCANAL
SHOHO
14
heavy
cloud
cover
9:30 a.m.
6 May
8
7:00 a.m.
4 May
noon
5 May
12
Jomard Passage
11
15
9:15 a.m.
8 May
RADM CRACE
3 cruisers
separates
from carriers
7:30 a.m.
7 May
15
9:00 a.m.
8 May
10
LEXINGTON
plus escorts
from Pearl Harbor
Coral
Sea
LEXINGTON
13
NEOSHO
SIMS
2
6:30 a.m.
1 May
YORKTOWN
retires
RADM FLETCHER
YORKTOWN
plus escorts
Great
Barrier
Reef
CHESTERFIELD I.
NEW CALEDONIA
Noumea
Rockhampton
AUSTRALIA
Brisbane
MacARTHUR's HQ
0
100
200
300
Nautical Miles
145°
150°
155°
160°
165°
5°
10°
15°
20°
25°

MAP 58

MIDWAY: THE JAPANESE ATTACK

4 JUNE 1942

Having missed the American carriers at Pearl Harbor, Yamamoto began almost at once to consider how he might complete the destruction of the U.S. fleet so that Japanese consolidation of its southern empire could continue without interference. He knew that Japanese superiority in the Pacific would not last beyond 1942, when the products of America's industrial mobilization would join the Pacific Fleet, so he was eager for an early showdown. Yamamoto ordered his staff to work out the details of an attack on the western Aleutians and Midway, the key objective of which would be to lure out the U.S. fleet and destroy it.

Yamamoto planned to leave little to chance. He would employ no fewer than 162 warships, including four fleet carriers and eleven battleships. He would have had six carriers, but the *Shokaku* and *Zuikaku* were undergoing repairs for damage sustained in the Coral Sea. Still, the force that Yamamoto assembled ought to have been sufficient. Despite his numerical superiority, however, Yamamoto would fail at Midway for three reasons: (a) an unnecessarily complicated plan; (b) American code breaking; and (c) fateful decisions made by the carrier group commanders on both sides.

THE PLAN

Yamamoto's plan was too clever by half. He divided his huge armada into no less than seven operational groups and deployed them in such a way as to make them incapable of providing mutual support. Three of the seven Japanese groups were to attack American outposts in the Aleutians, including sending an air raid to Dutch Harbor (1) and invading Attu (2) and Kiska (3). These diversions served mainly to keep the Japanese forces assigned to them out of the decisive battle. Likewise, Vice Admiral Kondo's Invasion Force (4), five thousand soldiers in twelve transports with a substantial surface escort, never got into the fight. Nor did Yamamoto's Main Force of seven battleships, including the super-battleship *Yamato* (5). Everything, then, depended on Vice Admiral Nagumo's Strike Force of four carriers with their escorts (6).

Yamamoto envisioned that the Japanese occupation of Midway would draw out the American fleet from Pearl Harbor. On its way to Midway, the U.S. fleet would run through a gauntlet of Japanese submarines (7), after which it would be jumped by Nagumo's carrier planes and land-based planes from occupied Midway. Only then would Yamamoto's Main Force close in to sink any survivors with gunfire. But Nimitz's advance knowledge of the Japanese objective rendered Yamamoto's vision obsolete from the start.

THE CODE

Once again Lieutenant Commander Rochefort's cryptanalysts were able to determine with some accuracy where and when the Japanese planned to strike. With this intelligence, Nimitz made two crucial decisions: He ordered round-the-clock repairs on the *Yorktown,* jury-rigged if necessary, so that it would be ready for the coming fight, thus increasing his available carrier force from two to three. His second decision was to order his three carriers to sea on 28 May, five days before the Japanese established their submarine cordon. The U.S. carriers took up positions three hundred miles north of Midway (8)—the last place (quite literally, as it turned out) that the Japanese would look for it.

THE DECISIONS

The third key to American victory was the effect of critical decisions made by the carrier-group commanders: VADM Nagumo Chuichi and RADM Raymond A. Spruance. Halsey, who would ordinarily have commanded the American carrier force, was in the hospital, laid up by a violent skin rash, and Nimitz, therefore, assigned the job to Fletcher, who would personally command the *Yorktown* group (TF 17), while Spruance, a surface officer, would command the *Hornet* and *Enterprise* group (TF 16). More than one American aviator considered it outrageous that a black shoe should command a carrier group, but with hindsight it is clear that the appointment was inspired.

Nagumo opened the battle just after dawn on 4 June by sending a 108-plane strike to assault Midway Island (9), retaining 93 planes armed with armor-piercing ordnance in case his scout planes spotted the American carriers. The defenders of Midway shot down thirty-eight of the attacking planes, and the Japanese commander of the attack force radioed back that Midway's airfields were still operational: another air strike was needed to finish the job. Japanese search aircraft had failed to report any American surface forces, and so Nagumo ordered the ninety-three reserve planes to be rearmed with fragmentation bombs for a second strike on Midway. This process was nearly complete when at 7:28 Nagumo received a startling report from a Japanese search plane whose flight had been delayed by an engine malfunction: American surface ships to the northeast! The news froze Nagumo—he halted the changeover of ordnance for ten minutes until the pilot could identify the ships. Meanwhile, he waited.

During this interlude, Nagumo's covering fighters shot down the majority of American land-based bombers from Midway, which were making their second attack without fighter cover (10). The American bombers scored no hits. A few minutes later the Japanese scout plane reported that one of the enemy ships to the northwest was a carrier! Nagumo had to decide: Should he launch a strike at once? To do so, he would have to send out his bombers without fighter escort, and he had just witnessed the results of such an attack on his own force. Better to wait, he thought, recover the planes returning from Midway, rearm and refuel, and then launch a balanced attack. For two hours, from 8:30 to 10:30, the Japanese flight crews worked feverishly to recover, refuel, and rearm the planes of the strike force.

While they worked, planes from the American carriers were already en route. Spruance had decided *not* to wait.

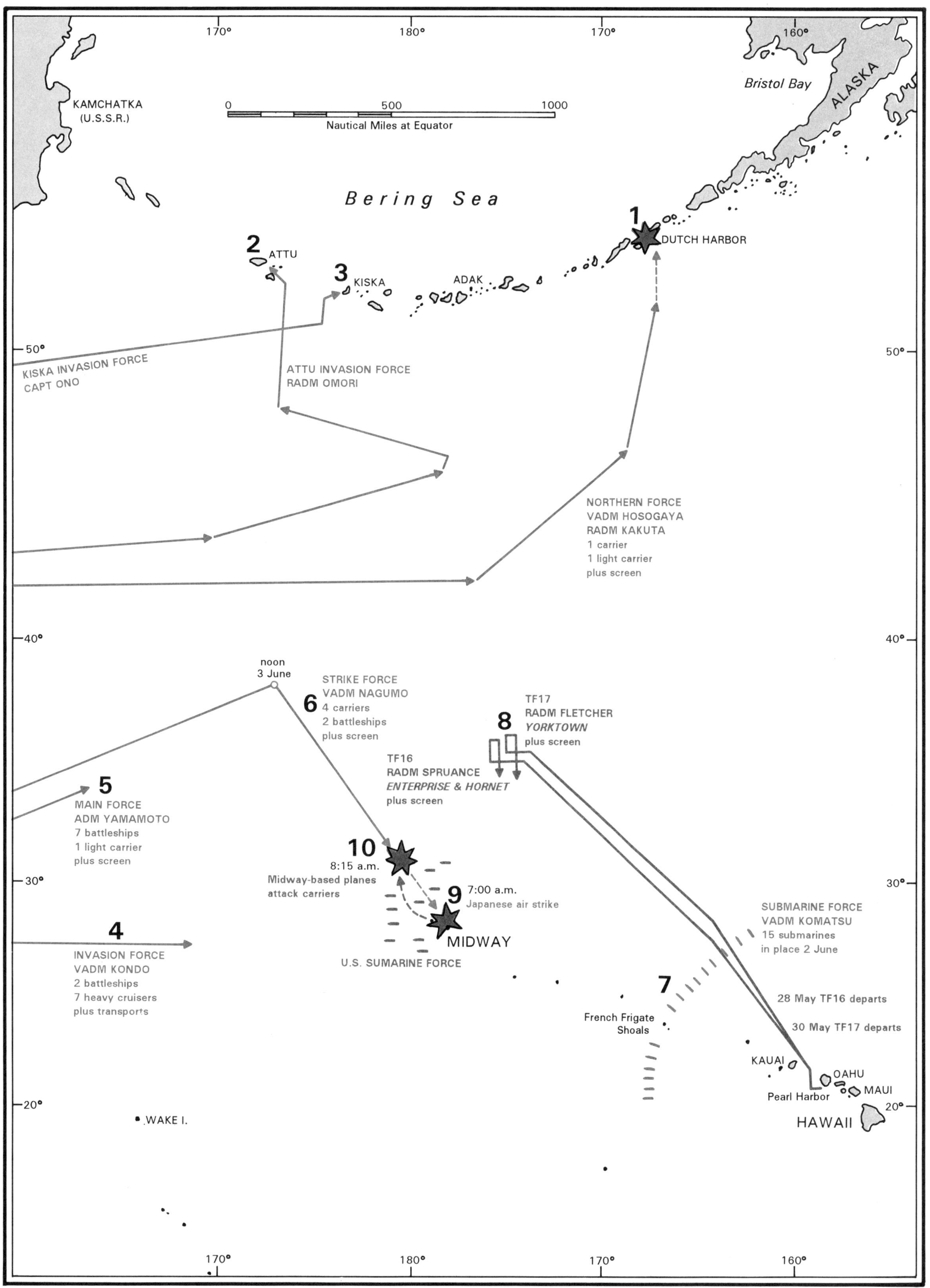

170°
180°
170°
160°
KAMCHATKA (U.S.S.R.)
0
500
1000
Nautical Miles at Equator
Bristol Bay
ALASKA
Bering Sea
1
DUTCH HARBOR
2
ATTU
3
KISKA
ADAK
50°
50°
KISKA INVASION FORCE
CAPT ONO
ATTU INVASION FORCE
RADM OMORI
NORTHERN FORCE
VADM HOSOGAYA
RADM KAKUTA
1 carrier
1 light carrier
plus screen
40°
40°
noon
3 June
STRIKE FORCE
6
VADM NAGUMO
4 carriers
2 battleships
plus screen
TF17
8
RADM FLETCHER
YORKTOWN
plus screen
TF16
RADM SPRUANCE
ENTERPRISE & HORNET
plus screen
5
MAIN FORCE
ADM YAMAMOTO
7 battleships
1 light carrier
plus screen
10
8:15 a.m.
Midway-based planes
attack carriers
9
7:00 a.m.
Japanese air strike
30°
30°
SUBMARINE FORCE
VADM KOMATSU
15 submarines
in place 2 June
4
MIDWAY
INVASION FORCE
VADM KONDO
2 battleships
7 heavy cruisers
plus transports
U.S. SUMARINE FORCE
7
28 May TF16 departs
French Frigate
Shoals
30 May TF17 departs
KAUAI
OAHU
MAUI
Pearl Harbor
20°
20°
WAKE I.
HAWAII
170°
180°
170°
160°

MAP 59

MIDWAY: THE AMERICAN COUNTERATTACK

4 JUNE 1942

While Japanese bombers were attacking Midway, Nagumo was unaware that the American carriers were some three hundred miles to the northwest (1). Unlike Nagumo, Spruance and Fletcher were alerted to the presence of the enemy carrier force by reports of American scout planes and bombers from Midway—though under radio silence themselves, they could eavesdrop on the reports to Midway. Just before 6:00 a PBY out of Midway reported the location of Nagumo's carriers (2), and Spruance and Fletcher steamed southwest to bring their air groups within striking range.

The optimum operational range of the American Dauntless dive-bomber and Devastator torpedo-bomber was approximately one hundred miles. Launching from such a distance would ensure sufficient time over the target and a margin of safety on the return flight. But it might take up to three hours for the U.S. carriers to close to optimum range, and in the meantime they might be discovered by the Japanese and lose the advantage of surprise. CAPT Miles Browning, Halsey's chief of staff serving Spruance in that same capacity, suggested that an early launch would catch the Japanese carriers in a vulnerable state—rearming and refueling for a second strike. Spruance took Browning's advice and ordered a 7:00 A.M. launch (3) despite the long range (some 175 miles), and he did not hedge his bet: he launched a full deck load, ninety-eight bombers and twenty fighters, retaining only a few fighters for air cover. Fletcher preferred to wait. The *Yorktown*'s bombers did not take off until 8:30, an hour and a half later (4).

The American attack pilots became separated en route, but they flew toward the reported location of the Japanese carriers (5) and found . . . nothing. At 9:15 Nagumo had turned his force northeast to open the range while he rearmed and refueled, and as a result the American attack planes found only empty seas where they had expected to find enemy carriers. Now the American pilots would have to search for the flattops.

The first to find them was Torpedo Squadron Eight from the *Hornet*—which consisted of fifteen Devastator torpedo-bombers commanded by LCDR John C. Waldron. Without waiting for support, Waldron ordered an immediate attack. The Japanese Zeros flying cover for the carriers swooped down on the American planes. The Devastator pilots pressed home their attack, but their courage and determination availed them nothing. They scored no hits, and Japanese fighters shot down all fifteen planes. The torpedo-bombers from the *Enterprise* and *Yorktown* arrived next and suffered a similar fate. Altogether, thirty-five of forty-one Devastators were shot from the sky, and the six U.S. planes that survived the strike retired to their carriers. The Japanese ships had not suffered a single hit.

It was approximately 10:25 A.M., and the course of the Pacific war was about to change.

To fight off the torpedo-bomber attacks, the Japanese fighters had descended to low altitude. Just as the last of the U.S. torpedo planes had been dispatched, the American dive-bombers appeared overhead at fourteen thousand feet. Their arrival at that time and place was a matter of the purest chance. The bomber pilots had been disappointed when they arrived at the coordinates they had been given and found nothing there. Spruance's decision to launch early meant that they would have little time for an extended search. LCDR Wade McClusky with thirty-seven Dauntless dive-bombers from the *Enterprise* guessed at the location of the enemy carriers by extrapolating the course of a lone enemy destroyer, and he found them at 10:25 (6). The Japanese had nearly completed the changeover of ordnance and refueling. In their haste, not all the ordnance had been re-stored; fuel lines snaked across the wooden decks. The Japanese fighter cover had descended to a few hundred feet to shoot down the torpedo-bombers. Unmolested by Zeros, and with the Japanese carriers in their most vulnerable state, the dive-bomber pilots pushed their sticks forward, sending their aircraft into a steep dive to execute a textbook attack on the four enemy carriers (see inset).

One of the first bombs hit Nagumo's flagship, the *Akagi*, penetrated to the hangar deck, and exploded among the discarded ammunition. Another bomb exploded among the fuel lines on the flight deck. Within minutes the *Akagi* was in a sinking condition. The *Kaga* suffered a similar fate, and it, too, went down. The *Yorktown*'s dive-bombers, which arrived over the target almost simultaneously, concentrated on the *Soryu*, hitting her with three bombs. The crew of the *Soryu* fought the ensuing fires, but their damage-control efforts were to no avail and the *Soryu*, too, went down. Only the *Hiryu* survived unscathed.

Despite the shock of this stunning reversal, Nagumo was still game for the fight, and he ordered the *Hiryu* to launch an attack against the American carriers (7). The Japanese pilots found the *Yorktown* and put three bombs and two torpedoes into her (8). (While being towed back to Pearl Harbor the next day the *Yorktown* finally succumbed to submarine-launched torpedoes and went down.) But the American pilots won the last round. Late in the afternoon they found the *Hiryu* and sent her to the bottom (9). Nagumo's entire carrier force had been annihilated. Yamamoto toyed with the idea of trying to close with his battleships, but with only one light carrier to provide air cover, he had to give it up and reverse course for Japan.

The American victory at Midway ended the six months of Japanese victories and marked a turning point in the Pacific war.

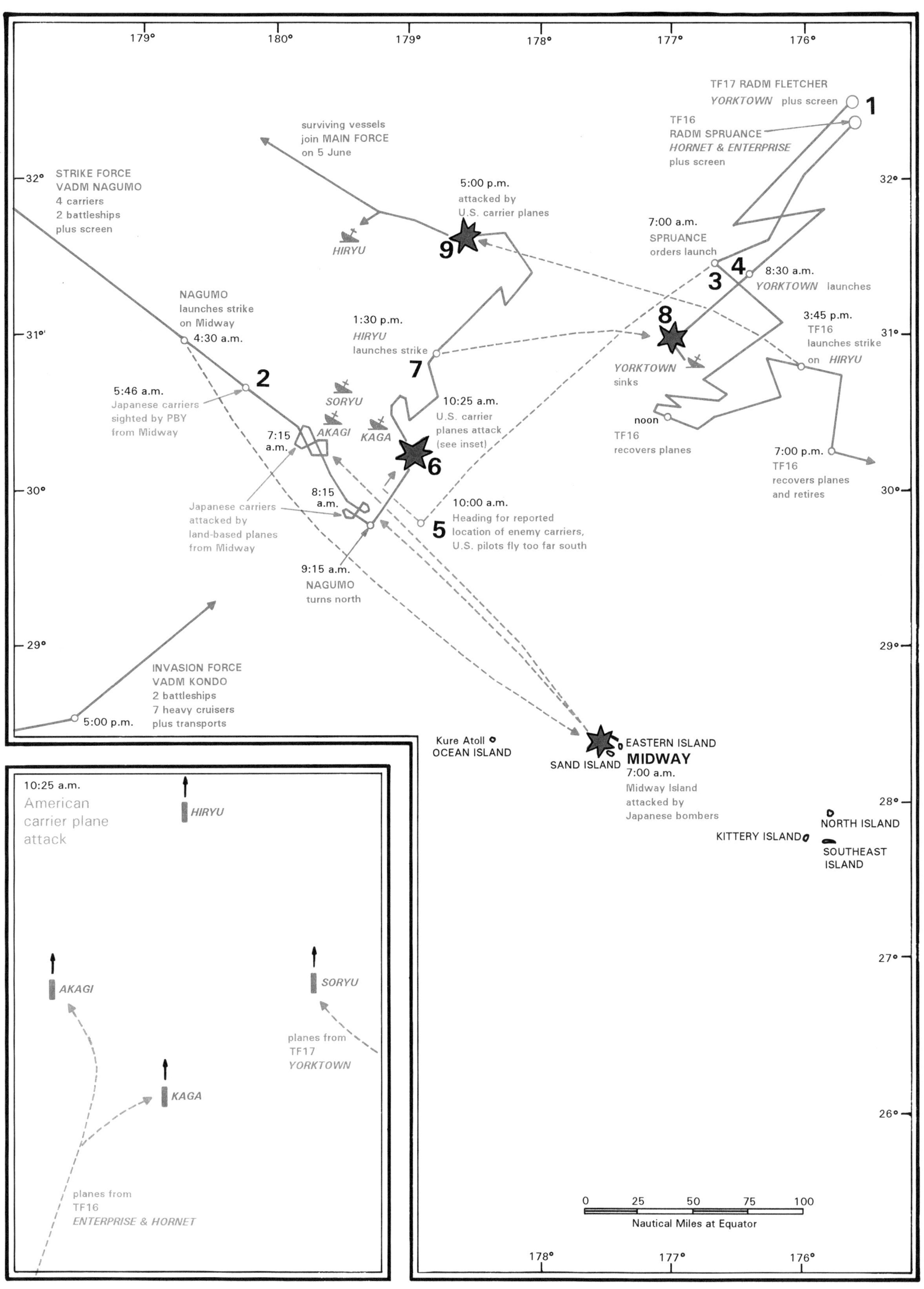
179°
180°
179°
178°
177°
176°
TF17 RADM FLETCHER
YORKTOWN plus screen
1
TF16
RADM SPRUANCE
HORNET & ENTERPRISE
plus screen
surviving vessels
join MAIN FORCE
on 5 June
32°
STRIKE FORCE
VADM NAGUMO
4 carriers
2 battleships
plus screen
5:00 p.m.
attacked by
U.S. carrier planes
HIRYU
9
7:00 a.m.
SPRUANCE
orders launch
3
4
8:30 a.m.
YORKTOWN launches
NAGUMO
launches strike
on Midway
4:30 a.m.
1:30 p.m.
HIRYU
launches strike
7
8
3:45 p.m.
TF16
launches strike
on HIRYU
31°
YORKTOWN
sinks
2
5:46 a.m.
Japanese carriers
sighted by PBY
from Midway
SORYU
AKAGI
KAGA
10:25 a.m.
U.S. carrier
planes attack
(see inset)
noon
TF16
recovers planes
7:15
a.m.
6
7:00 p.m.
TF16
recovers planes
and retires
30°
8:15
a.m.
Japanese carriers
attacked by
land-based planes
from Midway
10:00 a.m.
Heading for reported
location of enemy carriers,
U.S. pilots fly too far south
5
9:15 a.m.
NAGUMO
turns north
29°
INVASION FORCE
VADM KONDO
2 battleships
7 heavy cruisers
plus transports
5:00 p.m.
Kure Atoll
OCEAN ISLAND
EASTERN ISLAND
MIDWAY
SAND ISLAND
7:00 a.m.
Midway Island
attacked by
Japanese bombers
28°
NORTH ISLAND
KITTERY ISLAND
SOUTHEAST
ISLAND
10:25 a.m.
American
carrier plane
attack
HIRYU
AKAGI
SORYU
planes from
TF17
YORKTOWN
KAGA
planes from
TF16
ENTERPRISE & HORNET
27°
26°
0
25
50
75
100
Nautical Miles at Equator
178°
177°
176°

Map 60

Guadalcanal I

August–September 1942

On the day after the American victory at Midway, Admiral King learned that Churchill had declared a 1942 cross-channel invasion of occupied France to be impossible. King, therefore, transferred landing craft from the Atlantic to the Pacific and pushed plans to launch a counteroffensive in the Pacific to prevent the Japanese from consolidating their conquests. He was already planning an American initiative in the Solomons when he learned that the Japanese were building an airstrip on Guadalcanal. But Guadalcanal was in MacArthur's theater, and King did not want MacArthur to command the operation. A compromise solution, hammered out by the Joint Chiefs, moved the theater boundary one degree to the west (see map 56), putting Guadalcanal in the Navy's theater but confirming that MacArthur would command the subsequent advance to Rabaul.

The initial American landings near Lunga Point on Guadalcanal (1) were uncontested, but the Japanese soon responded to the challenge, gathering naval forces to assail the supporting fleet and sending in a steady stream of ground reinforcements by night. The result was an arduous six-month campaign on land and sea that was physically and emotionally exhausting both for the marines who defended their foothold on the island with its invaluable airstrip and for the sailors who sustained them there.

Savo Island (9 August 1942)

Learning of the American landing on Guadalcanal, VADM Mikawa Gunichi sortied from Rabaul with seven cruisers and a destroyer to attack the American support fleet. An Australian reconnaissance bomber spotted Mikawa's force, but the Allied command dismissed the report, and the news never reached the Allied ships guarding the approaches to what would soon become known as "Ironbottom Sound." Rear Admiral Fletcher had withdrawn the American carrier force because of the threat from Japanese land-based air. For defense of the beachhead, therefore, the Allies relied on three cruiser-destroyer groups under the overall command of Australian RADM Victor Crutchley: RADM Norman Scott commanded the eastern group in Sealark Channel (2); CAPT Frederick Riefkohl's force patrolled north of Savo Island (3); and Crutchley himself commanded the third group south of Savo (4). But on 9 August Crutchley took his flagship *Australia* to Lunga Roads (5) to confer with RADM Kelly Turner without telling CAPT Howard Bode in the *Chicago* that he was in temporary command.

Mikawa's cruisers arrived well after dark, slipping undetected past the picket destroyer *Blue* (6) an hour past midnight. The Japanese ships closed to within three miles of the southern Allied group and launched torpedoes, then broke into two groups and turned north (7), undetected until an American destroyer finally sounded the alarm at 1:43. Then all hell broke loose. Japanese floatplanes dropped flares that illuminated the Allied ships, and the Japanese opened fire. Hit by two dozen 8-inch shells, the Australian cruiser *Canberra* was knocked out of the battle almost at once. The *Chicago* took a torpedo hit but stayed afloat.

Steaming north, the Japanese opened fire on the northern Allied force with such effectiveness that all three U.S. cruisers eventually sank. By now the Japanese had expended all their torpedoes, and hoping to get beyond the range of U.S. air strikes by dawn, Mikawa decided to retire (8). With the exception of Pearl Harbor, the Battle of Savo Island was the worst defeat in American naval history.

Tenaru River (21 August 1942)

While Mikawa devastated the Allied surface force, the Japanese Army rounded up reinforcements for the ground war. The first one thousand Japanese reinforcements landed at Taivu Point (9) on 18 August. Moving west along the coast, they encountered the 2nd Battalion of the 2nd Marines behind Alligator Creek just beyond the Tenaru River (see lower map). Confident of the superior morale and fighting ability of his men, the Japanese commander, COL Ichiki Kiyono, decided to launch an immediate attack. On the night of 21 August Ichiki's soldiers made repeated assaults and took heavy losses (10). The next morning another U.S. Marine battalion crossed Alligator Creek upstream and pinned the Japanese against the sea (11). Before midday the marines had wiped out the entire Japanese landing force.

Bloody Ridge (12–14 September 1942)

Over the next two weeks the Japanese made regular night runs to drop more reinforcements on Guadalcanal. By mid-September they had six thousand troops at Taivu Point under MGEN Kawaguchi Kiyotaki, and though his force was still numerically inferior, he decided to attack. This time the Japanese target was a low ridge (12) south of Henderson Field defended by LCOL Merritt Edson's Raider Battalion, which was reinforced by the Marine Parachute Battalion—about 840 men altogether. During the night of 13–14 September some 2,400 Japanese repeatedly assaulted the American position, but though Edson's men were forced back, they held the ridge line and badly mauled the Japanese, who lost more than half their number.

Cape Esperance (11–12 October 1942)

In the second week of October the U.S. Navy partially avenged the humiliation of Savo Island in another night surface action (13). An American force of four cruisers and five destroyers under Rear Admiral Scott intercepted a Japanese surface force of three cruisers and two destroyers under RADM Goto Aritomo. This time it was the Japanese who were surprised, and the Americans sank a cruiser and a destroyer. The Americans lost the destroyer *Duncan,* and the cruiser *Boise* was badly damaged but remained afloat.

Far from ending the fight for Guadalcanal, these early battles merely set the stage for even more furious combat.

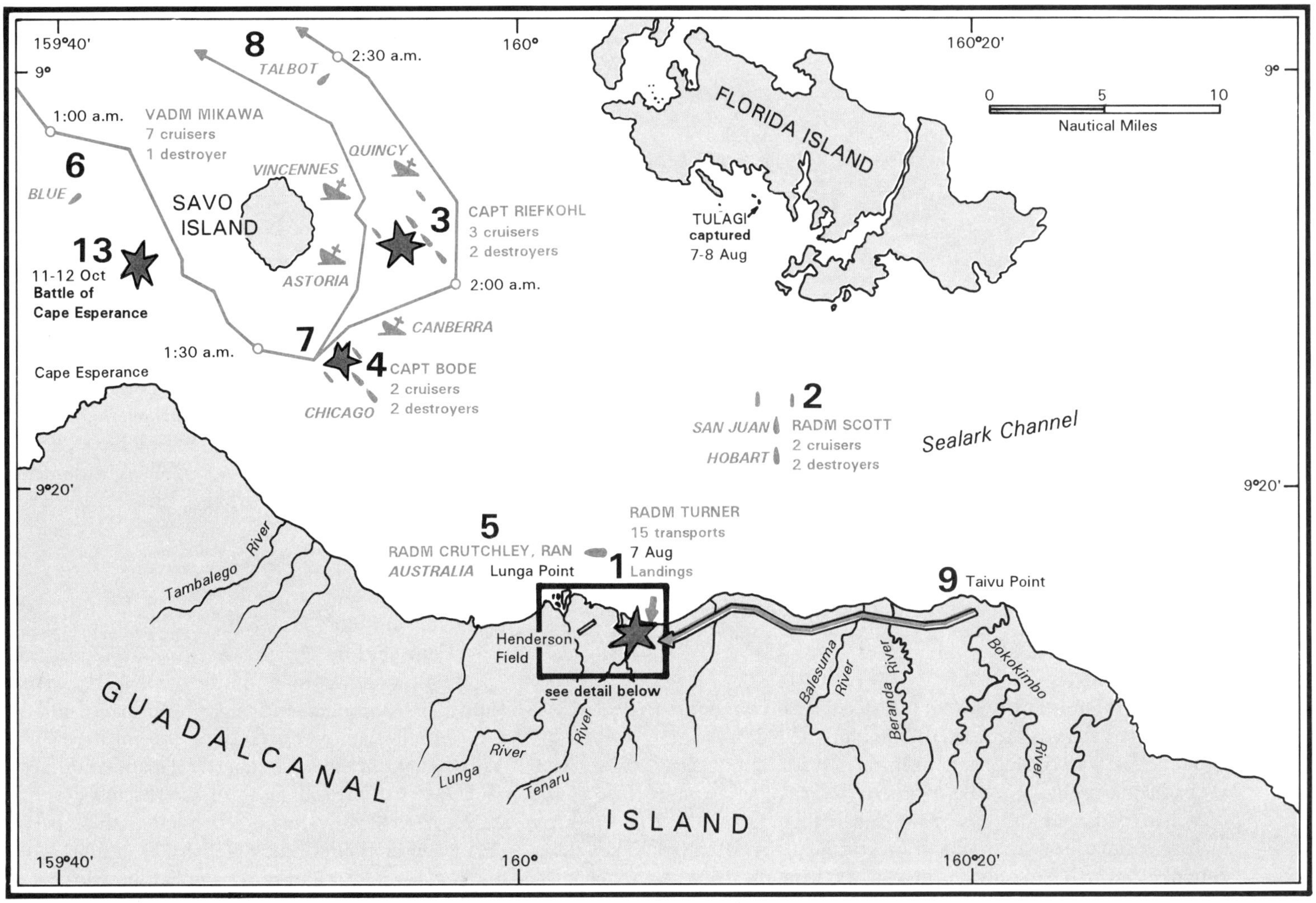

159°40'
160°
160°20'
9°
9°
0 5 10
Nautical Miles
8
TALBOT
2:30 a.m.
1:00 a.m.
VADM MIKAWA
7 cruisers
1 destroyer
QUINCY
FLORIDA ISLAND
6
BLUE
VINCENNES
SAVO
ISLAND
3
CAPT RIEFKOHL
3 cruisers
2 destroyers
TULAGI
captured
7-8 Aug
13
11-12 Oct
Battle of
Cape Esperance
ASTORIA
2:00 a.m.
CANBERRA
1:30 a.m.
7
4
CAPT BODE
2 cruisers
2 destroyers
Cape Esperance
CHICAGO
2
SAN JUAN
HOBART
RADM SCOTT
2 cruisers
2 destroyers
Sealark Channel
9°20'
9°20'
Tambalego River
5
RADM CRUTCHLEY, RAN
AUSTRALIA
Lunga Point
RADM TURNER
15 transports
7 Aug
Landings
1
9
Taivu Point
Henderson
Field
see detail below
Balesuma River
Beranda River
Bokokimbo River
Lunga River
Tenaru River
GUADALCANAL
ISLAND
159°40'
160°
160°20'

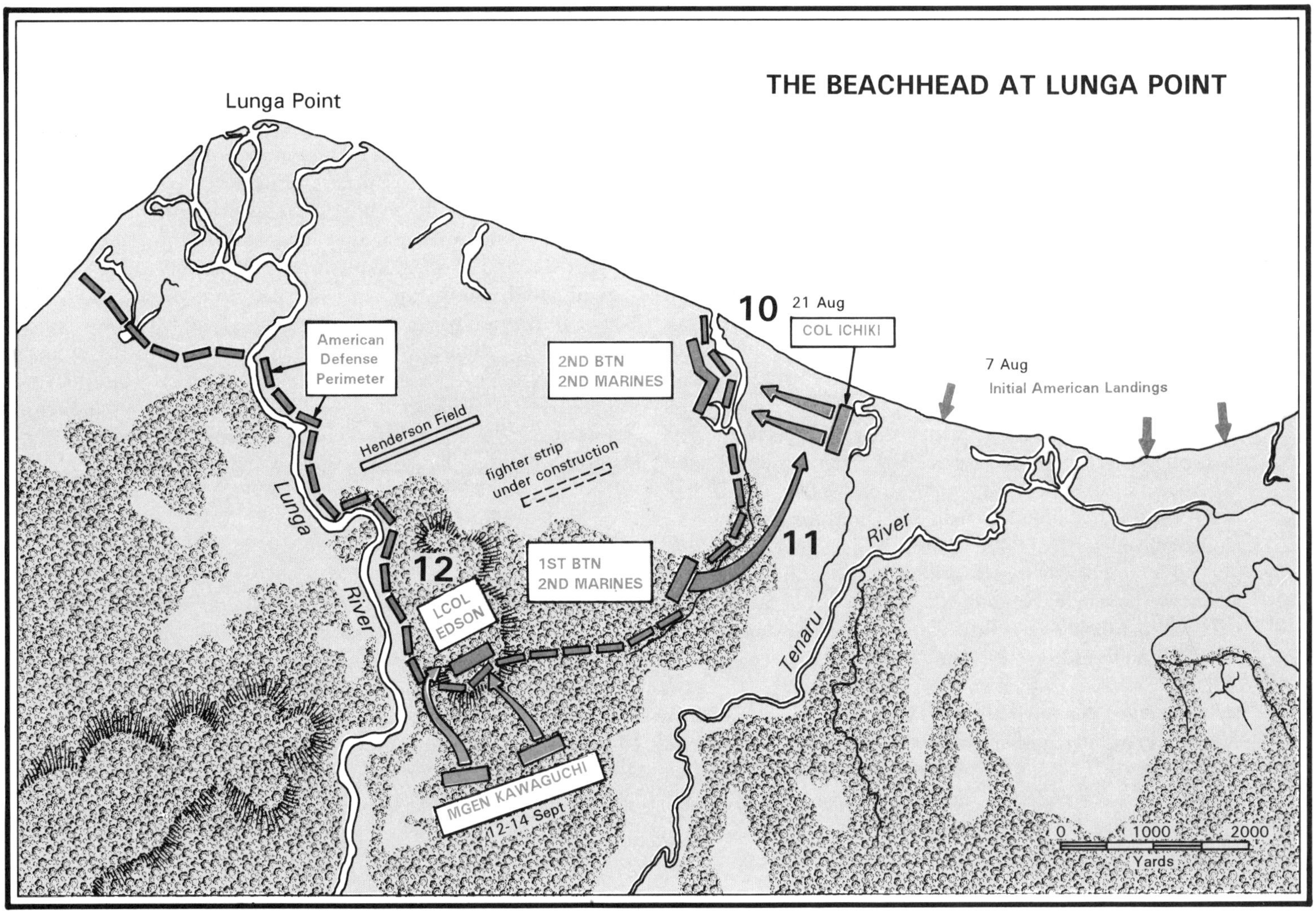

THE BEACHHEAD AT LUNGA POINT

Lunga Point
10
21 Aug
COL ICHIKI
American
Defense
Perimeter
2ND BTN
2ND MARINES
7 Aug
Initial American Landings
Henderson Field
fighter strip
under construction
Lunga
River
11
Tenaru River
12
1ST BTN
2ND MARINES
LCOL
EDSON
MGEN KAWAGUCHI
12-14 Sept
0 1000 2000
Yards

Map 61

Guadalcanal II

October 1942–February 1943

The failure of the first two Japanese attempts to drive the U.S. Marines from Guadalcanal led the Imperial high command to adjust its estimate of the effort that would be necessary to reclaim the island. For the third attempt the Japanese committed an entire army division. Meanwhile, an Imperial Japanese Navy strike force would act to prevent any U.S. interference at sea. On the ground, the Japanese fared no better than before, thrashing their way through dense jungle and hurling themselves to destruction on Bloody Ridge, manned in part by the 1st Battalion of the 7th Marines under LCOL "Chesty" Puller (see lower map). Meanwhile, the stage was set at sea for a major action between Japanese and American carrier forces.

Battle of the Santa Cruz Islands (26–27 October)

The opposing carrier forces had skirmished two months earlier in the Battle of the Eastern Solomons (24–25 August). In that action, American pilots from the *Enterprise* and *Saratoga* had sunk the Japanese light carrier *Ryujo,* while Japanese pilots had damaged the *Enterprise.* Since then, however, a Japanese submarine had sunk the American carrier *Wasp* (15 September), which had only recently arrived from the Atlantic, and two weeks later another Japanese submarine put a torpedo into the *Saratoga,* which had to return to Pearl Harbor for repair. These losses left the United States with only two active carriers in the Pacific. Hoping to achieve what he had failed to do at Midway, Yamamoto dispatched Vice Admiral Nagumo with four carriers and five battleships, along with no fewer than fifty-eight cruisers and destroyers, to get the American carriers.

Those carriers, the *Hornet* and *Enterprise,* were under the immediate command of RADM Thomas Kinkaid, but they were under the strategic direction of a new American commander at Noumea, VADM William F. "Bull" Halsey, an officer in the mold of Decatur and Farragut. When Halsey learned from the message traffic that Japanese carrier forces were in the area, he flashed Kinkaid a brief order: "Attack. Repeat. Attack."

American and Japanese search planes made nearly simultaneous sightings of enemy carriers a few minutes before 7:00 A.M. on 26 October (see upper map). Nagumo immediately launched a strike toward the American carriers, though U.S. pilots got in the first blow when an SBD from the scouting force landed a five hundred–pound bomb on the light carrier *Zuiho,* putting it temporarily out of action (1). When the Japanese pilots arrived over the American flattops at about 9:00 A.M., a rainsquall partially covered the *Enterprise,* so the Japanese concentrated on the *Hornet* (2). Four bombs and two torpedoes hit that hapless vessel, which suffered further damage when two Japanese pilots flew their airplanes into the crippled carrier. By 9:30, although twenty-five of twenty-seven enemy planes had been splashed, the *Hornet* was desperately wounded. Taken under tow, it suffered more hits later in the day and had to be abandoned, the fourth American carrier to be sunk in the Pacific war.

Meanwhile, American pilots had found Nagumo's force and damaged the *Shokaku* (3), which joined the crippled *Zuiho* and retired toward Truk (4). Soon afterward, however, Japanese pilots found the *Enterprise* and hit it with three bombs (5), leaving Kinkaid no choice but to retire south (6). These losses left the United States without a single undamaged carrier in the Pacific theater.

The Naval Battle of Guadalcanal (12–15 November)

The Japanese continued to pour reinforcements into Guadalcanal by night, and the Americans continued to try to intercept the convoys (see lower map). In the predawn darkness of 13 November five cruisers and eight destroyers under RADM Daniel J. Callaghan, whose flagship did not have surface-search radar, chanced upon a superior Japanese surface force under RADM Abe Hiroaki south of Savo Island (7). At 1:40 A.M. the destroyer *Cushing* swung hard left as the Japanese fleet suddenly appeared out of the night (8). From that moment the battle became, in the words of Samuel Eliot Morison, "an unplanned, wild and desperate melee in black darkness." In furious fighting the Americans lost two cruisers and four destroyers, while the Japanese lost two destroyers and suffered fatal damage to the battleship *Hiei,* which Allied airplanes sank the next day (9).

The very next night the new fast battleships *Washington* and *South Dakota,* under the command of RADM Willis Lee (10), tangled with a Japanese surface force under VADM Kondo Nobutake. In another midnight battle west of Savo Island (11) the Americans lost two more destroyers, but the radar-directed 16-inch guns of the American battleships so punished the battleship *Kirishima* that Kondo decided to retire. The next morning the *Kirishima* went down.

While the U.S. Marines clung to their perimeter around Henderson Field, the ubiquitous "Tokyo Express" continued to make night runs down "the Slot" to drop off supplies and reinforcements for the Japanese Army. On 30 November a U.S. surface force of five cruisers and six destroyers under RADM Carleton H. Wright attempted to intercept one such run by eight destroyers under RADM Tanaka Raizo. In the Battle of Tassafaronga, Tanaka proved once again the superiority of the Japanese Long Lance torpedoes and severely mauled Wright's force, sinking one cruiser and damaging three others.

By December 1942 reinforcements for the defenders of Henderson Field had raised U.S. ground strength to thirty-five thousand, and in January the Japanese high command decided that continued efforts to reclaim the island would be fruitless. The last Japanese ground troops were evacuated from Kamimbo Bay (12) on the night of 7–8 February, and the long campaign for Guadalcanal was over.

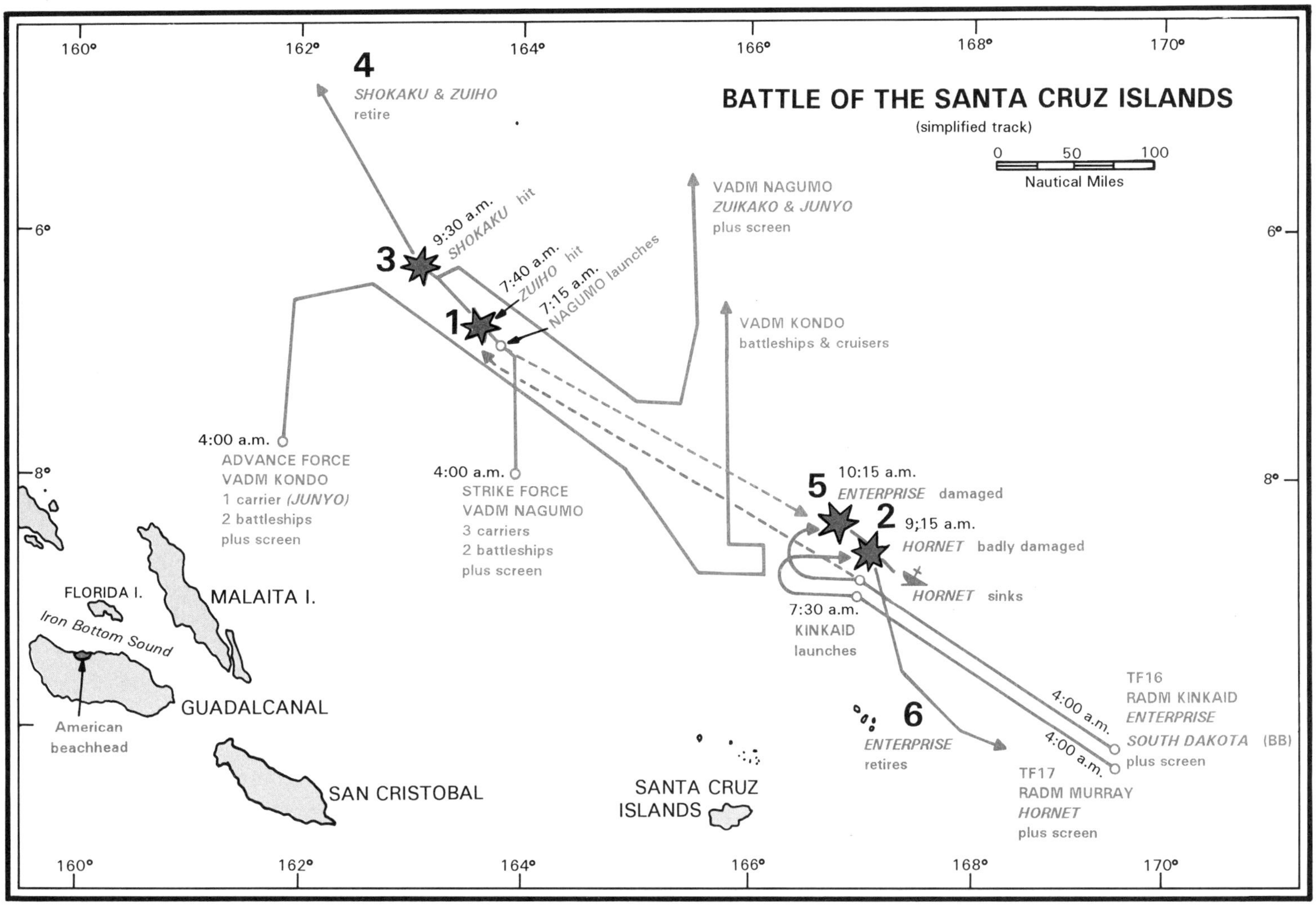

BATTLE OF THE SANTA CRUZ ISLANDS

(simplified track)

0 50 100
Nautical Miles

160° 162° 164° 166° 168° 170°

6° 8°

4
SHOKAKU & ZUIHO
retire

3
9:30 a.m.
SHOKAKU hit

1
7:40 a.m.
ZUIHO hit

7:15 a.m.
NAGUMO launches

VADM NAGUMO
ZUIKAKO & JUNYO
plus screen

VADM KONDO
battleships & cruisers

4:00 a.m.
ADVANCE FORCE
VADM KONDO
1 carrier *(JUNYO)*
2 battleships
plus screen

4:00 a.m.
STRIKE FORCE
VADM NAGUMO
3 carriers
2 battleships
plus screen

5
10:15 a.m.
ENTERPRISE damaged

2
9;15 a.m.
HORNET badly damaged

HORNET sinks

7:30 a.m.
KINKAID
launches

6
ENTERPRISE
retires

4:00 a.m.
TF16
RADM KINKAID
ENTERPRISE
SOUTH DAKOTA (BB)
plus screen

4:00 a.m.
TF17
RADM MURRAY
HORNET
plus screen

FLORIDA I.

MALAITA I.

Iron Bottom Sound

American
beachhead

GUADALCANAL

SAN CRISTOBAL

SANTA CRUZ
ISLANDS

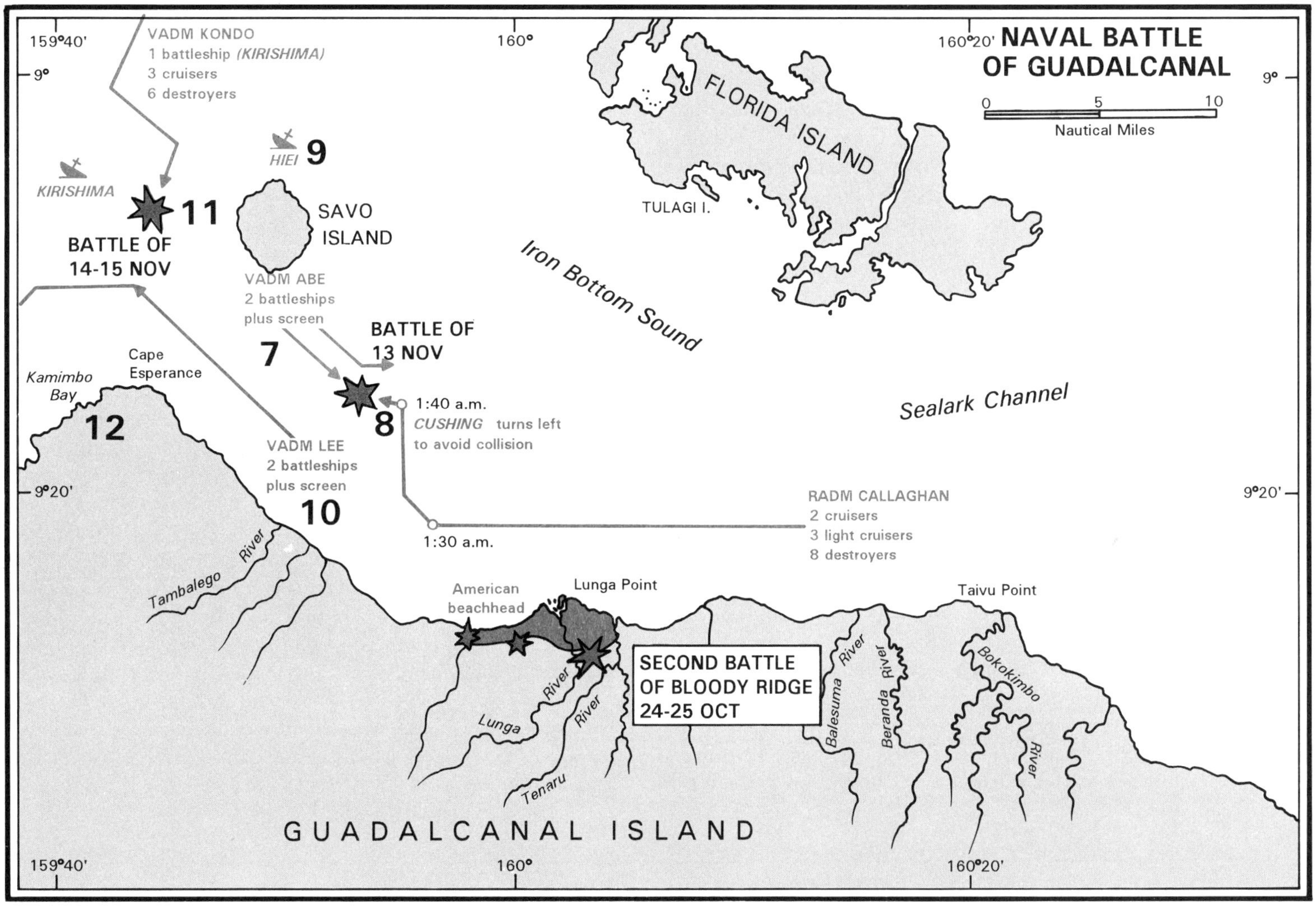

NAVAL BATTLE OF GUADALCANAL

0 5 10
Nautical Miles

159°40' 160° 160°20'

9° 9°20'

VADM KONDO
1 battleship *(KIRISHIMA)*
3 cruisers
6 destroyers

KIRISHIMA

11
BATTLE OF
14-15 NOV

HIEI 9

SAVO
ISLAND

FLORIDA ISLAND

TULAGI I.

Iron Bottom Sound

VADM ABE
2 battleships
plus screen

7

BATTLE OF
13 NOV

8
1:40 a.m.
CUSHING turns left
to avoid collision

Sealark Channel

Kamimbo
Bay

Cape
Esperance

12

VADM LEE
2 battleships
plus screen

10

1:30 a.m.

RADM CALLAGHAN
2 cruisers
3 light cruisers
8 destroyers

Tambalego River

American
beachhead

Lunga Point

Lunga River

Tenaru River

SECOND BATTLE
OF BLOODY RIDGE
24-25 OCT

Balesuma River

Beranda River

Taivu Point

Bokokimbo River

GUADALCANAL ISLAND

MAP 62

BATTLE OF THE ATLANTIC

DECEMBER 1941–DECEMBER 1942

Midway and Guadalcanal notwithstanding, the vital element of the naval war against the Axis powers was the maintenance of the transatlantic lifeline to Britain. The man who orchestrated the U-boat war against the Atlantic convoys was ADM Karl Dönitz, who contrived a "tonnage strategy" aimed at destroying the maximum amount of Allied gross merchant tonnage—which, he argued, would not only weaken Britain's ability to sustain the war effort but would also force the Allies to reallocate their resources to make up the losses. In the prewar years, Dönitz had pleaded with Gross Admiral Erich Raeder, head of the German Navy, to make U-boat construction the highest wartime priority, but Raeder had built a balanced fleet around the capital ships *Tirpitz* and *Bismarck.* Raeder's decision seemed to be vindicated in May 1941 when the *Bismarck* broke out into the Atlantic, sank the British battlecruiser *Hood* (1), and provoked panic in Whitehall before a dramatic pursuit by the Royal Navy ended with the destruction of the *Bismarck* (2) on 27 May.

To pursue his strategy of tonnage warfare, Dönitz had fewer than one hundred U-boats in 1941, only a third of which could be on station at any given time, and many of which were deployed in the Mediterranean or off Norway. But thanks to the victory of the German Army in France, U-boats were able to operate from ports on the Bay of Biscay after June 1940—which meant they had much shorter runs to their prime hunting ground off Ireland. When the United States became a belligerent in December 1941, Dönitz faced an embarrassment of targets. He sent an initial force of five boats to the American coast in December and increased the number to twenty by the spring of 1942. Many American coastal cities continued to burn their peacetime lights, silhouetting coastal merchantmen for U-boat skippers. Lacking an adequate number of effective escorts, and pressed by demands from two oceans, Admiral King declined to establish coastal convoys until he could institute an integrated system of interlocking convoys.

The map at right depicts the pattern of sinkings in the Atlantic during the first eight months of U.S. participation in the war—from 7 December 1941 to 1 August 1942. Each symbol represents *three* Allied vessels sunk by U-boats. In the first two weeks of 1942, U-boats destroyed more than one hundred thousand tons of Allied shipping along the American coast, and the numbers only got worse in February and March as the U-boats extended their operations to the Caribbean. King came under enormous pressure from Roosevelt and Marshall to do something, but until adequate escorts became available, there was little he could do. By spring he had assembled enough escorts to complete an interlocking coastal convoy system, and the number of coastal sinkings fell off dramatically. By the end of June he was able to extend convoy protection to the Caribbean as well.

But even as the crisis eased in the western Atlantic, it suddenly grew much worse in mid-ocean. In May and June 1942 total Allied losses in the Atlantic reached an astonishing 1.2 *million* tons. In part this was due to an increase in the number of operational U-boats in the Atlantic (from twenty-two in January to eighty-six in August), but the German success also resulted from a dramatic shift in fortunes in a clandestine duel between code breakers in England and Germany.

Through 1940 and 1941 British code breakers in Bletchley Park outside London had been reading the German message traffic, thanks in large part to their possession of a so-called Enigma machine—a captured German encryption device. The intelligence gathered from this source (the very existence of which was the most closely guarded secret of the war) was appropriately called "Ultra." The British had made use of Ultra intelligence in support of the convoys by determining the location of Dönitz's U-boat "wolf packs" and then rerouting convoys to avoid them. But in February 1942 the Germans added another wheel to the Enigma machine, so complicating the job of the code breakers that this intelligence source was temporarily lost. Worse, the same month that the Allies went "blind," the Germans cracked the Allied convoy codes so that Dönitz could now vector his wolf packs directly to the Atlantic convoys.

As a result, the German war on Allied commerce seemed on the verge of decisive success in the late summer of 1942 (see graph). By the fall, half of the raw materials consumed in Britain came from stockpiles. At such a rate, some feared that Britain could be forced to its knees by mid-1943. Then, suddenly, at the end of the year the outlook began to improve. December losses totaled "only" 262,135 tons, less than half that of the summer months. Part of the reason was the weather. The small U-boats (750 tons), which tracked the convoys on the surface, were more vulnerable to Atlantic gales than their larger prey. Another reason was increased air cover for the convoys. Though the air forces of both the United States and Britain preferred to use their aircraft to bomb Germany, the desperate situation in the Atlantic forced them to agree to increase the number of planes devoted to convoy protection. Finally, American naval shipyards began to turn out new vessels at a rate previously unimaginable. Even while the U-boats tracked and torpedoed their quarry, in the last six months of 1942 the Allies actually *increased* their available tonnage at a rate of 160,000 tons per month because of the ability of American yards to build ships faster than the Germans could sink them.

By the end of 1942 the battle against the U-boats had not been won, and U-boats would continue to constitute a serious threat to Allied convoys, but the transatlantic lifeline to Britain remained intact.

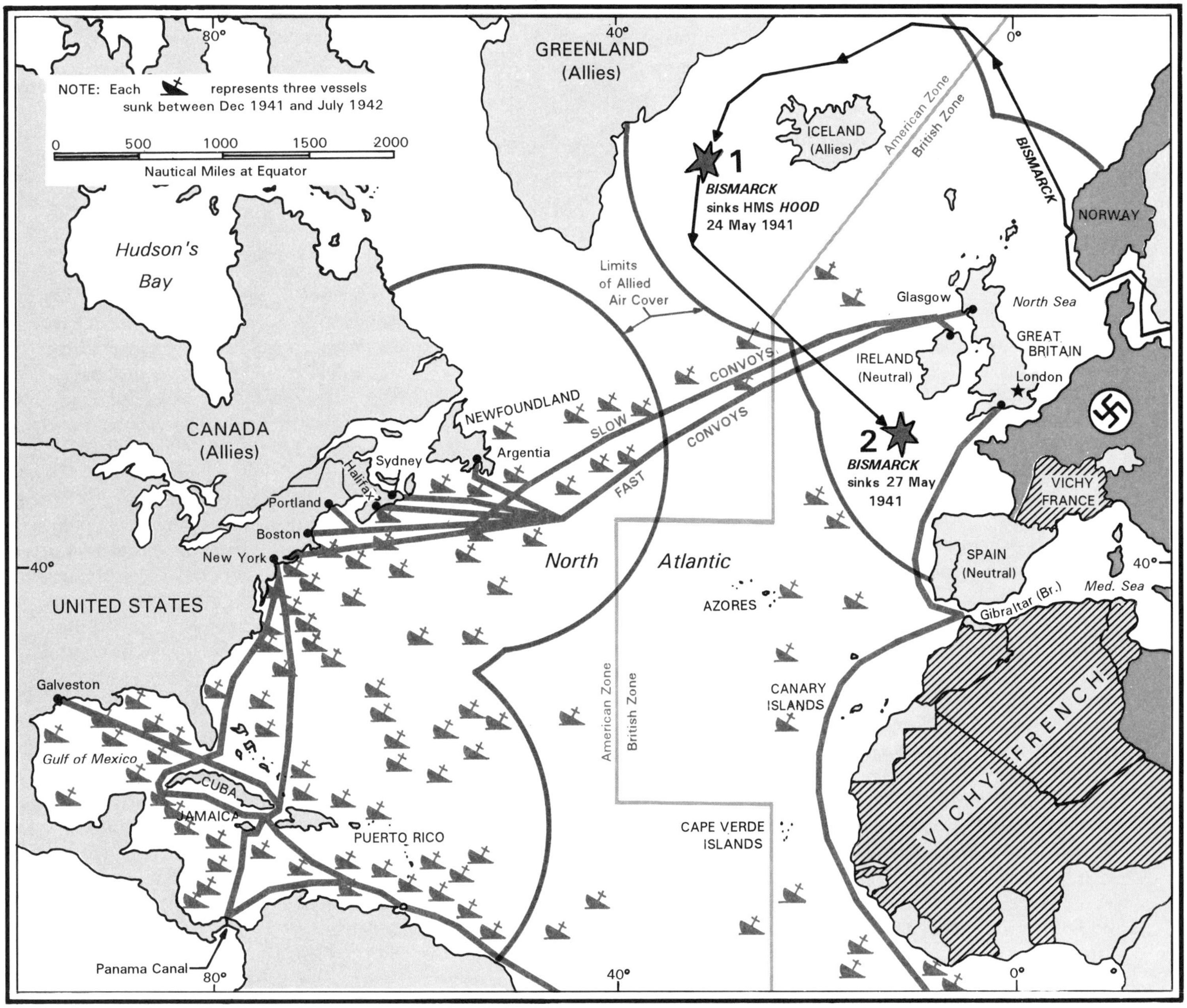

NOTE: Each [ship symbol] represents three vessels sunk between Dec 1941 and July 1942
0 500 1000 1500 2000
Nautical Miles at Equator
GREENLAND (Allies)
ICELAND (Allies)
American Zone
British Zone
BISMARCK
1 BISMARCK sinks HMS HOOD 24 May 1941
2 BISMARCK sinks 27 May 1941
NORWAY
Hudson's Bay
CANADA (Allies)
Limits of Allied Air Cover
Glasgow
North Sea
GREAT BRITAIN
IRELAND (Neutral)
London
NEWFOUNDLAND
SLOW CONVOYS
FAST CONVOYS
Argentia
Sydney
Halifax
Portland
Boston
New York
North Atlantic
VICHY FRANCE
SPAIN (Neutral)
Gibraltar (Br.)
Med. Sea
AZORES
UNITED STATES
Galveston
Gulf of Mexico
CUBA
JAMAICA
PUERTO RICO
CANARY ISLANDS
CAPE VERDE ISLANDS
VICHY FRENCH
Panama Canal
80°
40°
0°

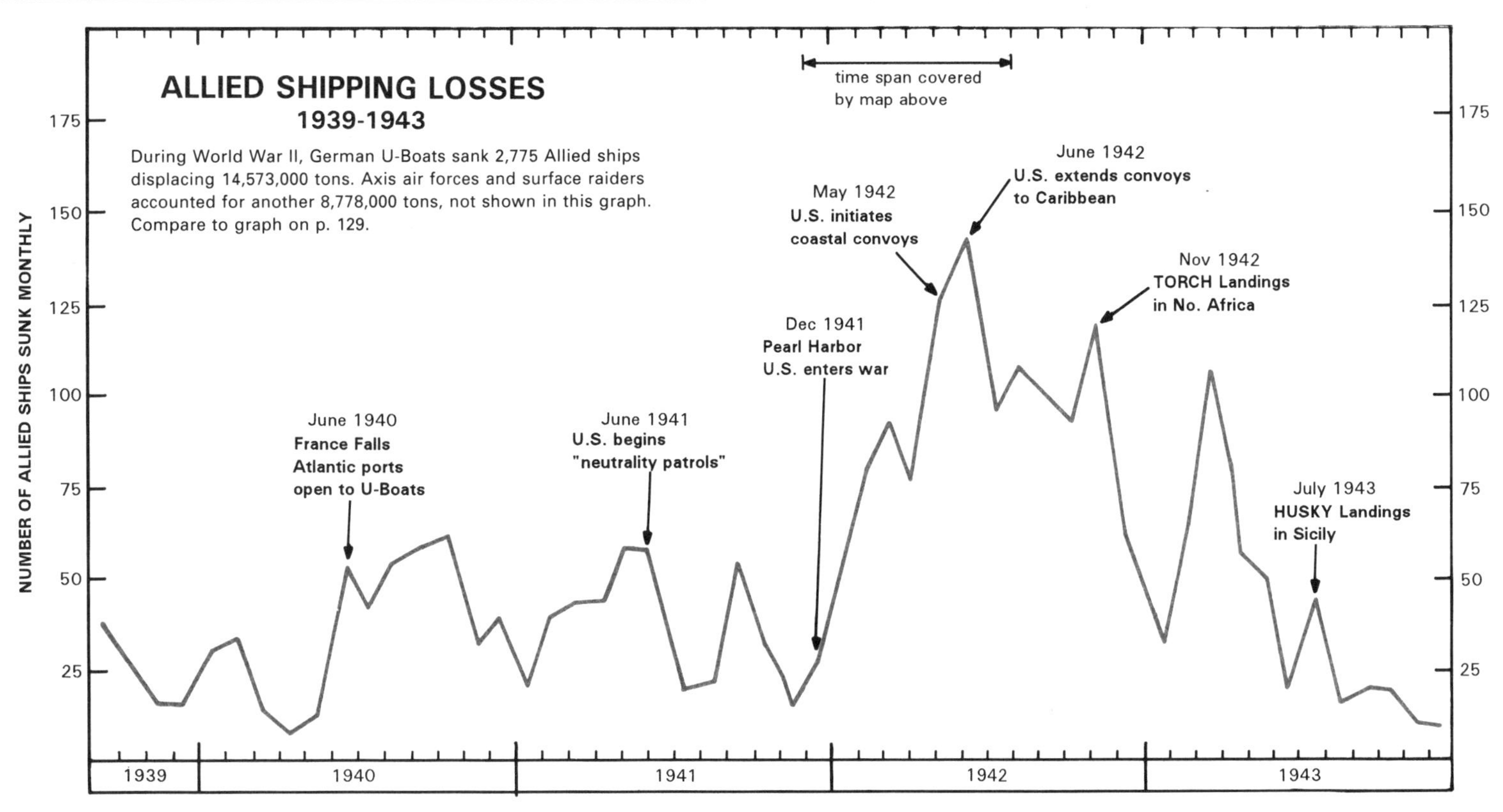
ALLIED SHIPPING LOSSES
1939-1943
During World War II, German U-Boats sank 2,775 Allied ships displacing 14,573,000 tons. Axis air forces and surface raiders accounted for another 8,778,000 tons, not shown in this graph. Compare to graph on p. 129.
time span covered by map above
NUMBER OF ALLIED SHIPS SUNK MONTHLY
175
150
125
100
75
50
25
June 1940
France Falls
Atlantic ports open to U-Boats
June 1941
U.S. begins "neutrality patrols"
Dec 1941
Pearl Harbor
U.S. enters war
May 1942
U.S. initiates coastal convoys
June 1942
U.S. extends convoys to Caribbean
Nov 1942
TORCH Landings in No. Africa
July 1943
HUSKY Landings in Sicily
1939
1940
1941
1942
1943

MAP 63

TORCH: THE LANDINGS IN NORTH AFRICA

8–11 NOVEMBER 1942

Significantly, the one aspect of Anglo-American shipping that survived unscathed during 1942 was the movement of U.S. troops to Britain for an eventual offensive against the Germans. More than a quarter million U.S. troops crossed the Atlantic in fast liners that, at twenty-eight knots, could outrace any submarine and most escorts. But what were these soldiers to do? Because the Germans were masters of the continent, any assault against western Europe would require a cross-channel attack on an unprecedented scale. The timing of that operation soon became a divisive issue in an otherwise cooperative Anglo-American relationship.

Only days after the United States entered the war, at a conference in Washington code-named ARCADIA, Winston Churchill had proposed that the Allies mount an invasion of French-held Morocco and Algeria as an alternative to a direct attack against German-occupied western Europe. Like most Britons of his generation, Churchill had vivid memories of the carnage of World War I, and he was determined to avoid a precipitate invasion of France that might force another generation of Englishmen to die in the trenches. Churchill was not insensitive to the claim that the Soviets were carrying the burden of the ground war, but he was unwilling to sacrifice British soldiers to ensure the survival of the Soviet regime by launching what he, at least, considered a premature invasion.

The American attitude was far different. Eager to come to grips with the enemy, the American Joint Chiefs in March argued for a small-scale cross-channel attack in 1942 (SLEDGEHAMMER) to be followed by an all-out assault in 1943 (ROUNDUP). George Marshall, among others, feared that a North African operation would necessarily postpone any cross-channel attack until 1943 or even 1944. The western Allies were uncertain that the Soviet Union could hold out until then; Roosevelt remembered that Lenin's government had pulled out of the war against Germany in 1917 and did not doubt that Stalin might do the same. Accordingly, in May Roosevelt reassured Stalin's emissary that the Allies planned to establish a second front that year—that is, in 1942.

But despite American eagerness and assurances, British troops would have to bear much of the burden of any cross-channel attack in 1942, and in June Churchill informed Roosevelt that such an attack was simply impossible. As if to prove their point, the British (using Canadian troops) carried out a large-scale raid on the French seacoast town of Dieppe in August 1942. Its disastrous failure seemed to underscore British objections to a premature invasion. This left the Americans with two alternatives: abandon the Germany-first policy and focus on the war in the Pacific, or accept Churchill's proposal to invade North Africa. Though the American Joint Chiefs favored the first alternative (partly as a gambit to encourage the British to reconsider), Roosevelt sided with Churchill and chose the second.

Ironically, the "enemy" in an Allied invasion of North Africa would not be Germans, but Frenchmen. Though many Frenchmen despised the collaborationist Vichy regime, France was officially neutral. Allied planners believed that the attack would nevertheless provoke a swift German response, and in particular they expected that it would draw *Luftwaffe* aircraft from the Russian front. Still, an Allied invasion of French North Africa would be almost literally a shot in the dark, for no one was quite certain how the French defenders of Morocco and Algeria would interpret their duty. Would they fight for Vichy? Or would they welcome the American invaders as partners in a campaign to lift the burden of German occupation off their homeland?

The TORCH operational plan called for British and American troops, escorted by Royal Navy vessels, to land at Oran and Algeria on the Mediterranean coast (1), while U.S. forces assailed French Morocco on the Atlantic coast. An American, LGEN Dwight D. Eisenhower, commanded the overall operation, and MGEN George S. Patton commanded the American landing force of thirty-five thousand Army troops. The American naval force collected for the operation consisted of more than one hundred vessels under the command of RADM H. Kent Hewitt. The Western Task Force sailed from Norfolk on 23 October, arriving off the Moroccan coast on 7 November. At dawn the next morning, while the guns of the covering force took out the French batteries and planes from the carrier *Ranger* shot up French aircraft on the ground, American landing craft headed for the beaches at three locations: Mehedia (2), Fedalla (3), and Safi (4).

At first the French did not know who was attacking, and they fought back with some vigor. At Casablanca (see inset), the French battleship *Jean Bart* employed its 15-inch guns with effect, and seven French destroyers that made a rush at the U.S. transport fleet were driven back only after gunfire sank two of them (5). Elsewhere, the Americans encountered only modest resistance. At Mehedia, the destroyer *Dallas* forced its way up the Sebou River to seize the airfield at Port Lyautey (6), and at Safi two U.S. four-stack destroyers, specially modified for the operation and loaded with troops, steamed into the harbor and seized the port in a *coup de main.*

Even while these battles were being fought, American negotiators were attempting to convince ADM J. L. F. Darlan, the senior French commander in Africa and the number two man in the Vichy government, to agree to a cease-fire. On 10 November an agreement was struck, and the next day the fighting stopped, replaced almost at once by Franco-American cooperation. The Allies now had a foothold in North Africa, but the hard part was still ahead.

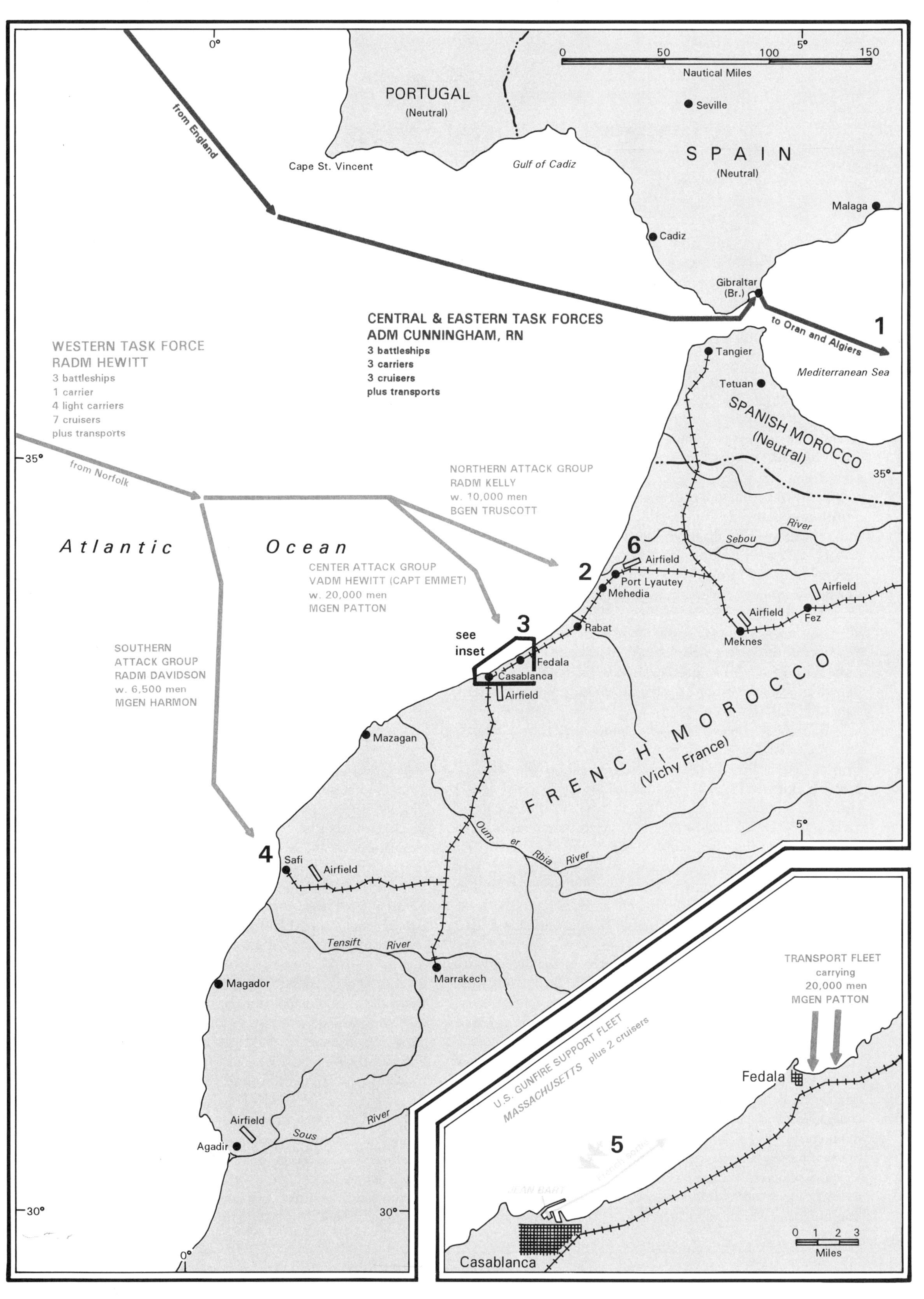

0°
0
50
100
150
5°
Nautical Miles
PORTUGAL
(Neutral)
Seville
from England
S P A I N
(Neutral)
Cape St. Vincent
Gulf of Cadiz
Malaga
Cadiz
Gibraltar
(Br.)
to Oran and Algiers
1
CENTRAL & EASTERN TASK FORCES
ADM CUNNINGHAM, RN
3 battleships
3 carriers
3 cruisers
plus transports
WESTERN TASK FORCE
RADM HEWITT
3 battleships
1 carrier
4 light carriers
7 cruisers
plus transports
Tangier
Mediterranean Sea
Tetuan
SPANISH MOROCCO
(Neutral)
35°
from Norfolk
NORTHERN ATTACK GROUP
RADM KELLY
w. 10,000 men
BGEN TRUSCOTT
35°
River
Sebou
A t l a n t i c
O c e a n
6
Airfield
CENTER ATTACK GROUP
VADM HEWITT (CAPT EMMET)
w. 20,000 men
MGEN PATTON
2
Port Lyautey
Mehedia
Airfield
Airfield
Fez
Rabat
Meknes
3
see
inset
SOUTHERN
ATTACK GROUP
RADM DAVIDSON
w. 6,500 men
MGEN HARMON
Fedala
Casablanca
Airfield
FRENCH MOROCCO
(Vichy France)
Mazagan
5°
Oum
er
Rbia
River
4
Safi
Airfield
Tensift
River
Marrakech
Magador
TRANSPORT FLEET
carrying
20,000 men
MGEN PATTON
U.S. GUNFIRE SUPPORT FLEET
MASSACHUSETTS plus 2 cruisers
Fedala
Airfield
River
Sous
Agadir
5
30°
30°
0°
0 1 2 3
Miles
Casablanca

Map 64

The Med: HUSKY, AVALANCHE, and SHINGLE

January 1943–January 1944

A week before the Allies landed in Morocco and Algeria, the British Eighth Army under GEN Bernard Montgomery defeated Field Marshall Irwin Rommel, the erstwhile "Desert Fox," in the second battle of El Alamein (October–November 1942). Combined with the success of TORCH, this made it possible for the Allies to consider their next strategic move once North Africa was secured. To discuss their options, Roosevelt, Churchill, and the Combined Chiefs of Staff met in Casablanca in January 1943. The British were eager to continue the pressure in the Mediterranean; they argued for an amphibious operation into Sicily or Sardinia to knock Italy out of the war. This could be achieved, of course, only by abandoning any hope of a cross-channel attack in 1943. Despite American objections, the inertia of events in North Africa led to the adoption of the British proposal.

First, however, Rommel had to be dispatched. Despite a setback at Kasserine Pass in February, Allied forces on the ground gradually pinned the Germans into a small enclave in Tunisia. Rommel went home sick in March, but his successor fought on until 12 May when he was forced to surrender his entire command, some 230,000 men, thanks to Allied naval superiority in the Mediterranean, which prevented their evacuation. With North Africa in Allied hands, the Combined Chiefs of Staff prepared to execute the planned invasion of Sicily, code-named HUSKY.

Eisenhower once again commanded the combined operation, with ADM Sir Andrew Cunningham, RN, as the naval commander. The U.S. Navy contingent, dubbed the Western Naval Task Force (1), was commanded by Kent Hewitt, now a vice admiral, while ADM Bertram Ramsay, RN, commanded the Eastern Naval Task Force (2). Hewitt's command had grown to more than five hundred ships, including significant numbers of new landing craft: the 1,500-ton landing ship tank (LST), the 550-ton landing craft tank (LCT), and the 200-ton landing craft infantry (LCI). These new vessels, plus the small amphibious DUKWs (amphibious truck, duck, troop), proved invaluable.

Despite a fierce storm on the night of 9 July, Hewitt's force successfully escorted transports carrying three Army divisions, each of about twenty-four thousand men, to the southern coast of Sicily, landing them at Licata (3), Gela (4), and Scoglitti (5). At Gela, the cruisers of RADM John L. Hall's covering task force repelled two enemy tank attacks with naval gunfire. In the air, it was a different story. Because no escort carriers were available, U.S. Army Air Corps planes had been charged with providing air cover for the landing. But the commander, GEN Carl Spaatz, was so wedded to strategic bombing that he failed to provide sufficient forces for this vital task. Without air cover, the ships had to rely on antiaircraft (AA) fire to repel more than twenty-four *Luftwaffe* attacks in as many hours. Worse, when American transport planes arrived over the task force only moments after a German air raid, Navy AA gunners shot down twenty-two of them, which were towing gliders filled with Allied paratroopers.

On the ground, Patton's Seventh Army drove west then north, taking Palermo (6) on 22 July, then sped east toward Messina (7), while General Montgomery's British Eighth Army moved up the east coast. Patton's movement was much swifter, not only because of that officer's aggressive temperament but because he took advantage of superior sea power, employing Navy vessels for gunfire support and leapfrogging past Axis strong points with amphibious landings (8). Meanwhile, Montgomery became bogged down in a lengthy fight for Catania (9).

The Allied landings in Sicily eroded whatever Italian support there had been for participation in Hitler's war. In July the Italian Fascist Council stripped Mussolini of his power and incarcerated him on Ponza Island (10). His replacement was Marshall Pietro Badoglio, who immediately put out feelers to the Allies, suggesting that Italy was willing to change sides. To support these developments, the Allies determined to extend the campaign into Italy. On 3 September the British Eighth Army landed on the Italian toe (11), and a week later Vice Admiral Hewitt's Western Task Force delivered LGEN Mark Clark's mostly American Fifth Army to Salerno (12) in an operation code-named AVALANCHE.

The German defenders under Field Marshall Albert Kesselring were waiting for the Allies at Salerno and turned it into a pocket of death. Hoping to achieve surprise, Clark had decided to land without a preliminary naval bombardment. But once ashore, gunfire from American and British cruisers and destroyers was all that kept the Germans from driving the Allies into the sea. At one point Clark seriously contemplated evacuation. In the end, Eisenhower had to order Montgomery to fight his way up the coast to relieve Clark's forces (13). With the arrival of the lead elements of the British Eighth Army, Kesselring fell back to the Gustav Line (14), and the Allies occupied Naples on 1 October.

Far from ending the war in the Mediterranean, the landings in Italy, like those in North Africa, bogged the Allies down in a secondary theater, with the prospect of an early cross-channel attack growing dimmer all the time. In January 1944 the Allies decided to try yet another leap past the Gustav Line to secure an open road to Rome. Code-named Operation SHINGLE, this effort was similar in both planning and result to AVALANCHE. This time two divisions of Clark's Fifth Army, again transported by Hewitt's Western Task Force, landed at Anzio (15) south of Rome, with the idea that Allied forces would dash inland to cut German lines of supply and communication. The landings went well enough, but MGEN John Lucas, commanding the ground forces, failed to push inland quickly, and the Anzio beachhead became another cul-de-sac. With that, the Italian front turned into an uneasy stalemate.

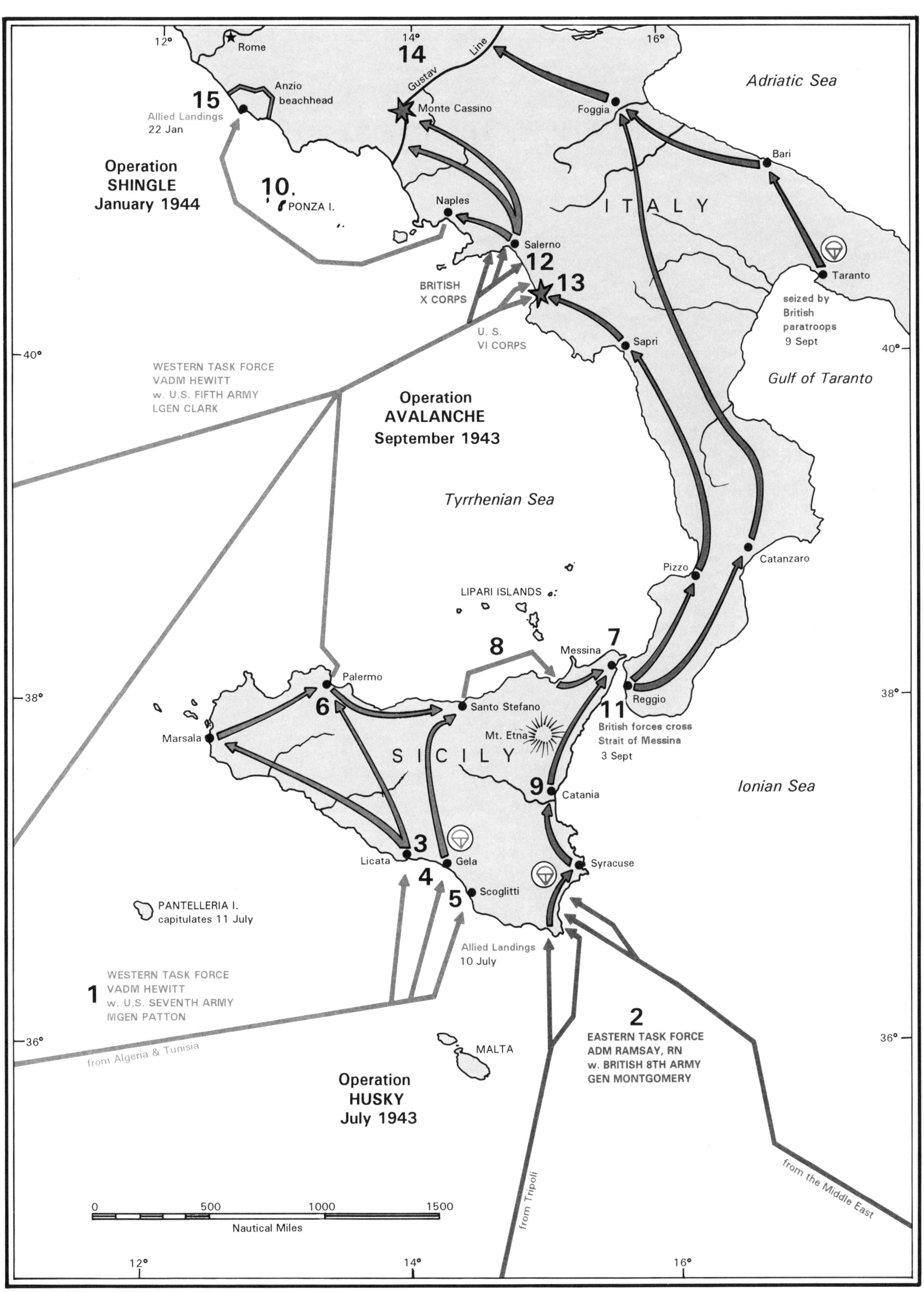

12°
14°
16°
Rome
14
Gustav Line
Adriatic Sea
15
Anzio beachhead
Allied Landings
22 Jan
Monte Cassino
Foggia
Bari
Operation SHINGLE January 1944
10.
PONZA I.
Naples
I T A L Y
Salerno
12
13
BRITISH X CORPS
U. S. VI CORPS
Taranto
seized by British paratroops 9 Sept
Sapri
40°
WESTERN TASK FORCE
VADM HEWITT
w. U.S. FIFTH ARMY
LGEN CLARK
Operation AVALANCHE September 1943
Gulf of Taranto
Tyrrhenian Sea
Pizzo
Catanzaro
LIPARI ISLANDS
8
7
Messina
Palermo
Reggio
38°
6
Santo Stefano
11
British forces cross Strait of Messina
3 Sept
Marsala
Mt. Etna
S I C I L Y
9
Catania
Ionian Sea
3
Licata
Gela
4
Syracuse
5
Scoglitti
PANTELLERIA I.
capitulates 11 July
Allied Landings
10 July
1
WESTERN TASK FORCE
VADM HEWITT
w. U.S. SEVENTH ARMY
MGEN PATTON
from Algeria & Tunisia
2
EASTERN TASK FORCE
ADM RAMSAY, RN
w. BRITISH 8TH ARMY
GEN MONTGOMERY
36°
MALTA
Operation HUSKY July 1943
from Tripoli
from the Middle East
0
500
1000
1500
Nautical Miles

MAP 65

CARTWHEEL: THE ADVANCE TO RABAUL

JULY–NOVEMBER 1943

While Allied forces in the Mediterranean conquered Sicily, U.S. forces in the Pacific inaugurated a staged advance toward the Japanese citadel of Rabaul (1). In July 1942 Admiral King had agreed that once Guadalcanal had been secured, the advance to Rabaul would fall under MacArthur's command, but now that it was imminent, King balked. He proposed instead the establishment of a unified command under Nimitz. This time the Army insisted that the agreement stand. Forces under MacArthur's overall direction would conduct simultaneous advances toward Rabaul from both the south and the east. After securing the Trobriand Islands (2), forces under MacArthur's direct command would conduct a series of leaps across northeastern New Guinea from Buna (3) to Salamaua and Lae on the Huon Gulf (4), to Finschhafen, and finally to Cape Gloucester on New Britain (5). At the same time, forces under Admiral Halsey (but reporting to MacArthur) would "climb the ladder" of the Solomon Island chain: from Guadalcanal to New Georgia, and finally to Bougainville. This dual operation was code-named CARTWHEEL.

Halsey's campaign in particular was characterized by a series of violent naval battles (see lower map). His first target was Munda Airfield on the New Georgia Island (6), some one hundred nautical miles west of Guadalcanal. U.S. soldiers and marines landed on Rendova Island (7), then were sea-lifted across Blanche Strait to New Georgia. As at Guadalcanal, the Japanese reaction was twofold: to ferry reinforcements to New Georgia from nearby islands in a reprise of the "Tokyo Express," and to attack the Allied support force with cruisers and destroyers. The result was a series of furious night surface actions.

BATTLE OF KULA GULF (5–6 JULY)

The first such action pitted a Japanese force of ten destroyers against RADM Walden Ainsworth's force of three light cruisers and four destroyers in Kula Gulf (8). Ainsworth's vessels dispatched two Japanese destroyers, sinking one and running the other aground, though the Japanese claimed the cruiser *Helena,* which succumbed to a Long Lance torpedo.

BATTLE OF KOLOMBANGARA (12–13 JULY)

Exactly a week later the opposing forces clashed again in virtually the same waters (9). This time Ainsworth had three light cruisers (a New Zealand cruiser having replaced the lost *Helena*) and ten destroyers; the Japanese force consisted of one cruiser, the *Jintsu,* five destroyers, and four destroyer-transports. U.S. gunners concentrated on the *Jintsu* and sank it, but Japanese torpedoes crippled all three U.S. light cruisers and sank the destroyer *Gwin.*

BATTLE OF VELLA GULF (6–7 AUGUST)

In yet another confrontation with a Japanese reinforcement convoy, the Americans took advantage of their superiority in radar and employed improved torpedo tactics as six U.S. destroyers under CDR Frederick Moosbrugger intercepted four Japanese destroyers in Vella Gulf (10). Thanks to his surface-search radar, which most Japanese destroyers did not yet have, Moosbrugger could track his targets from more than ten miles away, and he ambushed the Japanese destroyers with torpedoes launched from just beyond six thousand yards. One Japanese destroyer went down almost at once; two others went dead in the water and were finished off by American gunfire. Hundreds of embarked Japanese soldiers drowned. Only one Japanese vessel escaped, retiring north at high speed.

Japanese resistance on New Georgia ended on 5 August. The next target, Kolombangara (11), promised to be even tougher because of its larger garrison. Encouraged by Nimitz, however, Halsey decided to skip Kolombangara and jump to Vella Lavella. Such a move violated the hoary military principle that one should never leave a fortified enemy base in his rear, but without command of the air or sea, the twelve thousand Japanese soldiers on Kolombangara were effectively cut off and rendered impotent.

BATTLE OF VELLA LAVELLA (6–7 OCTOBER)

U.S. and New Zealand forces landed on Vella Lavella on 15 August. Within six weeks the surviving Japanese defenders, about six hundred men, were pinned into a small corner of the island. Six destroyers under CAPT Frank Walker intercepted the nine destroyers plus some smaller craft that the Japanese high command sent to evacuate the survivors (12). Walker's force sank one Japanese destroyer, but he lost two of his own destroyers, and he could not prevent the successful evacuation of the beleaguered Japanese garrison.

BATTLE OF EMPRESS AUGUSTA BAY (2 NOVEMBER)

Halsey's next leap was to Bougainville, the largest of the Solomon Islands. On 1 November a Marine division, an Army division, and a brigade of New Zealand troops went ashore in Empress Augusta Bay (13). The very next day the Japanese sent a scratch force of two heavy cruisers, two light cruisers, and six destroyers under VADM Omori Sentaro to break up the landing. This time a force of four light cruisers and six destroyers under RADM "Tip" Merrill intercepted the enemy force, fighting the battle beyond the effective range of the Long Lance torpedoes (approximately twenty thousand yards), and used radar-directed gunnery to batter Omori's ships. After losing a cruiser and a destroyer, Omori retired.

By now, Halsey and MacArthur had advanced by separate routes to Rabaul's doorstep. MacArthur was eager to kick in the door and assault the Japanese citadel, but U.S. strategic planners in Washington, including both Marshall and King, determined that Rabaul was no longer so dangerous as it once was. Like Kolombangara, it was left to wither on the vine. It was just as well, for even as Halsey's surface vessels fought the last battle of CARTWHEEL, the grand Central Pacific Drive was getting under way 1,400 miles to the northeast—at Tarawa.

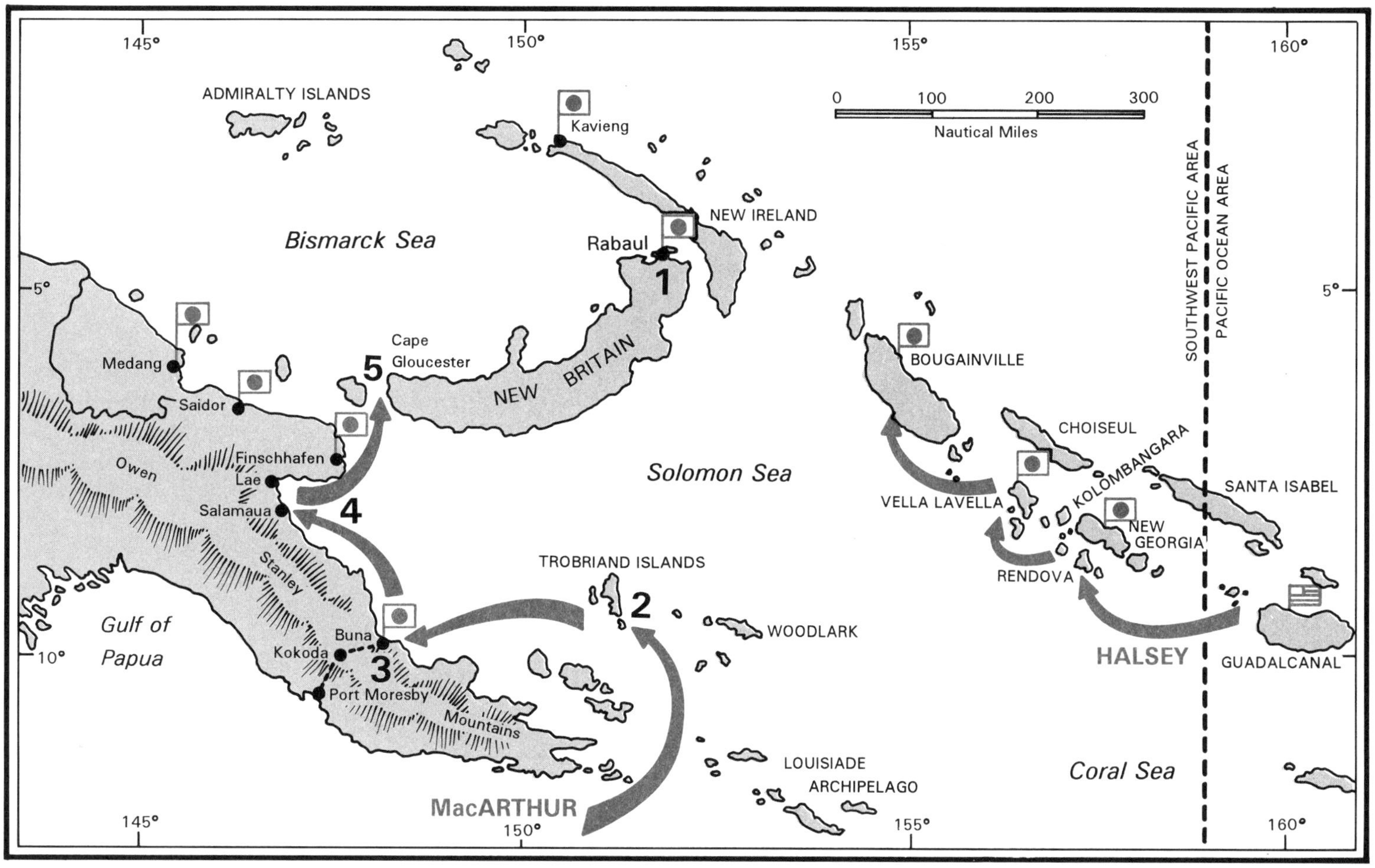

145°
150°
155°
160°
ADMIRALTY ISLANDS
Kavieng
0 100 200 300
Nautical Miles
SOUTHWEST PACIFIC AREA
PACIFIC OCEAN AREA
NEW IRELAND
Bismarck Sea
Rabaul
1
5°
Medang
Cape Gloucester
5
BOUGAINVILLE
Saidor
NEW BRITAIN
CHOISEUL
Owen
Finschhafen
Lae
Salamaua
4
Solomon Sea
KOLOMBANGARA
SANTA ISABEL
VELLA LAVELLA
NEW GEORGIA
RENDOVA
Stanley
TROBRIAND ISLANDS
2
WOODLARK
Gulf of Papua
Buna
Kokoda
3
Port Moresby
Mountains
HALSEY
GUADALCANAL
10°
LOUISIADE ARCHIPELAGO
Coral Sea
MacARTHUR

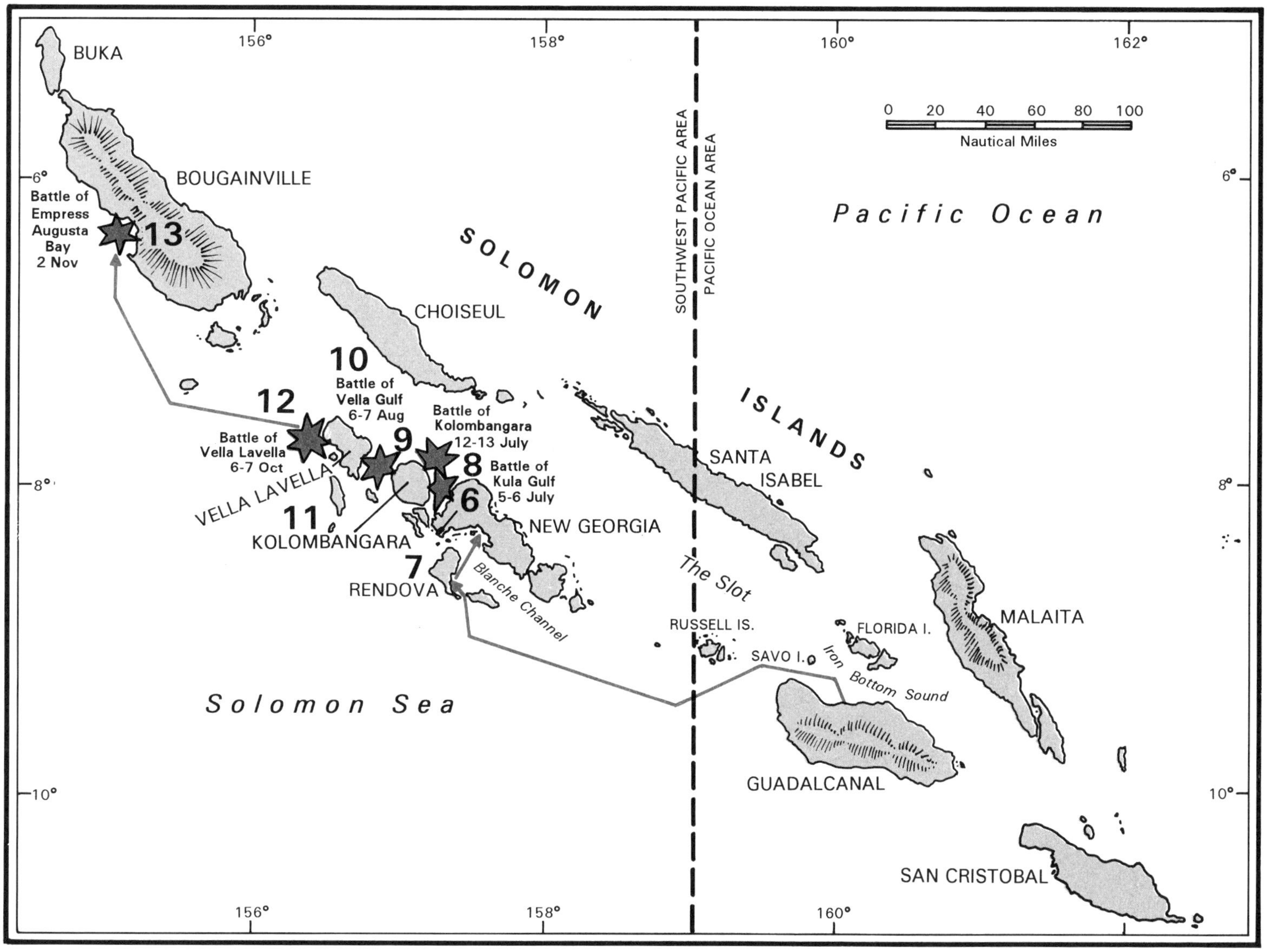

156°
158°
160°
162°
BUKA
0 20 40 60 80 100
Nautical Miles
6°
BOUGAINVILLE
SOUTHWEST PACIFIC AREA
PACIFIC OCEAN AREA
Pacific Ocean
Battle of Empress Augusta Bay 2 Nov
13
SOLOMON
CHOISEUL
10
Battle of Vella Gulf 6-7 Aug
12
Battle of Kolombangara 12-13 July
ISLANDS
Battle of Vella Lavella 6-7 Oct
9
8
Battle of Kula Gulf 5-6 July
SANTA ISABEL
8°
VELLA LAVELLA
11
6
KOLOMBANGARA
NEW GEORGIA
7
RENDOVA
The Slot
Blanche Channel
RUSSELL IS.
FLORIDA I.
MALAITA
SAVO I.
Iron Bottom Sound
Solomon Sea
GUADALCANAL
10°
SAN CRISTOBAL

MAP 66

CENTRAL PACIFIC DRIVE: THE GILBERTS (TARAWA)

20–23 NOVEMBER 1943

Throughout the campaign for Guadalcanal (WATCHTOWER) and the advance to Rabaul (CARTWHEEL), Navy planners in Washington had never forgotten Plan Orange—the prewar contingency plan for the defeat of Japan, the principal element of which was a drive across the Central Pacific. Admiral King had always thought of WATCHTOWER and CARTWHEEL as blocking moves to prevent further Japanese initiatives rather than as the first steps of an American offensive. Moreover, he was keenly aware that a continuation of the campaign in the southwestern Pacific would, in effect, turn the war over to MacArthur. He was, therefore, doubly eager to launch a Central Pacific campaign where the Navy's carriers had sea room to operate effectively. Though the British worried that opening another front in the Pacific would absorb resources that might otherwise go to Europe, the Combined Chiefs of Staff at the TRIDENT conference in Washington in May 1943 gave King a grudging go-ahead to initiate a Central Pacific campaign in the fall.

A Central Pacific campaign was possible at all due largely to the appearance in 1943 of the first products of an astonishing number of new-construction warships pouring out of America's shipyards. No fewer than a dozen new carriers—six *Essex*-class fleet carriers and six *Independence*-class light carriers—joined the Pacific fleet in August and September. To command this growing armada, King created a new fleet organization. VADM Raymond Spruance, heretofore serving as Nimitz's chief of staff, assumed command of what was now designated the Fifth Fleet. Under him, a trio of distinguished officers would direct the various elements of American sea power (see schematic at right). RADM Richmond Kelly Turner assumed command of the assault force—the amphibious, transport, and assorted support vessels of the fleet; RADM Charles A. Pownall commanded the fast carrier force, which would provide both the striking power and defensive air cover; and MGEN Holland M. Smith (known as "Howling Mad" Smith only partly because of his initials) commanded the embarked marines who would take the beaches.

The initial target of this force was supposed to be the Marshall Islands (1), which had been under Japanese control as a League of Nations Mandate since World War I. But an assault on the Marshalls seemed overly ambitious in the fall of 1943, and King was unwilling to postpone the campaign further. He, therefore, directed that the initial assault be directed at the Gilberts. Specifically, the Fifth Fleet would strike first at Makin Island in the northern Gilberts (2) and Betio Island in the central Gilberts atoll of Tarawa (3). Seizing the airstrip on Betio would provide a base for air cover for future operations and would allow the U.S. Navy–Marine Corps team to perfect its amphibious tactics. In short, it would be a good warm-up for the main event.

Makin proved to be relatively easy, though the slow pace of the Army National Guardsmen charged with its capture meant that naval forces had to remain offshore longer than planned, allowing a Japanese submarine to arrive on scene and sink the light carrier *Liscomb Bay.* Still, the real nightmare was on Betio (see inset). The Japanese commander, RADM Shibasaki Keiji, had turned the tiny island into a virtual fortress. His five thousand crack troops were well entrenched and manned more than two hundred gun emplacements protected by pillboxes of concrete or shock-absorbing coconut logs. Shibasaki boasted that Tarawa could not be taken by a million men in a hundred years.

As daunting as the enemy defenses were, the major obstacle to American success on Betio turned out to be the coral reefs that surrounded the island. The LCVP landing craft that would carry the marines ashore drew four feet of water. Though the best available charts showed a five-foot clearance over the reefs at high tide, locals claimed that neap tides, characteristic of the season, would yield only a three-foot clearance. Weighing the available evidence, RADM Harry Hill, commander of the task force covering the landing, decided that the LCVPs could clear the reefs. But MGEN Julian Smith, who commanded the 2nd Marine Division, warned his men to be prepared to wade ashore if necessary.

The assault took place at dawn on 20 November. The preinvasion bombardment was furious but brief in the hope that the Japanese would be caught by surprise. But not only was the bombardment inadequate, it was lifted too early owing to inaccurate estimates of how long it would take the landing craft to reach the shore. In addition, the jarring salvos of the 16-inch guns of the *Maryland,* which Hill was using as his flagship, temporarily knocked out the ship's communications, preventing him from making last-minute changes to the bombardment schedule. As a result, the Japanese on Tarawa had a short but crucial respite to sight their guns and prepare a murderous welcome for the marines as they came ashore. Worse, many of the U.S. landing craft grounded on the reef, some as far as eight hundred yards from the beach. The marines took horrible casualties as they waded ashore under heavy fire (4).

The fight for Betio Island took three days and cost the marines more than three thousand casualties, including one thousand dead. The Japanese fought—almost literally—to the last man; only seventeen of five thousand were taken alive. The American public was shocked. MacArthur adopted an "I-told-you-so" attitude, claiming that such assaults were not only wasteful but also strategically insignificant. With the example of Tarawa before them, more than a few Americans were prepared to agree. If the next assault proved as costly, support for a continuation of the Central Pacific drive might disappear altogether.

THE FIFTH FLEET COMMAND TEAM

VADM Raymond A. Spruance (National Archives)

RADM C. Pownall (National Archives)

RADM R. K. Turner (Official U.S. Navy photo)

MGEN H. M. Smith (Official U.S. Marine Corps photo)

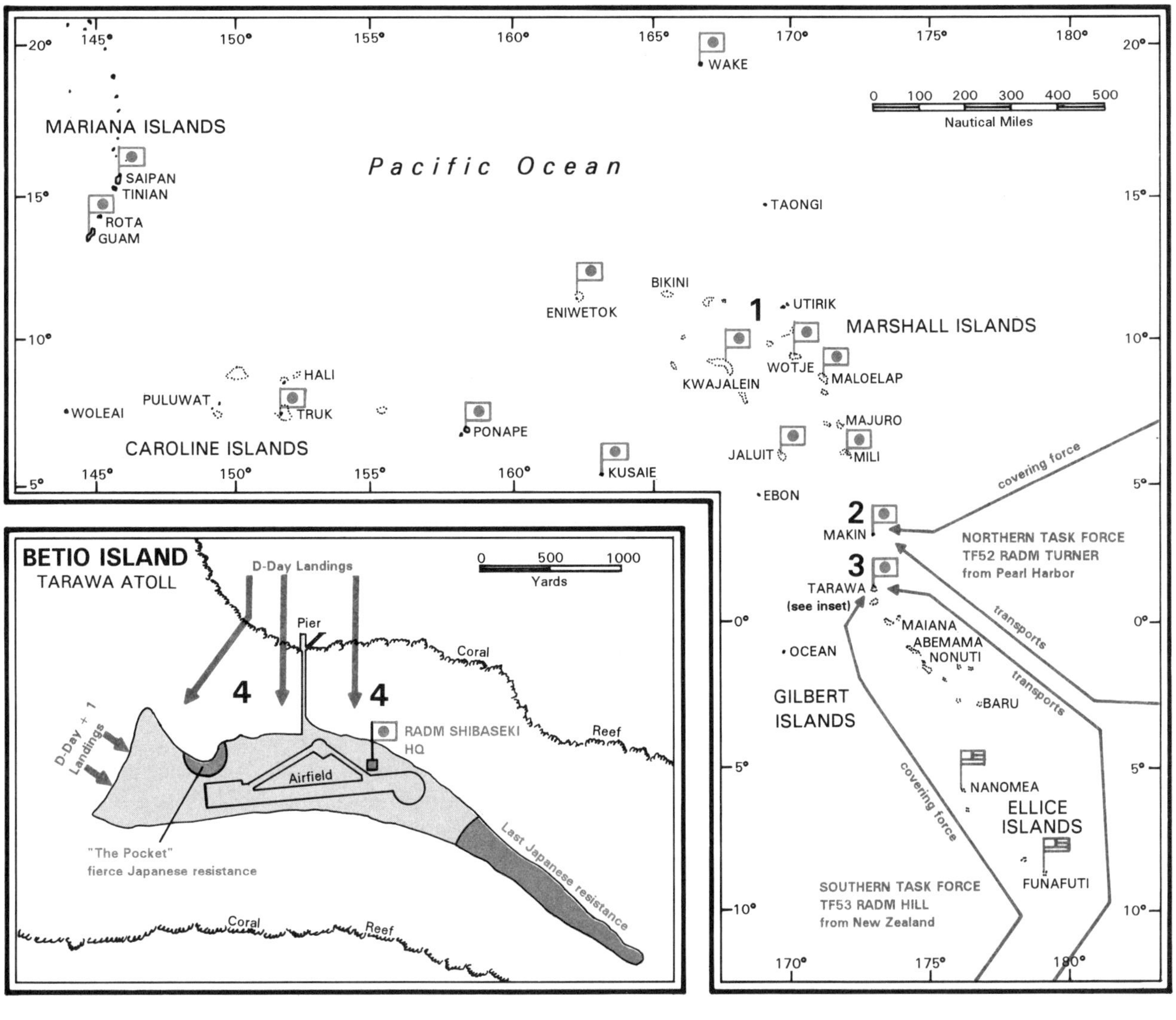

MAP 67

CENTRAL PACIFIC DRIVE: THE MARSHALLS

FEBRUARY 1944

Unlike the Gilberts, which the Japanese had occupied at the outbreak of the war, the Marshall Islands had been in Japanese hands since 1914. Rather than the one airstrip they had built in the Gilberts, the Japanese had a ring of air bases on half a dozen islands in the Marshalls, including two on Kwajalein (1) at the center of the archipelago. If Tarawa had cost 3,300 American casualties, the cost of Kwajalein might be prohibitive. Though Nimitz was confident that the lessons learned at Tarawa could be applied effectively in an amphibious operation against Kwajalein, his staff was unconvinced. Spruance, Turner, and Smith all urged him to consider seizing two of the outer islands—Wotje and Maloelap (2)—as a preliminary step to a subsequent attack on Kwajalein. But Nimitz again demonstrated his willingness to make difficult decisions by declaring that the next assault would be on Kwajalein and that if his commanders were unwilling to conduct it, he would find other commanders. Events would prove that his bold decision to proceed was correct.

Among the lessons learned at Tarawa was the need for longer and more accurate naval gunfire support. It was evident that the preliminary bombing and shelling at Tarawa had been inadequate and that ships and planes would have to target specific objectives rather than merely lobbing ordnance onto the targeted island. Another lesson was the need for better command and control of the task force. Rather than relying on battleships or cruisers as flagships, task force and task group commanders instead would fly their flags on specialized command ships whose primary function was communication. Finally, the nightmare of the reefs off Tarawa led to more conscientious intelligence gathering, eventually including teams of Navy frogmen who gathered sand samples from targeted beaches. All these lessons were applied with deadly efficiency in the American invasion of the Marshall Islands.

In the last month of 1943 U.S. planes from the Gilberts and from Rear Admiral Pownall's carrier task force began bombing Japanese bases in the Marshalls. Many prewar analysts had doubted the ability of carrier-based air to challenge land-based air. Airfields, after all, were unsinkable aircraft carriers. Though the Japanese had squandered many of their air assets in the defense of Rabaul, Pownall was sensitive to this conventional wisdom, and he failed to press home his initial raid. As a result, Japanese bombers from Kwajalein struck back at his task force as it was retiring, damaging the new carrier *Lexington.* Displeased by Pownall's lack of aggressiveness, Nimitz replaced him with VADM Marc Mitscher, a weathered, gaunt, and fearless naval aviator who would command the fast carrier task force for most of the war (see photo, page 139). From 29 January to 6 February Mitscher's carrier pilots flew more than six thousand sorties, virtually annihilating Japanese air power in the Marshalls (3).

Kwajalein is the world's largest coral atoll (see lower map), but only four of its several score islands are large enough to host major military facilities: Ebadon (4) at the western end, which the Japanese had not developed; the twin islands of Roi and Namur (5) at the northern salient; and Kwajalein (6) at the southern tip. U.S. forces targeted both Roi-Namur and Kwajalein for a 1 February landing. RADM Richard L. Conolly, recently transferred from the Mediterranean, commanded the Northern Attack Force escorting the 4th Marine Division, which went ashore on Roi and Namur, while Rear Admiral Turner commanded the Southern Attack Force for the landing on Kwajalein, where the Army's 7th Division went ashore.

The Marines on Roi-Namur executed their assignment with characteristic aggressiveness, relying on their own rapid advance to keep the defenders back on their heels, and they secured their objective in just over a day. Army troops on Kwajalein advanced more methodically, taking three days to complete their assignment. Throughout the operation, U.S. surface ships provided effective gunfire support for both forces, the battleships closing to within 1,500 yards of the beach to fire their 16-inch projectiles. By the time all three islands were secured, the Japanese had lost a total of 8,800 men, while U.S. casualties were just over 400 killed and 1,800 wounded.

So effective was the U.S. attack on these islands that the on-scene commanders recommended an immediate assault on Eniwetok (7), the westernmost atoll in the Marshalls and target of the original Orange Plan (see map 53). But Eniwetok was within air-strike range of the Japanese citadel of Truk in the Carolines (8). To take Eniwetok, therefore, Truk would have to be neutralized. Again Mitscher's fast carrier force (TF 58) was called upon to neutralize Japanese land-based air. Mitscher's twelve carriers launched a total of thirty air strikes, first against the airfields on Truk, then against the ships in Truk's commodious lagoon. His planes not only annihilated Japanese air power in the Carolines, destroying more than two hundred planes, but also sank six combatants and more than thirty other vessels.

On 19 February the Marines waded ashore at Engebi, the northernmost island of Eniwetok atoll, while two Army battalions landed on Eniwetok itself. After two and a half days, the atoll was declared secure. Other Japanese bases in the Marshalls—Wotje, Maloelap, Jaluit, and Mili—were simply bypassed and cut off. The Marshalls had been conquered at less cost than that experienced by the 2nd Marine Division in its first *day* on Tarawa. Moreover, the neutralization of Truk by Mitscher's carrier task force led King to direct that the U.S. Navy–Marine Corps team bypass the Carolines altogether and leap 1,200 miles to the west to the Marianas (9), to assail Japan's inner ring of defenses.

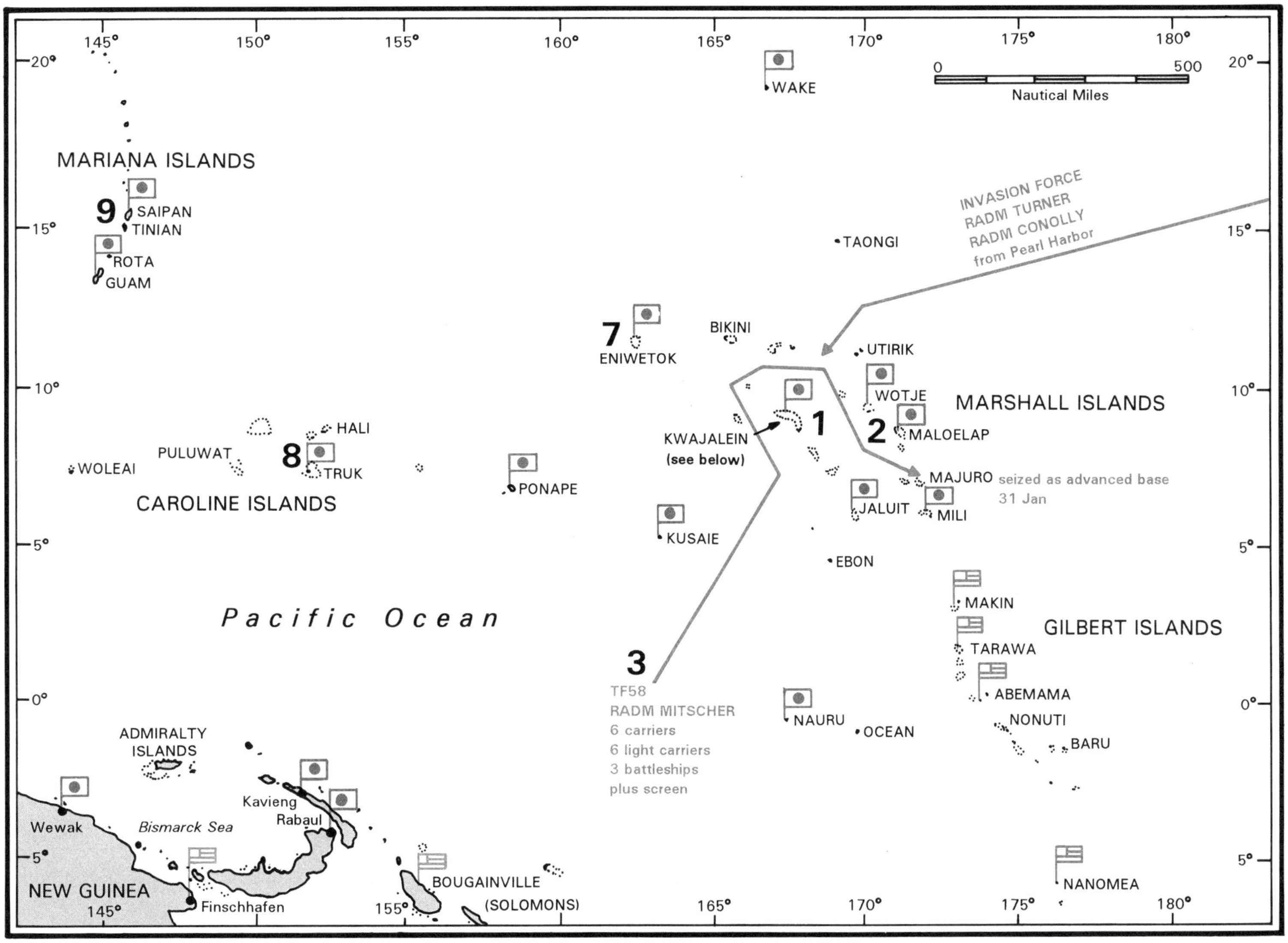

MARIANA ISLANDS
9 SAIPAN
TINIAN
ROTA
GUAM
WAKE
0 500
Nautical Miles
INVASION FORCE
RADM TURNER
RADM CONOLLY
from Pearl Harbor
TAONGI
7 ENIWETOK
BIKINI
UTIRIK
WOTJE
MARSHALL ISLANDS
KWAJALEIN
(see below)
1
2 MALOELAP
MAJURO seized as advanced base
31 Jan
JALUIT
MILI
HALI
PULUWAT
8 TRUK
WOLEAI
CAROLINE ISLANDS
PONAPE
KUSAIE
EBON
MAKIN
GILBERT ISLANDS
TARAWA
ABEMAMA
NONUTI
BARU
Pacific Ocean
3
TF58
RADM MITSCHER
6 carriers
6 light carriers
3 battleships
plus screen
NAURU
OCEAN
ADMIRALTY
ISLANDS
Kavieng
Rabaul
Wewak
Bismarck Sea
NEW GUINEA
Finschhafen
BOUGAINVILLE
(SOLOMONS)
NANOMEA
145° 150° 155° 160° 165° 170° 175° 180°
20° 15° 10° 5° 0° 5°

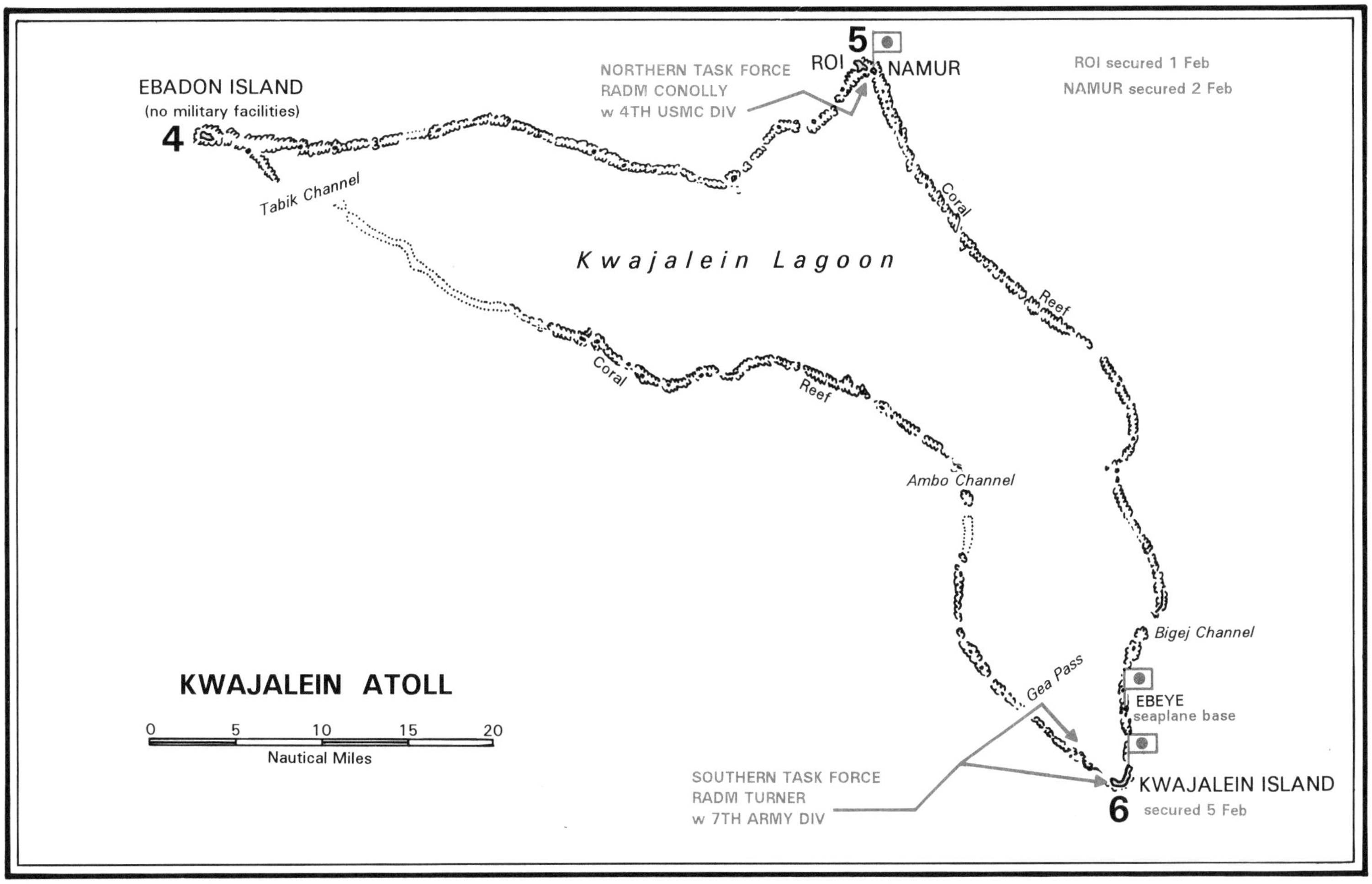

5 ROI NAMUR
NORTHERN TASK FORCE
RADM CONOLLY
w 4TH USMC DIV
ROI secured 1 Feb
NAMUR secured 2 Feb
EBADON ISLAND
(no military facilities)
4
Tabik Channel
Kwajalein Lagoon
Coral Reef
Coral Reef
Ambo Channel
Bigej Channel
Gea Pass
EBEYE
seaplane base
KWAJALEIN ISLAND
6 secured 5 Feb
SOUTHERN TASK FORCE
RADM TURNER
w 7TH ARMY DIV

KWAJALEIN ATOLL

0 5 10 15 20
Nautical Miles

MAP 68

CENTRAL PACIFIC DRIVE: THE MARIANAS

15–18 JUNE 1944

The American decision to leap from the Marshalls to the Marianas was a bold one, not only because it meant bypassing Japanese bases in the Carolines and leaving Truk on the American flank, but because of the distances involved. The Marianas were more than a thousand miles from the nearest Allied base and more than twice that from the staging bases in Hawaii and the Solomon Islands (see map A). At such distances, a shuttle transport system was impractical: everything necessary for the entire operation would have to be carried at one time. It would require a huge fleet—more than seven hundred vessels, from the fast carriers of Marc Mitscher's Task Force 58 to the LSTs and LCTs of Kelly Turner's amphibious force. The U.S. Navy would have to carry not only the 127,000 men of three and a half Marine divisions and an Army infantry division but also all the associated supporting equipment, including tanks, guns, trucks, food, fuel, ammunition, and supplies. As impressive as it was that the United States could assemble such an armada, it was doubly so in light of the fact that the Marianas campaign coincided with an even larger operation in the European theater: the long-awaited cross-channel invasion into occupied France (see map 70).

Of the fifteen islands in the Marianas archipelago, only the southernmost four had any military significance: Saipan, Tinian, Rota, and Guam (see map B). The first three had been Japanese since World War I; Guam had been a U.S. possession since the Spanish-American War and had been seized by the Japanese only days after the Pearl Harbor attack. The Japanese attached special importance to the defense of these islands. For one thing, it would be the first time the Americans had attacked an island with a significant Japanese civilian population. For another, the Marianas were only 1,200 miles from the home islands of Japan, within range of U.S. Army Air Corps B-29 Superfortress bombers. Though Guam was the largest of the Marianas, Saipan was the most important because it was the most heavily defended and the closest to Japan. Saipan, then, was the primary American target.

The 2nd and 4th Marine Divisions went ashore on Saipan on 15 June 1944 (see map C). The plan was to use amphtracs, tracked landing vehicles or LVTs, to move inland quickly so as to avoid becoming bogged down on the beach. That proved impossible, due partly to Japanese artillery and partly to unfriendly terrain. Though some twenty thousand U.S. Marines were ashore by nightfall of D-day, they had moved only about one thousand yards inland. That night the Japanese counterattacked, using tanks for the first time in the island-hopping campaign, though their assaults were poorly coordinated and characterized more by determination than effectiveness. The marines held their ground, and reinforced the next day, they began to fight their way inland, along with the 27th Infantry Division, against a force of thirty-two thousand Japanese.

Initially, the Japanese high command had decided that the Imperial Japanese Army would have to bear sole responsibility for the defense of the Marianas. Though Japanese naval officers still hoped for a decisive victory that would turn the war around, their fleet simply lacked the ability to challenge the Americans so far from Japanese bases in the southwestern Pacific. The reason was oil. American submarines had so devastated the Japanese tanker fleet that the Imperial Japanese Navy simply did not have enough fuel to maneuver beyond the western Pacific. In May, however, the commander of the Combined Fleet, Admiral Toyoda Soemu, ordered the commander of the newly reorganized First Mobile Fleet, ADM Ozawa Jisaburo, to top off his tanks with unprocessed crude oil straight from the East Indies wellheads and prepare to sortie for a showdown engagement with the enemy fleet.

On paper, Ozawa's force was impressive: nine carriers, six battleships (including the superbattleships *Yamato* and *Musashi*), eleven heavy cruisers, and thirty light cruisers and destroyers. But fuel was only one of Ozawa's problems. Two more were planes and pilots. Ozawa's nine carriers embarked just over four hundred airplanes, evenly divided between fighters and bombers. In comparison, Mitscher's Task Force 58 operated more than nine hundred planes off of fifteen carriers. Moreover, most of the Japanese pilots were novices compared to the veteran American flyers—even some of the "experienced" Japanese aviators had only six months of training. To compensate for these disadvantages, Ozawa relied heavily on two factors: the cooperation of land-based planes from Japanese airfields in the Marianas and other nearby islands, and the superior range of his carrier-based planes. Because Japanese aircraft were unarmored, they had a significantly greater range than comparable American planes—three hundred miles to two hundred miles. (Of course, the lack of armor was one reason the Japanese were so short of skilled pilots by 1944.) Ozawa calculated that he could launch his carrier-based fighters and bombers outside the range of U.S. carrier planes and, if necessary, have them land and refuel at airfields on Guam.

Ozawa's sortie presented Spruance with both a problem and an opportunity. On the one hand his orders specified that covering the Saipan beachhead was his primary responsibility. To perform that task, he had to position the carriers of Mitscher's TF 58 within two hundred miles of Saipan—the effective range of the American fighters and bombers. On the other hand, Spruance had learned at Midway that in a carrier battle, the side that got in the first strike had a tremendous advantage. Tethering TF 58 to Saipan would restrict Mitscher's freedom of movement and leave the initiative to Ozawa. Though Mitscher was eager to go on the offensive, the responsibility of choosing between these options belonged to the Fifth Fleet commander, Raymond A. Spruance.

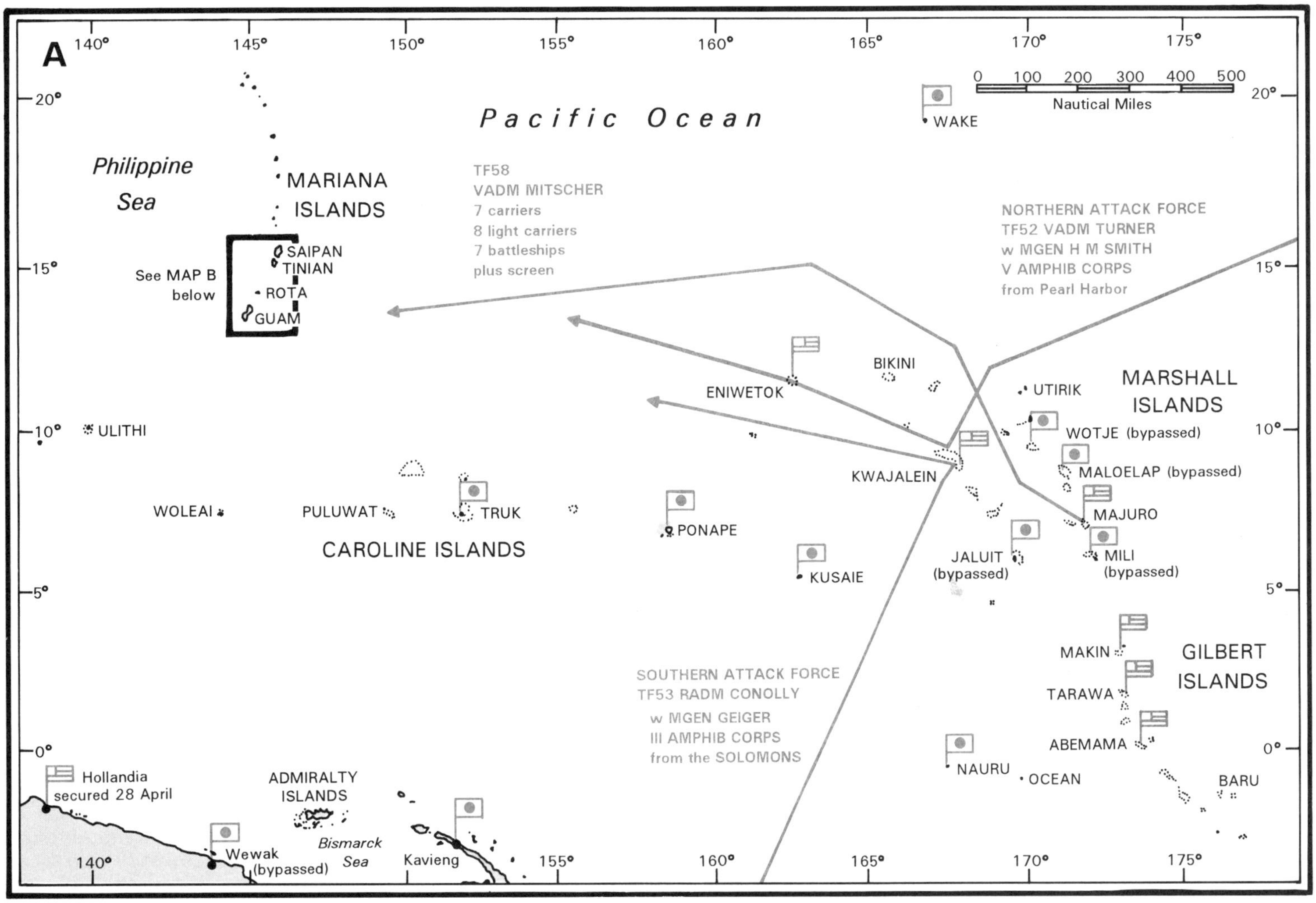

A
Pacific Ocean
Philippine Sea
MARIANA ISLANDS
SAIPAN
TINIAN
ROTA
GUAM
See MAP B below
TF58
VADM MITSCHER
7 carriers
8 light carriers
7 battleships
plus screen
NORTHERN ATTACK FORCE
TF52 VADM TURNER
w MGEN H M SMITH
V AMPHIB CORPS
from Pearl Harbor
WAKE
0 100 200 300 400 500
Nautical Miles
BIKINI
ENIWETOK
UTIRIK
MARSHALL ISLANDS
WOTJE (bypassed)
KWAJALEIN
MALOELAP (bypassed)
MAJURO
JALUIT (bypassed)
MILI (bypassed)
ULITHI
WOLEAI
PULUWAT
TRUK
PONAPE
CAROLINE ISLANDS
KUSAIE
MAKIN
TARAWA
ABEMAMA
GILBERT ISLANDS
SOUTHERN ATTACK FORCE
TF53 RADM CONOLLY
w MGEN GEIGER
III AMPHIB CORPS
from the SOLOMONS
NAURU
OCEAN
BARU
Hollandia secured 28 April
ADMIRALTY ISLANDS
Wewak (bypassed)
Bismarck Sea
Kavieng
140° 145° 150° 155° 160° 165° 170° 175°
20° 15° 10° 5° 0°

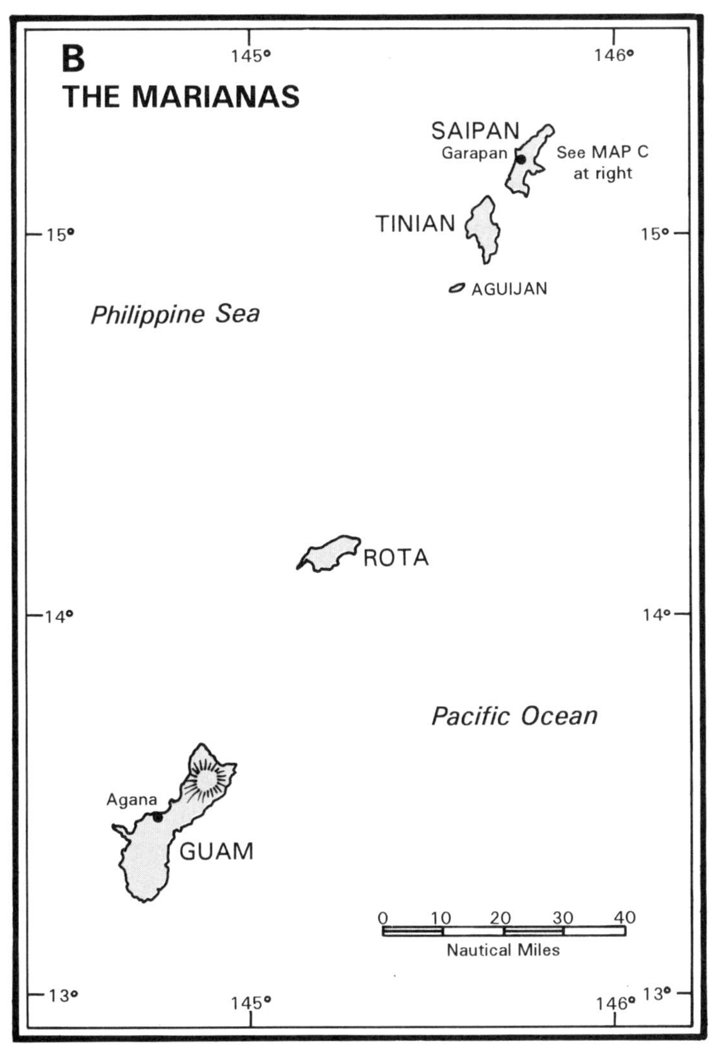
B
THE MARIANAS
145°
146°
SAIPAN
Garapan
See MAP C at right
TINIAN
AGUIJAN
Philippine Sea
ROTA
Pacific Ocean
Agana
GUAM
0 10 20 30 40
Nautical Miles
15°
14°
13°

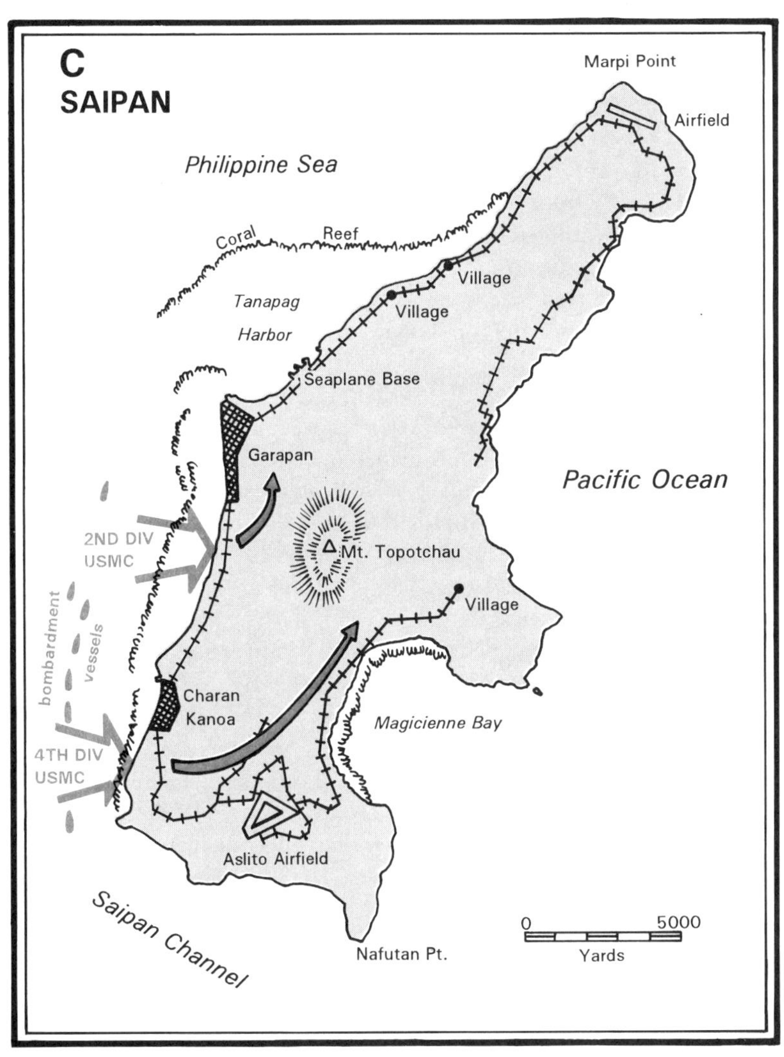
C
SAIPAN
Marpi Point
Airfield
Philippine Sea
Coral Reef
Tanapag Harbor
Village
Village
Seaplane Base
Garapan
Pacific Ocean
Mt. Topotchau
2ND DIV USMC
bombardment vessels
Village
Charan Kanoa
Magicienne Bay
4TH DIV USMC
Aslito Airfield
Saipan Channel
Nafutan Pt.
0 5000
Yards

MAP 69

BATTLE OF THE PHILIPPINE SEA (THE MARIANAS TURKEY SHOOT)

19–20 JUNE 1944

The same morning that the Marines went ashore on Saipan, Spruance received two reports from American submarine commanders. At 6:35 A.M. the *Albacore* reported the location and composition of Ozawa's force debouching from San Bernardino Strait (1); then only a hour later the *Seahorse* reported a *second* fleet approaching from the south (2). This was VADM Ugaki Matome's battleship force bound for a rendezvous with Ozawa. These reports proved that there were at least two Japanese forces at sea. Spruance postponed the planned American landing on Guam until the situation clarified itself, and after detaching seven battleships and eight other warships for duty off Saipan, he concentrated Mitscher's Task Force 58 and RADM Willis Lee's battleship force 180 miles to the west (3).

On 17 June the submarine *Cavalla* updated Ozawa's location (4) but reported seeing only fifteen ships. Fifteen! Where were the rest? Spruance was well aware of the Japanese predilection for complicated operational plans. It seemed likely to him that Ozawa's carrier force was a feint to draw TF 58 away from the beachhead and allow an "end run" by Japanese surface forces. To take care of that possibility, Spruance ordered Mitscher's carriers, arrayed in four groups, to remain within supporting distance of Saipan. Fifteen miles west of the carriers, Spruance deployed Lee's fast battleship group to provide an AA screen and an advance warning of enemy raids. The entire armada would steam west (toward the enemy) in daylight, then east (away from the enemy) at night, all the time within a two hundred–mile radius of the beachheads on Saipan.

These dispositions seemed to offer Ozawa a rare opportunity. The longer range of his planes, combined with the availability of air bases on Guam, meant that he could remain outside the range of the American bombers and attack Mitscher's "tethered" fleet with impunity. But Ozawa's confidence was based on unrealistic expectations of support from VADM Kakuta Kakuji's planes on Guam. Though Imperial Japanese Navy Headquarters had led Ozawa to expect help from as many as five hundred land-based planes, Kakuta could put fewer than one hundred in the air. Moreover, Spruance had ordered a series of strikes against Guam's airfields (5) to render them virtually unusable.

Ozawa launched his first strike, consisting of fifty-three bombers and torpedo planes and sixteen fighters, at 8:30 A.M. on 19 June (6). A half hour later he launched another, even larger, strike. At 10:30 Mitscher's F6F Hellcats met the Japanese planes approaching TF 58 (7). The seasoned American pilots shot down all but seventeen of the enemy planes in the first wave, while Japanese bombers scored only one hit—on the battleship *South Dakota.* An hour later the American fighters pounced on the planes of the second strike force. Hellcat pilots downed seventy more enemy planes, and accurate AA fire accounted for another twenty-seven. One Japanese pilot crashed his torpedo-bomber into the *Indiana,* and near bomb misses caused casualties on several American warships, but no ships were seriously damaged. To the experienced American pilots, it was a "turkey shoot."

Ozawa launched two more raids before the day was over—forty-seven Japanese planes attacked from the north at 1:00 in the afternoon (8), and an hour or so later eighty-two planes flew toward a false sighting south of the American fleet and failed to make contact (9). Meanwhile, American bombers plastered the runways at Orote Airfield so that when a few survivors from Ozawa's strikes tried to land on the damaged runways, they either crashed or were shot down. The day-long air battle finally ended after dusk with the Japanese having lost some 315 aircraft; the Americans lost a total of 30.

While American naval aviators shot down Japanese planes, the Navy's submarines sank enemy carriers. Having fulfilled their task of shadowing Ozawa's force and reporting its progress, the American subs now became hunters. At 9:00 that morning, just as Ozawa was launching his second strike, the *Albacore* put one torpedo into his flagship, the brand-new 33,000-ton *Taiho,* and three hours later the *Cavalla* pumped three torpedoes into the *Shokaku* (10). The *Shokaku* went down almost at once, but remarkably, so did the *Taiho* when the volatility of the unrefined crude petroleum the Japanese were forced to use as fuel caused a huge internal explosion.

Still, the American carrier-based bombers had not yet had their innings, and having been forced to stand on the defense all day, they were eager to strike back. By nightfall Spruance was satisfied that there were no other enemy surface units preparing an "end run," and he gave Mitscher the go-ahead to pursue. All night TF 58 steamed west at twenty-three knots. A dawn search revealed only empty seas, but at 3:40 that afternoon (20 June) a search plane from the *Enterprise* spotted the Japanese fleet retiring to the northwest 275 miles away. Despite the hour and the range, Mitscher launched more than two hundred planes toward the enemy (11). Only then was it determined that the true distance was closer to 350 miles. Still, the U.S. pilots pressed on, and in the gathering dusk they sank the light carrier *Hiyo* and damaged several other ships (12). Then they had to return to their own carriers in the dark and low on fuel. Mitscher ordered the U.S. carriers to turn on their lights despite the danger of attracting the attention of Japanese subs. Some eighty American planes were lost due to either insufficient fuel or accidents during recovery, but most of their pilots were recovered.

Despite these losses, and despite Mitscher's expressed disappointment that "the enemy had escaped," the Battle of the Philippine Sea was a decisive American victory. Japanese naval air power had ceased to exist.

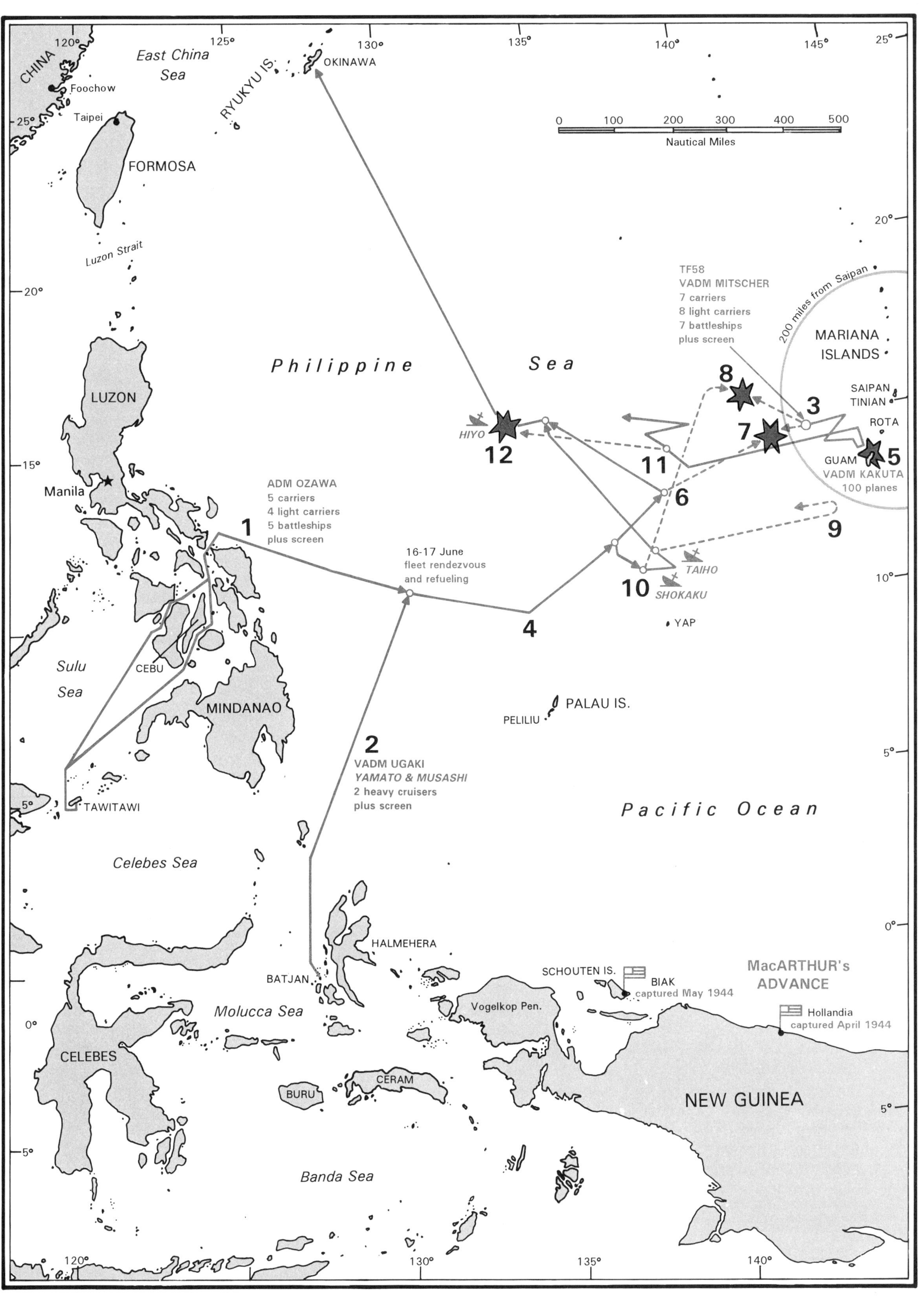
CHINA
Foochow
Taipei
FORMOSA
East China Sea
RYUKYU IS.
OKINAWA
Luzon Strait
LUZON
Manila
Philippine Sea
TF58
VADM MITSCHER
7 carriers
8 light carriers
7 battleships
plus screen
200 miles from Saipan
MARIANA ISLANDS
SAIPAN
TINIAN
ROTA
GUAM
VADM KAKUTA
100 planes
0 100 200 300 400 500
Nautical Miles
HIYO
TAIHO
SHOKAKU
ADM OZAWA
5 carriers
4 light carriers
5 battleships
plus screen
16-17 June
fleet rendezvous
and refueling
1
2
3
4
5
6
7
8
9
10
11
12
YAP
CEBU
Sulu Sea
MINDANAO
PALAU IS.
PELILIU
VADM UGAKI
YAMATO & MUSASHI
2 heavy cruisers
plus screen
TAWITAWI
Pacific Ocean
Celebes Sea
HALMEHERA
BATJAN
SCHOUTEN IS.
BIAK
captured May 1944
MacARTHUR's ADVANCE
Hollandia
captured April 1944
Vogelkop Pen.
Molucca Sea
CELEBES
BURU
CERAM
NEW GUINEA
Banda Sea

MAP 70

NEPTUNE AND OVERLORD: THE LANDINGS IN NORMANDY

6 JUNE 1944

While U.S. forces in the Pacific were leaping a thousand miles westward, Allied forces in Europe embarked on the most important amphibious operation in the history of warfare: the long-awaited invasion of German-occupied France. The salient characteristic of NEPTUNE (the naval and amphibious phase) and OVERLORD (the overall invasion plan) was the enormous scale of the operation. During NEPTUNE, which lasted from 6 to 24 June, more than 4,000 Allied vessels landed 714,000 men, more than 111,000 vehicles, and more than 250,000 tons of supplies in France. In terms of manpower and resources, it was the single largest undertaking in American military-naval history.

The man tasked with overall command responsibility for OVERLORD was an American, GEN Dwight D. Eisenhower. But all three of his senior subordinates were British officers: GEN Sir Bernard Montgomery commanded the ground troops, Air Chief Marshall Sir Tafford Leigh-Mallory commanded the air forces, and ADM Sir Bertram Ramsay commanded the naval forces with responsibility for NEPTUNE.

For more than a year the Allies had participated in an elaborate scheme to keep the Germans from guessing the site of the cross-channel invasion. In the end, Normandy was selected over the Pas de Calais (1) because the Allies needed the port facilities at Cherbourg (2) and Le Havre (3). Until those ports were secured, however, the Allies would have to rely on supplies arriving over the beach, and to facilitate that effort, British planners devised innovative floating docks called "mulberries" and an offshore breakwater of sunken hulks to create a temporary harbor.

The weather provided some last-minute drama. Originally planned for May, D-Day was finally set for 5 June. But on 4 June the channel blew up into a gale, forcing Eisenhower to postpone the attack, and ships already at sea had to be recalled. Though the meteorologists called for improved conditions on the sixth, the outlook was still uncertain. Nevertheless, at 4:15 A.M. on 5 June Eisenhower made his decision, announcing, "O.K. We'll go."

The minesweepers cleared a channel (the Spout) through the German mine fields (4) and marked the channel with buoys, while ships from nearly every port in southern England assembled at Area Zebra (5) for the push south. The Germans, assuming that the poor weather would keep the Allies in port, were unaware that the Allied armada had sailed; Field Marshall Irwin Rommel, the German Army Group B commander, went home to attend his wife's birthday party. At 1:30 A.M. on 6 June one thousand Allied planes dropped one British and two American paratroop divisions (the 82nd and 101st) behind the targeted beachheads (see lower map). Even now, the Germans hesitated. Finally, at 5:00 A.M. Allied warships opened fire on the German beach defenses, and Allied bombers rained ordnance on the nearby countryside. (Alas, fearful of hitting the landing forces on an overcast day, most of the Allied planes dropped their ordnance too far inland, leaving the German strong points undamaged.)

Even before the battleships opened fire, Allied soldiers in the invasion force had begun to clamber into their landing craft, bobbing violently in the choppy waters of the Bay of the Seine. Five Allied divisions would go ashore on D-Day: two divisions of the American First Army (LGEN Omar Bradley) landed on Utah (6) and Omaha (7) Beaches, while two British divisions and one Canadian division of the British Second Army (LGEN Sir Miles Dempsey) headed toward three beaches (8) north of Caen (Gold, Juno, and Sword). A naval task force backed each army. The bombardment group of RADM Alan Kirk's Western Task Force, including the old 14-inch–gun battlewagons *Texas* and *Arkansas* and a dozen cruisers, provided gunfire support for Utah and Omaha Beaches, while another bombardment group from RADM Sir Philip Vian's Eastern Task Force, which included the Pearl Harbor survivor *Nevada,* performed the same service for the British and Canadians.

On the British and Canadian beaches, opposition was relatively light. The same was true on Utah Beach where, by fortuitous chance, the set of the tide carried the landing boats some two thousand yards south of their targeted beaches and deposited the invaders in a weakly defended area (9). On Omaha Beach, however, it was a different story. As at Tarawa, astonishing personal bravery amidst confusion and unforeseen disasters characterized the American landings. A majority of the amphibious tanks that were supposed to be able to "swim" ashore went straight to the bottom with their crews inside. Likewise, most of the field artillery loaded into the generally reliable DUKWs failed to make it to shore through the heavy seas and enemy gunfire. The men of the 1st and 29th Infantry Divisions found themselves trapped on the narrow strip of Omaha Beach under heavy fire, with little tank or artillery support. By persistence and the sheer press of numbers, plus some crucial gunfire support from the destroyers of Kirk's Western Task Force, the Americans managed to secure the beach and work their way to the high ground to establish a toehold on the coast.

By the end of D-Day the Allied foothold was secure enough that Eisenhower could discard the press release he had prepared in case the landings had failed. Moreover, the ability of the Allied navies to sustain the men on the beach with a continuous flow of reinforcements and supplies allowed the invaders to expand their lodgement in the coming days and weeks. In the end, it was this ability to sustain and supply the Allied armies that made the campaign in Europe possible.

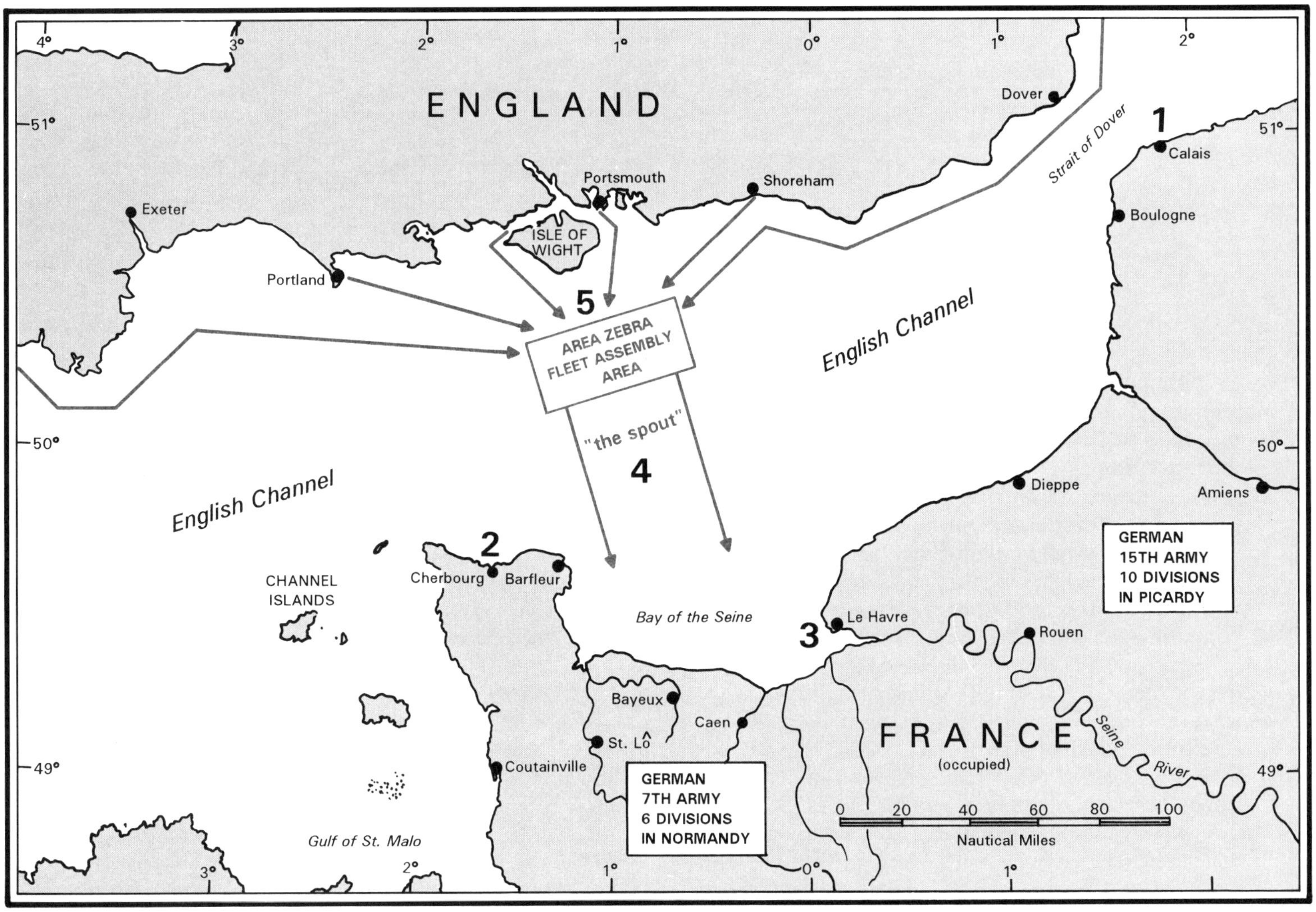

4° 3° 2° 1° 0° 1° 2°

ENGLAND

Dover

51°

1

Calais

Strait of Dover

Portsmouth

Shoreham

Exeter

Boulogne

ISLE OF WIGHT

Portland

5

AREA ZEBRA
FLEET ASSEMBLY
AREA

English Channel

"the spout"

4

50°

English Channel

Dieppe

Amiens

2

Cherbourg

Barfleur

CHANNEL
ISLANDS

GERMAN
15TH ARMY
10 DIVISIONS
IN PICARDY

Bay of the Seine

Le Havre

3

Rouen

Bayeux

Caen

St. Lô

Coutainville

FRANCE
(occupied)

Seine River

49°

GERMAN
7TH ARMY
6 DIVISIONS
IN NORMANDY

0 20 40 60 80 100
Nautical Miles

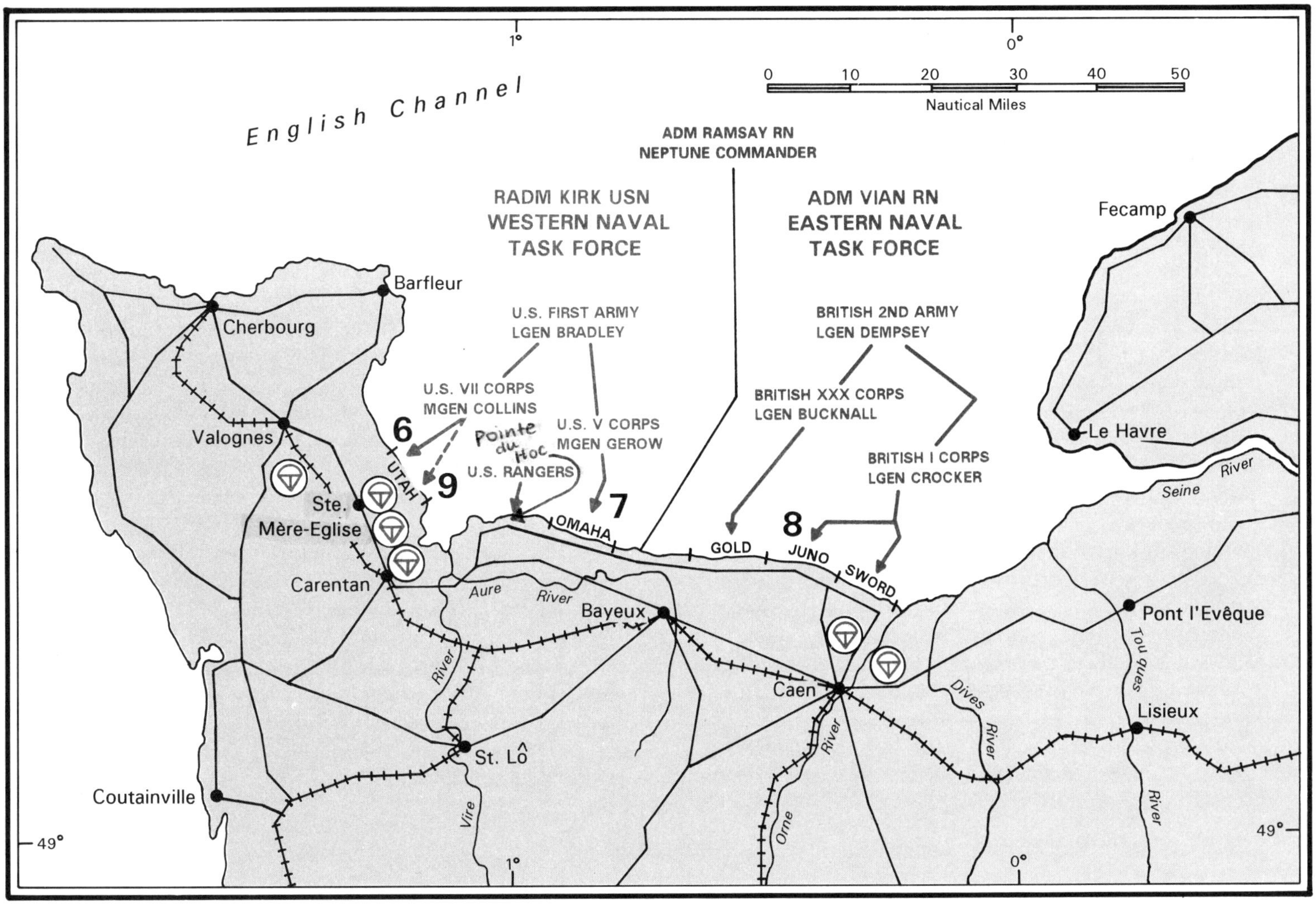

Gulf of St. Malo

3° 2° 1° 0° 1°

1° 0°

0 10 20 30 40 50
Nautical Miles

English Channel

ADM RAMSAY RN
NEPTUNE COMMANDER

RADM KIRK USN
WESTERN NAVAL
TASK FORCE

ADM VIAN RN
EASTERN NAVAL
TASK FORCE

Fecamp

Barfleur

Cherbourg

U.S. FIRST ARMY
LGEN BRADLEY

BRITISH 2ND ARMY
LGEN DEMPSEY

U.S. VII CORPS
MGEN COLLINS

BRITISH XXX CORPS
LGEN BUCKNALL

Valognes

6

Pointe du Hoc

U.S. V CORPS
MGEN GEROW

Le Havre

UTAH

9

U.S. RANGERS

BRITISH I CORPS
LGEN CROCKER

Seine River

Ste. Mère-Eglise

7

8

OMAHA

GOLD

JUNO

SWORD

Carentan

Aure River

Bayeux

Pont l'Evêque

Touques River

Caen

Dives River

Lisieux

Vire River

Orne River

St. Lô

Coutainville

49°

1° 0°

49°

Map 71

The Allied Breakout and ANVIL (DRAGOON)

July–August 1944

Despite the Allied success in gaining a lodgement on the northwestern coast of France, the battle for Normandy hung in precarious balance for most of a month. After their initial surprise, the Germans counterattacked with ferocity and skill despite a complete lack of air cover. Worse yet, from the Allied viewpoint, was the storm that nature unleashed on 18 June. For four days high winds and heavy seas battered the ships of the invasion armada, wrecking the "mulberry" off Omaha Beach. To secure reliable logistic support, the seizure of the Cherbourg port facilities became the highest Allied priority.

Hitler had ordered the forty thousand Germans defending Cherbourg (1) under the command of GEN Karl-Wilhelm von Schlieben to hold the port at all costs. Hitler still hoped to contain the Allied lodgement by denying a port facility to the invaders. The American VII Corps of MGEN J. Lawton Collins began the attack on Cherbourg on 22 June. The Germans fell back into the inner defenses, and the Americans had to fight their way pillbox-by-pillbox into the city, aided by naval gunfire from the old battleships *Texas* and *Arkansas*. After five days the Allies declared the city secure.

The Anglo-American forces devoted the next several weeks to building up their resources in Normandy in preparation for the drive to the Seine River. The one millionth American soldier came ashore in Normandy on the Fourth of July, and two days later LGEN George S. Patton flew in to take command of a newly organized Third Army (2). By the end of the month the Third Army was operational, and almost immediately it achieved a breakout near Avranches (3) and began to drive south and east, fanning out across the French countryside as German resistance weakened. At the same time, British and Canadian forces advanced south from Caen, and soon the Germans were caught in a pocket (the Falaise Gap) that closed on 21 August and trapped fifty thousand German soldiers and more than a thousand tanks and guns (4).

Meanwhile, the Allies pressed ahead with a plan to invade southern France. Originally code-named ANVIL, Churchill insisted the operation be called DRAGOON, claiming the Americans had dragooned him into it. Churchill opposed the landings near Toulon and Marseille because he was once again urging consideration of a favorite theme: an advance through Trieste at the head of the Adriatic Sea, and then north through the Ljubljana Gap into eastern Europe. In part this was a reflection of Churchill's penchant for sideshow operations, but his motives were also political: he wanted to ensure the occupation of eastern Europe by Anglo-American armies before the arrival of the Red Army advancing through Poland from the east. But his scheme was both militarily and logistically unrealistic; the Americans never considered it a serious military alternative. Instead, the Allies would go ahead with ANVIL-DRAGOON.

The troops for DRAGOON came from the Italian front, where the Allies had captured Rome on 4 June after a long siege. The landing craft and gunfire-support ships, commanded by RADM Morton Deyo, were mostly veterans of NEPTUNE released after the fall of Cherbourg. A group of escort carriers commanded by RADM Calvin Durgin provided air cover. D-day was set for 15 August, just as the Falaise Gap was closing.

In contrast with the landings in Normandy, DRAGOON's were a model of timing and efficiency. It helped considerably that the enemy forces in this case were mostly conscripts—including many reluctant warriors from Poland and Czechoslovakia whom the Germans had pressed into service. Moreover, the beaches and the weather on the French Riviera were close to ideal. Finally, the invaders benefited from the experiences of their colleagues in Normandy. This combination of circumstances made the DRAGOON landings a textbook model of amphibious operations.

Before dawn on 15 August five thousand paratroopers landed behind the beaches to seal them off from any enemy reinforcements. Beginning at 6:00 A.M., 1,300 Allied planes bombed the three targeted beaches—Alpha, Delta, and Camel—along a thirty-mile stretch of the French Riviera from Cannes to Toulon (5). Then at 7:30 A.M. the naval gunfire took over, targeting specific objectives and strong points with the aid of aerial spotters from the escort carriers. As the Allied landing craft approached the beach, the naval gunfire lifted or moved inland, and at 8:00 the infantrymen stepped ashore. There were remarkably few casualties against light opposition, especially when compared with the heavy losses at Omaha Beach.

Once ashore, three divisions of the American 7th Army (LGEN Alexander Patch), under the command of MGEN Lucian K. Truscott, began to drive inland up the Rhône River Valley. At the same time, Free French forces under Général d'Armée de Lattre de Tassigny headed west along the coast to capture Marseille and Toulon (7). These ports capitulated on 28 August, and two weeks later the Franco-American forces met elements of Patton's Third Army at Dijon (6). Independent of this campaign, Paris (8) surrendered on 25 August.

The war in Europe was not over. There was still the Battle of the Bulge in December, the siege at Bastogne (9), and the crossing of the Rhine, another movement that involved Army-Navy cooperation, in March 1945. But from August of 1944 to V-E Day on 8 May 1945, the war in Europe was an Army war. The popular celebrations that followed news of the German surrender in May were muted because of the death of Franklin Roosevelt on 12 April and the knowledge that the war in the Pacific was far from over.

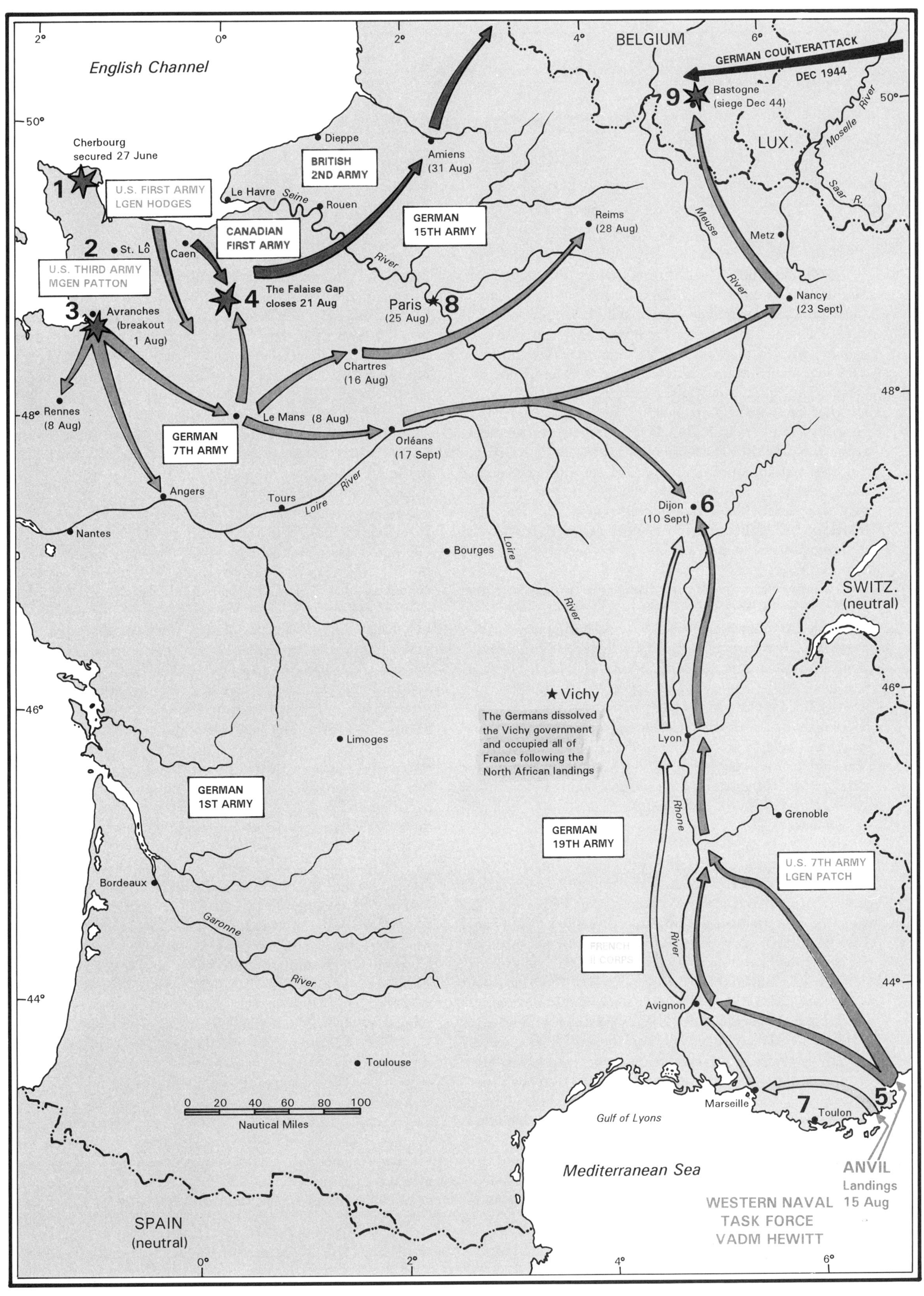
English Channel
BELGIUM
GERMAN COUNTERATTACK
DEC 1944
9
Bastogne
(siege Dec 44)
LUX.
Moselle
River
Saar R.
Meuse
River
Metz
Nancy
(23 Sept)
Cherbourg
secured 27 June
1
U.S. FIRST ARMY
LGEN HODGES
Dieppe
BRITISH
2ND ARMY
Amiens
(31 Aug)
Le Havre
Seine
Rouen
GERMAN
15TH ARMY
Reims
(28 Aug)
CANADIAN
FIRST ARMY
2
St. Lô
Caen
River
U.S. THIRD ARMY
MGEN PATTON
4
The Falaise Gap
closes 21 Aug
Paris
(25 Aug)
8
3
Avranches
(breakout
1 Aug)
Chartres
(16 Aug)
Rennes
(8 Aug)
Le Mans (8 Aug)
GERMAN
7TH ARMY
Orléans
(17 Sept)
Angers
Tours
Loire
River
Nantes
Dijon
(10 Sept)
6
Bourges
Loire
River
SWITZ.
(neutral)
Vichy
The Germans dissolved
the Vichy government
and occupied all of
France following the
North African landings
Limoges
Lyon
GERMAN
1ST ARMY
Rhone
Grenoble
GERMAN
19TH ARMY
U.S. 7TH ARMY
LGEN PATCH
Bordeaux
Garonne
River
River
Avignon
Toulouse
0 20 40 60 80 100
Nautical Miles
Marseille
7
Toulon
5
Gulf of Lyons
Mediterranean Sea
ANVIL
Landings
15 Aug
WESTERN NAVAL
TASK FORCE
VADM HEWITT
SPAIN
(neutral)
2°
0°
2°
4°
6°
50°
48°
46°
44°

MAP 72

RETURN TO THE PHILIPPINES

JULY–OCTOBER 1944

Following the capture of the Marianas, the commanders who had engineered the Central Pacific Drive—Raymond Spruance, Richmond Kelly Turner, and Holland M. Smith—were recalled to Pearl Harbor to plan the next step in the war against Japan. In their place, King installed a new command team and redesignated the Fifth Fleet as the Third Fleet, with VADM William F. "Bull" Halsey in overall command (see inset). Mitscher stayed on as commander of the fast carrier force, now designated as TF 38 instead of TF 58. (Intercepting references to the U.S. Third Fleet, the Japanese assumed the Americans had deployed an entirely new force. What kind of hydralike enemy was this, they wondered, that grew whole new fleets after each battle?) The change in fleet command bred a change in style as well. Whereas Spruance's great strength was his calculating coolness, Halsey was known to the public as a bold, even reckless, fighter.

Meanwhile, U.S. planners contemplated their next step. The Philippine Islands had been at the core of American strategy in the Pacific even before the first bombs dropped on Pearl Harbor. With the seizure of the Marianas, however, some Navy planners, and in particular Admiral King, doubted the strategic necessity of an attack on the Philippines. Why not bypass these well-defended islands, King asked, and instead invade Formosa (1), which could provide equally valuable anchorages and would also be a stepping-stone to the coast of China, whose mainland airfields could be used to bomb the Japanese home islands? Such a suggestion was pure anathema to MacArthur, who had made his promise to return to the Philippines a personal mantra.

To resolve the issue, MacArthur and Nimitz met with President Roosevelt in Hawaii in July. At their meeting MacArthur argued that a reconquest of the Philippines was not only good strategy, it was also good politics, for otherwise Asians would never again trust the word or the resolve of the United States. Roosevelt found MacArthur's arguments compelling, but he left the final decision to the Joint Chiefs. The JCS subsequently determined that Mindanao, and not Formosa, would be the next Allied target, a decision confirmed at a meeting of the Combined Chiefs of Staff (CSS) at the Quebec Conference in September. There, Allied planners approved a series of preliminary landings in the Palaus (2), in the western Carolines (3), and on Morotai (4) during September and October, a landing on Mindanao (5) in November, and finally a landing on Leyte (6) in December. But even as the Combined Chiefs were ratifying these decisions, they received a message from Halsey that led them to scrap these plans and accelerate the timetable.

In a series of raids against Japanese bases in the Philippines in early September, Halsey's carriers encountered an almost inexplicably weak response from the defenders. What Halsey did not know was that Admiral Toyoda had ordered his commanders to conserve their airplanes for the coming naval battle. Unaware of this, Halsey wrote to Nimitz to suggest that U.S. forces ought to skip the attack on Mindanao and strike directly at Leyte. He recommended a landing on 20 October, a full two months ahead of the schedule that had just been devised. Nimitz relayed Halsey's recommendations on to the CCS, still meeting in Quebec, who after obtaining MacArthur's approval revised the timetable. Not all the preliminary landings were scrapped, however. Nimitz decided to go ahead with the landings in the Palau Group, five hundred miles west of Mindanao, mainly because the invasion fleet was already at sea. It was arguably Nimitz's only major error of the war.

On 15 September the 1st Marine Division landed on Peleliu, the southernmost island of the Palau Group (2), while five hundred miles to the southwest the 31st Infantry Division landed on Morotai (4). Because the initial landings on Peleliu were uncontested, the U.S. commanders hoped for a walkover. But those hopes were soon dashed. An island dominated by a series of limestone ridges pockmarked by phosphate mines, Peleliu was a labyrinth of caves and man-made tunnels, some quite elaborate, which the Japanese had turned into a defensive maze impervious to aerial bombing or naval gunfire. The 1st Marines, later joined by elements of the U.S. Army's 81st Division, had to go into the caves and tunnels and take out the enemy one at a time. Before the island was secured more than two months later, U.S. losses totaled one thousand killed and five thousand wounded. The only strategic advantage gained for this sacrifice was a foretaste of the kind of fighting that Americans would encounter on Iwo Jima and Okinawa.

While the Marines fought the enemy hand-to-hand on Peleliu, the U.S. Seventh Fleet, commanded by VADM Thomas Kinkaid, steamed into Leyte Gulf, where four U.S. Army divisions went ashore on Leyte at 10:00 A.M. on 21 October (6). It was MacArthur's hour. He splashed ashore from a landing craft in the afternoon, toured the beachhead, and later at a carefully staged ceremony in Tacloban stepped up to a radio microphone to announce: "This is the voice of freedom, General MacArthur speaking. People of the Philippines, I have returned!"

The American return to the Philippines would not go unchallenged. The Japanese perception of the strategic value of those islands, situated astride Japan's line of communications with the oil-rich southwestern Pacific, had been Japan's reason for going to war in the first place, and Japan would not give them up without a desperate struggle. As soon as news of the American landings on Leyte reached him, Admiral Toyoda issued orders to initiate SHO-1, thus touching off the greatest naval battle in history: the Battle for Leyte Gulf.

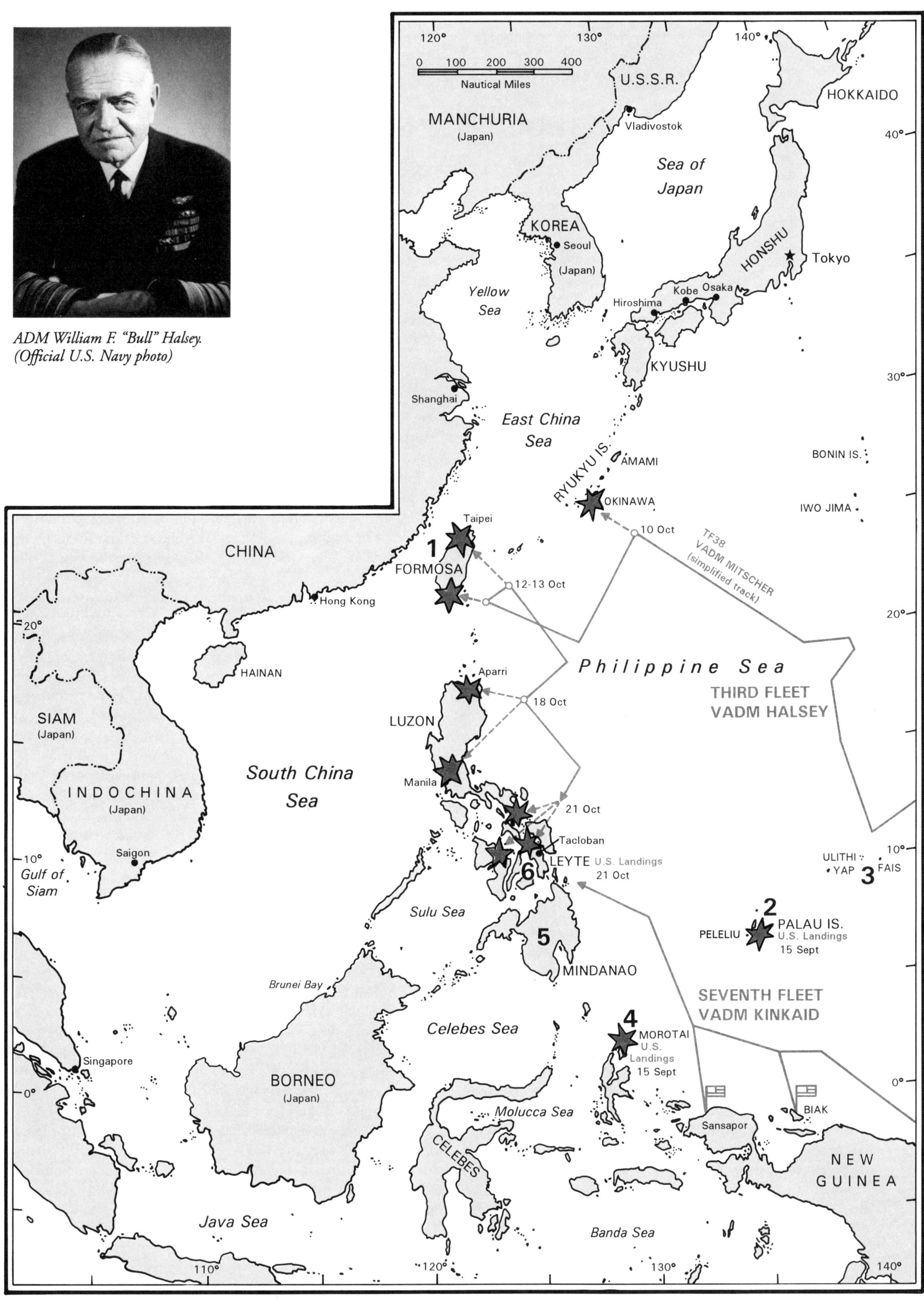

ADM William F. "Bull" Halsey. (Official U.S. Navy photo)

MAP 73

LEYTE GULF: THE SIBUYAN SEA

23 OCTOBER 1944

Determined as they were to strike at the American invasion armada, the Japanese were constrained by their greatly diminished naval assets. Ozawa's First Mobile Fleet, licking its wounds in the Inland Sea (1) after the Marianas Turkey Shoot, still boasted ten aircraft carriers, but those carriers had few airplanes and still fewer experienced pilots. It was doubtful that this force could even defend itself effectively in a fleet engagement, much less drive off the combined strength of the American Third and Seventh Fleets. A more lethal strike force was the substantial fleet of battleships and heavy cruisers at Linga Roads (2) near Singapore. Once he determined that Leyte was the target of the American armada gathering in the southern Philippine Sea, Admiral Toyoda ordered this force to sortie.

The Japanese ships at Linga put to sea on 18 October and shaped a course for Brunei Bay (3) on Borneo's western coast, where they refueled—again relying on unrefined crude straight from the wellheads. Four days later (22 October), with fuel tanks topped off, this fleet left Brunei and headed for the Philippines in two formations: ADM Kurita Takeo commanded the stronger of the two groups, five battleships (including the superbattleships *Yamato* and *Musashi*), ten heavy and two light cruisers, and fifteen destroyers. The second group, commanded by VADM Nishimura Shoji, consisted of two battleships, one cruiser, and four destroyers. To strengthen this smaller force, Toyoda ordered a cruiser-destroyer force under VADM Shima Kiyohide from the Ryukyus to support Nishimura (4). In Toyoda's concept, these forces would constitute the hammer and the anvil of a double envelopment of Leyte Gulf. While Nishimura's Southern Force, reinforced by Shima, transited Surigao Strait to attack the Americans from the south (5), Kurita's fleet would charge out of San Bernardino Strait (6) to destroy the U.S. invasion fleet.

One problem with this plan was that these Japanese surface forces could not reasonably expect to get within gunnery range of the American invasion force without air cover. Toyoda's solution to this dilemma was creative but also desperate. First of all, Kurita and Nishimura would approach the landing beaches from the west, passing through straits in the Philippine archipelago where they could call upon support from Japanese land-based air. This was something of a slender reed, however. Land-based air support had proved disappointing in the Marianas campaign, and Toyoda was not altogether sure he could rely upon the Army's full cooperation. He, therefore, counted even more on deception and distraction. The key to his plan was a gambit to lure Halsey and his fast carrier force away from the beachhead. To do this, Toyoda ordered Admiral Ozawa (7) to steam south through the Philippine Sea and launch air strikes against the American carrier force. Ozawa's mission was to attract Halsey's attention and entice him to attack. His task force consisted of only one fleet carrier (the *Zuikaku*) and three light carriers, plus two converted battleships fitted with flight decks aft, and about one hundred planes. It was not a strike force; it was a sacrificial offering.

At Leyte Gulf, American naval forces from both MacArthur's and Nimitz's commands had come together to support the Leyte landings. The Seventh Fleet, under the direct command of VADM Thomas C. Kinkaid, was part of MacArthur's Southwest Pacific command; the Third Fleet, under Halsey, was part of Nimitz's command. Kinkaid, charged with direct support of the landings, had no fleet carriers, but he did have sixteen escort carriers arranged in three groups (designated Taffy 1, 2, and 3) under RADM Thomas L. Sprague. Halsey's four carrier groups patrolled the waters east of the landing site, providing air cover and seeking an opportunity to engage the Japanese fleet.

Halsey and Kinkaid first learned about the approaching Japanese strike force at 6:00 A.M. on 23 October when two American submarines, the *Darter* and *Dace,* reported the location, course, and speed of Kurita's force in the South China Sea (8). After dutifully reporting, the two subs attacked, sinking two cruisers (including Kurita's flagship) and so badly damaging a third that two destroyers had to escort it back to Brunei. Having lost five of his thirty-two ships in the first twenty-four hours, Kurita nevertheless steamed on toward the Sibuyan Sea.

Warned by the submarines, Halsey sent out search planes at dawn on 24 October, and soon thereafter American pilots located and inflicted minor damage on Nishimura's force in the Sulu Sea (9). Then just after 8:00 A.M. other search planes reported Kurita's presence in the Sibuyan Sea (10). His ships were without the promised air cover because the Japanese commander in the Philippines chose to support Kurita by attacking Halsey's carriers. These attackers managed to sink the light carrier *Princeton,* but they failed to distract Halsey's attention or diminish his striking power.

In the confined waters of the Sibuyan Sea, and with no air cover, Kurita's warships were sitting ducks. Though the Japanese had added scores of new AA guns to their surface ships, these proved little more than a nuisance to the American pilots, who delivered their ordnance on the most valuable targets. Four of Kurita's five battleships were badly crippled, including the *Musashi,* which was hit by nineteen torpedoes and seventeen bombs and later sank, taking more than 1,100 men with it. Disgusted by the absence of air support, Kurita ordered the remainder of his fleet to reverse course.

But though Kurita did not know it, Toyoda's plan was about to bear fruit. Even as Kurita turned away, Ozawa was launching an air strike of some seventy-six planes—all he had—in a desperate effort to attract Halsey's attention. It did.

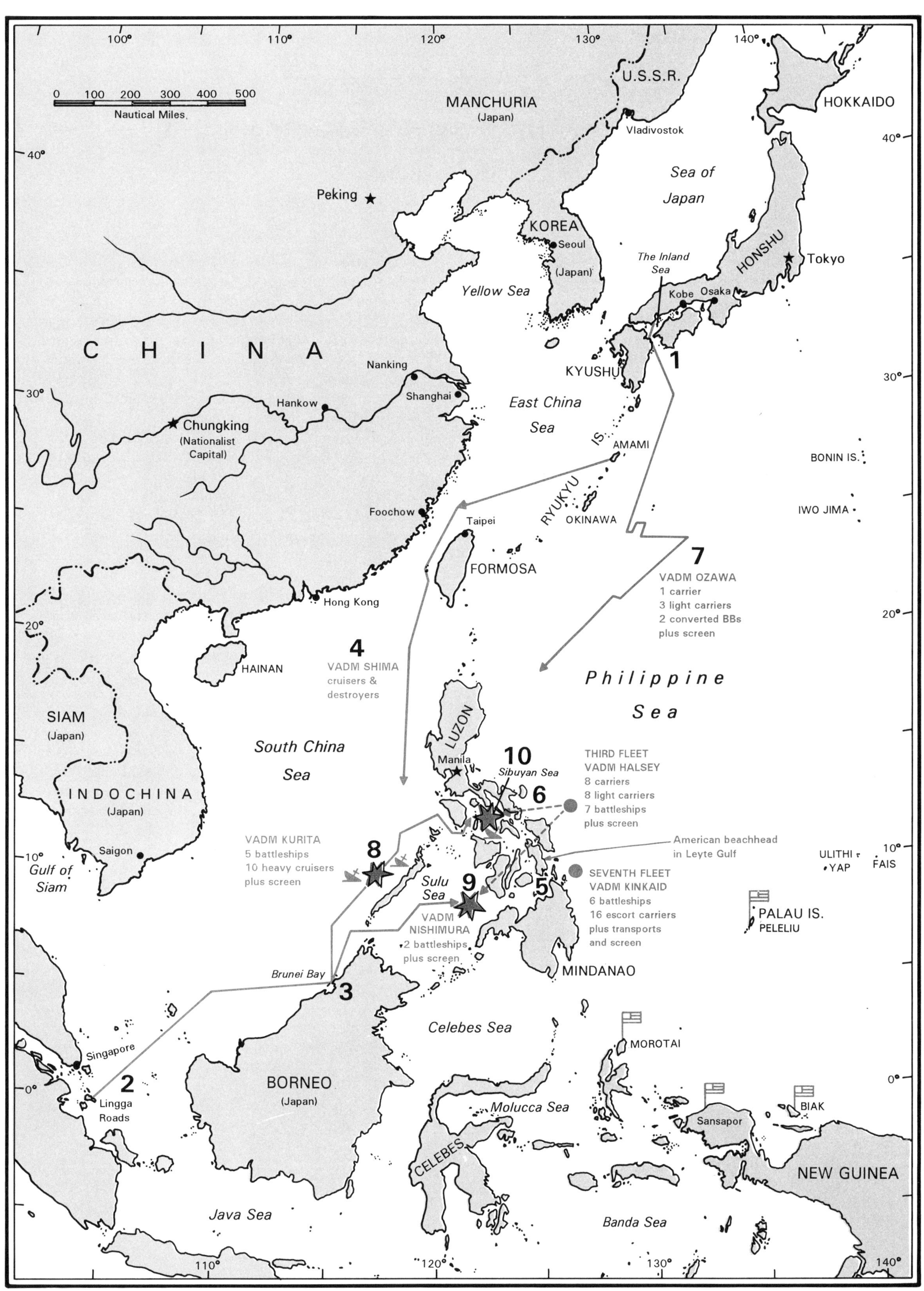

0 100 200 300 400 500
Nautical Miles
MANCHURIA
(Japan)
U.S.S.R.
Vladivostok
HOKKAIDO
Sea of
Japan
Peking
KOREA
Seoul
(Japan)
Yellow Sea
The Inland
Sea
HONSHU
Tokyo
Kobe
Osaka
C H I N A
Nanking
Shanghai
Hankow
Chungking
(Nationalist
Capital)
KYUSHU
1
East China
Sea
IS.
AMAMI
BONIN IS.
RYUKYU
OKINAWA
IWO JIMA
Foochow
Taipei
FORMOSA
7
VADM OZAWA
1 carrier
3 light carriers
2 converted BBs
plus screen
Hong Kong
HAINAN
4
VADM SHIMA
cruisers &
destroyers
Philippine
Sea
SIAM
(Japan)
LUZON
South China
Sea
Manila
10
Sibuyan Sea
THIRD FLEET
VADM HALSEY
8 carriers
8 light carriers
7 battleships
plus screen
6
INDOCHINA
(Japan)
VADM KURITA
5 battleships
10 heavy cruisers
plus screen
8
American beachhead
in Leyte Gulf
Saigon
Gulf of
Siam
Sulu
Sea
9
5
SEVENTH FLEET
VADM KINKAID
6 battleships
16 escort carriers
plus transports
and screen
ULITHI
YAP
FAIS
VADM
NISHIMURA
2 battleships
plus screen
PALAU IS.
PELELIU
Brunei Bay
3
MINDANAO
Celebes Sea
MOROTAI
Singapore
2
Lingga
Roads
BORNEO
(Japan)
Molucca Sea
Sansapor
BIAK
CELEBES
NEW GUINEA
Java Sea
Banda Sea
100°
110°
120°
130°
140°
40°
30°
20°
10°
0°

MAP 74

LEYTE GULF: THE BATTLE OF SURIGAO STRAIT

25 OCTOBER 1944

The twenty-fifth of October 1944 was the most violent day in the history of the U.S. Navy. From the predawn darkness until late in the evening, three geographically separate but strategically linked naval battles took place within three hundred miles of Leyte Gulf. The Americans emerged victorious in all three battles, but one of them was a very near thing, and controversial decisions by the opposing admirals played key roles in the outcome.

The stage was set in the afternoon and evening hours of 24 October. Halsey's pilots returning from the Sibuyan Sea reported their success against Kurita's Center Force and the fact that his ships had reversed course and were steaming west. Even accounting for pilot exaggeration, it was evident that the Center Force had been badly damaged. Halsey reasonably assumed that Kinkaid's Seventh Fleet could handle the Japanese Southern Force (Nishimura and Shima) advancing toward Surigao Strait (1). That left the enemy carriers (Ozawa's Northern Force), which the Americans had not yet spotted. In anticipation of an opportunity to take on the enemy's main fleet, Halsey at 3:00 P.M. announced the formation of a task force of four battleships, six cruisers, and fourteen destroyers to be assembled from the carrier screens. This would constitute Task Force 34 (TF 34) and would be commanded by VADM Willis Lee. But Halsey did not follow this preliminary order with an "execute," and so the fast battleships remained with their carrier groups. Admiral Kinkaid, however, who received some of Halsey's message traffic, assumed that TF 34 was a fact—that this strong surface force had been detached to guard the outlet of San Bernardino Strait. That left him free to concentrate all of his own surface forces to the south to welcome the Japanese Southern Force under Nishimura.

Instead of watching San Bernardino Strait, as Kinkaid believed, TF 34 was with Halsey going after bigger fish. At 5:00 P.M. when search planes from RADM Frederick Sherman's task force reported sighting enemy carriers to the north, Halsey decided to go after them. At 8:00 P.M. he notified Kinkaid: "Central Force [Kurita] heavily damaged according to strike reports. Am proceeding north with three groups to attack carrier forces at dawn." Alas, this message was subject to misinterpretation. Halsey had four carrier groups plus TF 34. He had sent RADM John S. McCain's carrier group off to refuel, so presumably Halsey was taking the other three carrier groups north. But what about TF 34? Kinkaid reasoned erroneously, with no firm evidence, that this force was being left behind to watch Kurita.

As Halsey steamed toward Ozawa at a speed designed to bring him within striking range of the Japanese carriers by dawn, he was notified that Kurita's Center Force had turned around and was once again heading east (2). Some members of his command hinted that this was significant, but the news did not concern him. He knew that Kurita had been badly hurt in the Sibuyan Sea and believed that Kinkaid's force was strong enough to take care of itself. He continued steaming north.

Just past midnight Kurita's surface force emerged from San Bernardino Strait into the Philippine Sea (3). He could hardly believe there were no enemy vessels there to contest his advance. Mystified, he turned south and began to steam along the coast of Samar in the darkness. Though he did not know it, the only American combat vessels between him and the transports, tankers, and landing ships in Leyte Gulf were the unarmored escort carriers under RADM Thomas L. Sprague (4). The heavies of the Seventh Fleet—Kinkaid's battleships and cruisers—were all watching Surigao Strait (see lower map).

BATTLE OF SURIGAO STRAIT

Mostly veterans of Pearl Harbor, Kinkaid's six old battleships, four heavy and four light cruisers, and twenty-one destroyers were commanded by RADM Jesse Oldendorf. Knowing that Nishimura's Southern Force could approach Leyte Gulf only via the narrow Surigao Strait between Leyte and Dinagat Islands, Oldendorf laid an elegant trap. He ordered his PT boats to take up positions inside Surigao Strait (5). Their job was to race out of the darkness and loose their torpedoes at the enemy fleet as it passed. Farther up the strait, Oldendorf placed his destroyers, which were also to launch torpedo attacks (6). Should any enemy ships survive this gauntlet, they would find Oldendorf's cruisers and battleships in a position to "cap the T" of the Japanese battle line (7).

Nishimura entered the southern end of Surigao Strait at 11:00 P.M. on 24 October. For three hours his ships ran the gauntlet of PT boats and destroyers. The PT boats did no damage, but the destroyers unleashed a furious torpedo attack, sinking one Japanese destroyer and hitting both of Nishimura's battleships. The battleship *Fuso* actually blew in half, the two halves each burning brilliantly in the pitch darkness. A second destroyer attack put three torpedoes into Nishimura's other battleship, the *Yamashiro,* and sank another destroyer. Then Oldendorf's battle line opened fire, raining shells on the few Japanese ships still afloat. Shima's cruiser-destroyer force steamed into the middle of this massacre a few minutes after 4:00 A.M. Shima accurately assessed the circumstances, and after launching a half-hearted torpedo attack, he withdrew, covering Nishimura's surviving cripples. Oldendorf sent his cruisers in pursuit, and they sank two more stragglers. Of Nishimura's surface force, only one badly damaged destroyer survived. It was as one-sided and complete a naval victory as has ever been recorded.

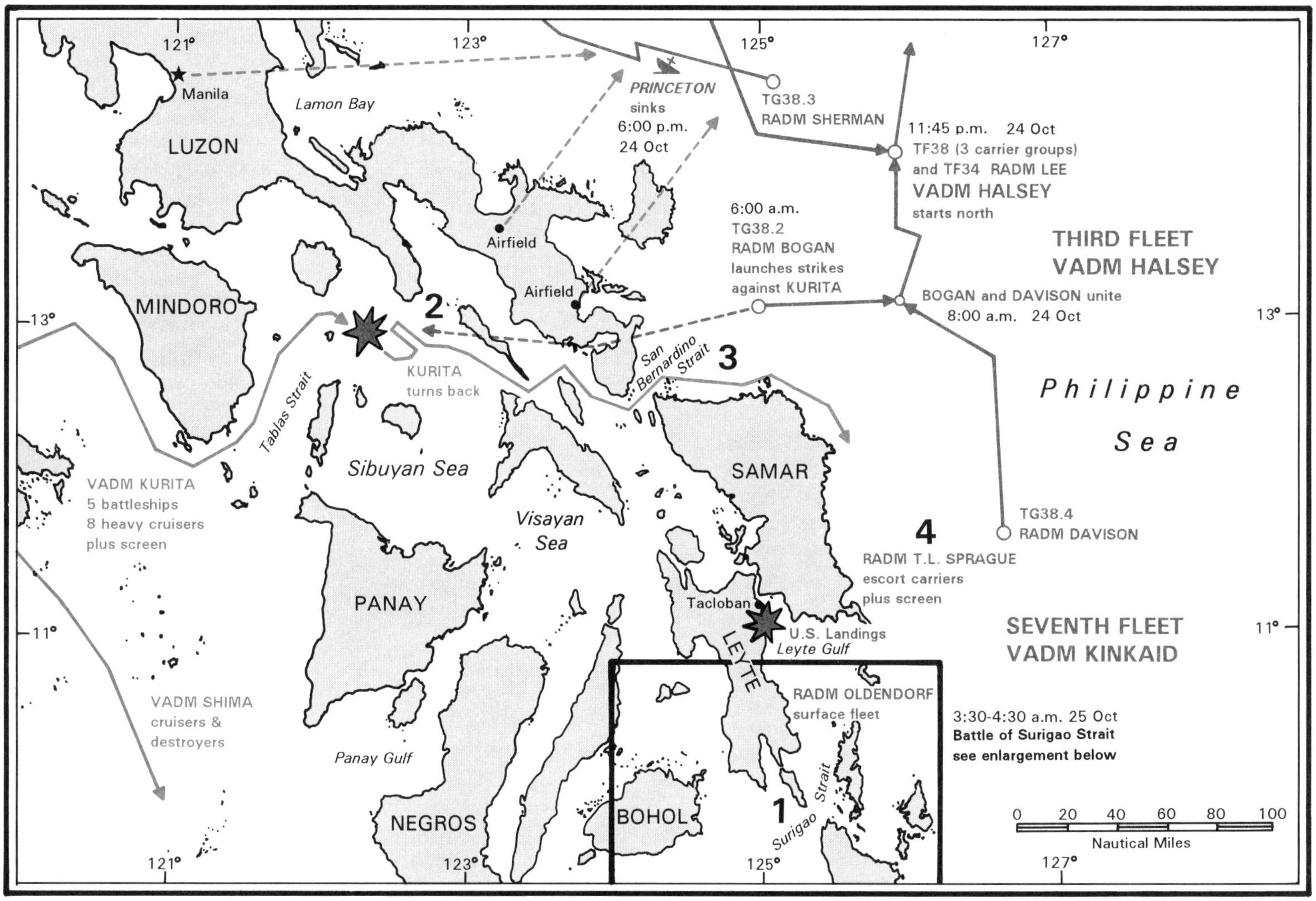

121° 123° 125° 127°

Manila

Lamon Bay

LUZON

PRINCETON sinks 6:00 p.m. 24 Oct

TG38.3 RADM SHERMAN

11:45 p.m. 24 Oct TF38 (3 carrier groups) and TF34 RADM LEE
VADM HALSEY starts north

Airfield

Airfield

6:00 a.m. TG38.2 RADM BOGAN launches strikes against KURITA

THIRD FLEET
VADM HALSEY

MINDORO

2

BOGAN and DAVISON unite 8:00 a.m. 24 Oct

13°

KURITA turns back

San Bernardino Strait

3

Tablas Strait

Philippine Sea

Sibuyan Sea

SAMAR

VADM KURITA
5 battleships
8 heavy cruisers
plus screen

Visayan Sea

TG38.4 RADM DAVISON

4

RADM T.L. SPRAGUE escort carriers plus screen

PANAY

Tacloban

U.S. Landings

Leyte Gulf

LEYTE

SEVENTH FLEET
VADM KINKAID

11°

RADM OLDENDORF surface fleet

VADM SHIMA cruisers & destroyers

3:30-4:30 a.m. 25 Oct
Battle of Surigao Strait
see enlargement below

Panay Gulf

Surigao Strait

1

NEGROS

BOHOL

0 20 40 60 80 100
Nautical Miles

121° 123° 125° 127°

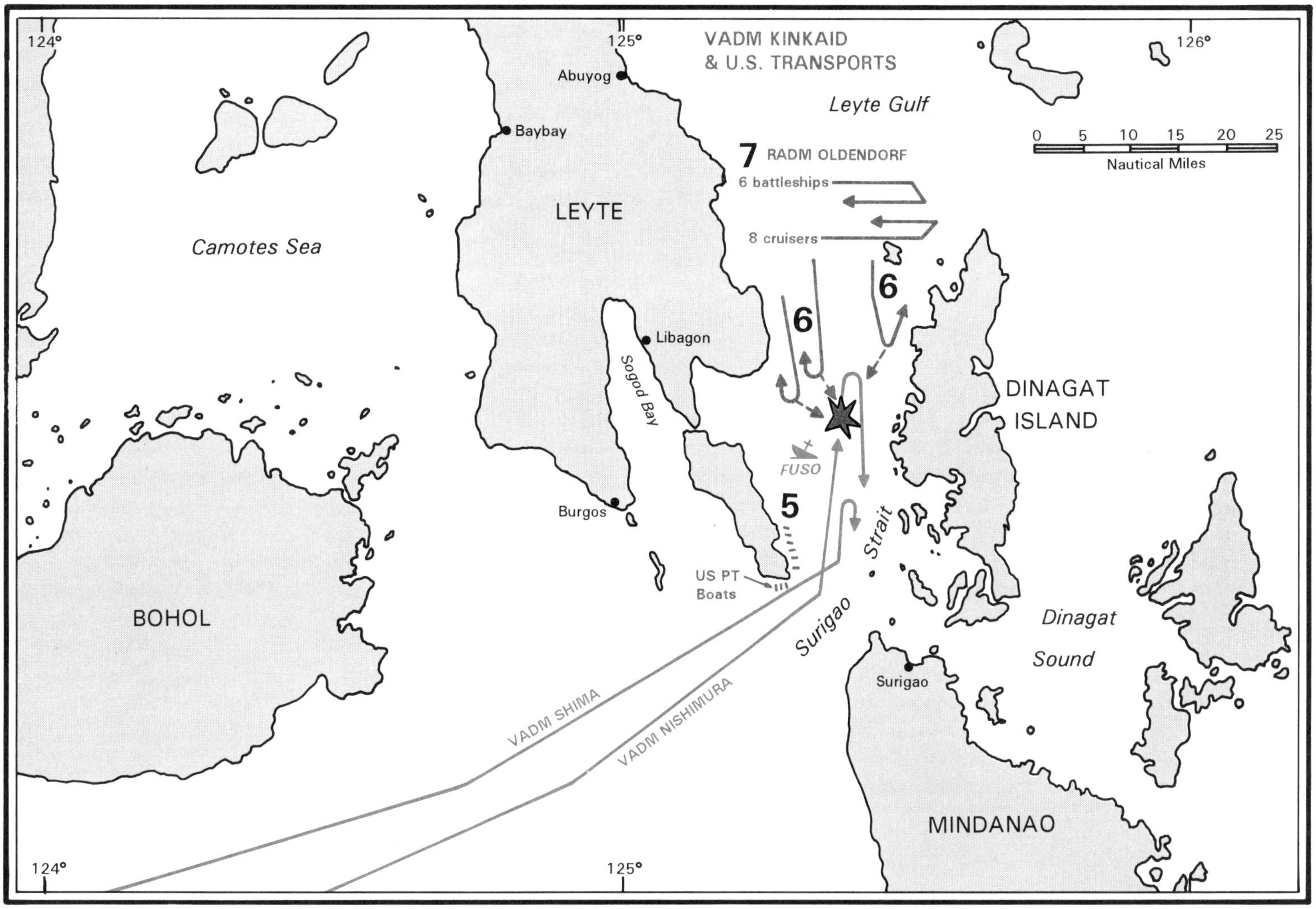

124° 125° 126°

VADM KINKAID & U.S. TRANSPORTS

Abuyog

Leyte Gulf

Baybay

0 5 10 15 20 25
Nautical Miles

7 RADM OLDENDORF

6 battleships

8 cruisers

LEYTE

Camotes Sea

6

6

Libagon

Sogod Bay

DINAGAT ISLAND

FUSO

5

Burgos

US PT Boats

Surigao Strait

BOHOL

Dinagat Sound

Surigao

VADM SHIMA

VADM NISHIMURA

MINDANAO

124° 125°

MAP 75

LEYTE GULF: THE BATTLE OFF SAMAR AND CAPE ENGAÑO

25 OCTOBER 1944

In the predawn darkness of 25 October, while Oldendorf's destroyers savaged Nishimura's battleships and Halsey steamed north for a rendezvous with Ozawa, Kurita's Center Force was closing Leyte Gulf. Kurita was unaware that Halsey had taken Ozawa's bait, but having intercepted a report from Shima, he *did* know that Nishimura's force had come to grief in Surigao Strait. For all he knew, he was now on his own, with the U.S. Third and Seventh Fleets lying in wait. As if to confirm that thought, when the sun came up over the Philippine Sea, lookouts on Kurita's flagship spotted American carriers and escorts on the southern horizon. They were the jeep carriers of RADM Clifton Sprague's Taffy 3. (RADM Thomas L. Sprague commanded Taffy 1 and was the senior officer among Taffy group commanders; RADM Clifton Sprague [no relation] commanded Taffy 3.) These vessels were a far cry from the fast fleet carriers of TF 38. Small (eight thousand tons), slow (eighteen knots), and unarmored, they were fragile shells compared to Kurita's battleships and cruisers. But because Kurita expected to see Halsey's fast fleet carriers, that is what he thought he saw.

BATTLE OFF SAMAR

At about 6:45 A.M. Kurita ordered, "General Attack," and his ships opened fire (1). Sprague turned east, into the wind, to launch planes, then he fled south, all the while calling for support. Sprague's pilots attacked Kurita's vessels willingly, but many flew fighters and none of them had armor-piercing ordnance. Their attacks served a purpose, however. Japanese doctrine called for vessels to maneuver independently under air attack, so the Japanese fleet lost forward progress as its ships wheeled and turned individually.

Sprague's destroyers, too, flung themselves into the fight, charging toward Kurita's advancing behemoths to launch torpedoes. They put one heavy cruiser out of action, damaged several other vessels, and won valuable time when Kurita ordered the *Yamato* to turn away to comb the torpedoes (2). Even after expending all its torpedoes, the destroyer *Johnston* fought on, defiantly firing its 5-inch guns at the battleship *Kongo* before it was overwhelmed by enemy shell fire and went down. Two other American destroyers, the *Hoel* and *Samuel B. Roberts,* suffered a similar fate. While his planes and destroyers fought heroically against impossible odds, Sprague steered into a nearby rainsquall, then turned west toward Leyte Gulf, hoping to meet Oldendorf's battleships coming to his aid.

All the while Kurita's surface forces were closing the range; by 9:00 A.M. shells began to strike home on the American flattops. The *Gambier Bay,* repeatedly struck by high-caliber shells, capsized and sank (3). It seemed that within minutes the entire task force must be destroyed, leaving the way open for Kurita to enter Leyte Gulf itself and attack the transports. Then, astonishingly, at 9:15 the Japanese ships reversed course and headed north.

Put simply, Kurita had lost his nerve. When air groups from Taffy 1 and 2 arrived overhead just after 8:00, the sky seemed filled with American planes. Two of Kurita's cruisers went down to American torpedo bombers (4), and even when the U.S. planes had no ordnance to drop, they made repeated dry runs at the Japanese ships, hoping to throw them off track. Kurita believed he had already pressed his luck as far as he could. At 9:11 he ordered his fleet to regroup and retire (5).

There was a tragic postscript. Later that morning Japanese kamikaze planes from the Philippines attacked U.S. ships off Samar and damaged two light carriers, sinking the *St. Lô* (6).

BATTLE OF CAPE ENGAÑO

Throughout the desperate Battle off Samar, Sprague sent out repeated plain-language calls for help to anyone listening, including both Kinkaid and Halsey. There was little either man could do, though Halsey did order McCain's task group to cease refueling and head to Sprague's assistance. But where was Task Force 34? One interested eavesdropper on the message traffic was Admiral Nimitz in Pearl Harbor. Like Kinkaid, he assumed that Halsey had left TF 34 behind when he started north, but when Kinkaid asked Halsey that morning, "Is TF 34 guarding San Bernardino Strait?" Halsey replied, "Negative. TF 34 is with carrier groups. . . ." Though Nimitz did not like to interfere in a commander's conduct of battle, he could not resist prodding Halsey to action by asking him: "Where is, repeat where is, Task Force 34?"

Stung by the implied rebuke, Halsey nevertheless continued on course for an hour before ordering TF 34 and one carrier group to reverse course and steam south at 11:00 A.M. (7), though by then Kurita was in retreat from Leyte Gulf. Planes from Halsey's other two carrier groups continued to attack Ozawa's decoy carriers (8), and before the end of the day all four Japanese flattops had been sunk in what was dubbed the Battle of Cape Engaño. Still, Halsey bitterly regretted that he had lost his chance to destroy Ozawa's entire fleet, especially because by the time TF 34 arrived in the vicinity of San Bernardino Strait, Kurita had made good his escape.

Though Leyte Gulf was the greatest naval victory in American history, the battle remains controversial. Some attributed the mistakes of the day to a simple communications problem, not surprising when the command structure was so complicated. Kinkaid assumed that TF 34 was guarding San Bernardino Strait, and Halsey assumed that Kinkaid had sufficient resources to guard the landing beaches without help. Halsey's orders made destruction of the Japanese fleet his top priority, but his behavior at Leyte Gulf was also due to his own pugnacious temperament, which led him to lunge at Ozawa's bait with insufficient consideration for the larger strategic picture.

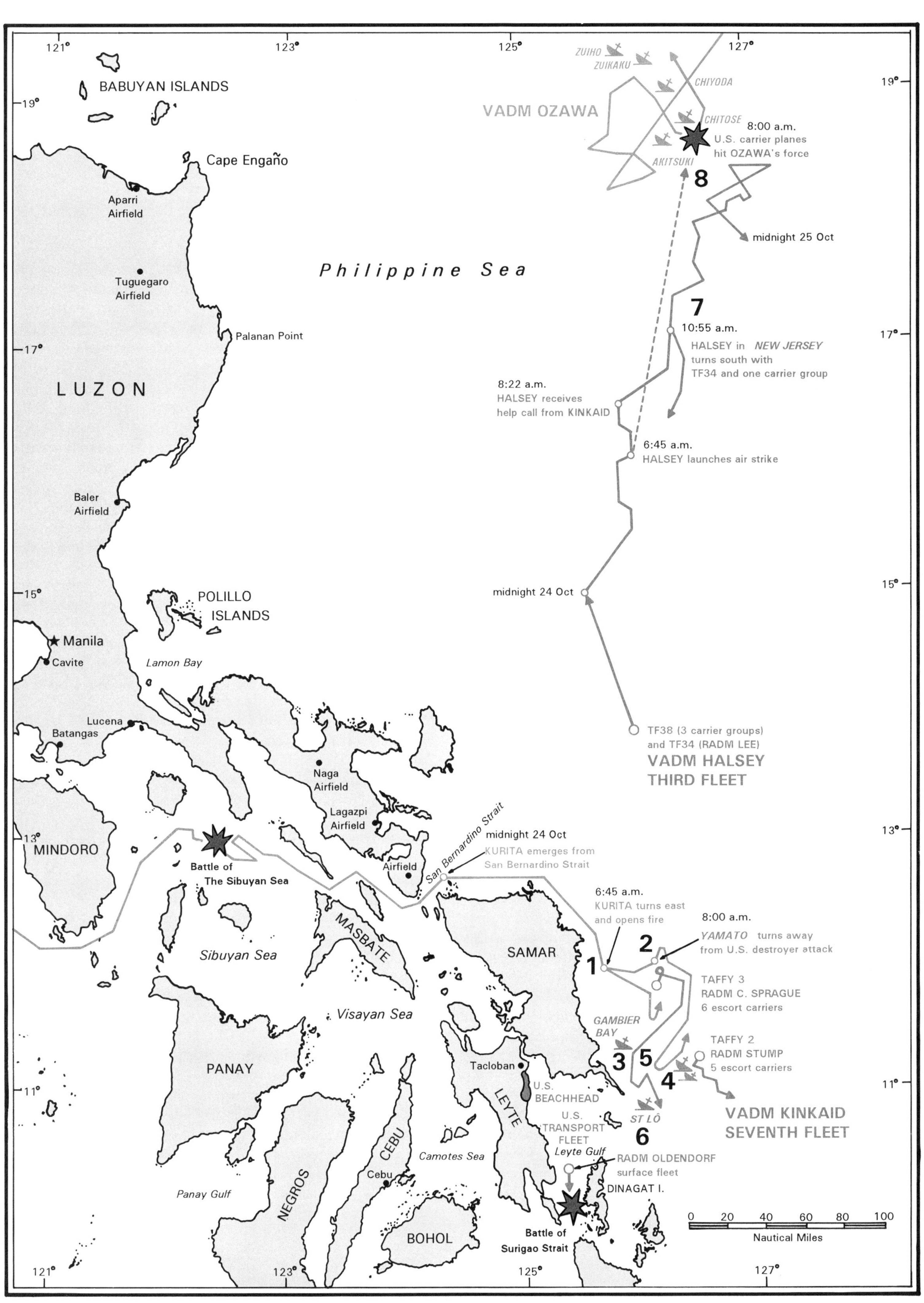

BABUYAN ISLANDS
Cape Engaño
Aparri Airfield
Tuguegaro Airfield
Palanan Point
LUZON
Philippine Sea
Baler Airfield
POLILLO ISLANDS
Manila
Cavite
Lamon Bay
Lucena
Batangas
Naga Airfield
Lagazpi Airfield
Airfield
MINDORO
Battle of The Sibuyan Sea
San Bernardino Strait
midnight 24 Oct
KURITA emerges from San Bernardino Strait
Sibuyan Sea
MASBATE
Visayan Sea
SAMAR
PANAY
Tacloban
U.S. BEACHHEAD
LEYTE
U.S. TRANSPORT FLEET
Leyte Gulf
CEBU
Cebu
Camotes Sea
NEGROS
Panay Gulf
BOHOL
Battle of Surigao Strait
DINAGAT I.
RADM OLDENDORF surface fleet
VADM OZAWA
ZUIHO
ZUIKAKU
CHIYODA
CHITOSE
AKITSUKI
8:00 a.m.
U.S. carrier planes hit OZAWA's force
8
midnight 25 Oct
7
10:55 a.m.
HALSEY in NEW JERSEY turns south with TF34 and one carrier group
8:22 a.m.
HALSEY receives help call from KINKAID
6:45 a.m.
HALSEY launches air strike
midnight 24 Oct
TF38 (3 carrier groups) and TF34 (RADM LEE)
VADM HALSEY
THIRD FLEET
6:45 a.m.
KURITA turns east and opens fire
8:00 a.m.
YAMATO turns away from U.S. destroyer attack
1
2
TAFFY 3
RADM C. SPRAGUE
6 escort carriers
GAMBIER BAY
3
5
TAFFY 2
RADM STUMP
5 escort carriers
4
ST LÔ
6
VADM KINKAID
SEVENTH FLEET
0 20 40 60 80 100
Nautical Miles
121°
123°
125°
127°
19°
17°
15°
13°
11°

MAP 76

IWO JIMA

19 FEBRUARY–16 MARCH 1945

American victory in the Battle of Leyte Gulf did not secure the Philippines—it meant only that the American landings could proceed. The fight for the Philippines, carried on by the soldiers of MacArthur's ground forces aided by Kinkaid's Seventh Fleet, lasted eight months and resulted in casualties numbering into the hundreds of thousands.

Meanwhile, U.S. Army Air Force planes began a studied bombing campaign of Japan's home islands. The key instrument in this campaign was the B-29 Superfortress bomber, which could fly more than three thousand miles at 360 mph, carrying a bomb load three times that of the B-17. The first B-29 raids on Japan, launched from bases in China in June, were disappointing. Early raids from Saipan (1), which began in November, also achieved little. One reason, air-power advocates insisted, was that U.S. planes were subject to interdiction by Japanese fighters on Iwo Jima (2). They, therefore, had to fly a long eastward dogleg to their targets—both ways—using up fuel and limiting their payload. Moreover, planes damaged in the air raids on Japan had no emergency landing fields en route back to the Marianas. The capture of Iwo Jima would solve both these problems.

The geography of Iwo Jima is the stuff of nightmares (see inset). Twelve square miles of volcanic ash, the island is appropriately teardrop-shaped and boasts only one piece of high ground—the dominating hump of Mount Suribachi, at the southern tip. The commander of the Japanese garrison, LGEN Kuribayashi Tadamichi, believing that earlier campaigns in the Pacific had proven that a defense at the water's edge was ineffective, planned a defense in depth from inland strong points. He could not hope to hold Iwo Jima, but he was determined to sell his island dearly. He did not exhort his twenty-one thousand men to victory; instead, he ordered each of them to kill ten of the enemy before dying.

The Third Fleet became the Fifth Fleet again in January 1945 when Spruance and his command team replaced Halsey and his team. Kelly Turner again commanded the amphibs, and MGEN Harry Schmidt commanded the III Amphib Corps consisting of three Marine divisions (3rd, 4th, and 5th) charged with seizing and holding the island. Army Air Force planes had bombed Iwo Jima from high altitude for seventy-four days, and Schmidt asked Spruance for ten days of concentrated naval gunfire prior to the landing. Alas, Spruance had scheduled carrier strikes on Japan's homeland (3) to take place simultaneously with the Iwo Jima landings, so he told Schmidt that the Marines would have to make do with three days of preliminary gunfire, and a fourth only "if necessary." Spruance may have been eager to prove that carrier strikes could be more effective in destroying Japan's industrial infrastructure than high-altitude B-29 raids. Whatever his motive, the shortened preliminary gunfire preparation at Iwo Jima was tragically inadequate.

Marines hit the beach at 9:00 A.M. on 19 February (4) and stepped into the mushy volcanic dust of Iwo Jima. A few dozen yards inland the beach rose to a slight crest and then leveled off to expose a black, barren plain, devoid of any vegetation, which emitted spumes of subterranean gasses like the effluence of hell. Japanese guns on Mount Suribachi utterly commanded that plain, and the American beachhead became congested as incoming troops crowded into those in the first wave who could not get off the beach. The amphtracs could not grip the soft volcanic dust and bogged down on the lip of the crest. Japanese mortar shells landed among troops on the crowded beach, falling indiscriminately among the living and dead. American naval gunfire support took out a number of important enemy positions, but the slaughter on the landing beaches continued. Despite these difficult conditions, some thirty thousand marines had come ashore by nightfall.

Once off the beach, U.S. Marines had to go into the underground bunkers and fight it out with an enemy who fully expected to die and wanted only to take some Americans with him. In combat with such an enemy, the flame-thrower and the grenade proved to be the marines' most effective weapons. Also important in this struggle was the close cooperation between Marine units ashore and U.S. destroyers. Each regimental combat team was assigned a specific vessel for its support, and Navy fire-control personnel communicated directly with the marines ashore to ensure accurate and timely naval gunfire against hardened shore positions.

On 23 February a Marine unit fought its way to the top of Mount Suribachi and raised a small flag as a token of conquest (5). A larger flag borrowed from an LST soon replaced the small flag, and the photograph of that second flag-raising became a symbol for American, and particularly Marine Corps, valor and determination.

The ceremony on Suribachi notwithstanding, the fight for Iwo Jima occupied another full month. Major General Schmidt declared the island to be secured on 16 March, but "mopping up" operations continued for several weeks. Of Kuribayashi's 21,000 men, only 216 were taken alive, though another 800 were discovered hiding out in remote caves in April and May. The Americans lost more than 6,800 killed and 20,000 wounded—a high price to pay for an emergency landing field.

Even before the island was declared secure, planes of the reorganized XX Air Force (MGEN Curtis LeMay) were using its airfields to inflict unimaginable destruction on the Japanese homeland with massive fire-bombing raids. On a single night (9 March) LeMay's B-29s killed more than eighty thousand Japanese civilians and made more than a million others homeless. No country could absorb such punishment indefinitely.

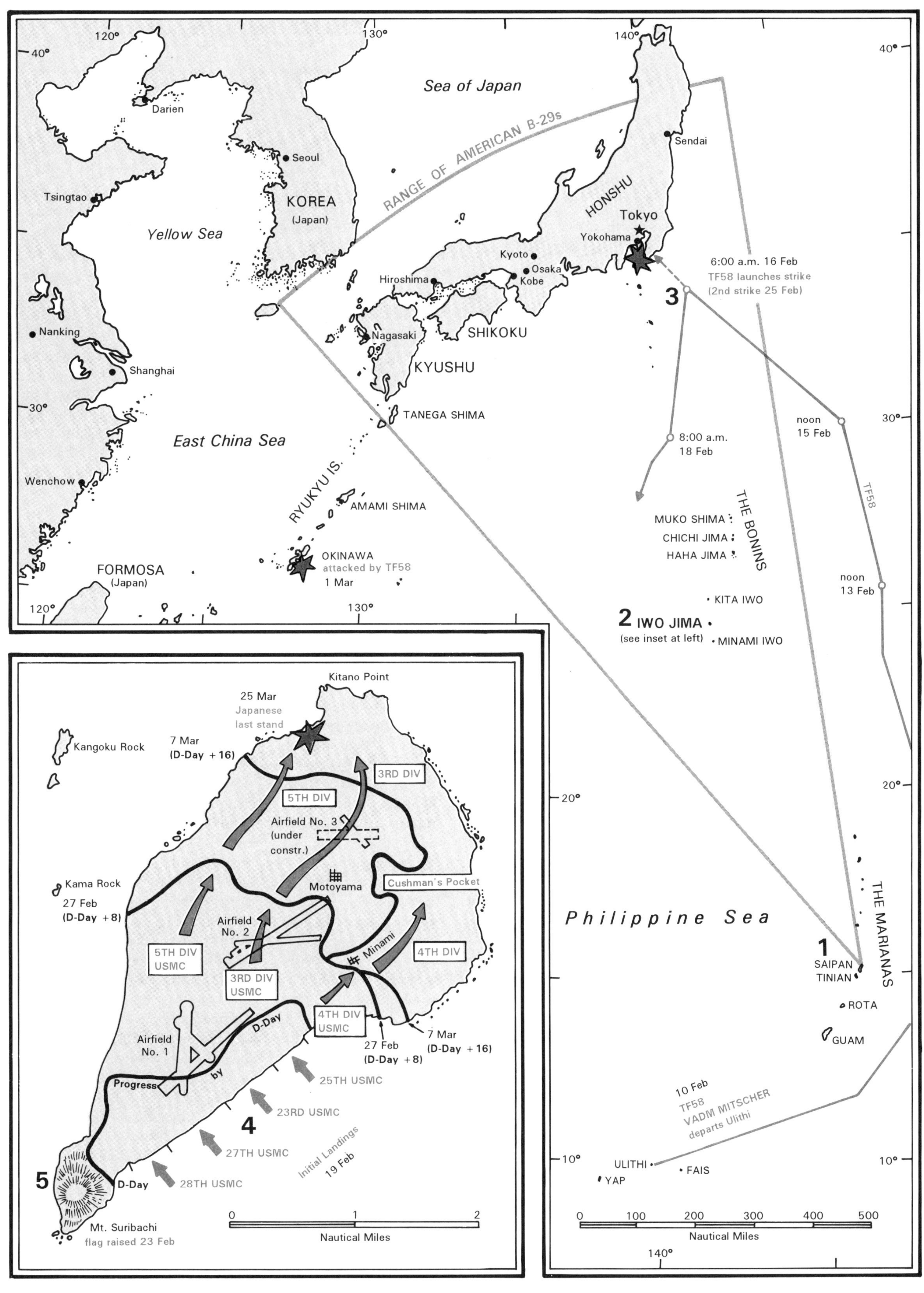
Sea of Japan
RANGE OF AMERICAN B-29s
Darien
Seoul
KOREA
(Japan)
Tsingtao
Yellow Sea
HONSHU
Sendai
Tokyo
Yokohama
Kyoto
Osaka
Kobe
Hiroshima
6:00 a.m. 16 Feb
TF58 launches strike
(2nd strike 25 Feb)
3
SHIKOKU
Nagasaki
KYUSHU
Nanking
Shanghai
TANEGA SHIMA
East China Sea
noon
15 Feb
8:00 a.m.
18 Feb
Wenchow
RYUKYU IS.
AMAMI SHIMA
TF58
THE BONINS
MUKO SHIMA
CHICHI JIMA
HAHA JIMA
FORMOSA
(Japan)
OKINAWA
attacked by TF58
1 Mar
noon
13 Feb
KITA IWO
2 IWO JIMA
(see inset at left)
MINAMI IWO
Kitano Point
25 Mar
Japanese
last stand
Kangoku Rock
7 Mar
(D-Day +16)
3RD DIV
5TH DIV
Airfield No. 3
(under
constr.)
Kama Rock
27 Feb
(D-Day +8)
Motoyama
Cushman's Pocket
Airfield
No. 2
Minami
5TH DIV
USMC
4TH DIV
3RD DIV
USMC
4TH DIV
USMC
D-Day
27 Feb
(D-Day +8)
7 Mar
(D-Day +16)
Airfield
No. 1
Progress
by
25TH USMC
23RD USMC
4
27TH USMC
Initial Landings
19 Feb
5
D-Day
28TH USMC
Mt. Suribachi
flag raised 23 Feb
Nautical Miles
Philippine Sea
1
SAIPAN
TINIAN
THE MARIANAS
ROTA
GUAM
10 Feb
TF58
VADM MITSCHER
departs Ulithi
ULITHI
FAIS
YAP
Nautical Miles

MAP 77

OKINAWA

1 APRIL–21 JUNE 1945

Two days after the Americans landed on Iwo Jima, Japanese suicide planes, or kamikazes, crashed into two American carriers, knocking the *Saratoga* temporarily out of action and sinking the light carrier *Bismarck Sea.* Kamikazes also took a heavy toll among the ships supporting MacArthur's Philippine operations. But it was in the battle for Okinawa that the kamikazes demonstrated their terrible potential.

Having lost so many planes, carriers, and surface warships in defending the edges of their Pacific empire, the Japanese found themselves in desperate straits now that U.S. forces were penetrating the inner ring. Japan's greatest military asset was its 2.8 million–man Kwantung Army in China and Manchuria. But American command of the sea and the air meant that those forces could not easily be brought to bear in a defense of the homeland. Lacking any viable alternatives, the Japanese would now rely upon a stubborn yard-by-yard defense of their home islands and hope that the Americans would yet grow weary of their losses. What the Japanese needed was a miracle.

At least once before when they had needed such a miracle, it was supplied to them. In 1570 when the Chinese emperor dispatched an overwhelming invasion force to conquer Japan, a terrible storm blew up and scattered the Chinese fleet, virtually destroying it. Such a storm—known in Japanese legend as the divine wind, or kamikaze—was the kind of miracle the Japanese needed now. Indeed, a typhoon had battered the American fleet in December of 1944, sinking three U.S. destroyers and damaging many vessels. But this time the Japanese would have to create their own divine wind, and thus "kamikaze" became the inspiration for Japan's young suicide pilots.

Japan's air defenses lacked both experienced pilots and aviation fuel. Relying on kamikazes solved both problems. Suicide pilots needed little training, and their planes required only enough fuel for a one-way flight. In defense of Okinawa, the Japanese high command would hurl some two thousand kamikaze planes at the American invasion force—some of them obsolete biplanes. From the very day of Pearl Harbor, the Japanese had believed that their greatest advantage over the Americans was that they were willing to accept the price of victory, whereas their opponents were not. Japan's hope now was to inflict so much damage on the Okinawa invasion force that the Americans would be forced to call off the landings.

Japanese opposition ashore was deceptively light when the vanguard of the U.S. Tenth Army (LGEN Simon B. Buckner) landed on Okinawa on Easter Sunday, 1 April 1945. U.S. planners had expected to encounter fierce resistance and had calculated that three days would be needed for the capture of the Yontan and Kadena airfields (1). Instead, both airfields were secured by the end of the first day. The reason for this surprising early success was that the Japanese defender, LGEN Ushijima Mitsuru, had entrenched his one hundred thousand–man army into limestone caves and tunnels in the southern quarter of the island (2). Like Kiyabayashi on Iwo Jima, he would avoid costly counterattacks and make the Americans pay in blood for their gains. Meanwhile, he would rely on the divine wind—the kamikazes—to destroy the invader's fleet.

The Japanese had one more arrow in their quiver: the superbattleship *Yamato,* a 72,000-ton behemoth with nine 18.1-inch guns capable of throwing shells weighing 3,500 pounds a distance of 22.5 miles. In the Japanese plan, the *Yamato* would sweep up whatever vessels were left afloat after the attack of the kamikazes.

The first large-scale kamikaze attack took place on 6 April. Nearly seven hundred planes from Kyushu and Formosa, half of them kamikazes, struck at the U.S. fleet near Okinawa (3). The attackers sank six ships and severely damaged seventeen others. That same day the *Yamato* sortied from the Inland Sea, escorted by one light cruiser and eight destroyers (4), but with only enough fuel for a one-way trip to Okinawa, and with no air cover. Planes from Mitscher's TF 58 spotted it at 8:23 A.M. on 7 April (5). At 10:00 A.M. Mitscher launched more than two hundred American bombers toward the *Yamato's* reported position. Pounded by numerous bombs and torpedoes, the *Yamato* went down at 2:23 P.M., taking more than 1,400 Japanese sailors with it (6).

The loss of the *Yamato* had no perceptible impact on the determination of Japan's kamikaze pilots. More than 380 planes attacked the U.S. fleet on 12 April, sinking two more ships and damaging nine. Other attacks followed: 315 planes on 15 April; 215 more on 27 April; 235 on 3 May; 275 on 10 May. The American picket destroyers got the worst of it. Stationed fifty to one hundred miles out from Okinawa to give warning of the Japanese attacks, these vessels were the first sighted by the attackers and thus became the initial targets. Altogether the Japanese sank 34 ships during the fight for Okinawa and damaged 368 others, many so severely that they had to leave the theater. Nearly 5,000 sailors were killed and another 4,800 wounded.

Ashore, the soldiers and marines were having a tough time, too. Having discovered the Japanese in their fortified positions, the Americans fought their way forward, taking heavy losses and inflicting even heavier casualties. In the third week of June the U.S. troops cornered the last defenders in the southernmost toe of the island. On 21 June Lieutenant General Ushijima killed himself, and the island was declared secured the next day. In the bloodiest battle of the Pacific War, U.S. forces ashore lost 7,613 killed, including Lieutenant General Buckner, and 31,800 wounded; the Japanese lost more than 80,000 killed.

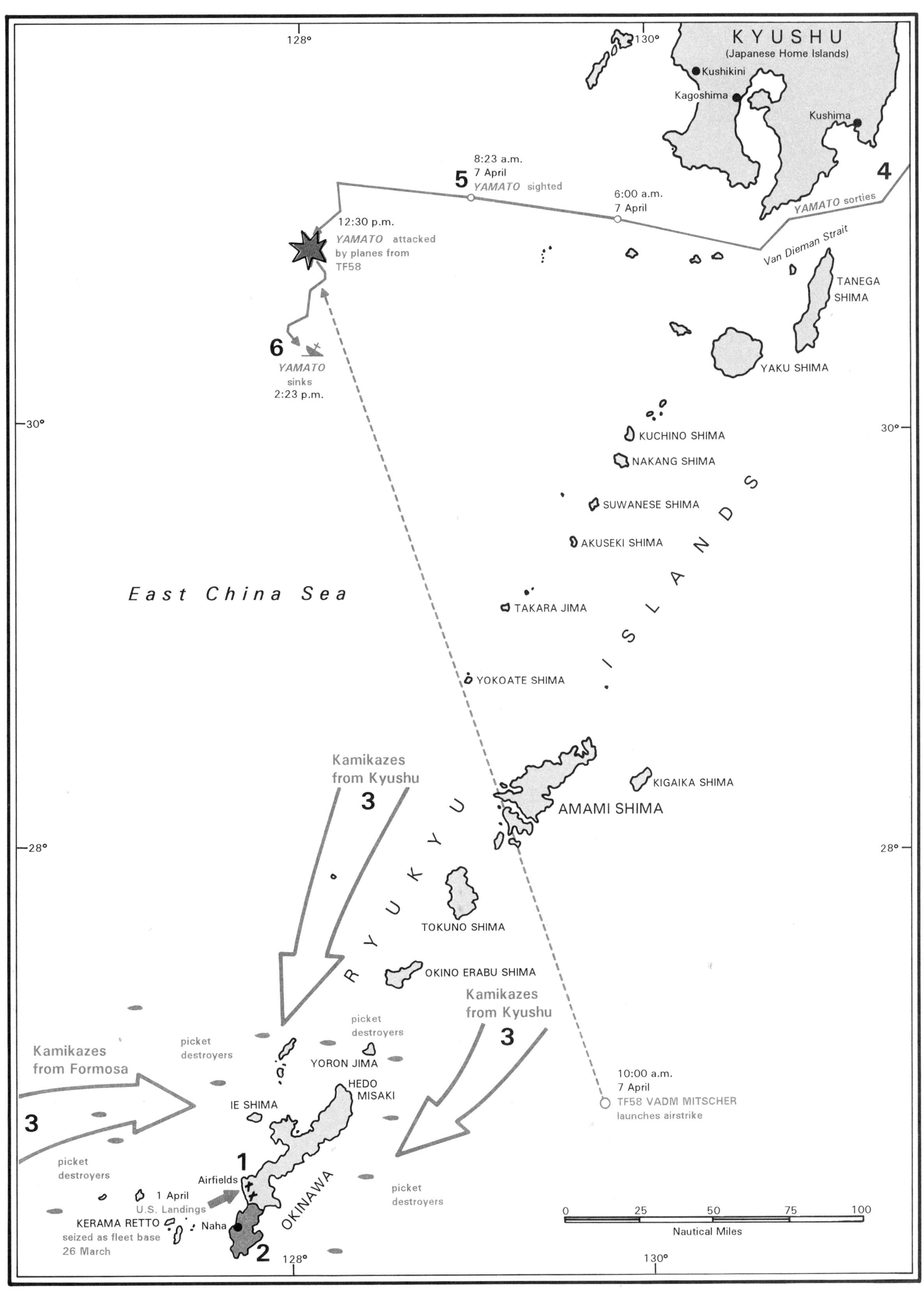

KYUSHU
(Japanese Home Islands)
Kushikini
Kagoshima
Kushima
4
YAMATO sorties
Van Dieman Strait
TANEGA SHIMA
YAKU SHIMA
8:23 a.m.
7 April
5
YAMATO sighted
6:00 a.m.
7 April
12:30 p.m.
YAMATO attacked by planes from TF58
6
YAMATO sinks 2:23 p.m.
KUCHINO SHIMA
NAKANG SHIMA
SUWANESE SHIMA
AKUSEKI SHIMA
TAKARA JIMA
YOKOATE SHIMA
East China Sea
RYUKYU ISLANDS
AMAMI SHIMA
KIGAIKA SHIMA
Kamikazes from Kyushu
3
TOKUNO SHIMA
OKINO ERABU SHIMA
Kamikazes from Kyushu
3
picket destroyers
picket destroyers
YORON JIMA
HEDO MISAKI
Kamikazes from Formosa
3
IE SHIMA
10:00 a.m.
7 April
TF58 VADM MITSCHER launches airstrike
picket destroyers
1
Airfields
1 April
U.S. Landings
KERAMA RETTO
seized as fleet base
26 March
Naha
2
OKINAWA
picket destroyers
0 25 50 75 100
Nautical Miles
128°
130°
30°
28°

Map 78

The Final Assault

July–August 1945

While MacArthur's forces reconquered the Philippines and the Navy–Marine Corps team seized Iwo Jima and Okinawa, American submarines continued to ravage Japanese shipping. As an island nation, Japan was wholly dependent on imports to sustain its industrial economy. In particular, the Japanese imported most of their steel and virtually all of their oil. As American submarines devastated Japan's merchant fleet, shortages in these two crucial materials threatened to shut down the nation's industry altogether.

The United States had 112 small submarines when the war began, but added more than 200 newer and larger boats during the war. After a slow start—due almost completely to defects in the American Mark XIV torpedo, which ran too deep and often failed to detonate—by 1944 U.S. submarines began to have a decisive impact on the war. That year U.S. submarines sank 603 Japanese ships totaling 2.7 million tons; in November alone U.S. subs sank some 340,000 tons of enemy shipping, including the 60,000-ton carrier *Shinano,* sunk on its maiden voyage. American submarine skippers especially targeted tankers, sinking more than a half million tons of them in the last two months of 1944. So efficient were the American subs that by 1945 they were literally running out of targets. In June the Pacific Fleet Submarine Force commander, VADM Charles Lockwood, sent nine subs—Hydeman's Hellcats—into the previously inviolate Sea of Japan (1), thus completing a virtual blockade of Japan's home islands. In twenty days those nine submarines sank twenty-eight Japanese vessels. Daring submarine skippers entered enemy harbors to torpedo ships at anchor or surfaced to shell coastal facilities. In July CDR Gene "Lucky" Fluckey in the *Barb* landed a shore party on the eastern coast of Sakhalin Island, planted explosives on a railroad track, and watched a passing train blow up. Though submarines constituted a relatively small percentage of American assets in the Pacific war, they accounted for more than 50 percent of all enemy losses at sea, sinking more than 1,300 Japanese ships.

The American fast carriers, now once again under Halsey's command as TF 38, began a new series of raids on Japanese cities in July (2). While Army Air Corps B-29s rained death in high-altitude terror-bombing raids, Navy planes from TF 38 sought out Japan's few remaining military assets, especially enemy aircraft. Japan still had more than five thousand planes, but instead of committing them to a defense against American raids, the Japanese high command withheld them to defend the home islands against the expected American invasion. When planes from TF 38 appeared over Tokyo on 10 July (3), no enemy planes rose to contest the skies. Throughout July and August Halsey's carrier-based planes ranged up and down the coasts of Honshu and Hokkaido, striking the enemy at will and destroying the few remaining warships of the once-proud Imperial Japanese Navy in the Inland Sea (4).

Meanwhile, American strategic planners had decided on the next American assault. Code-named OLYMPIC, it was to be an invasion of Kyushu in November, followed by an invasion of Honshu (CORONET) in March of 1946. Staffers estimated that OLYMPIC could result in casualties exceeding a quarter of a million Americans killed and wounded. With this somber prediction in his mind, President Truman headed for Potsdam, outside Allied-occupied Berlin, to meet with Churchill and Stalin and discuss the fate of the postwar world.

On 16 July scientists of the top-secret Manhattan Project successfully detonated an atomic device at Alamagordo, New Mexico. News of the successful test quickly reached President Truman in Potsdam and gave added bite to the Potsdam Declaration, released by the Allies on 26 July, which called for Japan's "unconditional surrender" lest it face "prompt and utter destruction." With atomic weapons at hand, this was no idle threat. Of course, American possession of such a weapon was not spelled out in the declaration, and some have wondered if a clearer explanation of the alternatives—or even a demonstration of the bomb's terrifying potential—might have convinced Japan to surrender at once. After all, even discounting the bomb, it was evident to anyone by August 1945 that Japan had no hope of winning. Cut off by American sea power, bombed daily by American air power, Japan had become a passive target, absorbing punishment, incapable of offering effective resistance.

But Japan's military leaders, bred in the code of Bushido, believed that annihilation was preferable to surrender. While the United States would surely have won a conventional war by relying on a prolonged blockade and continued air assault, it would likely have meant another year of war and resulted in far more casualties than those caused by the use of atomic weapons.

At 9:15 A.M. on 6 August 1945 COL Paul Tibbets piloted a lone B-29, the *Enola Gay,* over Hiroshima and released his single bomb (5). Three days later, on 9 August, a second bomb leveled Nagasaki (6); that same day the Soviet Union declared war on Japan. The sudden impact of these dramatic and unprecedented events gave Emperor Hirohito the leverage to override his military commanders' determination to continue to fight on to the hopeless end. He told his people that they must bear the unbearable and accept surrender.

The final instrument of peace was signed, appropriately enough, on board the American battleship *Missouri* in Tokyo Harbor on 2 September 1945. That morning at colors the *Missouri* hoisted the flag that had flown over the nation's Capitol on 7 December 1941. The largest and most powerful naval force ever created had won the greatest naval war in history.

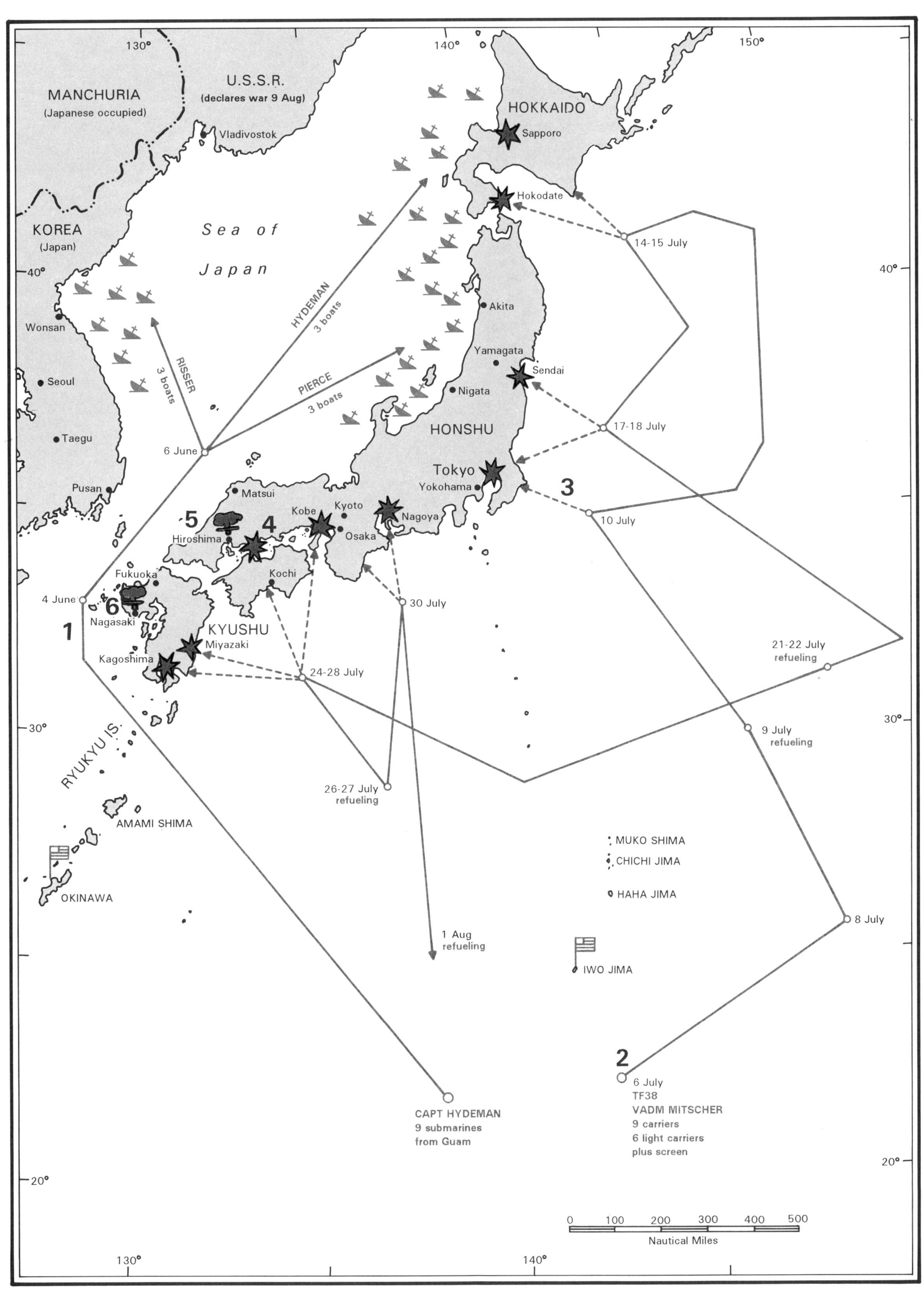

MANCHURIA
(Japanese occupied)
U.S.S.R.
(declares war 9 Aug)
Vladivostok
HOKKAIDO
Sapporo
Hokodate
KOREA
(Japan)
Sea of Japan
Wonsan
Seoul
Taegu
Pusan
HYDEMAN
3 boats
RISSER
3 boats
PIERCE
3 boats
6 June
14-15 July
Akita
Yamagata
Sendai
Nigata
17-18 July
HONSHU
Tokyo
Yokohama
3
10 July
Matsui
Kobe
Kyoto
Nagoya
Osaka
5
4
Hiroshima
Fukuoka
Kochi
4 June
6
Nagasaki
1
KYUSHU
Miyazaki
Kagoshima
30 July
24-28 July
21-22 July
refueling
9 July
refueling
RYUKYU IS.
26-27 July
refueling
AMAMI SHIMA
OKINAWA
MUKO SHIMA
CHICHI JIMA
HAHA JIMA
8 July
1 Aug
refueling
IWO JIMA
2
6 July
TF38
VADM MITSCHER
9 carriers
6 light carriers
plus screen
CAPT HYDEMAN
9 submarines
from Guam
0 100 200 300 400 500
Nautical Miles
130°
140°
150°
40°
30°
20°

PART IX

The Cold War Navy 1946–1980

IT IS ALMOST AN UNDERSTATEMENT to say that at the end of World War II the United States possessed the greatest navy in the history of the world. It was a force so large and powerful it would have been unimaginable to Alfred Thayer Mahan; indeed, it is almost unimaginable now. Having started the war with seven carriers and seventeen battleships, the U.S. Navy four years later boasted nearly *100* fleet and escort carriers, as well as 120 battleships and cruisers, more than 440 destroyers, and several hundred submarines. Counting armed landing craft, the Navy List in 1945 contained more than sixty-five thousand combatant vessels manned by more than four million naval personnel. It was twice as large as all of the rest of the world's navies combined.

With the war over, America's servicemen were eager to go home. It is a peculiarly American characteristic to enter wars less than fully prepared and to exit from them with almost frenetic haste. In the fall of 1945 the men who had fought the war perceived that their job was done, and they wanted to go home—at once. Explanations that these things take time provoked skepticism and bitter comments about government inefficiency. But although many soldiers and sailors complained about foot-dragging, the demobilization progressed with remarkable speed. Appropriately titled Operation MAGIC CARPET, the transportation of American military men from the fighting fronts back to the United States was a logistic achievement equivalent to a major amphibious operation. Not only transports but warships, too, were pressed into service to carry the troops home. Carriers proved to be especially suited for this task, equipped as they were with galleys and bunks to feed and sleep thousands of men at a time. By the end of 1946 the Navy had processed out three and a half million officers and men.

U.S. Marines in North Korea watch as planes from American carriers in the Sea of Japan provide close air support. Fighting under the auspices of the United Nations, U.S. forces in Korea found themselves in a different kind of war, one where the rules of engagement reflected the ambiguities of the Cold War era (see maps 79–81). (Official U.S. Marine Corps photo)

The ships, too, were "processed out." By the end of 1946 there were just over one thousand combatant warships still on active service. But the Navy did not enter another period of naval "retrenchment" characterized by obsolescence and inactivity as it had in the years following the end of the Civil War. To be sure, hundreds of ships were mothballed, and hundreds more sent to the breakers for scrap, but the Navy that survived—though only a shadow of what it had been in 1945—remained the greatest naval power on earth.

What saved the Navy from a more complete demobilization was the growing American belief in the Soviet Union's determination to extend its influence and control over as much of the globe as possible. The Red Army had borne much of the burden of the war against Hitler's Germany, but after "liberating" Eastern Europe, it stayed on as an occupying force while "an iron curtain" (to use Winston Churchill's phrase) descended across the continent. Meanwhile, in China, Mao Tse-tung's communist forces pressured a weakening nationalist regime under Chiang Kai-shek.

The Soviet threat forced Americans to abandon their traditional peacetime insularity. Fearing that the Soviet Union would fill the vacuum of power in a Europe exhausted by war, President Truman announced in March 1947 that the United States would support free peoples threatened by internal insurgency or external invasion (the Truman Doctrine). That same year Secretary of State George Marshall announced a U.S. program to extend economic aid to most of Europe (the Marshall Plan), a policy designed partly for humanitarian reasons but also to forestall the kind of economic chaos that might prove fertile ground for communist rebellion. Finally, in 1949 the United States sponsored a peacetime alliance aimed at deterring a conventional Soviet attack in Europe—the North Atlantic Treaty Organization (NATO). These policy decisions marked a dramatic break from the past and

A nest of mothballed destroyers lined up in San Diego Harbor in July 1950. The swift American demobilization after World War II reduced the Navy from nearly 1,200 major combatants in 1945 to only 267 by 1948. Though the Navy's hierarchy protested this dramatic reduction, the absence of a credible overseas threat and American possession of the atomic bomb seemed to make a powerful conventional Navy unnecessary. (Official U.S. Navy photo)

characterized American foreign and defense policy for the next forty years. In those Cold War years, the United States provided a "nuclear umbrella" of strategic deterrence to discourage overt Soviet aggression, while its conventional forces engaged in two hot wars against Soviet-supported regimes in Korea (1950–1953) and Vietnam (1959–1973).

At the beginning of the Cold War, however, it was unclear what role the U.S. Navy would play in this gray twilight war. The Soviet Navy posed no credible threat in 1945, and with the onset of the atomic era and the emergence of an independent Air Force, Navy leaders feared that the Navy's traditional role as the nation's sword point in diplomacy and its first line of defense in time of war was being threatened. Advocates of air power claimed that the strategic bombing of Germany and Japan had been largely responsible for American victory, and they asserted that in the future the traditional roles previously played by land and naval forces would all but disappear. Navy leaders did not object to the creation of an independent Air Force, but they did object to the idea, forwarded by some, that the Air Force should assume control of the Navy and Marine Corps air forces.

The issue was apparently resolved in 1947 with the passage of the National Security Act. That law created a National Security Council (NSC) and a Central Intelligence Agency (CIA), and it reorganized the armed services into three independent branches—Army, Navy, and Air Force—with the cabinet-level office of Secretary of Defense to preside over all three. This was a compromise between the advocates of complete "service unification" and traditionalists who fought to retain the existing system. The Navy survived intact. Not only did the Navy and Marine Corps retain control over their own air forces, but the Secretary of the Navy, James V. Forrestal, became the first Secretary of Defense.

In March 1949, however, Forrestal resigned as Secretary of Defense; only days later he threw himself from the sixteenth-floor window of the Bethesda Naval Hospital. His successor was a particularly unfortunate choice—especially from the Navy's point of view. Louis Johnson was a strong advocate of air power who believed that the Air Force should control Navy air, and that the Army should absorb the Marine Corps. Such an agenda would have been daunting to the most skilled politician or diplomat. But Johnson was neither. From his first days in office it was evident that he lacked the personal and political skills necessary to deal effectively with the professional officers over whom he was supposed to preside.

One of Johnson's first acts was to announce that he was killing the Navy's single most important postwar project—the construction of the sixty thousand–ton carrier *United States.* Both the manner and the content of Johnson's bombshell shocked the Navy high command. Johnson had not sought advice from, or even informed, the chief of naval operations, ADM Louis Denfeld, before announcing the decision. Moreover, the *United States* was of special importance to the Navy, for off its broad flight deck were to have flown the Navy planes capable of delivering the atomic bomb, thus ensuring a role for the Navy in atomic deterrence. As far as Johnson was concerned, strategic deterrence was to be the exclusive province of the Air Force. To underscore the point, the money saved from the cancellation of the *United States* would be spent on a long-range Air Force bomber—the B-36.

All this was too much for naval aviators, especially the vice chief of naval operations (VCNO), ADM Arthur Radford, who testified before a congressional committee in October 1949 that strategic bombing could not achieve the quick and easy victory promised by many of its advocates, and that the B-36 was a "billion dollar blunder." Other Navy and Marine Corps officers testified similarly in an episode that has come to be known as "the revolt of the admirals." When Admiral Denfeld added his voice to that of the other critics, Secretary of the Navy Francis P. Matthews removed him as CNO.

The Navy lost the battle but won the war. The subsequent report of the Naval Affairs Committee criticized Denfeld's removal from office and recommended the construction of a supercarrier in the next budget. Moreover, within the year the Navy and Marine Corps would have ample opportunity to demonstrate the continued relevance of both carrier-based naval air and amphibious warfare, with the outbreak of the Korean War (see maps 79–81). Finally, within a decade the Navy would claim a role in strategic deterrence as well with the deployment of the A-3D Skywarrior heavy attack aircraft and the development of the nuclear-powered submarine and the submarine-launched ballistic missile (see map 83). Indeed, during much of the Cold War era the Navy remained the nation's key instrument of both diplomacy and warfare from the Mediterranean (map 82) to East Asia (maps 85–87), as well as in the Caribbean only ninety miles from the United States (map 84).

The 16-inch guns of the USS New Jersey *fire on North Korean troops from the Sea of Japan. The* New Jersey *was one of several World War II–vintage battleships called up for duty in the postwar era. In an extended Cold War career, she fired her big guns into Vietnam and Lebanon as well as Korea. (Official U.S. Navy photo)*

On duty at Yankee Station in the Gulf of Tonkin, the U.S. carrier Coral Sea *launches planes for a strike against targets in North Vietnam in March 1965 (see map 86). Though the air campaign against North Vietnam was the heaviest in history, the resilience of the enemy (or, as some argued, the limitations of the rules of engagement) made the campaign indecisive. (Official U.S. Navy photo)*

MAP 79

THE KOREAN WAR

JUNE–SEPTEMBER 1950

Like Poland—itself the victim of many wars across its borders—Korea's geography has been largely responsible for its precarious political existence. Invaded by the Japanese in the sixteenth century and by the Manchus in the seventeenth century, Korea adopted a policy of deliberate isolation and came to be known as the "Hermit Kingdom." The Korean government signed commercial agreements with Japan (in 1876) and the United States (in 1882), but after the Russo-Japanese War the victorious Japanese claimed Korea as a "protectorate" in 1905, and five years later they annexed it outright, ending a dynasty that had ruled since 1392.

When World War II came to an end in August of 1945, Koreans looked forward to liberation from Japanese occupation and the reestablishment of Korean independence. First, however, the Allies had to determine the administrative apparatus for the surrender of Japanese forces throughout Asia. In addition to the formal surrender ceremonies on board the *Missouri* in Tokyo Bay, the Chinese were delegated to accept the surrender of Japan's 2.8 million–man Kwantung Army, which had occupied much of China since 1937; the British would preside over surrender ceremonies in Burma and Siam; and the French would re-occupy Indochina. But what of Japanese forces in Korea? The question was complicated by the fact that the closest Allied power other than China was the Soviet Union, which had entered the war, as promised, precisely three months after V-E Day, but only four days before V-J Day. Suspicious of Soviet territorial ambitions, some Americans did not believe the brief Soviet campaign against Japanese forces in Manchuria justified their participation in the surrender of Korea.

The compromise, worked out hurriedly as the Pacific war rushed to a close, was that the Soviets would supervise Japanese capitulation in the northern half of Korea while American forces did so in the southern half. More or less arbitrarily, the thirty-eighth parallel was selected as a dividing line because it was about midpoint on the Korean peninsula (see map A). Soviet troops marched into Korea from the north, and the Seventh Fleet brought two U.S. Army divisions to Korea by sea. Both occupying forces established societies molded in their own image. The Soviets encouraged the development of "Provisional People's Committees" in North Korea, while the United States promoted the candidacy of Princeton-graduate Syngman Rhee as president of South Korea. The countrywide elections projected for 1948 never took place, and what had been intended as a temporary division for administrative convenience became a de facto political boundary. The Soviets and Americans withdrew their occupation forces within a few years, though each left behind a number of military advisers.

The United States was not entirely sure how important Korea was to the successful defense of freedom and democracy in Asia. When in January 1950 Secretary of State Dean Acheson briefed the National Press Club in Washington about the nation's new forward-defense policy, he did not mention Korea (see map B). America's defensive shield, he said, ran from the Aleutians archipelago through Japan and the trailing chain of the Ryukyus to Okinawa, and then south to the Philippines. By implication, this did not include either Korea (1) or the nationalist Chinese island of Formosa (2), to which the armies of Chiang Kai-shek had withdrawn after being driven from the mainland by the Chinese Communists under Mao Tse-tung in 1949.

Acheson's remarks may have convinced the North Korean government of Kim Il-sung that the United States would not fight for South Korea. In any event, at dawn on 25 June 1950 the North Korean Army of more than one hundred thousand men, bolstered by two hundred Soviet-made T-34 tanks and two hundred military aircraft, charged across the thirty-eighth parallel with the obvious intention of unifying Korea by force (see map C). The United States assumed at once that this was part of a coordinated communist strategy for world conquest. Following hard on the heels of the fall of China and the successful testing of a Soviet atomic bomb, Americans saw this overt aggression as a direct challenge.

President Truman reacted quickly, directing U.S. naval forces in the Pacific to provide air and gunfire support for the outnumbered South Korean forces as they fell back before the North Korean onslaught, and sponsoring a United Nations resolution condemning the invasion. Meanwhile, Task Force 96, consisting of the cruiser *Juneau* and four destroyers under RADM John Higgins, provided offshore gunfire support to the retreating South Korean Army (3), and Task Force 77, consisting of the *Essex*-class carrier *Valley Forge* and its escorts under the command of VADM Arthur Struble (4), flew sorties against the advancing North Korean columns. In the first week of July aviators from the *Valley Forge* struck at the North Korean capital of Pyongyang (5), and planes from HMS *Triumph* attacked Haeju. Two weeks later, after refueling at Okinawa, Struble took TF 77 into the Sea of Japan and struck targets along Korea's northeastern coast (6).

Meanwhile, the South Korean forces and their American allies continued to fall back until they defended only a small toehold on the peninsula around the southern seaport of Pusan (7). There they were bolstered by the arrival of the first elements of American ground forces from Japan that would eventually make up the U.S. 8th Army. The First Provisional Marine Brigade arrived from Camp Pendleton on 2 August, and by the end of the month U.S. forces at Pusan outnumbered those of the enemy. It was now evident that the South Koreans and their American allies would not be pushed into the sea. It was time for a counterattack.

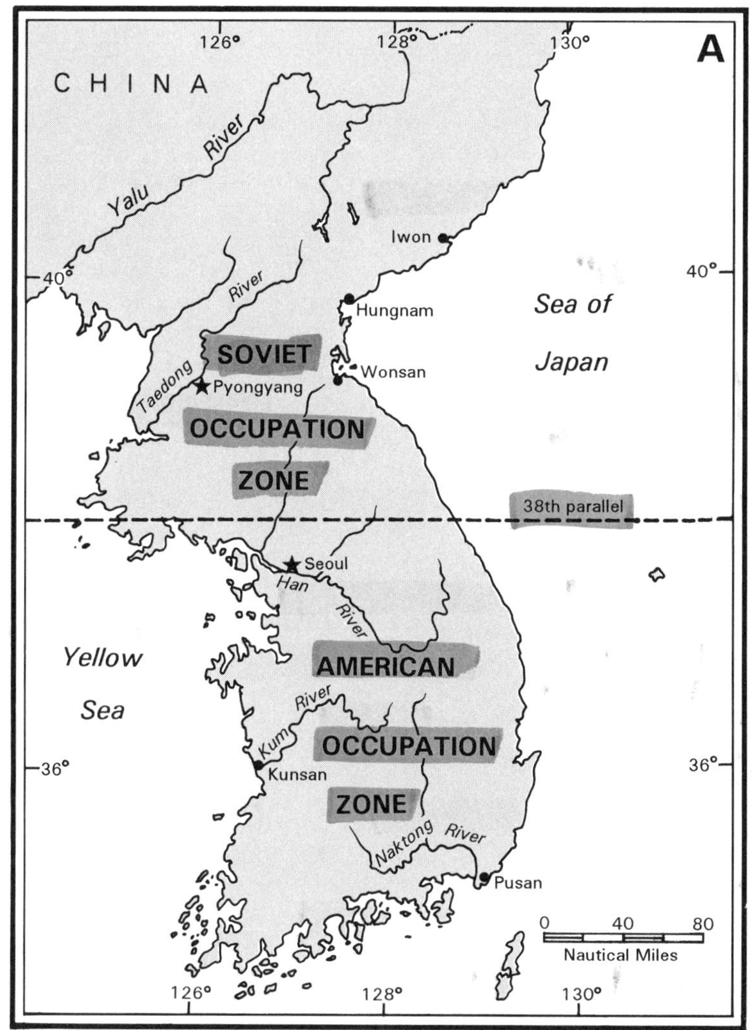
A
CHINA
Yalu River
Iwon
Hungnam
Sea of Japan
River
Taedong
SOVIET
OCCUPATION
ZONE
Pyongyang
Wonsan
38th parallel
Seoul
Han River
Yellow Sea
AMERICAN
OCCUPATION
ZONE
Kum River
Kunsan
Naktong River
Pusan
0 40 80
Nautical Miles
126° 128° 130°
40° 36°

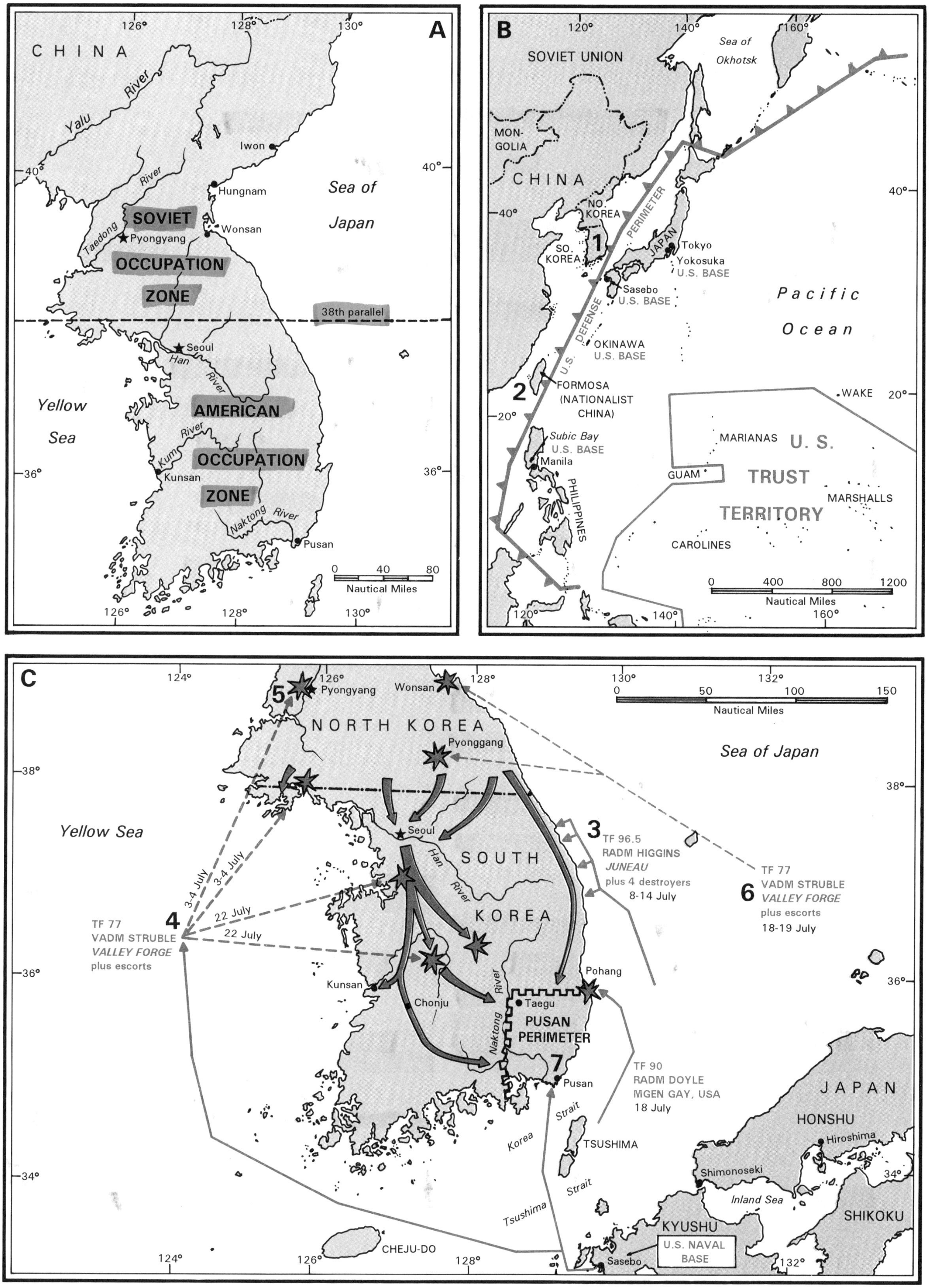

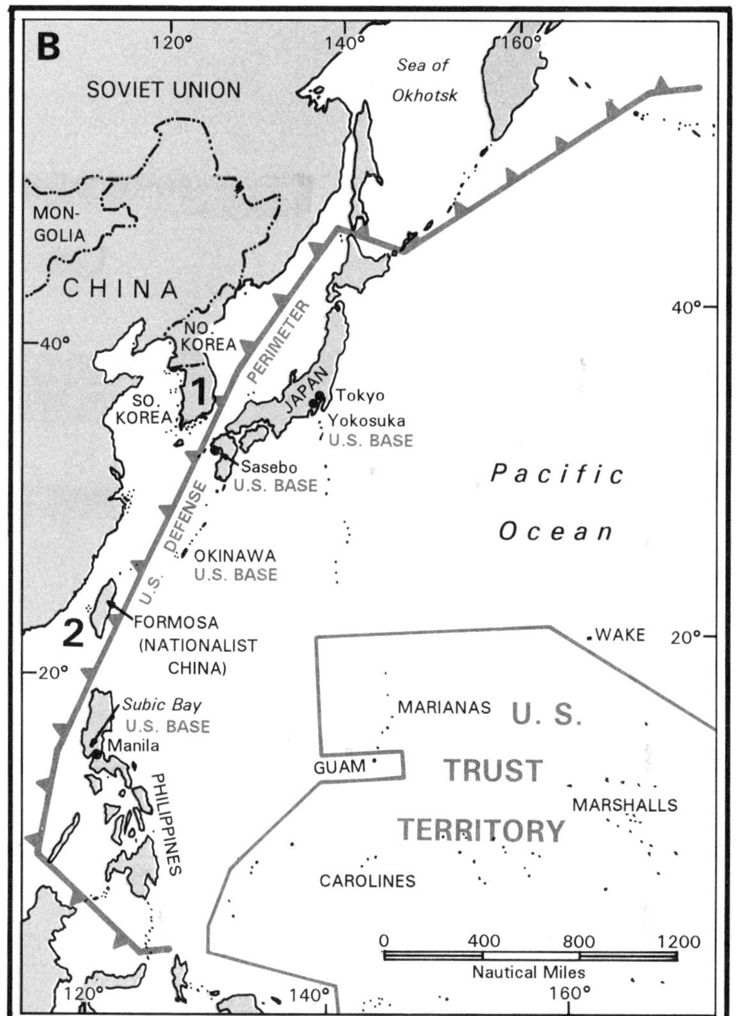
B
SOVIET UNION
Sea of Okhotsk
MONGOLIA
CHINA
NO. KOREA
SO. KOREA
1
PERIMETER
JAPAN
Tokyo
Yokosuka U.S. BASE
Sasebo U.S. BASE
U.S. DEFENSE
Pacific Ocean
OKINAWA U.S. BASE
2
FORMOSA (NATIONALIST CHINA)
WAKE
Subic Bay U.S. BASE
Manila
PHILIPPINES
MARIANAS
U. S.
GUAM
TRUST
TERRITORY
MARSHALLS
CAROLINES
0 400 800 1200
Nautical Miles
120° 140° 160°
40° 20°

C
5
Pyongyang
Wonsan
NORTH KOREA
Pyonggang
Sea of Japan
Yellow Sea
Seoul
3
TF 96.5
RADM HIGGINS
JUNEAU
plus 4 destroyers
8-14 July
SOUTH
Han River
KOREA
6
TF 77
VADM STRUBLE
VALLEY FORGE
plus escorts
18-19 July
3-4 July
3-4 July
22 July
22 July
4
TF 77
VADM STRUBLE
VALLEY FORGE
plus escorts
Kunsan
Chonju
Naktong River
Pohang
Taegu
PUSAN PERIMETER
7
Pusan
TF 90
RADM DOYLE
MGEN GAY, USA
18 July
Korea Strait
TSUSHIMA
Tsushima Strait
JAPAN
HONSHU
Hiroshima
Shimonoseki
Inland Sea
KYUSHU
SHIKOKU
CHEJU-DO
U.S. NAVAL BASE
Sasebo
0 50 100 150
Nautical Miles
124° 126° 128° 130° 132°
38° 36° 34°

MAP 80

CHROMITE: THE INCHON LANDING

15 SEPTEMBER 1950

In addition to ordering U.S. forces into Korea, President Truman also sought U.N. condemnation of the North Korean aggression. On 27 June the United Nations adopted an American-sponsored resolution authorizing member nations to "furnish such assistance to the Republic of Korea as may be necessary to repel the armed attack. . . ." The Soviet Union could not exercise its veto power because Soviet representatives were boycotting Security Council meetings in protest of the United Nation's failure to recognize Mao Tse-tung's Chinese communist government. Though U.S. forces in Korea fought under the auspices of the United Nations, as did units of many other U.N. member nations, the Korean conflict was predominantly an American war. The vast majority of U.N. combat troops were Americans, as was the commander, GEN Douglas MacArthur.

With U.N. forces pinned into the Pusan perimeter, the obvious strategy for regaining the initiative in Korea was an amphibious landing behind North Korean lines. The real question was where? The three most likely sites (see map A) were Kunsan (1), Inchon (2), and Pyongyang (3). Kunsan was the best landing beach, but because it was only one hundred miles behind the front, a landing there could achieve only tactical success. Pyongyang offered the greatest chance for a decisive blow, but it was north of the thirty-eighth parallel, and the U.N. mandate was not to conquer North Korea but only "to repel the armed attack."

That seemed to point to Inchon by default. But Inchon had problems of its own, most of which were a product of its unique geography and hydrography (see map B). The entrance to Inchon Harbor via Flying Fish Channel was narrow and treacherous, flanked by shallows that became mud flats at low tide. If a ship were damaged in the channel, it could block access to the beach for reinforcements or supplies or, in a worst-case scenario, make evacuation impossible. The tides themselves averaged twenty-three feet, with a maximum of thirty-three feet, so that access by deep-draft vessels like LSTs was possible only at high tide. Moreover, the tidal current averaged more than five knots, making navigation tricky even for a single ship and vastly complicating the deployment of hundreds of ships. In short, Inchon Harbor was a narrow cul-de-sac where, quite literally, it would be necessary to conquer or die. Finally, since an assault would have to be made at full tide to accommodate the LSTs that drew sixteen feet of water, it would have to be executed on 15 September or 3 October, and the latter date was too late in the season to ensure an opportunity to exploit a successful landing.

Such facts seemed to disqualify Inchon as a landing site, and most high-ranking officers preferred Kunsan even though a landing there was unlikely to be decisive. MacArthur, however, wanted Inchon. When the top U.S. commanders met in Tokyo on 23–24 August, MacArthur was at his dramatic best. Pushing back from the table, he strode around the room, gesturing with his pipe and speaking of the importance of surprise and audacity. He recalled Wolfe's landing at Quebec and declared that he could sense the hand of destiny. His performance carried the day. Despite all its problems, Inchon was selected as the landing site, and 15 September—only twenty-two days away—was designated as D-day. The landing would be known officially as Operation CHROMITE.

The fleet assembled for CHROMITE was Joint Task Force 7 under the U.S. Seventh Fleet commander, VADM Arthur Struble. The fast carrier force (TF 77) of RADM Edward C. Ewen provided air cover; RADM James Doyle commanded the attack force (TF 90) of 180 surface ships scraped together from across the Pacific; and the First Marine Division under MGEN Oliver P. Smith spearheaded the landing force of seventy thousand men under MGEN Edward Almond.

Air strikes against Inchon began on 10 September, and three days later six U.S. destroyers threaded their way up Flying Fish Channel at low tide (see map C) to shell the fortified island of Wolmi do (4) at a range of only eight hundred yards. For most of two days ships and planes took turns in blasting the island. Then at 6:30 A.M. on 15 September two waves of LCVPs carried the men of the 5th Marine regiment to Green Beach (5) on Wolmi do. By 7:15 A.M. they had secured the island, raising an American flag at the crest of Radio Hill. Spotting the flag through his field glasses, MacArthur announced, "That's it. Let's go down and have a cup of coffee."

But the fight for Inchon was not over—indeed, it was not yet fully started. The attack on the city itself began that afternoon at Red Beach (6), which was not a "beach" at all but a seawall that separated the city of Inchon from the harbor, and at Blue Beach (7) south of the city. Marines began the assault at 5:30 P.M., an hour before high tide and just before dusk. They had to secure a foothold in an unknown city before full dark, and to sustain them there eight LSTs remained offshore, unloading throughout the night, even though the falling tide left them sitting high and dry on the mud flats by morning. By dawn, American forces held the city and began to move inland. Even while the landing was in progress, MacArthur sent Vice Admiral Struble a message: "The Navy and the Marines have never shone more brightly than this morning."

MacArthur's determination to land at Inchon was an audacious gamble and it yielded dramatic success (see map D). Supported by the 7th Division of the U.S. Army, Marines moved inland and captured Seoul (8) on 28 September, severing the lines of communication to the North Korean forces in the south. At the same time, Lieutenant General Walker's 8th Army broke out of Pusan (9). Outnumbered, their supply lines cut, the North Koreans fled north in a disorganized mass. The war had been turned around in a single stroke.

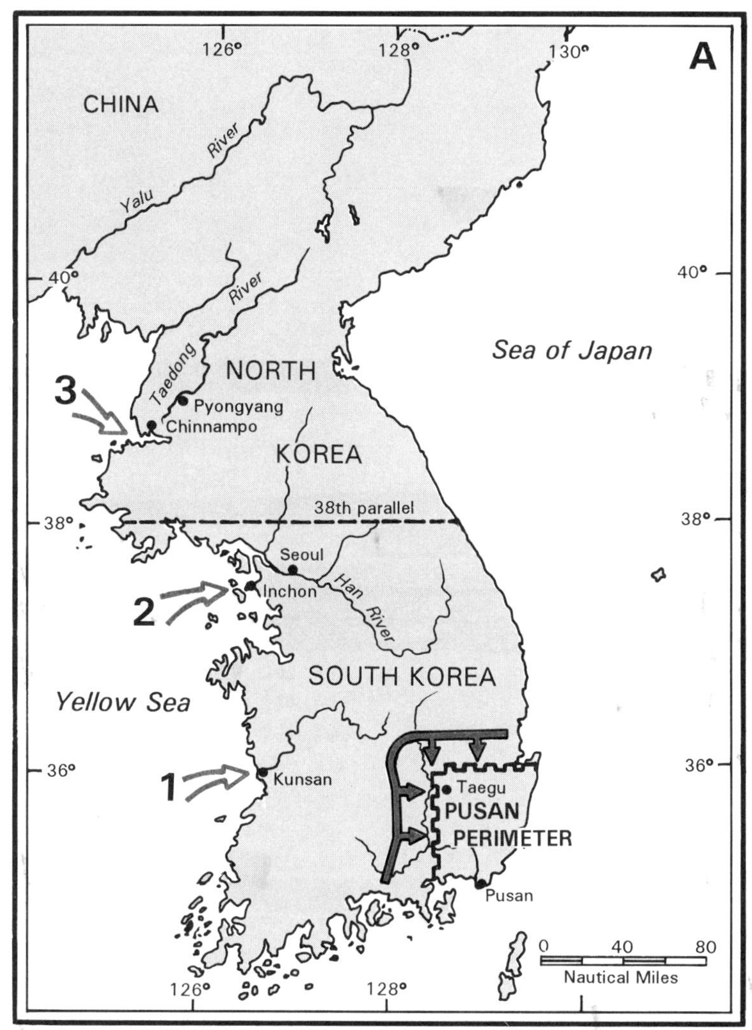
A
CHINA
Yalu River
Taedong River
NORTH
KOREA
Pyongyang
Chinnampo
3
38th parallel
Seoul
Inchon
2
Han River
SOUTH KOREA
Yellow Sea
Sea of Japan
1
Kunsan
Taegu
PUSAN
PERIMETER
Pusan
Nautical Miles

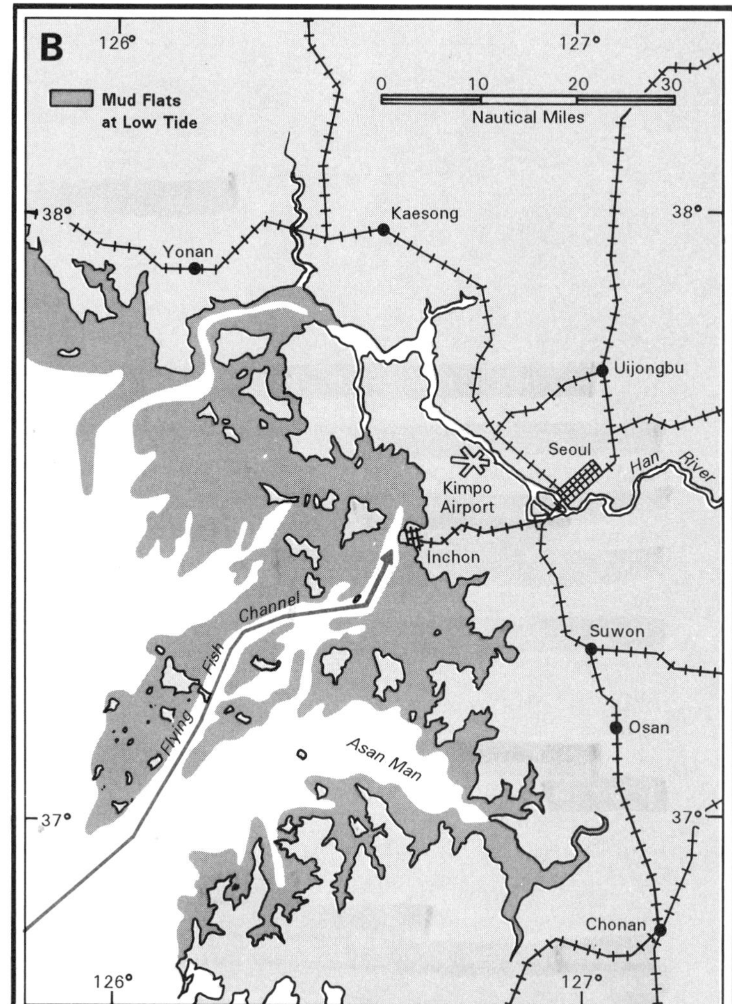
B
Mud Flats
at Low Tide
Nautical Miles
Kaesong
Yonan
Uijongbu
Seoul
Han River
Kimpo
Airport
Inchon
Flying Fish Channel
Suwon
Osan
Asan Man
Chonan

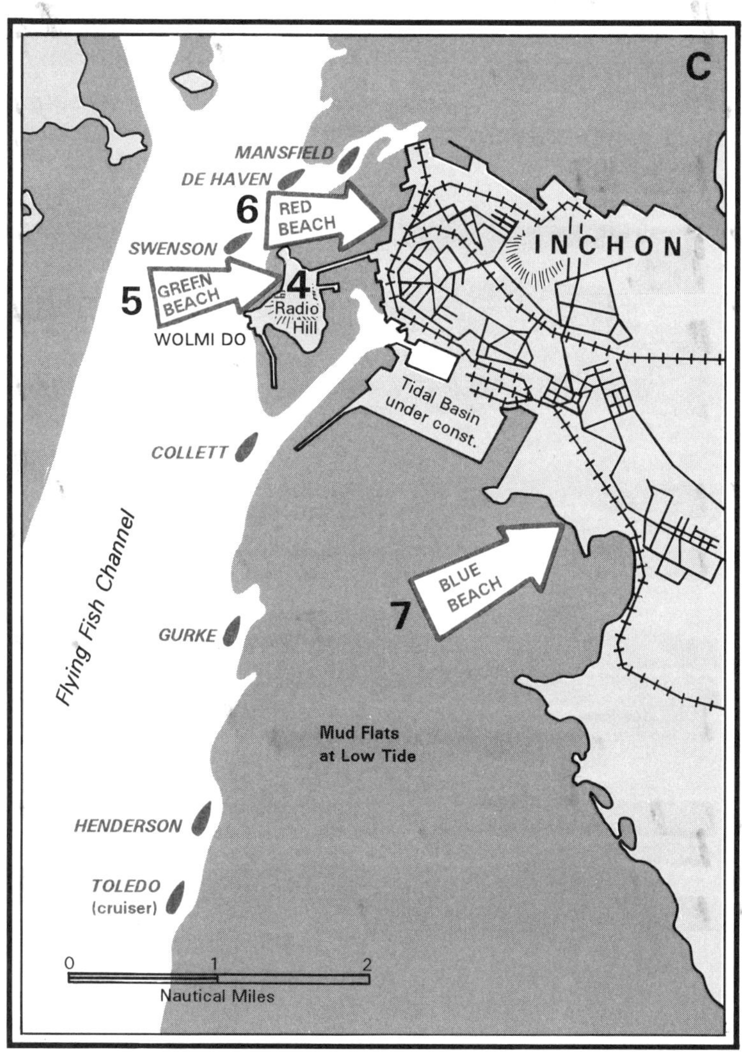
C
MANSFIELD
DE HAVEN
6
RED
BEACH
SWENSON
INCHON
5
GREEN
BEACH
4
Radio
Hill
WOLMI DO
Tidal Basin
under const.
COLLETT
Flying Fish Channel
BLUE
BEACH
7
GURKE
Mud Flats
at Low Tide
HENDERSON
TOLEDO
(cruiser)
Nautical Miles

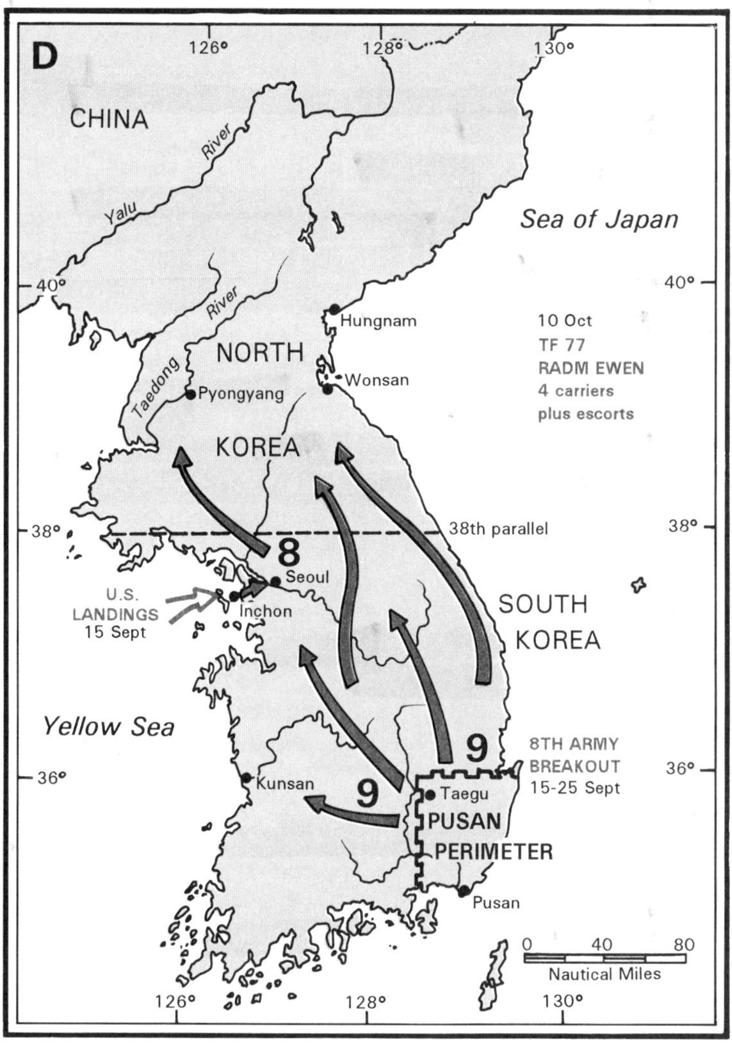
D
CHINA
Yalu River
Taedong River
Sea of Japan
Hungnam
10 Oct
TF 77
RADM EWEN
4 carriers
plus escorts
NORTH
Wonsan
Pyongyang
KOREA
38th parallel
8
Seoul
U.S.
LANDINGS
15 Sept
Inchon
SOUTH
KOREA
Yellow Sea
9
8TH ARMY
BREAKOUT
15-25 Sept
Kunsan
9
Taegu
PUSAN
PERIMETER
Pusan
Nautical Miles

MAP 81

THE HUNGNAM EVACUATION

OCTOBER–DECEMBER 1950

U.S. forces turned control of Seoul over to South Korean authorities on 29 September. That same day General MacArthur outlined his plan to extend the war into the north. His plan was consistent with U.S. and U.N. directives that authorized him to move beyond the thirty-eighth parallel "provided that . . . there has been no entry into North Korea by major Soviet or Chinese Communist forces." After Chinese Prime Minister Chou En-lai announced that China would intervene in the war if non-Korean troops attempted to conquer North Korea, MacArthur was advised to employ only Korean troops in those provinces bordering China and the U.S.S.R.—advice he did not heed.

MacArthur called for a dual advance up the Korean peninsula (see map A). While LGEN Walton H. Walker's 8th Army advanced north from Seoul toward Pyongyang (1), MGEN Edward M. Almond's 10th Corps, including the First Marine Division, would land at Wonsan (2) and advance up Korea's eastern coast. South Korean forces would support both advances. A major flaw in this plan was that an imposing mountain range would separate the two prongs of the advance, but MacArthur believed that he was pursuing a defeated enemy, and he discounted the possibility of Chinese intervention.

On 5–7 October the 10th Corps was relieved at Inchon and reembarked for a strike at Wonsan (see map B). Joint Task Force 7 was reconstituted with Vice Admiral Struble again in overall command. The first U.S. Navy unit to arrive at Wonsan was Mine Squadron Three under CAPT Richard T. Spofford, whose job was to clear a channel for the landing fleet. He soon discovered that his six minesweepers were wholly inadequate for the task. Soviet technicians had assisted the North Koreans in sowing more than three thousand magnetic and contact mines in Wonsan Harbor, and on 12 October mines sank two of Spofford's largest minesweepers (3). Three more sweepers were sent to Wonsan, but it was a full week before a clear channel could be swept, and in the meantime, forces of the South Korean Army captured Wonsan from the landward side (4).

The First Marine Division landed unopposed at Wonsan on 18 October, and the U.S. 7th Infantry Division went ashore at Iwon (5, map C) on 29 October. Marines advanced northwest toward the Chosin Reservoir (6), while the 7th Infantry Division moved north toward the Manchurian border. In the first week of November U.S. forces began to encounter elements of the Chinese Army. The 7th Marine Regiment fought an entire division of Chinese Communists at Chinhung-ni (7) on 7 November but continued its advance. On 15 November elements of the 7th Infantry Division reached the Manchurian border at Hyesanjin (8). Then on 27 November eight full corps of Chinese Communist forces struck simultaneously at Walker's 8th Army in the west and at the 5th and 7th Marine Regiments at Yadam-ni near the Chosin Reservoir. Hopelessly outnumbered, the Marines began a fighting withdrawal—attacking in the other direction—to fight their way out of the trap. Aided by close air support from TF 77, the Marines fought their way south for twelve days in bitter cold before linking up with other U.N. forces at Chinhung-ni on 9 December. That same day MacArthur authorized the evacuation of the 10th Corps from Hungnam (9).

The withdrawal of U.N. forces from Hungnam and Wonsan was a logistic achievement comparable to the evacuation of the British Army from Dunkirk in 1940. U.S. and allied vessels gathered from across the Pacific evacuated 105,000 soldiers, 91,000 civilians, and 17,500 vehicles from Hungnam. From Wonsan U.S. Navy ships evacuated another 3,800 soldiers and 7,000 civilians, plus 1,146 vehicles. At the same time, some 69,000 men of the 8th Army were evacuated from Inchon on the western coast.

Through December and January Communist Chinese forces pushed U.N. forces south of the thirty-eighth parallel. Though in March a U.N. counteroffensive regained the thirty-eighth parallel and recaptured Seoul, MacArthur grew frustrated by what he considered restraints placed on his freedom of action. He argued for a naval blockade of China, air strikes against Chinese cities, and an invasion of mainland China by Chiang Kai-shek's nationalists on Formosa. These suggestions found little favor among the Joint Chiefs and horrified America's U.N. partners. But MacArthur's pronouncements won support from Truman's political foes. Republican congressman Joe Martin charged that "the Truman administration should be indicted for the murder of thousands of American boys." When MacArthur wrote Martin a letter that seemed to endorse those views, the congressman read the letter into the Congressional Record. Having previously ordered MacArthur to communicate his opinions only through channels, Truman was unable to tolerate such public insubordination, and the president stripped MacArthur of all his commands and replaced him with GEN Matthew B. Ridgeway.

In May 1951 Ridgeway coordinated a U.N. offensive that pushed communist forces beyond the thirty-eighth parallel and inflicted terrible casualties, prompting the Soviet delegate to the U.N. to propose a negotiated settlement. The ensuing peace talks lasted most of two years. Meanwhile, planes from TF 77 conducted Operation STRANGLE, which targeted railroads and highways supporting the communist ground forces, and Navy ships off Wonsan maintained a blockade so constrictive that it constituted a virtual siege of the city. Finally, on 27 July 1953 the two sides signed an armistice at Panmunjon (10), establishing a cease-fire line just north of the thirty-eighth parallel. That cease-fire line became the new de facto border between North and South Korea. Under the auspices of the United Nations, American forces had successfully halted the first overt aggression of the Cold War era.

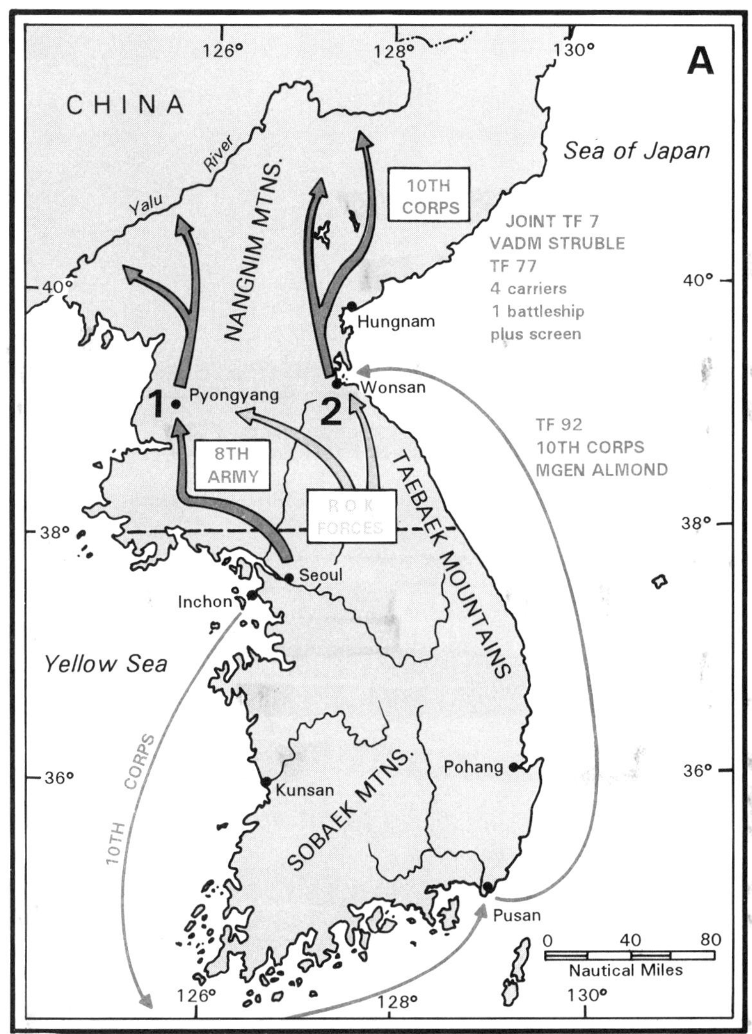
A
CHINA
126°
128°
130°
Sea of Japan
Yalu River
NANGNIM MTNS.
10TH CORPS
JOINT TF 7
VADM STRUBLE
TF 77
4 carriers
1 battleship
plus screen
40°
Hungnam
Wonsan
1
Pyongyang
2
TF 92
10TH CORPS
MGEN ALMOND
8TH ARMY
R O K FORCES
TAEBAEK MOUNTAINS
38°
Seoul
Inchon
Yellow Sea
10TH CORPS
36°
Kunsan
SOBAEK MTNS.
Pohang
Pusan
0 40 80
Nautical Miles

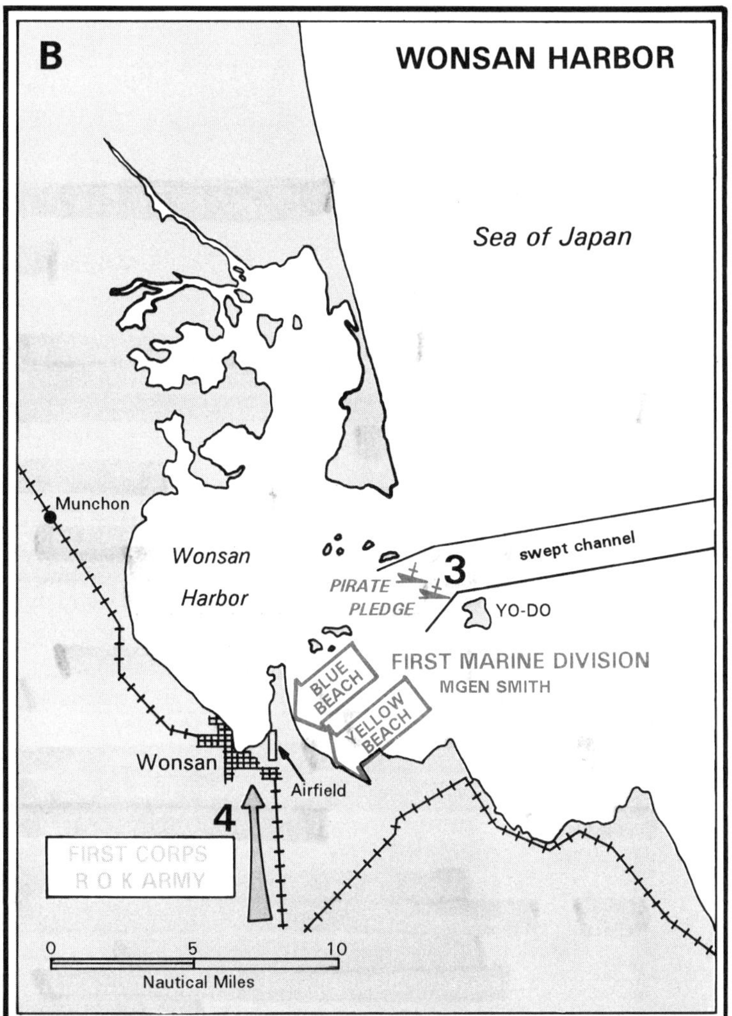
B
WONSAN HARBOR
Sea of Japan
Munchon
Wonsan Harbor
swept channel
3
PIRATE
PLEDGE
YO-DO
FIRST MARINE DIVISION
MGEN SMITH
BLUE BEACH
YELLOW BEACH
Wonsan
Airfield
4
FIRST CORPS
R O K ARMY
0 5 10
Nautical Miles

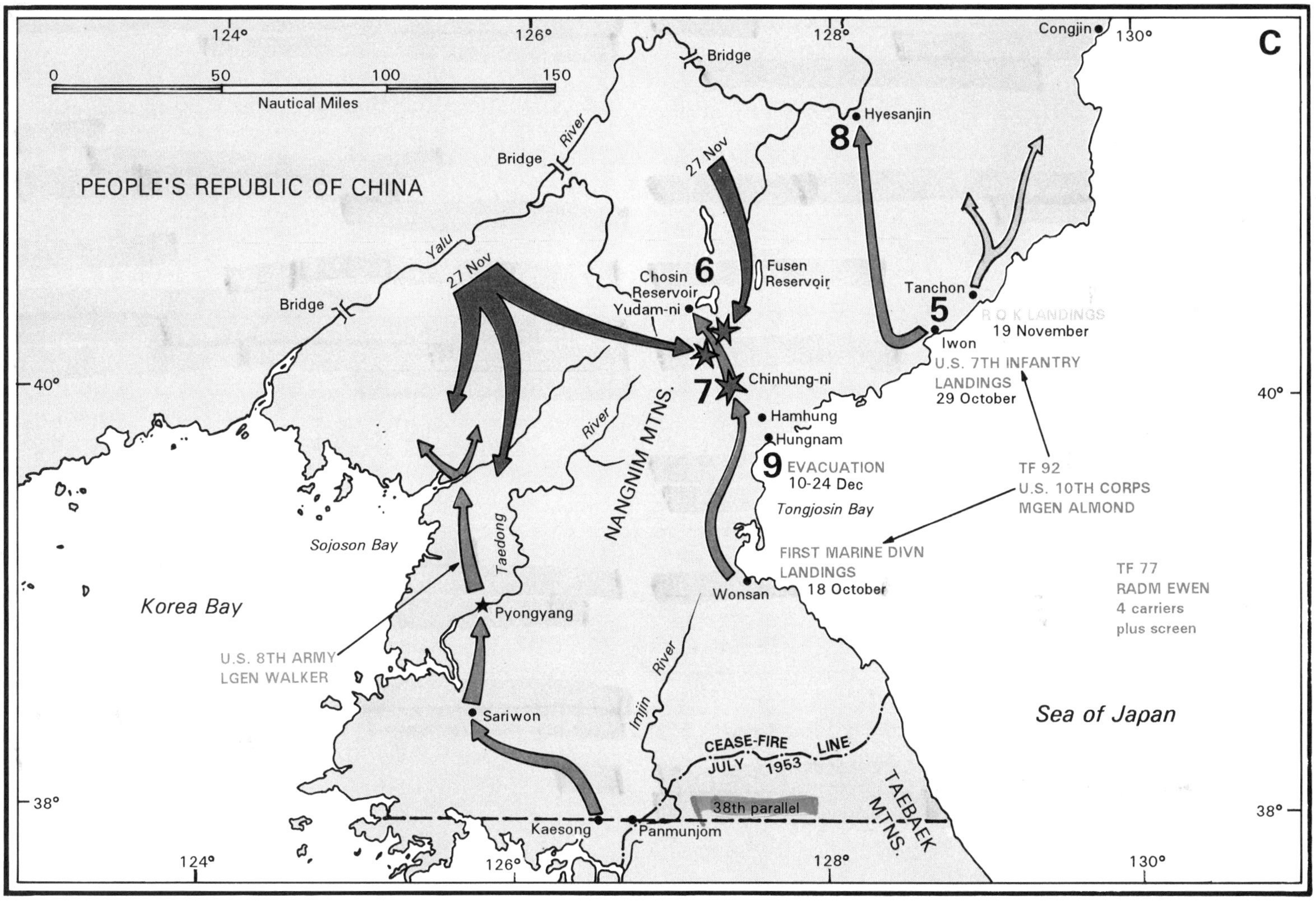

C
124°
126°
128°
130°
Congjin
Bridge
0 50 100 150
Nautical Miles
Hyesanjin
8
Bridge
River
27 Nov
PEOPLE'S REPUBLIC OF CHINA
Yalu
27 Nov
Chosin Reservoir
6
Fusen Reservoir
Tanchon
Bridge
Yudam-ni
5
R O K LANDINGS
19 November
Iwon
U.S. 7TH INFANTRY
LANDINGS
29 October
40°
Chinhung-ni
7
Hamhung
Hungnam
River
NANGNIM MTNS.
9
EVACUATION
10-24 Dec
TF 92
U.S. 10TH CORPS
MGEN ALMOND
Tongjosin Bay
Sojoson Bay
Taedong
FIRST MARINE DIVN
LANDINGS
18 October
TF 77
RADM EWEN
4 carriers
plus screen
Korea Bay
Pyongyang
Wonsan
U.S. 8TH ARMY
LGEN WALKER
River
Imjin
Sariwon
Sea of Japan
CEASE-FIRE LINE
JULY 1953
38th parallel
TAEBAEK MTNS.
38°
Kaesong
Panmunjom

MAP 82

THE EASTERN MED: SUEZ AND LEBANON

JULY–DECEMBER 1956 AND JULY–OCTOBER 1958

In addition to full-scale wars like the one in Korea, the Cold War was also marked by more-ambiguous confrontations. The eastern Mediterranean and the Middle East proved to be a particularly volatile region, partly because of its geographic and economic significance, but also because of its quilt-work of religious and nationalist sentiments. One element of that volatility was the creation of the state of Israel in May 1948, and another was the resurgence of Arab nationalism, personified in the 1950s by Egypt's COL Gamal Abdel Nasser (see map A).

Nasser came to power in Egypt via a 1952 revolution, and by 1954 he had established himself as a virtual dictator. He was primarily an Arab nationalist, but when he concluded an arms deal with the Soviet Union, the United States began to see him as a potential Soviet satellite. As a result, the United States backed out of a project to fund the Aswan High Dam on the Nile River (1). (Eventually, the Soviet Union provided the loans necessary to finance the dam.) Then on 26 July 1956 Nasser declared that the Egyptians would nationalize and run the Suez Canal (2), which a British-French investment company owned.

For both economic and strategic reasons, Nasser's announcement shocked and angered the British and French. Economically important to both nations, the Suez Canal was vital for Britain because 65 percent of its oil came through the canal. The French reaction was influenced by the fact that Nasser was a vocal supporter of rebels in Algeria, where France was fighting to hold onto the last remnant of its colonial empire. Thus Nasser's bold move prompted both protests and military preparations in Britain and France.

A fourth nation became involved in the crisis on 29 October when the Israeli Army crossed into Sinai and began driving toward the Suez Canal (see map B). By prearrangement, the British and French called for a cease-fire, and when their demand was ignored, they used that as a pretext to invade Egypt. The Israeli Army made quick work of the Egyptian forces, completing a conquest of Sinai when Sharm al-Shaykh surrendered on 3 November (3). Two days later British and French paratroopers seized key sites near Port Said (4), and Anglo-French seaborne forces landed on 6 November.

The escalating war placed the United States in a curious position. Though Nasser was clearly the victim of a coordinated assault, he was also vaguely associated with the Soviet Union. Should the United States take a stand against aggression as it had in Korea, or side with its traditional allies against a potential Soviet client? On 30 October the chief of naval operations, ADM Arleigh Burke, flashed a message to VADM Charles R. Brown, the Sixth Fleet commander: "Situation tense; prepare for imminent hostilities." Brown responded, "Am prepared for imminent hostilities, but which side are we on?" Burke's reply showed that he, too, was unsure: "If U.S. citizens are in danger, protect them. Take no guff from anyone."

Eventually, the United States supported a U.N. resolution calling on all sides to withdraw. U.N. troops replaced British and French forces in December, and the following spring Israeli forces evacuated the Sinai. Egypt assumed control of the canal in July 1958. Throughout the Arab world the outcome was viewed as a triumph over Western imperialism, and British prestige suffered a heavy blow. The United States began to perceive that it would have to fill the power vacuum in the eastern Mediterranean or risk the spread of a pro-Soviet pan-Arab movement that could eliminate Western influence in the Middle East. In 1957, therefore, President Eisenhower announced what became known as the Eisenhower Doctrine: the United States would provide military and economic aid to any Middle Eastern nation threatened by communism. The first test of this doctrine came in Lebanon.

Half Christian and half Moslem, Lebanon is an oddity among Middle Eastern nations. In 1958 the Christian president, Kamil Shamun, was nearing the end of a six-year term and hoped to amend the constitution to allow himself another term. When the murder of an opposition newspaper editor in May 1958 provoked riots in Beirut, Shamun invoked the Eisenhower Doctrine and asked for U.S. troops. The United States viewed the Lebanese crisis as an internal dispute until 14 July, when another pan-Arab nationalist overthrew the moderate government of Iraq. Fearful that this was part of a growing regional movement, Eisenhower decided to comply with Shamun's request and send in the Marines.

The U.S. landing took place the next day (see map C). A combat-ready battalion landing team went ashore at 3:00 P.M. on Red Beach (5) near the airport south of Beirut. Marines found themselves confronting swimsuit-clad tourists and ice cream vendors on the popular swimming beach, but they secured the airport perimeter and awaited further orders. Then the situation became very complicated. The Lebanese Army commander, GEN Fuad Shihab, feared that in spite of President Shamun's invitation, his own forces would look upon the Marines as invaders and ignite a full-scale war. He asked the U.S. ambassador, Robert McClintock, to stop or postpone a U.S. advance into Beirut. McClintock tried, but he had no command authority. When a U.S. armored column advancing toward Beirut encountered a Lebanese armored unit only a mile beyond the airport (6), the two sides faced each other at point-blank range. Meeting in a nearby schoolhouse, ADM James Holloway, General Shihab, and Ambassador McClintock agreed that the U.S. advance could continue, but with Lebanese officers accompanying and preceding each unit.

The U.S. Marines occupied Beirut for about two months and departed in the fall after General Shihab was elected president. Despite the comic opera of the initial landings, the Lebanon crisis of 1958 showed just how complicated the U.S. role was likely to be during the Cold War, and how difficult it would be for Navy and Marine Corps officers to ascertain their duty.

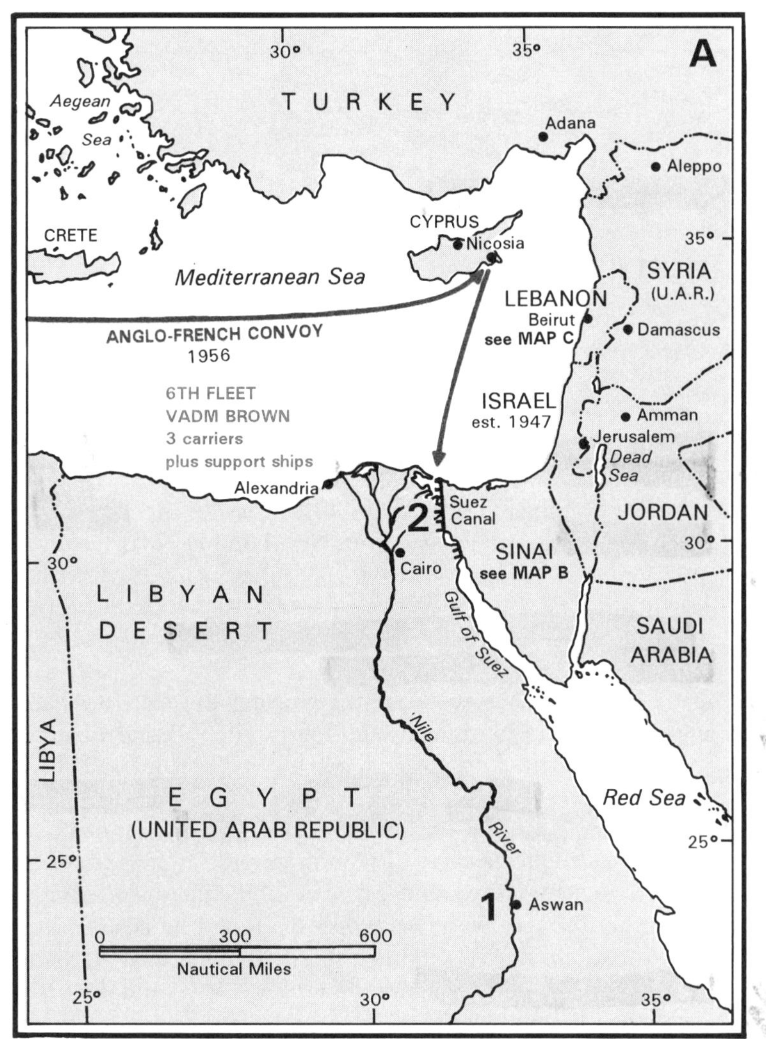

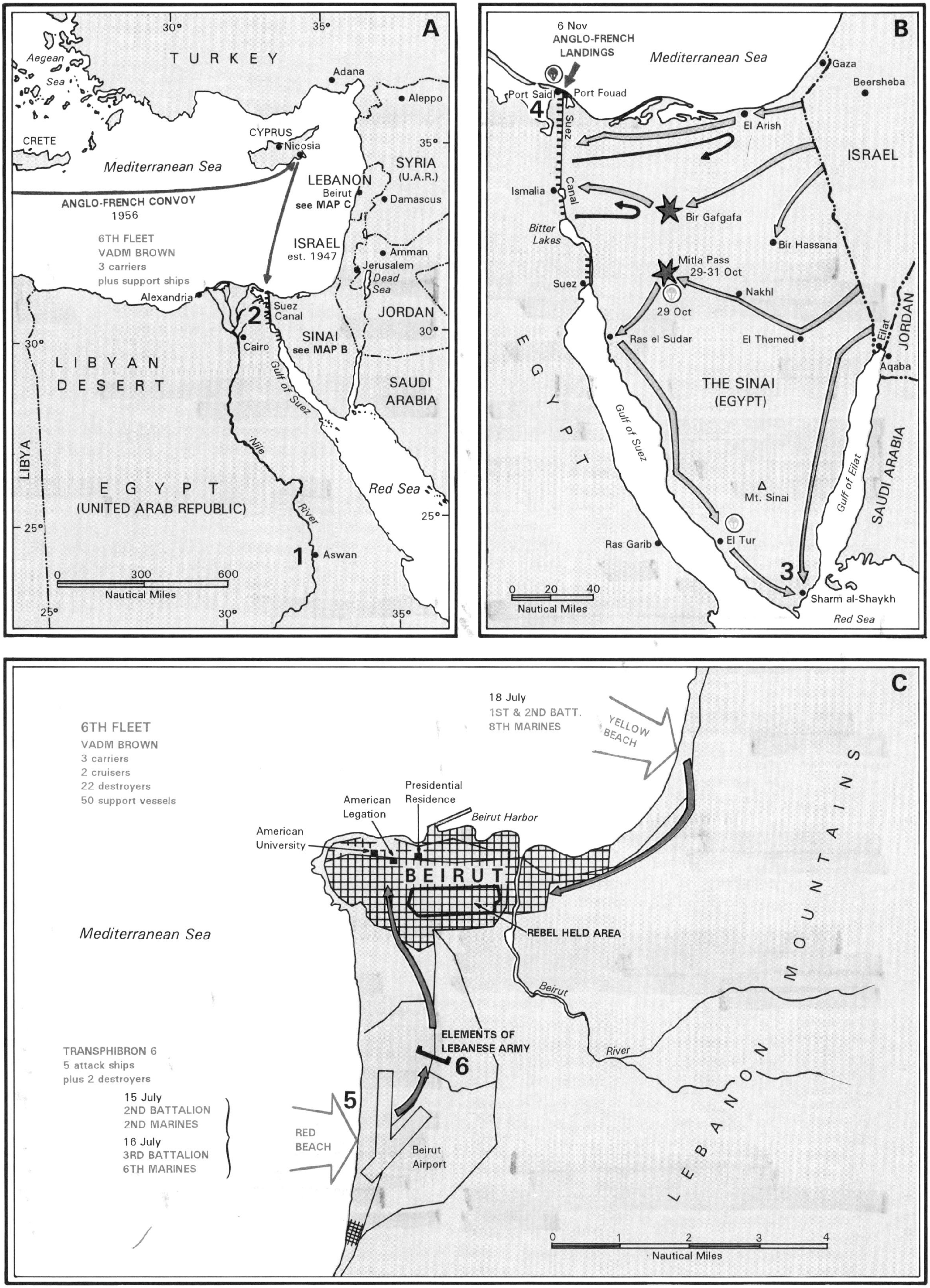

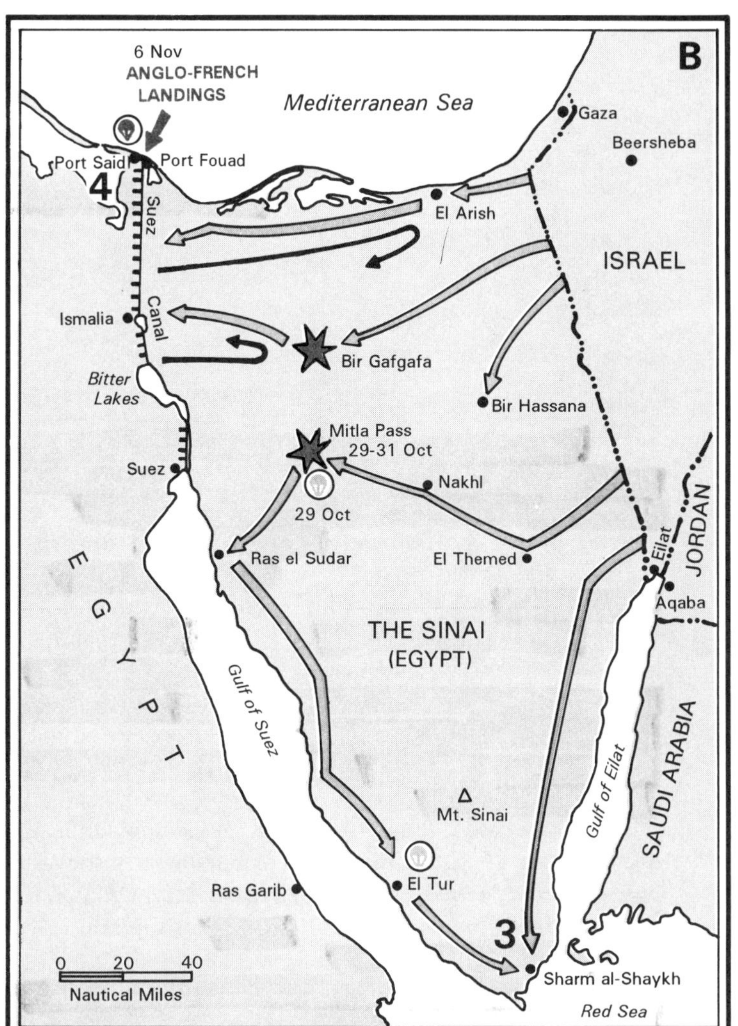

C

18 July
1ST & 2ND BATT.
8TH MARINES

YELLOW BEACH

6TH FLEET
VADM BROWN
3 carriers
2 cruisers
22 destroyers
50 support vessels

Presidential Residence
American Legation
Beirut Harbor
American University
BEIRUT
REBEL HELD AREA
Mediterranean Sea
LEBANON MOUNTAINS
Beirut River

ELEMENTS OF LEBANESE ARMY
6

TRANSPHIBRON 6
5 attack ships
plus 2 destroyers

15 July
2ND BATTALION
2ND MARINES
16 July
3RD BATTALION
6TH MARINES

5
RED BEACH
Beirut Airport

0 1 2 3 4
Nautical Miles

MAP 83

"UNDERWAY ON NUCLEAR POWER"

JANUARY 1955–JULY 1960

The single most important technological development of the Cold War era was the application of nuclear power to naval propulsion, and specifically to submarine propulsion. It was a revolution that occurred with remarkable speed—only six and a half years elapsed between the establishment of a Nuclear Power Branch in BuShips in July 1948 and the maiden cruise of the nuclear-powered *Nautilus* in January 1955. That this revolution took place so quickly and with no major accidents was due to one man: RADM Hyman Rickover. It was Rickover's personal drive and determination, fueled by an acerbic and uncompromising personality, that midwifed the nuclear revolution in the U.S. Navy. In 1949 Rickover predicted that the U.S. Navy would have a fully operational nuclear submarine at sea by 1 January 1955. He missed his prediction by just over two weeks. As the *Nautilus* got under way from New London, Connecticut, on 17 January 1955, it signaled its tug as it cast off: "Underway on nuclear power."

Nuclear power made submarines true submersibles; no longer did they have to surface and fire up their diesel engines to recharge the electric batteries. The *Nautilus* steamed more than 62,000 miles without refueling, then steamed another 91,000 miles after receiving a new core. To measure the boat's capabilities, the *Nautilus* left San Francisco in July 1958 under the command of CDR William Anderson, on a secret mission to the North Pole (see upper map). After an aborted attempt in June, the *Nautilus* left Pearl Harbor for a second try in July. It passed through the Bering Strait (1) on 29 July, where its navigator took one last fix before submerging. In the Chukchi Sea (2) the water was only 150 feet deep, leaving little room for the *Nautilus* to navigate the space between the ocean floor below and the sea ice above. After several attempts, Commander Anderson finally found sea room in the Barrow Sea Valley (3), and he turned the *Nautilus* due north for the run to the pole.

Among the new equipment supplied to the *Nautilus* for this voyage was a sonar mounted upside down on the boat's upper hull so that the crew could monitor the ice above as well as the ocean floor below. At 11:15 P.M. on 3 August 1958 Commander Anderson announced to the crew over the 1-MC that they had reached the North Pole (4). The *Nautilus* did not tarry there, though there was plenty of deep water under its hull, but pressed onward—due south now—into the Greenland Sea. There the *Nautilus* surfaced (5), and Commander Anderson was picked up by helicopter for a trip to Washington and a ceremony in the White House. The boat continued south to Portsmouth (6). Within days the nuclear-powered *Skate* (CDR James Calvert) duplicated the feat of the *Nautilus*, this time breaking through the polar ice cap to surface at the North Pole.

As impressive as these feats were, they were soon eclipsed by the voyage of the much larger nuclear-powered *Triton*, commanded by CDR Edward Beach (see lower map). This giant submersible, which displaced 6,500 tons and boasted two nuclear reactors, got under way from New London on 16 February 1960 and headed south for St. Paul Rocks (7), which it reached on 24 February. From that landmark the *Triton* began a global circumnavigation that lasted two months and covered 26,723 miles—all of it submerged.

The *Triton*'s crew celebrated crossing the equator that night, as the ship continued south toward the Falkland Islands (8), where it arrived on 3 March precisely on schedule. At this point, however, Chief Radarman J. R. Poole suffered a severe kidney-stone attack that required hospitalization. Commander Beach directed the *Triton* to turn north toward Montevideo (9). On 5 March a hundred nautical miles off the South American coast, the *Triton* came to periscope depth and broached—its narrow conning tower only slightly exposed. Chief Poole was transferred to a motorboat from the cruiser *Macon*, and the *Triton* slipped back under the surface.

The *Triton* passed through Le Maire Strait off Cape Horn on 7 March and steered northwest for Easter Island (10), which it passed—submerged—on 13 March. Ten days later the *Triton* crossed the international date line, and on 28 March the *Triton* conducted a submerged photo reconnaissance of Guam before heading for the Philippines. Attempting to duplicate Magellan's route as much as possible, the *Triton* transited Surigao Strait on 31 March, then backtracked up the Bohol Strait to Magellan Bay on Mactan Island (11), where Magellan lost his life in 1521. From there the *Triton* headed south into the Sulu Sea, passed through the Makassar Strait to the Java Sea, and through the Lombok Strait into the Indian Ocean (12). The *Triton* passed Capetown on 17 April, Easter Sunday, then headed northwest to St. Paul Rocks, where it arrived on 25 April, completing the first underwater circumnavigation of the world 440 years after Magellan's voyage.

Four months before the *Triton* completed its historic voyage, the Navy commissioned its first ballistic-missile submarine (SSBN), the *George Washington*. Combining the submerged sea-keeping abilities of the *Nautilus* and *Triton* and the new design shape of the *Albacore* class of diesel boats, the *George Washington* was an invisible missile platform and thus established for the Navy a key role in the nation's strategic-defense program. On 20 July 1960 the *George Washington* fired a Polaris missile while submerged. In the 1960s it became common to speak of a "triad" of American nuclear deterrence: land-based missiles, bombers, and nuclear-powered ballistic-missile submarines. The presumed survivability of these SSBNs gave the United States a credible second-strike capability and greatly enhanced the nation's deterrence posture throughout the Cold War era.

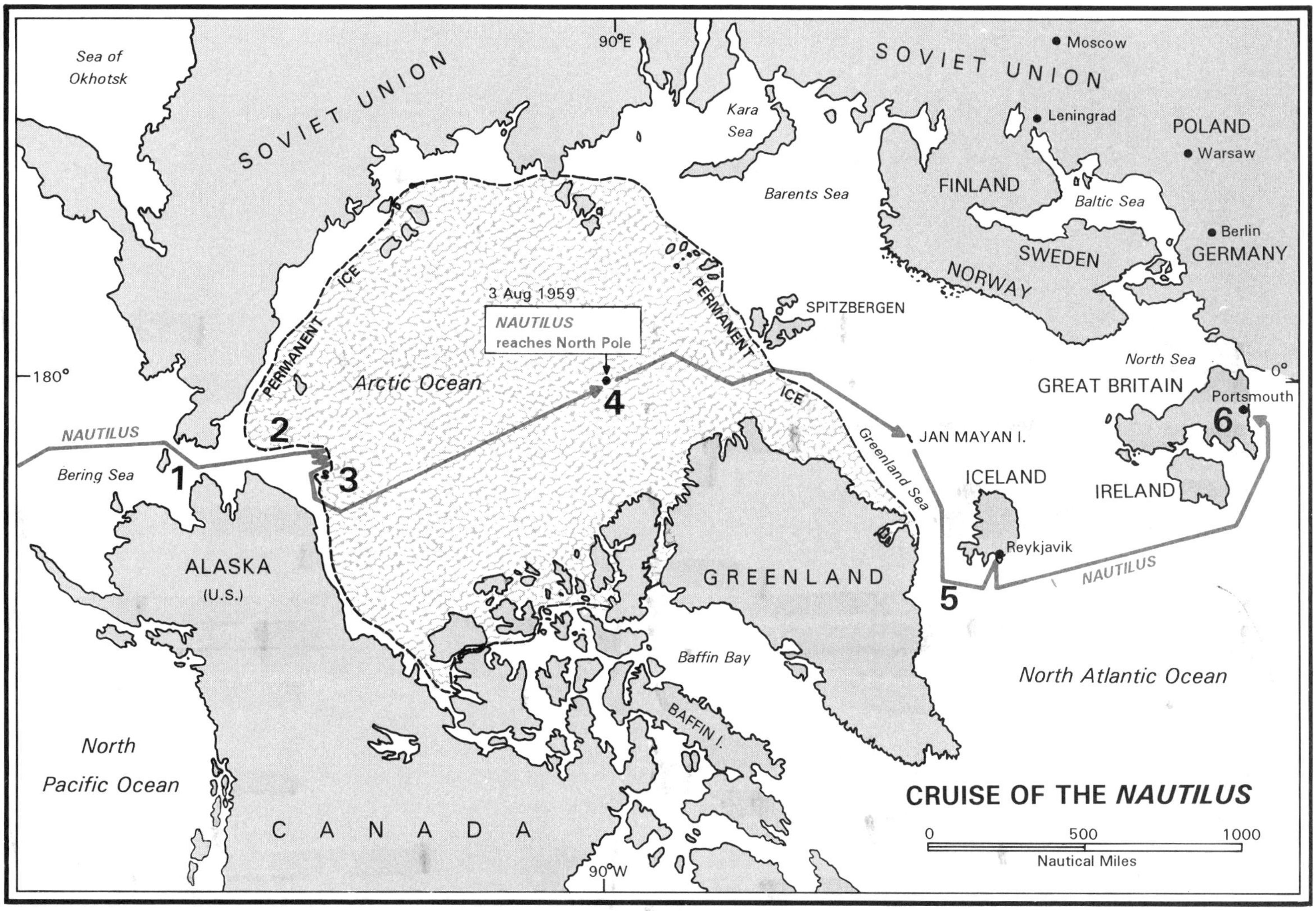

Sea of Okhotsk
SOVIET UNION
90°E
Kara Sea
SOVIET UNION
Moscow
Leningrad
POLAND
Warsaw
FINLAND
Baltic Sea
Berlin
GERMANY
SWEDEN
NORWAY
Barents Sea
PERMANENT ICE
PERMANENT ICE
3 Aug 1959
NAUTILUS reaches North Pole
SPITZBERGEN
North Sea
0°
180°
Arctic Ocean
4
GREAT BRITAIN
Portsmouth
6
ICE
NAUTILUS
2
JAN MAYAN I.
Greenland Sea
Bering Sea
1
3
ICELAND
IRELAND
Reykjavik
NAUTILUS
5
ALASKA (U.S.)
GREENLAND
Baffin Bay
North Atlantic Ocean
BAFFIN I.
North Pacific Ocean
CANADA
90°W

CRUISE OF THE *NAUTILUS*

0 500 1000
Nautical Miles

120° 180° 120° 60° 0° 60°
GREENLAND
SOVIET UNION
ALASKA (U.S.)
ICELAND
60°
CANADA
GREAT BRITAIN
North Atlantic Ocean
ALEUTIANS
EUROPE
CHINA
North Pacific Ocean
New London
JAPAN
UNITED STATES
TRITON departs 16 Feb 1960
30°
BONINS
MIDWAY
HAWAII
TRITON
PHILIPPINES
28 March
AFRICA
11
GUAM
CAROLINES
MARSHALLS
7
ST. PAUL ROCKS
NEW GUINEA
GILBERTS
TRITON
SOUTH AMERICA
0°
12
South Atlantic Ocean
10
AUSTRALIA
EASTER ISLAND
Indian Ocean
South Pacific Ocean
13 March
Monte-video
9
Capetown
5 March
TRITON broaches to send RDC Poole ashore
NEW ZEALAND
FALKLAND ISLANDS
8

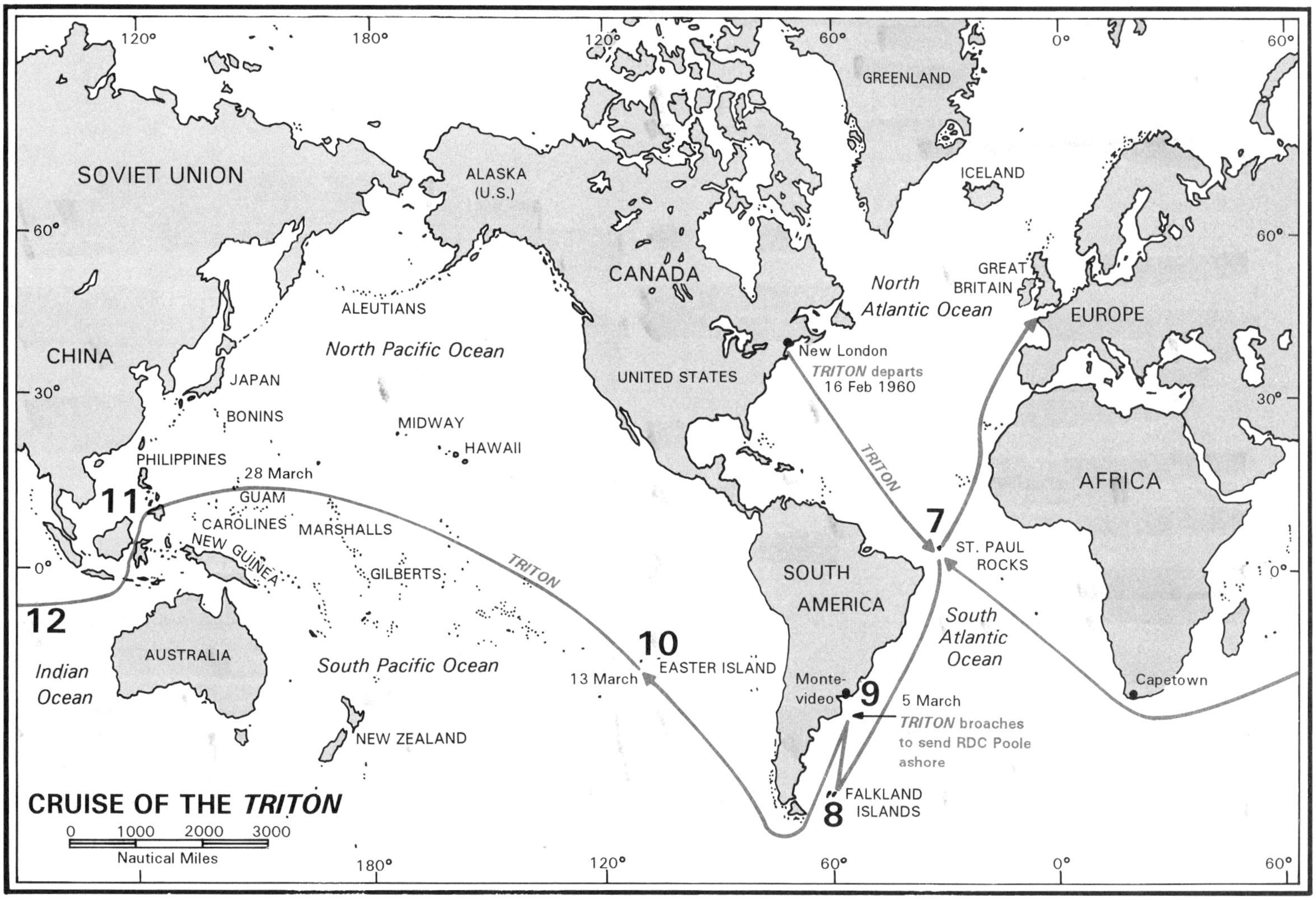

CRUISE OF THE *TRITON*

0 1000 2000 3000
Nautical Miles
180° 120° 60° 0° 60°

MAP 84

THE CUBAN MISSILE CRISIS

16–28 OCTOBER 1962

During the presidential election of 1960 John Kennedy charged that the Republicans had allowed the Soviets to surpass the United States in missile technology. The charge seemed credible because of the stunning Soviet success in launching the world's first man-made earth satellite, *Sputnik,* in 1957. Only after he had been elected did Kennedy learn the extent of America's lead in nuclear warheads, which was so great that the Soviet premier, Nikita Khrushchev, was desperately seeking a way to close the gap.

Three months after Kennedy's inauguration, 1,500 anti-communist Cuban exiles stormed ashore on the southern coast of Cuba at the Bay of Pigs (1). Its leaders hoped the landing would provoke a spontaneous anti-Castro uprising in Cuba. Instead, twenty thousand Cuban soldiers attacked the invaders and killed or captured all of them within two days. Though Kennedy had given his approval, the CIA had planned and sponsored the bungled operation, and it was particularly humiliating because Castro had been claiming for months that the United States was planning an invasion, and the United States had righteously denied it.

If the United States had backed one invasion, might it not try again? The question prompted Castro to ask his new Soviet ally for more military aid so that he could defend his small country against Yankee imperialism. Thus Khrushchev's desire for a quick fix to the strategic imbalance and Castro's need for military support came together in 1962 to create the Cuban Missile Crisis, the closest the United States and the Soviet Union ever came to nuclear war.

On 16 October 1962 Kennedy was awakened by his National Security Adviser, McGeorge Bundy, at 7:30 A.M. Bundy got right to the point: the Soviets had placed intermediate-range nuclear missiles in Cuba. He could make this statement with some certainty because of the remarkable resolution of photographs taken by high-altitude U-2 planes flying over Cuba (see photo at upper right). The only good news was that the missiles were not yet operational so that the United States had a few days to decide what action to take.

While Navy Crusader jets flew low-level reconnaissance over Cuba to gather more detailed information, Kennedy established an Executive Committee (EXCOM) of top administration officials to consider U.S. options. Debate quickly narrowed those options to three alternatives: official protest and political pressure (which no one thought was sufficient); an air strike followed by invasion (which could provoke a Soviet retaliation); or a naval blockade. Eventually the idea of a naval blockade won a majority of support, and the EXCOM recommended it to the president on 18 October. Like Lincoln one hundred years earlier, Kennedy was loath to use the word "blockade" because blockade was an act of war. The president called it a "quarantine." When President Kennedy told the CNO, ADM George Anderson, that "it looks as though this is up to the Navy," Anderson responded, "Mr. President, the Navy will not let you down."

ADM Robert Dennison ran the overall operation from Norfolk, and VADM Alfred Ward took command of the Second Fleet, which would execute the blockade. The fleet was deployed in two major units. Task Force 135, built around the carriers *Enterprise* and *Independence,* operated from a position south of Cuba (2), ready to strike in case the blockade failed. North of Cuba, Task Force 136 deployed along two intersecting arcs five hundred miles from Havana and Point Maisi (3), and thus beyond the range of land-based MiG fighters in Cuba, to interdict vessels headed for Cuba. A cruiser-destroyer group anchored each end of the interdiction line, and thirteen destroyers positioned themselves at sixty-mile intervals along the arc. U.S. destroyers also patrolled the Florida Strait south of Key West and the Windward Passage east of Point Maisi.

The days that followed were extraordinarily tense. No one was quite sure how the Soviet government would react if a U.S. Navy destroyer stopped one of its ships. Secretary of Defense Robert McNamara also worried about what U.S. destroyer skippers might do if a Soviet vessel refused to stop. McNamara was often present in Flag Plot in the Pentagon, looking (both figuratively and literally) over Admiral Anderson's shoulder as he tracked vessels bound for Cuba. With the stakes so high, the tension led to some friction and a few shouted exchanges.

The quarantine went into effect at 10:00 A.M. on 24 October. Several ships were allowed through the quarantine line after being visually inspected and photographed, but not until 26 October did the U.S. Navy stop and search a vessel. The ship was the Panamanian-owned, Lebanese-registered *Marucla,* chosen less because it was suspicious than to demonstrate U.S. resolve. The *Marucla* stopped as ordered, was searched, and was allowed to continue (4). But the next day the Soviet tanker *Groznyy* refused to acknowledge the orders of an American destroyer to stop. Other destroyers arrived on the scene, but the *Groznyy* plowed onward. It was a game of "chicken" with the highest possible stakes. Admiral Dennison ordered the U.S. destroyers to "clear their guns" by firing *away* from the *Groznyy.* This demonstration had the desired effect. The *Groznyy* stopped, radioed Moscow for instructions, and retired beyond the quarantine line (5).

The two superpowers avoided war when the Soviets agreed to remove their missiles from Cuba in exchange for an American pledge that the United States would not invade Cuba and an unwritten understanding that the United States would remove its Jupiter missiles from Turkey. American military strength and the evident determination of the Kennedy administration to stand firm were the crucial factors in convincing Khrushchev to retreat. The outcome was a particular victory for the U.S. Navy, which had demonstrated its operational skill and its flexibility as an instrument of national pressure.

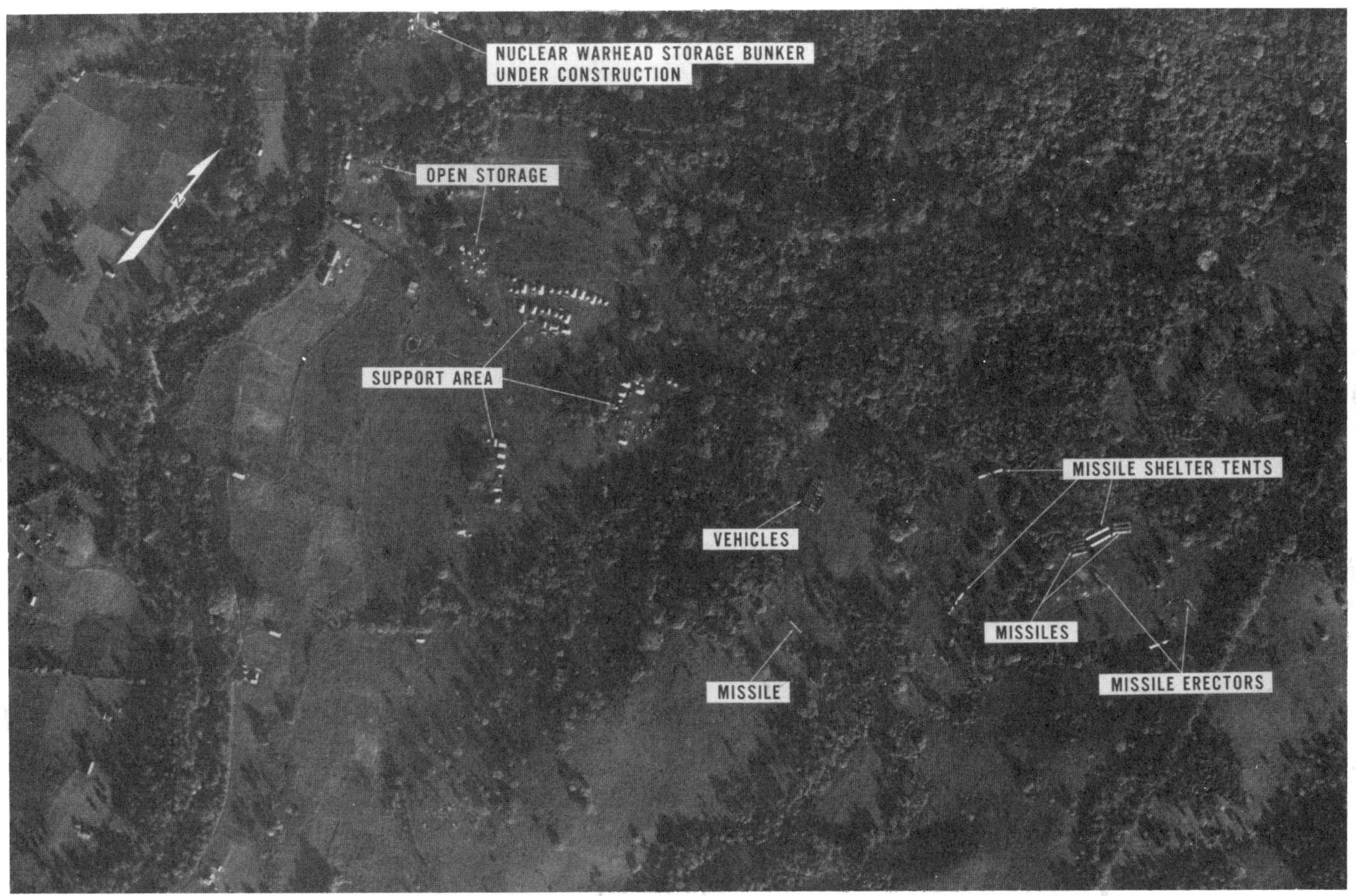

Russian missiles in Cuba: One of the remarkable satellite photos taken on 14 October 1962 that proved the Soviets were installing what the United States defined as "offensive" missiles on the island of Cuba—sparking what became known as the Cuban Missile Crisis. (Official U.S. Navy photo)

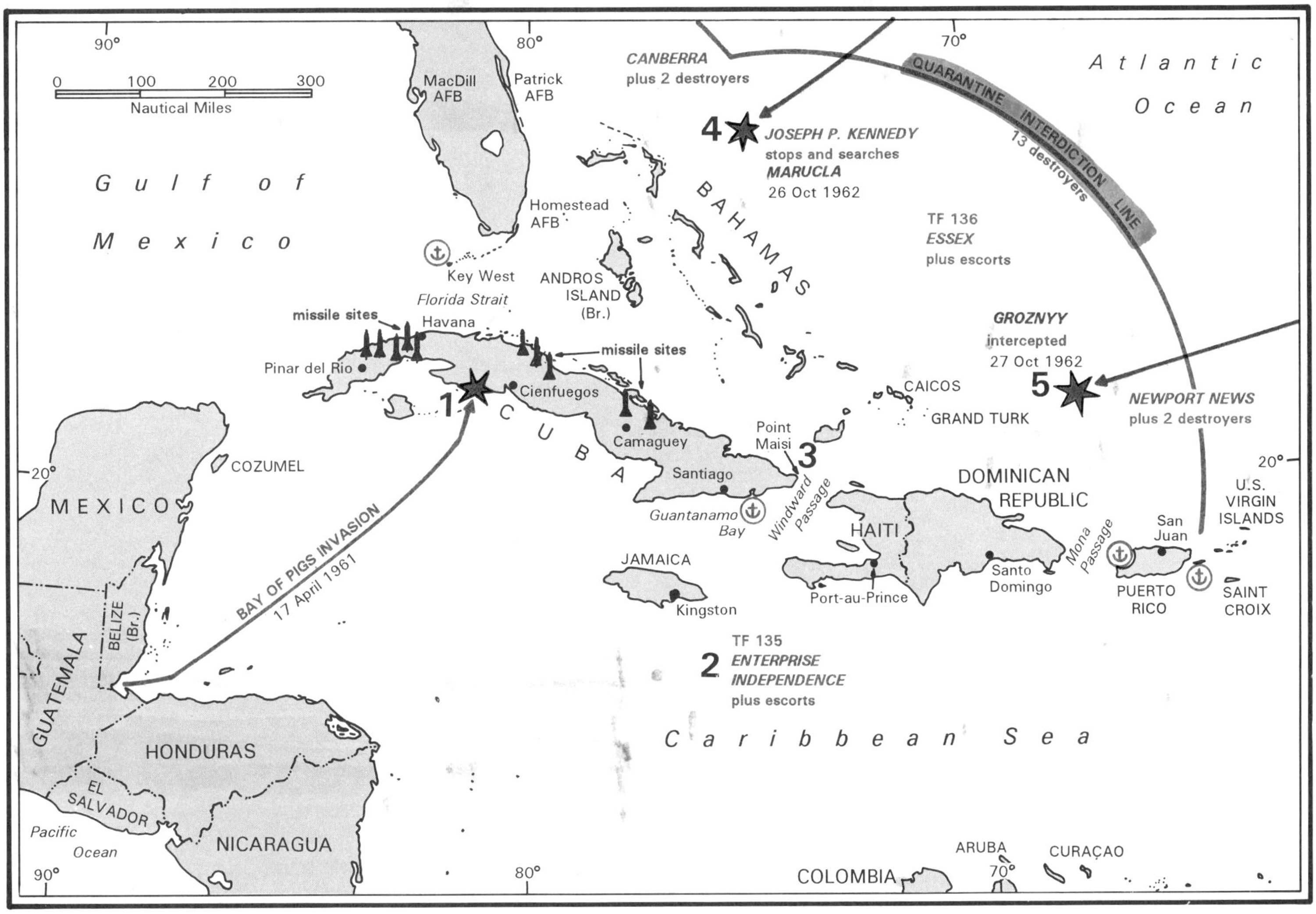

MAP 85

THE VIETNAM WAR: THE TONKIN GULF INCIDENT

AUGUST 1964

The Vietnam War (1959–1973) was a draining experience for the United States—physically, economically, and emotionally. Its roots, like those of the Korean War, lay in the politics of the Cold War. During World War II the United States had avowed a policy of supporting national liberation movements throughout Japanese-occupied South Asia, including the Philippines, which received its independence in 1946. But that same year the United States declined to support the independence movement of Ho Chi Minh in French Indochina, partly because he was a communist and partly because the United States was eager to placate the French to ensure their adherence to an anti-Soviet front in Europe. Ho Chi Minh, however, initiated a war for Vietnamese independence that lasted eight years and climaxed in a humiliating French defeat at Dien Bien Phu (1) in May of 1954. Subsequent peace talks in Geneva led to the partition of Indochina into three states: Laos in the northwest, Cambodia in the southwest, and Vietnam along the coast.

But Vietnam had two governments claiming a right to rule: Ho Chi Minh's "Democratic Republic of Vietnam" and the French puppet government of the Emperor Bao Dai. As a compromise, the delegates at Geneva agreed to divide Vietnam—temporarily—near the seventeenth parallel (2), thus creating a North Vietnam with its capital at Hanoi (3) and a South Vietnam with its capital at Saigon (4). Elections were to be held within two years to determine which government would rule a unified Vietnam. Those elections were never held because the man who emerged as president of South Vietnam, Ngo Dinh Diem, was unwilling to risk a nationwide election against Ho Chi Minh. Diem maintained a fervently anticommunist (though not thoroughly democratic) government for most of a decade while fending off a continued communist insurgency supported by North Vietnam.

When John Kennedy took office in January 1961, he was eager to reverse what he saw as a string of American defeats since Korea. Rather than depend on nuclear deterrence, Kennedy opted for a more "flexible response" to the communist challenge. The new president was particularly interested in counterinsurgency warfare, and the jungle of Southeast Asia seemed a suitable testing ground for such a policy. In April Kennedy sent one hundred additional military advisers to South Vietnam, raising the total to eight hundred, and over the next two years he authorized additional units until by the time of his death in November 1963 there were more than twenty-three thousand U.S. "advisers" in South Vietnam.

Kennedy's assassination in November 1963 made Lyndon Johnson president. Johnson was eager to embark on a program of domestic reforms and had little interest in foreign policy. By keeping virtually all of Kennedy's foreign policy advisers, he ensured that the confrontational policy in Vietnam would continue to run on autopilot. In addition, Johnson was determined not to be blamed for "losing" South Vietnam as Truman had been blamed for "losing" China in 1949. He got an opportunity to demonstrate his firmness in August 1964.

During 1964 the U.S. government began directing the South Vietnamese Navy in a series of covert sabotage operations (code-named 34A) against North Vietnam. To support these operations, U.S. Navy destroyers conducted intelligence-gathering (DeSoto) patrols in the Gulf of Tonkin off the North Vietnamese coast. The first such patrol, by the destroyer *John R. Craig* in February–March, went off without incident, but the second, by the destroyer *Maddox* (CAPT John Herrick), had profound consequences. Near midnight on 30–31 July South Vietnamese Navy fast patrol boats conducted a 34A attack against North Vietnamese facilities on Hon Me Island (5). That same day the *Maddox* began a DeSoto patrol along the North Vietnamese coast (6). Nearing Hon Me at 3:20 A.M. on 2 August, Captain Herrick learned from radio-intelligence intercepts that the North Vietnamese were scrambling their PT boats. He, therefore, turned out to sea (7) until daylight, returning to coastal waters at 10:45 A.M. At 3:00 that afternoon his radar picked up the blips of several PT boats moving parallel to his track. Anticipating an attack, Herrick requested air support from the *Ticonderoga* (8). At 4:00 P.M. three PT boats approached the *Maddox* at high speed. Herrick ordered several warning shots, but the boats continued to close. At three thousand yards they launched torpedoes, which missed. The *Maddox* then fired on the targets, which quickly retired, one of them severely damaged (9). At 4:30 aircraft from the *Ticonderoga* arrived overhead and attacked, sinking the damaged PT boat.

ADM Tom Moorer, commander in chief of the Pacific Fleet, ordered the destroyer *Turner Joy* to join the *Maddox* and directed that the DeSoto patrol continue. Meanwhile, on 3 August the South Vietnamese Navy made another 34A attack near Vinh Son (10). Presumably, the North Vietnamese again scrambled their PT boats, for late the next evening both the *Maddox* and *Turner Joy* made radar contact with small surface units well beyond North Vietnamese waters (11). At 10:39 P.M. the *Turner Joy* opened fire. With both ships running blacked out under low overcast skies and in a heavy sea, the sequence of events became confused. Many of the subsequent PT boat sightings, which went on for hours, may have been the product of nerves, and Captain Herrick later reported that "freak weather effects on radar and overeager sonarmen may have accounted for many reports." Even so, the North Vietnamese attacks on American destroyers in the Gulf of Tonkin took on an importance out of proportion to their military significance three days later (7 August) when Congress passed the Gulf of Tonkin Resolution, granting President Johnson broad authority to take retaliatory measures against North Vietnam. It marked the beginning of official American involvement in the war.

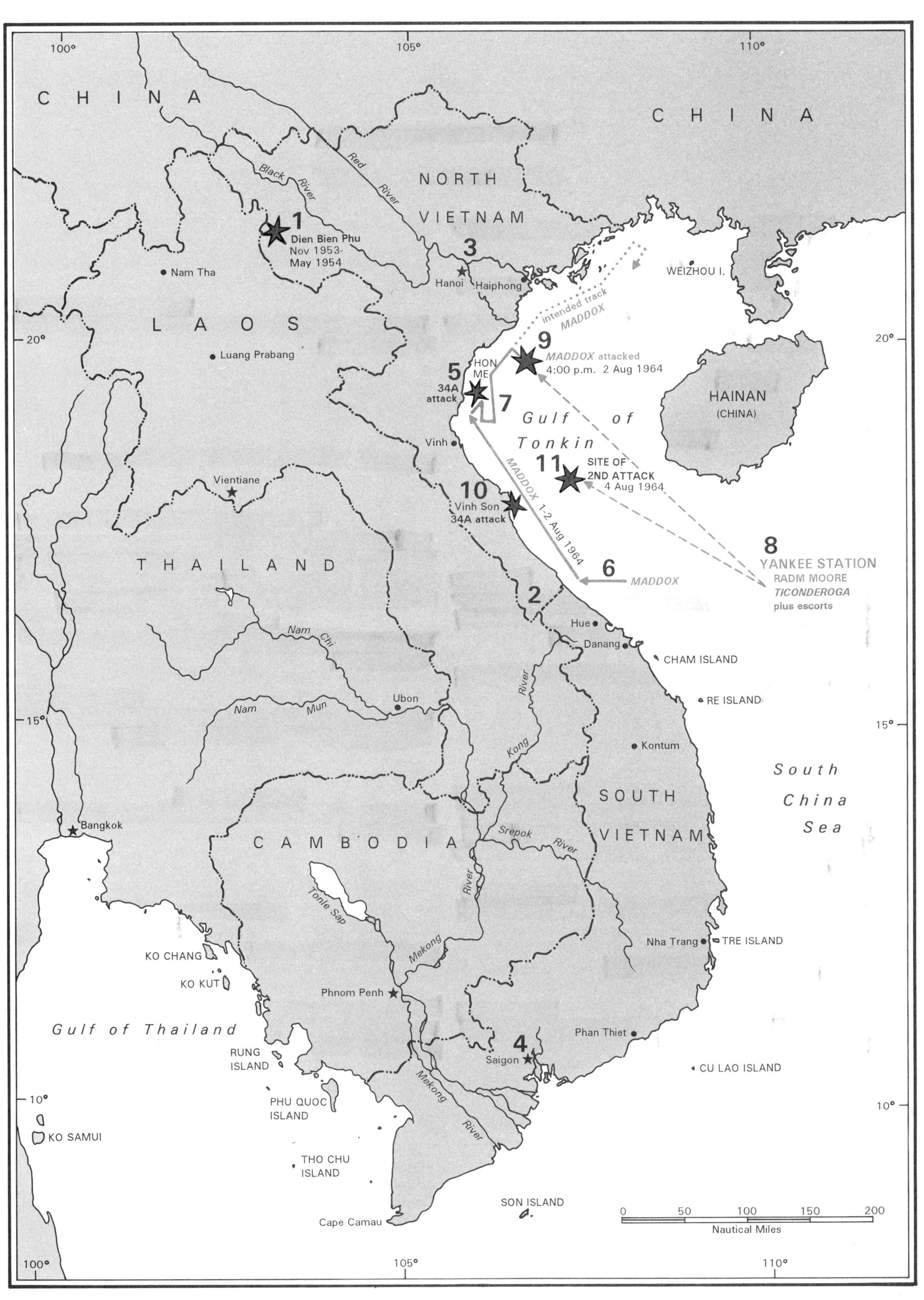

100°
105°
110°
CHINA
CHINA
NORTH VIETNAM
Black River
Red River
1
Dien Bien Phu
Nov 1953-
May 1954
3
Hanoi
Haiphong
Nam Tha
WEIZHOU I.
intended track
MADDOX
LAOS
20°
Luang Prabang
9
MADDOX attacked
4:00 p.m. 2 Aug 1964
5
HON ME
34A attack
7
HAINAN
(CHINA)
Gulf of Tonkin
Vinh
11
SITE OF
2ND ATTACK
4 Aug 1964
Vientiane
10
Vinh Son
34A attack
MADDOX 1-2 Aug 1964
8
YANKEE STATION
RADM MOORE
TICONDEROGA
plus escorts
THAILAND
6
MADDOX
2
Hue
Danang
CHAM ISLAND
Nam Chi
River
RE ISLAND
Ubon
Nam Mun
15°
Kong
Kontum
South China Sea
SOUTH VIETNAM
Bangkok
Srepok River
CAMBODIA
River
Tonle Sap
Nha Trang
TRE ISLAND
Mekong
KO CHANG
KO KUT
Phnom Penh
Gulf of Thailand
Phan Thiet
4
Saigon
RUNG ISLAND
CU LAO ISLAND
10°
Mekong River
PHU QUOC ISLAND
KO SAMUI
THO CHU ISLAND
SON ISLAND
Cape Camau
0 50 100 150 200
Nautical Miles

MAP 86

THE NAVAL AIR WAR

AUGUST 1964–MARCH 1968

President Johnson reacted swiftly to the Tonkin Gulf Incident. Even before Congress passed the Gulf of Tonkin Resolution, he ordered planes from the *Constellation* and *Ticonderoga* to strike at a variety of targets along the North Vietnamese coast. Two planes were lost in these first naval air strikes, and LT (jg) Everett Alvarez became the first American POW of the war.

For the first six months of active American involvement in Vietnam, air strikes from Task Force 77, the carrier strike force at Yankee Station (1), were conducted as deliberate and measured retaliations for provocations by communist forces. On 7 February 1965 a Viet Cong mortar attack on the South Vietnamese air base at Pleiku (2) killed eight Americans, and that same day eighty-three planes from the *Coral Sea, Hancock,* and *Ranger* retaliated by attacking Dong Hoi (3). Three days later the Viet Cong exploded a bomb at the U.S. advisers' base at Qui Nhon, and the next day ninety-nine U.S. planes from TF 77 hit Chanh Hoa (4).

Then in March the United States inaugurated Operation ROLLING THUNDER, a major bombing campaign of North Vietnam, involving both carrier-based Navy planes and Air Force B-52s flying from bases in South Vietnam and Thailand. For the purpose of coordinating targets between the two services, North Vietnam was divided up into six Route Packages, or "Route Packs." The Navy had primary responsibility within Route Packs II, III, and IV, while the Air Force carried the load in Route Packs I and V. Route Pack VI, which included both North Vietnam's capital of Hanoi (5) and its major seaport at Haiphong (6), was divided between the two services.

The purpose of ROLLING THUNDER was not so much to achieve either tactical or strategic success as it was gradually to increase the pain of the war on North Vietnam until its leaders acknowledged the ill wisdom of challenging the United States. It was the national equivalent of twisting a nation's arm behind its back until it hollered "uncle." With occasional bombing halts to give the North Vietnamese a chance to reconsider (or, perhaps, to placate the growing antiwar movement in the United States), ROLLING THUNDER lasted until late 1968—more than two and a half years. But North Vietnam never hollered uncle, and the war continued to escalate.

Some naval aviators complained that the restrictive rules of engagement made it difficult to apply the kind of pressure that might have been effective. At first, bombing strikes were prohibited above a line drawn across Vietnam at 18° 30' north (7). In April 1965 the line was moved north to the twentieth parallel (8). Then it moved steadily northward until by the summer of 1966 only Zone VI was off limits. In July 1966 only a thirty-mile radius around Hanoi and a ten-mile radius around Haiphong were off limits to American bombers (9).

Soon even these geographical restrictions were eased. On 29 June 1966 forty-six planes from the *Ranger* hit oil-storage tanks on the outskirts of Haiphong, returning to hit that target again on 3 August. On 20 April 1967 planes from the *Kitty Hawk* struck at electrical power plants only a mile from downtown Haiphong, and on 19 May 1967 planes from the *Bon Homme Richard* struck at a plant a mile from downtown Hanoi. In late August 1967 planes from TF 77 began bombing the bridges between Haiphong and Hanoi in an effort to isolate the capital from its seaport.

Over the months of nearly continuous flight operations from Yankee Station, scores of American planes were lost, and hundreds of pilots and crew members became POWs and MIAs. Then, too, flight operations are inherently dangerous, and accidents added to the cost of the lengthy bombing campaign. The worst accidents of the war involved fires on board carriers. On 26 October 1966 a fire on board the *Oriskany* killed 44, and another fire on the *Forrestal* in July 1967 killed 134.

Given the high human and materiel cost of these operations, it was a source of frustration to naval aviators that U.S. policy makers frequently "interfered" in what the flyers thought were purely tactical decisions, such as determining a plane's bomb load or defining the angle of approach to bridges. Then, too, because of the immense volume of ordnance being dropped on North Vietnam, aviators began to run out of high-value targets and were often ordered to hit truck parks or unpaved roads.

The real dilemma was that by 1967 policy makers were already becoming aware that the air and ground campaign in Vietnam was not achieving the expected results. Unable to back away from the war they had created, but equally unable to effect the outcome they had predicted, they could think of nothing else to do but continue bombing. At the same time, they feared expanding the war into something they could not control at all, and so they stopped short of authorizing an unrestricted air or ground war.

On 31 March 1968 President Johnson announced to a shocked television audience that he would not seek reelection. He also announced an immediate bombing halt in North Vietnam above the twentieth parallel and called for the opening of peace talks to end the war. But the end of the war was still five years away. Before it came, Navy planes would be called upon to mine Haiphong Harbor in May 1972, and that December President Nixon would order Operation LINEBACKER II, the heaviest concentrated bombing of the war. Operationally more successful than ROLLING THUNDER, these air assaults may also have had an important impact on the peace negotiations. Throughout the eight years of active American involvement in Vietnam, U.S. Navy and Air Force planes dropped a total of 7.4 million tons of bombs, more than in all of America's previous wars combined. During that same time the United States suffered losses of 3,700 aircraft and 2,000 American airmen, plus another 2,500 missing in action. It was a high price to pay for results that were, at best, uncertain.

104°
106°
108°
Gejiu
Nanning
BOMBING PROHIBITED
BUFFER ZONE
CHINA
Red River
Qinzhou
22°
VI-A USAF
Yen Bai
Black River
Thai Nguyen
V USAF
Phuc Yen
5
VI-B USN
WEIZHOU I.
Hanoi
Cam Pha
Haiphong
Hon Gai
Hoa Lac
Gia Lam
6
Dong Song
Cat Bi
9
Nam Dinh
Restricted Bombing Zone July 1966
IV USN
8
Northern Bombing Limit April 1965
20°
Mekong R.
Quan Lang
Luang Prabang
Thanh Hoa
Bai Thuang
LAOS
Tonkin Gulf
HAINAN ISLAND (CHINA)
III USN
Vinh
7
Northern Bombing Limit March 1965
II USN
18°
Vientiane
Mekong River
Cape Dao
I USAF
Chanh Hoa
first air strikes February 1965
4
1
YANKEE STATION
Dong Hoi
3
TF 77
CORAL SEA
HANCOCK
RANGER
plus escorts
Udorn
USAF 1965-76
DMZ
LAOS
Dong Ha
Quang Tri
Hue
Khon Kaen
Banghiang R.
Danang
USAF 1962-72
16°
THAILAND
Nam Chi
SOUTH
USAF 1964-74
Nam Mun
Ubon
Mekong River
Kong River
Quang Ngai
Khorat
USAF 1964-76
VIETNAM
0 30 60 90 120
Nautical Miles
2
USAF 1962-70
104°
CAMBODIA
106°
CAMBODIA
108°
Pleiku

MAP 87

MARKET TIME

MARCH 1965–DECEMBER 1972

Six months after the Gulf of Tonkin Incident, on 16 February 1965, Army helicopter pilot LT James Bowers was on routine patrol south of Qui Nhon when he spotted what appeared to be a camouflaged oceangoing vessel anchored in Vung Ro Bay (1). He radioed in a report, and soon afterward surface and air units of the South Vietnamese Navy closed on the bay and took the vessel under fire. Harassing return fire kept them at a respectful distance for most of three days before they finally succeeded in seizing the vessel. It proved to be an armed 130-foot trawler loaded with weapons and ordnance, carrying papers identifying it as part of North Vietnamese Naval Transportation Group 125. The incident proved that the North Vietnamese were bringing military supplies into the south not only on the famous Ho Chi Minh Trail through Laos (2) but also by sea. Moreover, the tentative South Vietnamese response suggested to some U.S. Navy observers that American naval forces would be a more reliable weapon to interdict this traffic than the South Vietnamese Navy.

As a result, on 11 March the U.S. Navy created the Coastal Patrol Force, later designated as Task Force 115, whose objective was to interdict enemy efforts to move supplies to South Vietnam by sea: Operation MARKET TIME. This assignment was as difficult and tedious as a full coastal blockade but even more frustrating, for *this* blockade was selective, and it was often very difficult to tell friend from foe among the hundreds of wooden junks trading and fishing along the South Vietnamese coast.

By April 1965 the Navy had committed a dozen destroyers, destroyer escorts, and ocean minesweepers, which patrolled the Tonkin Gulf near the seventeenth parallel. But the Navy lacked sufficient shallow-draft vessels for the important inshore work. As a result, Secretary of the Navy Paul Nitze requested help from the Coast Guard, and the first of seventeen 82-foot Coast Guard cutters, beefed up with five .50-caliber machine guns and an 81-mm mortar, arrived in Vietnamese waters in July. In addition, the Navy contracted for eighty-four small (fifty-foot) twin-engine patrol craft that were officially known as PCFs (patrol craft, fast), but which everyone called swift boats due to their top speed of twenty-eight knots. These shallow-draft vessels (the cutters drew five feet and the swift boats only three and a half) were organized into five coastal squadrons and stationed along the South Vietnamese coast (3).

Much of the enemy effort to smuggle arms and supplies into the South was conducted by means of wooden junks, indistinguishable from the hundreds of other junks that had traded or fished along the South Vietnamese coast for a hundred years. Less frequently, the North Vietnamese employed oceangoing trawlers such as the one spotted in Vung Ro Bay. Typically, these larger vessels stayed out beyond the forty-mile limit of U.S. surface patrols during the day and then made a dash for a predetermined landing site after dark. To foil these efforts, land-based Navy planes conducted coastal patrols out of several airfields, including Tan Son Nhut air base near Saigon (4) and Cam Ranh Bay (5), as well as Sangley Point Airfield in the Philippines and Utapao Airfield in Thailand. Twin engine SP-2H Neptunes, P-3 Orions, and for a time P-5 Martin seaplanes conducted regular offshore patrols. Pilots sighting a suspicious vessel would radio its location to Navy and Coast Guard surface units, which closed in for a closer inspection.

For the most part, duty on MARKET TIME was boring routine patrol, much of it conducted in oppressive heat. U.S. Navy and Coast Guard vessels, as well as Vietnamese Navy vessels, cruised up and down the coast, stopping to examine or board occasional vessels, either randomly or because of suspicious behavior. Since most of the vessels searched turned out to be friendly, it required a careful combination of watchful diligence and diplomatic courtesy. Only occasionally did the cutters and swift boats find it necessary to employ their weapons. Of fifty trawlers discovered trying to infiltrate South Vietnamese waters between 1965 and 1972, all but two were either destroyed or forced to abort their mission.

The most tangible success of MARKET TIME—and the only major sea battle—took place in February–March 1968 during the Tet Offensive. Worn thin by their profligate expenditure of lives and equipment in a bold offensive during January (see map 89), the North Vietnamese attempted to run four trawlers into the South on a single night in the predawn hours of 1 March. One trawler off Binh Dinh (6) assessed the odds and turned back. Two others, one off Quang Ngai (7) and one off Khanh Hoa (8), were taken under fire by USCG cutters and Navy swift boats and were forced to run themselves ashore, where they blew up in spectacular explosions that occurred nearly simultaneously at 2:30 A.M.—even though they were nearly one hundred miles apart. The Coast Guard cutter *Winona* sank the fourth trawler off An Xuyen (9) before it could reach the shore.

Just as it is difficult to assess the effectiveness of the Union blockade of the Confederacy, it is also difficult to determine with any precision the effectiveness of MARKET TIME. Statistics can testify to the number of vessels stopped, examined, boarded, searched, and seized. The numbers are impressive and prove how monumental the task was. But while MARKET TIME successfully interdicted a substantial amount of arms and other supplies, a great deal nevertheless found its way through the naval net. There are no statistics to show what MARKET TIME did *not* interdict. At the very least, MARKET TIME forced the enemy to be even more inventive and creative in bringing into the South the tools of war that sustained their long and bitter conflict with the South Vietnamese government and its powerful ally.

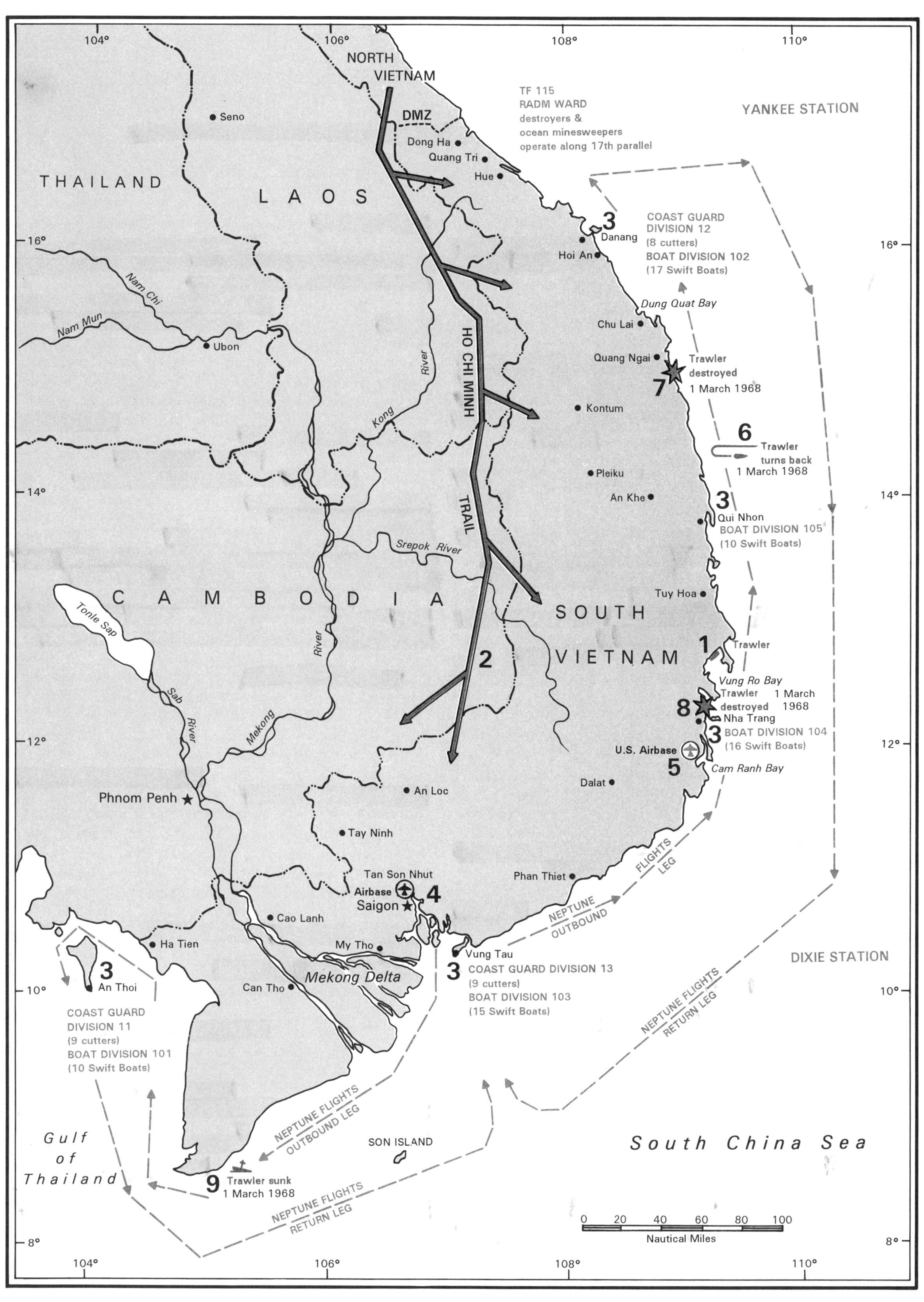

NORTH VIETNAM
DMZ
TF 115
RADM WARD
destroyers &
ocean minesweepers
operate along 17th parallel
YANKEE STATION
Seno
Dong Ha
Quang Tri
Hue
THAILAND
LAOS
3
Danang
COAST GUARD DIVISION 12
(8 cutters)
BOAT DIVISION 102
(17 Swift Boats)
Hoi An
Nam Chi
Nam Mun
Ubon
Dung Quat Bay
Chu Lai
HO CHI MINH TRAIL
Kong River
Quang Ngai
7
Trawler destroyed
1 March 1968
Kontum
6
Trawler turns back
1 March 1968
Pleiku
An Khe
3
Qui Nhon
BOAT DIVISION 105
(10 Swift Boats)
Srepok River
Tuy Hoa
CAMBODIA
Tonle Sap
SOUTH VIETNAM
1
Trawler
Vung Ro Bay
2
8
Trawler destroyed
1 March 1968
Nha Trang
3
BOAT DIVISION 104
(16 Swift Boats)
U.S. Airbase
5
Cam Ranh Bay
Sab River
Mekong River
Dalat
Phnom Penh
An Loc
Tay Ninh
Phan Thiet
FLIGHTS LEG
Tan Son Nhut
Airbase
4
Saigon
Cao Lanh
NEPTUNE OUTBOUND
Ha Tien
My Tho
Vung Tau
3
COAST GUARD DIVISION 13
(9 cutters)
BOAT DIVISION 103
(15 Swift Boats)
DIXIE STATION
3
An Thoi
Mekong Delta
Can Tho
COAST GUARD DIVISION 11
(9 cutters)
BOAT DIVISION 101
(10 Swift Boats)
NEPTUNE FLIGHTS RETURN LEG
NEPTUNE FLIGHTS OUTBOUND LEG
Gulf of Thailand
SON ISLAND
South China Sea
9
Trawler sunk
1 March 1968
NEPTUNE FLIGHTS RETURN LEG
0 20 40 60 80 100
Nautical Miles
104° 106° 108° 110°
16° 14° 12° 10° 8°

MAP 88

GAME WARDEN AND THE MOBILE RIVERINE FORCE

DECEMBER 1965–SEPTEMBER 1968

In addition to interdicting enemy traffic along the seacoast, the U.S. Navy took on the job of halting the enemy's use of the labyrinth of waterways known collectively as the Mekong Delta. As the Mekong River enters Vietnam from Cambodia, it fans out over a marshy alluvial plain and divides into four outlets, which are (north to south) the My Tho, the Ham Luong, the Co Chien, and the Hau Giang, also known as the Bassac River. These outlets are connected with one another by navigable canals that cut through marshy plains and wetlands, much of which are themselves navigable to shallow-draft barges and sampans. To the communist rebels (called Viet Cong or VC), much of the Mekong Delta was a sanctuary, just as the Everglades was a sanctuary to the Seminole Indians in the nineteenth century. In particular, the Viet Cong were strong in the Rung Sat Special Zone (1) southeast of Saigon and the Plain of Reeds (2) west of Saigon.

The Navy's effort to interdict enemy traffic in the Mekong Delta was dubbed Operation GAME WARDEN and was conducted by a variety of specially designed small craft. The mainstay of the River Patrol Force (Task Force 116) was the thirty-one–foot PBR (river patrol boat), a fiberglass-hulled vessel propelled by diesel-powered water jets so that it could speed along at twenty-five knots in less than a foot of water. The first PBRs arrived in Vietnam in April 1966, and they began to patrol the Mekong Delta in May. By June there were eighty such boats in operation, and in August they established an effective partnership with Huey (UH-1B) helicopters borrowed from the Army and called "Seawolves" by their Navy crews.

The PBRs operated out of a half dozen bases throughout the delta: Nha Be and Cat Lo in the Rung Sat Special Zone; My Tho (3), Vinh Long (4), Can Tho (5), Sa Dec (6), and Long Xuyen (7) in the delta. Like their colleagues who patrolled the coast, sailors on the PBRs spent most of their time in stopping and searching sampans for contraband—in a typical month, the PBRs of GAME WARDEN would stop and inspect an average of one hundred thousand vessels. Unlike the sailors off the coast, however, PBR patrols were conducted along rivers, sloughs, and canals where ten-foot-high grasses along the shoreline could hide enemy units with machine guns or recoilless rifles. Most of the vessels the patrols stopped and searched proved innocent, but they could never be sure when a sampan might be bait for an ambush. The PBR sailors of GAME WARDEN engaged in an average of eighty firefights a month during 1966–1968, and one out of every three GAME WARDEN sailors was wounded in action. GAME WARDEN gradually expanded its area of responsibility until by July 1968 it covered the entire network of rivers and sloughs from the Cambodian border to the South China Sea.

One of the largest firefights of Operation GAME WARDEN took place on 31 October 1966 ten miles west of My Tho (8). On routine patrol, BM1 James Williams, in command of a two-boat PBR squadron, stumbled upon a major Viet Cong troop movement involving more than three score junks and sampans. Because he was maneuvering at high speed up a narrow canal, Williams chose to charge directly into the concentration of vessels, with all guns blazing. After running through the enemy fleet, Williams called up support from Seawolf helicopters, turned around, and ran through the enemy fleet a second time. His two PBRs and the helicopters destroyed more than fifty enemy vessels and captured a half dozen more. For his conduct, Williams was awarded the Medal of Honor. A month later two more PBRs encountered another concentration of enemy forces in the same area. Once again the PBRs succeeded in disrupting the movement, sinking twenty-eight sampans.

In addition to the lightly armored PBRs, the Navy also employed monitors, armored troop carriers (ATCs), and armored support patrol boats in the Mekong Delta as part of the Mobile Riverine Force (Task Force 117). These vessels were built atop the hulls of old landing craft (LCMs) and equipped with bar armor designed to detonate enemy ordnance, especially rockets, before it could penetrate. Heavy, slow, and ungainly, the ATCs were the exact opposite of the speedy little PBRs. Their function was to carry soldiers to enemy strong points and provide fire support during ground operations.

The first such operation took place in February 1967 in the Rung Sat Special Zone. Four months later more than fifty ATCs, accompanied by ten monitors (LCMs converted to armored fire-support vessels) and several command vessels, transported seven hundred men of the Army's 9th Infantry Division to a suspected Viet Cong strong point near the small village of Ap Bac (9). In a two-day fight the ATCs and monitors provided fire support for the infantry as the Viet Cong was driven from the area. The VC left 225 dead behind on the ground. American losses totaled 46 killed and 150 wounded. A similar action in December left another 235 Viet Cong dead.

Dramatic as such battles were, most of the work done by the brown-water sailors of GAME WARDEN and the Mobile Riverine Force was more mundane, though just as dangerous. PBRs patrolling in pairs occasionally encountered well-laid ambushes; ATCs, and even their LST mother ships, were occasional victims of enemy mines. In November 1968 a mine severely damaged the *Westchester County* (LST 1167), killing eighteen sailors.

That same month Richard Nixon was elected president to succeed an exhausted and frustrated Lyndon Johnson. During the campaign Nixon had claimed that he had a secret plan to end the war. That plan had two elements: first, Nixon would mix the carrot of negotiations with the stick of renewed heavy bombing in North Vietnam, and second, he would inaugurate a program to turn the war back over to the South Vietnamese—a program that came to be called Vietnamization. In one of the first manifestations of this new policy, the U.S. Navy turned twenty-five riverine vessels over to the South Vietnamese Navy in February 1969.

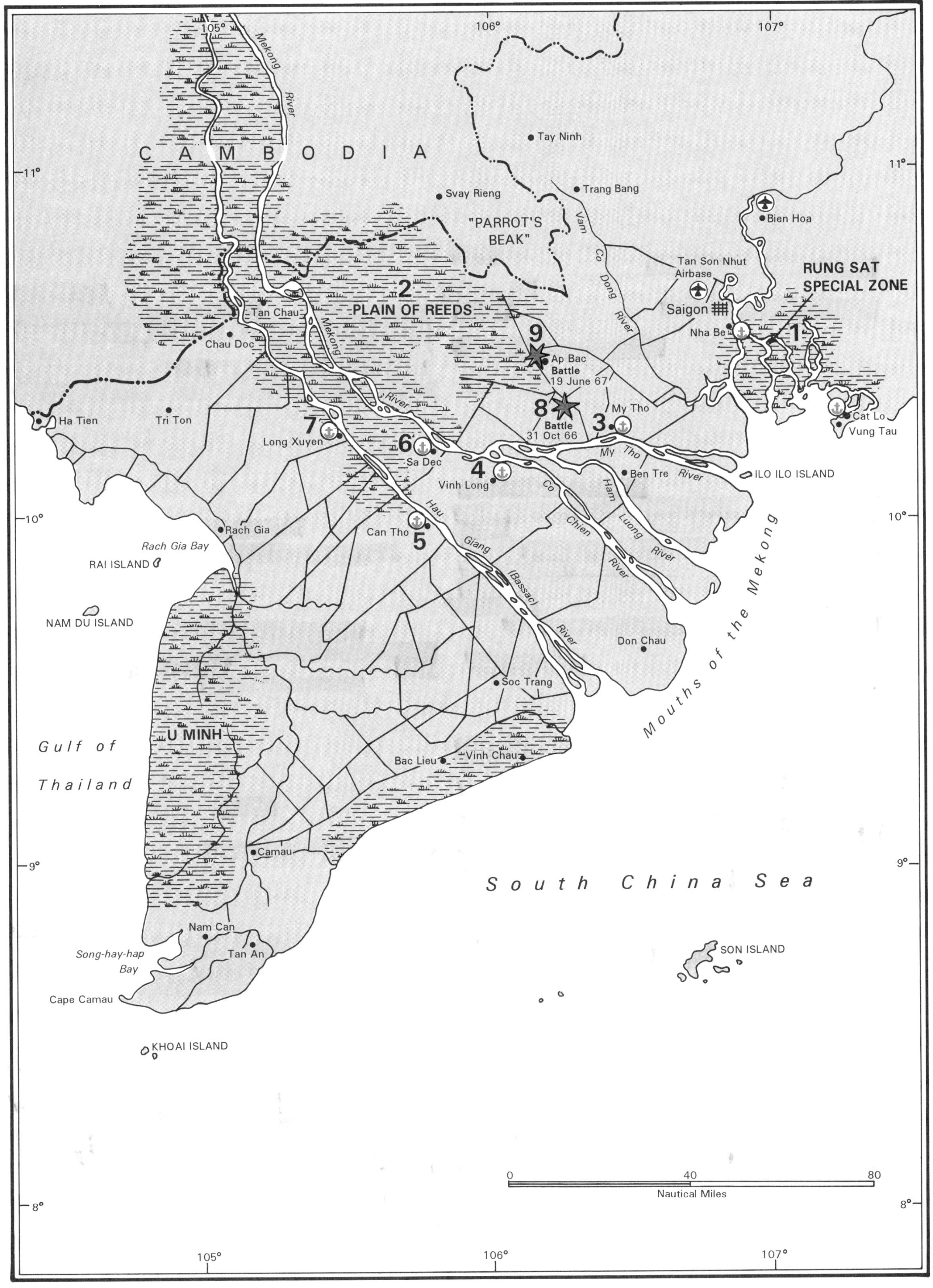
CAMBODIA
Mekong River
Tay Ninh
Trang Bang
Svay Rieng
"PARROT'S BEAK"
Vam Co Dong River
Tan Son Nhut Airbase
Bien Hoa
RUNG SAT SPECIAL ZONE
Saigon
Nha Be
1
2
PLAIN OF REEDS
Tan Chau
Chau Doc
9
Ap Bac
Battle 19 June 67
8
Battle 31 Oct 66
3
My Tho
Cat Lo
Vung Tau
Ha Tien
Tri Ton
7
Long Xuyen
6
Sa Dec
4
Vinh Long
My Tho River
Ben Tre
ILO ILO ISLAND
Ham Luong River
Co Chien River
Hau Giang (Bassac) River
Can Tho
5
Rach Gia
Rach Gia Bay
RAI ISLAND
NAM DU ISLAND
Mouths of the Mekong
Don Chau
Soc Trang
U MINH
Gulf of Thailand
Bac Lieu
Vinh Chau
Camau
South China Sea
Nam Can
Tan An
Song-hay-hap Bay
Cape Camau
SON ISLAND
KHOAI ISLAND
0
40
80
Nautical Miles
105°
106°
107°
11°
10°
9°
8°

MAP 89

I CORPS: THE MARINES IN VIETNAM

MARCH 1965–JUNE 1971

Despite the millions of tons of bombs dropped from the air and the thousands of stop-and-search missions at sea, Vietnam was essentially a ground war. And no part of that war was more important or violent than the combat in the five northern provinces of South Vietnam collectively known as I Corps (pronounced "Eye" Corps by those who fought there), which was the responsibility of the III Marine Amphibious Force (III MAF).

U.S. Marine ground troops first came ashore in Vietnam on 8 March 1965 when the 9th Marine Expeditionary Brigade from Okinawa landed at Da Nang (1) to provide security for the airfield. In May the marines at Da Nang were reinforced and reorganized as the III Marine Amphibious Force under the command of LGEN Lewis Walt. Originally, the marines were to provide base security at key locations to free up units of the South Vietnamese Army (ARVN) to go into the field. But effective base security required active patrols, and the U.S. Military Assistance Command, Vietnam (MACV) did not believe that ARVN troops were as effective in the field as American forces. As a result, it was not long before the marines of III MAF began active field operations against the enemy. Moreover, since I Corps was the closest command area to North Vietnam, it became the scene of some of the fiercest fighting of the war.

Besides Da Nang, U.S. Marines established enclaves at Phu Bai (2), south of the old Imperial capital of Hue, and Chu Lai (3), in southern Quang Tin Province. The Marines planned to conduct a long-term pacification program based on a partnership with ARVN forces and the local populations that would gradually expand progovernment influence through the five provinces. But this strategy clashed with the determination of GEN William Westmoreland at MACV headquarters to defeat Viet Cong and North Vietnamese units in the field with large-scale operations that would wear down both the capability and the will of the communists.

Bowing to this strategic blueprint, III MAF conducted a number of large-scale operations within I Corps. The first of them was Operation STARLITE in August of 1965. Four battalions (four thousand marines) landed fourteen miles south of Chu Lai to attack the 1st Viet Cong regiment (4). In a campaign lasting most of a month, the marines counted 964 enemy soldiers killed at a loss of 50 marines killed and 125 wounded. No further large-scale operations were attempted during the rainy monsoon season (September–February), but in March 1966 the First Marine Division arrived in Vietnam to join the Third as part of III MAF, and that summer eight thousand marines and three thousand ARVN troops conducted Operation HASTINGS III just south of the Demilitarized Zone (DMZ) near Dong Ha (5), where they intercepted a North Vietnamese Division. Over the next two years the Marines conducted other major operations in Quang Tri Province, including Operations PRAIRIE FIRE (February–March 1967), SCOTLAND II (April 1968–February 1969), and NAPOLEON SALINE (November–December 1968).

The war in Quang Tri Province began to resemble conventional warfare as the Marines occupied a series of armed camps (marked with blue squares) to defend a political and military border (the DMZ). In this role, the Marines often had to leave the initiative to the enemy, who operated from a sanctuary and was, therefore, able to control the timing of operations. The westernmost of the armed camps guarding the DMZ was at Khe Sanh (6), where in late 1967 two full North Vietnamese divisions assaulted the 26th Marine regiment reinforced by an ARVN ranger battalion and some artillery. For nine weeks the North Vietnamese besieged Khe Sanh, hitting the base with as many as one thousand rounds of artillery or rockets every day. At the same time, Navy and Marine Corps close air support, plus heavy bombing by Air Force B-52s, took a heavy toll on the attackers. By the time the North Vietnamese gave up and withdrew, they had lost an estimated ten thousand men. The Marines lost 205 killed and 800 wounded.

The most famous, and in the end the most important, communist offensive of the war in I Corps came in January 1968 as part of the nationwide Tet Offensive. During that campaign the communists seized Hue (7), committing seven battalions to the attack. The U.S. Marines and their ARVN allies took a month to recapture the city, and once again the enemy paid dearly, losing at least five thousand killed at Hue alone. In the whole of Vietnam the communists may have lost as many as eighty thousand men during the Tet Offensive.

Even though the Marines nearly always inflicted greater casualties on the enemy than they suffered themselves, they too paid a very dear price in Vietnam. Quite apart from the loss of morale that accompanied the frustrations of war in the jungles of I Corps, where rainfall averaged 120 inches per year and the temperature in the summer seldom dropped below 100, and quite apart from the loss of prestige at home, where a war-weary public was often unwilling to recognize or appreciate the efforts marines were making in Vietnam—apart from all that, the Marines also paid a heavy price in casualties. The U.S. Marine Corps suffered more than 103,000 casualties in Vietnam—killed and wounded—more than in World War I and World War II *combined.*

The Marines left Vietnam the way they had come—in increments—taking their equipment with them. The last of them left in June 1971, turning the war back over to the ARVN forces as part of the Vietnamization program. In January 1973 the United States and North Vietnam signed the Paris Peace Accords, ending direct U.S. participation in the war, and two years later, in April 1975, Saigon fell to North Vietnamese forces. After three decades of nearly constant warfare, Vietnam was unified, independent . . . and communist.

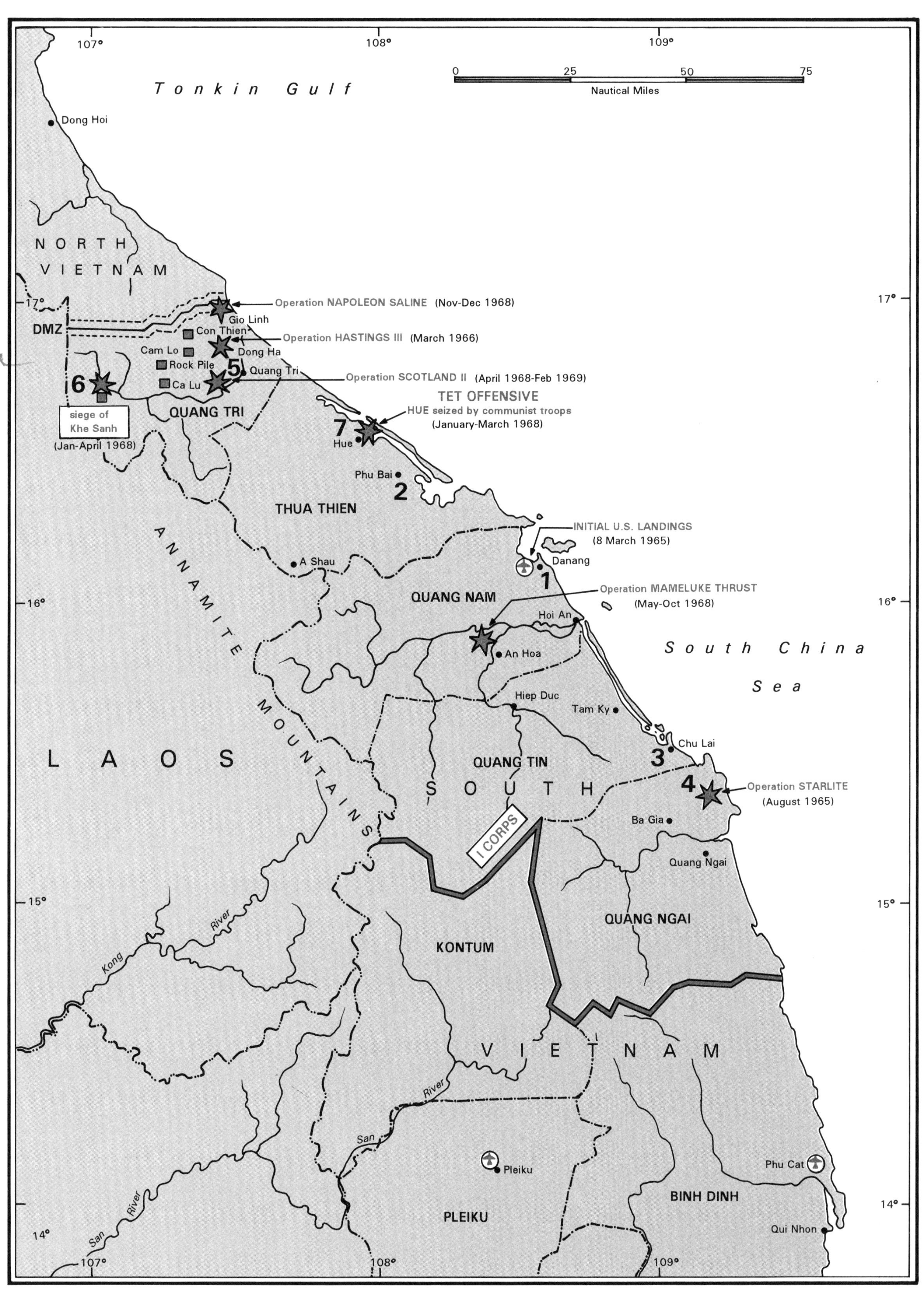

107°
108°
109°
0
25
50
75
Nautical Miles
Tonkin Gulf
Dong Hoi
NORTH VIETNAM
17°
DMZ
Operation NAPOLEON SALINE (Nov-Dec 1968)
Gio Linh
Con Thien
Operation HASTINGS III (March 1966)
Cam Lo
Dong Ha
Rock Pile
5
Quang Tri
Operation SCOTLAND II (April 1968-Feb 1969)
6
Ca Lu
siege of Khe Sanh
(Jan-April 1968)
QUANG TRI
TET OFFENSIVE
HUE seized by communist troops
(January-March 1968)
7
Hue
Phu Bai
2
THUA THIEN
INITIAL U.S. LANDINGS
(8 March 1965)
Danang
1
A Shau
ANNAMITE MOUNTAINS
Operation MAMELUKE THRUST
(May-Oct 1968)
16°
QUANG NAM
Hoi An
An Hoa
South China Sea
Hiep Duc
Tam Ky
Chu Lai
3
LAOS
QUANG TIN
SOUTH
4
Operation STARLITE
(August 1965)
I CORPS
Ba Gia
Quang Ngai
15°
Kong
River
QUANG NGAI
KONTUM
VIETNAM
River
San
Pleiku
Phu Cat
BINH DINH
14°
PLEIKU
San
River
Qui Nhon

PART X

The Pax Americana 1980–1994

THE WAR IN VIETNAM bitterly divided Americans, and it left a conspicuous legacy. Even while the war was still in progress, the nation began to retreat from the commitments it had made at the height of the Cold War. In January 1970 President Nixon announced what became known as the Nixon Doctrine: that henceforth Asian nations would have to be responsible for their own defense. "The nations of each part of the world," Nixon told Congress, "should assume the primary responsibility for their own well being." In part, this new doctrine provided the underpinning for Nixon's Vietnamization program, then under way, but in part, too, it reflected the prevailing mood of Americans who were no longer willing to endorse John Kennedy's promise to "pay any price, bear any burden, support any friend, oppose any foe. . . ."

After Vietnam, American policy shifted away from concerns about overt communist aggression in Asia and focused on ensuring regional stability in other parts of the world, especially in the Caribbean and the Middle East. In both these regions, local antagonisms and economic issues frequently overshadowed the Cold War paradigm of democracy vs. communism. The United States was naturally concerned about political and economic stability in the Caribbean, long an "American lake" (see map 48). But in the 1970s and 1980s the United States also grew increasingly concerned about events in the Middle East, which produced a majority of the world's oil, and where feuds between Arabs and Israelis, Moslems and Christians, and Sunni and Shiite Moslems ensured almost constant turmoil. There the United States found itself caught in the middle of local wars and forced to play the role of mediator—sometimes as conciliator, sometimes as enforcer.

The nuclear-powered carrier Eisenhower *transits the Suez Canal on its way to the Persian Gulf in 1990 during the Iran-Iraq War (see map 92). In the age of the Pax Americana, the carrier battle group and the amphibious attack ship (LPH), with its embarked marine amphibious unit (MAU), constituted the spear points of American policy and power. (Official U.S. Navy photo)*

The Nixon Doctrine, with its suggestion of an American retreat from the precepts of the Truman Doctrine, lasted barely a decade. During that decade, however, the United States sought to build up regional powers to assume the role previously played by the United States and Britain. In the Middle East, the primary candidate for this assignment was Iran, with Saudi Arabia playing a junior role. Ruled by Shah Mohammed Reza Pahlavi, who had come to power with U.S. support in 1953, Iran seemed large enough and stable enough to assume the role of regional power. Through the 1970s, therefore, the United States sold massive amounts of arms to the shah—in 1978 alone Iran imported more than $10.5 billion worth of arms. Then in 1979 the shah's government collapsed, and the religious leader of the fundamentalist Shiite Moslems, the bitterly anti-American Ayatollah Ruhollah Khomeini, came to power.

With the collapse of the shah's government and the hostage crisis that followed the seizure of the American embassy in Tehran, the United States effectively abandoned the Nixon Doctrine. Exactly ten years after Nixon had proclaimed that the nations of the world would have to look out for their own security, President Jimmy Carter used the same forum, a State of the Union Address, to announce the Carter Doctrine: "Let our position be absolutely clear: An attempt by any outside force to gain control of the Persian Gulf region will be regarded as an assault on the vital interests of the United States. . . ."

In part, Carter's declaration was aimed at the Soviet Union, which invaded Afghanistan in December of 1979. But in part, too, Carter was signaling America's unwillingness to allow the Middle East to descend into chaos, whatever its origin. The Persian Gulf in particular, through which flowed much of the world's oil (though only 15 percent of America's oil), was of vital importance, and Carter's declaration made it clear that the United States would not allow it to fall victim to either communist expansion or fundamentalist extremism. The Carter Doctrine, therefore, marked not only a renewal of the

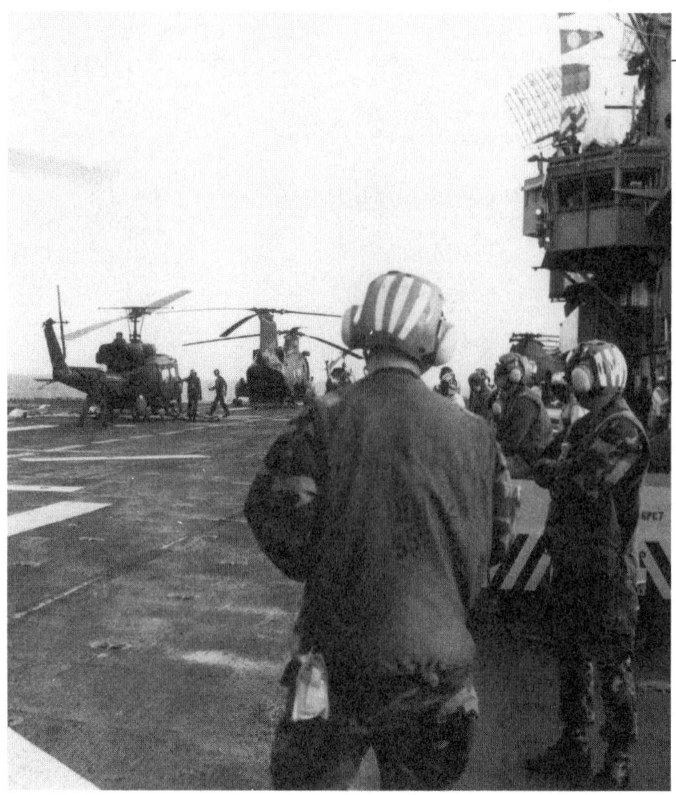

The deck of the amphibious assault ship Guam *during the U.S. invasion of Grenada. U.S. Marines conducted a helicopter-borne assault from the* Guam *to Pearls Airfield on 25 October 1983 to initiate Operation URGENT FURY, which deposed the pro-Cuban government of Grenada (see map 90). (Department of Defense photo)*

U.S. commitment to the use of force but also the emergence of a policy that, under Carter's successors, would make the United States a kind of global policeman.

In November 1980 Ronald Reagan was swept into office on a wave of popular discontent with both the stagnant domestic economy and Carter's perceived inability to deal effectively with the hostage crisis in Iran. Evoking a nostalgia for simpler times, the new president promised to return America to greatness both at home and abroad. The policy he employed to achieve this goal was straightforward: a dramatic increase in military spending, which provided an artificial stimulus to the economy at home, and a tough, assertive foreign policy. In the first months of his administration Reagan obtained a supplemental $2.9 billion for the Navy, and for fiscal year 1982 the president virtually doubled the Navy's budget. This did wonders for materiel readiness and morale in the Navy as the fleet expanded to fifteen carrier battle groups by 1986 under the aggressive stewardship of Navy Secretary John Lehman. Moreover, it is likely that the increased military spending, which the Soviets could not hope to match, accelerated the collapse of the Soviet empire. On the other hand, the increased military spending was executed by means of deficit financing and contributed to an enormous national debt that would eventually constitute an anchor on the U.S. economy.

By the end of the decade the Cold War was over. The roots of this dramatic event were more evident in hindsight than at the time. The Soviet Union had been fighting a losing battle to maintain a minimal standard of living for its population while at the same time pouring the bulk of its gross national product into defense. Despite its headline-grabbing space program and massive land army, the pressure of attempting to maintain military and technological parity with the United States, including the construction of a blue-water navy, put such pressure on the Soviet economy that a collapse was perhaps inevitable. Experts on the Soviet Union had long recognized its inner weaknesses and even referred to it mockingly as "Upper Volta with Rockets." Even so, when the collapse came, it caught most of the world by surprise. The events of the late 1980s astonished the world as the Berlin Wall came down and the Soviet Union broke apart.

At the height of the Roman Empire, when it had occupied most of the known world, the Roman legions no longer had to concern themselves with set piece battles against enemy armies and instead assumed the responsibility of maintaining stability and security in the far corners of the empire. Their job, in short, was to enforce the peace—a Roman peace or, in Latin, a *Pax Romana.* In the nineteenth century, when Britain was at the height of its power, British citizens spoke proudly of a *Pax Britannica.* In the post–Cold War years under Presidents Ronald Reagan and George Bush, America embarked on a period that could suitably be entitled a *Pax Americana.* The threat in this era came not so much from the Soviet Union, already in the throes of the economic difficulties that would lead to its collapse, as from regional instability caused by emotional nationalism, religious fanaticism, local rebellion, and, most frustrating of all, international terrorism.

The U.S. Navy had to adjust to what President Bush called "a new world order." In a post–Cold War environment, the development of antisubmarine tactics, for example, became less urgent than issues such as counterterrorism, drug interdiction, and rapid response to local crises. In December 1979 Carter had authorized the creation of a joint services Rapid Deployment Force (RDF), and in the post–Cold War era this concept was expanded and refined. For the Navy, the instrument of rapid response was the nuclear-powered carrier battle group. For the Marine Corps, the instrument was the marine amphibious unit (MAU), a battalion-sized infantry force with its own armor, air, and artillery support embarked on an amphibious assault ship (LPH) ready to go wherever needed.

Having the capability to respond was one thing; deciding when and where to do so was another. In the Caribbean the United States continued to worry about the spread of communism from Cuba, where Castro presided over a tottering economy, into Central America, where civil wars between pro-American and leftist forces led to informal (and controversial) American intervention in both Nicaragua and El Salvador. In a more direct exercise of American power, the United States sent Army and Marine forces to the tiny Caribbean island nation of Grenada in 1983 to protect American citizens there and to forestall the development of a pro-Cuban communist government (see map 90).

While most Americans supported the exercise of military power in the Caribbean, there was less agreement about American intervention elsewhere in the world. The bleeding ulcer of Vietnam had made Americans wary of overseas commitment. Africa, the Middle East, and the Balkans all offered opportunities for the exercise of American power in the name of stability or humanity, but U.S. forces generally became involved only when the American national interest was directly affected, a policy officially articulated by Secretary of Defense Caspar

A Marine F/A-18 Hornet flies over Kuwait, with oil fires burning on the ground. Marine pilots in particular felt unreasonably constrained by the air tasking order used during the air war against Iraq, and they lobbied to be excluded from the carefully preplanned ATO in order to strike at targets of opportunity (see map 93). (Department of Defense photo)

Weinberger in November 1984. In 1986 President Reagan ordered an attack on Libya after a string of terrorist activities directed at American citizens (see map 91). Two years later, during the war between Iran and Iraq, the United States accepted the job of regional policeman as U.S. Navy ships escorted neutral tankers through the Persian Gulf (see map 92). And in the 1990s the United States assumed the leadership role in the first major conflict of the post–Cold War world, one in which the United States and Russia acted—officially at least—as partners. In a dramatic demonstration of America's logistic and military capability, the United States humbled Iraq in the Gulf War—Operation DESERT STORM (see maps 93–94).

A Tomahawk missile is launched from the U.S. battleship Missouri *in the Persian Gulf during the air war against Iraq in February 1991. The Tomahawk was one of several precision weapons that demolished the Iraqi air-defense system and demonstrated the extent of American technological superiority. (Official U.S. Navy photo)*

MAP 90

THE CARIBBEAN: OPERATION URGENT FURY

25–31 OCTOBER 1983

The Caribbean remained a central concern of American foreign policy into the post–Cold War era (see map A). Castro's Cuba was a constant irritant, and much of Central America was economically underdeveloped and, therefore, fertile ground for revolution. Communist rebels threatened the stability of the government in El Salvador, while just to the south another revolutionary movement attempted to overthrow the socialist government of Nicaragua. In both cases, the Reagan administration sought to influence the outcome through overt and covert means.

Both Cuba and Nicaragua supplied and encouraged the leftist guerrillas in El Salvador (1). But because the Salvadoran military boasted a number of so-called "death squads" that routinely murdered opponents of the government, there was little congressional enthusiasm to vote substantial military aid for El Salvador. Nevertheless, the United States did send military advisers there in 1981, and in February 1983, 1,600 American troops participated in military exercises in nearby Honduras (2). That summer two American naval task forces—first the *Ranger* battle group, and then the refurbished battleship *New Jersey*—maneuvered off the coast of El Salvador in a demonstration of American interest and concern.

The situation in Nicaragua (3) was more complicated. There a socialist government with close ties to Cuba played the role of regional provocateur by encouraging rebellion in neighboring states. Supporters of the Nicaraguan government were decidedly anti-American and called themselves "Sandinistas" in memory of Augusto Sandino, who had fought against the U.S. Marines during the American occupation of 1927–1933. The Reagan administration, therefore, supported the antigovernment rebels, known as "Contras." But once again Congress was not enthusiastic about providing direct American aid to underwrite a rebellion, especially because there was no clear evidence that the Sandinista government was unpopular with the majority of Nicaraguans. Undeterred by congressional qualms, the Reagan administration sought to funnel support to the Contras by covert means, including a notorious arms-for-hostages arrangement by which the administration secretly sold arms to Iran, then used the money to support the Contras in Nicaragua (see map 92).

These foreign-policy frustrations reached a climax on 23 October 1983 when an Arab terrorist willing to give up his life drove a truck filled with explosives into the U.S. Marine barracks in Beirut. The ensuing explosion killed 241 marines and sailors and wounded 71 more. Then, just two days later (though the timing was entirely coincidental), the Reagan administration scored a dramatic success in the small Caribbean-island nation of Grenada (4).

Discovered in 1498 by Columbus, who named it Concepción, Grenada is the southernmost of the Windward Islands and is only twenty-one miles long and twelve miles wide (see map B). A British colony until 1974 when it became independent, Grenada remained part of the British Commonwealth even after 1979, when the so-called "New Jewel" movement came to power and established friendly relations with Castro's Cuba. Later that year Cuban engineers began constructing an airfield at Point Salinas (5), and in 1980 Grenada signed a treaty with the Soviet Union that authorized use of the airfield by Soviet long-range reconnaissance planes. Over the next two years Soviet, Cuban, and East German technicians arrived in Grenada to provide technical assistance. Disconcerting as these developments were, things took a dramatic turn for the worse in October 1983 when a military junta headed by GEN Hudson Austin executed the civilian prime minister, Maurice Bishop, and announced the formation of a Revolutionary Military Council. These events triggered social unrest and a crackdown by General Austin's forces that appeared to threaten the safety of American students at the Medical School near St. George's (6).

In response to these events and an appeal from the Organization of Eastern Caribbean States (OECS), the United States quickly assembled a twelve-ship task force under the command of VADM Joseph Metcalf. The task force was built around the carrier *Independence* and the amphibious assault ship *Guam* carrying 1,900 marines of the 22nd MAU under COL J. P. Faulkner. At 5:00 A.M. on 25 October a Navy SEAL team infiltrated St. Georges and took control of Government House (7, map C), holding it against several attempts by Cuban troops to retake it. A half hour later helicopters from the *Guam* landed four hundred marines at Pearls Airport (8, map B). One company secured the airport, and another took control of the harbor at Grenville (9, map B). At 6:00 A.M. planes from the *Independence* struck at Fort Frederick (10, map C) while troops of the Army's 82nd Airborne Division parachuted onto the runways at the Point Salinas Airfield and Army Rangers assaulted the western coast of the island.

Shortly after dawn on 26 October marines landed on the western coast of the island near St. Georges, and soon thereafter they relieved the SEAL team holding Government House. The British Governor General, Sir Paul Scoon, was evacuated to the *Guam* along with the American students, and the vast majority of Grenadans welcomed the Americans as liberators. On 29 October the Marines and the 82nd Airborne linked up near Anse Bay and eliminated Cuban resistance. The entire operation was achieved with a total American loss of 18 killed and 116 wounded.

The events in the Caribbean and in Lebanon in October 1983 proved that the possession of power did not guarantee foreign-policy success. The lesson was not that military force was ineffective in a post–Cold War world, only that it had to be applied selectively, and that overwhelming force was more likely to be effective than gestures of concern.

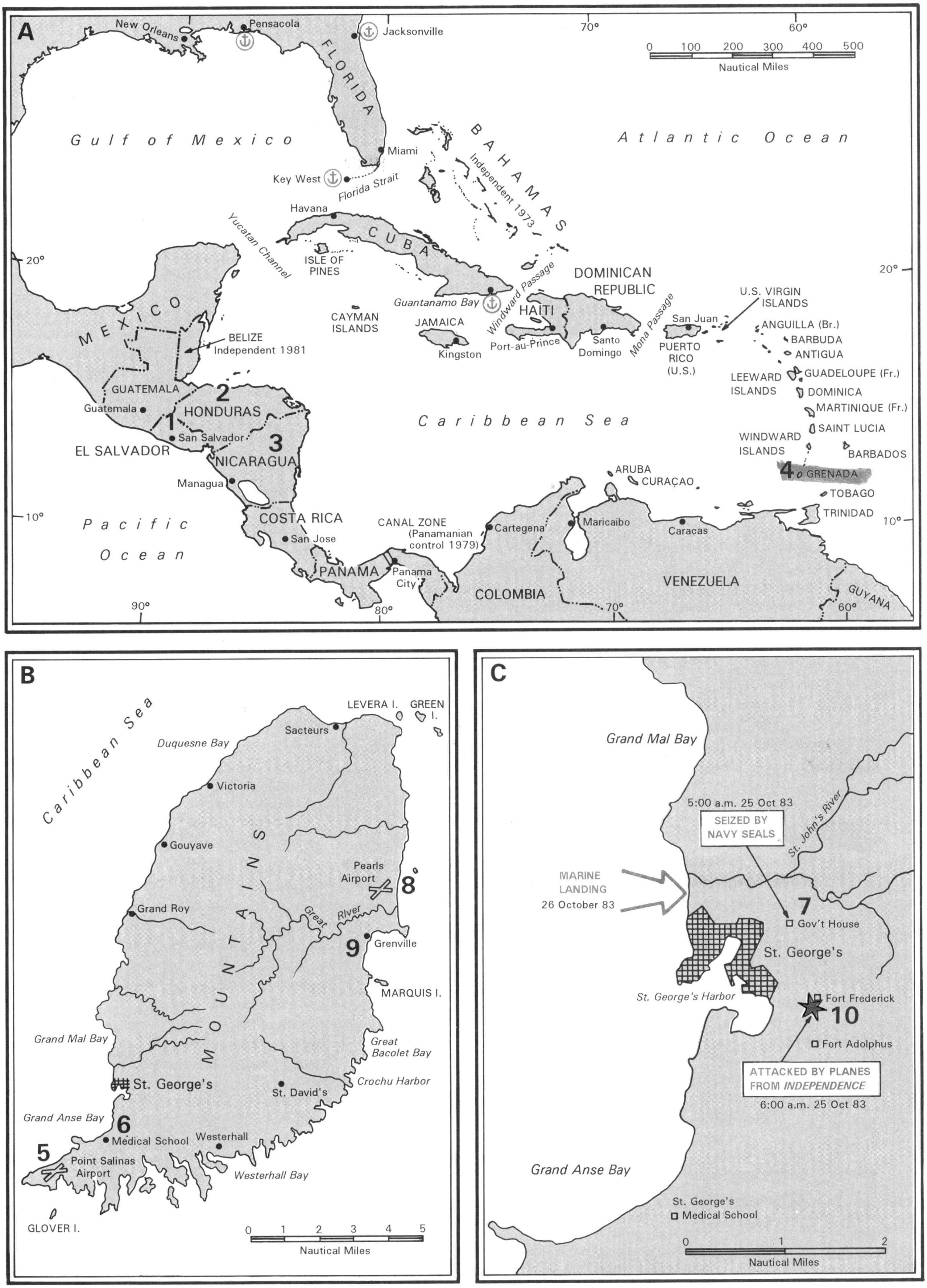

A
New Orleans
Pensacola
Jacksonville
FLORIDA
70°
60°
0 100 200 300 400 500
Nautical Miles
Gulf of Mexico
Atlantic Ocean
Miami
Key West
Florida Strait
BAHAMAS
Independent 1973
Havana
CUBA
Yucatan Channel
ISLE OF PINES
20°
MEXICO
BELIZE
Independent 1981
CAYMAN ISLANDS
JAMAICA
Kingston
Guantanamo Bay
Windward Passage
HAITI
Port-au-Prince
DOMINICAN REPUBLIC
Santo Domingo
Mona Passage
San Juan
PUERTO RICO (U.S.)
U.S. VIRGIN ISLANDS
ANGUILLA (Br.)
BARBUDA
ANTIGUA
LEEWARD ISLANDS
GUADELOUPE (Fr.)
DOMINICA
MARTINIQUE (Fr.)
SAINT LUCIA
WINDWARD ISLANDS
BARBADOS
4 GRENADA
TOBAGO
TRINIDAD
GUATEMALA
Guatemala
2
HONDURAS
1
San Salvador
EL SALVADOR
3
NICARAGUA
Managua
Caribbean Sea
ARUBA
CURAÇAO
10°
Pacific Ocean
COSTA RICA
San Jose
CANAL ZONE
(Panamanian control 1979)
Cartegena
Maricaibo
Caracas
PANAMA
Panama City
COLOMBIA
VENEZUELA
GUYANA
90°
80°
B
Caribbean Sea
Duquesne Bay
LEVERA I.
GREEN I.
Sacteurs
Victoria
Gouyave
MOUNTAINS
Pearls Airport
8
Grand Roy
Great River
9
Grenville
MARQUIS I.
Grand Mal Bay
Great Bacolet Bay
St. George's
Crochu Harbor
St. David's
Grand Anse Bay
6
Medical School
Westerhall
5
Point Salinas Airport
Westerhall Bay
GLOVER I.
0 1 2 3 4 5
Nautical Miles
C
Grand Mal Bay
5:00 a.m. 25 Oct 83
SEIZED BY NAVY SEALS
St. John's River
MARINE LANDING
26 October 83
7
Gov't House
St. George's
St. George's Harbor
Fort Frederick
10
Fort Adolphus
ATTACKED BY PLANES FROM INDEPENDENCE
6:00 a.m. 25 Oct 83
Grand Anse Bay
St. George's Medical School
0 1 2
Nautical Miles

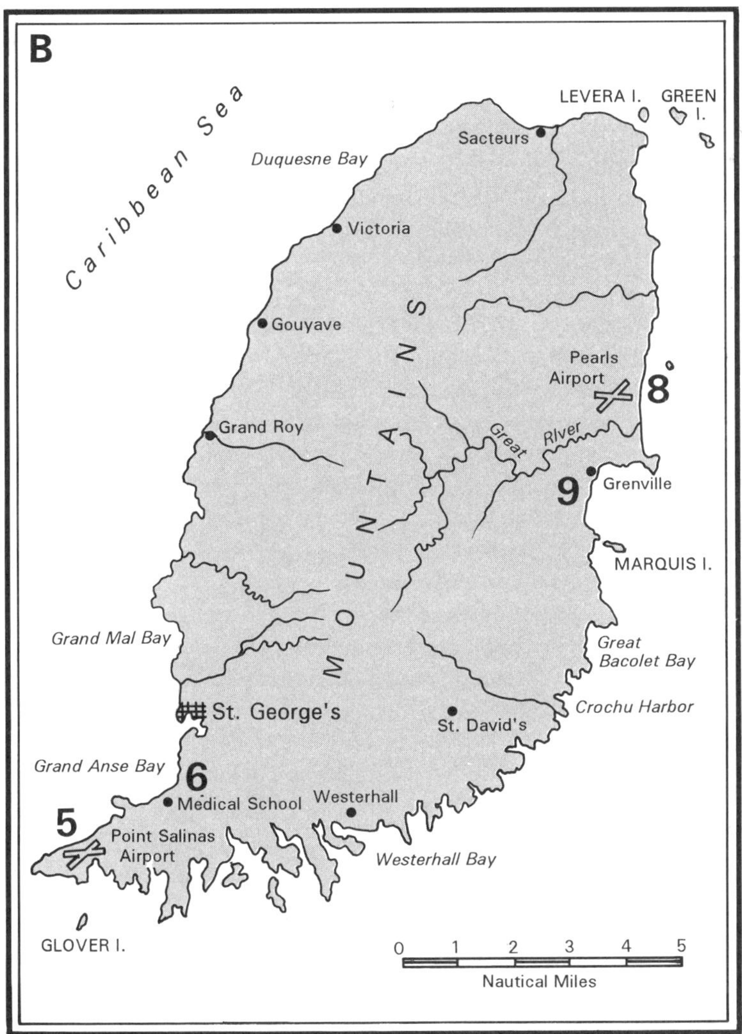

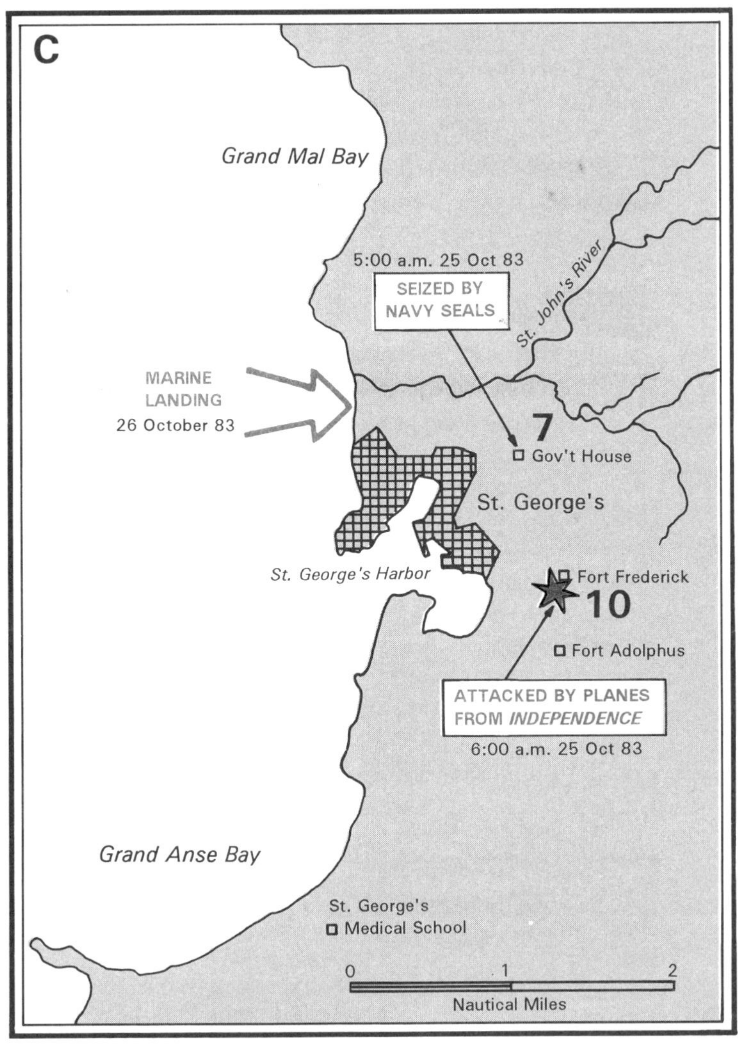

THE MEDITERRANEAN: OPERATION EL DORADO CANYON

MARCH–APRIL 1986

Four months after the disastrous truck bombing of the Marine barracks in Beirut, the United States withdrew its forces from Lebanon, though Navy ships off the coast, including the *New Jersey*, continued to pound away at rebel positions in the mountains. For their part, Lebanese and Palestinian rebels continued their campaign against the symbols of U.S. power, especially banks, airlines, and embassies. In September 1984 another truck bomb exploded outside the U.S. embassy in Beirut, killing twenty-three and wounding the U.S. ambassador. In June 1985 Palestinian terrorists hijacked a TWA plane from Athens and ordered the pilot to Beirut, where they killed an American passenger. After lengthy negotiations the hijackers escaped into the war-torn city, taking several American hostages with them. The military ruler of Libya, COL Muammar Qaddafi, both encouraged and applauded all this terrorist activity.

Four months after the TWA hijacking, in October 1985, four Palestinians hijacked the passenger liner *Achille Lauro* off the coast of Egypt, held the ship's company and its passengers hostage for three days, and killed an elderly American citizen. Failing to coerce the release of Palestinian prisoners, the terrorists agreed to release their hostages in exchange for free passage to Tunis. The United States, however, discovered the terrorists' itinerary, and four F-14 Tomcats from the *Saratoga* forced their plane to divert to Sigonella, Sicily, where Italian police took the terrorists into custody. Partly as a result of this incident, in January 1986 the United States severed all economic ties with Libya, and President Reagan ordered U.S. citizens to leave the country.

Libya had long claimed the Gulf of Sidra south of 32° 30' north latitude as territorial waters (see map A). Qaddafi had decreed that any enemy who violated this "line of death" would be destroyed. The rest of the world rejected the Libyan claim, and the United States conducted occasional flights over the Gulf to validate its status as international waters. In August 1981 Libyan jets had fired on two Navy F-14 Tomcats inside the Gulf, and the Tomcats had shot down both Libyan planes. Now in response to the acceleration of Libyan-sponsored terrorism, President Reagan ordered the Navy to conduct a series of exercises in the vicinity to demonstrate the nation's capability and determination.

The *Coral Sea* and *Saratoga* carrier battle groups conducted Operation ATTAIN DOCUMENT I during six days in late January 1986, remaining just north of the so-called line of death. The same two carriers returned for five days in February (ATTAIN DOCUMENT II), and in March they were joined by the *America* battle group for ATTAIN DOCUMENT III (see map A).

On 24 March the cruiser *Ticonderoga* and two destroyers crossed the "line of death" into the Gulf, and the Libyans reacted by firing five missiles from Sirte (1) at U.S. planes flying cover for the surface ships. VADM Frank Kelso, Sixth Fleet commander, authorized American forces to return fire, and planes from the *America* struck at two Libyan vessels in the Gulf of Sidra, sinking a patrol boat out of Misratah (2) and damaging a missile-firing corvette out of Benghazi (3). That night planes from the *Saratoga* twice attacked the Libyan missile site at Sirte that had fired at American planes earlier in the day. Another Libyan corvette was destroyed the next day (25 March). Having made their point, U.S. forces withdrew from the Gulf on 27 March.

The Libyan response to these activities was not long in coming. In the first week of April a bomb exploded on a TWA flight from Rome to Athens, after which Qaddafi announced, "We shall escalate the violence against American targets, civilian and non-civilian, throughout the world." Two days later a bomb in a West Berlin nightclub killed an American serviceman, and President Reagan directed a retaliatory strike on Libya itself—Operation EL DORADO CANYON.

American planners targeted three sites in the capital city of Tripoli and two in Benghazi. The plan called for a night attack, but the Sixth Fleet had only eighteen planes (A-6E Intruders) capable of conducting the kind of precision night bombing called for in the plan. It was, therefore, determined that night-capable Air Force F-111 fighter-bombers from England would attack the targets in Tripoli while Navy planes struck at those in Benghazi. Prime Minister Margaret Thatcher gave permission for the United States to use bases in England, but France and Spain denied the American request for overflight privileges. This necessitated a six thousand–mile roundabout flight path and four in-flight refuelings en route to the target (see map B).

OPERATION EL DORADO CANYON (SEE MAP C)

At 5:30 P.M. (local time) on 14 April twenty-nine Air Force planes (twenty-four attack planes and five electronic suppression planes) took off from Lakenheath and Upper Heyford Airfields in England. Six and a half hours later (2:00 A.M. [local time] on 15 April), as the Air Force planes neared Tripoli (4), the *America* and *Coral Sea* launched their planes (5). Navy Corsairs and Hornets struck at nearby surface-to-air missile (SAM) sites, while the Intruders headed for their targets in Benghazi (6). Six planes from the *America* hit the al-Jumahiriya Military Barracks in Benghazi, while six others from the *Coral Sea* hit nearby Benina Airfield (7), where they destroyed several planes on the ground, including three MiGs.

One F-111 was lost in the strike. Libya later announced that the raid had killed thirty-seven Libyans and wounded ninety-three others, mostly in Tripoli. Though the military value of the attack was modest at best, as a signal of American willingness to retaliate for terrorism it was apparently successful because Libyan-directed terrorist attacks declined over the next several years.

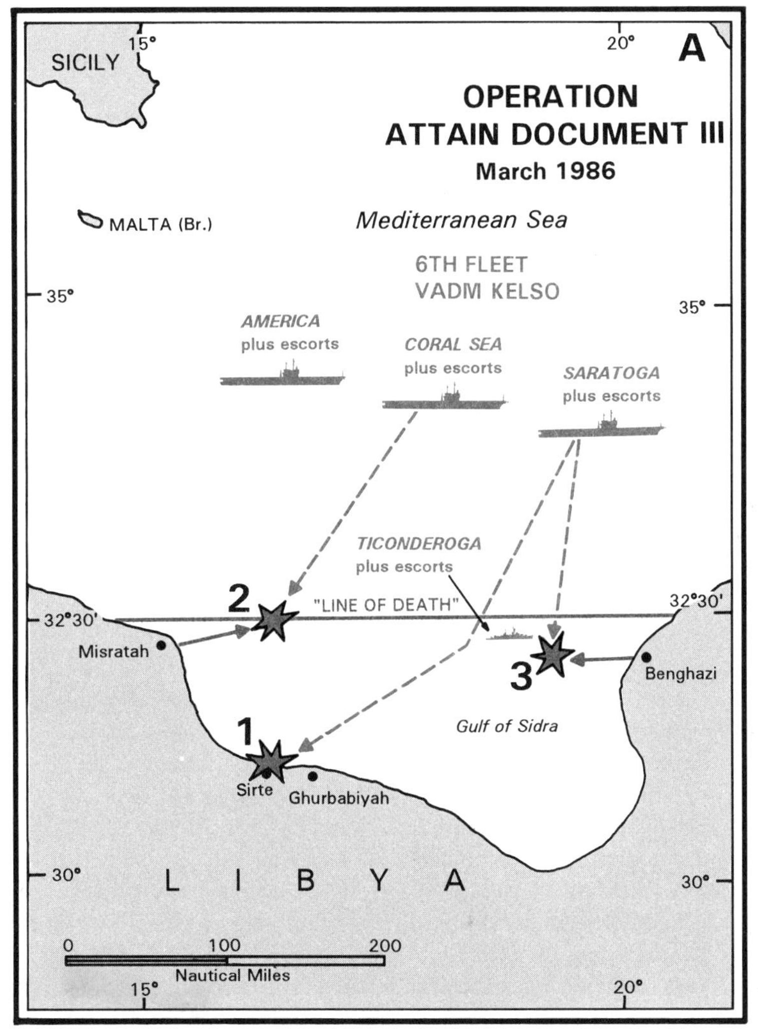

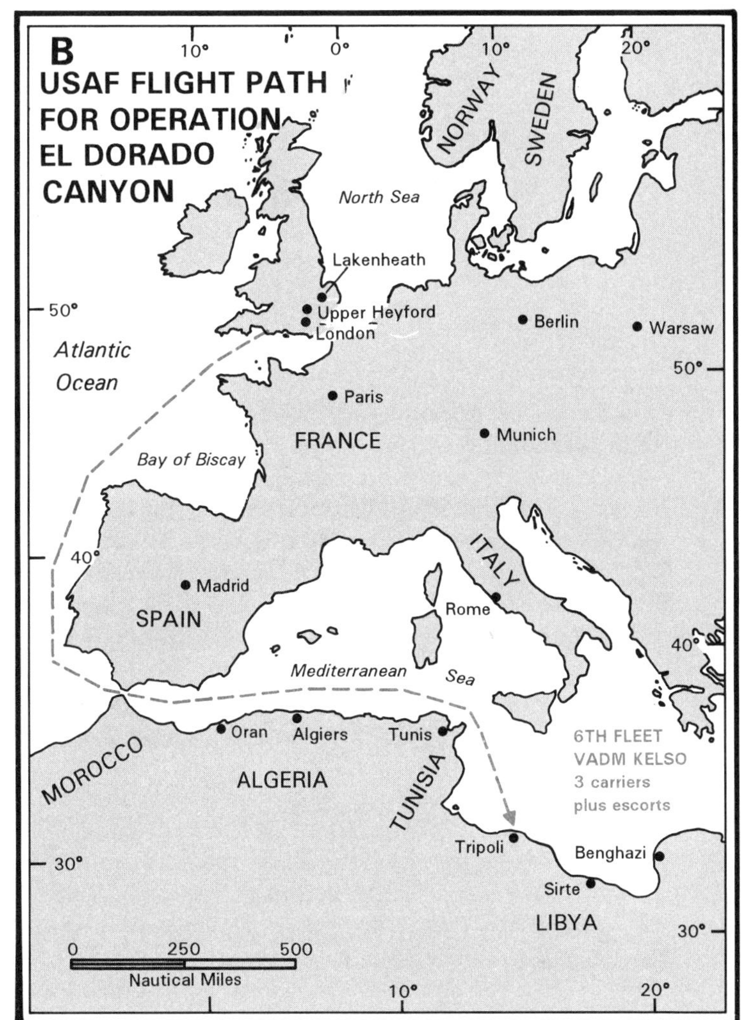

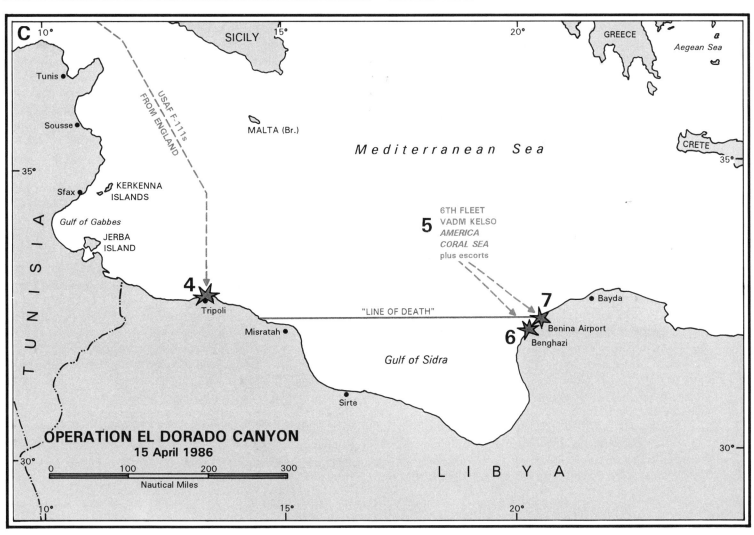

C
10°
SICILY
15°
20°
GREECE
Aegean Sea
Tunis
USAF F-111s
FROM ENGLAND
Sousse
MALTA (Br.)
CRETE
Mediterranean Sea
35°
35°
Sfax
KERKENNA
ISLANDS
Gulf of Gabbes
5
6TH FLEET
VADM KELSO
AMERICA
CORAL SEA
plus escorts
JERBA
ISLAND
TUNISIA
4
Tripoli
7
Bayda
"LINE OF DEATH"
Misratah
Benina Airport
6
Benghazi
Gulf of Sidra
Sirte
OPERATION EL DORADO CANYON
15 April 1986
30°
30°
0
100
200
300
Nautical Miles
L I B Y A
10°
15°
20°

Map 92

The Persian Gulf: Operation PRAYING MANTIS

March 1987–August 1988

With the possible exception of Lebanon, no part of the world was more volatile in the 1980s than Southwest Asia and the Persian Gulf (see upper map). While the Soviets remained bogged down in their war against the U.S.-supported rebels in Afghanistan, a war in the Persian Gulf between Iraq and Iran escalated dramatically in 1984, threatening the free passage of shipping through the Gulf. Iraq had begun the war in September 1980, expecting an easy victory over its larger but disorganized neighbor. Instead, Iran had proved remarkably resilient, and the enormous human and materiel cost of the war led Iraq to resort to the use of chemical weapons and Scud missiles as well as stepping up attacks on Iranian shipping in the Persian Gulf (see lower map).

Iran had difficulty responding, for Iraq exported most of its oil via a pipeline to Turkey; and because its major port in the Shatt al-Arab (1) was closed due to the war, Iraq's imports generally came by neutral shipping through Kuwait or Saudi Arabia. Iran's only means of interrupting that trade, therefore, was to attack those neutral vessels, even though the United Nations had formally condemned attacks on neutral shipping in the Persian Gulf.

The Reagan administration found itself in an awkward position during this developing crisis. Officially, the United States was neutral in the Persian Gulf war, but unofficially it "tilted" toward Iraq and had declared an embargo on arms to Iran. Yet at the same time it was secretly selling arms to Iran in the hope of obtaining Iran's support for the release of American hostages in Lebanon (and using the money thus obtained to support the Contra rebels in Nicaragua). These arrangements became public in November 1986 just as the Gulf crisis was escalating.

In December, after Iranian forces had attacked three Kuwaiti ships, Kuwait asked the United States about the possibility of reflagging its ships as American vessels. On 7 March 1987 the United States agreed to escort eleven Kuwaiti supertankers through the Gulf, thus initiating Operation EARNEST WILL. Before the first convoy could get under way, however, the situation was further complicated on 17 May when an Iraqi Mirage fighter fired two Exocet missiles into the American frigate *Stark* (2), killing thirty-seven American sailors. Iraq apologized for its error, and the Reagan administration refused to allow the incident to derail its pro-Iraqi policy. On 21 July the first escorted tanker convoy got under way from Fujaira in the United Arab Emirates (3), bound for Kuwait. The convoy safely passed through the Strait of Hormuz, but on 24 July the tanker *Bridgeton* was severely damaged when it struck a mine west of Farsi Island (4).

In the wake of the *Stark* and *Bridgeton* incidents, the United States strengthened its forces in the Persian Gulf. Minesweeping helicopters and ships were rushed to the Gulf; the Middle East Force at Bahrain (5) grew from six to thirteen ships; and the *Enterprise* battle group steamed into the Gulf of Oman (6). In September a helicopter from the American frigate *Jarrett* surprised the *Iran Ajr,* a modified landing craft laying mines north of Bahrain (7). Rockets and machine-gun fire from the helicopter disabled the vessel, and the next day a SEAL team boarded, photographed, and impounded the ship.

The Iranians tried a new tack on 15 and 16 October when they fired several Silkworm missiles from the Fao Peninsula into the tanker anchorage off Kuwait, hitting the *Sea Isle City* (8). In retaliation, U.S. naval forces shelled two Iranian-owned oil platforms. This game of provocation and retaliation escalated on 14 April when the U.S. guided-missile frigate *Samuel B. Roberts* struck an Iranian mine (9), which blasted a twenty-one-foot hole in its hull and wounded ten Americans. Effective damage control saved the ship, but the United States decided to turn up the heat.

On 18 April 1988 the U.S. Navy executed Operation PRAYING MANTIS. The immediate objective was the destruction of two more Iranian oil platforms, but when Iranian surface forces sortied in response, the result was the largest surface naval action since Leyte Gulf in World War II. The U.S. attack began at 8:00 A.M. when two U.S. destroyers and an amphibious ship warned the crew of the Sassan oil platform (10) to evacuate. About half of the sixty men on the platform did so, and after the destroyers opened fire and silenced the Iranian guns, the rest of the Iranians evacuated as well. Navy and Marine Corps personnel fast-roped down from helicopters and set explosive charges that destroyed the platform. Meanwhile, the cruiser *Wainwright* and two frigates assailed the Sirri platform (11), where a similar scenario was enacted except that the platform was so devastated by shell fire that explosive charges were not necessary or even possible.

Thus provoked, several Iranian gunboats and the missile patrol boat *Joshan* sortied and shot up a few nearby American-flag tankers. The *Wainwright* and its two frigates attacked, firing five missiles at the *Joshan,* all of which hit, leaving it a sinking wreck (12). Showing more courage than wisdom, two Iranian frigates sortied—one at a time—and each fell victim to superior American firepower. The *Sahand* was sunk after being hit with two missiles and four bombs, and the *Sabalan* went dead in the water after taking a laser-guided bomb amidships, and it had to be towed back to Bandar Abbas (13).

The events of 18 April, and successful counterattacks that summer by Iraqi forces ashore, convinced Iran to accept a U.N. cease-fire resolution, which went into effect on 20 August. In December Operation EARNEST WILL ended. U.S. Navy ships had assumed a huge responsibility; over the life of EARNEST WILL the Navy escorted 270 neutral ships through the Persian Gulf, where mines and shore-based Silkworm missiles covered every square mile, yet only the unlucky *Bridgeton* had suffered any damage.

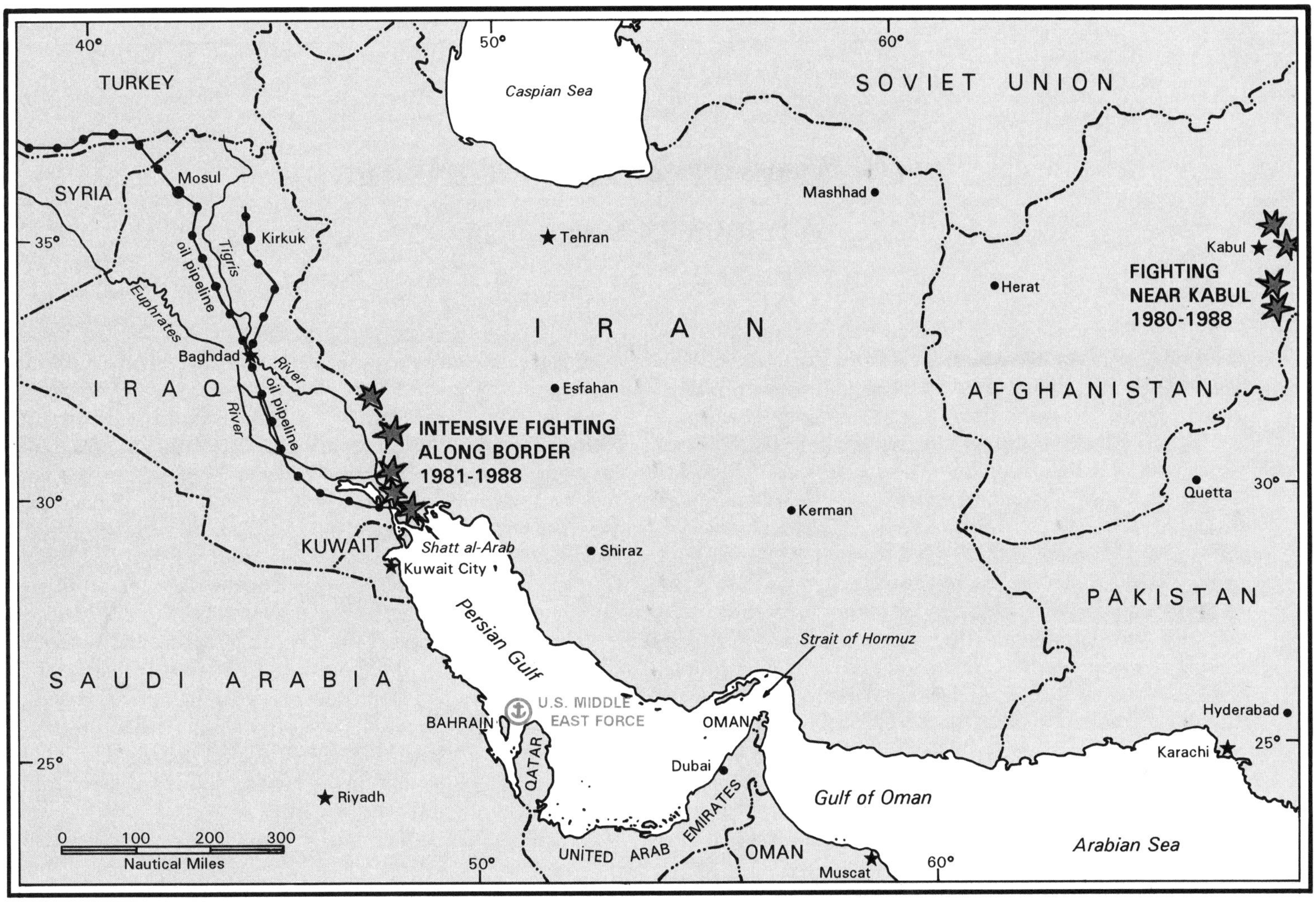

40° 50° 60°
TURKEY
Caspian Sea
SOVIET UNION
SYRIA
Mosul
Kirkuk
oil pipeline
Tigris
Euphrates
Tehran
Mashhad
Herat
Kabul
FIGHTING NEAR KABUL 1980-1988
35°
I R A N
Baghdad
River
oil pipeline
River
I R A Q
Esfahan
AFGHANISTAN
INTENSIVE FIGHTING ALONG BORDER 1981-1988
30°
Quetta
Kerman
KUWAIT
Shatt al-Arab
Kuwait City
Shiraz
PAKISTAN
Persian Gulf
Strait of Hormuz
SAUDI ARABIA
U.S. MIDDLE EAST FORCE
BAHRAIN
OMAN
Hyderabad
Karachi
25°
QATAR
Dubai
Riyadh
Gulf of Oman
EMIRATES
0 100 200 300
Nautical Miles
UNITED ARAB
OMAN
Arabian Sea
Muscat
50° 60°

46° 50° 54° 58°
Tigris
Euphrates
River
Ahvaz
ZAGROS MOUNTAINS
Abadan
Basra
Kerman
30°
IRAQ
Fao
1
Shatt al-Arab
KUWAIT
8 *SEA ISLE CITY* hit by missile 16 Oct 87
Kuwait City
Shiraz
Bushire
I R A N
BRIDGETON hits mine 24 July 87
4
FARSI ISLAND
Persian Gulf
SUMMAN PLATEAU (DESERT)
13
Bandar Abbas
2 *STARK* attacked 17 May 87
7 *IRAN AJR* discovered laying mines
9 *ROBERTS* hits mine 14 Apr 88
Jubayl
SABALAN damaged
SAHAND
5 BAHRAIN
U.S. MIDDLE EAST FORCE
12 *JOSHAN*
26°
SAUDI ARABIA
11 SIRRI oil platform attacked 18 Apr 88
OMAN
Strait of Hormuz
10 SASSAN oil platform attacked 18 Apr 88
3
Fujaira
Gulf of Bahrain
Doha
QATAR
DAS
Dubai
6 *ENTERPRISE* battle group
Riyadh
Abu Dhabi
EMIRATES
Gulf of Oman
0 100 200
Nautical Miles
UNITED ARAB
OMAN
46° 50° 54° 58°

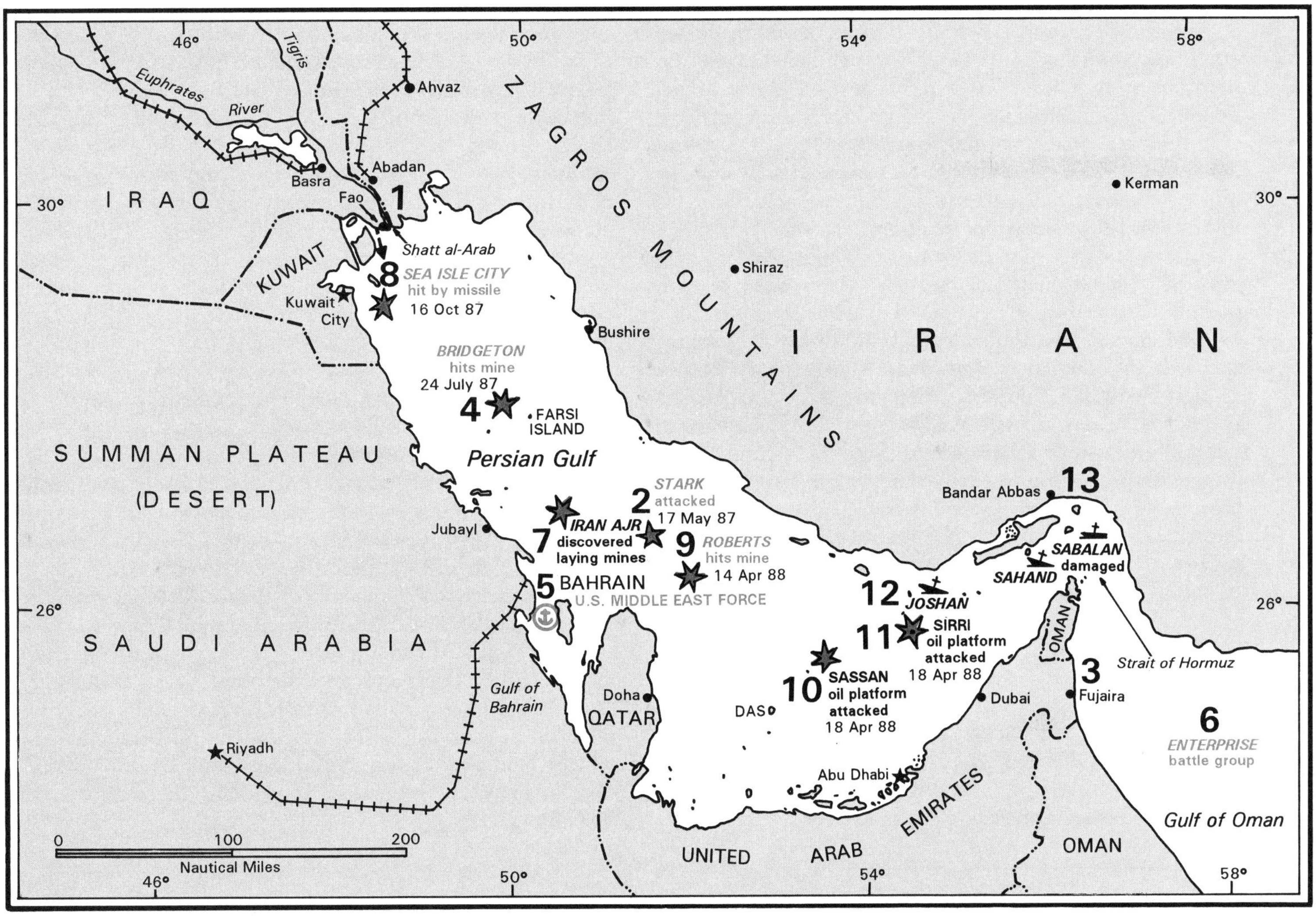

MAP 93

DESERT STORM: THE AIR WAR

16 JANUARY–24 FEBRUARY 1991

On 2 August 1990 more than one hundred thousand Iraqi troops, bolstered by 350 tanks, invaded the emirate of Kuwait (1). The attack came as a surprise in part because Kuwait had been a loyal ally to Iraq in its war with Iran. Calling the act "naked aggression," President George Bush acted quickly, freezing Iraqi assets in the United States and launching a diplomatic offensive to forge an international coalition to oppose Iraq's takeover. U.S. initiatives led to U.N. resolutions imposing sanctions on Iraq, a U.N. embargo of Iraq, and even a joint U.S.–U.S.S.R. declaration condemning the Iraqi invasion. None of these initiatives convinced the Iraqis to withdraw, however, and on 6 August the government of Saudi Arabia, fearing it might be the next to be targeted by Iraq's unpredictable leader, Saddam Hussein, formally requested U.S. assistance. Then began a dramatic and remarkable buildup of U.S. and allied forces in Saudi Arabia known as Operation DESERT SHIELD.

The first unit to be sent to the Gulf was the 7th Marine Expeditionary Brigade (MEB) commanded by MGEN John Hopkins. The Marines arrived at Dhahran, Saudi Arabia (2), on 14 August, and despite delays occasioned by the cultural differences between Americans and Saudis, they were in position by 25 August. That same day planes carrying the Marines of the 4th MEB, commanded by MGEN Harry Jenkins, took off from Hawaii to join the 7th. On 3 September LGEN Walter Boomer set up his headquarters at Riyadh (3), and by the end of the month there were thirty thousand fully armed and equipped marines in place along the Saudi-Kuwaiti border. The influx of U.S. and allied, particularly British, forces continued through the fall, including the deployment of some 125,000 reservists, and by the end of the year the United States and its allies had achieved numerical superiority, with allied strength peaking at more than seven hundred thousand.

Meanwhile, the United States continued with economic and diplomatic initiatives. Turkey and Saudi Arabia agreed to shut off the pipelines through which most of Iraq's oil exports flowed, and because the U.S. Navy controlled the Persian Gulf, Iraq had no way to export its oil. Other OPEC countries agreed to increase production to compensate for the loss of Iraqi oil from the world market. Even this had no effect on Saddam Hussein, however, nor did a U.S.-sponsored U.N. resolution passed in November to authorize the use of military force if Iraqi troops did not withdraw from Kuwait by 15 January.

Following the failure of a last-minute conference between U.S. Secretary of State James Baker and Iraq's Foreign Minister Tariq Aziz (9 January), and a congressional authorization for the use of U.S. military force (12 January), the war began on 16 January 1991. DESERT SHIELD became DESERT STORM as the allies launched a massive air offensive against Iraq. U.S. Air Force F-117 "Stealth" fighter-bombers and U.S. Navy sea-launched Tomahawk cruise missiles conducted the first strikes and specifically targeted Iraqi radar and air-defense systems. In the first twenty-four hours of the war, allied planes flew 1,400 sorties and U.S. Navy ships fired 104 Tomahawk cruise missiles. The destruction of Iraqi air defenses and the inability of Iraqi fighters to mount an effective challenge to allied air power gave the allies undisputed command of the skies. For five weeks the allies flew an average of 1,200 sorties per day, destroying the Iraqi military infrastructure and shattering the morale of Iraqi soldiers. Iraq could respond only by firing Scud-B missiles at Israel in the hope of changing the character of the war and disrupting the allied coalition.

As in the air war against North Vietnam, the U.S. Air Force and Navy shared responsibilities. But rather than applying a geographical division (Route Packs) as in Vietnam, bombing assignments for each day's strikes were determined in advance by a complicated air tasking order (ATO). The ATO was so lengthy (the plan for 17 January was more than seven hundred pages long) that it had to be flown out to the carriers daily. This system worked well enough against an enemy that had been rendered passive by the destruction of its air-defense system, but it left little room for adjustments to changing tactical circumstances. For that reason, helicopter operations and anti–surface ship operations in the Persian Gulf were not included in the ATO. Even so, many Navy and Marine Corps pilots felt handcuffed by the ATO system.

U.S. carriers in the Red Sea (4) concentrated on Iraqi air bases in western Iraq (5). Such missions required a five-and-a-half-hour flight and an in-flight refueling from Air Force tankers, but it also allowed the Navy planes to reach their targets without passing over enemy air defenses. Launching twenty to thirty planes per strike, the carriers in the Red Sea generally conducted two strikes per day and operated eighteen out of every twenty-four hours. The carriers in the Persian Gulf (6) were closer to targets in Kuwait and Iraq than any shore-based planes and were able to deliver regular and repeated attacks against Basra and the Republican Guard concentration points (7).

Over the thirty-eight days of the air campaign, allied planes flew a total of 94,000 sorties and delivered more than 60,000 tons of ordnance. Postwar assessment indicated that this campaign was instrumental in wrecking the morale of the enemy army before the ground war even began. Much of the allied ordnance was composed of "smart bombs," many of which hit their targets with pinpoint accuracy. Film of these strikes was repeatedly shown on news programs in America and made high-technology ordnance the media star of the air war.

The allies lost a total of forty-one airplanes and forty-three killed, including twenty-four Americans. Iraqi losses can only be estimated, but one authority set them at 9,000 killed, 17,000 wounded, and more than 150,000 deserted from the Iraqi Army.

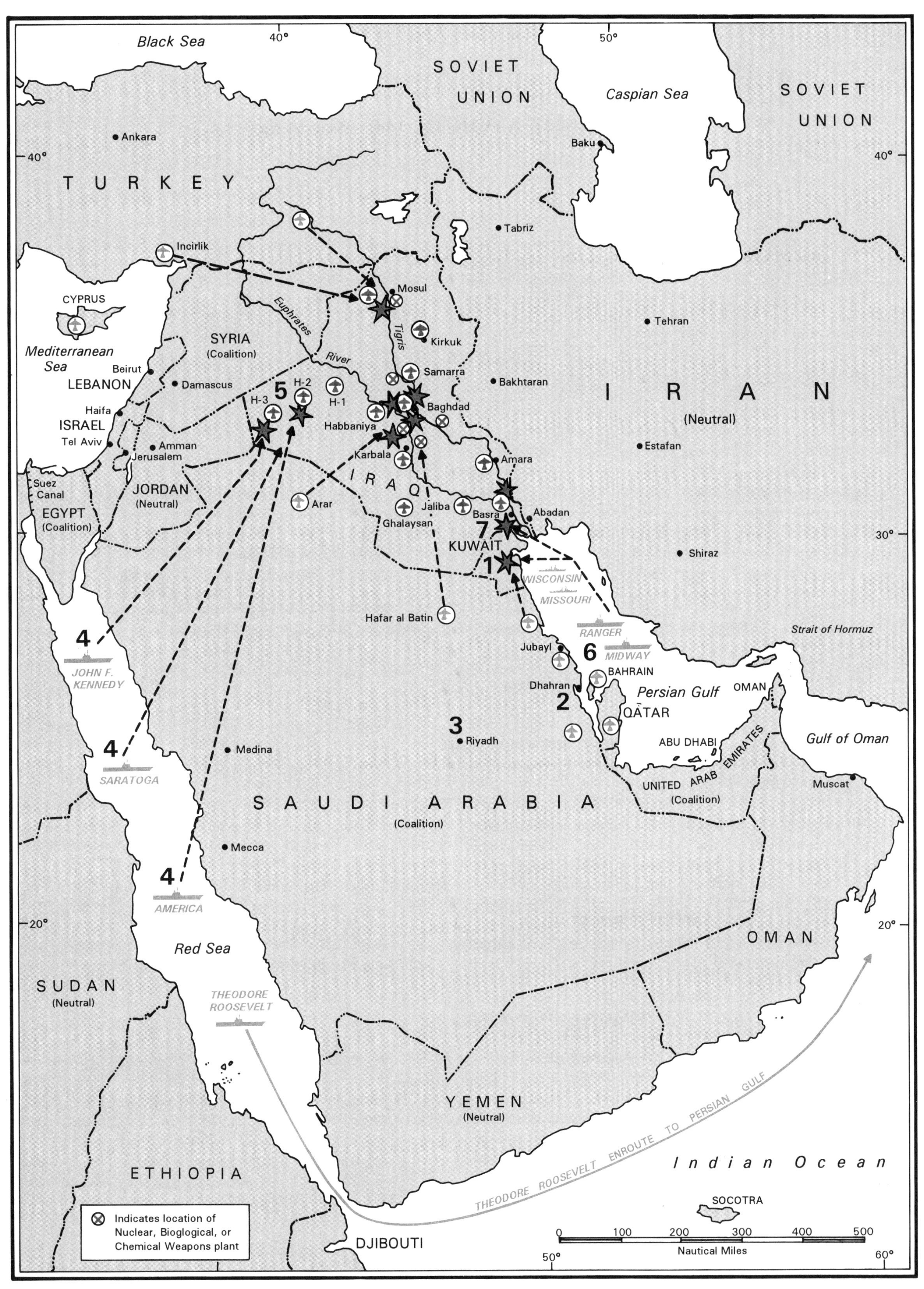
Black Sea
SOVIET UNION
Caspian Sea
SOVIET UNION
Ankara
Baku
TURKEY
Tabriz
Incirlik
Mosul
CYPRUS
Euphrates River
Tigris
Kirkuk
Tehran
SYRIA (Coalition)
Mediterranean Sea
Beirut
LEBANON
Damascus
Samarra
Bakhtaran
IRAN (Neutral)
H-3
H-2
H-1
Baghdad
Haifa
ISRAEL
Tel Aviv
Habbaniya
Amman
Jerusalem
Estafan
Karbala
Amara
IRAQ
Suez Canal
JORDAN (Neutral)
EGYPT (Coalition)
Arar
Jaliba
Basra
Ghalaysan
Abadan
KUWAIT
Shiraz
WISCONSIN
MISSOURI
Hafar al Batin
RANGER
MIDWAY
Strait of Hormuz
JOHN F. KENNEDY
Jubayl
BAHRAIN
Dhahran
Persian Gulf
OMAN
QATAR
Riyadh
Medina
ABU DHABI
UNITED ARAB EMIRATES (Coalition)
Gulf of Oman
Muscat
SARATOGA
SAUDI ARABIA (Coalition)
Mecca
AMERICA
Red Sea
OMAN
SUDAN (Neutral)
THEODORE ROOSEVELT
YEMEN (Neutral)
ETHIOPIA
Indian Ocean
THEODORE ROOSEVELT ENROUTE TO PERSIAN GULF
SOCOTRA
DJIBOUTI
Indicates location of Nuclear, Bioglogical, or Chemical Weapons plant
0 100 200 300 400 500
Nautical Miles
1
2
3
4
4
4
5
6
7
40°
50°
60°
20°
30°

Map 94

Desert Storm: The Ground War

24 February–6 May 1991

Though the air war over Iraq took a heavy toll on Iraqi defenses and severely eroded the morale of Iraqi troops, only a ground campaign could bring the war to a conclusion. Iraq's ruler, Saddam Hussein, had promised that an allied attack would provoke "the mother of all battles" and that the Americans would "swim in their own blood." Given that Iraq had the fourth largest army in the world, such boasts could not be ignored. The Iraqis had three army corps (sixteen divisions) in southern Kuwait plus another eight divisions to the west (see upper map). Iraq's best troops, the Republican Guard, were held as a mobile reserve near the Iraqi-Kuwaiti border (1).

Rather than assail this force in a frontal attack, allied planners, headed by U.S. Army GEN Norman Schwarzkopf, preferred an end run. This meant either an amphibious landing behind the Iraqi lines or a deep left hook through the Iraqi desert west of Kuwait where Iraq had positioned only two divisions. The Iraqis discounted the possibility of an allied offensive through the western desert because they believed the allies would encounter irresolvable logistic, mechanical, and navigational problems. Establishing several giant supply depots in the desert solved the logistic problem; preventive maintenance kept the tanks running despite the desert sand; and global positioning satellites solved the problem of navigation in a virtually trackless terrain. Though the Marines continued to support the notion of an amphibious attack up the Shatt al-Arab to Basra (2), General Schwarzkopf decided to employ the 4th MEB in the Persian Gulf as a decoy and to rely instead on the left hook through the desert.

Though the Marines were denied the chance to execute the amphibious plan they had prepared, they did spearhead the first ground attack of the war. At 4:00 A.M. local time on 24 February the 1st Marine Expeditionary Force crossed the border into Kuwait to assail the Iraqi defense line (3). Intended to draw Iraqi attention away from the main allied thrust farther west, the Marine offensive nevertheless achieved surprising success and almost at once began to produce a startling number of prisoners. Three Iraqi divisions broke apart after only a cursory resistance, and the Marines pushed forward while six mechanized brigades from Saudi Arabia, Qatar, and Oman attacked northward along the coast (4). The allied feint turned into a full-scale thrust deep into Kuwait.

While the Marines and Arab forces penetrated the Iraqi lines into Kuwait, the giant left hook of the allied main offensive also got under way. On the extreme left the French 6th Light Armored Division, reinforced by a brigade of the 82nd U.S. Airborne, struck northeast to Salman (5) to establish a flank guard for the main offensive. To their right, three hundred helicopters lifted two thousand men and fifty vehicles of the 101st Airborne to the Iraqi air base at Ubayyid to establish advance base COBRA (6). Then this force leaped forward again to establish base GOLD (7), from which point it advanced to cut Highway 8. These movements secured the allied left flank and cut off one possible Iraqi avenue of escape. At the same time the U.S. 24th Mechanized Infantry Division (8) literally raced across the sand toward Jaliba Airfield (9), where it encountered the first serious resistance of the war from elements of the Republican Guard.

With the stage set, the armored and mechanized divisions of the VII Corps (see lower map) struck the hammer blow. Allied tanks sliced through the Iraqi lines and raced north to Busayya (10) and then turned east in a blitzkrieg campaign that kept the enemy confused and off balance. The Iraqi defense was spotty and uncoordinated, and the allies took prisoners by the thousands. On 27–28 February the Hammurabi Division of the Republican Guards attempted to fight a delaying action (11) to hold off the allied advance but was badly routed.

Finally recognizing the extent of the unfolding disaster, Saddam Hussein attempted to salvage at least part of his army by announcing that he would evacuate Kuwait. Apparently, he hoped that this would appease the allies, who would allow his remaining forces to leave unmolested. Instead, the allies announced that military units moving in formation would be considered appropriate military targets. Iraqi units that sought to escape up the road to Basra became the victims of repeated allied air strikes that turned the road into a "highway of death" (12).

As allied armored columns closed in from the west, the U.S. Marines and Saudi troops continued to advance on Kuwait City from the south. The 1st Marine Division attacked the city through burning oil fields while the 2nd Marine Division destroyed an Iraqi counterattack and drove toward Jahrah. On 26 February the Marines paused to let Arab forces pass through their lines and lead the way into Kuwait City (13). During the campaign the Marine Expeditionary Force destroyed a total of 1,040 enemy tanks, 608 armored personnel carriers, and 432 artillery pieces while inflicting heavy casualties and taking uncounted thousands of prisoners. All of this was achieved at a cost of twenty-four killed and ninety-two wounded. In the entire war, only 147 allied soldiers were killed, 88 of them Americans. Of those eighty-eight, twenty-eight died as the result of a Scud-missile attack on Dhahran.

The astonishing success of the allied war against Iraq in January–February 1991 demonstrated both the impressive capability of the new generation of sophisticated weapons and the new American role as world policeman. President Bush spared no effort to ensure both international cooperation and congressional support. Having defined the objective clearly, he allowed time for a thorough buildup of forces and the application of overwhelming strength.

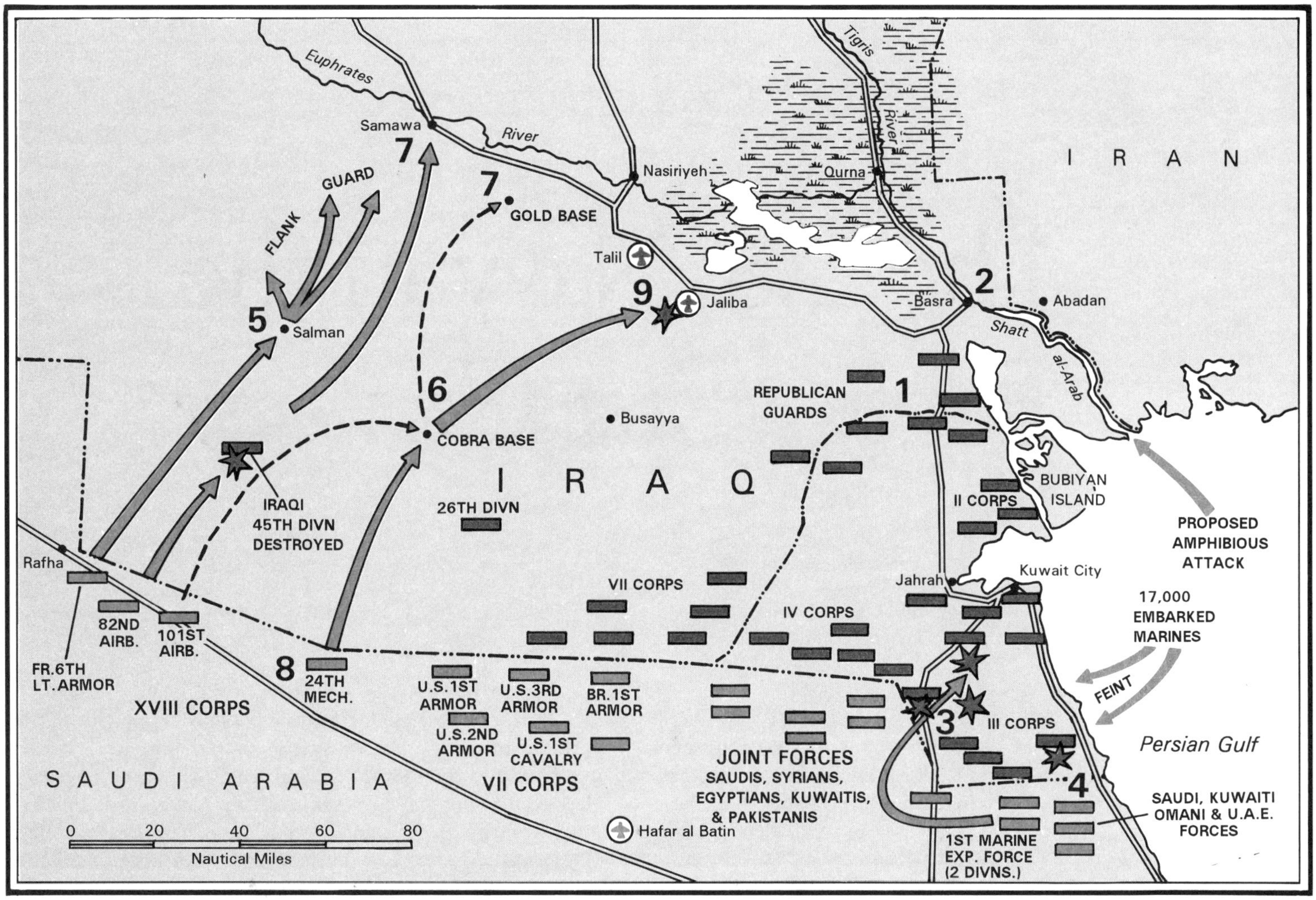

Euphrates
River
Tigris
River
Samawa
Nasiriyeh
Qurna
I R A N
7
FLANK
GUARD
7
GOLD BASE
Talil
9
Jaliba
Basra
2
Abadan
Shatt
al-Arab
5
Salman
6
REPUBLICAN
GUARDS
1
Busayya
COBRA BASE
IRAQI
45TH DIVN
DESTROYED
I R A Q
26TH DIVN
II CORPS
BUBIYAN
ISLAND
PROPOSED
AMPHIBIOUS
ATTACK
Rafha
Jahrah
Kuwait City
VII CORPS
17,000
EMBARKED
MARINES
IV CORPS
82ND
AIRB.
101ST
AIRB.
FR.6TH
LT. ARMOR
8
24TH
MECH.
U.S.1ST
ARMOR
U.S.3RD
ARMOR
BR.1ST
ARMOR
FEINT
3
III CORPS
XVIII CORPS
U.S.2ND
ARMOR
U.S.1ST
CAVALRY
Persian Gulf
JOINT FORCES
SAUDIS, SYRIANS,
EGYPTIANS, KUWAITIS,
& PAKISTANIS
SAUDI ARABIA
VII CORPS
4
SAUDI, KUWAITI
OMANI & U.A.E.
FORCES
0 20 40 60 80
Nautical Miles
Hafar al Batin
1ST MARINE
EXP. FORCE
(2 DIVNS.)

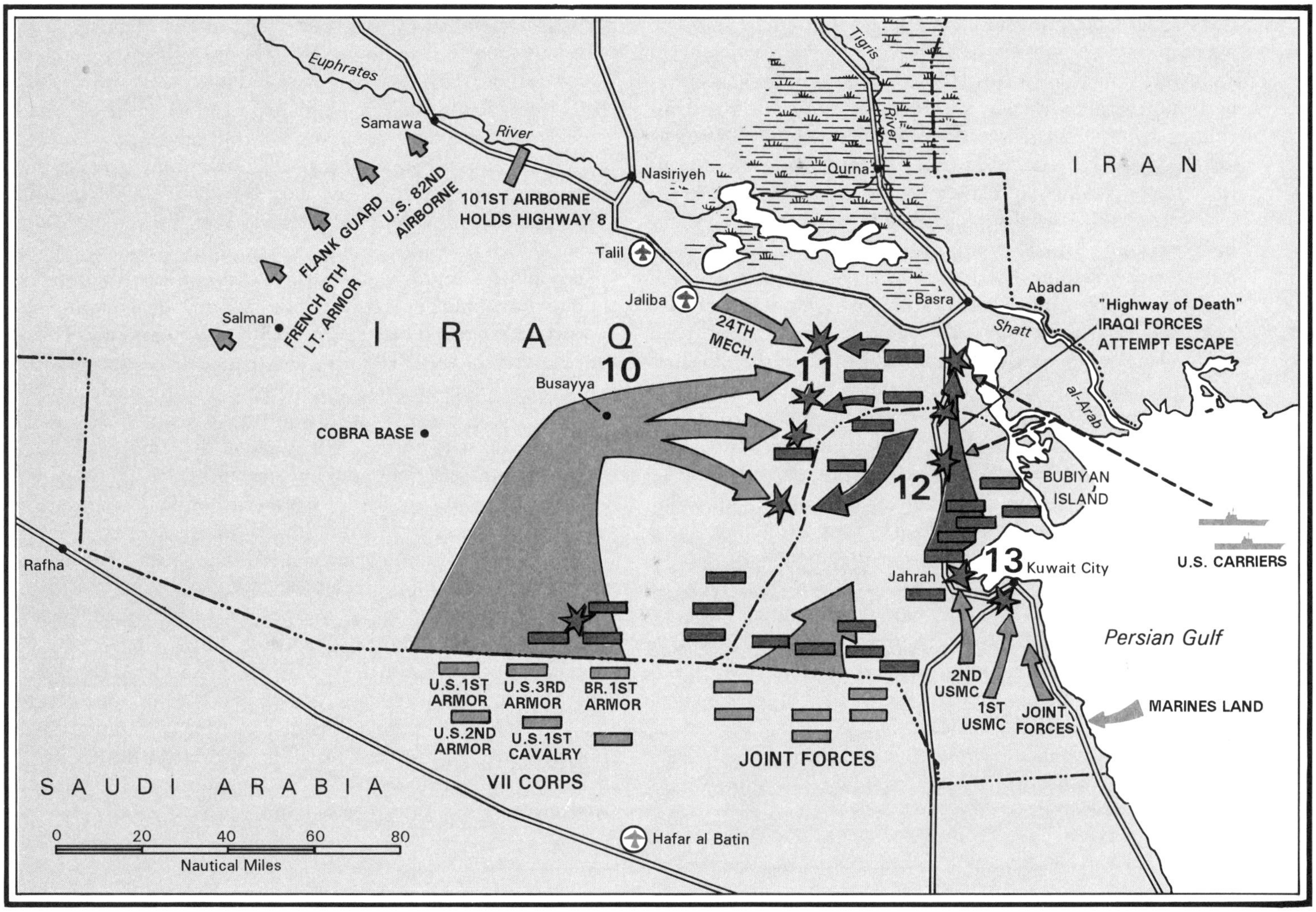

Euphrates
River
Tigris
River
Samawa
Nasiriyeh
Qurna
I R A N
101ST AIRBORNE
HOLDS HIGHWAY 8
U.S. 82ND
AIRBORNE
FLANK GUARD
FRENCH 6TH
LT. ARMOR
Talil
Jaliba
Basra
Abadan
"Highway of Death"
IRAQI FORCES
ATTEMPT ESCAPE
Shatt
al-Arab
Salman
I R A Q
24TH
MECH.
11
Busayya
10
COBRA BASE
12
BUBIYAN
ISLAND
U.S. CARRIERS
Rafha
13
Jahrah
Kuwait City
Persian Gulf
2ND
USMC
1ST
USMC
JOINT
FORCES
MARINES LAND
U.S.1ST
ARMOR
U.S.3RD
ARMOR
BR.1ST
ARMOR
U.S.2ND
ARMOR
U.S.1ST
CAVALRY
JOINT FORCES
VII CORPS
SAUDI ARABIA
0 20 40 60 80
Nautical Miles
Hafar al Batin

EPILOGUE

The U.S. Navy in the Twenty-first Century

DESPITE THE DRAMATIC success of DESERT STORM, even that war left an ambiguous legacy. A chastened but defiant Saddam Hussein continued to rule Iraq despite U.S. encouragement to Iraqi Kurds in the north and Shiite Moslems in the south to overthrow him. Then, too, the need to protect the Kurds and Shiites from Saddam's wrath prompted the United States to declare and enforce "no-fly zones" in Iraq. Thus did the American determination to drive Saddam Hussein's forces from Kuwait become another open-ended commitment, one which proved costly in April 1994 when two Air Force F-15s accidentally shot down two U.S. Army Blackhawk helicopters in the northern no-fly zone, killing all twenty-two on board, including fifteen Americans. The burden of enforcing a Pax Americana was also demonstrated in Somalia, where President Bush sent a Marine force in late 1992 to establish a stable environment so that relief supplies could be delivered to a starving population. Initially greeted as saviors, the Marines became caught in the middle of local power struggles and eventually became the target of resentment and even violence before they evacuated Somalia in 1994.

These events provided ample evidence that the world remained a dangerous place. The dissolution of the Soviet Union had removed the putative enemy from the game boards of the nation's war colleges, but it also opened a Pandora's box of long-dormant national rivalries as regional violence broke out in South Asia and the Balkans. Such an international environment confronted U.S. policy makers with a more complex game board and some very difficult decisions. Even as the nation was liberated from the threat of a nuclear holocaust, Americans were uncertain about what responsibility, if any, the United States should bear for ensuring peace and stability in these regional wars. Television crews filmed starving children in Somalia, wounded children in Sarajevo, and victims of tribal warfare in Rwanda and South Africa. Such footage created pressure for the greatest power in the world to do something. In the new world order, which of these conflicts, if any, called for American intervention?

It may be that the United States will back away from the burden of maintaining a Pax Americana in the twenty-first century. Or it may be that the United States will apply its power selectively, opting for involvement only when American national interests are directly affected. In either case, the U.S. Navy of the future, characterized by a continued reliance on high-technology weapons and a small but highly skilled enlisted and officer corps, will almost certainly continue to be the spear point of American power. The economic pressure to reduce spending in the post–Cold War era will mean that the Navy cannot have everything it would like to have to guarantee success in this role, and to maintain its ability to react quickly and effectively around the world it will have to scale back its commitment to many of the weapons systems that dominated the era of the Cold War. But then the history of the U.S. Navy is, after all, the story of adjustment to change.

Mahan notwithstanding, no one policy—no single naval philosophy—has proved satisfactory to meet the needs of the republic throughout its 220-year history. Some generations supported an expanded Navy, others allowed it to atrophy. This is not because some generations were smarter than others but because what was appropriate to one age was either inadequate or unnecessary to another. The Navy of the Barbary Wars was obviously inadequate for the Civil War, and the Navy of the Civil War was unnecessary for the circumstances the United States faced in the 1870s. Similarly, a naval-arms-limitation agreement was a good idea in 1922, even though twenty years later American industry was running at full speed to produce a fleet of unprecedented size and power. Such change is inevitable because the very purpose of the U.S. Navy is to support the national interests, and those interests change. Of course, change is often wrenching. Captains of the age of sail hated to see the squat, ugly little steamships replace their elegant frigates; members of the gun club wept as the last battleships were decommissioned. But change is the one certainty in predicting the future; and if the past is any predictor the U.S. Navy will adjust, survive, and continue to serve as the guardian of the nation.

INDEX

References to maps are printed in boldface type. Numbers in italics refer to photographs.

About the Author

Craig L. Symonds is Professor of History at the U.S. Naval Academy, where he has taught naval history and Civil War history since 1976. Dr. Symonds previously taught in the Department of Strategy and Policy at the U.S. Naval War College in Newport (1972–75), and in 1994–95 he taught in the Department of Strategic Studies at Britannia Royal Naval College in Dartmouth, England. A former History Department chair at the Naval Academy (1988–92) and winner of the Naval Academy's teaching-excellence award (1988), Dr. Symonds is the author of six other books, including historical atlases of both the American Revolution and the Civil War, as well as an award-winning biography of Confederate General Joseph E. Johnston.

About the Cartographer

William J. Clipson, former head of the graphic-arts department at the U.S. Naval Academy, is a freelance cartographer who has illustrated more than five hundred books, including *A Battlefield Atlas of the American Revolution, A Battlefield Atlas of the Civil War,* and *Gettysburg: A Battlefield Atlas* in collaboration with Craig L. Symonds.

The Naval Institute Press is the book-publishing arm of the U.S. Naval Institute, a private, nonprofit, membership society for sea service professionals and others who share an interest in naval and maritime affairs. Established in 1873 at the U.S. Naval Academy in Annapolis, Maryland, where its offices remain today, the Naval Institute has members worldwide.

Members of the Naval Institute support the education programs of the society and receive the influential monthly magazine *Proceedings* and discounts on fine nautical prints and on ship and aircraft photos. They also have access to the transcripts of the Institute's Oral History Program and get discounted admission to any of the Institute-sponsored seminars offered around the country.

The Naval Institute also publishes *Naval History* magazine. This colorful bimonthly is filled with entertaining and thought-provoking articles, first-person reminiscences, and dramatic art and photography. Members receive a discount on *Naval History* subscriptions.

The Naval Institute's book-publishing program, begun in 1898 with basic guides to naval practices, has broadened its scope to include books of more general interest. Now the Naval Institute Press publishes about one hundred titles each year, ranging from how-to books on boating and navigation to battle histories, biographies, ship and aircraft guides, and novels. Institute members receive significant discounts on the Press's more than eight hundred books in print.

Full-time students are eligible for special half-price membership rates. Life memberships are also available.

For a free catalog describing Naval Institute Press books currently available, and for further information about subscribing to *Naval History* magazine or about joining the U.S. Naval Institute, please write to:

Membership Department
U.S. Naval Institute
291 Wood Road
Annapolis, MD 21402-5034
Telephone: (800) 233-8764
Fax: (410) 269-7940
Web address: www.usni.org